Religion in the Mirror of Law

Eastern European Perspectives from the Early Modern Period to 1939

edited by Yvonne Kleinmann
Stephan Stach
Tracie L. Wilson

Studien zur
europäischen Rechtsgeschichte

Veröffentlichungen des
Max-Planck-Instituts
für europäische Rechtsgeschichte
Frankfurt am Main

Band 280

Vittorio Klostermann
Frankfurt am Main
2016

Religion in the Mirror of Law

Eastern European Perspectives from the Early Modern Period to 1939

Edited by
Yvonne Kleinmann
Stephan Stach
Tracie L. Wilson

Copy-edited by
David Dichelle

Vittorio Klostermann
Frankfurt am Main
2016

Bibliographische Information der Deutschen Nationalbibliothek
Die Deutsche Nationalbibliothek verzeichnet diese Publikation in der Deutschen Nationalbibliographie; detaillierte bibliographische Daten sind im Internet über *http://dnb.dnb.de* abrufbar.

Druck und Bindung: docupoint GmbH, Barleben
Typographie: Elmar Lixenfeld, Frankfurt am Main

Gedruckt auf Alster Werkdruck der Firma Geese, Hamburg.
Alterungsbeständig ISO 9706 und PEFC-zertifiziert

Printed in Germany
ISSN 1610-6040
ISBN 978-3-465-04181-8

Contents

Acknowledgements

This volume has its roots in the international conference *Religion in the Mirror of Law. Research on Early Modern Poland-Lithuania and its Successor States in the 19th and Early 20th Centuries* held in Lviv at the Center for Urban History of East-Central Europe in 2010. This interdisciplinary meeting included perspectives from history, legal studies, literature, and ethnology, with participants from Austria, Germany, Israel, Poland, Ukraine, and the United States. The articles presented here are extensively reworked versions of most of the papers presented.

The conference was the initiative of the research group *Pathways of Law in Ethno-Religiously Mixed Societies: Resources of Experience in Poland-Lithuania and its Successor States* based at the Institute for Slavic Studies at Leipzig University, the members of which are also the editors of this volume. The German Research Foundation (Emmy Noether Program, GZ KL 2201/1-1) acted as primary sponsor of the conference as well as of this volume. Additional partners and sponsoring institutions are the Center for Urban History of East-Central Europe in Lviv, which hosted the conference, as well as the German Historical Institute in Warsaw and the Max Planck Institute for European Legal History in Frankfurt am Main, both of which generously contributed to the conference budget.

The editors would like to take this occasion to thank all those who participated in the conference and especially those who braved the editing process in discussing and revising their articles. We offer special thanks to Harald Binder, Director of the Center for Urban History of East-Central Europe and the center's coordinator, Iryna Matsevko. We wish to thank Eduard Mühle, Director of the German Historical Institute in Warsaw from 2008 through 2013, and especially Deputy Director, Ruth Leiserowitz, who represented the institute at the conference. We wish to express our gratitude to the Director of the Max Planck Institute for European Legal History, Thomas Duve, and to Stefan Ruppert who took part in the conference. We are particularly grateful to the Max Planck Institute for integrating our book into the series *Studien zur europäischen Rechtsgeschichte* (Studies in European Legal History) and we extend special thanks to Karl-Heinz Lingens, the coordinator of the series for his steady encouragement and patience. Finally, we would like to thank Nadja Mitzkat, Magda Wlostowska, Sven Jaros and Anja Schyma, the students whose efforts have also contributed to the conference and the editing of this volume.

The editors

Note on Transliteration

The transliteration of Belarusian, Russian, and Ukrainian in this book follows the Library of Congress system with the exception that for the sake of readability the many »ь« (soft signs) in Ukrainian are represented as »'« only in the footnotes but not in the main text.

Hebrew is transliterated according to a simplified version of the Library of Congress system with the aim to reflect the pronunciation of Modern Hebrew: *alef* and *ayin* are both depicted as »′,« *tet* and *taf* as »t,« and *kaf* and *kuf* as »k,« whereas the distinction between *ḥet* and *khaf* has been retained in the form of »ḥ « and »kh.«

The transliteration of Yiddish follows the YIVO-style.

Reflections on the Meanings of Religious Belonging in Eastern European Legal Culture: An Introduction

This book is about the interconnections of religion and law in East Central European legal culture – or more precisely cultures. It delves into the role of religion in legal thought, in political constitutions, legal practice and performance, as well as in understandings of justice from the 16th century to 1939. During this long period the Polish, Lithuanian, Belorusian and Ukrainian lands that are at the core of our common project were continuously inhabited by multiple religious communities and settlers of various religious belongings.[1] This continuity notwithstanding, many political, social and cultural changes occurred, one of them being essential shifts in the understanding of religion and the religious community itself.

While being part of a religious community during the early modern period, apart from common worship and rites, went hand in hand with a specific legal, social, and economic status,[2] from the late 18th century on, the all-encompassing

1 This historical fact is testified by many publications, among others Adam Kaźmierczyk, Andrzej K. Link-Lenczowki, Mariusz Markiewicz, Krystyn Matwijowski, eds., *Rzeczpospolita wielu wyznań.* (Kraków: Księgarnia Akademicka, 2004); Tomasz Ciesielski and Anna Filipczak-Kocur, eds., *Rzeczpospolita państwem wielu narodowości i wyznań. XVI–XVII wiek* (Warszawa-Opole: DiG, 2008); Jerzy Tomaszewski, *Ojczyzna nie tylko Polaków. Mniejszości narodowe w Polsce w latach 1918–1939* (Warszawa: Młodzieżowa Agencja Wydawnicza, 1985); idem, *Rzeczpospolita wielu narodów* (Warszawa: Czytelnik, 1985); Christhardt Henschel and Stephan Stach, eds., *Nationalisierung und Pragmatismus. Staatliche Institutionen und Minderheiten in Polen 1918–1939* (Marburg: Herder-Institut, 2013) = *Zeitschrift für Ostmitteleuropaforschung* 62, no. 2.

2 Myron M. Kapral', *Natsional'ni gromadi L'vova XVI–XVIII st.* (L'viv: Literaturna agencia Piramida, 2003); Leszek Ćwikła, »Sytuacja prawna mieszczan wyznania prawosławnego Rzeczypospolitej po unii brzeskiej (1595–1596 r.),« *Prace historyczno-archiwalne* 17 (2006): 5–26; Wojciech Kriegseisen, *Stosunki wyznaniowe w relacjach państwo-kościół między reformacją a oświeceniem (Rzesza Niemiecka – Niderlandy Północne – Rzeczpospolita polsko-litewska)* (Warszawa: Wydawnictwo Naukowe Semper, 2010), esp. 533–660; idem, *Ewangelicy polscy i litewscy w epoce saskiej (1696–1763). Sytuacja prawna, organizacja i stosunki międzywyznaniowe*

competences of the religious community were heavily contested by internal schisms, new types of leaders, state authorities, as well as secular social institutions.[3] Such re-evaluations occurred similarly in other European countries. Yet, in terms of statehood, Poland in particular, from the early modern Polish-Lithuanian Commonwealth to the so-called Second Republic between 1918 and 1939 underwent radical territorial and political reconfigurations – namely the integration into three different empires in the late 18th century[4] and the re-building of statehood after 1918 – which implied reconfigurations in the status of the various religious communities as well as their individual members.[5] For a *longue durée* study of the interaction of religion and law, this means that there is no continuous status of religious minority vs. majority, but constellations in flux, as can be exemplified with the development of the previously underprivileged Uniate Church in Austrian-ruled Galicia in the long 19th century.[6]

(Warszawa: Semper, 1996), esp. 19–49; Tomasz Kempa, *Wobec Kontrreformacji: Protestanci i prawosławni w obronie swobód wyznaniowych w Rzeczypospolitej w końcu XVI i w pierwszej połowie XVII wieku* (Toruń: Wydawnictwo Adam Marszałek, 2007); Gershon D. Hundert, *Jews in Poland-Lithuania in the 18th Century: A Genealogy of Modernity* (Berkeley–Los Angeles: University of California Press, 2004); Adam Kaźmierczyk, *Żydzi w dobrach prywatnych w świetle sądowniczej i administracyjnej praktyki dóbr magnackich w wiekach XVI–XVIII* (Kraków: Uniwersytet Jagielloński, Katedra Judaistyki, 2002); Eli Lederhendler, *The Road to Modern Jewish Politics: Political Tradition and Political Reconstruction in the Jewish Community of Tsarist Russia* (New York–Oxford, 1989), 11–12, 26–28.

3 Helmut Reinalter, »Einleitung. Der Josephinismus als Variante des Aufgeklärten Absolutismus und seine Reformkomplexe,« in: Josephinismus als Aufgeklärter Absolutismus, ed. Helmut Reinalter (Wien–Köln–Weimar: Böhlau, 2008), 9–16; Lederhendler, *The Road to Modern Jewish Politics*, 36–57; Yvonne Kleinmann, *Neue Orte – neue Menschen. Jüdische Lebensformen in St. Petersburg und Moskau im 19. Jahrhundert* (Göttingen: Vandenhoeck & Ruprecht, 2006), 70–75, 290–302.

4 The initial phase is intensely analysed in Hans-Jürgen Bömelburg, Andreas Gestrich, Helga Schnabel-Schüle, eds., *Die Teilungen Polen-Litauens. Inklusions- und Exklusionsmechanismen, Traditionsbildung – Vergleichsebenen* (Osnabrück: fibre, 2013).

5 See the recent study by Stephan Stach, *Nationalitätenpolitik aus der zweiten Reihe. Konzepte und Praktiken zur Einbindung nationaler und ethnoreligiöser Minderheiten in Piłsudskis Polen* (1926–1939), Ph.D. thesis, Martin-Luther-Universität Halle-Wittenberg, 2014.

6 Larry Wolff, »The Uniate Church and the Partitions of Poland: Religious Survival in an Age of Enlightened Absolutism,« *Harvard Ukrainian Studies* 16, no. 1–4 (2002–2003): 153–244; Oleh Turiy, *Hreko-katolyts'ka tserkva v suspil'no-politychnomu zhytti Halychyny, 1848–1867*, Ph.D. thesis, Ivan Franko National University of Lviv, 1994; John-Paul Himka, *Religion and Nationality in Western Ukraine: The Greek Catholic Church and the Ruthenian National Movement in Galicia, 1867–1900* (Montreal: McGill-Queen's University Press, 1999).

Although research on the coexistence of ethno-religious communities in the outlined region is abundant, some aspects are underrepresented. Most studies are conceptually based on minority studies and focus on inferior legal status;[7] another research branch concentrates on ethno-religious conflict.[8] In contrast to these tendencies, two basic ideas were at the origins of this collection: First, a withdrawal from the ideological aspect of religious coexistence, particularly from the concentration on interreligious conflict. We departed from the simple observation that, over the centuries, severe juridical confrontation as well as mass violence occurred rather rarely[9] compared to the extended periods of unspectacular coexistence. We therefore paid special attention to the legal tools that formed the basis for cooperation, negotiation, mediation, and compromise between different religious communities and between individuals of different confessions. From this angle, conflict is seen as a dysfunctional moment or phase in a functioning system. Taking the above-mentioned political and economic aspects of religious communities into account, it also must be stressed that conflict between different religious groups or individuals did not necessarily occur for religious reasons.[10]

Secondly, we decided to adopt a concept of law beyond the examination of its normative and juridical aspects that are traditionally expressed in constitutions,

7 E. g. Adam Kaźmierczyk, Andrzej K. Link-Lenczowski, Mariusz Markiewicz and Krystyn Matwijowski, eds., *Rzeczpospolita wielu wyznań* (Kraków: Księgarnia Akademicka, 2004), esp. 391–495; Tomasz Ciesielski and Anna Filipczak-Kocur, eds., *Rzeczpospolita państwem wielu narodowości i wyznań, XVI–XVIII wiek* (Warszawa–Opole: Wydawnictwo DiG, 2008), esp. 263–380.

8 E. g. Barbara Skinner, *The Western Front of the Eastern Church: Uniate and Orthodox Conflict in 18th-Century Poland, Ukraine, Belarus, and Russia* (DeKalb, IL: Northern Illinois University Press, 2009); Magda Teter, *Jews and Heretics in Catholic Poland: A Beleaguered Church in the Post-Reformation Era* (Cambridge et al.: Cambridge University Press, 2006); Erich Fröschl, Maria Mesner, Uri Ra'anan, eds., *Staat und Nation in multi-ethnischen Gesellschaften* (Wien: Passagen Verlag, 1991), esp. 23–168.

9 The most prominent examples being the so-called Chmelnicki (Khmelnytsky) massacres in the mid-seventeenth century and the pogroms in the Ukrainian governments of tsarist Russia in 1881/1882 and 1905/1906. See e. g. Frank E. Sysyn, »The Jewish Factor in the Khmelnytsky Uprising,« in *Ukrainian-Jewish Relations in Historical Perspective*, eds. Howard Aster and Peter. J. Potichnyj (Edmonton: Canadian Institute of Ukrainian Studies Press, 1990), 43–53; John D. Klier and Shlomo Lambroza, eds., *Pogroms: Anti-Jewish Violence in Modern Russian History* (Cambridge: Cambridge University Press, 1992); Edward H. Judge, *Easter in Kishinev: Anatomy of a Pogrom* (New York: New York University Press, 1992); Jonathan Dekel-Chen, David Gaunt, Natan M. Meir, and Israel Bartal, eds., *Anti-Jewish Violence: Rethinking the Pogrom in East European History* (Bloomington: Indiana University Press, 2010).

10 See the articles by Jürgen Heyde and Yvonne Kleinmann in this volume.

laws and court proceedings. Some of the articles presented in this volume take narrative aspects of normative texts into account; others look at law as a cultural field that is closely interlinked with other social fields like politics, economy, and the arts. Legal anthropologist Lawrence Rosen has stressed that law is inextricably bound up with culture and that it should not merely be seen as a »mechanism for attending to disputes or enforcing decisions« but »as a framework for ordering relationships, an orderliness that is itself dependent on its attachment to all other realms of its adherents' lives.«[11] Another inspiration comes from Law and Society Studies, an approach that frequently stresses the links between law, institutions, and the public sphere.[12]

On this basis we look at law as a phenomenon that is often disconnected from the existence of a state and based in much smaller units. Therefore, various understandings of justice, the establishment of social institutions, the settling of disagreements beyond courts, etc. are considered as law. This kind of inquiry begins to look at law long before the establishment of legal norms by political rulers or governments and pays special attention to the evolutionary and dynamic character of law, the »pathways of law«.[13] Some of the articles therefore focus on »emergent« and »imagined« law rather than on law as a fixed norm or legal corpus.

The book assembles a great variety of approaches reaching from a close reading of normative texts, interpretations of legal theory, literature and press, biographical research, the analysis of institutions, through local and micro-studies. The individual articles are arranged into four clusters: *Imagining Law – Imagining Society* focuses on symbolic and idealistic functions of law rather than on its practical aspects, whereas the contributions to *Shifts in Political Rule and the Reorganization of Law* delve into the concrete consequences of establishing a new political power for different religious communities and their representatives. The authors of the section *Competing Laws – Competing Loyalties* scrutinize the fields of conflict between the state and religious communities as well as the legal

11 Lawrence Rosen, *Law as Culture: An Invitation* (Princeton–Oxford: Princeton University Press, 2008), 4–5, 7.

12 See for example, Lawrence M. Friedman, »The Law and Society Movement,« *Stanford Law Review* 38, no. 3 (1986): 763–780 and Alan Hunt, *Explorations in Law and Society: Toward a Constitutive Theory of Law* (London: Routledge, 1993). In addition, the Law and Society Association has published the *Law and Society Review* since 1966, and the British-based *Journal of Law and Society* has been published since 1982.

13 The term is based on the project *Pathways of Law in Ethno-Religiously Mixed Societies: Resources of Experience in Poland-Lithuania and Its Successor States*, funded by the German Research Foundation: http://www.religion-and-law-in-east-central-europe.de; http://gepris.dfg.de/gepris/projekt/56603816.

antagonism between different factions within religious communities. *Ethno-Religious Coexistence in Legal Norm and Practice* concentrates on regional and local studies on neighborly interaction, and forms of mediation between different religious groups.

Imagining law – imagining society

In recent decades, scholars of legal anthropology have analyzed how in a comparative sense specific contexts and expressions of law are linked to larger macro-level systems. They have conceptualized relationships between law, state and society at various levels and have acknowledged the important role that ideology plays as a cultural framework in which law is presented and practiced.[14] The sub-field of legal anthropology includes a range of perspectives and approaches to the study of law, in particular approaches that stress legal pluralism, performative aspects of law, and ideology that are especially useful for the study of religion and law in historical contexts. Nevertheless, very few scholars in the field have addressed historical topics.[15] One of the more compelling ways that legal anthropology is connected to law and religion in historical Eastern Europe is through frameworks that express ideology as well as the language and practices of empire.

The first section of this book examines various ways of thinking about law and what it means in specific contexts. One goal is to suggest more flexible concepts as a means of expanding the ways that scholars approach the study of law. This flexibility includes examining the connections of law to other aspects of life. In this regard it is also significant that the articles cross disciplinary boundaries and include approaches from literature, history, legal studies, and ethnography. The themes that the authors address include entanglements of law, society, and culture, the role of social networks and activism, and the concept of performance. In this regard they are close to approaches espoused by Austrian legal

14 Franz and Keebet von Benda-Beckmann, »How Communal is Communal and Whose Communal is it? Lessons from Minangkabau,« in *Changing Properties of Property*, eds. Franz and Keebet von Benda-Beckmann and Melanie Wiber (Oxford: Berghahn, 2006), 194–217; Franz and Keebet von Benda-Beckmann, »Einleitung,« in *Gesellschaftliche Wirkung von Recht. Rechtsethnologische Perspektiven*, eds. Idem (Berlin: Reimer, 2007), 7–19.

15 Some exceptions include Andrea L. Smith, »Citizenship in the Colony: Naturalization Law and Legal Assimilation in 19th Century Algeria,« Political and Legal Anthropology Review 19, no. 1 (1996): 34–49; Jean and John Commaroff, *Of Revelation and Revolution: The Dialectics of Modernity on a South African Frontier* (Chicago et al.: University of Chicago Press, 1997); the above-mentioned text by Lawrence Rosen also includes analysis of historical contexts.

scholar Eugen Ehrlich, writing at the turn of the 20th century in Czernowitz, Bukovina at the eastern periphery of the Austrian Empire. Ehrlich, often regarded as the founder of the field of the sociology of law,[16] stressed the importance of studying law as a component of society. He also emphasized the importance of examining how law functioned in life rather than merely regarding law that existed in written texts.[17]

The idea of »performance« is central in this section, though interpretations of this concept vary.[18] Studies which focus on the performative aspect of law and analyze the processes by which legal disputes are negotiated are especially useful in revealing the everyday workings of law and often provide a counter to more abstract notions of the ways in which law works. Performance approaches can also demonstrate the ways that the negotiation and implementation of law take on theatrical qualities and provide contexts for the performance and display of power.[19]

In addition, this section underscores the notion that law exists beyond normative categories of law. For example, it shows that imperial authorities were well aware of the important role that art and social institutions played in lending legitimacy to or to undermining the empire. Each of the authors addresses law and its connections to ethnic and religious identity. A common theme is how concepts of religious identity changed over time, and how social activism and networks challenged previous categories and shaped new ones.

Jürgen Heyde's article deals with legal discourse and its political functions in 16th-century Poland, namely with the Sejm's anti-Jewish legislation around 1538. The author stresses that although at first glance the legislation appears to have endangered the legal, social, and economic position of the Jews, later documentation reveals that the laws were never put into practice. A closer interpretation demonstrates that the anti-Jewish legislation of the Sejm in actual fact mirrored the nobles' effort to reduce the king's power. Heyde points to the

16 See among others Marc Hertogh. *Living Law: Reconsidering Eugen Ehrlich* (Oxford: Hart, 2009).

17 Eugen Ehrlich, *Fundamental Principles of the Sociology of Law* (New Brunswick: Transaction Publishers, 2001 [1913]).

18 Key texts include Richard Bauman, *Verbal Art as Performance* (Prospect Heights, IL: Waveland Press, 1977); idem, *Let Your Words Be Few: Symbolism of Speaking and Silence among Seventeenth Century Quakers* (London: Cambridge University Press, 1998); Richard Bauman and Charles L. Briggs, »Poetics and Performance as Critical Perspectives on Language and Social Life,« *Annual Review of Anthropology* 19 (1990), 59–88; Judith Butler, *Bodies That Matter: On the Discursive Limits of Sex* (London: Routledge, 1993) and *Gender Trouble: Feminism and the Subversion of Identity* (London: Routledge, 1990).

19 See for example, Beverly J. Stoeltje, »Gender Ideologies and Discursive Practices in Asante,« PoLAR: Political and Legal Anthropology Review 23 (2000): 77–88.

performative aspects of law-making in the Polish Sejm and claims that political discourse on a religious group functioned as a means of negotiating social hierarchies between other actors and setting standards for social discipline. Judaism in the sense of theological positions and ritual, he argues, was not the object of attack. His analysis considers discrepancies between the law on the books and what occurred in actual practice – an aspect of what Ehrlich has described as »the living law.« He explains these gaps as expressions of the nobles' striving to compete against the king for sovereignty over the Jews.

Anna Juraschek's article on the reinterpretation of Shakespeare's character Shylock in the *Merchant of Venice* by the Austrian novelist Karl Emil Franzos in the late 19th century explores the connections between legal scholarship and literature. The focus is on various depictions of Shylock and the influence of the ideas of legal scholar Rudolf von Jhering on Franzos' work. Juraschek demonstrates changes in the author's depiction of the problematic character, shifting from ambivalence in *Der Shylock von Barnow* (1868–1872) to portraying him as a more positive force in *Der Pojaz* (1895). In fact, in his later work, due to the impact of Jhering's legal thinking and elaboration of the famous court case in Shakespeare's *The Merchant of Venice*, Franzos ultimately recast his Shylock as a Jewish civil rights activist. Juraschek addresses the ways that literary and theatrical representations are reframed to comment on the situation of Habsburg Jewry in the 19th century, demonstrating that literature can be both inspired by and play a role in promoting legal concepts.[20]

According to *Jana Osterkamp*, historical debates over legal reforms provide an ideal context in which to explore both the constructedness of confessional communities and the normativeness of law. Referring to Benedict Anderson's concept of »imagined communities,«[21] she introduces the concept of »imagined law,« which she defines as »law that cannot yet be implemented.« More specifically, she examines the promise that federalization might have held for the Habsburg Empire, arguing that it had the potential of allowing ethnic and religious groups to develop into new political and legal territorial bodies. The text explores how collectives are formed and how they change the state and legal order. For example, Osterkamp claims that municipal self-government changed the Jewish community from merely a religious institution to a »political corporative body,« allowing for personal autonomy. However, even as the legal

20 Another example of connections between literature and legal concepts is Lynn Hunt's *Inventing Human Rights: A History* (London: W. W. Norton & Co., 2007), which makes the case that emergence of the novel as an influential literary genre played an significant role in expanding support for the concept of human rights.

21 Benedict R. Anderson, *Imagined Communities: Reflections on the Origin and Spread of Nationalism* (London: Verso, 2006), originally published in 1983.

position of Austrian Jewry became more negotiable, the Austrian administration and courts were not prepared to fully alter its status.

Tracie Wilson's article on women's charity and anti-sex-trafficking associations in Lviv explores changing legal concepts in the context of social activism at the turn of the 20th century. Drawing on the work of Eugen Ehrlich, she introduces the concept of »emergent law« to refer to institutional shifts and innovative thinking about law and social practices that were undergoing change and becoming increasingly accepted. The author analyses legal aspects of changes taking place regarding categories of membership, increased participation of women in public life, the development of supra-ethnic and religious consciousness with regard to charity, and the influence of charity organizations in enforcing morality and law. Based on an ethnographic perspective, Wilson's article examines the processes through which institutions were made more inclusive and examines the role of legal concepts in shaping the practices of religious institutions and social activist networks. Such examples demonstrate that the social acceptance of new concepts and practices was also rooted in culture.

Shifts in political rule and the reorganization of law

As law is and has always been highly dependent on political rulers or representatives who codify law and are responsible in their executive role for its organization and enforcement, changes in political rule often result in legal reorganization of society. This holds true for the territories of Poland-Lithuania that were incorporated into the Habsburg, Prussian, and Russian Empires as the result of the partitions of Poland-Lithuania in the late 18th century, as well as for the creation of an independent Polish state following World War I, when largely the same territories formed the new Republic. In both processes, the integration of annexed territories into the three empires, as well as the reunion of most of these territories into one state, legal regulation and law had to be reshaped in order to fit the new political and social situations. These processes took place at various levels of society.

Helga Schnabel-Schüle has pointed out in her considerations of shifts in political rule (*Herrschaftswechsel*) that, to begin with, the new ruler had to legitimize his or her authority.[22] She draws on the typology of rule by Max Weber who observed that legitimacy can be derived from three sources:

22 Helga Schnabel-Schüle, »Herrschaftswechsel – zum Potential einer Forschungskategorie,« in *Fremde Herrscher – fremdes Volk. Inklusions- und Exklusionsfiguren bei Herrschaftswechseln in Europa*, eds. eadem and Andreas Gestrich (Frankfurt a. M. et al.: Lang, 2006), 5–20, here 6–7.

charismatic, traditional, and rational-legal rule. In his view charismatic rule is based on emotional devotion to a person considered to be exceptionally able to lead, whereas traditional rule derives its power from the supposed holiness (*Heiligkeit*) of the ruling order. In turn, rational-legal rule draws its legitimacy from the popular perception that authority is based on commonly accepted laws and customs.[23]

If rule was based on holiness it necessarily related to religion as well so that religious difference between the ruler and his new subjects could pose a threat to his legitimacy. In practice, however, both the Romanov and the Habsburg administrations generally proved to be able to integrate religious difference into their imperial rule. While the status of a religion could change – as in the case of Catholicism in the former Polish territories coming under Tsarist rule – the imperial bureaucracies were willing to cooperate with religious communities, and integrated religious elites into their system of state administration.[24] The Austrian Empire, for instance, raised the status of the Uniate Church in Galicia, renaming it Greek-Catholic and cultivating a loyal clergy in the process.[25] Authorities of the Tsarist Empire also made use of religious communities under the »spiritual administration« of the state to strengthen their rule.[26] Nevertheless, as the case of the Uniate Church shows, which was abolished in the Russian Empire in 1839, imperial tolerance ended if a religious community that was considered to be inferior challenged the position of the monarch's faith.[27] The major source of legitimacy for a ruler was not to be called into question. However, empires not only drew their legitimacy from the religion of the ruler himself, but in cases where no direct conflict between his religion and that of his subjects occurred, religious communities were usually integrated into the administrational framework of the state, as for instance in the registry of births

23 Max Weber, *Wirtschaft und Gesellschaft, Grundriss der verstehenden Soziologie* (Tübingen: Mohr, ^{5}1972), 124.

24 Mikhail D. Dolbilov, *Russkii krai, chuzhaia vera: Etnokonfessional'naia politika imperii v Litve i Belorussii pri Aleksandre II* (Moskva: Novoe literaturnoe obozrenie, 2010), 17.

25 John Paul Himka, »The Greek Catholic Church and Nation-Building in Galicia, 1772–1918,« *Harvard Ukrainian Studies* 8, nos. 3/4 (1984): 426–452; Ivan L. Rudnytsky, »Galicia under Austrian Rule,« in *Essays in Modern Ukrainian History*, ed. idem (Edmonton: CIUS, 1987), 325–352.

26 Heinz-Dietrich Löwe, »Poles, Jews, and Tartars: Religion, Ethnicity, and Social Structure in Tsarist Nationality Policies,« *Jewish Social Studies* 6, no. 3 (2000): 52–96.

27 Theodore R. Weeks, »Between Rome and Tsargrad: The Uniate Church in Imperial Russia,« in *Of Religion and Empire, Missions, Conversions, and Tolerance in Tsarist Russia*, eds. Robert P. Geraci, and Michael Khodarkovsky (Ithaca, NY: Cornell University Press: 2001), 70–91, here 75.

and deaths, and helped to uphold the social order. In exchange, the clergy of these communities received certain material benefits, education, as well as high social status.[28] This privileged position, in turn, could lead to alienation and thus to conflicts between the clergy and the communities they were meant to serve.[29]

The emergence of new self-appointed ethno-religious elites who became integrated into the imperial administration also led to re-negotiations of power within the different communities. During changes in governance, the ruling elites struggled to hold on to their positions, while new groups sought the support of the new rulers to advance their standing.[30] Religious communities were one arena where such struggles took place.[31]

When in the second half of the 19th century national movements in Eastern Europe gained momentum, many religious practices were adapted by national cults. Frequently national movements integrated religion into their vision of the nation, thus providing a modern justification for religion.[32] Religious communities became objects of nationalization and often even vehicles of national movements. Especially in multinational empires, but also in young nation states, where national minority movements had limited opportunities for institutionalization, nationalized religious communities served as their organizational backbone. This development is particularly evident in the close connection of

28 Himka, »The Greek-Catholic Church,« 428–429; Oleh Turij, »Die griechisch-katholische Kirche und die ukrainische nationale Identität in Galizien im 19. Jahrhundert,« in *Konfessionelle Identität und Nationsbildung. Die griechisch-katholischen Kirchen in Ostmittel- und Südosteuropa im 19. und 20. Jahrhundert*, eds. Hans-Christian Maner and Norbert Spannenberger (Stuttgart: Franz-Steiner-Verlag, 2007), 41–49, here 43; Löwe, »Poles, Jews, and Tatars,« 65–67.

29 See the article by Oksana Leskiv in this volume.

30 On old and new Jewish elites see Eli Lederhendler, *The Road to Modern Jewish Politics: Political Tradition and Political Reconstruction in the Jewish Community of Tsarist Russia* (New York–Oxford: Oxford University Press, 1989), 84–110; Isaac Levitats, *The Jewish Community in Russia, 1772–1844* (New York: Columbia University Press, 1943), 69–86.

31 On the concept of *arenas* see Karsten Holste, Dietlind Hüchtker, and Michal G. Müller, »Aufsteigen und Obenbleiben in europäischen Gesellschaften des 19. Jahrhunderts. Akteure – Arenen – Aushandlungsprozesse,« in *Aufsteigen und Obenbleiben in europäischen Gesellschaften des 19. Jahrhunderts. Akteure – Arenen – Aushandlungsprozesse*, eds. idem (Berlin: Akademie-Verlag, 2009), 9–19, here 9–11. On the competition of different groups within one religious community see Yvonne Kleinmann, »Jüdische Eliten, polnische Traditionen, westliche Modelle und russische Herrschaft. Kulminationen in den Jahren 1804, 1844, 1869 und 1881,« in *Ibid.*, 193–222.

32 Martin Schulze Wessel, »Einleitung,« in *Nationalisierung der Religion und Sakralisierung der Nation im östlichen Europa* (Stuttgart: Franz Steiner Verlag, 2006), 7–14.

the Polish national movement with the Roman Catholic Church during the 19th century[33] as well as in the entanglement of Ukrainian nationalism with the Greek Catholic Church.[34] It accompanied a direct interconnection of national and religious affiliation in 19th century imperial discourses, where Roman Catholic and Polish or Greek Catholic and Ruthenian/Ukrainian became largely synonymous.[35]

The interconnection of religion and nationality became even more powerful in independent Poland, when the state administration used religion, along with the people's native languages, to determine the nationality of the state's population.[36] Thus, while the nation, in some ways, replaced religion as a source of legitimacy of rule, religion still remained an important component of national belonging. In this context religious communities were seen as a kind of natural mediator between the state and the various national groups. Therefore, confessional politics became an important part of the state's nationality policy and ongoing legal regulation of one's religious community became of vital importance for the respective nation or nationality.[37]

The articles in this section focus on changes in the legal position of religious communities evoked by changes in political rule from different perspectives. *Angela Rustemeyer* analyses the limits of the tsarist administration's ability to integrate religious communities into the new imperial framework. She delves into confessional, legal, and institutional conflict following the annexation of the eastern parts of Poland-Lithuania, using the example of a court case involving alleged blasphemy in the Belarusian territories after the first partition of Poland-Lithuania. According to the author, Catherine II deepened the already existing lines of religious and ethnic conflict in the cities by integrating the Jews into the urban community in a reform of urban law, and also provoked new conflicts between Uniate burghers and the Orthodox Church. Rustemeyer demonstrates how this development led the tsarist government to withdraw from its conventional strategy of integrating religious authorities of the various

33 Jerzy Kloczowski, *A History of Polish Christianity* (Cambridge: Cambridge University Press, 2000), 215–252.

34 On the role of the Greek Catholic Church in the Ukrainian movement see Turij, »Die griechisch-katholische Kirche,« and John-Paul Himka, »The place of Religion in the Ukrainian National Revival,« in *Nationalisierung der Religion*, ed. Schulze Wessel, 89–99. On the role of the Orthodox Church see Ricarda Vulpius, »Kirchenkampf in der Ukraine als Beispiel für die Sakralisierung der Religion und die Nationalsierung der Religion (1917–1921),« in *Ibid.*, 101–118.

35 Weeks, »Between Rome and Tsargrad«.

36 Henschel and Stach, *Nationalisierung und Pragmatismus*.

37 On the example of the Jewish communities see Stach, *Nationalitätenpolitik aus der zweiten Reihe*, 225–239.

confessions into state government, and to criminalize adherents of the Uniate Church. As she argues, the reasons for this were mainly rooted in the proximity of the Orthodox and the Uniate Churches. The Uniate Church was thus suppressed because it was not different enough to fit into the imperial Russian system that tolerated controlled diversity.

In the Austrian Empire the fate of the Uniate Church was completely different as *Oksana Leskiv* demonstrates in her biographical article on the priest and Ukrainian national figure Iosif Levytskyi: Renamed as Greek-Catholic, its status was elevated under the new ruler which in turn provoked conflicts between the privileged priests and their communities. In her microstudy, Leskiv examines how the relation of Greek-Catholic priests and peasants in Galicia changed as a consequence of enlightened absolutist rule under Maria Theresa and Joseph II. Due to their reforms, she argues, in the medium term, priests became part of the imperial administration and received academic training which led to an improvement of their social status, but also often resulted in their alienation from rural society. Therefore, the claim of many Greek-Catholic priests to take a leading position in the emerging Ukrainian national movement was thwarted by their growing personal distance to the peasants, the nucleus of that nation. In addition, the abolishment of serfdom strengthened the self-confidence of the peasants who began to question the privileges of the clergy. In her analysis of the trial against Iosyf Levytskyi in the mid-19th century, Leskiv exemplifies the economic conflicts and the struggle for dominance that emerged from these developments.

Hanna Kozińska-Witt, who delves into municipal self-government in Austrian Krakow in the second half of the 19th century, exemplifies to what extent the new imperial order stimulated changes in the local legal system, in the division of urban space, and the emergence of new elites: The integration of the former free city of Krakow into the Habsburg Empire went along with several changes, such as the emancipation of the Jewish population and reforms of communal law that materialized in a new municipal statute. At the same time, the spatial division between Jewish and Christian areas in the city decreased. Under these circumstances, the author argues, the newly consolidated »progressive« Jews – a secularly educated, rather marginalized group within the Jewish community – used the implementation of federal law to increase their influence in municipal politics as well as in the Jewish Community vis-à-vis its Orthodox majority.

The rising interference between religious communities and national groups is addressed by *Stephan Stach*, who examines the Institute for Nationality Research in independent Poland after World War I: Initially founded as an institution that was meant to provide the government with scholarly-based policy advice on nationality questions, after Józef Piłsudski's coup d'état in 1926 it became an important forum of communication between the state administration, politicians, and representatives of the national minorities. Due to the weakening of the parliament, Stach claims, the institute served as a mediator between the national minorities and the government: While the latter sought information and advice for its projects on the legal regulation of religious communities, the minorities' representatives used this channel to promote their propositions and shape such regulations. Using the examples of the Orthodox Church and the Jewish communities the author demonstrates that even though the government was interested in the minorities' opinion on these issues, it only considered concessions to the minorities' demands when they went along with other political benefits.

Competing laws – competing loyalties

Shifts in political rule always led to the reorganization of law, at times also to competition between legal systems and – at least temporarily – to legal pluralism, as understood according to John Griffiths' classical definition as a »state of affairs, for any social field, in which behavior pursuant to more than one legal order occurs.«[38] In the phase immediately after annexation, the continental empires of the 19th century, for the sake of social peace, relied strongly on the cooperation with traditional elites in their newly conquered territories. The imposition of political control depended on mediators in the annexed societies who were ready and able to communicate the rulers' expectations to their newly acquired subjects, and to explain the latter's traditions to the new rulers. Imperial administrations needed time to begin to grasp foreign cultures, namely languages and legal traditions. Jane Burbank has analyzed this ratio of the empire using the example of tsarist Russia;[39] she has also studied how non-Russian local elites developed into junior partners of and even merged with the imperial administration practicing ethno-religious legal traditions, while at the same time accepting the superior authority of tsarist rule. As a result initial legal pluralism turned into a differentiated »imperial rights regime«[40] or in other words into a system of derivative power.

Religious elites – in the Russian as well as in the Austrian Empire – played a prominent role as holders of derivative power. In the annexed non-Christian

38 John Griffiths, »What is legal pluralism?« in *Journal of Legal Pluralism* 24 (1986): 1–55, here 2.

39 Jane Burbank, »Thinking like an Empire: Estate, Law, and Rights in the Early Twentieth Century,« in *Russian Empire: Space, People, Power, 1700–1930*, eds. Jane Burbank, Mark von Hagen, and Anatolyi Remnev (Bloomington: Indiana University Press, 2007), 196–217.

40 Eadem, »An Imperial Rights Regime: Law and Citizenship in the Russian Empire,« *Kritika* 7, no. 3 (2006), 397–431, here 400–402.

societies, namely the Jewish society at the western periphery of tsarist Russia and the northeastern periphery of the Habsburg Empire, law and jurisdiction originated in religious law. The same was true for Muslim peoples in the southeastern regions of the Russian Empire whose legal system was rooted in *Sharia*.[41] The imperial administrations of the 19th century were essentially at ease with these traditions, as one of their principles was to »outsource« at least one legal sphere, namely marital law, to the various religious communities.[42] However, this decision was based on a rather homogeneous understanding of religion in these »traditional« societies whereas in the course of modernization – marked by industrialization, urbanization, the emergence of secular education and science – important changes took place. It was mainly enlightened thought and secular social movements that challenged the monopoly of religious authorities in this sphere. Competing with the established religious elites emerging secular elites also tried to win over the empires' rulers to gain their cooperation.[43] Therefore special attention has to be paid to competing understandings of law within the individual communities, which in some ways were turning from religious into increasingly ethno-national entities.

In the present volume two articles examine the partly concurring, partly competing understandings of law of the imperial administration, religious communities, and individual actors. *Dror Segev* delves into different interpretations of Jewish law (*Halakhah*) as well as into the competition of Jewish and imperial law in late tsarist Russia. His test case is the debate on Jewish burial, which according to orthodox rabbis, had to take place on the day of death whereas imperial law on the basis of medical expertise prescribed a wake of three days. Segev focuses on the evolution of this controversy on the pages of the Hebrew press of the 1880s that emerged as a new public sphere. He analyses the tactics of Jewish enlighteners (*Maskilim*) who, through press accounts, tried to discredit the practice of immediate burial as a dangerous superstitious custom before the tsarist authorities, as well as the response of orthodox rabbis who claimed that immediate burial was part and parcel of Jewish law and therefore not negotiable. At a second level, he examines the position of the imperial administration that considered immediate burial as intolerable interference into

41 Robert D. Crews, »Islamic Law, Imperial Order. Muslims, Jews, and the Russian State,« *Ab Imperio* 2004, no. 3: 467–490; idem, *For Prophet and Tsar: Islam and Empire in Russia and Central Asia* (Cambridge, Mass.: Harvard University Press, 2006).

42 Burbank, »An Imperial Rights Regime«, 407–410.

43 Kleinmann, »Jüdische Eliten, polnische Traditionen, westliche Modelle und russische Herrschaft«.

its legal sovereignty, but due to a lack of medical personnel and police officers was not able to control such circumventions.

Vladimir Levin analyses the interaction between orthodox rabbis and tsarist administrators in the sphere of law from 1908 to 1910. He focuses on the preparations, proceedings, and outcome of the sixth Rabbinical Commission, an irregular assembly of state-elected rabbis within the Ministry of the Interior that was established in 1848 in order to provide the government with expertise in Jewish religion and law. Levin describes the activities of the numerous Russian and Polish rabbis as an effort to achieve a coalition between Jewish Orthodoxy and the tsarist government against strong secularizing tendencies, and the revolutionary movement in particular. For the rabbis involved this mainly implied strengthening the power of *Halakhah* within the imperial system of law, which was consistent in part with Russian legislation that generally delegated the vast field of marital issues to the legal institutions of the various religious communities. Nevertheless, he claims, the interests of the rabbis did not match with those of the tsarist government, which, like other European imperial powers of the time, tried to increase control over its subjects and rejected any autonomous strivings. In legal practice, however, Levin observes that there was actually little friction between state law and Jewish law so that the Russian Empire was a relatively safe place for observant Jews.

The strong interconnection of religious and communal leadership with political power must be seen as principally accepted characteristics of the imperial system of the 19th century, which admitted concurring religious, ethno-national, as well as imperial loyalties.[44] This compatibility was called into question by at least some actors when national states were proclaimed and established beginning in 1918. If we consider nation, religion, confession, social group, and ideological adherence in the new nation states not as aspects of »identity« but as expressions of »loyalty«, the focus of analysis can be placed on the various relations within ethno-religious communities, between ethno-religious groups, between these groups and the new governments.[45] From this perspective the question arises as to how the multiple loyalties of the imperial

44 For the Habsburg Empire this has been verified by various case studies in Laurence Cole and Daniel L. Unowsky, eds., *The Limits of Loyalty: Imperial Symbolism, Popular Allegiances, and State Patriotism in the Late Habsburg Monarchy* (New York et al.: Berghahn Books, 2007).

45 On the concept of loyalty as a relational category see Martin Schulze Wessel, »Loyalität als geschichtlicher Grundbegriff und Forschungskonzept: Eine Einleitung,« in *Loyalitäten in der Tschechoslowakischen Republik 1918–1938. Politische, nationale und kulturelle Zugehörigkeiten*, ed. idem (München: Oldenbourg, 2004), 1–22.

period reconfigured during the shift of political rule, and whether they were compatible with the new understanding of the state and its monopolies.

Liliana Hentosh explores this question using the example of the Greek Catholic Church hierarchy's changing political and legal status in Galicia after the collapse of the Austrian Empire. Like Oksana Leskiv she takes a biographical approach analyzing the political career of Andrei Sheptytskyi who by appointment of the Vatican and the Austrian emperor in 1900 served for forty years as the Archbishop of Lviv and Metropolitan of Halych. Her investigation concentrates on the question of ambivalent loyalties during the shift from imperial rule to competing Ukrainian and Polish national states. Hentosh stresses that Sheptytskyi, who came from a Polish-Ruthenian family, had faced no choice of national belonging during imperial times and as the head of the Greek Catholic Church had enjoyed the status of a Habsburg official. After 1918, both his prominent political status as a cleric and his dual nationality, she claims, were unacceptable to the political leaders of the young nation states. Sheptytskyi's efforts to mediate between the competing national groups during the Ukrainian-Polish War (1918–1919) and at the international negotiations on the status of Eastern Galicia at the peace conference in Paris (1919–1923) were therefore to no avail. As a result, the metropolitan had to withdraw from political activity and through a symbolic oath swore loyalty to the Polish state while his Greek Catholic community drew him into the Ukrainian national movement.

Ethno-religious coexistence in legal norm and practice

Throughout the entire period under consideration, the various ethno-religious communities and their individual members did not enjoy equal legal status. During the early modern period, personality of law, which meant that everyone was treated before the court in accordance with the law of his or her religious community or social estate, was the norm.[46]

Throughout the long 19th century, the confession of the empires' monarchs and at the same time of the dominant ethno-religious group enjoyed a privileged status while other confessions were tolerated in principle, but in practice often played a subordinate role in public life. Access to higher education and to state service was granted to members of some minority groups only gradually and not always permanently.[47] Only the establishment of democratic states and the

46 Gillian R. Evans, *Law and Theology in the Middle Ages* (London et al.: Routledge, 2002), 87–90.

47 On the Jewish case see Benjamin Nathans, *Beyond the Pale: The Jewish Encounter with Late Imperial Russia* (Berkeley et al.: University of California Press, 2002), 201–309.

Soviet Union after World War I guaranteed full citizenship and equal rights to all residents regardless of their religious background. If we, however, take the example of Poland's March Constitution from 1921, Catholicism again received a leading position in the state, even though freedom of religion was generally granted.[48] In stark contrast, religious institutions of any confession were closed down in the early Soviet Union.[49]

But what happens when we dissociate ourselves from these macro-categories? Mainly two questions come to the fore: 1. How were legal norms concerning hierarchies of religious communities put into practice, particularly in places where quantitative proportions did not correlate with the legal minority status? In other words, what role should be attributed to local solutions of ethno-religious coexistence, and should they prevent us from making generalizations?[50] 2. Who were the mediators between coexisting, at times competing religious communities, and what legal instruments did they use or develop for the purpose of successful cohabitation and mutual benefit?

It is in this sense that the contributions to this section explore regional and local constellations and partly focus on sophisticated instruments of legal interaction. *Anat Vaturi* undertakes a thorough revision of the many juridical and administrative functions of the Krakow voivode, the most important royal office holder in the early modern city, particularly with regard to his role in Catholic-Jewish interaction. Whereas older studies have stressed the voivodes' responsibility for jurisdiction over the Jews and classified their judgements as partly anti-Jewish, Vaturi draws our attention to their less visible activities, namely their interventions on behalf of peaceful Catholic-Jewish coexistence. Through a re-reading of privileges, court decrees, and administrative regulations she comes to the conclusion that it was the voivodes' many functions which enabled them to act as successful mediators in conflicts between Catholics and Jews: In cases when their juridical authority could not reach into the Catholic sphere they used their administrative competences to arrange settlements between the competing groups. Another strategy, she claims, was the bi-religious composition of the voievode's court that protected Jews from exclusively Catholic jurisdiction. Therefore, one can conclude that the voievodes fostered

48 See esp. articles 111 and 114, http://libr.sejm.gov.pl/tek01/txt/kpol/e1921.html (accessed March 20, 2016).

49 William B. Husband, *»Godless Communists«: Atheism and Society in Soviet Russia, 1917–1932* (DeKalb: Northern Illinois University Press, 2000), 36–68.

50 An example was provided by Anna Reid who gave up writing a general history of Ukraine in favor of a history of the most prominent Ukrainian cities and towns. See Anna Reid, *Borderland: A Journey through the History of Ukraine* (New York: Basic Books, 2015).

interreligious dialogue through administrative means and soft skills rather than through normative law.

Yvonne Kleinmann also looks, in a different way, at instruments of mediation in a religiously heterogeneous setting. She undertakes a close reading of the town and guild privileges issued to the burghers and artisans in early modern Rzeszów, a medium-sized town under noble rule in Red Ruthenia, inquiring as to how religious diversity was reflected (or ignored) in these documents. First of all she states that, deviating from other towns, no privileges were addressed specifically at the Jewish population, whereas Jews, Roman Catholics, as well as small Protestant groups were the addressees of common general privileges. What sense could it make to the town lords, she asks, to integrate all groups into one privilege? In her further analysis she identifies the town privileges themselves as a means of maintaining the social peace between the Magdeburg law community of well-established Christian burghers and Jewish newcomers. The guiding principles, she claims, were proportional shares in taxation and maintenance of the town, mutual responsibility, the acceptance of the Magdeburg law courts in Christian-Jewish legal interaction, as well as neutrality in religious matters. In contrast, the privileges issued to the mixed guilds clearly expressed the Catholic artisans' efforts to impose Catholic symbols and rituals.

Maria Cieśla delves into the often neglected specifics of the early modern Grand Duchy of Lithuania. She raises the question whether there was legal equality between Jewish dwellers and Christian burghers in the cities and towns of the Grand Duchy. Though some sources claim that this was the case, using four issues, she demonstrates that the legal and social status of Jews differed substantially from that of Christians – both in normative law and in practice: On the basis of the privileges granted to them the Jews generally had no political rights within the cities, but did organize their own communities. As subjects of the king or of the magnate owning the city, they were subordinate to a different jurisdiction, which at least in some spheres granted them a higher legal status than the Christian burghers'. Cieśla acknowledges that a more or less equal treatment of Jews and Christians developed in terms of taxation whereas the economic activity of Jewish artisans and traders was much more restricted than that of their Christian peers. Differentiating between legal norm and practice, she points out that in everyday life the townsfolk tended toward cooperation, resulting, for example, in consultation with the Jewish communities by the towns' magistrates or in agreements to overlook restrictions imposed on Jewish artisans.

Moving our focus to the Russian imperial framework of the 19th century, *Eugene Avrutin* scrutinizes everyday legal disputes between neighbors of different religious and ethnic groups in the northwest provinces in the mid-nineteenth century. He argues that, although various minor quarrels occurred, archival documents reveal few cases of intense conflict between members of different ethno-religious groups. Instead, when neighbors were unable to broker disputes satisfactorily among themselves, they made use of legal resources available in the form of civil courts. Avrutin examines the ways that imperial law could serve individuals to address disputes in three key contact zones: the neighborhood, the noble estate, and the marketplace. The central focus is on the ways that Jews and their mostly Catholic and Russian Orthodox neighbors made use of conflicting aspects of imperial law to settle quarrels and disputes over property, contractual obligations, and debt. Through the analysis of a series of court cases Avrutin implements claims made by supporters of the *New Imperial History*[51] over the last decade, based in the exploration of regional interactions rather than top-down relations between the tsarist government and its imperial subjects.

Yvonne Kleinmann, Stephan Stach, Tracie L. Wilson

51 Among others Ilya Gerasimov, Sergey Glebov, Jan Kusber, Marina Mogilner, and Alexander Semyonov, »New Imperial History and the Challenges of Empire,« in *Empire Speaks Out: Languages of Rationalization and Self-Description in the Russian Empire*, eds. Ilya Gerasimow, Jan Kusber, and Alexander Semyonov (Leiden–Boston: Brill, 2009), 3–32.

Imagining Law – Imagining Society

Polemics and Participation: Anti-Jewish Legislation in the Polish Diet in the 16th Century and its Political Context

During the 16th century, religion and religious differences played a major role in political debates and in law-making in Poland. While these discussions were mainly centred on the Reformation and the Catholic Church's reaction to it, they were of a political and not a theological character and therefore focussed on the topics of rights, freedoms, and their potential or actual infringement in connection with religious arguments. During the sessions of the Polish Diet (*Sejm*), religious arguments served as a means of negotiating concepts of political order. This especially concerned the relations between the king and the estates, or – in other words – the range and limitations of royal power versus the personal and political liberties of the nobility.

Debates on religion also served as a means of negotiating the social order and delimitating social discipline – and in this regard they also affected Jews. The present paper addresses legislation concerning the Jewish population which was passed in an atmosphere of political as well as religious tension in the middle decades of the 16th century. I examine the social and political groups promoting these laws and the arguments they brought forward in the debates. While it is impossible to trace the specific actors, the persons responsible for drawing up the legislature, or the participants of the Sejm debates, one can attribute the arguments to certain social groups – burghers, clergy, middle nobility (*szlachta*) – and thus gain insight into the political agenda behind the laws.

The laws – known in early modern Polish political terminology as Constitution or *constitutio* – passed at the Sejm conventions in Piotrków 1538 and in Cracow 1539 both seem to indicate a major shift in the legal status of the Jewish population in the Kingdom of Poland. The Constitution of Piotrków included a number of regulations concerning the Jewish population that constricted their economic and social position in the Kingdom of Poland. Most surprisingly, although these laws were passed with the consent of the king and the nobility, after the Diet, neither the king nor the nobles took any measures to enforce them in practice. Nevertheless, during the following decades, the Sejm Constitution of 1538 was repeated several times by the Diet, only again to be neglected in legal practice. The Constitution of Cracow issued in 1539 did not show an anti-Jewish bias, as it chiefly involved the relations between the king and the nobility: King Sigismund (Zygmunt) I renounced his exclusive right to the highest jurisdiction over the Jewish population in the kingdom, granting the nobility the right to pass judgement over the Jews living on their property. While this constitution was put into practice, the Piotrków legislation of 1538 was not. This article attempts to provide an explanation for this fact.[1]

There were often cases of laws not being enforced in the early modern period, not only in Poland-Lithuania, but all over Europe. Michel Foucault identified a similar tendency in his study on the movement in favour of a reform of the juridical system in late 18th-century France. He pointed out that early modern law was characterized by intensive law-making processes, which differed significantly from law-making in modern times. In retrospect, early modern laws appear to have been lacking in efficiency and showed a considerable amount of arbitrariness in their application.[2] Jürgen Schlumbohm has drawn from Foucault's thought and – using examples from German territories – puts forward the proposition that non-abidance by the law might even be characteristic of early modern legal systems.[3] As he points out, the reasons for this well-known phenomenon are more complex than they might seem at first glance. He discusses problems of administrative organisation, i.e. the technical implementation of laws, the important question of the acceptance of legal norms in society, as well as performative aspects of law-making.

In this paper I would like to stress these last points – acceptance in society and the performative aspects of law-making. Unlike Schlumbohm, who discussed the performative character of law as a means for the authorities to demonstrate their power over their subjects, I will draw attention to aspects of negotiation in the course of law-making procedures, which leads to several further questions: Who are the actors of these negotiations, where do their main interests lie – even

1 For a closer analysis, including a discussion of older works, see Adam Kaźmierczyk, *Żydzi w dobrach prywatnych w świetle sądowniczej i administracyjnej praktyki dóbr magnackich w wiekach XVI–XVIII* (Kraków: Uniwersytet Jagielloński/Katedra Judaistyki, 2002), 21–27; Jürgen Heyde, »Polnischer Adel und jüdische Elite. Über rechtliche Oberhoheit und soziale Kontakte 1454–1539,« *Leipziger Beiträge zur jüdischen Geschichte und Kultur* 3 (2005): 103–115; Jürgen Heyde, *Transkulturelle Kommunikation und Verflechtung. Die jüdischen Wirtschaftseliten in Polen vom 14. bis zum 16. Jahrhundert* (Wiesbaden: Harrassowitz, 2014), 67–74, 211–220.

2 Michel Foucault, *Surveiller et punir. Naissance de la prison* (Paris: Gallimard, 1993 [1975]), especially 98–106.

3 Jürgen Schlumbohm, »Gesetze, die nicht durchgesetzt werden – ein Strukturmerkmal des frühneuzeitlichen Staates?« *Geschichte und Gesellschaft* 23 (1997): 647–663.

if they are not overtly expressed –, and why may such an incentive have seemed suitable in reaching an overarching goal?

Looking at the legislation from 1538 concerning the Jewish population, it seems at first difficult to understand why these charters were not implemented in practice. The estates convened at the Diet – the king, the envoys to the lower house (*izba poselska*) and the senators – passed regulations aimed at restricting the social and economic position of another group not represented politically, namely the Jews. The wording of the laws leaves little doubt: The prevailing legal, social, and economic position of the Jews constituted a wrong that urgently needed to be changed; therefore, appropriate legislation was to be passed at the Diet. Nevertheless, after the sessions were closed, neither the king nor the nobles undertook any effort to enforce these laws in practice. In the following paragraphs, I explore the reasons for this contradiction by examining the political context of the legislation on the Jews (*De Judaeis*).

First, I provide an introduction to the 1538 Sejm Constitution concerning the Jews. In the following section, I look into whether or not the various points of the Constitution were implemented, looking for clues and evidence – albeit circumstantial – indicating their implementation or lack thereof. This leads to an evaluation of such regulations within the context of other political and legal motivations in the first half of the 16th century, providing a clearer idea of the political significance of the legislation passed at the Sejm of Piotrków.

The chapter »De Judaeis« in the Piotrków Constitution of 1538

The chapter on the Jews[4] is the 13th of a total of 48 chapters passed by the Diet in 1538 »by mutual consent of the councillors of the kingdom and the envoys of the lands«.[5] The chapter's paragraphs do not comprise a concise legislative program, nor do they reflect the actual interests of the nobility, but include several well-known demands of burghers and clergy. Most of the points mentioned are characterized by thoroughly anti-Jewish phrases, whereas others simply repeated typical administrative provisions. The first paragraph forbade the Jews from running custom houses of any kind:

> We hereby state to be observed without fail that Jews shall not and cannot lead any type of custom house, as we deem it unworthy and against divine law that

4 »Konstytucje Sejmu walnego Piotrkowskiego 1538,« in *Volumina Constitutionum*, vol. 1, part 2: *1527–1549*, eds. Wacław Uruszczak, Stanisław Grodziski and Irena Dwornicka (Warszawa: Wydawnictwo Sejmowe, 2000), 160–192, especially 169–170.

5 Ibid., 164.

people of this sort should be allowed to hold any kind of honours and offices amongst Christians.[6]

Originally, a similar demand had already figured in a legislative proposal from 1505 for the Sejm of Radom, which had not ultimately been included in the debates and proceedings.[7]

The second paragraph determined that objects pawned to Jews should be recorded in the local court records.[8] This passage had already been approved by the Diet of 1532 upon the request of the Jewish communities. The Constitution claimed that it had become common practice to assign the supervision of pawned objects allocated to Jews to their elders, a custom that was, however, deemed impractical. The pawnbrokers dearly wished not to cause offence or to arouse distrust as the result of uncertainties connected to a pawn. Therefore, the Diet decreed that pawns and the day of their submission be inscribed into public court records (libri Iudaeorum), as had been customary in earlier times.[9]

The next part considers receiving and trading stolen goods. As thieves were potentially able to sell their loot to Jews, if stolen goods were found in a Jew's home, Jewish merchants would not be able to provide bailsmen and would be sentenced to the same punishment as the thieves.[10] This paragraph refers to a passage in the first general privilege issued to the Jews by Duke Bolesław the Pious of Kalisz back in 1264, freeing Jewish merchants from the obligation to give up stolen goods without compensation.[11] The Catholic Church had criticized this law as early as the 13th century, and the 1285 Synod of Łęczyca pressed the duke to nullify this privilege, because Christian creditors were not allowed to claim acquisition in good faith and had to return stolen pawns to their rightful owners without compensation.[12]

6 »Statuimus inviolabiliter observandum, Iudaeos teloneis quibuscunque praefici non debere neque posse, indignum et iuri divino contrarium censentes, eius generis homines aliquibus honoribus et officiis inter christianos fungi debere.« in »Konstytucje Sejmu walnego Piotrkowskiego 1538,« 169–170.

7 Ferdinand Bostel, »Tymczasowa ustawa radomska z r. 1505,« *Kwartalnik Historyczny* 3 (1889): 658–686, here 666, 679. A new edition of the project is printed in Stanisław Grodziski, Irena Dwornicka and Wacław Uruszczak, *Volumina Constitutionum*, vol. 1, part 1: *1493–1526* (Warszawa: Wydawnictwo Sejmowe,1996), 143–147.

8 »Konstytucje Sejmu walnego Piotrkowskiego 1538,« 169.

9 *Volumina Constitutionum*, vol. 1, part 2, no. 41: Sejm walny krakowski 1531–1532, 99.

10 »Konstytucje Sejmu walnego Piotrkowskiego 1538,« 169.

11 [I[gnacy] Zakrzewski and] F[ranciszek] Piekosiński, eds., *Kodeks dyplomatyczny Wielkopolski/Codex diplomaticus Poloniae Maioris*, vol. 1 (Poznań: Nakład Biblioteki Kórnickiej, 1877), 563–566 (no. 605), here 563.

12 Hanna Zaremska, »Rzecz skradziona w żydowskim zastawie,« in *Kościół, kultura, społeczeństwo. Studia z dziejów średniowiecza i czasów nowożytnych*, ed. Stanisław

In the following points the nobles adopted arguments brought into the political debate by town officials during their struggle with Jewish merchants in the large royal towns at the end of the 15th and the beginning of the 16th century. Paragraph 4 decreed an end to free commerce for Jewish merchants: They were to be obliged to abide by a new trading law which had yet to be issued, and adhere, in the meantime, to the agreements with the burghers that already existed in several towns.[13]

Paragraph 5 stated that the Jews had abandoned their old custom of marking themselves with a sign on their clothing so that they could be distinguished from the Christians. From now on they were obliged to wear a yellow hat, and if somebody reported a violation of this rule, the Jew was to pay half the fine to him and the other half to the king's official. An exception was made for Jews who were travelling; they were allowed to take off or hide the yellow sign, because wearing it might cause them danger.[14]

The following paragraph dealt with the treatment of bailment sums that were often issued by the king when conflicts between burghers and Jews turned violent. Even though such provisions usually had to be taken in order to guarantee the safety of the Jews against attacks by the burghers, the paragraph decreed that the entire Jewish community was to be held responsible for this deposit.[15] The last paragraph stated that Christian merchants were not allowed to trade in villages, and it was even less acceptable for Jews to do so. Therefore, the envoys prohibited Jews from trading beyond urban settlements upon the threat of severe punishment – in this case the confiscation of all merchandise.[16]

Jews in economic life before and after the Constitution of Piotrków

In the paragraphs of the chapter *De Judaeis* the Sejm addressed the most important fields of Jewish economic activity. Both regulations concerning the lease of public revenues and those on trade and merchandise were tied to political discussions that were consistently present in public debates at least since the beginning of the 16th century. The request to ban Jews from leasing tolls and customs had first been raised in the statutes of the Wrocław Synod of 1267. At the beginning of the 16th century this demand was raised again,[17] and even

Bylina (Warszawa: Semper, 2000), 337–350; Hanna Zaremska, *Żydzi w średniowiecznej Polsce. Gmina krakowska* (Warszawa: Instytut Historii PAN, 2011), 216–238.

13 »Konstytucje Sejmu walnego Piotrkowskiego 1538«, 169.

14 Ibid., 169–170.

15 Ibid., 170.

16 Ibid.

17 Ibid., 143–147; Bostel, »Tymczasowa ustawa radomska z r. 1505«.

though it had not been submitted for discussion by the parliament, it may be seen to have influenced the policy of the Polish king in the following years. After Sigismund I ascended to the Polish throne in 1507, most leases that had been in the hands of Jews and burghers were not renewed once the contracts expired. It is noteworthy, however, that not only Jews, but also burghers were affected by this policy. In fact, new contracts were almost exclusively issued to noblemen, who after 1520 gradually attained the remaining customs offices as well, so that there were no longer any Jewish leaseholders appointed by the king from the middle of the 1530s.

In practice however, Jews continued to manage customs offices, but were now appointed by the noblemen who leased them from the king. Unlike them, the Jews had the experience and the personnel to run customs offices successfully.[18] During the reign of Sigismund Augustus (Zygmunt August) in the middle of the century, the king began to assign public offices to Jews again, demonstratively neglecting the legislation of 1538. But he was not alone in his disregard of the Piotrków laws concerning Jews. During the great inspections (*lustracje*) of all royal estates and revenues in 1564 and 1570, it became apparent how many sources of public revenue were farmed out to Jews by the local officials (*starosta* and *wojewoda*) in the southern and eastern provinces of the kingdom, whether tolls and taxes, mills, fishponds, or taverns. There were occasional commentaries mentioning that many such leases had already belonged to Jews for a long time.[19]

Through 1538, the Polish nobility had never demanded that restrictions be made on Jewish trading rights. Paragraphs 4 and 5 of the Constitution referred to the conflicts between burghers and Jews in the large royal cities. From the end of the 15th century, the town councils of Lviv and Krakow had tried to marginalize Jews in local trade and to enforce the legal superiority of the municipality over the Jewish population. Several decades later – since the second decade of the 16th century – they were followed by Poznań, where the magistrate escalated the conflict even further.

In the beginning the burghers of Krakow had managed to achieve some manner of success: A treaty on Jewish trade in their city that was signed by the

18 Maurycy Horn, »Żydzi i mieszczanie w służbie celnej Zygmunta Starego i Zygmunta Augusta,« *Biuletyn Żydowskiego Instytutu Historycznego* 141 (1987): 3–20; idem »Mieszczanie i Żydzi na służbie królów polskich i wielkich książąt litewskich w latach 1506–1572 (w kopalnictwie i mennicach państwowych),« *Biuletyn Żydowskiego Instytutu Historycznego* 147–148 (1988): 3–20.

19 Maurycy Horn, »Działalność gospodarcza i pozycja materialna Żydów czerwonoruskich w świetle lustracji i inwentarzy z lat 1564–1570,« *Biuletyn Żydowskiego Instytutu Historycznego* 82 (1972): 15–26; idem, *Żydzi na Rusi Czerwonej w XVI i pierwszej połowie XVII wieku. Działalność gospodarcza na tle rozwoju demograficznego* (Warszawa: PWN, 1975), especially 223–250.

magistrate and the Jewish Elders in 1485 was about to eliminate almost all Jewish trade within the city and to give the burghers far-reaching control over Jewish economic activity. When, ten years later, Krakow's Jewish quarter burned down, the Jewish community opted to resettle in neighbouring Kazimierz. In Lviv during the 15th century, the Catholic burghers had managed to subordinate the Armenian and Ruthenian populations to the jurisdiction of the magistrate, but attempts to do the same with the Jewish population failed several times, being declined by the king himself. In the 16th century the burghers of Poznań used religiously founded anti-Jewish polemics in their attempts to convince the king of their ultimate goals: to marginalize the Jews in the city economically, rendering them dependent on the magistrate and – after the fire in the Jewish quarter of 1536 – to expel them altogether from the town. Similar to Jews in other towns, the Jews of Poznań were able to defend themselves against the pressure to exclude them, protecting not only their settlement within the town walls but also their trading rights.[20]

Just a few years after the Piotrków Constitution, the king, upon the initiative of noble town lords, signed privileges for several Jewish communities. In each case he emphasized the unrestricted trading rights for the Jewish population, e.g. in 1547 for Międzybóż and in 1550 for Komorno.[21] Similar provisions had been included into the medieval general privileges, but only in very general terms. Therefore, their inclusion into the new community privileges may be seen as a sign that the Jewish Elders were expecting resistance by the burghers and opted to have their trading rights explicitly guaranteed by the town lord and the king.[22]

20 Hanna Zaremska, »Crossing The River: How and Why the Jews of Cracow Settled in Kazimierz at the End of the Fifteenth Century,« in *Polin 22* (2010): 174–192; Zaremska, *Żydzi w średniowiecznej Polsce*, 493–504; Bożena Wyrozumska, »Did King Olbracht Banish the Jews from Cracow?« in *The Jews in Poland*, vol. 1, ed. Andrzej K. Paluch (Cracow: Jagiellonian University, 1992), 27–37; Heidemarie Petersen, *Judengemeinde und Stadtgemeinde in Polen. Lemberg 1356–1581* (Wiesbaden: Harassowitz, 2003), especially 57–79; Majer Bałaban, *Historia Żydów w Krakowie i na Kazimierzu 1304–1868*, vol. 1 (Kraków: Nadzieja, 1931), 55–66; Rex Rexheuser, »Zurückdrängen oder Aussiedeln. Die Stadt Posen und ihre Juden 1518–1538,« in idem, *Kulturen und Gedächtnis. Studien und Reflexionen zur Geschichte des östlichen Europas* (Wiesbaden: Harassowitz, 2008), 13–38.

21 Jacob Goldberg, ed., *Jewish Privileges in the Polish Commonwealth*, vol. 2 (Jerusalem: Israel Academy of Sciences and Humanities, 2001), 139–140; Mathias Bersohn, *Dyplomatariusz dotyczący Żydów w Polsce na źródłach archiwalnych osnuty (1388–1782)* (Warszawa: Drukarnia Edward Nycz, 1910), 49 (no. 53).

22 On the conflicts between burghers and Jews in the large royal cities of Krakow, Lviv, and Poznań, see Jürgen Heyde, »Topographie und Kommunikation. Zur Entwicklung der jüdischen Viertel im spätmittelalterlichen Polen,« in *Frühneu-*

The third chapter of the 1538 Constitution dealt with compulsory clothing marks for Jewish merchants. Such a demand had been voiced in synod statutes as far back as the 13th century. However, the Polish bishops had always pointed out that – in contrast to other countries – this request had never been enforced in Poland. And that was not about to change after 1538. When in 1565 a papal diplomat travelled through Poland, he remarked:

> In these principalities one still comes upon masses of Jews who are not disdained as much as in some other lands. They do not live here under pitiful conditions and do not engage in lowly pursuits [...] But rather, they possess land, engage in commerce, and devote themselves to study, especially medicine and astrology [...] They possess considerable wealth and they are not only among the respectable citizens, but occasionally even dominate them. They wear no special marks to distinguish them from Christians and are even permitted to wear the sword and to go about armed. In general, they enjoy equal rights.[23]

The envoy listed all the points usually involved in anti-Jewish legislative discrimination and, on the whole, they matched the provisions of the 1538 Constitution concerning the Jews. But in his conclusion referring to »equal rights« he voiced the impression that there was no legal discrimination against the Jews in Poland. It was not the absence of discriminatory legislation, however, but the absence of discriminatory practice that defined the situation of Jews within Polish society.

The legal position of the Jews in the political debates of the early 16th century

The crucial question is: Why was the discriminatory legislation of 1538 not translated into practice? Polish and Jewish historiography alike have traditionally posited that the king was too powerless to enforce his own legislation.[24] Upon closer inspection, however, such an assumption does not seem to fit the role of the king in 16th century Poland, as no crisis of royal power had as yet unfolded as would be the case in the late 17th or 18th century. It was not a lack of power, but apparently a lack of will to enforce the legislation of Piotrków that emerges from the actions of the king, as well as the nobility, towards the Jews in the following

zeitliche Ghettos in Europa im Vergleich, ed. Fritz Backhaus, (Berlin: trafo, 2012), 405–429.

23 Cited after Gershon David Hundert, *Jews in Poland-Lithuania in the Eighteenth Century: A Genealogy of Modernity* (Berkeley: University of California Press, 2004), 7.

24 Salo Wittmayer Baron, *A Social and Religious History of the Jews*, vol. 16: *Poland-Lithuania 1500–1650* (New York: Columbia University Press, 1973), 25–29; Rexheuser, »Zurückdrängen oder Aussiedeln«.

decades. The practical manifestations of a policy aimed at integrating the Jews, but not discriminating against them, showed clearly during the reign of Sigismund's son, Sigismund II. Augustus (1548–1572). Looking at the political debates from the early 16th century on, one may find characteristics more reminiscent of later political practice than of the Piotrków Constitution.

In 1506, King Alexander explained to the Magistrate of Lviv why he was not willing to tolerate any discrimination against the Jewish population by the burghers of the town: »It is true that the Jews of Lviv share the same civil burdens as the Christians and persons of other faiths [...] and therefore they are to enjoy the same freedoms as their fellow citizens«.[25] In 1532, King Sigismund I issued two decrees confirming Jewish trading rights – one directed at the royal towns of the kingdom, and one especially for the towns in Royal Prussia. In the last document the king referred to a complaint brought before the Diet that had just ended, made by »the entirety of the Jews, ours [i.e. the king's] as well as our subjects' [i.e. the nobles'] in our kingdom,«[26] because the Prussian towns had denied Jewish merchants entry. At the request of all the estates of the kingdom the king ordered the Prussian towns to grant the Jews – again explicitly the king's as well as the nobles' – access to their towns and the ability to conduct trade unhindered.[27]

The attitude of the king and the nobility towards the Jews at that time was also reflected in a law passed at the Diet in 1532 concerning the recording of objects deposited with Jewish pawnbrokers. These pawns were traditionally recorded in Jewish communal records, but from then on were to be recorded in the local court records. The law claimed that this was for the sake of the Jewish elders who wished to avoid uncertainty and conflict in these delicate matters. Although the law partly restricted Jewish communal autonomy, it did so at the initiative of Jews and without any polemical undertones.

25 »verum cum judei Leopolienses cum cristianis et aliorum rituum personis illuc commorantibus equaliter civilia ferunt onera sumptusque pares ad reformacionem civilem tribuunt et impendunt, merito eadem libertate cum concolis sunt potituri.« Sergei A. Bershadskii, ed., *Russko-evreiskii arkhiv. Dokumenty i materialy dlia istorii evreev Rossii*, vol. 3: *Dokumenty k istorii pol'skikh i litovskikh evreev v 1364–1569 gg.* (St. Petersburg, 1903), 71–72 (no. 48); Miron Kapral, ed., *Privilei natsional'nykh hromad mista L'vova XIV–XVIII st.* (Lviv: Mis'ke Hromads'ko-Kul'turne Ob'iednannia »Dokumental'na Skarbnytsia L'vova«, 2000), 400–401 (no. 118).

26 »accepimus querelam universitatis Judaeorum tam nostrorum quam subditorum nostrorum Regni nostri«. Vladislaus Pociecha, ed., *Acta Tomiciana per Stanislaum Gorski Canonicum ejusdem Petri Tomicii, post Serenissem Bone Sforce Regine Polonie Secretarium collecte*, vol. 14 (Poznań: Bibliotheca Kornicensis, 1952), 89–90 (no. 49).

27 A similar decree was issued to all royal dignitaries and town magistrates in the kingdom. See ibid., 89 (no. 48).

The Diet of 1532 discussed another project that might have affected the Jews, but was not passed. This so-called »correction of laws« (*korektura praw*) was meant to provide an amendment and unification of law throughout the whole kingdom. This was based on general privileges in the passages concerning the Jews, although it did revoke some of the economic rights granted exclusively to Jews but not to Christians, such as the release from responsibility in accepting stolen objects as pawns. On the other hand, the project underscored, among other things, paragraphs providing for Jewish homes to be protected from attack and for Jewish children to be protected from being abducted for baptism.[28] In these clauses, as well as in the general wording, the bill of 1532 differed substantially from the way that this subject was handled six years later at the Sejm of Piotrków.

By the following Diet in 1534, something already seemed to have changed in the political climate towards the Jews – the tone had ceased to be balanced and objective, but had become confrontational. King Sigismund himself was absent, remaining in the Grand Duchy of Lithuania due to the war between Lithuania and Muscovy, with the senators representing him instead during the deliberations. They were presented with a submission of noble envoys attacking Jewish trade, with the words:

> Thus, the unbridled Jewish trading rights, which have brought severe danger upon all the estates of the kingdom for a long time, are to be restricted. It has come to a situation, in which almost all trade is in the hands of the Jews. They corrupt and spoil all goods, especially those destined for human usage. Furthermore they have commercial ties to foreigners, as no Christian was allowed, thus depriving the king's treasure of due income and evading taxes. There is no place they would not penetrate. They go to Wallachia to buy cattle, exporting skins and other goods from the kingdom and thus causing a great increase in the price of everything. If they would limit themselves to usury and just live from the interest, the price increases, from which almost the entire kingdom is affected, would cease as well. They are, in fact, of no use to the Republic whatsoever und do not contribute to its defence either. According to ancient custom, Jews should be made to wear a sign on their clothing and to provide witnesses, if in one of their houses stolen goods were to be found. They should not enjoy greater rights than the Christians, because they [the Jews] themselves are often stealing.[29]

28 Waclaw Uruszczak, *Korektura praw z 1532 roku. Studium historycznoprawne*, vol. 1 (Warszawa: PWN/Kraków: Nakład Uniwersytetu Jagiellońskiego, 1990), 117–119; ibid., vol. 2 (Kraków: Nakład Uniwersytetu Jagiellońskiego, 1991), 91–92.

29 »Item, ut cohibeatur infrenata Iudaeorum in negotiando licentia, quae omnibus ordinibus Regni longe est perniciosissima. Nam eo ventum est, quod omnibus fere negotiatio a Iudaeorum manibus pendeat. Illi merces omnes, praesertim humanibus usibus destinatas, corrumpunt vitiantque et quod nemini christianorum licet, commercia habent cum externis, fiscum principis nostri clementissimi et vectigalia defraudantes. Nullus est locus, quem Iudaei non

The authors of this interpellation are not known, but they seem to have prepared it thoroughly in advance. The wording of this paragraph conveys a very emotional message, leaving little room for discussion. It combined the polemical views of burghers with ecclesiastical writings and new allegations referring to the ongoing war, accusing Jews not only of being useless for the defence of the kingdom, but also of conspiring with the enemy.

Never had a similar attack on the legal, economic, and social position of the Jews been launched in a Diet while the king was present. The interpellation seems to have taken the senators by surprise. They did, however, reject the main point of the interpellation quite clearly:

> To prohibit Jewish trade completely, as the envoys demand in their third article, did not appear appropriate to the senators at present, above all as the voivodes [*domini Palatini*] had said that they [the Jews] were in possession of privileges allowing them to engage in trade, and that they paid the king both regular and extraordinary contributions. Furthermore, one could not decide anything in this matter without consulting the king, whose subjects they [the Jews] are. So that there should be a differentiation between them [the Jews] and Christians, it is agreeable to everybody that they should wear yellow hats or caps.[30]

The senators were not the only ones who were surprised by the envoys' initiative. Even among their fellow noblemen, the demands presented at the Diet were not accepted as self-evident, and the reaction was in fact unequivocally negative. When the envoys returned home from the Diet they convened at regional dietines (*sejmiki*) to give an account of their activity. When the envoys of Lesser Poland related the initiative concerning Jewish trade to the *Sejmik* of Parczów, they were greeted with rejection and disbelief. The nobles of Lesser Poland supported the opinion that the Diet had to encourage Jewish trade, especially in

penetrent. Illi ad Valachiam euntes coemunt boves, cutes et alia eius generis extra Regnum educunt atque inde oboritur tanta rerum omnium caristia. Quod si suis usuris suoque fenore contenti viverent, a negotiatione abstinentes, cessaret haec, de qua omnes queruntur, caristia, quae calamitas totum fere regnum affligit. Neque vero alicui sunt usui reipublicae nec pro defensione aliquid impendunt. Signa rotarum more solito portent et cum res furto ablatae apud eos repertae fuerunt, evictores statuant nec maiori quam christiani praerogativa gaudeant, quoniam ipsi soli saepius furantur.« *Acta Tomiciana*, vol. 16, part 1, 100–107 (no. 51), here 102 (§ 3).

30 »Mercaturam Iudaeorum in totum prohibere, ut petunt nuntii in suo tertio articulo, non fuit visum dominis in praesens, praesertim cum domini palatini dicerent habere illos privilegia, quibus mercatura illis permitteretur, pendereque illos M[aiestati] regiae tributa ordinaria et extraordinaria et ob hoc non videbatur statui posse aliquid contra illos inconsulta M[aiestate] sua, cuius sunt subditi. Ut autem discrimen sit inter illos et christianos, placuit omnibus, ut gestarent pileos aut birreta crocei coloris.« *Acta Tomiciana*, vol. 16, part 1, 111–116 (no. 53), here 113–114 (§ 3).

Cracow, because the Jews provided goods at better prices than Christian merchants. For the nobles it was not the Jews but the Christian merchants of Cracow who were to blame for the ruin of the nobility.[31]

As the interpellation of the nobles had not been signed, the authors cannot be traced, but taking the responses of the senators at the Diet and the local nobles at the *sejmik* into account, one may still draw a rough sketch of the groups involved: The demands did not reflect the economic interests of the nobility, but especially in the sections phrased most harshly, followed the lines of argument in the burghers' anti-Jewish polemics. From the reaction of the *sejmik* in Lesser Poland it becomes clear that their position did not have much of a following among the broader noble public. The envoys most probably belonged to a group of politically active noblemen, very likely belonging to the upper stratum of the *szlachta*, well acquainted with Sejm politics, connected to church circles and townspeople, but not overly dependent on the king, whose authority they challenged.

The nobility's struggle for political participation

If the anti-Jewish polemics displayed at the Diets of 1534 and 1538 were not representative of the nobility's interests – at least not on a broader scale –, the question arises as to why such a program was devised at all? A general line of conflict emerges at the Diet of 1534: The envoys to the lower house (*izba poselska)* demanded changes while the senators defended the *status quo* – in the name of the king. This line of conflict was nothing new; it dated back to the very origins of Polish parliamentarism and formed the essence of the debates on the state of the monarchy, labelled at the time as the »execution of rights«, i.e. the enforcement of the nobility's participation rights.[32] The Diet of 1538 ended with an informal settlement, as the king acknowledged the demands posed by the Chamber of Envoys.

Since the Statutes of Nieszawa of the middle of the 15th century the question of the *szlachta*'s rights and opportunities for political participation had re-

31 *Acta Tomiciana*, vol. 16, part 2, 358–361 (no. 573), here 360.

32 Igor Kąkolewski, »Sozialverfassung und adelige Privilegiensicherung,« in *Polen in der europäischen Geschichte. Ein Handbuch*, vol. 2: *Der ständische Unionsstaat in der Frühen Neuzeit*, ed. Hans-Jürgen Bömelburg (Stuttgart: Hiersemann, 2011), 61–90; Anna Sucheni-Grabowska, »Przeobrażenia ustrojowe od Kazimierza Wielkiego do Henryka Walezego,« in *Tradycje polityczne dawnej Polski*, ed. Anna Sucheni-Grabowska and Alicja Dybkowska (Warszawa: Ed Spotkania, 1993), 16–74; Anna Sucheni-Grabowska, *Monarchia dwu ostatnich Jagiellonów a ruch egzekucyjny*, part 1: *Geneza egzekucji dóbr* (Wrocław: Zakład narodowy im. Ossolińskich, 1974).

peatedly dominated political discussions. When, in 1493, the Chamber of Envoys was installed as a continual representative body of the middle and lesser nobility, the *szlachta*, it was an institutional acknowledgement of their participation rights. Another milestone was the Constitution *nihil novi* at the Diet of 1505, setting up the legal ramifications of royal power: From now on, the king could not introduce any new legislation without consent of the two chambers of parliament representing the aristocracy and the *szlachta*.

During the early reign of Sigismund I, it became clear, however, that further adjustments were necessary because the king still was able to outmanoeuvre the *szlachta* while relying on the aristocracy, as represented in the king's council and the senate.[33] During King Sigismund's rule, which was based almost exclusively on the support of the aristocracy, the representatives of the *szlachta* presented him with a program of the »execution of rights« at the Diets of 1519 and 1520. It was agreed that a special reform Diet would be held to discuss the demands that had yet to be implemented. When this promise was not fulfilled, tensions arose between the monarch and the nobles of the Chamber of Envoys.

After Sigismund's marriage to Bona Sforza and the birth of their son, Sigismund Augustus, it became increasingly evident that the monarch would seek to base his rule on dynastic rights rather than parliamentary representation. When, in 1529, the nine-year-old Sigismund Augustus was declared Grand Duke of Lithuania and elected and crowned king of Poland *vivente rege* the following year, fears grew that the king might seek to abolish what had come to be called the concept of *Corona Regni Poloniae*, and subsequently diminish the *szlachta*'s parliamentary participation. At the Diet of 1530, Sigismund I made a first step toward mitigating these concerns, assuring the nobility that its right to elect the king would remain unabated in the future.

At that time the Commonwealth was involved in a war between Lithuania and Muscovy and faced the lingering danger of a war against the Ottoman Empire, so that there was no opportunity for an open debate about the constitutional shape of the kingdom. On the contrary, in the face of possible military action the monarch's position was strengthened even more, because as commander-in-chief the estates were obliged to follow his order.

33 There is no recent biography of Sigismund I. For a short overview, see Andrzej Wyczański, *Zygmunt Stary* (Warszawa: Zamek Królewski, 1985); on the political developments and conflicts in the first half of the 16th century, see especially idem, *Polska Rzeczą Pospolitą szlachecką* (Warszawa: PWN, 1991), especially 58–122; idem, *Szlachta polska XVI wieku* (Warszawa: PWN, 2001), especially 159–212; Sucheni-Grabowska, »Przeobrażenia ustrojowe od Kazimierza Wielkiego do Henryka Walezego«; Wacław Uruszczak, »Sejm w latach 1506–1540«, in *Historia sejmu polskiego*, vol 1: *Do schyłku szlacheckiej Rzeczypospolitej*, ed. Jerzy Michalski (Warszawa: PWN, 1984), 63–113.

The king and the Jews – a staged proxy-conflict

In this particular situation, the political debates at the following Diet engaged in secondary topics, where both sides could stake out their positions without paralysing the kingdom in a constitutional conflict. Such a secondary topic was the status of the Jews within the society of the kingdom, one which was connected to the role of the monarch as their overlord. There were several reasons why precisely this topic seemed appropriate at that particular time. For example, in persuading the Polish nobility of the need to engage in the wars against Muscovy and the Ottoman Empire the royal propaganda referred to the concept of the *Antemurale Christianitatis*, which assigned the role of defender of Christianity against »schismatics« and »infidels« to Poland-Lithuania under the leadership of the Polish king.[34]

Religious arguments were used in domestic debates as well, albeit at the inner-Christian, confessional level, i.e. defending the Catholic faith against the teachings of Martin Luther. From the very beginning of the Reformation movement, Sigismund I emphatically countered the new doctrine and already issued a ban against Luther's writings in 1520 – even before Emperor Charles V decided to take a similar step in the Holy Roman Empire.

From the late 15th century, representatives of the burghers, especially in the leading royal towns, repeatedly took to anti-Jewish polemics in order to weaken the economic position of the Jews and strengthen that of the Christian merchants. In the 1520s, for example, the magistrate in Poznań used religious arguments in its struggle against Jewish merchants, and even displayed religious symbols on the market square in order to make it a »holy space« where Jews had no business to be.[35]

Every nobleman in Poland was well acquainted with the basic structure of anti-Jewish polemics, as the chronicles of Wincenty Kadłubek and especially Jan Długosz were the most important books used in rhetoric lessons in their academic education. These works were known to advocate a ›republican‹ ideology and a critical stance toward dynastic politics, but they also conveyed a decidedly negative image of the Jews.[36]

34 Urszula Borkowska, »The Ideology of Antemurale in the Sphere of Slavic Culture 13th–17th century,« in *The Common Christian Roots of the European Nations: An International Colloquium in the Vatican* (Florence: Le Monnier, 1983), 1206–1221; Paul Srodeckij, *Antemurale Christianitatis. Zur Genese der Bollwerksrhetorik im östlichen Mitteleuropa an der Schwelle vom Mittelalter zur Frühen Neuzeit* (Husum: Matthiesen, 2015), 217–265.

35 Rexheuser, »Zurückdrängen oder Aussiedeln«, 26–38.

36 Hans-Jürgen Bömelburg, *Frühneuzeitliche Nationen im östlichen Europa. Das polnische Geschichtsdenken und die Reichweite einer humanistischen Nationalge-*

The Polish monarchs had ultimately defined their position as the sole overlords of the Jews in the general privileges, and in 1505 the Diet had formally accepted that position, which involved the inclusion of the first general privilege of 1264 into the collection of laws of the kingdom *Commune incliti Poloniae Regni privilegium constitutionum ed indultuum*, which was the last step toward the legal unification of the Polish lands after the reconsolidation of the kingdom in the early 14th century. As the highest legal instance over the Jews, the monarch delegated his authority to the voivodes and to the judges appointed by them (*Iudex Iudeorum*),[37] but declined to grant the magistrates any juridical power over the Jewish population living in their towns. In a general privilege issued to Jews of Greater Poland in 1453, the same reservation was made in respect to ecclesiastical courts. Sigismund I confirmed this in 1539 upon the request of the Jewish community of Poznań, with the confirmation included into the records of the castle court.[38]

Only the nobility had a particular role to play in the juridical authority over the Jews – as a representative of the king through the institution of the voivode's court and the *Iudex Iudeorum*. In his letter to the Prussian towns in 1532, King Sigismund acknowledged this, speaking about his own Jews and the Jews of the nobility. However, this phrase could not yet be interpreted as a formal acceptance of the nobility as legal overlords of the Jews in Poland in their own right. In 1534, however, the senate clearly indicated in its answer to the envoys that Jewish privileges could not be altered without the consent of the king, as his was the highest authority.

The anti-Jewish polemics were a secondary issue in yet another respect. In the 1530s, discussions between the reform movement and the king appeared to have reached a dead end. The conflict became more vigorous and the political atmosphere nearly hostile. When the »correction of laws« was presented to the Diet in 1532 the envoys did not discuss it right away, doing so only in 1534 when they largely rejected the project. In his absence, the king was criticized more vehemently and openly than before. Nevertheless, even in the aftermath, Sigismund I and his followers were not willing to make substantial concessions

schichte (1500–1700) (Wiesbaden: Harassowitz, 2006), 33–41; Urszula Borkowska, *Treści ideowe w dziełach Jana Długosza. Kościół i świat poza kościołem* (Lublin: KUL, 1983).

37 A close analysis of the office of *Iudex Iudeorum* is provided by Anat Vaturi in this volume.

38 Sh[muel] A. Cygielman: »The Basic Privileges of the Jews of Great Poland as reflected in Polish Historiography,« *Polin* 2 (1987): 117–149; Heidemarie Petersen, »Zwischen Geschichte und Politik. Das Privileg für die Juden Großpolens aus dem Jahre 1453 in der polnischen Historiographie,« *Kwartalnik Historii Żydów/Jewish History Quarterly* 212, no. 4 (2004): 519–527.

regarding constitutional reforms. Only in 1537, when the combined forces of the kingdom, which were convened near Lviv to march against Moldavia, refused their obedience to the king and disbanded, did the political controversy escalate into a military defeat for Sigismund I. He was now forced to send a signal that he was indeed willing to reach a compromise. The Diets in Piotrków 1538 and in Krakow 1539 were meant to deescalate and reduce the tensions between the monarch and the nobility. Even then, neither side was able to achieve meaningful progress on the reform agenda, while the legislation on the Jews sent a clear signal that the king accepted the participation rights of the nobility as a matter of principle. After the escalation in the army camp near Lviv the two sides thus managed to re-establish the groundwork for further talks.

Taking up the long-disputed demands of burghers and clergy, the envoys demonstrated the amount of popular support they could mobilize, creating a sort of common front of all the estates against the king. They could be sure that the burghers and clergy would back their efforts, even if this meant questioning the king's authority. In addition, they challenged the king on what seemed to be a marginal topic, i.e. the legal and economic status of the Jews, so that it would not be interpreted as an assault on the majesty of the king himself. By granting the Constitutions of 1538 and 1539, King Sigismund I showed that he understood the message sent by the envoys without being forced to make concessions on core points of his policy.

The Constitution of Piotrków against the Jews in 1538 was therefore not intended to mark a shift in the attitude of the king or nobility towards the Jews. As one can see in the following years, the policy was indeed not about to change – but it was an element of symbolic politics, aimed at facilitating negotiations on another and more important topic. Even as the efforts toward introducing constitutional reforms and the movement for the »execution of rights« did not reach a conclusion for another three decades, the Diet twice referred to the anti-Jewish provisions of Piotrków during the decisive and difficult phase of negotiations in the 1560s. After the Union of Lublin of 1569, when the reforms were translated into a new constitutional framework for the Commonwealth, this kind of anti-Jewish polemics vanished from the agenda and the discussions of the Polish-Lithuanian parliament for more than a century.[39]

39 Stanisław Grodziski, Irena Dwornicka and Wacław Uruszczak, ed., *Volumina Constitutionum*, vol. 2, part 1: *1550–1585* (Warszawa: Wydawnictwo Sejmowe, 2005), 172 (no. 68: Sejm of Piotrków 1565); ibid., 200 (no. 70: Sejm of Piotrków 1567); Anna Michałowska-Mycielska, ed., *Sejmy i sejmiki koronne wobec Żydów. Wybór tekstów źrodłowych* (Warszawa: Wydawnictwo Uniwersytetu Warszawskiego, 2006), 196–110 (no. 116: Sejm of Grodno 1678/1679), here 109.

Conclusion: Law-making and politics – a case of domestic diplomacy

The constitutions of the Polish Diet represent a model of law-making based on a political consensus between the monarch and the nobility. The Constitution *De Judaeis* of 1538 represents a political consensus, yet not a consensus that referred to the legal and economic situation of the Jews in the Kingdom of Poland, but a consensus at a different level. In signing the Constitution both sides signalled their will to reach a compromise on a far more principal issue – the question of noble participation in governing the kingdom. This topic, however, affected the role of the king as supreme ruler and thus could not be discussed openly without the risk of damaging the king's authority and evoking accusations of *lèse majesté*.

As the Polish king traditionally considered himself the supreme and sole overlord of the Jews of his kingdom, the attack on their legal and economic position was ultimately directed at the king as well. The nobles' initiative aimed to shift the constitutional balance of power, as did the »execution of rights«-movement. In the 1530s, it became clear that the differences between Sigismund I and the politically active part of the *szlachta* would be difficult to overcome, and the incidents of 1537 showed that the conflict was gradually escalating. Not being able to address the core issues of the reform movement directly, the envoys at the Diet of 1534 decided to attack just one aspect of Sigismund's authority. The Jews' position looked like a suitable target as the king had also traditionally been seen as the highest defender of the church. Sigismund had asserted this position before, against Muscovy, the Ottoman Empire, as well as domestically at the beginning of the Reformation. The nobles therefore took the ecclesiastical rhetoric of social exclusion, mixed it with the burghers' demands for the Jews to be marginalized economically and presented the king with their demand to share in his sovereignty over the Jewish population. The alliance with representatives of the church and the burghers was meant to underline the importance of their stance – and King Sigismund clearly understood the message. He approved the Constitution of Piotrków in 1538 and, in 1539, even granted the nobility legal authority over the Jews living on their estates.

In this way the king resolved the political tension that had led to the incidents of Lviv in 1537 and cleared the way for further talks on political reforms. The nobility had achieved its objective, and there was no further need to satisfy demands that were important to the Catholic Church and the burghers, but had little to do with the interests of the nobility. Once the hidden political agenda of the Piotrków Constitution was achieved, there was no longer a need to enforce its concrete points. From the very beginning they were not meant to be put into practice. The Piotrków Constitution was a showcase for domestic diplomacy, in which law-making functioned as an indication of the state of negotiations. At a symbolic level, it represented a sort of truce between the king and the nobles after years of a lingering open conflict.

Jürgen Heyde

Shylock as a Symbol of the Disenfranchised Jew – A Comparative Study of Karl Emil Franzos' and Rudolf von Jhering's Legal Thinking

It would, at first glance, seem difficult to imagine Shakespeare's Shylock as a positive character, one with whom you could identify. That he could be promoted to the status of a Jewish civil rights activist seems even more incredible. But both phenomena arose in the 19th-century Habsburg Empire in a wide range of cultural events, in the fine arts, and in political thought.[1] This essay will concentrate on the interaction between literature and legal theory, mainly represented by the Galician author Karl Emil Franzos and the Prussian professor of law Rudolf von Jhering. Both discussed the fate of Shakespeare's Shylock in their texts and treated him as a symbol for the judicial and religious persecution of Jews in 19th-century Galicia. While Jhering focused on anti-Jewish discrimination, Franzos delved, moreover, into the different inner-Jewish conflicts between the Haskalah[2] and Hasidism.[3] Franzos knew Jhering's publications and adapted his teacher's ideas to the specific situation in Galicia.

1 Maria Kłańska, »Shylock im Osten,« in Renate Heuer, *Verborgene Lesarten. Neue Interpretationen jüdisch-deutscher Texte von Heine bis Rosenzweig*, vol. 20 (Frankfurt a. M.: Campus Judaica, 2003), 73–97, and Ezra Mendelsohn, *Painting a People. Maurycy Gottlieb and Jewish Art* (Hanover, NH: Brandeis University Press, 2002).

2 The Haskalah, also called the Jewish Enlightenment, was a social and religious movement. It was founded by Moses Mendelssohn in Germany in the 18th century. In Eastern Europe it developed in the 19th century and competed later with other religious, cultural, and political movements such as Zionism, Communism, and especially Hasidism. Important social aims of the Maskilim, the members of the Haskalah movement, included the integration of the Jewish population into mainstream society, and laying better foundations for economic growth and cultural development. *YIVO Encyclopedia of Jews in Eastern Europe*, s.v. »Haskalah«.

3 Hasidism is a movement of religious revival, which developed in Eastern Europe in the late 18th century and especially spread in the poorer regions of the Habsburg and Russian Empires. Founded by the religious leader Yisra'el ben Eli'ezer, known as Ba'al Shem Tov (»Master of the Good Name« – also abbreviated as Besht) it was connected to a magical and spiritual movement, strongly linked to his person and other so called Tsadikim (righteous), who seemed to have a closer link to the divine sphere. The followers of Hasidism

Why exactly the authors assigned Shylock this role is an intriguing question, since the most common interpretation of his character is rather negative. Ezra Mendelsohn writes that

> Shylock, Shakespeare's Jewish moneylender, is surely the most famous Jewish character in all of European literature. He has been viewed, traditionally, as the stereotypical Jew, obsessed with filthy lucre and driven by revenge, a hater of Christians and Christianity, whose tragicomic fate at the hands of Christian Venice is fully justified.[4]

Shylock's behaviour is certainly questionable. He not only desires the death of his Christian competitor Antonio, but also of his own daughter Jessica, who ran away with a Christian.[5] In accordance with the common anti-Jewish prejudice, he is avaricious and sly.

It might therefore appear surprising that Karl Emil Franzos reinterpreted the role of this dramatic figure. He directly treated the subject of Shylock twice. In his novel *Der Shylock von Barnow* (»Shylock of Barnow«), written in the late 1860s and published in 1877 in the volume of stories *Die Juden von Barnow* (»The Jews of Barnow«), Franzos still supported a rather negative interpretation. This changed within his key novel *Der Pojaz* (The Pojaz), written in the late 1880s. In this novel Shylock as a symbol is used to denounce the deprivation of the rights of the Jews in his native country. This shift in Franzos' Shylock interpretation is the topic of this paper.

I argue that the influence of Jhering's thoughts actually evoked this change of view in Franzos' writing. To follow this idea one needs, first of all, to outline Shakespeare's drama, focusing on the paragraphs relevant to the new interpretation of the play, especially the legal case. Afterwards, I will look into Karl Emil Franzos' life and analyze his two works *Der Shylock von Barnow* and *Der Pojaz*, as well as Rudolf von Jhering's legal philosophy and its connection to Franzos' work and thought. Subsequently, I will outline the political ideas Franzos expressed in his literature.

Shakespeare's Shylock

Shakespeare's play *The Merchant of Venice*, written at the end of the 16th century,[6] takes place in medieval Venice. The play is about the downturn in the merchant

were generally conservative and did not only oppose the Haskalah but secularisation, nationalism, and Zionism. *YIVO Encyclopedia*, s.v. »Hasidism.«

4 Mendelsohn, *Painting a People*, 124.

5 William Shakespeare, *The Merchant of Venice* (New York: American Library, 1965), 88.

6 Gustav Landauer, *Shakespeare. Dargestellt in Vorträgen* (Frankfurt a. M.: Literarische Anstalt Rütten & Loening, 1923), 43.

Antonio's fate.[7] Although Antonio is the title figure, the emerging conflict is fought between the Jewish moneylender Shylock and the rich countess Portia. As only the court scene is important for Jhering's and Franzos' interpretations, I will concentrate on that part of the play.

The Jewish moneylender Shylock lends 3000 ducats to his Christian competitor Antonio on the condition that he would have to give him one pound of his own flesh if he could not pay back the money in time. It is actually not Antonio who needs the money, as he lends it to his friend Bassiano, who wants to marry the rich countess Portia. The way the contract is written expresses Shylock's desire for revenge against this Christian, who had until then despised him for being a Jew. Bassiano even warns Antonio against accepting this obviously immoral contract.

Shylock could not foresee that he had a realistic chance of getting the flesh, since Antonio was a very rich merchant who seemed to have wide influence in Venice.[8] However, Antonio surprisingly becomes insolvent and Bassiano forgets about his friend's debt. After the expiration of the deadline, Shylock demands »his right« before the Venetian court on the basis of their contract. The court allows the plaintiff to take a pound of Antonio's flesh with evident displeasure.[9] Not even the offering of a higher compensatory payment can turn Shylock away from his intentions. Antonio already seems lost, when Portia, the wife of Bassiano, enters the stage dressed as a judge. She too declares the contract to be valid and appeals to Shylock's mercy. He leaves no doubt in his response, however, that he seeks revenge and his rights. Portia responds by allowing Shylock to cut out the flesh, but without taking an ounce more or less and without spilling a single drop of this »Christian's blood«.[10] Shylock is forced to give in and is later even convicted for the attempted murder of Antonio. He loses all of his property, one half to Antonio and the other to his own daughter, Jessica, who had run away with a Christian, stealing treasure from her father along the way.

After Shylock's conviction he is forced to convert to Christianity,[11] while for all the other characters the play has a happy ending. The further fate of Shylock is not mentioned.

7 I am grateful to Dorothee Gelhard for her advice concerning the interpretation of Shakespeare's *Merchant of Venice*.

8 Hermann Sinsheimer, *Shylock* (München: Ner-Tamid-Verlag, 1960), 129–132.

9 Shakespeare, *The Merchant of Venice*, 110.

10 Ibid., 120.

11 Ibid., 122–123.

Shylock in Franzos' work

Karl Emil Franzos revisited Shylock in two of his works, first referring to him in the late 1860s[12] in his novella *Der Shylock von Barnow*, and twenty years later in the novel *Der Pojaz*. However, as I demonstrate, the two depictions feature important differences that reflect the development of Franzos' thinking over time.

Karl Emil Franzos was most probably born in 1847 in the provincial Galician town of Czortkow[13] as the youngest son of a doctor in Hasidic surroundings. How much he was involved in the religious life of his town is not known.[14] Franzos went to high school in Chernivtsi and studied law in Vienna and Graz, with – amongst others – Professor Rudolf von Jhering.[15] However, after he finished his education, he followed his literary inclination rather than practising a law-related profession. He worked as a journalist, published the periodical *Deutsche Dichtung* (»German Poetry«), and became the author of several novels and many novellas. In both his literature and his social engagement he was particularly interested in the legal situation of minorities, which he also described in his works.[16]

In the preface to *Die Juden von Barnow*, Franzos was quite open about his educational aim. With his stories he wanted to positively influence the situation

12 See the preface to the 6th edition of *Die Juden von Barnow* in which he states that he wrote the novella between 1868 and 1872, and thus prior to Jhering's article. Karl Emil Franzos, *Die Juden von Barnow* (Stuttgart and Berlin: J.B. Cotta'sche Buchhandlung, 1929), v.

13 Anna-Dorothea Ludewig, *Zwischen Czernowitz und Berlin: Deutsch-jüdische Identitätskonstruktionen im Leben und Werk von Karl Emil Franzos (1847–1904)* (Hildesheim: Georg Olms Verlag, 2008), 16. Ludewig shows, that the birthdate and birthplace given by Franzos do not correspond to the dates on his birth certificate. According to her, Franzos reinterprets his own autobiography and changes some facts to fit in his own world-view. One should be very suspicious of his comments on his own life.

14 Franzos stated in his autobiographical essay *Mein Erstlingswerk*, first published in Leipzig in 1894, not to have been integrated into the Hasidic community. Chajim Bloch, however, quoted a school-friend Mose Sonnenschein, who told Bloch about his time together with Franzos in the *kheder*, the Hasidic primary school. Karl Emil Franzos, »Mein Erstlingswerk: Die Juden von Barnow,« in *Karl Emil Franzos. Kritik und Dichtung*, ed. Fred Sommer (New York: Peter Lang Verlag, 1992), 125–144, here 133 and Chajim Bloch, »Erinnerungen an Karl Emil Franzos,« in *Gemeindeblatt der Israelitischen Religionsgemeinde zu Leipzig*, no. 41 (1931), 1.

15 Karl Emil Franzos, *Deutsche Dichtung*, vol. 13 (1892/1893), (Berlin: Verlag Fontane, 1893), 50.

16 Horst Sendler, »Karl Emil Franzos (1848–1904): Ein Kämpfer ums Recht,« *Neue Juristische Wochenschrift*, vol. 23 (1987): 1361–1369.

of the Jews in the eastern regions of Europe.[17] His audience was to be »readers of the West«,[18] and he wanted to show them the living conditions of the Jews in »Semi-Asia«,[19] as he called the region of Galicia and Bukovina. But he also mentions a translation into Yiddish and Hebrew to cautiously win the Orthodox Jews over to a freer form of worship.[20] In addition to this introduction, the narrator often comments critically within his stories on the events he recounts.

The protagonist of the novella *Der Shylock von Barnow,* Moses Freudenthal, is described as a gentle and very rich man, who is devout to his religion and tradition. All his love is directed to his only daughter Esther, a very intelligent girl. Though it is quite unusual, her father allows her to pursue a secular education, until he becomes afraid of the emerging differences in her view of the world. He thus tries to force her back into the »normal« Hasidic way of life and marry her to a local man. After forbidding her from reading any more books, she begins to borrow them secretly. Formed by her readings, Esther then perceives the shtetl as narrow-minded and flees, together with a Christian, from an arranged marriage. Moses thereupon disowns his daughter and prefers her death to any repentant return – just like Shakespeare's Shylock.

Nevertheless, there is a significant difference between Esther and Shylock's Jessica. Jessica not only steals from her father, but betrays him in every aspect of her behaviour. She speaks badly of him, converts to Christianity, and gives away her mother's ring, which had meant a great deal to her father. Shylock therefore wishes Jessica to lay »dead at his foot«[21] as he counts the money she stole and the cost of finding her. This scene, in particular, supports a negative reading of the character Shylock, since Shakespeare refers here to one of the oldest anti-Semitic stereotypes of Jews as greedy usurers, where money counts more than one's own daughter.

This stereotype is not adopted in Franzos' novella, even though the Christian townsmen interpret Moses' behaviour in this way.[22] Moses, in contrast, is rich and generous. Esther did not steal an ounce of money and Moses does not stop loving her. But he still prays to God for her death, »so that I don't have to curse my only child, that she dies, my Lord and God, she or I ...!«[23] Even as Moses

17 Franzos, *Juden von Barnow*, viii.

18 »Der Leser des Westens«. Ibid., vii.

19 Ibid., vii. The term »Semi-Asia« [Halb-Asien] originates from his book entitled *Aus Halb-Asien: Culturbilder aus Galizien, der Bukovina, Südrußland und Rumänien* (Leipzig: Verlag Duncker und Humblot, 1876).

20 »[um] die orthodoxen Juden vorsichtig für eine freiere Glaubensrichtung zu gewinnen.« Franzos, *Juden von Barnow*, vi.

21 Shakespeare, *The Merchant of Venice*, 88.

22 Franzos, *Die Juden von Barnow*, 40.

23 »ich flehe nur, daß sie sterbe, damit ich meinem einzigen Kinde nicht fluchen muß, daß sie sterbe, mein Herr und Gott, sie oder ich! ...«. Ibid., 8.

suffers from his harsh judgement, he feels forced to treat her in this manner. His religious conviction and social surroundings demand this of him and he knows no other way. In contrast with Shakespeare's Shylock, Franzos emphasizes the force of circumstances in his novella. Moses' harsh judgement is due to the strict religious convictions of the community, and Franzos did not forget to mention in the foreword that the long-term causes should be sought in the exclusion of Jews from Christian society.[24] Within the novella, the Jewish doctor, a Maskil[25] with a broad secular education, explains the reasons for the tragic end: Moses and, to an even greater extent, his daughter Esther, are described by him as victims of both – Hasidic and Christian society.[26] In the end, Esther returns, but her father is no longer willing to welcome her back. She dies of starvation the same night in front of his house and Moses remains a broken man until the end of his life. His money is then bequeathed to the miracle Rabbi of Sadagora, the symbol of all backwardness and religious fanaticism in Franzos' literature.[27]

Comparing the novella *Der Shylock von Barnow* to *Der Pojaz*, the dubious element of Shylock's character still dominates in the first text. In *Der Shylock von Barnow* Moses is described in an ambivalent way: Even though he is blamed for Esther's death, his extraordinary narrow-mindedness is presented as a result of his upbringing, and he does not know any better. The saddest fact about this event is that nothing changes in the end, nobody learns from it, apart from the already educated Jewish doctor. None of the Christians want to hear his explanations. Moses, who after these events is called the Shylock of Barnow, dies rich, but isolated and broken.

This all changes in Franzos' second treatment of the Shylock figure. In his novel *Der Pojaz*, in which he also refers to the Shylock of Barnow, the character acquires a noteworthy and positive new interpretation to which I now turn.

Shylock in the novel Der Pojaz

Franzos' most famous work, *Der Pojaz*, also addresses legal questions. Its hero perishes, caught between the state's laws and the narrow-mindedness of his own religious community. The novel was first printed in a Russian translation and

24 Ibid., vii–viii.

25 Adherent of the Haskalah movement. See footnote 2.

26 Franzos, *Die Juden von Barnow*, 34 and 38.

27 The same collection of stories contains the novella *Das Kind der Sühne*, in which the »miracle Rabbi« of Sadagora plays a very unpleasant role. He gives bad advice, takes the money of the poorest and keeps them in mental backwardness. Ibid., 124–169.

appeared in the Jewish-Russian magazine *Voskhod* (sunrise).[28] Published as a novel in St Petersburg[29] in 1895, it was also printed posthumously in German in 1905. Why Franzos published it first in Russian is not clear, but there are different speculations on the matter.[30]

The novel describes the life of the protagonist Sender Glatteis, known as Pojaz, who is born in a Hasidic shtetl. The name Sender is a short form of Alexander and refers back to the glorious Hellenic era in Jewish history. However, the surname Glatteis (»black ice«) serves on the one hand as a symbol of the discriminating practice of naming in the Habsburg Empire, in which the administration could give Jews funny sounding or even insulting surnames.[31] On the other hand, his surname can also be associated with his very unstable path in life. The Yiddish word *payats* can be translated as »comedian«, »clown«, or »actor«, figures that play a vital role in the shtetl tradition.[32] From the beginning Pojaz is representative of the outsider. He lives in a non-conformist way and questions many of the proscriptions and prohibitions of shtetl life. He repeatedly comes into conflict with the community, which meets him alternately with great love and great resentment.

The Hasidic town is described as very backward, although benevolently so.[33] The narrator points out the religious fanaticism, the lack of secular education

28 The Russian-Jewish monthly *Voskhod* was published in St. Petersburg from 1881 to 1906. Its founder and editor was Adolph Landau and his assistant the historian Simon Dubnow. The journal promoted the Haskalah, a distinct Jewish identity, and advocated against total assimilation. Between 1881 and 1884 it called for Jewish self-defence against the anti-Jewish pogroms taking place in the western provinces of the Russian Empire. *Encyclopaedia Judaica*, 1st ed., s.v. »Voskhod.« *Voskhod* printed the novel in two parts, in a version that differs slightly from the German version published in 1905, one year after Franzos' death. Rudolf Mark and Dieter Kessler »›Sender Glatejz‹. Ein unbekannter Roman von Karl Emil Franzos?« in *Juden in Ostmitteleuropa von der Emanzipation bis zum ersten Weltkrieg*, ed. Gotthold Rhode (Marburg: J.G. Herder-Institut, 1989), 311–319, here 312.

29 Karl Emil Franzos, *Sender Glateyz: Roman iz evreiskoi narodnoi zhizni* (St. Petersburg: Tipografiia A. E. Landau, 1895).

30 For more about these speculations see Ludewig, *Zwischen Czernowitz und Berlin*, 269. In the foreword of his Russian version Franzos explains his reasons for wanting to write a novel to meet the needs of his Russian readers. As a second reason he names the legal situation, as well as a lack of agreements between the Russian Empire and Germany to protect intellectual property.

31 Franzos, *Der Pojaz*, 12.

32 Dorothee Gelhard, *Spuren des Sagens. Studien zur jüdischen Hermeneutik in der Literatur* (Frankfurt a. M.: Peter Lang, 2004), 92.

33 Right in the beginning the narrator explains that a pious Jew has to get married according to religious law. Even if he gets divorced the next day, it is still better

and the subordination of reason and morality to putative religious laws to be the greatest deficiency in the small town of Barnow, which was also the home of Moses and Esther in *Der Shylock von Barnow*. This is connected to the linguistic, economic, and social isolation, which the narrator addresses critically. The most severely attacked deficiency is connected to language. In Hasidic towns, Jews spoke and wrote Yiddish and Hebrew, with only some of them understanding and speaking Polish or Russian as well, but they did not learn the Latin alphabet or German, which was, according to the narrator, the language of high culture. Since most Hasidic Jews did not speak the languages of their neighbours or the state administration, they could not communicate or take part in political life. This depiction expressed what Franzos saw as the attitude of the Hasidim towards politics and law. They did not feel the need to participate as long as they could live according to their religious rules. The situation of legal and social discrimination appeared to them to be a normal state.[34]

Sender is a very positive character, though unstable in his interests. Since he is not willing to go to school or practise any proper trade, he becomes a carter and leaves his hometown. After encountering a theatre group in Chernivtsi, he discovers that it is his destiny to become an actor. His nickname Pojaz (*payats*) had indeed derived from his natural ability to imitate people and act in sketches. The play that kindles this wish, in a pivotal experience, is Shakespeare's *Merchant of Venice*.[35] Remarkably, Sender identifies with the tragic role of Shylock who stands alone in defence of his rights in opposition to the Christian world. Only a part of the play is described, that is until Shylock loses the trial and has to convert to Christianity. What happens afterwards is not described and seems to be of no interest to Sender.

The play is retold from Sender's point of view. He does not understand some scenes but all in all recognizes a number of situations which are familiar to him such as the lending of money, the injustice of Christian courts towards Jews, and the insulting behaviour of the neighbours and servants.[36] Decisive for Sender's identification is Shylock's famous speech in which he articulates the silently suffered grief of all Jews, including his own. The best known quotation of the famous Shylock monologue is: »If you prick us, do we not bleed? if you tickle us,

than staying single. The narrator comments on this religious law with his usual satire. Franzos, *Der Pojaz*, 29.

34 Philipp Theisohn, »Eruv. Herkunft an den Grenzen der Aufklärung. Karl Emil Franzos' *Der Pojaz*« in *Herkünfte. Historisch – ästhetisch – kulturell; Beiträge zu einer Tagung aus Anlass des 60. Geburtstags von Bernhard Greiner*, eds. Barbara Thums and Bernhard Greiner (Heidelberg: Winter, 2004), 171–190, here 177.

35 Franzos, *Der Pojaz*, 68.

36 Ibid., 62–66.

do we not laugh? if you poison us, do we not die? and if you wrong us, shall we not revenge?«[37]

Shakespeare's Shylock appeals to his Christian adversaries to recognize the equality of Jews and Christians, not only on a legal basis, but also in everyday life. If they treat him his whole life as a person worthy of hatred, he will behave as they expect him to. Sender compares the situation of Shylock and the Jews of Venice to his situation and the Jews of Galicia. After watching the play he feels the political and social injustice which is inflicted on the Jews by the Christians in his daily life. Pojaz resumes:

> »Yes,« the old man said, beginning to talk about Christians and Jews, and how we are so bitterly persecuted by the Christians – it goes straight into my bone and marrow and deep into my heart. Until now I never thought much about us and the Poles, I just thought that was the way it was, but now my eyes have been opened to the bloody injustice that we suffer.[38]

Shakespeare's Shylock points to the anti-Semitic behaviour of Venetian people, but obviously still believes in his legal equality, which is probably why he persists in the literal fulfilment of the sentence, whereas Sender views the contract and Shylock's obstinate insistence on the flesh as wrong. He, in contrast to Shylock, is convinced, based on his own Galician experience, that Jews have no hopes for justice in a Christian court.[39] Sender follows the development of the case with great curiosity. After Portia, the false judge, recognizes the contract and rules that Shylock is not allowed to spill a single drop of blood, or he will lose his entire capital, Sender still accepts the outcome of the case, because he hopes it could solve the situation and restore justice. He hopes for Shylock to only take his money and does not appreciate his decision to try to finish with three times as much as was offered him in the beginning. Only when Portia decides that Shylock will not get a single ducat, does Sender see this as the beginning of the »injustice of the Christians that just does not end.«[40]

Shakespeare's Shylock is indeed condemned for the attempted murder of a Christian. Sender sums it up in his disbelief that someone can first borrow money, is then not able to pay it back but receives ten times as much later, while the moneylender loses everything, even his religion. The accuser, who demands

37 Shakespeare, *The Merchant of Venice*, 87.

38 »›Ja‹ sagt der Alte und fängt an zu reden über Christen und Juden, und daß wir so bitter von den Christen verfolgt werden – durch Mark und Bein ist es mir gegangen und durch das tiefste Herz. Bis dahin hab' ich noch nicht so viel nachgedacht über uns und die Polen, und hab' geglaubt, es schickt sich so, aber jetzt haben sich mir die Augen aufgetan über das blutige Unrecht, das wir erdulden.« Franzos, *Der Pojaz*, 63.

39 Ibid., 64.

40 »und hier fängt das Unrecht der Christen an und hört gar nicht auf.« Ibid., 68.

his rights, ends up being the accused. Sender reacts with outrage. It may be a coincidence, but this is very similar to a reaction described by Heinrich Heine when he saw the play in England. He recounts that an English woman called out at the end that »the poor man is wronged.«[41] Sender also shares his emotions on the matter with an insightful analysis as well: »Threatened [Antonio's] life? Why did Antonio sign such a bond? Why did the court allow such a bond to be sued for? Now it occurs to them!«[42]

Here, Sender Glatteis, an apparently naive and poorly educated Hasid, shows an unusually sophisticated legal understanding. He not only, like Heine's female spectator, feels that the lawsuit is unfair. He also knows the exact reason for this: The immoral contract should never have been accepted by the judge as something enforceable. Therefore, although one could have stopped Shylock on legal grounds from the very beginning, they instead led him into a trap. Shylock is brought down by the deliberate misconstrual of the law and even accused of attempted murder,[43] thus changing positions from being the accuser to being the defendant. The false jurist is even impudent enough to say that »he« was being gracious towards Shylock by not ordering his execution.

The remarkable difference in the view of Shylock in Franzos' two works is thus quite evident. What made Franzos change his interpretation as strongly as he did within merely a decade? One answer can be found in the legal philosophy of Rudolf von Jhering, who in his essay *Der Kampf ums Recht* (»The Struggle for Law«) interprets the lawsuit in nearly the same way that the character Sender does, a few years before *Der Pojaz* was written. This common new understanding of Shylock's mischief is unlikely to be a coincidence. There are several connections between the intellectuals Franzos and Jhering, who indeed met one another at least at two different stages of their lives, as Franzos wrote in his article on Jhering in the *Deutsche Dichtung* monthly.[44] Their first meeting took place at the University of Vienna as professor and student;[45] their second twenty years later, after Franzos published his novel *Ein Kampf ums Recht* (»A Struggle for

41 »Als ich dieses Stück [Kaufmann von Venedig] in Drurylane aufführen sah, stand hinter mir, in der Loge, eine blasse Britin, welche am Ende des vierten Aktes heftig weinte und mehrmals ausrief: the poor man is wronged! (dem armen Mann geschieht Unrecht!).« Heinrich Heine, »Shakespeare's Mädchen und Frauen,« in *Heinrich Heines Sämtliche Werke*, vol. 8 (Leipzig: Insel-Verlag, 1913), 155–302, here 252.

42 »Nach dem Leben getrachtet? Warum hat Anton so einen Wechsel unterschrieben? Warum hat das Gericht erlaubt, daß so ein Wechsel eingeklagt wird? Jetzt fällt es ihnen ein!« Franzos, *Der Pojaz*, 64.

43 Sinsheimer, *Shylock*, 135.

44 Franzos, »Rudolf von Jhering«, in *Deutsche Dichtung*, 50–52.

45 Ibid., 50.

Law«). This novel refers to Jhering's ideas in its title, and explores his philosophy in literary form for the first time. Franzos' novel concentrates, however, on the Galician Hutsuls[46] and their struggle against a Polish nobleman.[47] Jhering read and even commented on the novel in later editions of his essay *The Struggle for Law*.[48]

Jhering and his article The Struggle for Law

In 1872 Rudolf von Jhering held a talk on his understanding of law during his farewell ceremony as professor of law in Vienna. He published it under the title *The Struggle for Law*[49] the same year. Jhering's work is not only of high literary quality, it is also an attempt to present his ideas to non-lawyers. His success is reflected in the high number of sales of his essay, which was translated into more than fourteen languages and was in its sixth German edition by 1880.[50]

In his article, Jhering advanced the view that a legal system only operates effectively if the individuals are ready to assert their rights. At the same time he defended the absolute validity of the law as the basis of these rights.[51] He accentuated the innovative power that a sense of justice can provide, as »without the suspension of existing rights [...] legal progress is inconceivable«.[52] According to him, the internal development of law was connected to the external – cultural and historical – development of the affected society.[53] He therefore pleaded for the responsible adoption of the law, which not only entails its application, but also the need to fight for one's rights, if one feels that they have been violated. Jhering accentuated the importance of having a sense of justice, arguing that law is not only an abstract norm to be followed; it is also connected to one's personality. If someone robs you, not only are your rights violated, but your welfare and honour are affected as well. According to Jhering, fighting for the law meant standing up for oneself, something that should also be an obligation with regard to one's community. For Jhering, it was the idea within

46 Ruthenian Greek-Catholic mountain dwellers of the Carpathians.
47 Karl Emil Franzos, *Ein Kampf ums Recht* (Berlin: Verlag Neues Leben, 1970).
48 Rudolf von Jhering, *Der Kampf um's Recht* (Wien: Manz, 1872), IX, 64–65.
49 Ibid.
50 See Jhering's preface to the 6th edition of his essay. Rudolf von Jhering, *Der Kampf um's Recht* (Wien: Manz, 1880), vii–viii.
51 Rudolf von Jhering, *Der Geist des Rechts*, ed. Fritz Buchenwald (Bremen: Carl Schünemann Verlag, 1965), 28.
52 »ohne Aufhebung bestehender Rechte [...] ist der Fortschritt des Rechts selber nicht denkbar.« Jhering, *Geist des Rechts*, 30.
53 Elias Hurwicz, *Rudolf von Ihering und die deutsche Rechtswissenschaft. Mit besonderer Berücksichtigung des Strafrechts* (Berlin: Guttentag Verlagsbuchhandlung, 1911), 2.

the law that was paramount. He believed that most people litigated for idealistic reasons, and not only as the result of a cost-benefit analysis.[54]

To explain his theses, he chose no lesser example than Shakespeare's drama *The Merchant of Venice* and polemicized against the contemporary interpretation of the case that »justice« is shown to Shylock. After having analysed the play briefly he came to the conclusion that the root of injustice lay in the recognition of the debenture by the court. Jhering argued: »The bond was in itself null and void because its provisions were contrary to good morals; the judge should, therefore, have refused to enforce its terms on this ground from the first.«[55] However, because the court had accepted the debenture, the next interpretation of the contract was, from a legal point of view, more than just simply wrong:

> But as he did not do so, as the »wise Daniel« admitted its validity, it was a wretched subterfuge, a miserable piece of pettifoggery, to deny the man whose right he had already admitted, to cut a pound of flesh from the living body, the right to the shedding of the blood which necessarily accompanied it.[56]

According to Josef Kohler, a contemporary colleague and professor of law at the University of Würzburg, Jhering, whom he deemed »one of the most prominent scholars of our time«, was the first ever to defend Shylock from a legal perspective, thus directing the attention of the legal community to Shakespeare. According to Kohler, Jhering broke with common opinion on the case and argued that Shylock, whose downfall had been glorified and celebrated to that point, had in fact been seriously wronged.[57]

Kohler harshly disagreed with Jhering's case interpretation. He dedicated to the Shylock case a large chapter of his book *Shakespeare vor dem Forum der Jurisprudenz* (»Shakespeare before the forum of jurisprudence«) and demonstrated a completely different understanding of the law and its evolution. According to Kohler, Portia's judgement was right, not due to any legal argumentation, however, but because Shylock's purposes were evil. His desire to abuse the law as a means of attaining malicious revenge thus warranted that any opportunity could be taken to stop him. Kohler argued that the spirit of justice is not on Shylock's side, but on that side of the judge, who is forced to bend the law for a higher good. This argumentation explains why the judge must convict Shylock with such harsh severity to create an example for the future.[58] As even Shylock

54 Jhering, *Der Kampf um's Recht* (Wien: Manz, 1884), 18.

55 Rudolf von Jhering, *The Struggle for Law*, trans. John J. Lalor (Chicago: Callaghan and Company, 1915), 87.

56 Jhering, *Struggle for Law*, 87–88.

57 Josef Kohler, *Shakespeare vor dem Forum der Jurisprudenz* (Würzburg: Verlag Stahel'sche Universitätsbuch- und Kunsthandlung, 1883), 12.

58 Kohler, *Shakespeare vor dem Forum*, 95.

does not appeal against the verdict, he shows that he accepts the outcome of the case to his disadvantage.

Kohler did not doubt for a second that Shylock was the villain in this play and every opportunity to defeat him was therefore good. He thus even praised the breaking of the law by the false lawyer as the epitome of progress.[59] Kohler also disagreed with Jhering's interpretation that the case revealed an anti-Semitic motivation. According to Kohler, Shylock was to be reviled as a usurer, not as a Jew. Furthermore, Kohler defended the judge's decision that Shylock had to convert to Christianity as a »historical« truth, as people were always forced to convert »under the sign of the executioner.«[60] The contrast in their interpretation of the play could not be starker.

According to Jhering, Shylock's case was so uniquely interesting because the law itself was addressed in the verdict. He quoted what was for him Shylock's most important remark:

> The pound of flesh, which I demand of him,
> is dearly bought, is mine, and I will have it;
> If you deny me, fie upon your law!
> There is no force in the decrees of Venice!
> – I crave the law
> – I stay here upon [sic!] my bond.[61]

Jhering argued that Shylock's concern is not for the flesh, but the principle:

> These four words [I crave the law] change Shylock's claim into a question of the law of Venice. To what mighty, giant dimensions does not the weak man grow, when he speaks these words! It is no longer the Jew demanding his pound of flesh; it is the law of Venice itself knocking at the door of Justice; for his rights and the law of Venice are one and the same; they both stand or fall together.[62]

According to Jhering, the whole tragedy of the play lay in the betrayal of Shylock's belief in his rights and the rights of all medieval Jews, when he called him »that pariah of society who cried in vain for justice.«[63] Using the example of Shylock, Jhering showed that he had to fail due to the unequal treatment of Jews and Christians and not because of the merits of the case. For him, the same legal system had to be equally valid for Christians and Jews – both in medieval Venice and, even more so, in the Habsburg Empire.

59 Ibid., 90.

60 »mit dem Winke des Henkers«. Ibid., 96.

61 Shakespeare cited by Jhering, *Struggle for Law*, 80. In the German version Jhering cites the translation by August W. Schlegel and Ludwig Tieck, retranslated into English by Lalor.

62 Jhering, *Struggle for Law*, 86–87.

63 Ibid., 82.

Legal equality is based on a very modern understanding of law, within the field of legal studies as well. It is linked to an acknowledgement of the equality of people within society, as the French Revolution established in Europe for the first time. With the growth of the Enlightenment, along with Napoleon's campaign, it spread over Europe.[64]

Jhering's interpretation of the Shylock case was by no means welcomed as a long overdue corrective, whether in legal literature or in Shakespearean research. Even in later interpretations, one can find different understandings of the case. Gustav Landauer (1870–1919), a German Jewish philosopher, writer, and political activist, preferred to support Kohler's argumentation and listed other Shakespeare scholars, who agreed with this view.[65] Landauer, like Kohler, wrote that Shylock accepted the shift in the case – the literary interpretation. This served for him as evidence that Portia's resolution was correct with respect to the contemporary understanding of contracts.[66] Landauer supported the opinion that the play represented a struggle for a milder understanding of law. The contract had been legal according to the old Roman law, but was no longer in accordance with the new understanding of morals, which is why Landauer supported the turn of the case: »If you take the contract so seriously, so literally, do not wonder and do not complain if the judge is as literal about it as you: blood is not flesh.«[67] Like Kohler, Landauer did not see a single reason to defend Shylock.

Shylock between Haskalah and Hasidism

There is no doubt that Franzos had read Jhering's article and discussed his legal philosophy in his novel *Der Pojaz*. Franzos addressed the particular problems of the Galician shtetl using the example of Shylock – but even more so, the example of Sender's fate. Since at least two different Jewish worldviews co-existed in the

64 *Handwörterbuch zur deutschen Rechtsgeschichte*, vol. 1, s.v. »Gleichheit«.

65 Landauer, *Shakespeare*, 46–47. Among Shylock interpretations of these days one can name the one by Dietrich Schwanitz, who contradicts Jhering directly, but does not even understand his argument. He tries to prove that only Portia was able to read the contract abstractly, but then beats Shylock with his own weapon and reads the contract even more literally than Shylock himself. Though his argumentation is self contradictory, he did not even take into account the possibility of refusing the contract. His Talmudic argument misses any scientific foundations. Dietrich Schwanitz, *Das Shylock-Syndrom oder die Dramaturgie der Barbarei* (Frankfurt a. M.: Eichborn, 1997), 104.

66 Landauer, *Shakespeare*, 49.

67 »Nimmst du's mit dem Vertrag so ernst, so buchstäblich, so wundre dich nicht und beklage dich nicht, daß auch der Richter es buchstäblich macht wie du: Blut ist kein Fleisch.« Ibid., 48.

region, Haskalah and Hasidism, neither of them could be without influence. Sender stands between the two and his personal conflict with his hometown also derives from his confrontation with the possibilities offered him by the Jewish Enlightenment. Through this text Franzos was »intent on furthering the Haskalah ideal of dual and compatible German national/cultural and Jewish religious identities among as yet unacculturated Central and Eastern European Jews.«[68]

In tracking the fate of Sender one can find different approaches to link the two perspectives. Sender carries in his heart both the heritage of the shtetl and the vision of a better life. He never wants to fight the Hasidim, but to open them to Western culture and secular education. By playing Shylock he wants to evoke the same change of view in his co-religionists, with the play serving to illustrate the injustice inflicted on the Jews in Galicia. Sender prefers this role even to Lessing's *Nathan der Weise* (»Nathan the Wise«),[69] which renders homage to reason. This gentle and wise man seems at first glance much more suitable to teach society to be more tolerant than the ambiguous Shylock. The distance felt by Sender towards Nathan and his rational world[70] may have been precipitated by the fact that his way of thinking, arguing, and acting is very different to the reasoning the Hasidim were used to. The play is instead geared more toward the Western European intelligentsia.[71] Sender chooses Shylock as the most interesting role because of his emotional nature. He is even ashamed by the fact that he prefers such a wild and vindictive character to the noble and mild Nathan.[72]

It is therefore likely that the points of reference of Franzos' novel were mainly the seemingly irrational and emotional Hasidim and their particular circumstances, with the author even perhaps slightly distancing his work from the intellectual perspective of the Haskalah.[73] The colourfully dramatized injustice in Shakespeare's drama was closer to the real situation at hand and evoked a great sense of injustice. Shylock wants revenge, is not mild and understanding,

68 Elizabeth Loentz, »Karl Emil Franzos and Bertha Papenheim's Portraits of the (Eastern European Jewish) Artist,« in *The Jews of Eastern Europe*, eds. Leonard Greenspoon, Ronald A. Simkins, and Brian J. Horowitz (Omaha: Creighton University Press, 2005), 81–82.

69 Lessing published the play *Nathan the Wise* in 1779. It was directly influenced by the thought of Moses Mendelssohn. The play teaches the equality of all religions and the character Nathan represents a wise, mild, intelligent, and enlightened Jew.

70 Franzos, *Der Pojaz*, 104.

71 Ibid., 95–99.

72 Ibid., 104.

73 Sybille Hubach, *Galizische Träume. Die jüdischen Erzählungen des Karl Emil Franzos* (Stuttgart: Verlag Hans-Dieter Heinz, 1986), 134.

but instead returns the hatred he was treated with throughout his life.[74] Perhaps Franzos saw the need for a rebellious Shylock to prepare the ground before anyone would be able to behave as mildly and understandingly as Nathan.

By comparing the fate of Moses, the »Shylock of Barnow«, and Sender's interpretation of Shylock, I will focus on the development in Franzos' interpretation of Shylock and his understanding of law. In the first story the narrator directly criticises Jewish religious and social laws as well as the narrow-mindedness and lack of education, with the narrator indirectly intimating that the situation was also a product of anti-Jewish behaviour and legislation. The novella reveals the inner conflict of the feelings and religious understanding of Moses, the father: Even if people are good, they do wrong because they do not know any better. The character Shylock is identified with Moses, a man who brings about his daughter's death, although it brings him suffering as well. He even senses the injustice of the matter, but he still hurts her due to his religious convictions.

As mentioned before, this text is connected to the novel *Der Pojaz* as both stories take place in the same fictional town of Barnow. Franzos used to link many of his stories and some of his characters appear in different works, which is why the figure Sender knows the figure Moses and his family tragedy. Even though Sender is a particularly moral and upright person in his Hasidic shtetl, he supports Moses' treatment of Esther and compares her to Shakespeare's Jessica, because she ran away with a Christian and left her father. Only later does he learn from his first love Malke, a very intelligent and educated »Germanized«[75] Jewish woman, to understand Esther's decision. Later, Sender helps Malke to run away with her beloved, whom she chose of her own accord.

In contrast to Franzos' first novella, Sender identifies with Shylock and, therefore can also be identified with him. Shylock as a symbol moves from being a perpetrator to a victim in two regards: Actively, because Sender interprets Shakespeare's Shylock as a victim of the anti-Semitic Christian court; passively, because Sender is the victim of Hasidic injustice, i.e. its intolerance towards his artistic needs.

Just like Esther, Sender receives a secular education and holds an unacceptable wish in his heart and mind. Both characters represent what Franzos considered to be modern and progressive – a change within society towards the integration of secular culture within the religious community. Sender appraises theatre the same way as he does religion: For him acting entails commitment to a service, and in it he sees his own calling and fulfilment. But this ostensibly harmless wish stands in contrast to his surroundings. For Hasidim, performing on a stage and

74 Shakespeare, *Merchant of Venice*, 87.

75 For Franzos, »Germanizing« means cultural nationalism, but not baptism. Like the Maskilim, he considers Judaism to be a religion, not a nation.

learning German to this purpose is a sin to be punished very severely in accordance with their religious law. That is why Sender has to learn German secretly in a Dominican monastery and falls ill with consumption. When the local rabbi finds out about it, he banishes him from the community. Even though Sender is later reintegrated into society, when the rabbi lifts his ban, he runs away from his hometown to pursue his life purpose, but in doing so exposes himself unprotected to the Galician winter, which wears down his already weakened body. Before he manages to escape completely, he is caught by his foster mother who, against all reason, forces him to return to the shtetl, where he ultimately dies.

In the end, the reader is left with a feeling of injustice. The death of Sender seems at first glance to be completely senseless and arbitrary. Reconsidered in connection with Jhering's thinking, however, it becomes clear that Sender died, in some way, on a mission for subjective rights. In German the word »Sender« is indeed associated with being sent, perhaps as a missionary or messenger. Sender's struggle can then be understood as his personal fight in the spirit of the Haskalah. By performing Shylock on stage, Sender seeks to change Christian-Jewish relations; in his struggle for his personal rights he fights against what he perceives as antiquated Hasidic customs and works to change Jewish society. The shtetl does not however allow him to follow his calling as an actor, thus robbing him of any chance at self-fulfillment. Sender's struggle to be able to perform theatre turns not only into a struggle for his rights – it involves, from Jhering's view, his very moral survival.[76] Sender never questions his religion, but he trusts in his God-given talent and fate. While he questions some of the antiquated laws of the Hasidim, he never questions his Jewishness or the law of God. But he seeks a new interpretation of these things that allows him to be who he is.

Until his death Sender remains true to himself and believes in the honesty of his subjective rights. But his concrete dream remains unfulfilled: he never has the chance to play Shylock on stage in front of an audience. Still, in the last days of his life, when death is already looming, he is allowed to see his Shylock role performed by the talented and world famous Jewish actor Bogumil Dawison,[77] who descended, just like him, from a poor family in a Galician shtetl. In contrast to the novel's character Sender, the very real Dawison had quite a successful

76 Jhering, *Der Kampf um's Recht*, 20.

77 Dawison, Bogumil (1818–1872), was a Jewish actor from Galicia, who began his career in Warsaw and achieved great success as an interpreter of Shakespeare, Goethe, and Schiller on the German stage. His greatest successes were the Shakespearean roles of Richard III, Shylock, Lear, and Othello. Dawison was regarded as one of the great actors of his time and one of the first of Jewish origin. *Encyclopaedia Judaica*, s.v. »Dawison«.

acting career. This suggests that Galicia was already changing, something that could be interpreted as a positive sign for the future for those Galician Jews, who wanted to take part in Western culture.[78]

Conclusion

If Jhering had been asked to write an essay on »religion in the mirror of law« he would have argued that, in the eye of the law, people are equal no matter which religion they belong to. Using the example of Shylock, he showed that it was neither the law of Venice nor the behaviour of Shylock that directly led to his conviction, but rather the intentional misconstrual of the law in support of the widespread anti-Semitism of the time. Furthermore, Jhering characterized Shylock as a symbol of civil-rights activism, since he had nothing to gain apart from justice. Shylock treats the law idealistically and believes in its power and his own rights. According to Jhering, this was the way that everyone should understand the law. Law is organically connected to society and is transformed as society changes. As Shylock's case shows, it is not only important to contend with the state as a means of shaping the law, but in private matters as well. Religious communities should thus adapt to the needs of their believers.

Franzos concentrated on this point and confronts his readership with law in the mirror of Hasidism. He sought to demonstrate that in many respects, its law is outdated, especially in questions of education, marriage, and possible participation in secular politics, culture, and society. Nevertheless, he also points out the interdependence between constitutional law and the cultural isolation of the Jewish minority of Eastern Europe.[79] As Franzos saw it, decades of judicial and social oppression of Jews had led to a need for them to create their own cultural system, and one which protected their identity as a defence mechanism against inhospitable Christian surroundings. Franzos therefore expanded the new symbolic role of Shakespeare's Shylock, who helps to understand the anti-Semitic prejudices in Europe and its courts, and to depict the effects of blind hatred and arrogance. The identification of Shylock with Sender also symbolizes

78 Another particularly famous example was the Galician actor and author Alexander Granach, who identified directly with Sender and his perception of Shylock. In his autobiography, *Da geht ein Mensch*, he fulfilled the wish and fate of the fictive character Sender. He not only plays Shylock on stage, but he also changes the end of Shylock's history within his text, both according to Sender's dream. The author born as Jessaja even changes his name to Alexander, the original Greek version of Sender, as explained on the first pages of Franzos' novel. Alexander Granach, *Da geht ein Mensch. Autobiographischer Roman* (Augsburg: Ölbaum Verlag, 2003).

79 Theisohn, Eruv. Herkunft, 173–178.

the struggle to define law within the Hasidic world. Sender does everything it takes to fulfil his existential wish to become an actor but, in doing so, comes again and again into conflict with the customary law of the Hasidim. His death – as Franzos sees it – is a direct consequence of the antiquated Hasidic system and their unwillingness to change to meet the needs of the younger generation.

The difference between Jhering and Franzos is one of perspective, not of intention: They both sought to educate people to be responsible in their treatment of the state, and of private and religious law, and to strengthen their sense of justice; both did this in their respective fields, Jhering in legal philosophy and Franzos in literature. In light of the legal reforms of the Habsburg Empire and the new, though still rather theoretical, equality of the Jews,[80] it was Franzos' view that the Jews needed to take an active role in their own equality, behaving as citizens and taking part in the new social order and thus in their own legal emancipation.

Without the application of legal knowledge, a law is worth as much as Shylock's contract with Antonio. The philosophy of *The Struggle for Law* is suggested as a solution to the »Jewish question« in Galicia, as an ethical and practical way out of isolation. As a learned lawyer and professional writer, Franzos can be understood in this regard, but also a messenger in that he transformed the theoretical ideas of Jhering into literature and used the example of a Hasidic town to illustrate how one should understand law and behave as a responsible citizen. In doing so, he did not suggest giving up tradition, but opening it and reforming it.

Anna Juraschek

80 Wolfdieter Bihl, »Die Juden,« in *Die Habsburgermonarchie 1848–1918*, vol. 3, part 2: *Die Völker des Reiches*, eds. Adam Wandruszka, Peter Urbanitsch and Helmut Rumpler (Wien: Verlag der Österreichischen Akademie der Wissenschaften 2003), 880–948, here 890–896.

»Imagined Law« and »Imagined Communities«: Confessional Collectives and their Ideas for a Federal Habsburg Partition of Galicia

Nations do not just exist, nations are »made«. For several decades, contemporary historiography has been stressing the constructed character of national collectives, ever since Benedict Anderson coined the term »imagined communities«.[1] The constructed character of communities does not apply only to the concept of the nation, but also to the social and religious arenas. What counts as characteristic and essential with regard to a certain confessional community is dependent, to a significant degree, on the practices of its members and is the result of a process of negotiating, arguing, and imagining. These attempts serve to distinguish the respective denomination from others and to form its self-image and self-perception. The borderlines of the confessional communities imagined in this way are negotiable and shifting.

In contrast to this perspective, I claim that the law, while also being constructive, is capable of drawing distinctive lines between different groups at least from a normative perspective. It constructs, creates, and delineates certain communities by way of its specific normative means, including statutes, patents, and administrative acts, and through legal practice as it is reflected in court decisions. The law is often flexible enough to integrate newly emerging communities into its framework; although it is often too inflexible to answer social or political challenges. The federal plans for Galicia in the 19th century serve as an example for this.

Historical debates over legal reforms serve as an ideal mirror to reflect and to merge both the constructedness of confessional communities and the norma-

1 Benedict Anderson, *Imagined Communities: Reflections on the Origin and Spread of Nationalism* (London: Verso, 2006); Idem, *Die Erfindung der Nation: Zur Karriere eines folgenreichen Konzepts* (Frankfurt am Main et al.: Campus, 1996). Compare also the introduction in Hans Peter Hye, Brigitte Mazohl and Jan Paul Niederkorn, eds., *Nationalgeschichte als Artefakt: Zum Paradigma »Nationalstaat« in den Historiographien Deutschlands, Italiens und Österreichs* (Wien: Verlag der Österreichischen Akademie der Wissenschaften, 2009), 3–19.

tiveness of law. In this context, law becomes a field of imagination in itself, in which the representatives of »imagined communities« construct a law that cannot yet be implemented. I refer to this, therefore, as *imagined law*.

However, the logics of both of these discourses differ. Modern law, once normatively set, never refers to any single community, always dealing instead with competing and overlapping collective structures. This attribute of modern law, its universality, has influenced the discourse on *imagined law*. In contrast to concepts of nation or religion that refer to a single community, concepts of law and attempts at legal reform have to be phrased in a more general manner in order to be perceived as legal arguments and to serve more than only one community. In this respect, *imagined law* appears to be rather inclusive, whereas the imagination of national and religious communities tends to be exclusive.

In the second half of the 19th century, the conflict between socially constructed, »imagined« communities in the Habsburg Empire with their blurred borderlines and their legal-normative status resulted in attempts to bring about legal renewal and plans for federalization. The Habsburg partition of Galicia serves as a good example for the national, social, political, and religious contexts of these federalization plans.[2] My paper will focus on the question of how the proposed *imagined law*, and thus the imagined federal state, would deal with religious diversity of the imagined communities in Galicia, and which religious implications these plans contained. The Galician Jews and their federal ideas serve as the main example for this, while the role of Roman and Greek Catholicism is examined briefly.

Although all of the attempts to federalize the Habsburg monarchy in the 19th century ultimately failed, interest in a federal and multilayer state structure persisted throughout the century, both in the dynastic centre in Vienna and in the imperial peripheries. Considering the failure to put federalization plans into political practice, the underlying reasons for the remaining popularity of federal ideas deserve our attention. In the course of the second half of 19th century, at the latest, the Habsburg monarchy shifted from being a pre-modern empire with dynastic structures to an empire with elements of a composite state that relied on legal unity, the rule of law, and a rationalized administrative body.[3] This attempt

2 Joachim Kühl, *Föderationspläne im Donauraum und in Ostmitteleuropa* (München: Oldenbourg 1958); Rudolf Wierer: *Der Föderalismus im Donauraum* (Graz–Köln: Böhlau, 1960).

3 I follow Osterhammel's opinion that the Habsburg monarchy can historically be regarded as an empire; see Jürgen Osterhammel, *Die Verwandlung der Welt: Eine Geschichte des 19. Jahrhunderts* (München: Beck, 2009), 624–627. For the debate on this question compare also Johannes Feichtinger, Ursula Prutsch, and Moritz Csáky, eds., *Habsburg postcolonial: Machtstrukturen und kollektives Gedächtnis* (Innsbruck et al.: Studienverlag 2003); Kerstin S. Jobst, Julia Obertreis, and

at legal unity was rather fragile, a fact that is best expressed with regard to the fragmentary character of Austrian constitutional law.[4] The dynastic unity was in fact also placed in question in the light of the historical formations to which the representatives of various national movements frequently referred, including former kingdoms, counties, and principalities.[5]

Attempts to rationalize and to centralize political governance through legal and administrative means, however, were mainly hindered by the lack of homogeneity within the society. Multi-ethnicity, different denominations and religious confessions, and social and economic divides did not provide the ideal ground for a homogenous national state – at least not in the case of the Empire – in accordance with what was perceived as the »Western model« realized for example in France. Federalism offered alternative ways to overcome this impasse, since it was based on decentralization and on a multilevel structure as befits a society with overlapping collective and individual identities and loyalties. Therefore, not only did parts of the Viennese bureaucracy favour federal models, but representatives of different social milieus participated in the debate on federalism as well.

The ideal of federalism as a viable alternative to both a centralized monarchy and the development of nation states led even to an overestimation of the federal model. Even today, especially in some national historiographies, the view has persisted that the thorough federalization of Austria could have successfully prevented the clash of nations that culminated in the breaking apart of the monarchy and the emergence of nation states in the aftermath of World War I. This perspective is caused by the prevailing national paradigm that still determines the historiography on federalism in the Habsburg Empire.[6] In this

Ricarda Vulpius, »Neuere Imperiumsforschung in der Osteuropäischen Geschichte: Die Habsburgermonarchie, das Russländische Reich und die Sowjetunion,« in *Ostmitteleuropa transnational*, ed. Peter Haslinger (Leipzig: Leipziger Universitätsverlag, 2008), 27–56; Pieter M. Judson, »L'Autriche-Hongrie était-elle un empire?,« *Annales, Histoire, Sciences sociales* 63 (2008): 563–596.

4 After the failure of Austrian constitutionalism, from December 21, 1867 on, Austrian constitutional law consisted of five special statutes known as the *Staatsgrundgesetze des Kaiserthums Österreich* or *Dezemberverfassung* that referred only to certain important aspects of the state's organization; they were not introduced through the usual set of general constitutional principles common to modern constitutionalism. For details, see the German version of the constitution at http://www.verfassungen.de/at/.

5 Rudolf Schlesinger, *Federalism in Central and Eastern Europe* (London: Kegan Paul, 1945), 155–158.

6 See Csilla Dömök, *Nationalitätenfrage und Verfassungsgeschichte in Österreich zwischen 1848–1867: Österreich und der Föderalismus* (Berlin: wvb, 2010). Compare also Helmut Rumpler, *Eine Chance für Mitteleuropa: Bürgerliche Emanzipation und Staatsverfall in der Habsburgermonarchie* (Wien: Ueberreuter 1997);

context federalization is seen as a legal mean of placating the demands of national movements and of creating nationally more or less homogenous spaces. Helmut Rumpler has depicted this perspective as naïve and called it a »myth« that a federal order in the Danube area would have served to »reconcile the nations«.[7]

In addition to the national aspect, however, one must not overlook the social, economic, and religious components of a federal order. Especially with regard to the history of the Habsburg Empire, federalism stands for an order that would integrate the vast social heterogeneity of the region, i.e. federalism is the organization of diversity.

The partition plan for Galicia, 1848–1849

Galicia played a major role in many of the discussions held on introducing federalism to the Habsburg Empire. One has to look at its social, ethnic-national, and religious settings in order to understand these attempts. The strong entanglement between religion and nationality or ethnicity in Galicia contrasted sharply with the situation in other Habsburg crownlands (*Kronländer*). In Galicia the degree of differentiation between one's national or ethnic identity and one's religious adherence could be quite significant. The largest ethnic groups in Galicia were the Poles, Ruthenians, and Jews,[8] whereby the Poles and Ruthenians also corresponded with the major denominations of Roman Catholics and Uniates, later Greek Catholics.[9] Uniatism was supported by the Ruthenian Palatinate at the beginning of the 18th century in opposition to Orthodoxy, although before the three partitions of Poland-Lithuania it had often been regarded as a form of second-class Catholicism by the Polish rulers and society. The name of the Uniate Church was thus changed to the Greek Catholic Church during the Habsburg period as a means of associating with it a higher status, and it was granted at least formal-legal equality with other denominations during the Enlightenment era under Maria Theresa and Joseph II. While the Roman

Robert A. Kann, *Das Nationalitätenproblem der Habsburgermonarchie: Geschichte und Ideengehalt der nationalen Bestrebungen vom Vormärz bis zur Auflösung des Reiches im Jahre 1918*, 2 vols., 2. ed. (Graz–Köln: Böhlau, 1964); Kühl, *Föderationspläne*; Wierer, *Föderalismus*.

7 Helmut Rumpler, *Das Völkermanifest Kaiser Karls vom 16. Oktober 1918: Letzter Versuch zur Rettung des Habsburgerreiches* (München: Oldenbourg, 1966), 5.

8 For more details, see Rudolf A. Mark, *Galizien unter österreichischer Herrschaft. Verwaltung-Kirche-Bevölkerung* (Marburg: Herder-Institut, 1994), 53–65.

9 For the following compare John-Paul Himka, »Confessional relations in Galicia,« in *Galicia: A multicultured land*, eds. Christopher Hann and Paul R. Magocsi (Toronto et al.: University of Toronto Press, 2005), 22–35.

Catholic Church clung to its lost privileges in Galicia, the Greek Catholics profited in the long run by the emergence of an educated Ruthenian clergy that later played an important role within the national movement.[10] After the failure of the revolution of 1848–1849 the antagonism between the Roman and the Greek Catholics increased further, and hence between Ruthenians and Poles.

The reasons for this confrontation were threefold. They were national, since the majority of Ruthenians gradually became pro-Russian or at least anti-Polish in orientation; they were social, since land ownership was predominantly the domain of the Polish Roman Catholic landlords, despite the abolition of serfdom in 1848 that had emancipated the Ruthenian Greek Catholic peasants; and they were religious, since the inter-confessional struggle for influence, dominance, and souls persisted between the Roman and Greek Catholics. Conflicts thus hardened along social, ethnic, and religious lines.

The situation was also aggravated by the fact that 19th-century Viennese politics relied mostly on the Poles and the Roman Catholic Church.[11] This is illustrated by the fact that a ministry was established, officially without portfolio, to deal with Galician affairs, but which was led exclusively by a Pole who acted more as a representative of his nation than of his region.[12] In the last decade of 19th century, Vienna intervened quite often in the internal matters of the Greek Catholic Church, e.g. by supporting the reforms of monastic life within the Basilian order that were implemented by the Vatican. It also took measures to further the process of Polonization and to nurture Roman Catholicism as a means of opposing religious Russophilism.[13]

This bi-confessional and bi-national conflict is reflected in the discussions on the creation of a federal order throughout the 19th century. One example can be found in the debates on a new constitution in the Kremsier Revolutionary Assembly (*Reichstag*) of 1848–1849. Although federalists were much the minority, both sides, Poles and Ruthenians, made efforts toward the federalization of the

10 Oleh Turij, »Die Griechisch-Katholische Kirche und die Entstehung der ukrainischen nationalen Bewegung in Galizien,« *Ostkirchliche Studien* 47 (1998): 3–21. Compare also Oksana Leskiv in this volume.

11 See Rumpler, *Chance für Mitteleuropa*, 287–289, 429–431; Himka, »Confessional Relations,« 29; compare also Idem, *Religion and Nationality in Western Ukraine: The Greek Catholic Church and the Ruthenian National Movement in Galicia, 1867–1900* (Montreal: McGill-Queen's University Press, 1999).

12 For details, see Christoph von Bieberstein, *Freiheit in der Unfreiheit: Die nationale Autonomie der Polen in Galizien nach dem österreichisch-ungarischen Ausgleich von 1867. Ein konservativer Aufbruch im mitteleuropäischen Vergleich* (Wiesbaden: Harrassowitz, 1993), 125–132.

13 For details, compare Himka, *Religion and Nationality*, 73–134, especially 79–84, 121–125.

Austrian monarchy. One interesting proposal for a federal partition of Galicia into two parts was made by one of the leading Ruthenian deputies, the Greek Catholic bishop of Przemyśl, Gregor Jachimowicz. His request was already widely supported by the Ruthenian inhabitants of Galicia before the elections to the Kremsier Reichstag, but was rejected by the Polish Galicians.[14] Jachimowicz was part of the Ruthenian clergy and intelligentsia that formed a parliamentary alliance with Ruthenian peasant deputies, representing an »awakening of national sentiment«.[15] With the support of Polish deputies, however, he was elected to the Constitutional Commission of the Kremsier Reichstag.[16]

While Florian Ziemialkowsky, the Polish Galician deputy of the Constitutional Commission in Kremsier, favoured the federal partition of the monarchy along the existing borders of the crownland and thus upheld the territorial unity of Galicia, Jachimowicz and his supporters in Ruthenian society sought the federal division of Galicia into Polish and Ruthenian parts. None of these attempts succeeded in the end.[17] Especially interesting at this point, however, are the roles that religion and nation played in the logic of the accompanying discourse. According to contemporary self-perception, the Ruthenian movement of 1848 was part of a national awakening, although from the perspective of *the other*, that is Polish politicians and representatives, the Ruthenians did not form a nation, but were bound together only by a common dialect and faith. The Ruthenians adamantly and emotionally argued against this point of view,[18] as illustrated in a speech given by Prokopczyk, a representative at Kremsier:

14 Anton Springer, *Protokolle des Verfassungs-Ausschusses im Österreichischen Reichstage 1848–1849* (Leipzig: Hirzel, 1885), 24; Wierer, *Föderalismus*, 38; Rudolf Wagner, *Die Revolutionsjahre 1848/49 im Königreich Galizien-Lodomerien (einschließlich Bukowina): Dokumente aus österreichischer Zeit* (München: Der Südostdeutsche, 1983), 54–73; Andreas Gottsmann, »Der Reichstag 1848/49 und der Reichsrat 1861–1865,« in *Die Habsburgermonarchie 1848–1918*, vol. 7/1/1, *Verfassung und Parlamentarismus: Verfassungsrecht, Verfassungswirklichkeit, zentrale Repräsentativkörperschaften*, eds. Helmut Rumpler and Peter Urbanitsch (Wien: Verlag der Österreichischen Akademie der Wissenschaften, 2000), 569–665, here 583; Jan Kozik, *The Ukrainian National Movement in Galicia, 1815–1849* (Edmonton: Univ. of Alberta, 1986).

15 Gottsmann, »Der Reichstag 1848/49,« 586–587; John-Paul Himka: *Galician villagers and the Ukrainian national movement in the nineteenth century* (New York: St. Martin's Press, 1988), 123–142.

16 Leopold Sacher-Masoch, *Polnische Revolutionen: Erinnerungen aus Galizien* (Prag: Credner 1863), 320.

17 Wierer, *Föderalismus*, 38; Larry Wolff, *The Idea of Galicia. History and Fantasy in Habsburg Political Culture* (Stanford: Stanford University Press, 2010), 191.

18 Bieberstein, *Freiheit in der Unfreiheit*, 40; Schlesinger, *Federalism*, 158. Schlesinger mentions the fact that, at the Prague Slavic Congress, left-wing Polish politicians agreed with the Ruthenians/Ukrainians on the basis of equal rights for both Galician peoples, ibid.

> I do not understand how religion is to be seen to define who is a Ruthenian; it is my view that ancestry alone accounts for a nation [...] I hope that these representatives do not follow this [...] as such a distinction only arises from a disposition towards persecution.[19]

Even if one agrees with Prokopczyk's argument, one has to admit that the Ruthenian nation-building process was nevertheless partly founded on the basis of the Greek Catholic clerical infrastructure, both institutional and intellectual. Jachimowicz explicitly stated at the Kremsier Constitutional Commission that it was natural for the Greek Catholic clergy to represent Ruthenian national interests.[20] This presages the processes of the nationalization of religion and sacralization of the nation that would take place later.[21] The Polish Galician representative Ziemialkowsky pointed to the fact that Ruthenian peasants who supported the partition of Galicia into two parts had signed the relevant declaration only after being asked by representatives of the Greek Catholic Church to do so.[22] Polish Galicians from Lviv, alarmed by the suggested partition and ready to weaken the increasing political power of the Greek Catholic Church, wrote to the Crown in November 1848:

> We thus dare to lay at the steps of the throne of His Majesty our plea that the decision about the partition of Galicia (into two provinces) not be made before public opinion is consulted via political avenues and not via the church.[23]

Although these concrete Ruthenian partition plans failed as did similar Polish attempts, federalization plans remained on the political agenda. After the Austrian-Hungarian Compromise they led to the »Resolution Campaign« of 1868 that was initiated in the Galician *Landtag* by the federalist and national democrat Frantiszek Smolka as a protest to centralistic Viennese politics.[24] These

19 Sacher-Masoch, *Polnische Revolutionen*, 322.

20 Springer, *Protokolle des Verfassungs-Ausschusses*, 25.

21 Compare Ricarda Vulpius, »Der Kirchenkampf in der Ukraine als Beispiel für Sakralisierung der Nation und Nationalisierung der Religion (1917–1921),« in *Nationalisierung der Religion und Sakralisierung der Nation im östlichen Europa*, ed. Martin Schulze Wessel (Stuttgart: Steiner, 2006), 101–118.

22 Springer, *Protokolle des Verfassungs-Ausschusses*, 20.

23 »So wagen wir es, an den Stufen des Thrones Eurer Majestät die Bitte niederzulegen, daß die Frage über die Theilung Galiziens (in zwei Provinzen), nicht entschieden werde, bis die Meinung der Bevölkerung auf politischem, nicht auf kirchlichem Wege eingeholt werden wird.« Wagner, *Revolutionsjahre 1848/49*, 60.

24 Compare Stanislaw Grodziski, »Der Landtag des Königreiches Galizien und Lodomerien,« in *Habsburgermonarchie 1848–1918*, vol. 8/2, *Politische Öffentlichkeit und Zivilgesellschaft: Die Presse als Faktor der politischen Mobilisierung*, 2163–2165; Hans-Christian Maner, *Galizien: Eine Grenzregion im Kalkül der Donaumonarchie im 18. und 19. Jahrhundert* (München: IKGS Verlag, 2007) 129–146; Bieberstein, *Freiheit in der Unfreiheit*.

and later attempts were crucial in the establishment of an elevated while not fully autonomous status of Galicia within the Empire.[25] However, church activity and nationalist politics had then ceased to be as intertwined.[26]

The concept of personal autonomy

The federalist concepts that were discussed at the Kremsier Reichstag in 1848–1849 and later debated in the Imperial Council (*Reichsrat*) by representatives of the emerging national movements[27] were founded on the premise of homogeneity within the imagined constituent states of the proposed federation. They were inspired by the examples of existing federal countries such as the United States of America and Switzerland and sought to draw new borders in accordance with presumed historical, national, and linguistic areas. The guiding idea behind these attempts was the creation of a set of homogeneous spaces within a heterogeneous unit, an idea that reflected the contemporary territorialization of national discourse.[28] As discussed above, the prevailing national, social, confessional, and economic diversity within the Habsburg monarchy – both at the micro- and macro-levels – contrasted with these visions of federal territorialization as based on such an assumption of homogeneity.

Beyond this national territorial discourse, however, that was taking place in parliamentary bodies such as the *Reichstag* and the *Reichsrat* as well as in regional assemblies (*Landtage*), important alternative ideas also evolved that did not adhere to a territorial paradigm of national discourse or, for that matter, to the traditional territorial view of federalism. The most intriguing concept, developed with regard to national diversity by the Social Democrats Karl Renner and Otto Bauer, was described as »autonomy based on the personality principle« or simply

25 Bieberstein, *Freiheit in der Unfreiheit.*

26 Himka, *Religion and Nationality,* 158–162.

27 Compare Wierer, *Föderalismus*; Erika Weinzierl, »Föderalismus und Zentralismus in den Verfassungskämpfen des 19. Jahrhunderts,« in *Der österreichische Föderalismus und seine historischen Grundlagen*, ed. Institut für Österreichkunde (Wien: Hirt, 1969); Robert A. Kann, *Das Nationalitätenproblem der Habsburgermonarchie: Geschichte und Ideengehalt der nationalen Bestrebungen vom Vormärz bis zur Auflösung des Reiches im Jahre 1918*, vol. 2, *Ideen und Pläne zur Reichsreform*, 2. ed. (Graz–Köln: Böhlau, 1964), 20–45; Josef Redlich, *Das österreichische Staats- und Reichsproblem: Geschichtliche Darstellung der inneren Politik der habsburgischen Monarchie von 1848 bis zum Untergang des Reiches*, vol. 1, *Der dynamische Reichsgedanke und die Entfaltung des Problems bis zur Verkündigung der Reichsverfassung von 1861* (Leipzig: Der Neue Geist Verlag, 1920), 221–323; Springer, *Protokolle des Verfassungs-Ausschusses*.

28 On this aspect of »imagined territories« and political discourse, see Peter Haslinger, *Nation und Territorium im tschechischen politischen Diskurs, 1880–1938* (München: Oldenboug, 2010), 1–33.

»personal autonomy« as a form of non-territorial ethnic autonomy.[29] This kind of *imagined law* creates boundaries among national cultural collectives, not according to territoriality, but on the basis of personal decisions. It was a consequence of Renner's insight that it was impossible to determine even county boundaries along national lines without seriously violating legitimate cultural, economic, and administrative interests.[30] His system of dual federalism involved two elements: first, the historical crownlands were recognized as the cornerstones of a classical form of territorial federalism; and second, within those component states, power would be devolved to the nations that made up the population of the Empire. Thus, the population within a certain territory was divided into different national cultural collectives available for individual citizens to choose. These individual cultural and linguistic rights were not tied to a certain place or territory, but portable throughout the Empire.

Issues that dealt with questions of nationality such as culture, education, and language were to be administered at the level of the *Kronländer*, whilst political, economic, and material affairs were to be handled at the central federal level. Both legislative bodies would be elected by direct, equal, and universal male suffrage, but also be internally divided into separate *curiae* of nationalities. To insure the highest possible degree of autonomy, moreover, there would be elected regional and local bodies for each ethnicity and each locality in order to raise taxes and funds for cultural and educational programs. After a modified version of *personal autonomy* had been established as a legal principle in the Moravian Compromise of 1906, its implementation was discussed for Galicia and Bukovina as well.[31] This concept did not only attract the attention of the

29 On the following, see Karl Renner, *Der Kampf der Oesterreichischen Nationen um den Staat* (Leipzig: Franz Deuticke, 1902); Otto Bauer, *Die Nationalitätenfrage und die Sozialdemokratie* (Vienna: Verlag der Wiener Volksbuchhandlung Ignaz Brand, 1908); Hans Mommsen, »Otto Bauer, Karl Renner und die sozialdemokratische Nationalitätenpolitik in Österreich 1905–1914,« in *Studies in East European Social History*, ed. Keith Hitchins, vol. 1 (Leiden: Brill, 1977), 3–32; John Coakley, »Approaches to the Resolution of Ethnic conflict: The strategy of non-territorial Autonomy,« *International Political Science Review* 3 (1994): 297–314; Börries Kuzmany, »Der Galizische Ausgleich als Beispiel moderner Nationalitätenpolitik?«, in *Galizien. Peripherie der Moderne – Moderne der Peripherie*, eds. Elisabeth Haid, Stephanie Weismann and Burkhard Wöller (Marburg: Herder-Institut, 2013), 123–141.

30 Schlesinger, *Federalism*, 215.

31 The Moravian Compromise of 1906 was meant to solve the problem of equality for nationalities without territorial autonomy. Each individual Moravian citizen had the opportunity to opt for a certain national cadastre, German or Czech. This cadastre formed a mutually exclusive corporative body from which members of the Moravian Diet were elected, each with powers for self-government in areas such as agriculture, commerce, and education. See Horst Glassl,

Polish and Ruthenian national movements there, but also served as an important intellectual inspiration for another group, whose legal definition shifted in line with various ethnic, national, and religious perceptions – the Jews.

The strong tradition of self-government: Jewish attempts at personal autonomy

After the partitions of Poland-Lithuania, the Habsburg Empire became home to the largest group of Jews living outside Russia. The Jewish population of Galicia of that period constituted the largest number of Jews within the Empire and outnumbered the Jews living in all the states of Western Europe.[32] However, the Galician Jewish community was not only remarkable in terms of its sheer number. For the question of federalism it is of greater relevance that Jews held special rights as a corporative body, inherited from the times of the Polish-Lithuanian *Rzeczpospolita*. From a legal-normative point of view this status had carved out a community with distinct boundaries. During the Polish era, this status did, however, have discriminating features involving prescriptions, duties, regulations, and interdictions in various social and economic respects; and it did not include citizenship. On the other hand, the status guaranteed self-administration, self-jurisdiction, and self-government within the existing network of Jewish communities; Jewish municipalities were not only in charge of cultural affairs but decided on judicial matters within the Jewish community as well.[33] This remained a central matter with regard to Jewish identity in Galicia even after the loss of the Jews' particular legal status during the Era of Enlightenment under Maria Theresa and Joseph II.[34] Due to their relative independence, the Galician Jews were not only regarded as a religious, but also as a »political group«.[35] John

Der mährische Ausgleich (München: Fides, 1967); Gerald Stourzh, Die Gleichberechtigung der Nationalitäten in der Verfassung und Verwaltung Österreichs 1848–1918 (Wien: Verlag der Österreichischen Akademie der Wissenschaften,1985), 213–228, 233–240; Tara Zahra, Kidnapped souls: National indifference and the battle for children in the Bohemian Lands, 1900–1948 (Ithaca, New York: Cornell University Press, 2008), 32–39.

32 Victor Karady, *The Jews of Europe in the Modern Era* (Budapest–New York: CEU Press, 2004), 149; Maner, *Galizien*, 233.

33 For details see *Österreichisches Staatswörterbuch: Handbuch des gesamten österreichischen öffentlichen Rechtes*, ed. Ernst Mitschler and Josef Ulbrich, vol. 2 (Wien: Hölder, 1906), s.v. »Juden«, 946–971, here 965–966; Wolfgang Häusler, *Das galizische Judentum in der Habsburgermonarchie: Im Lichte der zeitgenössischen Publizistik und Reiseliteratur von 1772–1848* (München: Oldenbourg, 1979).

34 Israel Bartal, *Geschichte der Juden im östlichen Europa 1772–1881* (Göttingen: Vandenhoeck & Ruprecht, 2010), 89.

35 *Österreichisches Staatswörterbuch*, vol. 2, s.v. »Juden – Israelitische Kultusangelegenheiten«, 971–981, here 972.

Coakley has called this status an »early form of non-territorial ethnic autonomy«.[36]

Within the Habsburg Empire, the situation changed drastically. The policies pursued towards the Galician Jewry under Maria Theresa had three aims: restricting the growth of the Jewish population; profiting from their economic activities; and centralizing the administration of Jewish affairs at the state level.[37] Formally, Jewish political and cultural autonomy as well as Jewish legal autonomy in religious affairs remained unquestioned. The Jewish institutions of self-government, however, were subjected to the control and authority of state officials and thus dismantled.[38] Joseph II took additional measures towards dismantling Jewish self-administration as part of his modernization policy. Its general aim was, first, to legally, politically, and culturally unify an Empire with few common constitutional and socio-political structures by way of integrating autonomous and corporate institutions into a centralized administration. Secondly, he attempted to implement his political vision of separating state politics and religion.[39] Thus, due to this new enlightened and integrationist approach based on Joseph's view of tolerance,[40] Jews gained a number of new political and civic rights and became subject to general laws, although a large number of discriminating statutes were not in fact abolished. In 1789, furthermore, the establishment of a new municipal order meant that the Galician Jews definitively lost their particular legal status as a separate political body and henceforth counted only as a religious group.[41] This development continued during the constitutional era after 1848, which provided for confessional equality and freedom of movement, even as this did not go into practice until 1867/1868. By 1868, the Jews of Galicia were fully emancipated, at least from a legal perspective.[42]

36 Coakley, »Resolution of ethnic conflict«, 299.

37 Karady, *Jews of Europe*, 151; Bartal, *Geschichte der Juden*, 81–83; Teresa Andlauer: Die jüdische Bevölkerung im Modernisierungsprozess Galiziens, 1867–1914 (Frankfurt am Main et al.: Lang, 2001), 63–68.

38 Maner, *Galizien*, 236. For a European perspective, see Philipp Lenhard, *Volk oder Religion? Die Entstehung moderner jüdischer Ethnizität in Frankreich und Deutschland 1782–1848* (Göttingen: Vandenhoeck & Ruprecht, 2014).

39 Bartal, *Geschichte der Juden*, 86; Andlauer, *Jüdische Bevölkerung Galiziens*, 63–68.

40 Dirk Sadowski, *Haskala und Lebenswelt: Herz Homberg und die jüdischen deutschen Schulen in Galizien 1782–1806* (Göttingen: Vandenhoeck & Ruprecht, 2010), 13–15.

41 Karady, *Jews of Europe*, 156; Maner, *Galizien*, 238. For further details, see *Österreichisches Staatswörterbuch*, vol. 2, s.v. »Juden«, 966–967, and s.v. »Juden – Israelitische Kultusangelegenheiten«, 973.

42 Himka, »Confessional relations,« 29; Maner, *Galizien*, 246; Andlauer, *Jüdische Bevölkerung Galiziens*, 75–80; Małgorzata Śliż, *Galicyjscy Żydzi na drodze do*

The case of Galician Jewry during the transition period from the early modern era to modernity brings greater clarity to the constructive and deconstructive power of the law. During the Polish era, the Jews' special legal status had normatively carved out a political community and had influenced its identity at least to a certain degree by way of both legal privileges and discriminative measures.

During the Habsburg era, however, the legal abolition of privileges and – although with a considerable delay – that of discriminative acts, removed the boundaries of what had formed a type of legally constituted »gated community«. Deprived of their special legal status, the Galician Jews found themselves integrated into the general legal order of the Empire, but reduced to the status of a religious community. Nevertheless, tearing down the normative boundaries of this collective as a political body led neither to the sacralization of the community nor to the individualization of its members. The Galician Jews were legally emancipated at a time when the national question had been coming to a head in a manner hitherto unknown. Jewish identity was thus shaken through the elimination of a Jewish special legal status in three ways: It was impossible to return to the early modern understanding of Jews as a corporative political body anchored in special rights, since that would have fully contradicted the contemporary modern ideal of law as a system of universal rules and civic equality. The Jews, however, did need to respond both to the official legal perception of Judaism as a religion and to the challenges of the national agenda of the time. Positively speaking, the shaking of Jewish identity and the removal of prohibitions and hindrances broadened the scope for new ideas, whether from legal-normative or socio-political perspectives.

Jewish intellectuals around the turn of the century were very productive in developing or modifying concepts to answer these challenges. While Samuel Bloch, a politician of Galician origin, imagined a transnational Austrian identity for the Jews against a religiously imprinted background, Simon Dubnow, a prominent historian and political leader of the Russian Jewish community,[43] transformed the tradition of self-government into a positive self-image for Jews. He claimed that Jews with their more personal rather than territorial ties to each other formed the »most historical nation« among nations, as they did not have to rely on territory to shape their national identity. This point became part of his concept of diaspora-nationalism. Like the Bundist movement that offered a secular concept of Jewishness, this view had a

równouprawienia 1848–1914. Aspekt prawny procesu emancypacji Żydów w Galicji (Kraków: Księgarnia Akad., 2006).

43 Viktor E. Kelner, *Simon Dubnow: Eine Biografie* (Göttingen: Vandenhoeck & Ruprecht, 2010).

preference for local *personal autonomy.* In the following I will set aside the strong assimilative tendencies of the Jewish liberals of the period, who aimed to merge Jewish identity into the national culture of surrounding peoples, as well as the branches of the Zionist movement that sought to bring about a Jewish national state beyond the borders of the empires. Instead I will focus on the intellectuals in question who dealt with an imagined form of federalization, i.e. with an imagined »personal autonomy« in a federal state.

These ideas of a renewed state order built on the principle of personal autonomy evoke a type of federalization without territory based on *personal autonomy.* Not surprisingly, there were no attempts to create a »Jewish crownland« within the Habsburg Empire. The lack of a Jewish core territory that could serve as part of a federal state was too glaring, even if one were to submit that there were cases of other nationalities and groups without as clear-cut a homogeneous homeland as might have been claimed by their national movements. These could also be seen to be historical and political constructs to some degree. However, even if some Jewish politicians like Samuel Bloch favoured the model of a federalized Austria at the macro-level, they stressed the non-territorial features of such an imagined federal state at the local level. Bloch supported the federal plans of the moderate democrat Adolf Fischhof and thus stood in contrast to many liberal Jews of western Austria who favoured a centralized, German-speaking governmental system.[44] The federalization of Austria was meant to assure reconciliation among the nationalities in connection with the idea of an Austrian identity.

Bloch's concept of an Austrian Jewish identity consisted of two elements that are more complementary than contradictory: an ethnic, cultural, and religious element that tied primarily to non-political contexts; and a civic Austrian element connected to the political arena that was based on equal rights and equality before the law as fundaments of a modern democratic Austrian state (*Rechtsstaat*).[45] Jewishness, as Bloch saw it, was thus more a question of ethnicity than nationality. In contrast to Fischhof's idea of an Austrian identity, Bloch pointed out that his conception was not only inspired by enlightenment, but also by Talmudic law and Jewish thought as well.[46] The federal legal state Fischhof and Bloch imagined was structured territorially along historic and national lines, but also provided for strong autonomy rights at the local level, comprising all matters of municipal nature, schooling, health, culture,

44 Ian Reifowitz, *Imagining an Austrian Nation: Joseph Samuel Bloch and the Search for a Multiethnic Austrian Identity, 1846–1919* (New York: Boulder, 2003), 39, 123–124.

45 Reifowitz, *Imagining an Austrian Nation*, 127, 161–162.

46 Ibid., *Imagining an Austrian Nation*, 162.

and police, while transnational matters were to be solved at the central level.[47] Not surprisingly, Bloch found his most receptive audience in Galicia and Bukovina.[48]

While Bloch did not directly tackle the problem of Jewish non-territoriality, Simon Dubnow re-interpreted the early modern history of Jewish self-government during the Polish-Lithuanian era, with its non-territorial aspects, as a specific Jewish path toward modernity. Jewish autonomy as it had been realized in Poland-Lithuania was, as he saw it, not so much a model for the future as a constructive element for his national narrative. He did not thus fall back upon ideas of a legal corporative status for the Jews with special rights and privileges that would have adhered more to the logic of an early modern legal system than to the modern legal ideals of universality and equality. The tradition of Jewish self-government became a cornerstone of his conception of nationalism within the diaspora and was combined with political visions of a pluralistic, democratic, multinational polity.[49]

Dubnow argued that the Jewish municipality, the *kahal*, was to be regarded as a surrogate for the territorial nation state, and went even further than that.[50] He distinguished among three stages in the evolution of nations: the first, a natural state, was defined by way of tribe or race; the second was characterized by territorial-political bodies; and the third, most recent and elaborate stage was defined spiritually, historically, and culturally.[51] In this last stage, a historically and spiritually defined nation would be virtually indestructible once freed of being anchored to a territory or state. In his view, only the Jews had taken this path of a spiritual-cultural nation by way of an uninterrupted chain of autonomous rule.[52] This tradition of autonomy thus represented a sociological basis for a Jewish national history. Dubnow's concept was not meant to proclaim a »religious nation«, as Judaism was defined as a cultural entity; nevertheless, adherence to the Jewish nation still remained deeply connected to Jewish faith.[53] The core of Dubnow's autonomist thinking displayed striking similarities with

47 Wierer, *Föderalismus*, 99–100. For similarities with Renner, see Reifowitz, *Imagining an Austrian nation*, 198–213.

48 Ibid., 127.

49 Anke Hilbrenner, *Diaspora-Nationalismus: Zur Geschichtskonstruktion Simon Dubnows* (Göttingen: Vandenhoeck & Ruprecht, 2007), 119–121.

50 Ibid., 121.

51 Ibid., 111–116; Simon Dubnow, »Essays on the Old and New Judaism,« in *Nationalism and History*, ed. Koppel S. Pinson (Philadelphia: Jewish Publication Society of America, 1958), 73–241.

52 Hilbrenner, *Diaspora-Nationalismus*, 114; Karady, *Jews of Europe*, 292.

53 Compare Dieter Langewiesche, *Reich, Nation, Föderation: Deutschland und Europa* (München: Beck, 2008), 78.

the Austrian Social Democratic view of *personal autonomy*.[54] Similarly, also branches of the Zionist movement, as demonstrated by the Zionist Krakow Programme of 1906 and its representative Hermann Kadisch, supported the implementation of »personal autonomy«, that is the idea of an Austrian federation of nationalities based on personal affiliation.[55]

Another definition of Galician Jewry was propagated by the Bundist movement, the General Jewish Workers' Union in Lithuania, Poland, and Russia (*Algemeyner Yidisher Arbeter Bund in Lite, Poyln un Rusland*), that had founded a Galician sister organization in 1905. The *Bund*, as a social class organization, at first represented the interests of Jewish workers but, as a reaction to anti-Semitic violence, soon moved toward a more general advocacy of Jewish interests. The organization's main demands were the cultivation of the Yiddish language, an autonomous secular and often even antireligious nationalism, and the recognition of Jews as a national minority.[56] In contrast to Bloch and Dubnow, the Bundists did not refer to religion as a constitutive element of Jewishness. Until 1901, they, moreover, partly rejected Dubnow's view of a global Jewish identity and nation.[57] Instead, the Bundists' »imagined community« continued to be defined primarily in ideological terms and in terms of class interest. They criticized Dubnow's concept of a Jewish nation for glossing over social struggles and differences. However, as it became inevitable that the national question needed to be addressed, the *Bund* fully adopted the ideas of *personal autonomy* within a federal state as proposed by Austrian Social Democrats such as Renner.[58]

These competing concepts of Jewish identity, ethnicity, and nationality represent only a small selection of the ideas on Jewishness at the time. However, all of these contrasted strongly with the legal status of the Jews as a mere religious community within the Habsburg Empire. The government and bureaucracy were, moreover, unwilling to accept the different Jewish factions as legal entities – even if they were ready to negotiate with all of them – but

54 Hilbrenner, *Diaspora-Nationalismus*, 124–126.

55 Marsha L. Rozenblit, »The Dilemma of Identity: The Impact of First World War on Habsburg Jewry,« in *The Habsburg Legacy: National Identity in Historical Perspective*, eds. Ritchie Robertson and Edward Timms (Edinburgh: Edinburgh University Press, 1994, 144–157, here 148–149.

56 Karady, *Jews of Europe*, 294–295.

57 Henri Minczeles, *Histoire générale du Bund: Un mouvement révolutionnaire juif* (Paris: Austral, 1995), 278–279; Enzo Traverso, *Die Marxisten und die jüdische Frage: Geschichte einer Debatte 1843–1943* (Mainz: Decaton, 1995), 108.

58 Minczeles, *Histoire générale du Bund*, 242–243; Traverso, *Marxisten und jüdische Frage*, 108.

referred to Judaism as to a religion only.[59] The *imagined law* of a federal state with strong elements of *personal autonomy* that was postulated by Jewish intelligentsia challenged the Viennese political centre; the arena where conflicts of collective status and identity were usually carried out was in fact language politics.

Confronted with national conflict, the central Habsburg administration tended to leave questions of nationality open, refraining from defining the evolving boundaries between nationalities or from making use of the constructive potential of the law and norms as a means of drawing distinctive lines among collectives. In line with this policy, none of the censuses that were carried out every ten years, beginning in 1880, raised data on nationality in order to prevent a sharpening of the conflict, referring instead to religion and language only. Much in contrast to the intentions of the government, however, the category of *language* was soon becoming a political substitute for the term *nationality* and language statistics were commonly used as a means of pursuing national politics.

The statistics are nevertheless to be read carefully with regard to the Jews.[60] While the census did not expressly deny the Jews a status as a nationality – as it did not refer to such a category in the first place – it also did not offer the opportunity to choose a language specific to the Jewish community as neither Yiddish nor Hebrew were recognized as official languages spoken in the Empire (*landesübliche Sprachen*).[61] The combination of the parameters of religion and language reveals that the Galician Jews moved, somewhat ambivalently, among the languages German, Polish, and Ruthenian in the official statistics. This can be interpreted in two ways – as a parameter for national, political, or cultural belonging, or as a declaration of political loyalty. In the eyes of contemporaries, however, this lack of homogeneity seemed rather suspicious.[62] Part of the Jewish intelligentsia wanted to have clear-cut categories and official recognition as a Yiddish-speaking linguistic community.[63] Further momentum toward these aims was provided by the aforementioned Moravian Compromise and the subsequent failure of similar negotiations in Galicia and Bukovina that would

59 Karady, *Jews of Europe*, 165–166; Andlauer, *Jüdische Bevölkerung Galiziens*, 326–327. This rule differed from the legal situation e.g. in Prussia, see *Österreichisches Staatswörterbuch*, vol. 2, s.v. »Juden – Israelitische Kultusangelegenheiten«, 975.

60 With respect to Galicia and for further details, compare Emil Brix, *Die Umgangssprachen in Altösterreich zwischen Agitation und Assimilation: Die Sprachenstatistik in den zisleithanischen Volkszählungen 1880–1910* (Wien–Köln–Graz: Böhlau, 1982), 353–389.

61 Brix, *Umgangssprachen*, 355.

62 Ibid.

63 Andlauer, *Jüdische Bevölkerung Galiziens*, 318–320.

have led to a Jewish electoral register and parliamentary representation. Such a compromise would have opened the possibility for the recognition of Jews as a national minority.

Negotiations collapsed, however, due to intervention of Galician Polish politicians in Vienna who feared the interruption of the ongoing pro-Polish assimilation process and the creation of a third competing ethnic and political group of appreciable strength.[64] Galician bishops also opposed an anticipated Jewish dominance in the administration of Galician towns.[65] Still, in 1908–1909, Bukovinian liberal electoral politics paved the way for Jewish deputies to join the *Landtag* and municipal councils. Electoral districts with Jewish majorities were subsequently represented by two deputies: one for the Jewish population and one for the non-Jewish minority.[66] This system provided the Jews of Bukovina with a degree of political recognition, albeit without any consequences for their recognition as a political-national entity at the central level.[67] In Galicia, electoral reform was introduced only in 1914; it remained without practical consequences due to the impending World War.[68]

The reluctant attitude of the government and administration in Vienna was supported by a decision of the Imperial Court (*Reichsgericht*) on the question of whether Yiddish was to be regarded as a language customary to the Galician crownland. As Gerald Stourzh explained in detail, it was not until 1909 that the Imperial Court explicitly dealt with the question of a Jewish nationality, although it had been confronted with similar issues before.[69] In 1909, Max Diamant, a Jewish attorney from Czernowitz appealed to the *Reichsgericht* to recognize the legal sufficiency of providing Yiddish documents in an application for permission to open a Yiddish theatre. The particular case was actually a pretext to raise the question of recognition for a common Jewish language and thus, as Diamant himself stated before the court, the »problem of nationality«.[70] Diamant's main argument was based on the constitutionally anchored equality of languages, following the logic used for the census. He argued that Yiddish should be regarded as customary in the Habsburg Empire the same way every

64 Gerald Stourzh, »Max Diamant and Jewish Diaspora Nationalism in the Bukovina,« in *From Vienna to Chicago and back: Essays on Intellectual History and Political Thought in Europe and America* (Chicago–London: University of Chicago Press, 2007), 200–201.

65 Andlauer, *Jüdische Bevölkerung Galiziens*, 321.

66 Stourzh, *Gleichberechtigung der Nationalitäten*, 235–336.

67 Maner, *Galizien*, 250; Andlauer, *Jüdische Bevölkerung Galiziens*, 321.

68 Stourzh, *Gleichberechtigung der Nationalitäten*, 239; Glassl, *Ausgleich*, 243.

69 For the following and further details, see Stourzh, »Max Diamant and Diaspora Nationalism,« 190–203; idem, »Galten die Juden als Nationalität Altösterreichs?,« *Studia Judaica Austriaca* 10 (1984): 73–117.

70 Stourzh, »Juden als Nationalität,« 83.

other major language was, such as German or Romanian. With regard to the question of nationality, Diamant named religion as the main characteristic of Jewish nationality that distinguished the group from others:

> The Jews of the East are the descendants of the Jews who lived in the Jewish kingdom, later in the province of Judaea, and were then scattered; they are part of the same culture and have the same traditions as those who had emigrated from Palestine. Like the Romans and Greeks, this nation was originally the purveyor of a cultural good of its own within the Mediterranean; just as the Romans gave us legal thinking and the Greeks gave us art, the Jews gave us religion [...]. However, this cultural good is of greater importance to the Jews than religion is to other peoples of the Occident, encompassing its entire view of life.[71]

Ultimately, however, in spite of heated internal debates, Yiddish was not accepted at the Imperial Court as a language common to all Jews, as it was argued that only the as yet unassimilated »Jews of the East« were using it, an argument that had been submitted by Diamant himself.[72] As the judge Leo Pininski pointed out: »Yiddish, though undoubtedly widely spoken in Galicia and the Bukovina, is not generally recognized by Jews in other countries«.[73] With the rejection of a common Jewish linguistic community and thus – as explicitly stated – of a Jewish national minority, one of the most important conditions for the introduction of federal structures and *personal autonomy* for Galician Jews remained unsatisfied. The upper administrative and judicial levels of the Habsburg monarchy apparently lacked the political will needed to resume the tradition of the early modern Jewish legal status and to transform it into a modern form of minority rights. While these visions of community and federal law held by representatives of the Jewish intelligentsia were thus not converted into practice, they did not lose any of their visionary strength.

Conclusion

I will conclude by returning to my central questions: How are collectives formed and how do they change the state and the legal orders? With regard to the

71 »Die Juden des Ostens seien Nachkommen der Juden, welche in dem jüdischen Reiche, später in der Provinz Judäa gewohnt haben und dann zerstreut worden seien; sie gehören demselben Kulturkreis an, besitzen dieselben Traditionen wie die aus Palästina Ausgewanderten. Gleich den Römern und Griechen sei nun dieses Volk zunächst am Mittelmeer der Vermittler eines eigenen Kultur-Produktes gewesen; so wie die Römer das Recht, die Griechen die Kunst gebracht haben, so die Juden die Religion. [...] Dieses Kulturprodukt bedeute aber für den Juden aber noch mehr als die Religion für die Völker des Okzidents, es umfasse seine ganze Lebensauffassung.« From the protocol of the Imperial Court as cited in ibid., 110.

72 An argument that was made by Diamant himself, ibid., 84–88.

73 Ibid., 112.

partition of Galicia in the Habsburg Empire, I have attempted to exemplify these questions with the Ruthenian plans for a federal union and Jewish attempts at a federal form of *personal autonomy*. I claim that the constructedness of a collective, the normativeness of the law, and propositions of legal reform, the *imagined law*, are strongly entangled. The debates on these legal reforms reveal that the normative legal structure that had once defined certain collectives was competing with the changing ideas, perceptions, and self-perceptions of the respective groups.

The Ruthenian plans for a partition of Galicia in 1848 show that a clerical infrastructure with an educated clergy and direct access to public opinion were conditions essential for legal negotiations to occur, due to a lack of secular representatives at the time. The alliance of the Greek Catholic Church with the emerging Ruthenian and Ukrainian nation-building movements, best expressed in terms of a nationalization of religion, eventually led to the official recognition of Ukrainian nationality. A particular community was thus officially re-interpreted that was previously classified as an exclusively religious community. Federalization plans show how the interaction between this national group and the church could have developed into a new political-legal territorial body as well. Although these plans failed, the »imagined community« did at least benefit later from national minority rights.

The case of the Galician Jews differs from this development in various ways. The early modern legal order of Poland was characterized by a number of special rights, privileges, and restrictions and thus stood in contrast to modern paradigms of universality and equality before the law. The Jewish community was carved out as a distinct body within society and the state. Municipal self-government had moved the Jewish community beyond being only a religious institution but also – from a legal point of view – a political corporative body. During the Habsburg era, however, the Galician Jews were deprived of their special legal status, and reduced to a religious community subject to the general legal order. This process of legal modernization along with the contemporary challenges of nationalism called the nature of Jewish identity into question. The search for a new form of self-perception inspired Jewish intellectuals to envision a federal future for the Empire with elements of *personal autonomy*. The Austrian bureaucracy and courts, however, were not ready to provide for the necessary conditions in terms of altering their legal status. This resulted in severe hindrances to the creation of a legal situation that would have broadened the scope for Jewish identity and culture, even as appeals to the Viennese Imperial Court demonstrated that this status did indeed remain negotiable.

Jana Osterkamp

Emergent Law: Women's Charity and Anti-Trafficking Associations as Sites for Enacting Social Reform

According to police and court records, in June 1911, twenty-five-year-old Hersh Günsberg, from Russian-controlled Zhytomir, was stopped in Lviv under suspicion of trafficking in women. He was described as travelling with two teenage girls, one who claimed to be his sister and the other a friend. They told others who would later become witnesses in the case that they were en route to America and were waiting in Lviv to receive money.

Among the points that appeared suspicious to authorities was that the three could not produce addresses for the relatives they said they would be joining in Argentina and that the girls appeared to have no money of their own. One of the young women in question, Lea Gochmann, claimed that a man in a neighboring house had tried to lure her inside and asserted that he had called the police as an act of retaliation when she refused to comply. Police reports also indicate that the individual responsible for calling the travelers to their attention was Lviv merchant Henryk Sprecher, identified as a member of the local Society for the Protection of Women (*Towarzystwo Ochrony Kobiet*). After being interrogated, the two girls were turned over to a local shelter run by this society. Police records indicate that at least one of the girls was later sent back to Russia. It is not clear how long Günsberg remained in custody.

The themes invoked in these documents are indicative of a set of concerns and discourse in turn-of-the-century Lviv and within activist circles in Europe and North America. During this time, efforts of the early women's movement coalesced with official and local concerns about prostitution and trafficking in women. Such anxieties were connected to tensions regarding ethnic and national identities, women's calls for emancipation, as well as fears about crime and stereotypes of the alleged predatory nature of Jews.[1] This incident occurred

1 For a discussion of predatory representations of Jews in the Warsaw press of this period, see Robert Blobaum, »›Panika moralna‹ w polskim wydaniu. Dewiacje seksualne i wizerunki przestępczości żydowskiej na początku XX wieku«, in *Kobieta i rewolucja obyczajowa*, eds. Anna Żarnowska and Andrzej Szwarc

during the height of activism against trafficking in women just prior to World War I.[2]

In this article, I examine transformation within institutions to gain insight into how societal change is mirrored in the development of legal concepts such as membership, access to public participation, and shifting notions of community. Analysis of social welfare institutions and their relationships to religious communities and the enactment of legal practices provides a sphere in which to explore shifts in structures and approaches to social problems. In this case, the relationship between existing institutions within the Jewish community in Lviv and newer, more secularly oriented initiatives is a central focus. With this in mind, I argue for the application of a broadened concept of »law« which draws from the work of turn-of-the-century legal scholar Eugen Ehrlich, as well as from more recent scholarship on legal anthropology.[3] Key to this perspective is the concept of »law as process,«[4] offering insight into institutions and groups as sites for the development, cultivation, and enactment of norms that ultimately have a broader impact on social practice.

(Warszawa: DiG, 2006), 265–276. For depictions in the Polish press of Jews preying on Christian women in coverage of the large Lviv anti-trafficking trial, see also Keely Stauter-Halsted, »›A Generation of Monsters‹: Jews, Prostitution, and Racial Purity in the 1892 L'viv White Slavery Trial,« *Austrian History Yearbook* 38 (2007): 25–35.

2 During this time, articles devoted to women's issues became increasingly prominent and a regular feature in the local liberal daily *Kurjer Lwowski*, for example, in the form of the bi-monthly column *Głos kobiet.* In addition, Lviv anti-trafficking efforts and assistance to women in need were becoming increasingly institutionalized, with more attempts to develop ties with and spread activities to other places in Galicia.

3 Eugen Ehrlich, *Fundamental Principles of the Sociology of Law* (New Brunswick: Transaction Publishers, 2001 [1913]). Key texts from the early decades of legal anthropology include Bronislaw Malinowski, *Crime and Custom in Savage Society* (Totowa, NJ: Rowman & Allanheld, 1985 [1926]); Karl N. Llewellyn and E. Adamson Hoebel, *The Cheyenne Way: Conflict and Case Law in Primitive Jurisprudence* (Norman, OK: University of Oklahoma Press, 1941) and Leopold Pospisil, *Anthropology of Law: A Comparative Theory* (New York: Harper and Row, 1971). More recent texts include Carol J. Greenhouse, *Praying for Justice: Faith, Order, and Community in an American Town* (Ithaca, NY: Cornell University Press 1986); Franz and Keebet von Benda-Beckmann, »The Dynamics of Change and Continuity in Plural Legal Orders,« *Journal of Legal Pluralism and Unofficial Law* 53/54 (2006): 1–44; Sally Engle Merry, *Human Rights and Gender Violence: Translating International Law into Local Justice* (Chicago: University of Chicago Press, 2006) and Lawrence Rosen, *Law as Culture: An Invitation* (Oxford: Princeton University Press, 2006).

4 Sally Falk Moore, *Law as Process: An Anthropological Approach* (London: Routledge, 1978).

To better understand how legal institutions function, Ehrlich advocated ethnographic research and detailed study of institutional documents.[5] As bodies which regulate human behavior, charity institutions also fall into this category. Since charity had long been tied to religion, insight into the processes by which changes within traditional religious communities came about is also relevant to the present discussion. This process includes examining how visions for making organizations more inclusive and providing new opportunities to women were institutionalized. Focusing on the practices of local associations reveals the complexity of networks that existed among activists across regions and within groups in the local context. At the same time, it is important to recognize that traditional and modern approaches are not necessarily opposites and often coexist. In fact, elements that are perceived as modern often reinforce certain pre-existing social practices and beliefs.

Ehrlich viewed law as a mental image (*Gedankenbild*) that resides in people's minds and could be gauged based on people's attitudes.[6] He saw law as a component of society, growing out of human associations. Therefore, he was not interested merely in normative law or the law on the books, but in the institutions that actually regulated human behavior, arguing that this approach required observing law in its social context.[7] He advocated »direct observation of life, of commerce, of customs and usages, and of all associations, not only of those that the law has recognized but also those that it has overlooked and passed by, indeed even of those that it has disapproved.«[8]

My approach combines historical research with ethnographic perspectives and analysis and is informed by ethnographic and performance studies scholarship, which stress the emergent quality of cultural practices.[9] Following such

5 Ehrlich, *Fundamental Principles*, 489 and 495.

6 Marc Hertogh, »A ›European‹ Conception of Legal Consciousness: Rediscovering Eugen Ehrlich,« *Journal of Law and Society* 31, no. 4 (2004): 457–481, here 474.

7 Klaus A. Ziegert, »Introduction,« in Eugen Ehrlich, *Fundamental Principles of the Sociology of Law* (New Brunswick: Transaction Publishers, 2001 [1913]): xiv–xlix, here xxxvii.

8 Ehrlich, *Fundamental Principles*, 499.

9 See for example, Richard Bauman, *Verbal Art as Performance* (Prospect Heights, IL: Waveland Press, 1977); idem, *Let Your Words Be Few: Symbolism of Speaking and Silence among Seventeenth Century Quakers* (London: Cambridge University Press, 1998); and Beverly Stoeltje and Richard Bauman, »Community Festival and the Enactment of Modernity,« in *The Old Traditional Way of Life: Essays in Honor of Warren E. Roberts*, eds. Robert Walls and George Shoemaker (Bloomington, IN: Trickster Press/Indiana University Folklore Institute, 1989), 159–171.

models, one could assert that all forms of law are »emergent;« however, here I use the term »emergent law« to highlight, more specifically, shifts in institutions and thinking about charity practices which were in the process of changing, with newer models becoming increasingly accepted in the late 19th and early 20th centuries.

In this context, I approach organizations combating prostitution and trafficking in women as manifestations of bourgeois sensibilities of the period,[10] including the efforts of many middle and upper class activists to promote what they saw as a proper moral code of conduct for women. I consider changes taking place in charity directed at women at the turn of the century, focusing on forms that were intended especially for young women. First, I examine dowry awards, a charity practice with a long tradition in both Christian and Jewish societies. The second form, already mentioned above, is the emergence of associations to fight trafficking in women at the turn of the century. In these contexts, I analyze legal aspects of discussions, including changes in categories of membership, calls for legal changes to allow women to participate in public life, the development of supra-ethnic and religious consciousness with regard to charity, as well as the influence and involvement of emerging charity organizations in enforcing morality and law. Finally, I examine discourse on trafficking in women and consider why this topic provoked such strong reactions at the turn of the century and why it was a central part of activist agendas.

Societies devoted to the protection of women were a growing phenomenon at the turn of the century and, provide examples of increasingly secular and international efforts to address social problems. In part, they resulted from perceived inadequacies of older, religiously based institutions and approaches to dealing with the poor and socially excluded, but were also an effort to reshape society and institutions according to the moral vision of activists. At the end of the 19th century, men and increasingly women from bourgeois classes, many of whom were already involved in religious charity, began to advocate new kinds of social welfare programs in urban contexts. This process included searching for new avenues and models for extending charity to those in need. At the same time, as the organizations' names sometimes suggest, they reinforced bourgeois images of women as helpless and in need of protection. Examples include the above-mentioned Lviv Society for the Protection of Women, in actuality a local chapter of the Austrian Girl and Child Protection League (*Österreichische Mädchen- und Kinderschutzliga*).

10 See, for example, Dietlind Hüchtker, *Geschichte als Performance. Politische Bewegungen in Galizien um 1900* (Frankfurt–New York: Campus, 2014).

Within this text, I generally use the term »trafficking in women« as closer to the Polish and German terms used during the period and as a more neutral alternative to the English »white slavery« which was more common at the turn of the century. I find the latter to be a loaded term, with ethnic or racial connotations – whether or not they are intended – that in themselves merit separate study. The equivalent Polish, *białe niewolnictwo* (»white slavery«) was less common, though I have come across it in the press of the women's movement of the turn of the century.[11] More frequently, activists and journalists used the Polish term *handel kobietami i dziewczętami* (literally, »trade in women and girls«). Another common Polish term was *handel żywym towarem* (»trade in live goods«).[12] In German the term *Mädchenhandel* (»trade in girls«) was most prevalent.

Concern about an increase in prostitution and trafficking came about due to the convergence of a range of circumstances. One factor was an increase in the flow of populations from rural to urban areas due to the collapse of previously existing socio-economic structures and increased opportunities in urban areas due to industrialization. This trend meant that many more women – and often young women – were travelling and living on their own or at least away from the protection and constraints of their families. These developments also coincided with new opportunities for women to participate in public life.

In addition, the above-mentioned case reveals the centrality of migration to this issue, including the flow of Jews from Russia. The points of suspicion, namely that the young women were without money of their own and were unable or unwilling to provide addresses for relatives in the New World, are concerns that are echoed in anti-trafficking literature. Moreover, the possibility that the authorities were notified out of spite reveals the complexity of relationships among various groups in Jewish society including the existence of competing interests and motivations. This potential also suggests the precarious situation of many migrants and immigrants, for whom Lviv served as a thoroughfare, pointing to the inequalities and diverse experiences of Jews from different classes, religious orientations, and regions. Migration and immigration was also a problem for Habsburg authorities who struggled to render populations more legible.[13] To this end, the imperial system employed religious leaders

11 See for example, H. Polańska, »Handel dziewczętami,« *Świat Płciowy*, October, 1905, 20–25.

12 See for example »Handel żywym towarem,« *Dziennik Polski*, November 16, 1902, 27.

13 I borrow the concept of legibility from James Scott, *Seeing like a State* (New Haven and London: Yale University Press, 1998), 2. For a similar discussion of Russian contexts during this period, see Eugene Avrutin, *Jews and the Imperial*

throughout the 19th and early 20th centuries as administrative agents of state authority.[14]

Within Jewish society in Galicia, on the one hand, there was an increased trend toward the centralization of administration, with efforts by the Lviv Jewish Community Council to expand their influence beyond the city. On the other hand, however, an increase in the size of the Jewish population of Lviv meant that it was more difficult for a small number of individuals to maintain tight control over the Jewish community, creating spaces for more actors to exert limited forms of influence over traditional charity structures, such as dowry awards. In addition, some associations, partly due to guidance from Vienna and international assistance networks, promoted models of charity that extended beyond earlier models, in which each religious or ethnic group was to provide for its own members.

With regard to Jewish communities living in Galicia, historians maintain that most Jews in the region were Orthodox and that many among this population were Hasidic.[15] However, few documents in Lviv remain from distinctly Hasidic institutions. Although Hasidic members, in all likelihood, are mentioned in documents, they are often not clearly identified as such, rendering them, in many ways invisible.[16] In contrast, the records and voices which prevail in the archive are largely those of professional elites, mainly individuals with a strong

State: Identification Politics in Tsarist Russia (Ithaca: Cornell University Press, 2010).

14 For other examples, see Liliana Hentosh and Oksana Leskiv in this volume, for examples from the Russian imperial context, see Levin, also in this volume. For a broader discussion of Habsburg contexts, see Ernst C. Hellbling, »Die Landesverwaltung in Cisleithanien,« in *Die Habsburgermonarchie 1848–1918*, vol. 2, eds. Adam Wandruszka and Peter Urbanitsch (Wien: Verlag der Österreichischen Akademie der Wissenschaften, 1975), 243–262; and Wolfgang Häusler, »Das österreichische Judentum zwischen Beharrung und Fortschritt,« in *Die Habsburgermonarchie 1848–1918*, vol. 4, eds. Adam Wandruszka and Peter Urbanitsch (Wien: Verlag der Österreichischen Akademie der Wissenschaften, 1985), 633–669, here 638 and 664.

15 Piotr Wróbel lists the Jewish population for Lviv in 1910 as 57,387; however, he also points out that statistics for Jewish communities are unreliable, due to resistance and distrust among Jews of censuses and other official state polls, as well as their frequent avoidance of registering newborn children. Piotr Wróbel, »The Jews of Galicia under Austrian-Polish Rule, 1869–1918,« *Polin* 12 (1999): 97–138, here 105, 110, 136. See also Wacław Wierzbieniec, »The Processes of Jewish Emancipation and Assimilation in the Multiethnic City of Lviv during the Nineteenth and Twentieth Centuries,« *Harvard Ukrainian Studies* 24, no. 1 (2000): 223–250, here 233.

16 Marcin Wodziński, »Where History and Geography of Religions Meet: The Case of the Jewish Mystical Movement of Hasidism« (lecture, Center for the History and Culture of East Central Europe (GWZO), Leipzig, Germany, February 29, 2012).

command of German and Polish and those most closely associated with ruling institutions, such as the Jewish Community Council (*Gmina Wyznaniowa Izraelicka*) and a range of activist and professional institutions. Many of these same professionals and their families were central to Lviv's most prominent Jewish charity organizations.[17] Several of these associations existed within the framework of the Jewish Community Council, an arrangement that reflects the integral historical connection between charity practices and the formal structures of the Jewish community.

Change in Jewish Charity Institutions and Assistance for Women

Charity was a significant part of Jewish life connected to many aspects of daily religious practice and both men and women were among the recipients of charity for the poor and sick. In the early modern period the position of *gabai* or *gabai tsdakah*, the supervisor of charity, was an important figure within the community. Women also played an important role in administering to those in need. In the early modern period, for example, in Poznań and Swarzędz, female charity collectors (*kwestarki*) engaged in providing charity to women and in collecting donations, though they were more constrained in the ways in which they were permitted to undertake such collections. These charity collectors were women of high status, often widows of prominent male members of the community.[18] In many Jewish communities during the early modern period, the task of addressing various forms of charity shifted from the community *gabaim* to fall increasingly on a variety of brotherhoods or *chevrot*.[19]

Dowry funds have a long history among east European Jews.[20] In the late medieval and early modern periods, dowry funds in east European Jewish communities were part of centralized institutions which also held broader

17 See for example the membership list of the Lviv Chapter of the League for Combating Trafficking in Women (Lwowski Oddział Ligi do Zwalczania Handlu Dziewczętami) and the list of members of various committees of the Jewish Community Council in Lviv. Tsentralnyi Derzhavnyi Istorychnyi Arkhiv Ukrainy u Lvovi/Central State Historical Archive of Ukraine in Lviv (hereafter TsDIAL), collection/coll. (fond) 701, inventory/inv. (opis) 2, file (sprava) 1745, folio/fol. (arkush) 29–32 and coll. 701, inv. 3, file 6, fol. 12–17.

18 Anna Michałowska-Mycielska, *The Jewish Community: Authority and Social Control in Poznan and Swarzędz, 1650–1793* (Wrocław: Wydawnictwo Uniwersytetu Wrocławskiego, 2008), 41–42.

19 Ibid., 143.

20 I use the terms »eastern« and »western«, as well as »east« and »west« in their lower case forms, since capitalization reifies concepts that are, in fact, unfixed and often contested.

cultural functions.[21] Such funds continued to function into the 20th century, even as more secularly organized charities for women began to emerge. In late-19th and early-20th-century Lviv there were a number of separate dowry foundations, usually based on a provision of a last will and testament. Despite such changes, young women continued to direct their applications to the central Jewish Community Council, indicating a degree of continuity with earlier practices. These circumstances gave individuals and donor families more latitude in determining the conditions of the dowry funds. Often competitions for awards were held on the anniversary of the death of the benefactor or another member of the family. For example, the Schulim Stoff Foundation, established in 1909, was created to honor the memory of the founder's deceased daughter Sara, though the fund bears the name of the father.[22]

Very often, funds favored applicants who demonstrated that they were related to the deceased founder. In some cases the provisions stipulate specifically that such applicants be given priority. For example, the documents pertaining to the applications of Mina Günsberg (1913) and Chaje Rosenfeld (1919) indicate that these women were chosen because they were related to the donor family.[23] Some applications include elaborate family trees to show kinship ties.

The documents which accompanied the creation of dowry funds often stipulated criteria, by which young women would be considered eligible. Applicants were required to be »poor« or living in poverty and to be of »Mosaic faith« (*wyznania mojżeszowego*). In some cases there were age limitations, for example 16 to 35 or sometimes 40, and requirements that applicants had led a »morally upstanding life«. In some cases it was also required that the recipient be from Lviv.[24] In one case, benefactors were allowed to exclude specific individuals from eligibility, demonstrating the degree of latitude donors possessed in delineating criteria.[25]

Dowry funds hinge on traditional models of social life, whereby marriage was seen as the key means for women to ensure their security. These funds were part

21 I am grateful to Moshe Rosman for this observation. See also Jacob Katz, *Tradition and Crisis: Jewish Society at the End of the Middle Ages* (New York: New York University Press, 1993), 116–117.

22 Correspondence in TsDIAL, coll. 701, inv. 3, file 56, fol. 2.

23 Documents from the Chaje vel Klara Rosenstein Foundation (*Fundacyi imienia Chaje vel Klary Rosenstein*), TsDIAL, coll. 701, inv. 3, file 114. See also eligibility criteria from the Szyfra Bina Nathansohn Foundation. TsDIAL, coll. 702, inv. 4, file 164, fol. 12.

24 Examples of such requirements are included in documents from the Szyfra Bina Nathansohn and Ignacy Lewkowicz funds, documents for which are in TsDIAL, coll. 702, inv. 4, file 164, fol. 1 and coll. 701, inv. 3, file 414, fol. 15, respectively.

25 See documents from Szyfra Bina Nathansohn in TsDIAL, coll. 702, inv. 4, file 164, fol. 7.

of the traditional social order and as such served to maintain established gender roles. For example, the letter to one award recipient, Klara Eva Lauer, in 1916, indicates that the funds were to be turned over directly to her future husband once documentation of the marriage was provided.[26]

The emergence of more secularly-oriented, reform-based approaches to assistance did not indicate a clear break from past traditions, but rather a parallel, and even interconnected development, which often overlapped with previously established forms of charity. In this context, Ehrlich's work is again worthy of note, as it provides insight into turn-of-the-century perspectives. Writing in early-20th-century Bukovina, a territory adjacent to Galicia, he viewed the actions of the emerging women's movement as an attack on the existing system of sexual morality on which the family was based. Therefore, he concluded that feminist activists must have the ulterior motive of »preparing the way for an entirely new order of the family.«[27]

However, at the turn of the century, many feminists incorporated models of assistance which reaffirmed many aspects of traditional roles for women. Within German-Jewish contexts, providing poor young women with dowries was also an approach favored by some activists. For example, the *Jüdischer Frauenbund* (»League of Jewish Women«) actively encouraged and provided funds to newly married couples as a way to encourage earlier marriages, which they claimed would decrease the demand for prostitutes.[28] Yet, by distributing dowries, they were challenging the authority of the religious institutions, which had traditionally acted in this capacity. In addition, the basic act of giving dowry funds, indeed, of gift giving in general, functioned as a means to convey power.[29] In this sense, women's rights activists used the distribution of dowry awards and the struggle against trafficking in women as ways to harness more authority to advance their broader social agendas.

26 Letter to Klara Eva Laurer from the leadership (*przełożeństwo*) of the Gmina Izraelicka in Lviv. TsDIAL, coll. 701, inv. 3, file 414, fol. 20.

27 Ehrlich, *Fundamental Principles*, 58.

28 Bertha Pappenheim and Sara Rabinowitsch, *Zur Lage der jüdischen Bevölkerung in Galizien: Reise-Eindrücke und Vorschläge zur Besserung der Verhältnisse* (Frankfurt am Main: Neuer Frankfurter Verlag, 1904). See also Marion Kaplan, *The Jewish Feminist Movement in Germany: The Campaigns of the Juedischer Frauenbund, 1904–1938* (Connecticut: Greenwood Press, 1979), 130.

29 Marion Kaplan makes this point with regard to dowries, especially those given by family members, Marion Kaplan, *The Marriage Bargain: Women and Dowries in European History* (New York: Institute for Research in History and the Haworth Press, 1985), 4. Sociologist and anthropologist Marcel Mauss argues that gift giving in general serves as a form of exerting power, Marcel Mauss, *The Gift* (New York: Routledge, 2006 [1924]).

At the same time, I have found no mention of women's activists in Galicia distributing dowries to poor women. In Lviv, dowry funds administered by the Jewish Community Council continued to function into the 1920s. This may suggest less willingness to openly challenge existing institutional authority, or it may also be that this approach was not deemed effective, or was never considered. With regard to the debate about trafficking in women, concerns certainly existed within local women's activist circles in Lviv, although they were strongly influenced by activist agendas in Germany and Vienna.

Anti-trafficking societies in Lviv: Emergent legal concepts and new forms of charity

Although concern about prostitution and trafficking in women emerged in the last decades of the 19th century in Galicia, most organized efforts to address such issues came about in the early 20th century. In 1902 Rabbi Leopold Rozenak of the liberal German Union of Rabbis made a journey to eastern Europe to enlist the help of Galician rabbis in the struggle against trafficking in women. The following year prominent Jewish women's activists Bertha Pappenheim and Sara Rabinowitsch undertook a tour of Galicia and wrote a report of their findings.[30] The activity surrounding such visits may have been the spark that prompted a group of prominent Jewish men in Lviv, the same year, to compose a letter to the Viceroy of Galicia seeking permission to found a Jewish association, called the Jewish Society for Combating the Trafficking of Girls (*Towarzystwo żydowskie dla zapobiegania handlowi dziewczętami*).[31]

In this letter, the geographic scope of the proposed association was significant: While the statutes indicated that its headquarters was to be in Lviv, its activities would include the Kingdom of Galicia and Lodomeria, Krakow, and Bukovina. The expansiveness of the founders' vision for the association's future activities

30 Pappenheim and Rabinowitsch, *Zur Lage der jüdischen Bevölkerung in Galizien*; Sara Rabinowitsch, »Zur Lage des jüdischen Proletariats in Mohilew am Dnjepr,« *Die Welt*, August 15, 1902, 6–7. Originally from Vienna, Pappenheim later relocated to Frankfurt am Main where she became an important figure in the Jewish feminist movement. The much younger Rabinowitsch was originally from Minsk province and had just completed a doctorate in economics in Freiburg. See also Elizabeth Loentz, *Let Me Continue to Speak the Truth: Bertha Pappenheim as Author and Activist* (Cincinnati, OH: Hebrew Union College Press, 2007).

31 The Polish name of the association mentioned in the letter is *Towaryzstwo żydowskie dla zapobiegania handlowi dziewczętami*. The German name for the association, mentioned in the statutes within the same archival file is *Jüdische Vereinigung zur Verhinderung des Mädchenhandels*. TsDIAL, coll. 146, inv. 58, file 41.

may express their impressions of the far-reaching nature of trafficking in women in the region. However, it also asserts Lviv's central role as the capital city of Galicia and as an important center for the dissemination of ideas and networks.[32] Documents from a decade earlier demonstrate that members of the Lviv Jewish Community Council endorsed the idea that their institution should serve as a spiritual center for Jews throughout the region.[33] In fact, this was part of a general effort to centralize administration of the Jewish community.[34] In addition, the statutes for the proposed anti-trafficking society indicate that a member could be any person regardless of sex, social class *(stan)*, and place of residence. By expanding membership to those living outside of Lviv, and to women, the request demonstrates elements of inclusivity, especially considering that all the signatories of the letter were men.

The very formulation of such an organization as comprising members, who could join, if so inclined, demonstrates an important shift in thinking among a growing number of Jewish elites in Lviv, thus suggesting a considerable change in legal thought. In the early modern period, membership in the Jewish community was determined by birth; yet, for most women and poor men this meant a largely passive form of membership, as they were excluded from participation in most governing structures.[35] At the turn of the century, this remained the case in many ways; however, at the same time, Jews also became increasingly involved in voluntary membership associations clustered around specific interests and causes. Jewish identities became more contested and offered new associations for individuals to identify with.[36] Such groups reflected changes in broader society during this period and provide an illustration of the ways in which legal thinking is linked to and becomes an expression of popular

32 Ukrainian writer Ivan Franko also observes the importance of Lviv as a center for political activism among Ukrainians or Ruthenians in Galicia. See for example, Ivan Franko, *Fateful Crossroads* (Winnipeg: Language Lanterns Publications, 2006), 211 and 273.

33 Letter dated March 3, 1890. TsDIAL, coll. 701, inv. 2, file 761.

34 In 1889 the Lviv and Krakow Jewish Community Councils undertook an initiative to create an alliance representing the interests of Jews living in Galician cities and to centralize their administration. These plans included establishing a central office for charity. TsDIAL, coll. 701, inv. 2, file 751, fol. 1.

35 See for example, Gershon David Hundert, *Jews in Poland-Lithuania in the Eighteenth Century: A Genealogy of Modernity* (Berkeley, CA: University of California Press, 2004).

36 For accounts of tensions among Jews in Lviv, see Ezra Mendelsohn, »From Assimilation to Zionism in Lvov: The Case of Alfred Nossig,« *Slavonic and East European Review* 49, no. 117 (1971): 521–534 and Joshua Shanes, »Neither Germans nor Poles: Jewish Nationalism in Galicia before Herzl, 1883–1897,« *Austrian History Yearbook* 34 (2003): 191–213.

consciousness.[37] Voluntary membership associations, many of which focused on charity and other social issues, sought to impact the existing legal and political systems, some through the initiation of charity programs that sought to enhance the status of women and others through more direct political engagement, including revolutionary activities.

The inclusion of women into such associations was another change taking place at the turn of the century. Women's participation in the public sphere was beginning to gain wider acceptance, though there was also considerable resistance to changes to existing gender roles. In this case, it may have seemed especially appropriate that women play a part in a society focused on helping women. Membership in such organizations was also a means of enhancing one's prestige for both women and men, especially as such associations had ties to regional and even international networks, but also provided local venues for performing respectability.[38]

In the case of the above-mentioned statutes, many of the objectives listed in this document are similar to efforts promoted by western activists, including the founding of housekeeping schools and kindergartens, and the publication of brochures and other materials intended to educate the public about trafficking in women. References to Austrian and foreign associations with similar goals indicate an awareness of and perhaps considerable contact with such organizations. From the records, it remains unclear whether or not the Jewish association was approved by regional authorities.

In addition to Pappenheim's tour of Galicia and the local appeal to the viceroy for permission to form a Jewish anti-trafficking society, an international conference was held on the topic in Lviv in mid-September 1903. This meeting was one of the earliest events intended to raise awareness of such issues in Galicia, with western activists playing an important role. In addition to Pappenheim, other prominent participants included Paul Nathan, head of the Berlin-based Relief Association of German Jews (*Hilfsverein der Deutschen Juden*), and Emil Byk, the Austrian *Reichsrat* member for Galicia. The conference organizers expressly targeted Galician rabbis as their audience, though reports mention that none from Hasidic communities attended.[39]

37 Ehrlich draws from the works of Georg Friedrich Puchta and Friedrich Carl von Savigny in developing this concept. Ehrlich, *Fundamental Principles*, 443–444.

38 On related concepts of performance and political participation, see Hüchtker, *Geschichte als Performance*, 18–27, 198–200.

39 Lloyd P. Gartner, »Anglo-Jewry and the Jewish International Traffic in Prostitution, 1885–1914,« *Association for Jewish Studies Review* 7/8 (1982/1983): 129–178, here 174–175 and »Delegierten-Tag zur Bekämpfung des Mädchenhandels,« *Allgemeine Zeitung des Judentums*, September 25, 1903, 461–464. Consulted at http://www.compactmemory.de (accessed November 10, 2014).

At this conference Meier Munk, a prominent member of the Lviv Jewish community, originally from the influential northern German Jewish community in Altona,[40] proposed the founding of an organization devoted to protecting women and girls. Reports suggest that Jecheskiel Caro and other rabbis, such as Chaim Horowitz of Krakow, conveyed doubts about the need for such an organization, expressing resentment at what they perceived as implications that Jewish communities in Galicia were morally inferior. Ultimately, however, the participants agreed that such an organization would in fact be created. Interestingly, Caro's is the first signature, among the group of men requesting permission to found the organization, on the aforementioned letter, which was written in June 1903, three months prior to the conference. The fact that Caro later expressed skepticism at this conference may indicate that, despite his doubts about the prevalence of a trafficking problem, he nevertheless felt pressured to act in a demonstrable way. Meier Munk, another signatory of the letter, mentioned above, made proposals at the September conference to expand the scope of the association and to increase collaboration with international institutions.[41] As indicated, Munk was originally from the Hamburg region, the site of many charity and reform efforts directed at east central Europe, which may have facilitated collaboration with western activists.

Earlier the same year, correspondence from the Government Councilor (*Radca Rządu*) and Director of Police to the Council of the Viceroy (*Prezydyum c.k. Namiestnictwa*) indicates that the latter made inquiries regarding whether or not an association dedicated to combating trafficking in women existed in Lviv. According to the response, there was no such institution in the city, though the letter mentions that a Roman Catholic association dedicated to providing material and moral support to girls did exist.[42] These inquiries and the considerable pull that imperial authorities had over city officials in Lviv suggest that the central authorities also played an important role in steering debate on this issue within the city. Due to the challenges posed by the various languages used in the region and efforts to control migration, Vienna was dependent on local religious authorities to administer populations that they could otherwise

40 Munk migrated from Altona to Lviv in the mid 1890s and married Pessel Rokach of the local Jewish community. Rabbi Issac Schmelkes performed the ceremony on September 15, 1897. Marriage certificate from the Digitized Collection of Jewish Records (DCJR), http://dcjr.org/index.php/jewish-vital-records/marriage-certificate/1262-munk-meier-rokach-pessel (accessed March 17, 2015).

41 Gartner, »Anglo-Jewry,« 174–175; »Delegierten-Tag zur Bekämpfung des Mädchenhandels,« 461–464.

42 The letter, dated January 17, 1903 is located in the TsDIAL, coll. 146, inv. 4, file 171, vol. 3097, fol. 31.

not control. In addition, by centralizing and overseeing activism, authorities could more easily monitor and guide activities as a means of keeping in check potentially subversive groups.

The lineage of Lviv's anti-trafficking organizations is slightly unclear, with somewhat conflicting narratives. According to Nancy Wingfeld, Jewish committees formed early in response to trade in Jewish girls from Galicia, but such groups were subsumed in 1902 under the interdenominational Austrian League to Combat Traffic in Women.[43] However, the fact that the above-mentioned letter was written in 1903 and proposes the founding of a specifically Jewish association, suggests that efforts were not yet as centralized or coordinated as other reports indicate.

Edward Bristow suggests that the Jewish association in Lviv – presumably that mentioned above – faltered in its early years due to lack of funds and volunteers. He also indicates that the work of anti-trafficking associations was undermined by other calamities, such as the Kishinev pogrom of 1903, which further burdened western aid agencies, as well as squabbles between Austrian and German officials regarding support for the effort.[44] An article from a 1905 issue of the feminist *Świat Płciowy* (»Sexual World«) asserts that »because non-German cities reacted with indifference toward initiatives from Vienna, the [Vienna anti-trafficking] league decided to decentralize its actions.«[45] However, local documents that provide a clear indication of developments between 1903 and 1908 are sparse.

In any case, five years later, in 1908, the Lviv Chapter of the Austrian League for Combating the Trafficking of Girls *(Österreichische Liga zur Bekämpfung des Mädchenhandels)*,[46] was established. The leaders of this association are different from those listed in the earlier document, with women playing a much more visible role. One reason may be that Habsburg laws were changed in 1908 to allow women to join political associations,[47] part of a trend toward rendering it

43 Nancy M. Wingfeld, »Destination: Alexandria, Buenos Aries, Constantinople: ›White Slavers‹ in Late Imperial Austria,« *Journal of the History of Sexuality* 20, no. 2 (2011): 291–311, here 297.

44 Edward J. Bristow, *Prostitution and Prejudice: The Jewish Fight against White Slavery, 1870–1939* (New York: Schocken, 1982), 262–263.

45 »Z kongresów,« *Świat Płciowy*, October, 1905, 51.

46 In subsequent years the organization's name was changed to the Austrian Girl and Child Protection League (*Österreichische Mädchen- und Kinderschutzliga*). See the organization's annual reports, http://www.literature.at/collection.alo?from=1to=50&orderby=author&sortorder=a&objid=11075&page= (accessed November 10, 2014).

47 *Jewish Women: A Comprehensive Historical Encyclopedia*, s.v. »Habsburg Monarchy: Nineteenth to Twentieth Centuries,« http://jwa.org/encyclopedia/article/habsburg-monarchy-nineteenth-to-twentieth-centuries (accessed March 17, 2015).

more acceptable for women to participate in a wider range of organizations. According to the association's annual reports, Lviv chapter president Emma Lilien was especially active in networking with local and regional officials and participating in international meetings. Yet, there were still important ties between this group and other local Jewish charity projects. For example, Meier Munk, who played a key role in the earlier initiative, and Emma Lilien were both members of other Jewish charity organizations assisting youth. Lilien and Marya Kalmus-Schneiderowa from the Lviv anti-trafficking chapter also served on the board of another charity association *Zdrowie* (»Health«) dedicated to supporting Jewish youth in poor health.[48]

Lilien is listed as a founding member of *Opieka* (»Care«), which offered support to poor middle school pupils.[49] Records also indicated that, in one case, the community turned over a ten-year-old girl to Lilien and the Office for the Protection of Women (*Biuro Ochrony Kobiet*) or BOK, as the Lviv chapter was often referred to in local Polish language publications. In this case it appears that officials believed that the organization could offer better guidance to the child than the local Jewish orphanage.[50] In its later years of existence (1910–1913) the Lviv Chapter also received limited financial support from the local Jewish Community Council, as well as from the Lviv City Council.[51]

Emil Byk, a prominent participant in the 1903 anti-trafficking conference was another founding member of *Opieka*. Earlier, he had served as chairman of the charity committee of the Jewish *Cultusrath*.[52] Such examples demonstrate the degree to which elites occupied positions in more secular, non-religiously based institutions, but also remained tied to those linked directly to Jewish communities. At the same time, the *Cultusrath* itself could be seen as an institution with closer links to the imperial and regional governments, operating within an urban context in the Galician capital, and clearly distinct from the smaller religious

48 *Szóste Sprawozdanie zarządu towarzystwa ku wspieraniu chorej uczącej się młodzieży żydowskiej szkół średnich i wyższych »Zdrowie« za rok administracyjny 1911/1912* (Lwów: Nakład Towarzystwa, 1913). I consulted this brochure at TsDIAL, coll. 701, inv. 2, file 1745, fol. 43.

49 »Opieka« *Stowarzyszenie dla Wspierania Ubogiej Żydowskiej Młodzieży szkół średnich we Lwowie* (»Care« The Society for the Support of Impoverished Jewish Youth of Lviv Middle Schools), records for 1910. TsDIAL, coll. 701, inv. 3, file 9.

50 Ibid.

51 In 1911, the chapter received 200 crowns from the Jewish Community Council and 500 crowns from the city. See »Sprawozdnanie z działalności Lwowskiego Oddziału Austryackiej Ligi dla zwalczania handlu dziewczętami z Biurem ›Ochrona Kobiet‹ za rok 1910–1911,« TsDIAL, coll. 701, inv. 2, file 1745, fol. 27.

52 The *Cultusrath* was an institution within the Jewish Community Council (*Israelitische Cultusgemeinde*), which was concerned with ritual practices. See statutes of the Lviv Jewish community. TsDIAL, coll. 701, inv. 3, file 8a.

communities found in many towns. These ties also reveal the degree to which the state delegated authority over Jews in the city and throughout Galicia, to the Jewish Community Council, signaling an expansion of its legal competence.

As the above-mentioned letter and statutes proposing a Jewish anti-trafficking association suggest, prominent individuals affiliated with the Jewish Community Council played an important role in transforming Jewish institutions. In addition to a move toward more voluntary, membership-based organizations, in some cases there was also a shift toward endorsement of associations that included other ethnic groups. Both Jews and Poles were members of the Lviv chapter of the Austrian Anti-Trafficking League, including some of the city's most prominent and best educated women such as Felicya Nossig,[53] Ada Kalmus-Reichensteinowa, Marya Kalmus-Schneiderowa,[54] and Anna Lewicka.[55] Several members also came from other cities in Galicia, and some from other regions in the Habsburg Empire.[56]

The attempt to be more inclusive demonstrates a shift toward a supra-ethnic or supra-religious consciousness. However, it is important to note that the initial push for this supra-ethnic institution in Lviv came from Vienna and activists in the west, and ran counter to the ideas which prevailed in an atmosphere highly charged by nationalist claims. At the same time not all social activists embraced the positions endorsed by western feminists. For example, at the turn of the century, women activists within the Zionist movement were especially critical of the approaches endorsed by Pappenheim.[57]

With regard to the Lviv Chapter of the Austrian League for Combating Trafficking in Girls, the association's annual reports to the main organization in

53 Felicya Nossig was a prominent socialist and women's rights activist, as well as the sister of Jewish social activist and artist Alfred Nossig. Her father was a secretary of the Lviv Jewish Community Council. Also known as Felicya Próchnikowa, in her 40s she travelled to Switzerland and earned a doctorate in philosophy. See *Polski słownik biograficzny*, vol. 28, s.v. »Próchnikowa,« 558–560.

54 Marya Kalmus was the first woman to be awarded a doctor of medicine degree from Lviv University, her sister Ada Kalmus earned a doctorate in philosophy the previous year. See »Pierwsza kobieta doktorem medycyny na uniwersytecie lwowskim,« *Kurjer Lwowski*, March 12, 1904.

55 Anna Lewicka was a writer, publicist, and teacher from a prominent local Polish family. *Polski słownik biograficzny*, vol. 17, s.v. »Lewicka, Anna,« 222–223.

56 Sprawozdanie z działalności Lwowskiego Oddziału Austryackiej Ligi dla zwalczania handlu dziewczętami z Biurem »Ochrona Kobiet« za rok 1910–1911. TsDIAL, coll. 701, inv. 2, file 1745, fol. 30–32.

57 For a discussion of prominent activist Rosa Pomeranz's criticism of Pappenheim, see Dietlind Hüchtker, »Rückständigkeit als Strategie oder Galizien als Zentrum europäischer Frauenpolitik« *Themenportal Europäische Geschichte* (2009), http://www.europa.clio-online.de/2009/Article=402 (accessed March 17, 2015).

Vienna provide an overview of the local society's activities. Most of the available reports, however, were published by the parent organization in German and may be summaries of longer reports. The Lviv chapter's 1908 report reveals during its first year the association was focused mostly on helping women from Lviv, rather than those newly arrived or passing through. The organization's emphasis was on job and skills training. According to the report, most of the women who received help were from the middle class, revealing the organization's links to broader agendas of improving women's education, training, and employment opportunities. The first report mentions that one woman was rescued from a life of prostitution and had become a valued employee at a laundry service.[58]

Reports from subsequent years focus more on the founding of a shelter where women could live while they sought work or received training. Later reports also document the number of women rescued from traffickers or from prostitution, including statistics about the ethnic or religious breakdown of the women receiving help, who were categorized as Christian or Jewish, and sometimes more precisely as Roman Catholic, Uniate, Protestant, or Jewish. This latter element is significant in that it underscores the organization's broad approach that included helping women from different religious backgrounds, demonstrating a commitment to new forms of organizations based on a supra-ethnic and -religious ideal. For example, the association reported that, in 1911, it had 531 protégées (*Schützlinge*) of whom 43 percent were Roman Catholic, 25 percent Greek Catholic, 30 percent Jewish, and two percent Protestant.[59] This designation does not indicate how many women were rescued from dangerous situations, from lives as prostitutes, and how many were women who needed other forms of help, such as training, and therefore might have been seen as potential future victims.

The statistics provided above indicate that the organization was multiethnic with regard to the women that it assisted. With regard to its membership it was somewhat less diverse, with most of its members being comprised of Jews and Polish Roman Catholics. Ukrainian Uniates were much less visible and perhaps virtually absent from among its membership.[60] Although those who identified

58 »Bericht des Lemberger Lokalkomittees über das Vereinsjahr 1908,« in *Bericht der Österreichischen Liga zur Bekämpfung des Mädchenhandels. Das Vereinsjahr 1908 und Generalversammlungs-Protokoll vom 18. Mai* (Wien: Selbstverlag des Vereins, 1909), 22–25, here 30.

59 »Auszug aus dem Bericht des Zweigvereines in Lemberg ›Liga für Frauen- und Kinderschutz‹ über das Vereinsjahr 1911,« in *Bericht des Vereins ›Österreichische Mädchen- und Kinderschutzliga‹ (Österreichische Liga zur Bekämpfung des Mädchenhandels) über das Vereinsjahr 1911* (Wien: Selbstverlag des Vereins, 1912), 23–24.

60 I draw this conclusion mainly from the names that are listed, though it is not entirely possible to discern how individuals self-identified from names alone. It is

as Ukrainians or Ruthenians[61] formed a majority in eastern Galicia, they tended to be mostly rural inhabitants, whereas the Lviv chapter was mainly an urban association. At the same time, ethnic and class tensions may have been further reasons for the small number of Ruthenians.

From 1908 to 1914, the annual reports of the Lviv chapter present an image of a group of individuals dedicated to fighting the trafficking of women, as well as expanding education and work opportunities to women. The complicated development of this association and its initiatives reveal significant changes in, as well as connections to, previously existing practices and concepts regarding charity. In particular, changes in thinking about membership, the expansion of women's rights and participation, and the cultivation of supra-ethnic and supra-religious inclusiveness carried important legal implications. At the same time, skeptics of the trafficking problem, including prominent figures in Galician Jewish communities, questioned whether or not their efforts were misplaced.

Discourse on Trafficking in Women: Galicia and Beyond

Prominent narratives of the period commonly portray the women involved in trafficking as naive innocents lured into a life of moral depravity by traffickers who could be both men and women. This image was recurrent in women's activist literature, fictional representations from the turn of the century,[62] as well as a theme in folk narratives.[63] These stories are relevant to Galician contexts

possible, that some members identified with Ukrainian or Ruthenian ethnicity. See »Sprawozdanie z działalności Lwowskiego Oddziału Austryackiej Ligi dla zwalczania handlu dziewczętami z Biurem ›Ochrona Kobiet‹ za rok 1910–1911,« TsDIAL, coll. 701, inv. 2, file 1745, fol. 30–32.

61 Most Ukrainians or Ruthenians in the region were Uniate (also known as Greek Catholic) or Orthodox. However, there were exceptions to these delineations, for example ethnic Poles who were Uniate and ethnic Ukrainians who were Roman Catholic.

62 See, for example, Sholem Aleichem, »The Man from Buenos Aires,« in idem, *Tevye the Dairyman and Railroad Stories* (New York: Schocken Books, 1987), 166–176 and Ivan Franko, »For the Home Hearth,« in *Behind Decorum's Veil*, ed. Sonia Morris (Winnipeg: Language Lanterns Publications, 2006), 9–167. In her introduction, editor Sonia Morris asserts that the themes and subject matter of this novella are not fictional, but depict real events that took place from 1887 to 1897 and are documented in transcriptions of criminal trials, which Franko covered while working as a journalist for the liberal Polish daily *Kurjer Lwowski*. See Sonia Morris, »Introduction,« in *Behind Decorum's Veil*, ed. Sonia Morris (Winnipeg: Language Lanterns Publications, 2006), http://www.languagelanterns.com/decorum.htm (accessed March 17, 2015).

63 »Captive Maiden, Abduction, Folk motif. R0-R10,« in Stith Thompson, *Folk Motif Index* (Bloomington: Indiana University Press, 1959). In addition, there are

because they influenced local narratives and interpretations of trafficking in women. In addition, many of the alleged victims from Galicia ended up in London, Cairo, New York, Buenos Aires, and other far-flung places.

However, there were also voices expressing skepticism about this depiction. For example, in 1914 a brief article in the *New York Times* cited a statement from a Berlin police investigator – identified as Dr. Kopp – who declared that after spending several years researching white slavery, he believed that the term was a misnomer, stating that the practice of trapping girls and forcing them into prostitution rarely happened. Kopp maintained that nearly all women immigrating in order to work as prostitutes did so willingly and had already engaged in prostitution before immigrating. He suggested that international philanthropy was off-track in its efforts to stamp out an evil that did not exist.[64]

Two years earlier, in 1912, labor and women's rights activist Teresa Billington-Greig published an article in the *English Review* entitled »The Truth about White Slavery.« In this text, she recounts her unsuccessful efforts to substantiate a single claim of any girl being trapped by use of drugs or other forms of coercion. The author was scathing in her condemnation of what she saw as a rush to adopt draconian legislation, namely the reintroduction of flogging in Britain, as a response to national hysteria. She argued that the sheer frequency of such accounts of young women being abducted rendered the stories, which she refers to as »rumors,« suspect.[65] Indeed, on this point, moving beyond the confines of the turn of the century and approaching this topic from an ethnographic perspective provides important insight. In this case, Billington-Greig's description of the way such narratives circulated, including the fact that they are almost always attributed to an inaccessible third party, corresponds very closely with

regional variations which include references to the historical figure Roxalana, a Ruthenian woman said to have been captured during the 16th century and sold in Constantinople as a concubine in the Sultan's harem. In an unprecedented act, the Sultan married his beloved concubine, whereby she rose to the position of sultana, thereby possessing considerable power. http://beshkan.de/journal/frauen-in-der-welt-des-orients/roxelane-der-aufstieg-einer-sklavin-zur-sultanin/index.html (accessed August 31, 2012). Slavic wedding rituals include a mock bridal capture, also said to refer to the times when brides were captured by their husbands. See for example, images from the Katrina Thomas Ethnic Wedding Photograph Collection, Bryn Mawr College Special Collections, http://triptych.brynmawr.edu/cdm/singleitem/collection/BMC_Weddings/id/166/rec/35 and http://triptych.brynmawr.edu/cdm/singleitem/collection/BMC_Weddings/id/176/rec/4 (accessed August 15, 2014).

64 »No White Slaves, He Says,« *New York Times*, July 22, 1914, query.nytimes.com/mem/archive-free/pdf?res=F00B13FB3F5A15738DDDAB0A94DF405B848DF1D3.

65 Teresa Billington-Greig, »The Truth about White Slavery,« *English Review* 14 (1913): 428–446.

what contemporary folklorists refer to as »urban legends.« Such narratives are often interpreted as expressions of specific fears existing in a given society, especially anxieties connected to changes in social and economic practices and technological innovation.[66] Therefore, the drastic social upheavals that Galician society experienced at the turn of the century provided especially fertile ground for dramatic narratives about trafficking in women.

In addition, the stories also bear certain similarities to blood libel or ritual murder accusations, charges, which, in European contexts, were most often made against Jews.[67] The purported victim in such cases was usually a child, though allegations of Jews killing young women for ritual purposes also occurred. In fact, in the late 19th century a blood libel case occurred in Habsburg Bohemia in which a Jew was accused of murdering a nineteen-year-old Czech girl for ritual purposes.[68] However, stories about trafficking in women from the turn of the century often follow a pattern similar to folk narratives that have existed for centuries, though the groups or individuals perceived as threatening changes. Urban legends about the abduction of children and young women persist in modern contexts and reemerge especially in times of heightened fear.[69]

Such narratives illustrate that traditional ideas are also at work in the emergence of modernizing trends. Sociologist Bernard Paillard argues that seemingly archaic psychological and cultural elements are not an indication of the absence of modernity, but in fact also develop within modern societies, in part due to a need to assign guilt.[70] The longevity of the motif of the captive

66 Jan Harold Brunvand, *The Vanishing Hitchhiker: American Urban Legends* (New York: Norton, 1981).

67 »Folk motif V361. Christian child killed to furnish blood for Jewish rite,« in Stith Thompson, *Motif-index of Folk-literature*, http://www.ruthenia.ru/folklore/thompson/v.htm (accessed August 15, 2012); Alan Dundes, *The Blood Libel Legend: A Casebook in Anti-Semitic Folklore* (Madison, WI: University of Wisconsin Press, 1991). For texts focusing on east central Europe, see also Hanna Węgrzynek, *›Czarna legenda‹ Żydów: Procesy o rzekome mordy rytualne w dawnej Polsce* (Warszawa: Bellona, 1995); Zenon Guldon and Jacek Wijaczka, *Procesy o mordy rytualne w Polsce w XVI–XVIII wieku* (Kielce: DCF, 1995); Albert S. Lindemann, *The Jew Accused: Three Anti-Semitic Affairs* (Cambridge: Cambridge University Press, 1991); and Laura Engelstein, *The Keys to Happiness: Sex and the Search for Modernity in Fin-de-Siècle Russia* (Ithaca, NY: Cornell University Press, 1992), 299–333.

68 František Červinka, »The Hilsner Affair,« in *The Blood Libel Legend: A Casebook in Anti-Semitic Folklore*, ed. Alan Dundes (Madison, WI: University of Wisconsin Press, 1991), 135–161.

69 Véronique Campion-Vincent, »Complots et avertissements: légendes urbaines dans la ville,« *Revue française de sociologie* 30, no. 1 (1989): 91–105, here 92–96.

70 Bernard Paillard, »L'écho de la rumeur,« *Communications* 52 (1990): 125–139, here 129.

maiden does not mean that there have not been cases of women being abducted and forced into prostitution, but the frequency of such stories in certain contexts, the fact that often their alleged victims cannot be found or identified, and that the suspected perpetrators are members of marginalized social groups are all elements which render their veracity suspect. Additionally, assigning categories of victim and perpetrator set the stage for enactments of legal dramas, which also shaped public consciousness. For example, the Lviv trial of 1892, in which officials tried 27 Jewish men and women for trafficking, contributed to perceptions of sex trade in the region.[71]

While at the turn of the century critics like Billington-Greig were adamant that common philanthropic efforts were misguided and even damaging, their voices in Germany and Britain were a minority. During the same period, however, skeptical voices in Galicia could also be found within Jewish communities. For example, as mentioned above, Rabbis Caro from Lviv and Horovitz from Krakow were unconvinced of the prevalence of the problem among Galician Jewry.[72] Although concern among Jews that more open discussion of trafficking of women might also spark an increase in expressions of anti-Semitism may also have been one reason that some Jewish leaders were not eager to embrace this cause.

In recent works that address sex trafficking in the late Habsburg Empire, perspectives also vary. Martin Pollack's acclaimed *Kaiser von Amerika* examines the extreme poverty and ensuing flight from Galicia, evoking dramatic scenes of traffickers preying on unfortunate teenage girls.[73] In contrast, Dietmar Jazbinsek asserts that criminologists and social scientists have clearly established that so-called white slavery did not exist. He argues that the belief was propagated in order to advance particular agendas, especially racist and nationalist causes.[74]

Other historians, who are also skeptical about the prevalence of women forced into prostitution, suggest that women were often aware of their fate and had already worked as prostitutes before immigrating.[75] Malte Fuhrmann's

71 Stauter-Halsted, »A Generation of Monsters,« 25.

72 »Delegierten-Tag zur Bekämpfung des Mädchenhandels,« 461–464.

73 For example, in one chapter entitled »Trade in Delicate Meat« (*Handel mit delikatem Fleisch*) Pollack describes the exploits of a female trafficker, Anna Strassberg, who returns to Europe to lure unsuspecting girls into the sex trade by promising good positions caring for children in Jewish families in Constantinople. Martin Pollack, *Kaiser von Amerika: Die große Flucht aus Galizien* (Wien: Zsolnay Verlag, 2010), 44–46.

74 Dietmar Jazbinsek, »Der internationale Mädchenhandel Biographie eines sozialen Problems,« *WZB-Papers* FS II 02-501 (2002), http://skylla.wzb.eu/pdf/2002/ii02-501.pdf (accessed August 15, 2014).

75 For example, Keely Stauter-Halsted points out that at least one of the witnesses and alleged victims in the famous Lviv »white slavery« trial in 1892 admitted that

study describes the dismay of Habsburg officials when one woman, after supposedly being rescued from her captors in Constantinople and returned to Galicia, very eloquently explained that it had been her choice to leave, that her life as a prostitute in the Ottoman Empire was a great improvement on the life of poverty she had previously led with her family, and that she would return at first opportunity.[76] The research of such scholars sheds important light on the dynamics of prostitution and trafficking in women in the late Habsburg Empire.[77] At the very least, their insights suggest that forced prostitution was less prevalent than anti-trafficking activists portrayed.[78]

With these complexities in mind, some scholars have speculated on the motivations of anti-trafficking activists. Marion Kaplan has suggested that, for Pappenheim, the issue served the instrumental purpose of galvanizing activism, which could be harnessed to advance broader claims for women's rights, indicating another area where this topic was linked to changes in legal consciousness.[79] Others are more convinced that her insistence on the importance had more to do with her adherence to bourgeois ideals. Pappenheim and other members of the Jewish Frauenbund were significantly shaped by German

she had »sold love« in Galicia before deciding to relocate to Constantinople in hopes of earning a better income. Stauter-Halsted, »A Generation of Monsters,« 30. In Nancy Wingfeld's research on police interviews with young women rescued from traffickers, she recounts statements of a teenager girl who, unhappy or frustrated with her living conditions, agreed to leave with a man who promised better circumstances elsewhere, without notifying their families. Wingfeld, »Destination: Alexandria,« 300–301.

76 Malte Fuhrmann, »›Western Perversions‹ at the Threshold of Felicity: The European Prostitutes of Galata-Pera (1870–1915),« *History and Anthropology* 21, no. 2 (2010): 159–172, here 163–164.

77 For a more extensive discussion of prostitution and social class in the lands of partitioned Poland see Keely Stauter-Halsted, *The Devil's Chain: Prostitution and Social Control in Partitioned Poland* (Ithaca: Cornell University Press, 2015).

78 In fact, this topic remains very much contested in present day contexts. During the 1990s, in the aftermath of the Cold War, new claims about a rapid increase in sex trafficking emerged. One new development is that sex workers have increasingly become more organized and vocal, often insisting that anti-trafficking campaigns are actually damaging to sex workers because they continue to pass judgment on those who choose to work as prostitutes and use the image of the forced innocent to deny that all prostitutes deserve human rights. For insightful discussions by activists and scholars, see Kamala Kempadoo and Jo Doezema, *Global Sex Workers: Rights, Resistance, and Redefinition* (London: Routledge, 1998).

79 Marion Kaplan, *The Jewish Feminist Movement: The Campaigns of the Jüdischer Frauenbund, 1904–1938* (Westport–London: Greenwood Press, 1979), 103–105.

bourgeois principles of *Bildung* (education) and *Sittlichkeit* (morality).[80] In particular, the need to strictly adhere to the latter was seen as of utmost importance in preventing contamination of bourgeois society from »perversity« often associated with the working classes.[81] Aside from Pappenheim's motivations for taking up the anti-trafficking cause, it is likely that concerns about the threat of »white slavery« were also linked to changes in social practices. For example, a large increase in the numbers of women traveling alone violated social tabus and provoked anxiety, as well as challenging the existing social and legal status of women, which made them dependent on men.

Similar to German-Jewish feminists, such as Pappenheim, it appears that the Lviv chapter also used the issue of trafficking in women as a strategy to promote broader feminist goals.[82] For example, its first annual report's emphasis on training and job placement for middle-class women suggest this tendency and the reference to the rescue of a single, perhaps token, former prostitute reinforces this image. However, it may also be that the association had limited resources during its first year and chose to concentrate on what its members saw as manageable objectives. Reports from subsequent years suggest that more attention and resources were focused on rescuing women from prostitution, including direct intervention.[83] This last practice of seeking to influence and directly engaging in law enforcement also served to enhance the status of activist groups, by allying themselves with other power structures and providing a field in which they became new experts or elites.[84]

80 Shulamit Volkov, »The ›Verbürgerlichung‹ of the Jews as a Paradigm,« in *Bourgeois Society in Nineteenth-Century Europe*, eds. Jürgen Kocka and Allen Mitchell (Oxford: Berg, 1993), 367–391, here 373-380. See also discussion in Sara E. Wobick, »Mädchenhandel between Antisemitism and Social Reform: Bertha Pappenheim and the Jüdischer Frauenbund,« *Sophie Journal* 1 (2004): 1–23, here 10; Hanna Kozinska-Witt, »Bertha Pappenheim and Jewish Women from Eastern Europe,« *The American Association for Polish-Jewish Studies*, 2012, http://www.aapjstudies.org/index.php?id=144 (accessed August 15, 2014).

81 George Mosse, *Nationalism and Sexuality: Middle-Class Morality and Sexual Norms in Modern Europe* (Madison: University of Wisconsin Press, 1985), 4–5.

82 Kaplan, *The Jewish Feminist Movement*, 103 and 113.

83 One association report refers to »unsere Agenten« (»our agents«) working in conjunction with police in Lviv, Krakow, and Drohobycz to apprehend an Argentinean trafficker. See, *Bericht des Vereins ›Österreichische Mädchen- und Kinderschutzliga‹ (Österreichische Liga zur Bekämpfung des Mädchenhandels) über das Vereinsjahr 1910 und Generalversammlungs-Protokolle vom 30. Mai und 26. Juni 1911* (Wien: Selbstverlag des Vereins, 1911), 30.

84 For example, in her research on three women's rights activists in Galicia, Dietlind Hüchtker discusses the ways that their activism gave them access to new knowledge which allowed them to emerge as a new elite and, in effect, as »world architects« (*Gestalter/innen der Welt*). Hüchtker, *Geschichte als Performance*, 315.

Despite the limitations of the Lviv Office for the Protection of Women, the organization appears to have been partly successful in providing a space where individuals could address social welfare issues in a context that spanned beyond categories of ethnicity and religion. In 1911 the *Kurjer lwowski* asserted that it »is one of the few venues where individuals from diverse religious and ethnic backgrounds can work together.« In this regard, the Lviv association could be seen as an expression of secularization, in its attempt to make social initiatives more inclusive and reach beyond narrow religious and ethnic communities, thereby demonstrating a new way of thinking about society and charity.

The apparent absence of Ukrainian women activists in the association underscores that attempts at inclusivity were only partly realized and often hinged on other forms of exclusion, including discrepancies between upper and middle-class women and those from lower classes, as well as between urban and rural women. Despite attempts to promote inclusivity, modern institutions in urban contexts often maintained rather than eliminated exclusion.[85]

Conclusions

Many changes at the turn of the century were driven by social movements that converged during this period, including labor and socialist movements, the women's movement, as well as nationalist causes. Such movements of contestation marked a key component in processes of modernization[86] and, as I have shown, were also an important source of »emergent law.« In this context, changes in legal thinking led to the creation of new institutions and modifications to existing structures. These shifts meant new ways of thinking about charity, identifying communities in need, and redefining who could play a prominent role in these debates.

At the turn of the century, Habsburg authorities in Vienna continued to rely on local religious leaders to better administer populations that would otherwise be difficult to reach. This policy played an important role in reordering legal competencies and promoting increased centralization. This strategy also suggests one potential reason why there was an effort to coordinate control over newly emerging types of activism, such as the anti-trafficking movement. In a period marked by increasing contestation, officials may have deemed it prudent to manage and guide activist agendas where possible.

Surviving documents do not provide a clear indication of whether or not Hersh Günsberg and the women he was travelling with were engaged in

85 Paillard discusses this tendency in more general terms in late-20th-century contexts. Paillard, »L'écho de la rumeur,« 129.

86 Shmuel N. Eisenstadt, »Multiple Modernities,« *Daedalus* 129, no. 1 (2000): 1–29.

trafficking or prostitution. However, the surviving narrative reveals themes that were a source of considerable concern at the turn of the century. Records also reveal that the allegation made by Henryk Sprecher – the merchant identified as a member of the local anti-trafficking society – was credible to police, or that it was important to treat it as though it were. Indeed, other reports suggest that there was considerable collaboration between such societies and the police during this period, bestowing these associations with a new status.

In addition to the disparity among social classes discussed above, the efforts of organizations and the attention that trafficking in women received are connected to the articulation of other cultural hierarchies, including perceived inequalities between east and west. A closer look at societies for the protection of women at the local level complicates assumptions about relationships between centers and peripheries. Officials and intellectuals in Vienna and German cities often saw Galicia as a half-civilized eastern borderland. Yet, Lviv itself functioned as an important center in the region and regional activists did not always accept the approaches propagated by western activists. A Polonized elite associated with the Jewish Community Council and with the Lviv anti-trafficking chapter largely aligned themselves with the perspectives of western activists. However, while these inhabitants played important roles in developing and implementing approaches that included new forms of charity, many also worked within previously existing Jewish charity institutions.

Although there appears to have been a strong movement toward new forms of social activism based on more secular models, a closer look reveals much greater complexity. Many traditional forms of charity were not falling away, but were changing, if in less dramatic ways. Incorporating a concept of »law as process« renders such developments more visible by highlighting the ways that existing practices and structures are reshaped by emerging contexts and expectations.

In this article I have identified key areas where legal concepts were in the process of being contested and renegotiated: membership; the admission of women as participants in public life; the development of supra-ethnic and supra-religious consciousness with regard to activism; as well as attempts by anti-trafficking associations to influence and even police morality. These spheres demonstrate the role that social movements – born of specific circumstances and times – play in reshaping legal landscapes. Many of the issues raised in this discussion remain relevant to present-day discourse and suggest areas of research relevant to the longue durée, including the challenges posed by large-scale migration, activist networks, and the task of helping those in need.

Tracie L. Wilson

Shifts in Political Rule and the Reorganization of Law

Blasphemy's Long Shadow: Confessional, Legal, and Institutional Conflict in the Tsarist Partition of Poland under Catherine II

In 1780, Prince Aleksandr Alekseevich Viazemskii, the prosecutor general (*general'nyi prokuror*) in St Petersburg, Empress Catherine's right hand in important matters concerning the dispensation of justice, received information concerning a number of difficult cases that had occurred in the newly acquired Belarusian territory. These cases shed light on the integration of this part of the Polish-Lithuanian Commonwealth into the Russian Empire, one which was anything but smooth. Tensions were high in the region, as demonstrated by information from the local authorities that a peasant had repeatedly uttered words of blasphemy against Christ and the mother of God.[1] The case file does not tell us what these words were, but it reports that a group of 35 peasant witnesses questioned by the court in charge had corroborated the blasphemy. The subsequent conflict revolved around who should then deal with it.

The case was supposed to be passed on to the magistrate of the town of Kopys'. However, the consistory in charge of the Greek Catholic population in the region protested against the move. The institution, which bore the responsibilities of a tribunal for cases in the competence of the church, had just been founded by the Tsarist authorities as a means of overseeing members of the Uniate Church.[2] In the case under consideration the consistory complained that

1 Rossiiskii gosudarstvennyi arkhiv drevnikh aktov/Russian State Archive of Historical Records (hereafter RGADA), fond/f. (collection) 7, opis/op. (inventory) 2, delo/d. (file) 2561, list/l. (folio) 1. Elena B. Smilianskaia was the first scholar to analyze this case, see Elena B. Smilianskaia, »O evree Girshe Notoviche, khulivshem Khrista; sudebnyi kazus ekaterinskogo vremeni,« in *Svoi ili chuzhoi? Evrei i slaviane glazami drug druga*, ed. Olga V. Belova (Moskva: Dom evreiskoi knigi, 2003), 151–160. Elena B. Smilianskaia is also the author of the only comprehensive work on blasphemy in Russia, see Elena B. Smilianskaia, *Volshebniki, bogokhul'niki, eretiki. Narodnaia religioznost' i »dukhovnye prestupleniia« v Rossii XVIII v.* (Moskva: Indrik, 2003).

2 About the foundation of the consistory for the Uniate Church in the Polotsk and Mogilev *namestnichestva*, see Uladzimir I. Navitski, ed., *Kanfesii na Belarusi (Kanets XVIII–XX st.)*(Minsk: Ekaperspektyva, 1998), 6. There had been a

both mayors and a member of the municipal council were Jews.[3] The consistory polemically stated that the individuals in question were »of the same false belief« as the delinquent himself. Their books were alleged to contain the blasphemies he was accused of.[4] The consistory insisted that they were therefore incapable of judging the case. Moreover, it also claimed that Jews had manipulated peasants to support the blasphemer by stating that he was innocent.[5] Given the growing sensitivity to testimony and proof in this age,[6] this was a serious accusation.

We are unable to verify how the local population actually felt about this case and to what degree the so-called delinquent, who had been denounced to the authorities by a priest, received any support. As it is, the story presents well-known stereotypes of a Jewish anti-Christian conspiracy. However, it was not only the Jews who were reproached as being too biased to be judges. According to Lieutenant Colonel (*podpolkovnik*) General Rebinder, the empress' representative in the Polatsk region, the Catholics who dominated the local institutions were considered no better: they could not be trusted properly to judge in critical cases.[7]

What were the cases this high official had in mind? Men of the area's nobility, who had recently challenged Russian hegemony,[8] verbally attacked converts to the Orthodox faith as »Muscovites« and »apostates«, as did Uniate burghers, peasants, and workers on peasant farms.[9] Confronted by the new authorities'

Catholic consistory in Mogilev since 1773. Ibid., 21. The Uniate consistory was founded after Archbishop Smohozhevs´kyi's departure for Poland, with the clear intention of replacing the authoritative representative of the Uniates by a mere institution of control. Barbara Skinner, *The Western Front of the Eastern Church. Uniate and Orthodox Conflict in 18th-century Poland, Ukraine, Belarus, and Russia* (DeKalb, IL: Northern Illinois University Press, 2009), 161; RGADA, f. 7, op. 2, d. 2561, l. 7.

3 After the Russian annexation, the Jews in the towns of the region had been integrated into the structures of municipal self-government and could hold offices.

4 RGADA, f. 7, op. 2, d. 2561, l. 11 oborotnyi/ob. (verso).

5 Ibid., l. 1 ob.

6 This growing sensitivity can at least be observed in cases concerning lese-majesty, which were also dealt with under the auspices of the procurator general, see Angela Rustemeyer, *Dissens und Ehre. Majestätsverbrechen in Russland 1600–1800* (Wiesbaden: Harrassowitz, 2006), 353–358.

7 RGADA, f. 7, op. 2, d. 2561, l. 5. Rebinder's function was the one of a vice-governor, but it is designated in different terms (*praviashchii dolzhnost' pravitelia polotskogo namestnichestva*).

8 Henads Sahanowitsch, »Die Agonie der Adelsrepublik,« in *Handbuch der Geschichte Weißrusslands*, eds. Dietrich Beyrau and Rainer Lindner (Göttingen: Vandenhoeck & Ruprecht, 2001), 93–105, here 115.

9 »The Uniates do not stop calling those who convert to Orthodoxy names: scoundrels, abominable Muscovites, damned apostates (Unity vstupaiushchikh

takeover of a Uniate church in Vitsebsk, assigning it to the Orthodox Church, one burgher, for instance, said they would not join the Orthodox priest even at the price of their heads. A priest tried to make this particular burgher enter the church that had been made Orthodox, provoking him to utter disrespectful words about the empress: »Damned one, why do you not become Orthodox? It is the will of our gracious sovereign«. The Uniate burgher, who feared being forced to swear an oath to Orthodoxy, silently told himself that he would rather die,[10] thus trying to make the oath invalid.

The actors in this complex story are thus from a mixed Uniate, Jewish, Roman Catholic, and Orthodox population, all claiming or being ascribed religious-based allegiances. The story's setting is an area with an ambiguous image, the far East of the former Polish-Lithuanian Commonwealth and the far West of the Russian Empire of the time. The plot involves a conflict over religion and law with local and imperial dimensions. What can the story tell us? The situations described in this case file are too specific to say to which degree religious conflicts dominated everyday life. We can, however, reliably interpret this source as an indicator of the limits of legal and institutional conflict management as the government conceived it. By doing so, we can see the outlines of some important topics of the period. Firstly, the case cited above provides hints regarding the contemporary perception of civic identity in Poland-Lithuania and Russia. It sheds light on how the contemporary understanding of the civic character of institutions and the transformation of the former East of the Polish-Lithuanian Commonwealth into the West of the Russian Empire were interrelated. Secondly, the case hints at strong and weak factors of religious diversity in the territories annexed by Russia in the third partition of Poland-Lithuania. It makes these factors visible against the background of tendencies both towards secularization and towards a new role of religion as an instrument employed to stabilize the order imposed by a monarchy claiming to be enlightened.

Both aspects, civic identity in the area under consideration and the way autocracy dealt with religious diversity in the region, have been treated in recent research. Referring extensively to the uses of law and the court system, Iauhen K. Anishchanka's study of the relations between the Belarusian gentry and its new Petersburg overlords comes to the conclusion that the gentry had in fact renounced the defence of the autonomous status of the region. This is indeed remarkable, for they could have done so by using the authority of the influential

v blagochestie ne perestaiut rugat' nazyvaia kanaliiami, skvernymi moskaliami, prokliatymi apostatami).« RGADA, f. 7, op. 2, d. 2561, l. 5 ob.

10 Ibid., l. 12–12 ob.

Lithuanian Statutes.[11] While the differing religious identities of the newly conquered subjects were clearly prone to encourage resistance to the conqueror, the gentry's propriety interests favoured accommodation.[12]

Useful hints at how to fruitfully look at civic identity in late 18th-century Belarus are given in Larry Wolff's study on the Uniate Church under Catherine II. Wolff avoids explicitly ascribing an attitude of accommodation or resistance to the actors. However, he does state that the Uniate faith prepared the ground for a popular Ruthenian national identity. He also discusses the point of view of the Petersburg authorities as well as other representatives of the secular and clerical European elites concerning the foundations of civic identity or, more precisely, civic obedience. The most explicit position the author cites is the perception of Uniate peasants in both Belarus and Ukraine as too underdeveloped to confess civic obedience independently of religious obedience.[13] In this article, I am most prominently interested in such perceptions by historical actors. As the case presented above shows, the perception of civic (or un-civic) behaviour by the authorities is easier to establish from the sources than any »real« attitude of resistance or accommodation held by the population. This perception is telling if not about the autocracy's subjects' action itself, then at least about the conditions in which their actions took place.

Wolff also refers to the autocracy's policies towards religion and the churches. In his opinion, a secularized understanding of religion during the last years of Catherine's reign was responsible for the repression of the Uniate Church: the autocracy »sponsored a missionary campaign, conceived in an aggressively modern spirit, to meet the modern challenge of national integration«.[14] In contrast to Wolff's view, Barbara Skinner argues that Catherine's repression of the Uniate Church from the late 1770s continued the autocracy's traditional policy of not recognizing the Uniates as a confession separate from Orthodoxy, ending a short period during which the empress' observance of international obligations had restricted her freedom of action.[15] According to Skinner,

11 The Lithuanian Statutes were a major law code edited in three versions: 1529, 1566, and 1588, see Iauhen K. Anishchanka, *Belarus' u chasy Katsiryny II (1772–1796)* (Minsk: Vedy, 1998), 184–187.

12 About propriety, see Anishchanka, *Belarus'*, 186.

13 This was a statement by the papal nuncio. Larry Wolff, »The Uniate Church and the Partitions of Poland: Religious Survival in an Age of Enlightened Absolutism,« *Harvard Ukrainian Studies* 16, no. 1–4 (2002–2003): 153–244, here 229. The former Polatsk archbishop's remark about the »rough people« (with reference to the allegedly ignorant and superstitious peasants) being the target of Orthodox harassment suggests a similar perception. Ibid., 173.

14 Wolff, »The Uniate Church,« 190.

15 Skinner, *Western Front*, 168.

Catherine's repression of the Uniates was a notorious case of deviation from the main direction of her imperial politics, with the empress following the path to forced cultural unification prepared by the Orthodox clergy in this particular case.

An approach to the conflicts in the area of the first partition focusing on the institutional order permits us to assess the scope of explanations that refer to confessional conflict and emerging national attitudes. The story told above sheds light on some largely unnoticed aspects of the conquest, which we may consider to be relevant factors leaning in the direction of repression. Religious policy cannot be regarded in terms of a transnational transfer of ideas or a continuity of tradition without taking into consideration its relations to the law and institutions of jurisdiction. I do not refute the significance of both tradition and modernization for policies toward the region's religious groups, but I suggest considering theses policies from a different perspective.

Referring to the development of the court system during the reign of Catherine II, the story discussed on the following pages demonstrates conflicts over a modernized understanding of institutions in Russia.[16] From this Enlightenment perspective the institutions of the state could not function without the subjects' trust in them. This understanding of institutions is crucial to the course of events referred to in the case file. I will first provide a brief overview of the developments which most conspicuously marked this course of events: the annexation of Belarus from the Polish-Lithuanian Commonwealth and Catherine's politics of law enforcement. I follow this with a discussion of two areas of government activity in Catherinean Russia: the prosecution of religious crime and the confirmation of rule through institution-building. In doing so, I show why the Uniates were considered the weakest element in a religiously diverse context and thus became the target of enlightened absolutism.

The Conflict and its Setting: Conquest and Law Enforcement

In order to build empires, the disciplinary and participatory institutions of imperial states had to interact with the modes of conquest of their respective periods. This was indeed the case for 18th-century Russia, which followed disciplinary and participatory models, and modes of conquest differing from those of the pre-Petrine era.

16 Jörg Baberowski dates this modernization of the understanding of institutions into a later period: Iorg [Jörg] Baberowski, »Doverie cherez prisutstvie: Domodernye praktiki vlasti v pozdnej rossiiskoi imperii,« *Ab Imperio* 2008, no. 3, 71–95.

This justifies a closer look at the time before the Petrine period. To ascertain the specific traits of Russia's second move into Belarus in the first partition, a massive move that was decisive in the long term, we shall turn to the first such move for comparison. Muscovy had annexed a part of the region in 1654 with the conquest of Smolensk. From the Muscovite viewpoint the task had then been to integrate a group of nobles, the Smolensk *szlachta*, into Muscovy. However, the annexation was not followed by any sort of transfer of institutions from the Polish-Lithuanian Commonwealth to Muscovy.

In contrast, the 18th-century annexation was conditioned by the necessity to integrate municipal communities with multiple confessional profiles. While the integration of the Smolensk *szlachta* had added a new facet to the Empire's multiconfessional and polyethnic elite without altering its principles of domination, the mode of integration applied to Belarusian towns 120 years later reflected the change the 18th century had brought about. According to the Petrine principle of borrowing from the West, Catherine introduced a new type of town administration into the Empire that would serve as an example for the reform of Russian towns that was accomplished in the 1780s.

But to what degree was the western model of town administration prone to stabilize a larger political, social and economic system? Unlike the cities and towns of central Russia, some important Belarusian towns lived under Magdeburg Law, which had been accorded to them in the late Middle Ages.[17] However, it is questionable whether the Belarusian towns with their different ethnic groups and confessions corresponded to the ideal of city autonomy and inner peace established by Magdeburg law. In the key period of the mid-17th century, the inner cohesion of the Belarusian towns had been rather limited.[18] During the 18th century there were no hints at a situation closer to the ideal described above. After its acquisition by Russia, the Jews of the newly annexed Belarusian province petitioned the central government for less discriminating terms for themselves against the resistance of the Christian municipalities. These

17 Stanisław Aleksandrowicz, »Städte in den weißrussischen Gebieten des Großfürstentums Litauen (15.–18. Jahrhundert),« in *Handbuch der Geschichte Weißrusslands*, eds. Dietrich Beyrau and Rainer Lindner (Göttingen: Vandenhoeck & Ruprecht, 2001), 276–290, especially 277.

18 The inhabitants of the cities of Mahilioŭ and Vitsebsk reacted differently to Muscovite military pressure in 1654, with Mahilioŭ surrendering and Vitsebsk resisting. Stefan Rohdewald characterizes the early-modern Belarusian city of Polatsk as an example of the coexistence of Jews and non-Jews, which had failed in the German-speaking territories of the Holy Roman Empire in the middle of the 14th century. Stefan Rohdewald, *Vom Polocker Venedig. Kollektives Handeln sozialer Gruppen in einer Stadt zwischen Ost- und Mitteleuropa* (Stuttgart: Steiner, 2005), 251. However, this does not mean that there was a coherent community.

local authorities, for their part, correctly assessing the government's strategy of preserving the status quo whenever this did not endanger the establishment of the empress' rule, insisted upon the discrimination of the Jews as justified by the Commonwealth's tradition.[19] In this situation law and law enforcement were crucial, both as a means for the central authorities to put down local conflicts, and as a field where participatory rights were gained and lost.

Law enforcement in Catherine's Russia was not untypical of the European context of the period, with limitations on torture changing interrogation procedures.[20] Furthermore, attempts were made to more clearly differentiate felonies from less serious crimes. Some of the latter were ascribed to the sphere of the everyday maintenance of the public order (*Policey*).[21] Not surprisingly, the discourse about the reform of criminal law and criminal justice in Europe, notably the restriction of the monarch's ability to interfere with jurisdiction,[22] had no political implications in the frame of Catherine's enlightened absolutism.[23]

The law cannot be considered without referring to the tribunals that had to apply it. They were the object of the interreligious conflict in the situation analysed here. Thus religious contradictions were not only present in the legal conflict under consideration, but even structurally enrooted in it. As the case demonstrates, four religious communities – Uniates, Orthodox, Roman Catholics, and Jews – were involved in these contradictions. Concerning the Jews, interreligious conflict played a prominent role in thwarting the autocracy's attempts to rebuild municipal institutions.

The reform of town life and municipal administration in the Russian Empire under Catherine II as carried out in the newly conquered area was, on the one hand, an adoption of the existing basic city model of that area. On the other hand, it was a step towards subordinating traditional religious discrimination to

19 E. K. Anishchenko [= Ia. K. Anishchanka], *Cherta osedlosti: belorusskaia sinagoga v carstvovanie Ekateriny II.* (Minsk: Art-Feks, 1998), 82–85.

20 Aleksandr B. Kamenskii, *Ot Petra I do Pavla I. Reformy v Rossii XVIII v.* (Moskva: Rossiiskii gosudarstvennyi gumanitarnyi universitet, 1999), 403–404.

21 Oleg A. Omel'chenko, *»Zakonnaia monarkhiia« Ekateriny Vtoroi: Prosveshchennyi absoliutizm v Rossii* (Moskva: Iurist, 1993), 308.

22 Karl Härter, »Die Entwicklung des Strafrechts in Mitteleuropa 1770–1848,« in *Verbrechen im Blick. Perspektiven der neuzeitlichen Kriminalitätsgeschichte*, eds. Rebekka Habermas and Gerd Schwerhoff (Frankfurt a. M.: Campus, 2009), 71–107, here 78.

23 Compare Wolff, »The Uniate Church«. The rejection of the term »absolutism« has not been accepted in the historiography of Eastern Europe. Recent studies use it with ease on a conceptual level, see, for example, Ralph Tuchtenhagen, *Zentralstaat und Provinz im frühneuzeitlichen Nordosteuropa* (Wiesbaden: Harrassowitz, 2008).

the needs of municipal institution-building, which was not a purpose in itself: It was conceived to open up fiscal resources and to create a local foundation for the state. Including the Jews into municipal self-government was a step towards secularization in a pragmatic style. Yet, at the same time the Orthodox claim on Uniate churches made the cities a place of traditional religious confrontation in a spatial dimension,[24] as a struggle over sacred places put its stamp on city life. I will demonstrate that, in spite of the tendency towards secularization, religion was preserved – or even revitalized – as a force marking city life in the era of Catherine II. It is significant that a religious institution, the consistory, played a particular role in the case cited above.

To sum up the setting underlying the case presented above, the existing lines of conflict between ethnic and religious groups in the town were presumably deepened by the tsarist government's urban reform, which legally integrated the Jews into the town administration as passive, or even as active members. These lines cut across those of the conflict between Uniate burghers, on the one hand, and the Orthodox Church and the central government, on the other. A third conflict occurred between the imperial state and the nobility, the social stratum which the autocracy relied on in core areas of the empire. This situation prompted the imperial state to introduce measures to settle the situation, as social strata with otherwise divergent interests[25] now held similar anti-government opinions.

Defining Crime

The conflicts under consideration were portrayed as scandalous in terms of religious crime. In the early modern era, religious crime had been largely applied as a mode of interpretation of what was perceived as deviant behaviour. Given the Enlightenment's call for religious tolerance, which entailed, all over Europe and including the Russian Empire, a ban on the criminalization of religious practice perceived as deviant or alien, the prosecution of religious crime at the turn of the 19th century is quite striking. A rather banal reason for the criminalization of religious behaviour that continued throughout the Enlightenment era lay in an enlightened absolutist government striving for control: Even while the empress was preaching tolerance, both she and the central authorities nevertheless claimed a monopoly on the power to determine how far tolerance should go.

24 Skinner hints at similarities with the age of the religious wars in Europe. Skinner, *Western Front,* 229.

25 About gentry, peasant, and clerical interests, see Anishchanka, *Belarus'*, 9 and 183.

However, the case I examine here shows that the initiative to criminalize religious behaviour could also emerge from a local constellation with the central authorities assuming a reactive role. Local actors representing Christian confessions accused Jewish members of the municipality of adhering to a blasphemous religion, and Uniate believers called those who adopted Orthodoxy apostates. In order to understand the semantics of these accusations of religious crime in the case at hand, one has to consider their transnational historical and contemporary background. The criminalization of religious behaviour at the end of the 18th century was bound to both traditions and contemporary circumstances which transcended state borders and thus the reach of a single monarch and her administration. The forms of religious crime alluded to in the case referred to the past and present of the Polish-Lithuanian and the Muscovite-Russian legal spaces. These spaces were interconnected in many ways, as a look at the legal definitions of religious crime in early-modern law demonstrates.

With regard to law codes, Muscovy[26] and the Lithuanian part of the Commonwealth were closely linked, with the Lithuanian Statute being the most systematic legal code in all of Poland-Lithuania. This is, for example, true for the definition of crimes against the sovereign, which reflected the political essence of early modern law-making. In the middle of the 17thcentury, when working out the first comprehensive treatment of crimes against the ruler to occur in a Muscovite law code, the tsar's law-makers could rely on the corresponding chapter of the Third Lithuanian Statute as their most important source.[27] With regard to religious crime, however, the Muscovite law-makers profited from the Statute only as far as the criminalizing of improper behaviour at church was concerned. The Statute did not reflect much concern about religious deviance: It had no particular chapter about crimes against God,[28] which the Muscovites felt they needed. On the one hand, this hints at the Grand Duchy's central authorities not being particularly eager to prosecute such deeds themselves. On the other hand, it might indicate that as far as secular law is concerned, the sanctioning of religious crimes was mostly delegated to the level of local or urban law.[29]

26 This is the correct name of »Russia« before Peter the Great: Only in the Petrine era is the term »Russia« systematically used in Russian sources to refer to the country and state.

27 Arkadii G. Man'kov, ed., *Sobornoe Ulozhenie 1649 g. Tekst, kommentarii* (Leningrad: Nauka, 1987), 144.

28 Ivan P. Shamiakin, ed., *Statut vialikaha knjastva Litouskaha 1588: teksty, davednik, kamentaryi* (Minsk: Belaruskaia Savetskaia Enciklopedyia, 1989).

29 Juliusz Bardach, *Historia państwa i prawa polskiego* (Warszawa: PWN, 1966), Vol. 2, 353.

Muscovy and subsequently the Russian Empire lacked the density of urban law that had been provided by the transfer of law from Central Europe to the Commonwealth. Definitions of religious crime in secular law were provided by the central law codes. One of the religious crimes that had been defined by secular law since the mid-17th century was apostasy.[30] Russia's legal system, just like the legal system of the Commonwealth, reflected being in a country with a great variety of religious communities, but one with an official state religion as well. Leaving the state religion for another religion was indeed defined as a crime deserving of capital punishment.

With regard to conversions to Judaism and Islam, the criminalization of abandoning the Orthodox faith in Russia and the Catholic faith in the Commonwealth was rather unambiguous. A denomination as close to both Roman Catholicism and Orthodoxy – although at different levels – as the Uniate faith was a more complicated case. In 17th-century Muscovy there had been strong reservations about both Uniates and Orthodox believers in Poland-Lithuania, including doubts about the validity of the baptisms of adherents to Orthodoxy living under the rule of a non-Orthodox monarch.[31] Such an attitude far less matched the Russian authorities' position in the 18th century, as it would have meant doubting the authenticity of the Orthodox in the Commonwealth, whose rights as Orthodox believers the emperors claimed to defend. By contrast, Orthodox and Uniates remained each other's religious rivals more so than they were those of Jews or Muslims. This also explains the depiction of the Orthodox as »apostates« by the Uniates, as cited by the aforementioned tsarist official Rebinder in the case in question.

The relative proximity of religious denominations also plays a role when we turn to the religious crime most prominent in the given case, which was blasphemy. Blasphemy was defined as a crime in the first chapter of the 1649 Muscovite law code. However, the law was not everything. A look across the borders of the Eastern European countries shows that blasphemy is the best example of a crime being defined not just by law codes, but also by community practices. It was to a considerable degree perceived and prosecuted according to the ways in which communities were organized and symbolically represented.

Gerd Schwerhoff distinguishes two types of accusations of blasphemy in medieval and early modern European societies. The first are accusations of blasphemy as a means of restoring God's honour within a culture of communication generally marked by a continually perceived need to defend one's own honour. Such accusations were levelled at persons who, driven by anguish or

30 About conversion to Islam, see Man'kov, *Sobornoe Ulozhenie*, 131.

31 Tatiana A. Oparina, *Inozemtsy v Rossii XVI–XVII vv. Ocherki istoricheskoi biografii i genealogii* (Moskva: Progress-Traditsiia, 2007), 5–21.

despair, or simply as a means of mockery, swore and took the name of the Lord in vain. The prosecution of this kind of blasphemy, closely linked to the authorities' efforts to impose discipline on early modern men and women, worked best in communities of persons that spoke the same religious language. Nevertheless, Schwerhoff supposes that it was also promoted by the juridical identity of the respective communities: in the late medieval Holy Roman Empire it was mainly the task of city authorities to prosecute run-of-the-mill blasphemy, as swearing at God was understood as an insult to the local Christian community, consolidated in the burghers' oath that constituted the city as a body politic.[32] There was nothing similar which could have promoted people being accused of this kind of blasphemy in early modern Russia, and that may be one reason why the prosecution of blasphemy was rare there.[33]

The quantitatively insignificant, but nevertheless highly important accusations occurring in the context of interreligious polemics provide the second type of the prosecution of blasphemy in the societies Schwerhoff refers to.[34] This use of blasphemy charges is notorious for having instigated excesses of anti-Jewish violence from the Middle Ages. It also occurred in the Polish-Lithuanian Commonwealth, for example during inter-confessional conflicts in early modern Polatsk.[35] It is no surprise that it played a role in the case under discussion as well.

The confessional tensions between Orthodox and Uniates crystallized in conflicts over Uniate churches which were assigned to the Orthodox: what was regarded as an act of legitimate transfer by the authorities was perceived as an act of desacralization by Uniate believers. As concrete instances of religious conflict, the Belarusian cities with their Uniate burghers, considered to be neither Orthodox nor completely un-Orthodox, must have been a greater challenge to the central authorities than the annexed Protestant cities in the Baltic provinces, the Russian Empire's most recent conquest of non-Orthodox Christian communities at the time: The deeper demarcation between the religious denominations there presumably made religious spaces less convertible and therefore less likely to generate conflict. By contrast, in the situation in question, the step towards claiming sacred places of the conquered for the

32 Gerd Schwerhoff, »Gotteslästerung,« in *Enzyklopädie der Neuzeit*, vol. 4, ed. Friedrich Jäger (Stuttgart: Metzler/Poeschel, 2006), 1054–1056, especially 1054. About blasphemy prosecuted as a mockery of the burghers' oath, see Gerd Schwerhoff, *Zungen wie Schwerter: Blasphemie in alteuropäischen Gesellschaften 1200–1650* (Konstanz: UVK, 2005), 184.

33 Smilianskaia found 133 case files for the 18th century, see Smilianskaia, *Volsheb-niki, bogokhul'niki, eretiki*, 209.

34 Schwerhoff, »Gotteslästerung«.

35 Rohdewald, *Vom Polocker Venedig*, 289.

religion of the conqueror was a small one. Under these circumstances, accusations of blasphemy, made in order to justify the occupation of the others' religious spaces or, conversely, to assert resistance to this occupation, were a convenient strategy.

These accusations made use of motives common to interreligious polemics, with both Jews and Catholics declared too biased to be proper judges. In the case of the Jews this was sharpened by the argument that they adhere to a religion blasphemous in itself.[36] The above-cited analysis of the role of accusations of blasphemy in communities also demonstrates that the definition and the use of this crime were closely connected to the political fundaments of these communities. In the present case the political substance of blasphemy becomes visible in the context of both legal traditions and the acute legal situation in the annexed territory. In spite of common interpretations underlining the sacral character of tsarist rule, religious crimes and crimes against the sovereign had generally been separated in Muscovy and in Petrine Russia. However, we may suspect that, in the eyes of the authorities, they drew close in the period and under the circumstances discussed here, with religious conflict and the problem of political allegiance being so closely linked.[37] If religious crime was understood as a negation of allegiance, the question of who was going to judge it and according to which law was a crucial one. It was, however, part of a more general problem which the Petersburg authorities faced in the Belarusian cities.

In spite of all the traditional links between Lithuanian and Muscovite law and all similarities in jurisdictional practice, it cannot be ignored that after the annexation of Belarus the tsarist government sharply distinguished which law was to be applied in which cases in the newly acquired territory. Generally speaking, while civil law matters continued to be resolved on the basis of Lithuanian law, criminal cases were to be judged according to Russian law.

36 RGADA, f. 7, op. 2, d. 2561, l. 11 ob.

37 Somewhat later, religious and political crime were to be closely linked even far beyond the areas with elevated interreligious tensions, when the autocracy took notice of the first people calling into question its very legitimacy as a political order and when the French Revolution offered an example of how efficiently anti-ecclesiastic attitudes could connect with anti-monarchic ones. See Skinner, *The Western Front*, 197. However, accusations of lese-majesty referring to religious dissent can already been seen in the area about 1780: Provocation could quickly turn religious invectives against Orthodox believers into insults against the Orthodox empress: An Orthodox dweller of one town quarter (*slobozhanin*) which had formerly belonged to or still belonged to the Vitsebsk Basilian monastery replied to the Uniates who called him a »Muscovite schismatic« (*moskal' syzmatyk*) that they were all subjects of the empress and owed obedience to her orders (*ukazy*). He was promptly told that »your *ukazy* are as important as kissing a dog's ass.« RGADA, f. 7, op. 2, d. 2561, l. 6.

Correspondingly, the Petersburg authorities accorded the local nobles the right to be judges in civil cases, but not in criminal ones.[38] So while legal pluralism existed, it did not question criminal justice as the core of the realization of the imperial state's presence in the Belarusian provinces.

This had consequences at two levels. In practical terms, central legal regulation gained considerable influence on the fate of the accused. The government could neither be tolerant of the lax treatment of criminal acts, which might be oppositional actions in disguise, nor of the overly harsh treatment of criminals, which would have contradicted the empress' enlightened image. On a more abstract level, one consequence of this form of legal pluralism was a sharp contrast between the government's abstention from defining adherence to an empire-wide legal order in terms of civil law and its readiness to define allegiance in terms of criminal law. The latter was presented as being crucial to the political stability of the conquered region.

Tsarist law did not interfere with civil law relations in the former part of Lithuania discussed here, an area with an agrarian order differing from the one in central Russia.[39] So the government did not construct the integrity of propriety and of public order, on the one hand, and political domination, on the other hand, along the same lines. Further research would be needed to indicate if the lack of this link affected legal practices and social life. In Catherine II's empire, legal pluralism was reflected in its institutional pluralism.

Local and Imperial Institution-Building as Regulators of Conflict

In the early 18th century, Russia reformed its institutions for the dispensation of justice, although the law remained stable in its 17th-century core. Modifications were brought about by Peter the Great's additional codes and several unsuccessful proposals for legal codes, which nevertheless served as a source of reference. With avenues of legal change being limited, the reform of tribunals was supposed to lead to the dispensation of justice according to principles of governance. In the age of Catherine II, just as during the reign of Peter the Great, the dispensation of justice was closely linked to the autocracy's distributing restricted local powers to particular social groups.

The city in Catherine's Russia was conceived of as an intersection of state action and a restricted municipal self-administration, while rural Russia remained the sphere of the nobles. The cities were supposed to be islands of productivity, but also centers of good order. To be sure, there was a tremendous discrepancy of lifestyle between the metropolis Petersburg and the provincial

38 Anishchanka, *Belarus'*, 184.

39 Ibid., 69–70, 185.

towns. There was no unique urban way of life that represented the civilizing mission ascribed to the city since Peter the Great. Instead that mission was accorded to reformed administrative structures, independent of lifestyle and thus of the great differences among the cities. This focus on administrative structure rather than on urbanism made the Belarusian towns in some respect useful models for the reform of urban life and urban administration that was undertaken from 1775 to 1785.

For this purpose the Belarusian towns first had to be reformed to expand their capacity to integrate a heterogeneous population. The Jews were recognized as burghers in 1779 and consequently received the right to participate in municipal self-government.[40] The transition brought about was no less sharp than that in Western Europe of the era. The decisive development in more western parts of Europe, beginning in the 18th century, was the dissolution of the old estate order. In the Belarusian towns, lacking both the classic structure of the traditional city and the ideal of the *bürgerliche Gesellschaft*[41] as well as any significant socio-economic developments that would encourage the rise of a new elite, that decisive step was the end of the exclusion of Jews from urban institutions. This also involved the dispensation of justice. At the threshold of a new era in the history of jurisdiction in Europe, one which was to be inaugurated by the French reform of 1790,[42] the dispensation of justice in the Belarusian towns was reformed within the framework of tradition, but with an enlightened approach. Trials were not, however, made public, nor was the judicial separated from executive power. The unification of jurisdiction, a strong element of 18th-century reform in Europe,[43] took place within the restricted scope of the city. However, even if practised within a narrow framework, the unification of the dispensation of justice implied a unified approach to religion and law. This corresponded with the Catherinean approach to mainstream religion as a guarantee of civic obedience without restricting this to the Christian religion.

40 Rohdewald, *Vom Polocker Venedig*, 372; John Klier, »Polish Shtetls under Russian Rule, 1772–1914,« *Polin* 17 (2004): 109–119, here 109.

41 A term denominating an ideal type of society based on political participation, civil rights, openness towards innovation as well as male hegemony, and according large competences to the state while restricting its means of intervention into the citizens' private sphere. For a comprehensive definition, see Wolfgang Schmale, »Bürgerliche Gesellschaft,« in *Enzyklopädie der Neuzeit*, vol. 2, ed. Friedrich Jäger (Stuttgart: Metzler/Poeschel, 2005), 558–563, especially 558–559.

42 Barbara Dölemeyer, »Justiz,« in *Enzyklopädie der Neuzeit*, vol. 6, ed. Friedrich Jäger (Stuttgart: Metzler/Poeschel, 2005), 203–226, here 211–212.

43 For a an example, see Robert Zaugg, »Judging Foreigners. Conflict Strategies, Consular Interventions and Institutional Change in Eighteenth-Century Naples,« *Journal of Modern Italian Studies* 13, no. 2 (2008): 171–195.

Evidence of the fragility of the reform and of its restricted reach is easy at hand, regarding both the towns themselves and the rural inhabitants of the area, who, as we have seen in the case cited, were involved in the religious conflict discussed above. The central government accorded privileges to potentially loyal people in the region whose allegiance they sought to gain.[44] But the situation remained insecure: How could one make sure that the dispensation of justice for peasants stayed within the framework of established estate-orientated discrimination while, at the same time, not leaving the decision in cases concerning the empress' vital interests to a possibly unreliable nobility?[45] Against this background, the secular dispensation of justice was not considered to be a sufficient guarantee of order.

Catherine not only reformed the administrative structure of towns, but also increased the number of places called towns. Ordering that the places newly established as the »urban« centres of larger administrative units should also be seats of a »spiritual administration« (*dukhovnoe upravlenie*),[46] she underlined that religious authority was an indispensable part of state authority and its administrative representation in the towns. As to Uniate believers in the annexed Belarusian provinces, the enlightened empress afforded them an ecclesiastic institution to control particular religious groups and enforce obedience through behaviour corresponding to the formal rules of the respective religious community: the above-mentioned consistory. Orthodox consistories had come to Russia from the Ukraine. Protestants in the Empire also had consistories. An actor in the everyday lives of believers, meant to provide for religious discipline, the consistory can be seen to be a factor that strengthened confessional identity. However, in the case of the Uniates, upon whom consistories were imposed by the Petersburg authorities, their effect was probably quite the opposite: the lack of Uniate clerics recognized as qualified legitimized their replacement by Orthodox clerics. This could make the consistories into agents of Orthodox influence on the Uniates' religious matters. As the empress' and the state religion's agents of discipline and control, the consistories harmonized well with the Orthodox clergy's activity in favour of the Crown in this newly annexed region.

44 In 1778 the empress allowed nobles holding offices (»vsem nachal'nikam, sud'iam«) to freely purchase and sell peasants. This permission also extended to Belarus, where nobles who held peasants on the basis of possession (*zastava-arenda*) could be elected as judges. Anishchanka, *Belarus'*, 83.

45 Ibid., 67.

46 *Pervoe polnoe sobranie zakonov rossiiskoi imperii*, vol. 21, (Moskva: Gosudarstvennaia publichnaia istoricheskaia biblioteka, Elektronnyi zapasnik, 2006), document no. 15.153.

Concerning Catherinean municipal institution-building, the consistories adopted a doubly complementary function. They paved the way for a complete administrative structure, including the administration of religion, a structure that made the cities, in the authorities' eyes, centres of a good order to be spread throughout the region. Yet, the consistories were also, in a way, an alternative to the institutions of urban self-government. Establishing clerical control of non-clerics, they would not uphold the idea of self-administration, which always entailed the risk of transcending the limits of autonomy drawn by the autocracy. They could be trusted to play an admonishing role such as the one they had in the case under consideration. Consistories could not, of course, replace secular tribunals in the judging of criminal acts, which was considered a core function of the state. However, as the case demonstrates, they could call into question the legitimacy of these tribunals. They were not easy to handle as an instrument of central secular power, especially in the above-mentioned situation. In the case cited, a spiritual matter turned a magistrate and a consistory into rivals.[47] The problem in the situation following the conquest was that it was hard to distinguish among the different forms of conflict and deviance, as religious conflicts were closely linked to political conflict, and religious deviance could be closely connected with behaviour questioning the legitimacy of the empress' rule.[48]

Just as the Belarusian territory was integrated into the Western flank of the Empire, the enlightened absolutism in Russia led to ideas about diversity and its consequences for state-building at a larger scale. New tribunals, an indispensable by-product of municipal institution-building, were also a form of »organizing difference«[49] in the empire. In this context, the Enlightenment was less about the rule of reason than about differences between ethnic groups and about perceived levels of civilization. This sense of difference at the time of Catherine II was the origin of specific imperial institutions for the dispensation of justice. The Bashkirs and the Mishars, two Muslim ethnic groups in the Southern Urals, as well as the Kazakhs all obtained their own judiciary bodies.[50] According to

47 On the particular status of »spiritual affairs«, see Anishchanko, *Cherta osedlosti*, 83.

48 See a case in which a religious epithet against a newly converted Orthodox (»Muscovite schismatic«) was immediately followed by an epithet against the empresses' orders. RGADA, f. 7, op. 2. d. 2561, l. 6.

49 Lauren A. Benton, *Law and Colonial Cultures. Legal Regimes in World History, 1400–1900* (Cambridge, UK: Cambridge University Press, 2002), passim.

50 Vitalii Voropanov, »Praktika mestnogo pravosudiia: gosudarstvennye sudy dlia sel'skikh obyvatelei orenburgskoi gubernii v poslednei chetverti XVIII – nachale XIX,« *Ab Imperio* 2002, no. 3, 137–160. The Ukrainian Cossacks also obtained particular organs for administration and the dispensation of justice. Voropanov,

Vitalii Voropanov, these special bodies were accorded staff who had to belong to or be familiar with the respective ethnic group and the respective confession. Oaths sworn on the Koran in legal proceedings added a Muslim version to the important part religion played in such matters.[51]

The role accorded religion in juridical procedure hints at the authorities' conviction that religion guaranteed civic obedience. The scope of this conviction, which was growing firmer, well exceeded the boundaries of Christian communities. The particular tribunals for specific ethnic groups reflected Catherine's 1767 confession to Voltaire that law-making for a country like Russia with differences in climate, mores, and ways of thinking (*de climat, d'habitude, d'idées mêmes*) was difficult.[52] Characteristically, the empress did not mention religion as an important factor at this early stage of her rule. Somewhat later, about the time of the conquest of the Crimea with its significant Muslim population, Catherine and her advisors came to the conclusion that different religions in their essence, that is, if not falsified by fanaticism, were apt to stabilize order.[53] However, as Larry Wolff has demonstrated, it was Orthodoxy which in the empress' opinion was best able to do so.[54]

Unlike secularization in revolutionary France or in Joseph's II Austria, Catherine's policies in matters of religion were thus marked more by pragmatic measures for a better organization of the heterogeneous population, than by ambitious attempts at reforming age-old ways of life and death. Ultimately, this meant ascribing a new role to religion rather than banning it altogether.[55] The empress' attitude toward cultures, in general, corresponds with this approach.

»Praktika mestnogo pravosudiia,« 141. This was probably less a measure of enlightened imperial policy than a measure introduced to calm the situation after the destruction of the last remaining symbol of Cossack autonomy, the Zaporozhian Sech, in 1775.

51 Voropanov, »Praktika mestnogo pravosudiia,« 148, 152. Kamenskii stresses the growing role accorded to the priests' appeals to the conscience of the accused when the use of torture, formerly permitted to attain confessions, was being limited. Kamenskii, *Ot Petra I do Pavla I*, 403.

52 Quoted in Maya Lavrinovich, »Sozdanie sotsial'nych osnov imperii v XVIII v.,« *Ab Imperio* 2002, no. 3, 117–136, here 118. Original text: *Sbornik Imperatorskogo russkogo istoricheskogo obshchestva*, vol. 10 (St. Petersburg: Imperatorskoe russkoe istoricheskoe obshchestvo, 1872), 204.

53 On such a view of Islam, see Kelly A. O'Neill, *Between Subversion and Submission: The Integration of the Crimean Khanate into the Russian Empire 1783–1853*, Ph.D. thesis, Harvard University, 2006, 49–51.

54 Wolff, »The Uniate Church,« 159.

55 For a characterization of secularization in Russia under Catherine II, see Gregory L. Bruess, »Religious Tolerance in the Reign of Catherine the Great,« in *International Perspectives on Church and State*, ed. Menachem Mor (Omaha, NE: Creighton University Press, 1993), 299–315.

Catherine was more tolerant of cultural diversity than were the representatives of the French Revolution: The empress tended more towards a well-calculated tolerance of controlled diversity rather than towards forced unification.[56] However, Catherine was strongly committed to the position of having a single Orthodox state religion. As Barbara Skinner has demonstrated, the repressions against the Uniates in the area of the first partition have to be considered in this light. Yet, the combination of a pragmatic approach to religion while upholding a firm adherence to the state religion can hardly be held responsible for this form of selective religious repression. In order to explain these policies, we have to take into consideration both the character of the conflict in the region and the logic of Catherinean institution-building.

Even though the empire implemented its ideas about diversity through the introduction of separate institutions for the dispensation of justice among nomadic Muslim groups, in the newly annexed Belarusian territory it pursued policies that were quite different. In the latter context, reforming the dispensation of justice was also on the agenda, but there was an inclination towards having a single tribunal for the entire polyethnic and multiconfessional population of a town. Taken together, the two approaches hint at a desire for the »organization of difference« in the East and the West of the empire. The key towards understanding Catherine's repression of the Uniates may lie here, for they were a particularly vulnerable element in a regional setting of interconfessional conflict, a state of affairs that cast doubt on the institutional structure which was at the very core of the empire that was to be built.

Conclusion

Lauren Benton's study of colonial law cites a North African Muslim legal scholar who condemned one of his coreligionists for remaining under the rule and jurisdiction of Christian Spain after the *Reconquista*. While the scholar did not consider contacts between Christians and Muslims to be »contaminating« in general, he did consider subordination to the jurisdiction of non-believers to be just that.[57] This underlines the significance of legal institutions as compared to the experience of religious diversity in non-institutional contexts, insofar as the experience expressed in this historically and geographically remote case can be transferred to the situation discussed here.

The conflicts described in the case presented have to be considered within the context of institution-building in its political sense. One important novelty of the era of Catherine II in Russia was an embryonic understanding that

56 Skinner, *Western Front*, 231.

57 Benton, *Law and Colonial Cultures*, 1.

institutions can gain legitimacy and function successfully only if they are believed in by the subjects. There are several indications of this new understanding such as Catherine's reluctance to accept the oath of allegiance of Polish noblemen if it did not reflect genuine loyalty[58] or the introduction of paper money, the stability of which was dependent on the subjects' trust in it.[59] From this point of view, institutions had to include a civic element, and in this sense, the Catherinean principle of state-building modernized the Petrine one.

Religious diversity presented a serious obstacle to state-building in the late 18th century when it weakened trust in institutions. In the period under consideration, religion was not a value that historians could define as »absolute«, but there were interrelated concepts of belief, faith, and trust both separating and reconnecting the spheres of religious and secular action. These concepts, and the related claims to authority, were essential to the political order. Authorities in the Belarusian territory doubted the ability of adherents to Judaism or Catholicism to be proper judges, telling the central authorities that such people could not be trusted. This meant that the core of enlightened institution-building was at stake in the newly conquered area. The hybrid idea of imposing and, if necessary, enforcing trust, a powerful contradiction in itself, which characterized Catherinean projects from monetary reform to urban reform and beyond, was seriously challenged.

The belief in the capacity of religious adherence to subvert enlightened absolutism's cherished legal institutions as expressed by official representatives of the empress' interests in the case discussed here, considerably heightened tensions in the area after the first partition. This was all the worse because the different legal institutions were part of an emerging concept of empire. If religious crime was in fact negotiable, enlightened order was much less so. If religious diversity questioned this order, the central authorities were not willing to tolerate it.

Abolishing Judaism or Roman Catholicism in the area was out of the question. The most vulnerable group were neither the Jews nor the Roman Catholics, but the Uniates, because of their proximity to Orthodoxy. As Wolff has stressed, the Uniates were also thought to be particularly underdeveloped in

58 After Kościuszko's uprising the empress gave the command for »only from those present and willing« to take the oath of allegiance. Nikolai Vasil'evich Repnin, Bumagi kn. N. V. Repnina za vremia upravleniia ego Litvoiu. *Sbornik imperatorskago russkago istoricheskago obshchestva*, vol. 16 (St. Petersburg: Imperatorskoe russkoe istoricheskoe obshchestvo, 1875), 62.

59 About money, counterfeiting and trust in the early modern era, see Ludovic Desmedt and Jérôme Blanc, »Counteracting Counterfeiting? Bodin, Mariana, and Locke on False Money as a Multidimensional Issue,« *History of Political Economy* 42, no. 2 (2010): 323–360.

terms of civic identity as the autocracy understood it, that is to say: civic obedience.[60] If the functioning of the key institutions of rule in the area of the first partition was uncertain, the consequence in the logic of the imperial authorities was to enlarge, at the cost of the Uniate Church, the number of adherents to Orthodoxy.

Finally, the presented story suggests that Russian imperial policy towards the various religious groups of conquered territories depended on how much the autocracy's wish for a controlled »organization of difference« was respected. Not ideology, but institution-building was the neuralgic point. Perceived obstacles to institution-building in the area of the first partition may well have motivated the tsarist authorities to act in a repressive way, which was not typical of their policies concerning the various religions in the empire as a whole.

Angela Rustemeyer

60 Wolff, »The Uniate Church,« 159.

Trust and Conflict: Relations between Ruthenian Priests and Peasants in 19th-Century Galicia

> If a stranger stopped to talk to a Ukrainian villager from Galicia and asked him about his life, he would, after the usual complaints about ›landlords and Jews‹, certainly hear no less severe reproaches against priests and the priests' exactions.[1]

Father Kvintilian hated Korda and Kost Dumiak so intensely that he called them names even during his Sunday sermons. Kvintilian did not hesitate to speak ill of the rest of the congregation either. He felt no pity for peasants, as he believed that they were themselves to blame for their difficulties and poverty: »Who will help them if they have become used to dehumanization since the dawn of time and are not willing to change anything for the better.«[2] The community was not surprised »that their priest disgraced them during sermons, and pointed a finger at them, using bad and inglorious nicknames, as for them it was not a novelty.«[3]

1 »Koly khto-nebud' postoronnyi rozhovorytsia z ukrains'kym muzhykom u Halychyni i pochne rozpytuvaty ioho pro zhyttia-buttia, to, bezperechno, pislia zvychainykh narikan' na ›paniv ta zhydiv‹ pochuie takozh ne menshe tiazhki narikannia na popiv i popivs'ke zdyrstvo.« Ivan Franko, »Popy i ekonomichne polozhennia ukrains'koho narodu v Halychyni,« in *Zibrannia tvoriv u 50 tomakh, Ekonomichni pratsi (1878–1887)*, vol. 44, ed. Ivan Franko (Kyiv: Naukova dumka, 1984), 155–160, here 155.

2 »Khto iim pomozhe, koly vony pryvykly spokonviku do svoho skotiachoho stanu i ne bazhaiut' sobi nichoho lipshoho.« Ivan Franko, »Velykyi shum,« in *Zibrannia tvoriv u 50 tomakh, Povisti ta opovidannia (1904–1913)*, vol. 22, ed. Ivan Franko (Kyiv: Naukova dumka, 1979), 208–317, here 264.

3 »Dlia nykh tse ne bula niiaka novyna, shcho iih panotets' han'byt' iih poimenno na propovidiakh, pokazuie na nykh paltsiamy ta prykladaie do nykh pohani abo i soromni prozvyshcha.« Ibid., 280.

This passage is taken from the novel *Great Uproar* (*Velykyi Shum*) by Ivan Franko, a poet and literary critic of the late 19th and early 20th century, and one of the most prominent Ukrainian writers to this day. Franko based this story, like many others, on the lives of the villagers of Nahuievychi, where he was born. According to literary critics, the heroes of his story were adapted from historical people in Nahuievychi: Franko did not even change the name of Kost Dumiak who served as the headman (*viit*) of the village in the middle of the 19th century. The fictitious priest Korda represents Lev Kordasevych, a priest of the Nahuievychi parish from 1846 to 1852, who became an activist in the Ruthenian national movement. Finally, Kvintilian must be considered to be a fictionalized portrait of Iosyf Levytskyi, the priest of the Nahuievychi parish from 1854 to 1860, and a leader of the Ruthenian national movement.[4]

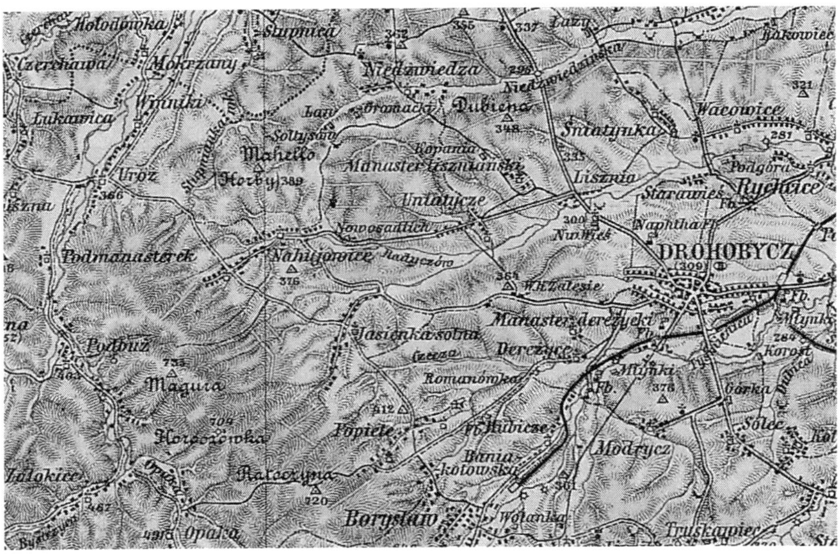

General map of Central Europe, folio 4149, Bundesamt für Eich- und Vermessungswesen, Vienna 1912. http://lazarus.elte.hu/hun/digkonyv/topo/200e/41-49.jpg.

4 Stepan Shchurat, »Kameniar i ioho ridne selo,« *Zhovten'* 11 (1966): 52–60, here 56.

Ivan Franko wrote in depth about Nahuievychi, the villagers, and Father Levytskyi. He was the first to use the protocols of the Levytskyi trial, transforming the accounts of peasants from this source into literature. The literary critic Stepan Shchurat (1909–1990), a specialist on Ivan Franko, likewise consulted the protocols and, on the basis of additional research, claimed that Franko was baptized by Levytskyi and heard much about him from his father and fellow villagers, who called him » a rude priest« (*ksiądz hruby*).[5] In his article translated as »The Stonecutter and His Native Village« (*Kameniar i ioho ridne selo*), Shchurat describes a number of events that emerged in the trial and provides his own opinion of the priest: »In order to take more money from peasants he complicated every affair, making up different obstacles. He artfully used canon and church laws, and the rulings of the secular authorities.«[6] While Shchurat, as a literary critic, tried to analyze the protocols, Franko used them as inspiration for his fiction, each in his own way fostering Levytskyi's negative image.

Still, the judgments are very straightforward and leave many questions unanswered, for example, why a priest who played an important role in the Ruthenian national movement would not receive recognition in his own parish. It is therefore my aim in this paper to re-examine the protocols of Levytskyi's trial, to delve into the relations inside the Nahuievychi community and especially to identify the motives of the conflict between the priest and the peasants. In a broader context it will be necessary to look at the transformation of church politics introduced by the Habsburg Empire and, as a consequence, at the changing role of the Greek Catholic clergy in the mid-19th century. Against this background, we will be able to distinguish continuous conflicts between priests and peasants from new ones that appeared after Enlightenment reforms.

Iosyf Levytskyi and the role of priests in Galician peasant communities

Iosyf Levytskyi, born in 1801 in the village of Baranchytsi in Eastern Galicia, was a representative of a new generation of educated clergy.[7] He studied in the *Barbareum* theological seminary in Vienna that had been founded during the reign of Maria Teresa and Joseph II along with another theological seminary, the

5 Ibid., 55. In the protocols *ksiądz* is used as either Ukrainian or Polish word to indicate a priest, for both Roman Catholic and Greek Catholic clergy.

6 »Shchob vytysnuty z selian iaknaibil'she hroshei, kozhnu spravu uskladniuvav, vyhaduvav riznomanitni trudnoshchi. Dlia tsioho khytro vykorystovuvav vsiaki kanonichni i tserkovni zakony, tsyrkuliary svits'koi i dukhovnoi vlady.« Ibid., 54.

7 In this article »clergy« is used synonymously with »priesthood« to the inclusion of deacons, priests, and bishops.

Studium Ruthenum in Lviv. After graduation, Levytskyi was a parish priest in the Galician villages of Shklo and then Hrushiv. He had also been teaching in the seminary of Peremyshl, when the Ruthenian language was established in all schools of Eastern Galicia in 1849.[8]

In Ukrainian historiography, the person of Iosyf Levytskyi is closely attached to the Ruthenian national movement. He is depicted as one of its leaders, and one of the priests who supported the movement and struggled to raise the national consciousness of the Ruthenian people. Together with other priests, he tried to convince the Ruthenians that they were a separate nation and at least worthy of cultural autonomy,[9] if not political independence.[10] These priests considered it to be their duty to gather songs, preserve local folklore, and publish grammars.[11] Scholars indeed claim that Iosyf Levytskyi was the author of the first printed grammar of the Ruthenian language in Galicia. He is also known as a writer, teacher, collector of folklore, and important public figure.[12] However, my research has also revealed that he was in fact a complicated figure and far from an entirely positive force in his local community.

Literary critics and historians have often depicted Levytskyi as an ill-tempered person with a sharp tongue.[13] It is reported that in the Peremyshl seminary he frequently quarreled with other priests on the matters of language, teaching, and national perspective, that he criticized the pastoral letters of the Metropolitan, and that he maintained a negative attitude towards Bishop Hryhoryi Iakhymovych (1792–1863). Due to these conflicts, the bishop ordered Levytskyi to leave the seminary and gave him a parish in Nahuievychi, where he could preach but was away from other priests and the students of the seminary in

8 Ivan Franko, »Do biohrafii Iosyfa Levyts'koho,« *Zoria* 11 (1886): 196; Idem, »Do zhyttiepysu Iosyfa Levyts'koho,« *Zoria* 5 (1886): 84.

9 For a discussion of the concept of cultural autonomy see the article by Jana Osterkamp in this volume.

10 Paul Robert Magocsi, *The Roots of Ukrainian Nationalism. Galicia as Ukraine's Piedmont* (Toronto: University of Toronto Press, 2002), 44.

11 Mykhailo Zubryts'kyi, Iurii Kmit, Ivan Kobylets'kyi, Ivan Levyts'kyi, and Ivan Franko, eds., *Materialy do kulturnoi istorii Halyts'koi Rusi XVIII i XIX viku* (L'viv: Drukarnia Naukovoho tovarystva imeni Shevchenka, 1902), 133; Michael Moser, »Iosyf Levyts'kyi iak borets' za kulturu ›rus'koi‹ (ukrains'koi) movy,« *Ukrayina: kulturna spadshchyna, natsional'na svidomist', derzhavnist'* 15 (2006/2007): 447–460, here 447.

12 Dmytro Blazheiovs'kyi, *Historical shematism of the eparchy of Peremyshl including the apostolic administration of Lemkivshchyna (1828–1939)* (L'viv: Kameniar, 1995), 741.

13 Franko, »Iosyfa Levyts'koho«; Hanna Hrom, *Nahuievychi* (Drohobych: Vidrodzhennia, 2002), 220; Hryhoryi Herbils'kyi, *Peredova suspil'na dumka v Halychyni (30-i – seredyna 40-ykh rr. XIX stolittia)* (Lviv: Vydavnytstvo L'vivs'koho universytetu, 1959), 86.

particular.[14] Iosyf Levytskyi and other Greek Catholic priests were indebted to the Habsburg Empire for their privileged position in society.[15] As a consequence of the imperial reforms of the 19th century, priests became a part of the state administration and a link between the empire's rulers and the common people of Galicia. They turned into guardians of order who controlled the peasants' activities and their attitude towards the empire.[16]

In the second half of the 18th century the situation had been very different. Priests often spent time in taverns together with the peasants drinking and fighting. In the times of Ivan Franko, peasants recalled these relations with sayings like »The head of a priest is blessed, respect it, but the buttocks are not, kick them as much as you want«.[17] The Supreme Ecclesiastical Authority tried to dissuade priests from going to taverns, urging them instead to care more for churches, education, and the parish. At that time many churches looked more like stables: chapels were covered with straw and lacked windows and finished floors or ceilings.[18] The new Habsburg authorities supported the fight against this with reforms and education – as was the general tendency during the Enlightenment – which contributed to economic and educational improvements in Galicia.

The Habsburg administration also introduced a code of behavior for priests, according to which they were entrusted with the task of educating their flock to be good Christians and good citizens.[19] They were then expected to perform the

14 Ibid., 220–222; Shchurat, »Kameniar i ioho ridne selo,« 54.

15 Ivan L. Rudnytsky, »The Ukrainians in Galicia under Austrian Rule,« in *Nationbuilding and the Politics of Nationalism. Essays on Austrian Galicia*, eds. Andrei S. Markovits and Frank E. Sysyn (Cambridge: Harvard University Press, 1989), 23–68, here 24–25; Marian Mudryi, »Avstrorusynstvo v Halychyni: sproba okreslennia problem,« *Visnyk L'vivs'koho Universytetu. Seriia istorychna* 35/36 (2000): 571–603, here 573.

16 Maksym Herasymenko, *Ahrarni vidnosyny v Halychyni v period kryzy panshchyznianoho hospodarstva* (Kyiv: AN URSR, 1959), 138–139.

17 »U popa holova pos'viachena, ale s-a ni, to holovu zaviazhy, a v s-u byi shcho si vlizy.« *Etnohrafichnyi zbirnyk*, vol. 24, part 2: *Halyts'ko-ruski narodnii prypovidky*, ed. Ivan Franko (L'viv: Naukove tovarystvo imeni Shevchenka, 1908), 539–544.

18 Melaniia Bordun, »Z zhyttia ukrains'koho dukhovenstva l'vivs'koi ieparkhii v druhyi pol. XVIII v.,« *Zapysky NTSH* 135, no. 13 (1924): 39–90, here 78.

19 John-Paul Himka, »Hreko-katolyts'ka tserkva i natsional'ne vidrodzhennia u Halychyni 1772–1918,« in *Kovcheh: Naukovyi zbirnyk iz tserkovnoi istorii*, vol. 1, eds. Iaroslav Hrytsak and Borys Gudziak (L'viv: Institute for Historical Research of the Ivan Franko National University of Lviv and Institute of Church History, 1993), 73–107, here 77; Andrii Zaiarniuk, *Idiomy emansypatsii. »Vyzvol'ni« proekty i halyts'ke selo u seredyni XIX stolittia* (Kyiv: Krytyka, 2007), 92.

duties not only of a chaplain, but also of a teacher and a state official.[20] At first priests were opposed to the reforms. It seems that they did not want to accept these new administrational tasks, viewing them as new obligations, but they would soon come to appreciate their new power and the connected benefits. Moreover it became hard to draw a line between secular and lay affairs once they received authority of the administration.[21] After but a few years of accommodation, Ruthenian priests eagerly proclaimed the emperor's patents and district headman's commands to the peasants.[22]

Portrait of Iosyf Levytskyi by W. Siffert, 1854 (Muzeum Narodowe Ziemi Przemyskiej, inv. no. MPS-632)

20 Oleh Turii, »Hreko-katolyts'kyi sviashchenyk v Avstriis'kyi monarkhii seredyny XIX st.: derzhavnyi sluzhbovets' chy dushpastyr?« in *Materialy II Mizhnarodnoho konhresu ukrainistiv: Istoriia*, vol. 1, eds. Iaroslav Isaievych and Iaroslav Hrytsak (L'viv: International Association of Ukrainian Studies, 1994), 56–62, here 57–58.

21 Shchurat, »Kameniar i ioho ridne selo,« 54.

22 Herasymenko, *Ahrarni vidnosyny v Halychyni*, 149–150.

Some community representatives claimed that priests were taking on too many official activities while neglecting their religious duties. For example, Dumiak, the above-mentioned village headman of Nahuievychi, complained that the pastors spent more time on administration instead of pursuing spiritual matters: »Our priests are so diligent, they piddle their time away like lawyers for no reason.«[23]

The interaction of priests and peasants reveals a paradox within the Ruthenian national movement. Although they were united as one nation with a common religion and common language, a great abyss remained between the leaders and the common people. Often the priests' better schooling and their administrational activities put them at a distance from the peasants and caused misunderstandings. The priests wanted to reeducate the people but did not support any public initiative towards a greater participation of peasants in community leadership. They often despised the rural community for its »barbarity« and lack of education, and opposed the peasants' folklore as superstitious practice and belief.[24] The peasants who felt disrespected by this developed, in turn, a distanced attitude towards the priests. They respected priests as educated and intelligent people but they rejected their absolute power.[25] Once priests began to believe in their common ethnicity with the Ruthenian peasantry and their religious unity, they started to speak up on behalf of the several million people of the Ruthenian nation. This position of primacy, however, also faced the resistance of many peasants.[26]

In his 19th century memoirs, the priest Philimon Tarnavskyi describes the tensions between the clergy and peasants: »When new priests from the Seminary came to the village, they were educated and had higher demands. That is why the people did not become accustomed to them quickly, did not like them, and called them ›German priests‹.«[27] We can only guess what the author meant by

23 »Taki to nashi dushpastyri zapopadlyvi, ony zaimaiutsia durnytsiamy, nache advokaty, bez niiakoi osnovy.« Fondy muzeiu imeni Ivana Franka u m. L'vovi/ Collection of the Ivan Franko Museum in Lviv (henceforth IFM), file (sprava) 1783: Protokoly dystsyplinarnoho slidstva proty Iosyfa Levyts'koho (1801–1860), Parokha sela Nahuievychi, letter 2, no. 538/32.

24 Herasymenko, *Ahrarni vidnosyny v Halychyni,* 150; Oleh Kryzhanivs'kyi and Serhii Plokhy, *Istoriia tserkvy ta relihiinoi dumky v Ukraini*, vol. 3. (Kyiv: Lybid', 1994), 250; Stanisław Nabywaniec, »Recepcja reform kościelnych cesarza Józefa II w greckokatolickiej diecezji przemyskiej,« in *Polska-Ukraina 1000 lat sąsiedztwa*, vol. 3, ed. Stanisław Stępień (Przemyśl: Poludniowo-Wschodni Instytut Naukowy, 1996), 127–165, here 165.

25 Herasymenko, *Ahrarni vidnosyny v Halychyni*, 150.

26 Himka, »Hreko-katolyts'ka tserkva,« 82–83.

27 »Koly pryishly novi sviashchennyky z Dukhovnoji Seminarii, to vony vzhe maly vyshchu osvitu i bil'shi vymohy, tak shcho narid ne skoro do nykh pryvyk, ne

high demands. In any case, his account gives us an idea of the changes in the relations between peasants and priests caused by Habsburg reforms. Based on the example of the village of Nahuievychi, I challenge Tarnavskyi's position by looking into the demands outlined in the protocols of the trial against Iosyf Levytskyi.

The protocols of the trial against Iosyf Levytskyi

The trial against Iosyf Levytskyi took place from February 23 to April 20, 1858, as documented on 943 pages of protocol accusations, justifications, and summaries.[28] It dealt with conflicts that had mainly occurred in the village of Nahuievychi, situated near the town of Drohobych, an important urban center of Galicia.[29] The villagers accused the priest of 17 disciplinary transgressions, including excessive fees, refusing to bury people, publicly insulting peasants, intervening in public affairs, and disgracing high church authorities before the people.[30]

The first to report Iosyf Levytskyi to the authorities was a villager by the name of Fedio Hlynka, involving an incident in 1856, when a pig owned by Hlynka was found in the fields of Levytskyi and taken by the priest to his household. The priest refused to give it back to the peasant, and when the animal died a few days later, he did not compensate him for the loss, thus refusing to comply with a court ruling. Later when Hlynka's father died, the priest refused to bury the body. Numerous insults followed from both sides.[31]

Stephan Shchurat has suggested that the appeal of Fedio Hlynka was disregarded at first as the consistory refused to take personal complaints into consideration.[32] The case only gained public momentum on August 9, 1857 when 37 residents of Nahuievychi sued the priest in the consistory of Peremyshl with regard to 17 disciplinary transgressions. This was the first case lodged by Nahuievychi villagers against a priest.[33]

At first glance it would appear that the trial was mainly caused by Levytskyi's arrogant behavior. As mentioned above, the priest was very demanding, some-

duzhe ikh liubyv i nazyvav ikh ›nimetskymy ksiandzamy‹. Philimon Tarnavs'kyi, *Spohady. Rodynna khronika Tarnavs'kykh iak prychynok istorii tserkovnykh, sviashchennyts'kykh, pobutovykh, ekonomichnykh i politychnykh vidnosyn u Halychyni v druhyi polovyni XIX st. i v pershyi dekadi XX st.* (Toronto: Dobra knyzhka, 1981), 35.

28 Shchurat, »Kameniar i ioho ridne selo,« 53.

29 Hrom, *Nahuievychi*, 13.

30 IFM, file 1783: Protokoly dystsyplinarnoho slidstva, protocol A, 5–6.

31 Ibid., General description, p. 169 (letter 1–2 of the Drohobych court case).

32 Shchurat, »Kameniar i ioho ridne selo,« 59.

33 IFM, file 1783: Protokoly dystsyplinarnoho slidstva, protocol A/28.

times rude, and dwelled on the social differences that existed between him and the peasants. The peasants were not willing to abide by his behavior any longer and decided to take Levytskyi to court. During the trial, however, other vital conflicts would also emerge.

A conflict over fees emerges most clearly from the protocols, and is mentioned in nine of 17 disciplinary transgressions. The economic situation indeed seems to have been difficult for both the priest and the peasants. Differences of religion and morality also played a role in the conflict between Levytskyi and the parish. These differences are vital to the understanding of the rural society and the interpretation of the interactions that took place in the community. There were, furthermore, clashes between Levytskyi and individual people, including Dumiak and Kmitsikevych. This reveals a struggle for dominance both within the secular administration and within the church hierarchy. Kost Dumiak was the village headman and representative of the secular authorities in Nahuievychi. Iurii Kmitsikevych was a priest in the village of Hai and the dean of Mokriany, who represented the church authorities in the district, which included the village of Nahuievychi.

In this paper I concentrate on three main lines of conflict: 1) fees and other forms of extortion; 2) differences in education and moral views; and 3) the struggle for control over the peasants. Although these issues are frequently intertwined in the protocols, I separate them here in order to provide an understanding of the needs of the rural society of the time and the context this created for the national movement in Galicia.

Economic background of the conflict

When he became a priest in Nahuievychi, he tripled fees and forced peasants to work on his fields without payment, to provide him with wood, to plant fruit trees in his garden, and to bring him hens, eggs and fish.[34]

The trial against Iosyf Levytskyi highlights the problems caused by the substantial fees introduced by the priest in Nahuievychi. The peasants complained extensively about different kinds of extortion. During the trial they testified that »the priest wanted to extract money from each godparent to baptize children [...], to procure payment for each singer in the christening ceremony [...], demanded money from women to bless them after childbirth [...], forced

34 »Stavshy nahuievyts'kym parokhom, vin vidrazu zh u troie pidvyshchyv oplaty za tserkovni posluhy, vymahav vid selian, shchob vony bezplatno praciuvaly v nioho na poli, zavozyly iomu drova, zasadzuvaly v ioho sadu fruktovi dereva, nosyly kurei, iaitsia, rybu [...].« Shchurat, »Kameniar i ioho ridne selo,« 54 (based on peasants' accusations during the trial against Iosyf Levytskyi).

payment for the blessing of Easter baskets«.[35] The villagers thus voiced their dissatisfaction with the requirement that they pay for each and every service.

In his defense, Iosyf Levytskyi argued that he did not want anything more than he deserved. He said that he only took money for services in amounts equal to the high prices he had had to pay for food and supplies. According to him, he had acted within the framework of the law, had taken what he had been due, receiving only some additional gifts from peasants.[36] He also explained that he had an income from services and a field, but he also needed to take care of the church, which reduced his personal fortune.[37] Levytskyi complained that the peasants »were making him a beggar« and could not imagine his real situation. For example, he testified in court that the peasants had run him into debt in the course of the previous year, as they had not supplied him with as many eggs as they had to for the Easter service.[38]

The case against Levytskyi reflects a general tendency: The Greek Catholic clergy in Galicia earned their living mostly from payments, both monetary and in form of natural products. Priests received land and salaries in return for their services. Pastoral perquisites (*jura stolae*) constituted their main source of income, mainly for performing church duties as baptizing, wedding ceremonies, funerals, and home blessings. These practices had been established by Joseph II on July 1, 1785, during the period of serfdom, and the payment rate had not changed since that time. Therefore, it did not meet the needs of the priests after serfdom was abolished, especially if one considers that most Greek Catholic priests had families. Priests therefore became more demanding about fees, which made the rural population unhappy. Both church and secular authorities received numerous complaints about priests from the peasants and lower middle class.[39]

The peasants, however, often refused to pay. Some of them simply did not have the means; others opposed any fee increases on principle. This practice had severe consequences for the priests' incomes, which they then tried to obtain by force, and very forceful words were indeed used in the protocols. Levytskyi did not deny that he had taken money or payment in kind from peasants. The core

35 »Pry spravuvanni tainy khreshchennia vymusyv vid kozhnoho khresnoho bat'ka hroshi [...], kazav tserkovnym spivakam pry nahodi odnykh khrestyn zaplatyty [...], vymusyv vid kozhnoi zhinky po porodi za blahoslovennia [...], vymusyv vzkhliadno vid kozhnoho sils'koho dvora za posviachennia velykodnikh pasok.« IFM, file 1783: Protokoly dystsyplinarnoho slidstva, letter 15.

36 Ibid., letter 23.

37 Ibid., letter 6, protocol a.

38 Ibid., letter 23, protocol e. § 22, p. 321.

39 Oleh Turii, *Hreko-katolyts'ka tserkva v suspil'no-politychnomu zhytti Halychyny, 1848–1867*, Ph.D. thesis, Ivan Franko National University Lviv, 1994, 39–41.

problem was that, according to the peasants, he had acted in a very aggressive way and thereby had provoked confrontation.

The above-mentioned complaint of peasants also states that Iosyf Levytskyi had not only been demanding money for himself, but also for singers who had helped during the ceremony. Consequently he was not exclusively taking care of his own interests but also sought fair payment for others. Further in the protocols, Levytskyi emphasized that he did not understand how peasants could even suggest that there should be an assistant priest in the village to assist Levytskyi if he did not earn enough to make a living himself.[40]

At another level, the trial mirrored the ramifications of imperial church politics in the local sphere: Levytskyi, representing the new type of educated priest, believed that he had to have better living conditions than the peasants. In contrast, the peasants were not ready to accept this change as they were used to priests who belonged to their social milieu, who ate the same kind of food, wore the same kinds of clothes, and shared the same social interests.

Perceptions of morality and religion

Iosyf Levytskyi thought of the peasants as »arrogant people«, and their complaints were for him all no more than an exhibition of a lack of religiosity, ignorance, and naivety. He believed that the peasants needed a strict priest, and that the lax preaching of his predecessors had led only to a decline in morals and faith:[41]

> Many villagers because of their godlessness, disbelief, and hardness of hearts have not gone to confession in years [...]. And the youth is so dedicated to pagan beliefs that it is afraid to study Christian Catholicism and does not want to come for catechesis on Sunday and holidays.[42]

Later he continued: »The landlords of Nahuievychi have not been going to church in years, dying without the sacraments, they rarely come to confession [...], what can I say – idlers.«[43] For him, the peasants were hopeless infidels, who could not accept God's teaching.

40 IFM, file 1783: Protokoly dystsyplinarnoho slidstva, letter 22.

41 Ibid., letter 27.

42 »Mnoho hospodariv po prychyni bezbozhnosti, neviry i zatverdilykh serts', ne spovidaiesia tsilymy rokamy, ne khodiat' do tserkvy [...] Vkintsy zovsim zanedbana molodizh pryv'iazana do pohanstva boit'sia khrystiiansko-katolyts'koi nauky, ne khoche znaty pro katekhizatsiiu v nedil'ni i sviatochni dny.« Ibid., letter 21.

43 »Rokamy ne khodiat' hospodari Nahuievych do tserkvy, umyraiut' bez pryiniattia sviatykh tayn, ridko prykhodiat' do spovidy [...], nema dumky – ledari.« Ibid., letter 26.

Ioannes Chaikovskyi, the priest from Iasenytsia Silna, a village not far from Nahuievychi, was of the same opinion. He described peasants as impudent people who needed »a vocal and strict leader.«[44] Taking Levytskyi's side, he claimed that he was just the right priest for the peasants of Nahuievychi. Most of the peasants did not agree with such a conclusion as they were disgusted by Levytskyi's behaviour. At the same time the official church was opposed to the physical and moral coercion that had been common in earlier centuries.[45] One very vivid example of Levytskyi's attitude to the peasants can be seen in the penance that he imposed on two villagers. The trial protocols indicate that he ordered them to lie down in the form of a cross during a church service.[46] Levytskyi himself claimed that this was a good way to punish sinners: »It [the punishment] is allowed, and sinners can either accept this atonement or not [...] there is no other way to frighten barbaric people away from sins.«[47]

The villagers found this form of penance to be very shameful. One of them refused to perform it, but described it during the trial.[48] Another peasant complained:

> We do not hear any good words and we are treated like wild animals; that is why most of our villagers, especially children, are not admitted to Easter confession. As a result of such a behaviour the people are in moral decline. Our children have quit going to Sunday school because Iosyf Levytskyi threatens them with beating.[49]

The peasants also accused Levytskyi of not carrying out his duties thoroughly and of not fulfilling them according to church prescriptions.[50] However, the peasants' understanding of the prescriptions was often confused with their own particular beliefs. For example, Fedio Klymko, the father of five children, complained that he had to light a candle three nights in succession because Levytskyi did not baptize his child when the newborn was brought to the church

44 Ibid., protocol a, § 25, p. 121.

45 Mykhailo Zubryts'kyi, »Prychynky do istorii rus'koho dukhovenstva v Halychyni vid 1820 do 1853 r.,« *Zapysky NTSH* 88, no. 2 (1909): 118–150, here 143.

46 IFM, file 1783: Protokoly dystsyplinarnoho slidstva, General description, p. 169 (letter 12, § 26).

47 »Tse dozvoleno, a hrishnyky mozhut' na tse pohodytys' abo ni. A iak pohodylys, to oboviazani tse vykonuvaty. Bo dlia neotesanykh liudei nema inshoho sposobu vidstrashyty ikh vid hrihiv.« Ibid. (letter 16).

48 Ibid.

49 »My ne chuiemo nikoly dobroho slova, i z namy obkhodiatsia iak z dykymy zviriamy, z tsiieii prychyny bil'sha chast' nashykh meshkantsiv a po bil'shii chasty ditei ne dopuskaiestia do sviatoi velykodnyoi spovidy. – Tomu cherez taku povedinku ie zdychinnia mizh hromadianamy. Nashi dity pokynuly v tserkvi katekhyzatsiiu nauky pro khrystyians'ku viru, bo pan parokh Iosyf Levyts'kyi hrozyt im, shcho zviazhe ikh, hrozyt' poboiamy.« Ibid. (letter 28).

50 IFM, file 1783: Protokoly dystsyplinarnoho slidstva, letter 2, no. 538/32.

on the Monday before Ascension Day.[51] This complaint suggests that the peasant was attempting to protect the child from evil before the baptism. In addition, he blamed Levytskyi for having given his son the rather unusual and ridiculous christening name Hermanovych: »The matter of my concern is that the priest has given the newborn such an odd name that I don't even know what to call my child now.«[52]

The conflict between the priest and the peasants was further aggravated by another matter. The peasants accused Levytskyi of having refused to deliver a sermon on the harmfulness of witchcraft in accordance with the suggestion of village headman Dumiak, who had in fact asked the priest to specifically mention the case of Olena Levych, whom the villagers believed to be a witch. According to the protocols, Levytskyi had refused to give a sermon saying only: »I am not near her house so I do not know who is visiting her and what they are doing there.«[53] Iurii Kmitsikevych, who led the trial, assumed that the priest did not want to accuse Olena Levych only because Dumiak, whom he disliked, had demanded support from him.[54]

The matter of witchcraft was very important for the peasants of Nahuievychi because they generally believed in witches and other supernatural creatures, though in an ambivalent way. In times of despair, they either used their help or blamed them for misfortunes.[55] An article by Ivan Franko, »*Upyri* burnt in Nahuievychi village in 1831«, describes the plague of the same year. Although Franko fictionalizes events and characters, he paints a vivid picture of the villagers' great fear of *upyri* – vampires or ghouls who in Slavonic mythology are half-human and half-demon. The peasants could therefore not be persuaded of the injustice of their beliefs by any priest or authority.[56]

The tense relations between priests and villagers was further aggravated by their gap in education. The peasants often did not even understand the prayers or doctrines. They had to learn them by heart but could not in fact say what they were about. The priests' reactions to this varied widely. Most of them contented themselves with the peasants' poor knowledge of religion. For example, the priest Iurii Kmitsykevych wrote that Marysia, the daughter of Ivan Kizhakovych,

51 Ibid., protocol e, § 5, p. 311.

52 »Zhaluiusia i na to, shcho Otets' tak moiu dytynu nazvav, shcho ne znaiu iak ii teper klykaty.« Ibid.

53 »Pry iei khati ne sydzhu, ne vydzhu kto tam khodyt' i shcho ona zi svoimi hist'my robyt'.« Ibid., protocol ee, § 8, p. 339.

54 IFM, file 1783: Protokoly dystsyplinarnoho slidstva, General description, p. 169 (letter 1, protocol ee).

55 Bordun, »Z zhyttia ukrains'koho dukhovenstva,« 78.

56 Franko, Ivan. »Sozhzheniie upyrei v sele Nahuievichakh v 1831 h.,« *Kievs'kaia staryna* 29, no. 4 (1890): 101–120, here 111–114.

»showed knowledge of everyday prayers during the exam and is prepared for confession although she forgets some words and misspells others.«[57]

While Iosyf Levytskyi does not appear in the court files to be very demanding of the peasants, the protocols do in fact document another problem: He did not miss any opportunity to mock the peasants' ignorance, and it was this humiliation in particular that led to the severe conflict. Other priests accepted the peasants' lack of education more easily or were at least able to guard their tongues.

Struggle for domination

Iosyf Levytskyi was shaped by the new educational system and administrational reform brought about by the Habsburg Empire. His involvement in secular affairs led to further escalation in the conflict with village headman Kost Dumiak. The question of hierarchy arose which was interpreted differently by the two sides. Dumiak believed in the legitimacy of his own power and claimed that a cleric should not intrude upon administrative affairs. By contrast, Levytskyi was convinced that he was chosen by God and the Empire to protect his community and to reign over it. Such antagonism and tensions regarding status find resonance in the saying: »Ever since the world has existed, priest and *viit* cannot be friends«.[58]

Dumiak was one of the few literate people around in his rural society. After 15 years of service in the army he joined at the age of 20, he returned home as a sergeant major of some education. He could therefore understand the juridical side of the conflict better than the rest of the community, and once he became a rural headman he was able to defend his community's interests and his own.[59] Dumiak appealed to the court and demanded a new priest for the villagers of Nahuievychi. He emphasized that this was a most urgent matter and announced that the villagers would seek help with »higher and the highest« authorities if the appeal were not taken into consideration.[60] The village headman thus often appeared to be the leading rebel among the peasants.[61]

57 »Po provedenomu z neiu ekzameni pokazalosia, shcho ona deiaki slova shchodennoi molytvy opustyla, a deiaki nenalezhyty vyskazuvala, odnak ie sposibna spovidatysia.« IFM, file 1783: Protokoly dystsyplinarnoho slidstva, letter 2b.

58 »Vid koly svit svitom, ne tantsiuvav shche pip z viitom.« Volodymyr S. Plaviuk, ed., *Prypovidky abo ukrayins'ko-narodnia filosofiia*, vol. 1 (Edmonton: Association of Ukrainian pioneers in Alberta, 1998), 250.

59 Hrom, *Nahuievychi*, 107.

60 IFM, file 1783: Protokoly dystsyplinarnoho slidstva, letter 29.

61 Iurii Kmit, »Z sils'kykh vidnosyn u Halychyni v ser. XIX v.« *Zapysky NTSH* 54/4 (1903): 1–8, here 7.

Levytskyi acknowledged Dumiak's influence on the village and defamed him as an immoral person who provided a negative example to others. By contrast, peasant witnesses in the trial admired Dumiak, who, according to them, had dared to stand up to the priest with his harsh and colorful sayings.[62] Levytskyi in turn demanded the suspension of the village headman from service. Apart from the personal insult, he blamed him of having shown disrespect to the religion and having frightened those villagers who supported the priest.[63] In this context it is worth mentioning that Vasyl Dumiak, the churchwarden (*palamar*) in Nahuievychi and a brother of the village headman, supported Levytskyi.

Another conflict arose between Iosyf Levytskyi and church dean Iurii Kmitsikevych, who led the investigation. The court documents indicate that they were rivals from earlier times and had no sympathy for each other.[64] This acknowledgement complicates the case, but it also provides insight into the relations between the two priests. Kmitsikevych seemed to be very displeased with Levytskyi's behavior, describing him as an immoral, rude, and high-handed priest who did not care about the spiritual state of his worshippers and who was interested only in his own financial gain. He even portrayed him as a mentally unstable person with an evil heart, who rejoiced in the misfortune of others, saying things such as: »During the last proceedings the priest [Levytskyi] turned into a madman and showed a display of anger that is not appropriate for a cleric, especially for a priest.«[65]

During the trial the dean repeatedly stressed how Levytskyi spoke ill of the bishop, which compelled Kmitsikevych to replace a number of bad words in the protocols with more appropriate language.[66] However, the document is still full of statements by Levytskyi such as »I am not some pushover, is the bishop going to beat me with a whip or something?«[67] and »I am playing with the bishop as with a ball.«[68]

62 E.g.: »Ja takiego księdza za włosy z błota wyciągał, i mnie taki ksiądz w ręke całował.« (The protocols are written in Cyrillic, although the language is Polish) IFM, file 1783: Protokoly dystsyplinarnoho slidstva, Drohobych court case, letter 3.

63 Ibid., letter 4.

64 Ibid., letters 3 and 7.

65 »Pry spysuvanniu tsioho ostannioho protokolu parokh formal'no pereminyvsia na furiiata i pokazav taku afektsyiu hnivu i zlobnosty, tak shcho tse ne lytsiuvalo osobi dukhovnyi a shche menshe parokhovi.« Ibid., letters 10–11.

66 Ibid., letter 9, § 19.

67 »A ia shcho smarkatyi, iepyskop bude mene tripachkoiu byty, chy shcho« IFM, file 1783: Protokoly dystsyplinarnoho slidstva, General description, p. 169 (letter 12, § 26).

68 »Ia tak hraiu sobi z iepyskopom iak miachem.« IFM, file 1783: Protokoly dystsyplinarnoho slidstva, letter 10, § 20.

During the trial, Levytskyi for his part accused Kmitsikevych of immorality, ascribing to him rancor, low cunning, mendaciousness, and even marital infidelity. He wrote a letter to the ecclesiastical consistory, accusing Kmitsikevych of a number of violations of his pastoral responsibilities. Levytskyi pointed out that the dean liked to travel on business, thus neglecting his parish, and noted that Kmitsikevych had personal enmity towards him and therefore depicted him in an unfavorable light. According to Levytskyi, this enmity was caused by the fact that he had accused Kmitsikevych in the past of abusing his wife and of marital infidelity with a Jewish woman.[69]

Taking into account the conflict between the dean and the priest, the bishop of Peremyshl entrusted Vasyl Haponovych, an investigator from Drohobych, to look into and confirm the case against Levytskyi. In light of the recent events, however, he deemed the conclusions drawn by the dean as too harsh, and Levytskyi remained in his post in Nahuievychi. Now finding himself in an advantageous position, the priest filed a reprimand against his fellow villagers to the district court, and on August 12, 1858, Fedio Hlynka was sentenced to a month's arrest, Nastia Didych to 14 days, and Anton Rurak and Maria Klymko to 8 days each as those who had taken the most active positions against Levytskyi in court.[70]

The fact that the priest remained in office after the trial, even though he had insulted the bishop during the investigation, indicates that church authorities, and presumably secular authorities as well, were reluctant to acknowledge any forthright criticism of the priesthood before the common people. Criticism of the clergy was in fact strongly censored and examined for expressions that were considered offensive, harmful, or dangerous. Both church and imperial authorities alike were afraid that the criticism of priests could lead to criticism of religious traditions that contradicted the basic principles of political rule and the administrative position of the clergy in the empire.[71]

The village community and the priest continued to argue even after Levytskyi returned to Nahuievychi. Within two years new conflicts had occurred, and seemingly for petty reasons. Headman Dumiak accused Levytskyi of using snuff during services, and stole his tobacco pouch, put it into an envelope, and sent it to the Supreme Ecclesiastical Authority. As a result, the priest was first to be sent away for six weeks of retreat, but managed to persuade Bishop Iakhymovych to

69 Ibid., letter 7, p. 52.

70 Shchurat, »Kameniar i ioho ridne selo,« 53.

71 Himka, John-Paul, *Galician Villagers and the Ukrainian National Movement in the Nineteenth Century* (Edmonton: Canadian Institute of Ukrainian Studies University of Alberta, 1988), 136–137.

allow him to return to Nahuievychi, and he did. Shortly thereafter, in 1860, however, Levytskyi died.[72]

Conclusion

With the establishment of Habsburg enlightened absolutism in Galicia, the Greek Catholic clergy began to enjoy the role of a new elite. Having more opportunities to acquire a good education, the social status of priests improved. This created a stronger division between priests and the common people. Clergy became part of officialdom, a link between the empire and the rural population that fostered increased control over peasants, and priests assumed an important role in social leadership and education. This, however, often led to them abusing their power and treating the peasants as inferiors. They were more ready to turn people into obedient laity than to promote their independent development. This became the main area of conflict between peasants and clergy. As shown in the case of Iosyf Levytskyi, peasants were even ready to take priests to court when quarrels escalated.

Following the lines of conflict in the trial against Iosyf Levytskyi, a variety of themes emerge, from economic matters to differences in the interpretation of religion and the struggle for political dominance. Finance in fact remained the most irksome problem for the villagers: While the priest viewed his perquisites as a regular payment for his services, the villagers saw them as a type of extortion. In terms of local power, Levytskyi's main rival was Dumiak, the village headman, who had both the power given him by the imperial administration and the opportunity to unite people and to speak in the name of all villagers in opposition to the priest.

Regarding religion and morality, the trial also shows how the perceptions of the peasants and Levytskyi differed. Due to their lack of education, peasants often adhered to their common local beliefs and did not understand the priest's demands for change. Levytskyi on his part was not one to seek a compromise with the villagers. He focused greatly on the educational gap between himself and the peasants while other priests were more reconciliatory in that regard. His considerable temper and rude behavior, moreover, only exacerbated the conflict with Dumiak and Kmitsikevych. With all the means available to him, Levytskyi strove to prove that he was right to take on a leading position in the community.

The trial presents a very vivid picture of a mid-19th century rural community in Galicia. It demonstrates what it meant for a priest not only to be a pastor and

72 Ibid., 220–221.

leader but to live alongside the people of his parish as well. The trial also exhibits the main conflicts and quarrels in Nahuievychi, as well as in many other Galician villages of the time. The analysis of such events is crucial to our understanding of the Ruthenian movement in the second half of the 19th century.

Oksana Leskiv

Austrian Law, Krakovian Habitus, and Jewish Community: The Construction of New Local Hierarchies in Habsburg Galicia

The dissolution of the estate system and the attempt to create a modern state constructed by a wider citizenship were reasons why both citizenship and confessional identity acquired new meaning and were newly negotiated in 19th-century Europe. In the eyes of the new liberal elites the traditional order was no longer suitable and became a »disorder« which had to be regulated in a newly defined way. The process of negotiating these new orders and hierarchies, and even the process of transforming and adjusting the traditional orders to the changing reality can be summarized under the term modernisation.

The tools to create the modern order included plans, maps, and statutes that stood for a new spatial and legal structure. Using the example of the city of Krakow, I will attempt to draw a connection between the relatively compact and clearly defined space that was perceived as belonging to one confession or one religious group and imperial law, which extended to everyone. My story will also be about how Christians and Jews became increasingly close to each other in urban space and in administration. In Krakow »Christian« almost exclusively meant Roman Catholic. At the end of the 19th century only two percent of the city inhabitants were Greek Catholic or Protestant.[1] In 1850, Jews made up about 33 and, in 1890, about 30 percent of the city inhabitants.[2] Up to the 19th century social intermingling with Christians was possible for Jews only for the sake of cultural assimilation. During the second half of the century the municipality made attempts to integrate Jews into the city's administration without removing them from their religious community.

1 Łukasz Tomasz Sroka, »The Jewish Community of Kraków in Autonomous Galicia,« *Polin* 23 (2010): 63–82, here 68.

2 Tomasz Gąsowski, *Między gettem a światem. Dylematy ideowe Żydów galicyjskich na przełomie XIX i XX wieku. Rozprawa habililitacyjna* (Kraków: Księgarnia Akademicka, 1996), 20; Ludwik Mroczka, *Krakowianie. Szkice do portretu zbiorowego w dobie industrialnej transformacji 1890–1939* (Kraków: Wydawnictwo Naukowe Akademii Pedagogicznej, 1999), 45.

I approach my topic in three steps. First, I describe the changes in the city articulated in urban space. Next, I present the structure of the Krakow municipality and the legal status of Jewish inhabitants in the municipal statutes. Lastly, I compare the Jewish legal position in Krakow to the one in Lviv.

Visible Religious Divisions in Urban Space

As Anna Jakimyszyn points out in her analysis of authoritative governmental acts in Krakow in the first half of the 19th century, Jews were perceived in the city as »an entirely different social group,« both by themselves and by Christians.[3] In the time under consideration, the 1850s through the 1870s, Krakow was still visibly divided by religious affiliation, a division that mostly ran along early modern lines between estates.[4] To be accurate, the Jews were not an official estate, but due to their administrative autonomy[5] and their professional characteristics, they functioned in this way. Therefore, some scholars indeed refer to them as an estate (*stan*)[6] or even caste (*kasta*).[7]

The centre of the city, *intra muros*, was Christian. The adjacent Kazimierz, a formerly independent city mostly inhabited by Jews, served as the centre of commerce and industry.[8] This visible, sharp division between the Christian and the Jewish world was perceived by contemporaries as rather exceptional and

3 Anna Jakimyszyn, *Żydzi krakowscy w dobie Rzeczypospolitej Krakowskiej. Status Prawny. Przeobrażenia Gminy. System edukacyjny* (Kraków–Budapest: Wydawnictwo Austeria, 2008), 259.

4 Jacek Purchla, *Matecznik polski. Pozaekonomiczne czynniki rozwoju Krakowa w okresie autonomii galicyjskiej* (Kraków: Znak, 1992), 34; Hanna Kozińska-Witt, *Die Krakauer jüdische Reformgemeinde 1864–1874* (Frankfurt a. M. et al.: Peter Lang, 1999), 61. See also Rudolf Jaworski, Christian Lübke, and Michael G. Müller, *Eine kleine Geschichte Polens* (Frankfurt a. M.: Suhrkamp, 2000), 206–207.

5 For a detailed analysis of the concept and practice of autonomy, see Michael Ausubel and Michael J. Broyde, »Legal institutions,« in *YIVO Encyclopedia of Jews in Eastern Europe*, http://www.yivoencyclopedia.org./article.aspx/Legal_Institutions (accessed April 24, 2012).

6 For a first reference see Ludwik Gumplowicz, »Stanisława Augusta projekt reformy żydowstwa polskiego«, in *Dwa życia Ludwika Gumplowicza. Wybór tekstów*, eds. Jan Surman and Gerald Mozetič (Warszawa: Oficyna Naukowa, 2010), 217–233, here 229–231; Małgorzata Śliż, *Galicyjscy Żydzi na drodze do równouprawnienie 1848–1914. Aspekt prawny procesu emancypacji Żydów w Galicji* (Kraków: Księgarnia Akademicka, 2006), 13–14.

7 Aleksander Hertz, *Żydzi w kulturze polskiej* (Warszawa: Biblioteka Więzi, 1988), 83–88.

8 Kazimierz was called *miasto żydowskie*, *zaułek żydowski*, or *siedlisko żydowskie*. The most recent, and concise history of Jewish Kazimierz in English provided Sean Martin, *Jewish Life in Krakow, 1918–1939* (London–Portland: Vallentine Mitchell, 2004), 31–47.

characteristic of Krakow. In Lviv, for example, Jews lived predominantly in religiously mixed areas.[9]

Although there were always Christian inhabitants in Kazimierz, the place was imagined by both groups to be exclusively Jewish. This perception was encouraged by the fact that the borderline between Krakow and Kazimierz consisted not only of constructed walls but in the 19th century still had a natural dimension: the branch of the Vistula River known as the Old Vistula along with swamps.[10] By the middle of the 19th century any idea of a strict division was more of a mental one, as the urban landscape had substantially changed.

At the very beginning of the century Kazimierz had been incorporated administratively into the city of Krakow.[11] In addition, the city walls were dismantled in 1822. The visible boundary between the city and its surroundings thus no longer existed, as the Old Vistula and the swamps dried out, and the remains of the river were filled in the 1870s. A new park, the *Planty Dietlowskie* as distinct from the *Planty Krakowskie* situated on the former city walls – would be later created in its place.[12] Stradomska Street, the road between the centre of Krakow and Kazimierz, became more important not only as the connecting road between the imagined Christian and Jewish areas, but also as a place for those Jews to live who could not find appropriate dwellings in overcrowded Kazimierz.[13] Some time later the area formerly known as the Sebastian Meadows was used to build modern houses for better-situated Jews.[14]

Strictly speaking, some privileged Jews did indeed live in Christian neighbourhoods in Krakow. If they had enough money to buy municipal citizenship and changed their traditional habit into urban dress they could leave Kazimierz legally. Andrea Schmidt-Rösler records some wealthy families living for years in Christian areas.[15] In contrast, the Jews of Stradomska Street ignored the legal

9 »Nicht zerstreut in verschiedenen Stadtvierteln, wie in der galizischen Hauptstadt, wohnt die Mehrheit der Israeliten Krakaus auf der Halbinsel Kazimierz […].» A. Allerhand, »Wird der galizische Juden je ein Pole werden?« *Neuzeit*, December 2, 1870, 563, quoted in Kozińska-Witt, *Die Krakauer jüdische Reformgemeinde*, 29; Andrzej Żbikowski, *Żydzi krakowscy i ich gmina w latach 1869–1919* (Warszawa: DiG, 1994), 40.

10 Nathaniel D. Wood, *Becoming Metropolitan. Urban Selfhood and the Making of Modern Krakow* (Illinois: Northern Illinois University Press, 2010), 30–31.

11 Bogusław Krasnowolski, *Ulice i place krakowskiego Kazimierza. Z dziejów Chrześcijan i Żydów w Polsce* (Kraków: Universitas, 1992), 26.

12 Krasnowolski, *Ulice i place*, 48–51.

13 Ibid., 202–215.

14 Ibid., 21–22.

15 In 1843, municipal citizenship was purchased by 196 Jews (Krakow had 13,000 Jewish inhabitants), see Andrea Schmidt-Rösler, »Gesetzgebung und Politik

restrictions and resettled without changing their traditional appearance. Over time, the street became an area with a religiously mixed population.[16]

Changes in Jewish Legal Status

At the beginning of 19th century the municipality had to be newly ordered and regulated. The inclusion of Kazimierz into the municipality of Krakow was therefore accompanied by attempts to modernize the new city district. The reorganisation began with mapping, the planning of new streets, the straightening of old ones, and the paving of the surfaces.[17] This also meant »cleaning« the Jewish areas and making them healthier. At the same time, the municipal authority worked to change the legal status of Jews through the introduction of new laws in order to bring it in line with the new legal system.

Since the end of 18th Century the autonomy of the Krakow *kahal*, the administration of the Jewish community,[18] was increasingly limited, while the governmental and municipal control of Jewish neighbourhoods and individuals was increased.[19] The Jewish community was eventually subordinated to the secular head of the municipal district (*wójt*). In turn, the municipal administration needed a number of officers who were adequately prepared to exercise power over the Jewish community. This was in fact the initial reason for allowing the restricted participation of some Jews in the secular municipal administration, a development that occurred during the period of the Krakovian Republic (1815–1846), when Krakow enjoyed the status of a free city. The basis for this Jewish participation was provided by the *Statute Organising the Followers of the Law of the Old Testament in the Free City of Krakow and its Environs*,[20] which took effect in 1817. The statute granted Jews a representation, known as the

gegenüber der jüdischen Bevölkerung in der Republik Krakau 1815–1846,« *Jahrbücher für Geschichte Osteuropas* 41 (1993): 210–241, here 219.

16 In 1880 39 % of the inhabitants of Stradom were Jewish, see Żbikowski, *Żydzi krakowscy i ich gmina*, 40.

17 Krasnowolski, *Ulice i place*, 20–23; Barbara Zbroja, *Miasto umarłych. Architektura publiczna Żydowskiej Gminy Wyznaniowej w Krakowie w latach 1868–1939* (Kraków: WAM, 2005), 17–19.

18 On the *kahal* see Michael Stanislawski, »Kahal,« in *YIVO Encyclopedia of Jews in Eastern Europe*, http://www.yivoencyclopedia.org./article.aspx/Kahal (accessed March 24, 2012).

19 Majer Bałaban, *Historia Żydów w Krakowie i na Kazimierzu 1304–1868*, vol. 2, (Kraków: Nadzieja, 1936) 565–566; Jakimyszyn, *Żydzi krakowscy*, 26–27 and 112–115; Śliż, *Galicyjscy Żydzi*, 20–21.

20 In Polish *Statut urządzający starozakonnych w Wolnym Mieście Krakowie i jego okręgu* see Michał Galas and Antony Polonsky, »Introduction,« *Polin* 23 (2010): 3–48, here 8; Sroka, *The Jewish Community of Kraków*, 72.

Committee for Jewish Affairs,[21] in the state's Senate.[22] The Committee was meant to replace the *kahal*, which had previously been abolished.

The Committee was initially headed by a Christian, although dominated by Orthodox Jews. Its main task was collecting municipal taxes from Jewish inhabitants. In addition, all acts affecting the institutions of the Jewish community had to be approved by the Committee. All religious duties and ceremonies carried out by the chief rabbi had to be practised in the presence of a Christian member of the Committee who acted as a translator – usually a converted Jew, whose influence was thus especially humiliating for the Jewish representatives. The municipal control over the Jewish community was therefore quite extensive. Although Andrzej Żbikowski asserts that the main task of the Committee was only to offer recommendations,[23] in practice its role appears to have been much more important.

Krakovian Jews were overwhelmingly Orthodox at the time, and interested in preserving their religious rites and way of life. In the first half of the 19th century, however, a new Jewish movement would emerge: Jews who called themselves Progressives,[24] had a secular education and were acculturated in non-Jewish society. They sought to reform religious habits to adapt them to the needs of modern life, establishing a new kind of worship in their own synagogue (*Tempel*) and sending their children to public schools. In this way, they created a new secular Jewish *intelligentsia* that supported the municipality in its regulatory endeavors. I use the word *Progressives* here as a descriptive term not intended to convey any judgement on their status or positions.

The Revolution of 1848 brought legal equality to all Jews of the Austrian Empire along with a new communal law (*Provisorisches Gemeindegesetz*). The situation in Krakow was more complex. After the defeat of the Krakovian Revolution in 1846, the free city of Krakow was incorporated into the territory

21 Bałaban, *Historia Żydów*, vol. 2, 598; Schmidt-Rösler, *Gesetzgebung und Politik*, 212–220; Łukasz Sroka, *Żydzi w Krakowie. Studium o elicie miasta 1850–1918* (Kraków: Wydawnictwo Naukowe Akademii Pedagogicznej, 2008), 42–44; Kozińska-Witt, *Die Krakauer Jüdische Reformgemeinde*, 113–114.

22 Janina Bieniarzówna, »Wolne Miasto Kraków«, in *Dzieje Krakowa. Kraków w latach 1796–1918*, vol. 3, eds. Janina Bieniarzówna and Jan. M. Małecki (Kraków: Wydawnictwo Literackie, 1994), 39–175, here 42.

23 Żbikowski, *Żydzi krakowscy i ich gmina*, 58

24 In Polish *postępowcy* or *Żydzi cywilizowani*, in German *Fortschrittler*. The shift from German to Polish in the official name in 1860s mirrored the Polonisation of the formerly German-oriented Reform Association. For more details, see Michael A. Meyer, »Religious Reform,« in *YIVO Encyclopedia of Jews in Eastern Europe*, http://www.yivoencyclopedia.org./article.aspx/Reform_Religious (accessed March 24, 2012). About the »new Jewish *intelligentsia*« and Orthodox Jews, see Rachel Manekin »Orthodox Jewry in Kraków at the Turn of the Twentieth Century,« *Polin* 23 (2010): 165–198, here 165–166 and 168.

of the Habsburg Monarchy under martial law, thus losing its previous autonomy. The administrative institutions of the Krakovian Republic were dissolved. In 1848, due to the liberalisation of the Habsburg Monarchy, a Municipal Council (*Rada Miejska*) could be elected, and of 40 councillors, 10 were Jewish.[25] The first Municipal Council was abolished in 1853 and replaced by a nominated Municipal Board (*Wydział Miejski*) consisting of 15 Christians and five Jews, most of whom had a secular education.[26]

It was the first time that Jews were equal members of the Municipal Council, and not only members of a subordinated committee. The simultaneous existence of the *Committee of Jewish Affairs* and Jewish representatives in the Municipal Council alarmed some Orthodox members of the Jewish community who perceived it as a useless doubling of authority.[27] Conflict thus loomed between the Orthodox Committee and the Municipal Council, dominated by the Progressives.

The continual presence of Progressives in the municipal administration also influenced the shape of the still overwhelmingly Orthodox committee. In 1864 the magistrate forced the committee to co-opt additional 20 members and to constitute a *Municipal Council Department for Jewish Matters*.[28] Those nominated included both Orthodox and Progressive Jews. The main task of the department was to prepare a new statute for the Jewish community. In the 1860s, political authorities thought such a project to be undesirable and indeed impossible without consulting representatives of both Jewish fractions. One can conclude that from the very beginning of the department's activities there was a strong representation of Progressives in the municipal hierarchy. Later they would even come to dominate the department.[29]

25 Łukasz Sroka, *Żydzi w Krakowie*, 113–114; also Zdzisław Noga, »Kraków – przestrzeń władzy,« in *Kraków dziedzictwo wieków*, eds. Karolina Grodzicka et al. (Kraków: Muzeum Historyczne Miasta Krakowa, 2006), 46–73, here 63.

26 Janina Bieniarzówna, »Od Wiosny Ludów do Powstania Styczniowego«, in Bieniarzówna and Małecki, *Dzieje Krakowa*, 177–224, here 200; Noga, *Kraków – przestrzeń władzy*, 64. According to Majer Bałaban in the Municipal Board, 12 Jews were in the group of 30 councillors, in: Bałaban, *Historia Żydów*, vol. 2, 686. The latter share corresponded with the percentage of Jews among city inhabitants, in 1850 about 33 percent. See Gąsowski, *Między gettem a światem*, 20.

27 Teofilia Mahler, *Walka między ortodoksją a postępowcami w Krakowie w latach 1843–1868*, unpublished MA thesis written under the supervision of Majer Bałaban in the 1930s, in: Archive of the Jewish Historical Institute/Żydowski Instytut Historyczny in Warsaw (AŻIH), sygn. 61, 26.

28 In Polish Wydział Rady Miejskiej dla Spraw Izraelickich. For more details on the Council see HAGLA [Abraham Gumplowicz], *Dawar baitto. Ein Wort zu seiner Zeit* (Kraków, 1868), 11; Żbikowski, *Żydzi krakowscy ich gmina*, 58.

29 Żbikowski, *Żydzi krakowscy i ich gmina*, 112–113; Kozińska-Witt, *Die Krakauer Jüdische Reformgemeinde*, 118.

In the aftermath of the defeat of the Krakovian Revolution in 1846 and the incorporation of Krakow into the Habsburg Monarchy, the task of Germanising the municipal administration intensified. The Jewish councillors who were nominated represented the Austrophile circles among the Jewish population. This Germanised Jewish *intelligentsia* was generally not very well integrated within the Jewish community (*kehila*). Its members led a rather isolated social life and were not accepted as representatives of local Jewry by the Orthodox majority. Some secularly educated Jews were foreigners, who had come to Krakow as professionals with the Austrian army, for example as physicians. They did not attain a strong position in the *kehila* of Krakow even as they fostered contacts with Austrian officials. Nevertheless, on the basis of their own assumed modernity and frequent interaction with Christian society they regarded themselves as the natural representatives of the Jewish community and were very sceptical about the political abilities of Orthodox Jews who lacked a secular education and were not respected as partners by the municipal elite.[30]

In spite of the self-perception of the Progressives, it was the Orthodox members of the magistrate whom the municipality regarded as official intermediaries between the *kehila* and secular power.[31] The Austrian authorities in Krakow had favourable opinions of the Progressives, but saw no advantage in supporting them. The Orthodox, who constituted the majority of Krakow Jewry, were known for their loyalty to the monarchy, which they proved by condemning the Polish national uprisings, as did, for example, the leader of Krakovian Orthodoxy, Salomon Deiches.[32] However, the Progressives tried, unsuccessfully, to humiliate the Orthodox by referring to them as »closet Hasidim«,[33] a group seen by enlightened Austrian officials as backward and dangerous.

The disintegration of the traditional social order – alongside the increase in religiously mixed neighbourhoods – produced an additional overlap of Jewish

30 This position is reflected in: *Neuzeit* October 12, 1866, 450, quoted in Kozińska-Witt, *Die Krakauer Jüdische Reformgemeinde*, 114.

31 One might speculate as to whether the contribution of Orthodox Jewish representatives to a programme of modernisation was the transmission of a pre-modern tradition of personal intermediation (*shtadlanut*) into the reformed institution of municipal administration. In contrast with early modern practice, not just an exceptional individual but the whole group of Jewish Orthodox councillors now served in the municipal administration.

32 Kozińska-Witt, *Die Krakauer Jüdische Reformgemeinde*, 87.

33 *Neuzeit*, November 21, 1867, 558. Hasidism is a movement of religious revival with a distinctive social profile. The followers of Hasidism, the *hasidim*, formed informal groups within Jewish communities. For more details see David Assaf, »Hasidism,« in *YIVO Encyclopedia of Jews in Eastern Europe*, http://www.yivoency clopedia.org./article.aspx/Hasidism/Historical_Overview (accessed March 24, 2012).

and Christian concerns. The new situation required a new definition of Jewish, non-Jewish and common domains. Notably the long-term presence of Jews within the Krakovian municipal administration brought about the necessity to regulate their status through written law and to define their competence with regard to the Jewish community. This need very soon found its expression in Krakow's administrative reform. Indeed, the very first Municipal Council elected after its implementation underlined the goal of »regulating the city«.[34] The new city order also stood for a clarification of the administrative relationship between Jewish and Christian inhabitants in an era of legal reform.

The Krakovian Municipal Statute

Both types of Jewish representation coexisted until the 1860s, when the Austrian Empire developed into a constitutional, federal monarchy, manifested in the Fundamental Law (*Staatsgrundgesetz*) of December 21, 1867.[35] In the same year new legislation formally suspended the *kahal* as an autonomous Jewish representation and replaced it by a committee that was subordinated to the municipality. In contrast, Jewish representation in form of Jewish municipal deputies in the Municipal Council was maintained. The constitution was liberal in spirit and upheld the equality of all citizens without regard for their religious affiliation. In November 1868, the Galician Provincial Parliament also confirmed the legal equality of the Jews.[36]

The constitution was known as the Framework Law (*Rahmengesetz*) as it created a general legal framework that integrated local law traditions, provided they did not contradict the constitution. The provincial laws (*Landesordnungen*) and municipal statutes could take on different forms due to social and economic specifics of each province or municipality. The Crown lands enjoyed home rule and self-government which in Galicia were in fact the basis for administrational Polonisation.[37] The Austrian officials, who rarely knew the regional languages, left Galicia, leaving their posts to Polish successors.

The Habsburg Monarchy allowed for self-government at many levels, from the provincial parliament (*Sejm Krajowy*) at the top, down through confessional

34 In the original »uporządkowanie miasta« / »in Ordnung-Bringen der Stadt.« See Beate Herget, *Die Selbstverwaltung Krakaus 1866–1915. Ein rechtshistorischer Beitrag zur Bedeutung der Statutarstädte in der Habsburger Monarchie* (Regensburg: Sophia-Verlag, 2005), 54.

35 Ibid., 24–26.

36 Żbikowski, *Żydzi krakowscy i ich gmina*, 109.

37 Harald Binder »Galizische Autonomie. Ein streitbarer Begriff und seine Karriere,« in *Moravské vyrovnání z roku 1905*, ed. Lukaš Fasora et al. (Brno: Matice moravská, 2006), 239–266.

associations at the bottom. Each of these levels had to be institutionalised and organised by individual statutes. Administrational Polonisation was an opportunity for anyone who mastered the Polish language. The Krakovian Progressives seized this occasion and began to Polonise their association and temple in the 1860s. By doing so they gained the support and esteem of the new Krakovian elite who had freshly entered office and was looking for allies.

The legal reform of the Austrian Monarchy, and the liberal constitution in particular, which granted home rule to the Crown lands, provided the basis for institutional reform in Galicia. It granted autonomy to the municipalities and to the Jewish communities, with both now governed by elected communal boards. Religious communities were autonomous in ritual and social concerns, but subordinate to local administrations in the domains of finance and secular jurisdiction. Elections to the Jewish community board thus had to be controlled and confirmed by the Municipal Council.

Modernisation in the Habsburg Empire was liberal in spirit and sought to erase the old estate system by introducing a new social hierarchy at every administrative level. In an enlightened vein, it stressed the economic and educational qualities of the individual. The liberal reformers supported anti-clericalism and aimed at the deconfessionalisation of politics, distinguishing between the public and the private sphere. All inhabitants were divided into privileged members of the city community (*Gemeindemitglieder*) and unprivileged foreigners (*Auswärtige*). Only members were eligible to vote and were divided into classes dependent on the amount of taxes paid.

Krakow and Lviv both belonged to a special category of 33 large cities (*Statutarstädte*) that had their own statutes within the Habsburg Monarchy.[38] They were removed from the administrative system of their provinces and subordinated directly to the provincial parliament and state administration. The statutes of these municipalities differed from those of other cities and included specific social characteristics. Their inhabitants were presumed to be wealthier than other municipal citizens in the monarchy, and therefore had to pay higher taxes for their individual right to participate in municipal elections. The financial status of the *Statutarstädte* was more favourable than that of other cities. After the introduction of municipal self-government, the revenues from direct taxes and indirect taxes (*akcyza*) were not passed on to higher administrative levels but were available to the local authorities. In addition, the municipal territories of the *Statutarstädte* were enlarged by incorporating suburbs and neighbouring communities.[39]

38 Herget, *Die Selbstverwaltung Krakaus 1866–1915*, 26–34; Hanna Kozińska-Witt, *Krakau in Warschaus langem Schatten* (Stuttgart: Franz Steiner, 2008), 40–42.

39 Herget, *Die Selbstverwaltung Krakaus 1866–1915*, 31.

Regarding the process of incorporation into one municipal administration, some exceptions from this practice were made for the Jewish communities of Brno, Prague, Krakow, and Lviv – the largest and most important of their respective provinces – communities that remained mostly independent of their municipalities. They were able to manage their properties by themselves and take care of their own religious, cultural, and social institutions.

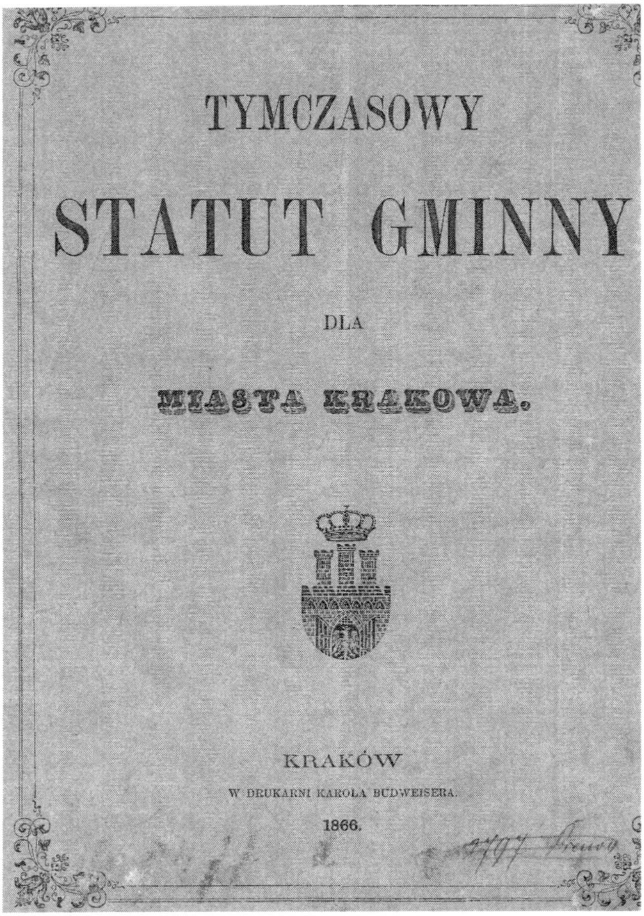
TYMCZASOWY

STATUT GMINNY

DLA

MIASTA KRAKOWA.

KRAKÓW

W DRUKARNI KAROLA BUDWEISERA.

1866.

Cover of the Provisional municipal statute of the capital city of Krakow, 1866.[40]

40 I would like to thank Alicja Maślak-Maciejewska for providing scans of this statute.

The *Provisional municipal statute of the capital city of Krakow*[41] was established in 1866 and remained in effect for 35 years. In 1866, approximately 4.4 percent of the city's inhabitants, or 2,086 of 47,500, belonged to the category of burghers and electors.[42] Electors were taxpayers and educated individuals, a group that included state and municipal officials, teachers, priests, rabbis, and Jewish preachers.[43] The statute thus differentiated between members of the traditional religious elite and those with a modern secular education. These burghers were divided into three classes (*curiae*) according to their educational level and share of governmental taxes. Each curia elected 20 city councillors of the total of 60. While councillors for the first curia could be elected by a rather small number of votes, candidates for the second and third needed much more support expressed by a larger number of electors.[44] The first curia in the city council was elected by the strongest taxpayers and those with a secular education. Because of the domination of the secularly educated it was called the »curia of the *intelligentsia*«. This supremacy of the *intelligentsia* was the peculiarity of Krakow in comparison with other municipalities, such as Lviv, that were instead dominated by strong economic elites. As a result of the new order, the Jewish councillors working in the municipal sphere were seen as Jewish representatives, but also as individuals representing the whole city.

The statute did not differentiate among burghers on the basis of their religious affiliation. As Nathaniel Wood claims, »Beginning in 1866, with the granting of self-government to the city, Jews were eligible to serve in municipal government so long as they met the criteria of the curia system, which discriminated in terms of sex, wealth, and education, but not religion«.[45] However, in the first sketch of the statute it was specified that only Christians could be elected to the offices of mayor and vice mayor.[46] The number of Jews on the Council was also limited to one third.[47] This suggestion originated in the traditional Krakovian election

41 *Statut tymczasowy królewskiego stołecznego miasta Krakowa / Provisorisches Gemeindestatut für die Kgl. Hauptstadt Krakau*, Kraków [1866]; reprinted in *Dziennik Ustaw krajowych*, nr. 7: *Zbiór ustaw i rozporządzeń administracyjnych*, ed. Jan Piwocki (Lwów, 1899), vol. 1, 584–607; Kozińska-Witt, *Krakau in Warschaus langem Schatten*, 65–67.

42 Herget, *Die Selbstverwaltung Krakaus 1866–1915*, 49.

43 Ibid., 40.

44 Jan M. Małecki, *W dobie autonomii galicyjskiej (1866–1918)*, in Bieniarzówna and Małecki, *Dzieje Krakowa*, 225–394, here 228.

45 Wood, *Becoming Metropolitan*, 31.

46 § 46 of the Municipal Statute abolished by the *Landesgesetz* of November 19, 1868 (Nr. 30). Landesgesetz, Blatt (folio) 1. Quoted in Herget, *Die Selbstverwaltung Krakaus 1866–1915*, 43–44 and 46; Małecki, *W dobie autonomii galicyjskiej*, 226.

47 Sroka, *Żydzi w Krakowie*, 115.

system which had excluded Jews from the office of mayor and vice mayor and limited their percentage on the Municipal Council.

There were continual attempts to limit the percentage of Jews in local self-government in Galicia. At the provincial level, some additional attempts to limit the percentage of Jewish councillors were made in the *Sejm Krajowy*, in the course of negotiations over municipal statutes. For example, it was postulated by the creators of the statutes that Jews generally could not make up more than two thirds of each curia.[48] The Austrian authorities refused to recognise this version of the Krakovian statute as not compatible with the constitution due to the postulated limitations.[49] The relevant paragraphs were removed, but, as memoirs of Krakovian politicians show, the limitation regarding the religious affiliation of the mayor remained valid as customary law.

Which areas of activity were determined by the Krakovian Statute? First of all, the statute regulated how later changes in municipal territory, as well as alterations of the statute would be handled. In the following, it established who belonged to the municipality, and defined the competences of the municipality and its officials.[50] It also decided on the form of representation, the electoral process, and the areas of competence of the Municipal Council. Only the last part of the statute concerned the »influence of municipal power on the affairs concerning diverse religious confessions«.[51] Due to the imperial regulations mentioned above, for the *Statutarstädte*, the Christian and Jewish spaces of activity in the Krakovian City Council were strictly divided. Each religious community possessed its own funds that were invested exclusively in its own institutions like schools and social welfare (§ 119). Only Christian deputies could make decisions about affairs concerning Christians, just as Jewish deputies decided on Jewish affairs (§ 120). If the number of Jews on the City Council failed to reach 21, the quorum needed to make decisions, it had to call upon further representatives of the Jewish community (*mężów zaufania*) for support (§ 123).[52] In this way, the participation of Jewish representatives in the municipal administration was affirmed and even prescribed by secular law. The body was to become a connecting link between confessional and secular authorities.[53]

48 Śliż, *Galicyjscy Żydzi*, 36.
49 Sroka, *Żydzi w Krakowie*, 115–116; Herget, *Die Selbstverwaltung Krakaus 1866–1915*, 46
50 Herget, *Die Selbstverwaltung Krakaus 1866–1915*, 41.
51 »O wpływie władzy gminnej na sprawy dotyczące różnych wyznań religijnych« / »Von der Versorgung der speciellen Angelegenheiten der christlichen und der israelitischen Bevölkerung.« *Statut tymczasowy / Provisorisches Statut*, Part (*Dział/ Hauptstück*) VI, §§ 119–123, 43–44. For more details see Herget, *Die Selbstverwaltung Krakaus 1866–1915*, 46–47.
52 There was no equivalent to this rule for the Christian members of the council.
53 Kozińska-Witt, *Die Krakauer Jüdische Reformgemeinde*, 121.

Dział VI.

Tytuł 17.

O wpływie władzy gminnéj na sprawy dotyczące różnych wyznań religijnych.

§. 119.

Każde wyznanie religijne pozostaje w posiadaniu i używaniu zakładów, fundacyj i funduszów przeznaczonych na jego cele duchowne, naukowe i dobroczynne, i opędza wydatki swe z własnych zasobów.

Każdy członek gminy miasta Krakowa przyczynia się do wydatków tego tylko wyznania religijnego, do którego sam należy, o ile takowe według ustaw administracyjnych nie są ciężarem realności przez niego posiadanych.

§. 120.

Specyalne sprawy chrześciańskie zostają pod wyłącznym zarządem chrześciańskich członków gminy krakowskiéj.

Sprawy te są:

a) dotyczące przedmiotów duchownych, szkolnych i dobroczynnych, tudzież zakładów wyłącznie z funduszów chrześciańskich dotowanych;

b) wykonywanie praw patronatu, prezentowania i mianowania pasterzy dusz i nauczycieli jakotéż nadawanie stypendyów.

§. 121.

W zarządzie spraw w paragrafie powyższym wymienionych zastępują gminę członkowie Rady miejskiéj chrześciańskiego wyznania.

Do wydania ważnéj uchwały w sprawach tego rodzaju obecność $^2/_3$ części członków Rady miejskiéj wyznania chrześciańskiego jest konieczną.

§. 122.

O ile zakłady na cele niżéj wyrażone w przyszłości z majątku gminy miasta Krakowa fundowane nie będą, gmina izraelicka pokrywa z własnych swoich zasobów wydatki:

a) na swoje cele religijne;

b) na zaopatrzenie swoich ubogich i chorych;

c) na utrzymanie swoich szkół i szpitalów;

d) na zaspokojenie innych właściwych swoich potrzeb.

Dochody jednakże, które na zaspokojenie potrzeb tego rodzaju przez ogół mieszkańców wnoszoneby były, rozłożone zostaną na użytek każdego wyznania, w stosunku przykładania się jego wyznawców.

§. 123.

W sprawach dotyczących przedmiotów w powyższym paragrafie wymienionych, o ile takowe pod rozpoznanie gminy przychodzić będą, stanowić mają pod przewodnictwem prezydenta członkowie Rady miejskiéj wyznania izraelickiego, w komplecie przynajmniéj $^2/_3$ części członków tego wyznania.

Gdyby liczba wybranych członków Rady miejskiéj wyznania izraelickiego 21 nie wynosiła, natedy liczba ta powołaniem do obrad mężów zaufania przez członków Rady miejskiéj wyznania izraelickiego uzupełnioną będzie.

The 6th part of the Krakow statute: »On the influence of municipal power on the affairs concerning diverse religious confessions«.

The Krakovian Statute was the basis for the first election to the Municipal Council. Among 60 elected councillors, 12 were Jewish.[54] Their percentage was within the stipulated limit and was even lower than in the analogue institutions of the past, the Municipal Council and the Municipal Board. Following the Municipal Statute, a mediating institution for Jewish concerns was established under the name Municipal Department for Jewish Affairs (*Wydział Miejski do Spraw Izraelickich*).[55] It consisted of twenty-one Jewish members and supervised the financial affairs of the Jewish community, the appointment of doctors to the Jewish hospital, and of teachers to the Jewish school in Kazimierz.

Regarding municipal law, Beate Herget asserts that Jews and Christians generally enjoyed an equal status, and emphasizes the influence of the constitution of December 1867, which brought an equal legal status to all the inhabitants of Krakow, irrespective of their religion.[56] Even though these »foreign« principles of equality conflicted with traditional Krakovian practice, the integration of Krakow into the Austrian Empire was closely tied to the implementation of imperial law.

The evolution of the statute illustrates the potential of imperial law with regard to the abolishment of discriminatory habits. Additionally, it demonstrates how »foreign« imperial law was adapted by local groups to take a changing reality into account: It was the Krakow conservatives (*konserwatyści krakowscy*), a Polish elitist group, who influenced the local shape of the statute. They exercised real power in the municipality and proclaimed a programme of social solidarity (*solidaryzm społeczny*). This slogan entailed imagining society as a joint organism, in which every social class and religious community has its own duties to fulfil. Jews were seen as an integral part of this organism. They were meant to assume specific functions that no other group was able to assume, and therefore were not necessarily perceived as competitors of the Christian population. The programme of the Krakovian conservatives intended to promote solidarity, stressing the peaceful cooperation of all social groups led by the conservative elite.[57]

54 Małecki, *W dobie autonomii galicyjskiej*, 227.

55 On the department see Galas and Polonsky, »Introduction,« 14. The authors claim that the department consisted of only 12 Jews, but this was contradictory to the stipulations of the statute. The 12 Jews mentioned were probably the regular municipal council members.

56 Herget, *Die Selbstverwaltung Krakaus 1866–1915*, 46–47.

57 Philip Pajakowski, »Ambiguities of Assimilation. The Kraków Conservatives and the Jews,« *Polin* 23 (2010): 83–102, here 83–85; Hanna Kozińska-Witt »Wielkomiejska Galicja w oczach konserwatystów krakowskich: Kraków i Lwów w ›Przeglądzie Polskim‹ (1866–1913),« *Kwartalnik Historyczny* 68 (2011): 453–479, here 459–460.

The statute as a written law differentiated between municipal domains, for which the religious affiliation of city councillors did not play a role, and confessional affairs, for which religion was of substantial importance. This division between Jewish and Christian spheres corresponded with the customary spatial order of the estates in Krakow. The Christian »collective« property was mostly located in the city centre – with some important exceptions in Kazimierz –, while the Jewish »collective« property was exclusively in Kazimierz. The Christian property included the property of Christian institutions, such as hospitals, schools, and social welfare institutions that were managed mostly by churches and convents.[58] By contrast »Jewish property« in the city centre belonged exclusively to individuals, while the Jewish community did not possess anything corporately.

Even though the Municipal Statute was indeed a means to adjust the municipality to a changed reality, it paradoxically built on Krakow's traditional social order. The new legal order, dissolving the formerly clear-cut Christian and Jewish neighbourhoods and merging Krakow and Kazimierz into a single municipal administrative unit, however, created the basis for new problems.[59] The process of municipalizing confessional institutions with the aim of religiously »neutralising« them was part of a series of reforms that had already begun throughout Galicia in the 1860s. This was marked by conflicts that lasted for years.[60] This municipalization was strongly interconnected with the financial system, as the costs of institutions were no longer covered by religious communities, but by the municipalities, who generally provided more money and better standards for schools and social welfare.[61] Each confessional group was meant to contribute to the municipal funds proportionally to its percentage of city inhabitants or taxes paid.[62]

As a result of the law, the boards of religious communities lost control over municipalized institutions, which the established religious authorities naturally disliked. In addition, some areas financed traditionally by the municipality, i.e.

58 A later comment on this paragraph mentioned that Christians and Jews continued to keep property of this kind. For institutions, which in the past had been financed by municipal funds, this financing was to be continued.

59 Śliż, *Galicyjscy Żydzi*, 36.

60 About the municipalizing of hospitals, see Kozińska-Witt, *Die Krakauer jüdische Reformgemeinde*, 139 and 259–260. Żbikowski mentions the hospital taxes covered by individual Jews or the Jewish community during the 1870s. Żbikowski, *Żydzi krakowscy i ich gmina*, 138–139.

61 Żbikowski, *Żydzi krakowscy i ich gmina*, 204.

62 The meaning of this sentence was not clear and it was postponed to the following version of the Statute (§ 122: *w stosunku przekładania się jego wyznawców*).

Hebrew and Jewish religion lessons in schools, were now declared to be a confessional matter and meant to be financed by the Jewish community.[63] Despite these limitations, the legal differentiation between Christian and Jewish spaces and competences can be seen as an improvement over the past, when Jewish affairs were conducted by Christians and converts. The division between Jewish and Christian funds also had a positive impact, as Jews could not be legally forced to cover the costs of Christian institutions. The consequences in legal practice can be illustrated by the protests of Jewish councillors against the municipal financing of the Association for Affordable Housing for Catholic Workers (*Towarzystwo tanich mieszkań dla robotników katolików w Krakowie*) in 1904. They successfully withheld their support for the association because of its confessional exclusiveness.[64]

Comparisons with the Municipal Statute in Lviv

The other *Statutarstadt* in Galicia was Lviv, the political capital, which is therefore of special interest in terms of comparison. The debates accompanying the preparation of the municipal statute in Lviv involved a general attempt to limit the percentage of Jewish councillors and to exclusively admit Christians to the office of mayor and deputy mayor.[65] The debate between the imperial administration and the municipality of Lviv on these limitations lasted for four years and delayed the enacting of the statute, which only came into power in 1870. As in Krakow it was ultimately the imperial government that imposed the removal of some restrictive paragraphs from the statute as not compatible with the Imperial Constitution of 1867. The ultimately approved version of the Lviv Municipal Statute did not explicitly exclude non-Christians from the office of mayor or vice mayor; it only specified that non-Christian office holders were prohibited from dealing with Christian concerns.[66] On the other hand, paragraph 27 introduced a limitation of another kind: In a spirit of secularisation it excluded clergymen of any religion from the office of mayor. Similar to the Krakovian statute, the liberal election regulations connected the right to vote with a tax census, thus privileging the wealthy and educated. In contrast to the

63 Kozińska-Witt, *Die Krakauer Jüdische Reformgemeinde*, 145.

64 Sroka, *Żydzi w Krakowie*, 122.

65 Heidi Hein-Kircher, »Concerning the Legal Status and Extent of Jewish Participation in the Lemberg Local Self Government: The Provisions of the Lemberg Statute of 1870,« *Simon Dubnow Institute Yearbook* 10 (2011): 237–254.

66 »Statut królewskiego stołecznego miasta Lwowa«, *Dziennik ustaw krajowych*, no. 79, 515.

three-curia structure of the Krakovian Municipal Council, the Lvivian structure consisted of only one curia.

The Lviv statute, like its Krakovian counterpart, differentiated between general municipal and specific religious concerns. In the sixth part it touched upon religious affairs.[67] The division between Jewish and Christian spaces and areas of activity was similar to the one in Krakow: each religious community possessed its own institutions and funds. However, in Lviv, »Christian« not only meant Roman Catholic, but could also refer to the significant Greek Catholic minority.[68] The main difference between the two statutes consisted in the paragraphs involving the bodies responsible for decisions about specific religious affairs. While the Krakovian statute created an informal body consisting of Jewish municipal deputies and some representatives of the Jewish *kehila*, the Lviv statute concentrated on defending Christian interests through the establishment of a special Christian board. In Paragraph 97 it excluded Jewish deputies from dealing with specific concerns of the Christian inhabitants and ordered:

> In case less than 80 deputies of Christian confession are among the members of the Municipal Council, according to § 24 of the election regulations, a Christian administrative board should be created to administrate the special concerns of the Christian people on the basis of this statute.[69]

Paragraph 24 also prescribed that the members of the Christian administrative board should be elected from the Christian elector lists of the previous elections.[70] Therefore, the provision for 80 Christian members in the statute did not concern the Municipal Council as a whole, as postulated during the previous debates, but the specific Christian administrative board consisting of the municipal deputies and the electors of Christian confession. The option to include external members mirrored the Christian fear of being outnumbered by Jewish peers on the Municipal Council. This apprehension seemed to be absent in Krakow where Jews were more likely to be outnumbered by Christians. In this point, the Krakovian elites seemed generally more self-assured and less afraid

67 In the original *O zawiadywaniu specyalnemi sprawami ludności chrześcijańskiej i izraelickiej / Von der Versorgung der speciellen Angelegenheiten der christlichen und israelitischen Bevölkerung*. Ibid., 503–505.

68 In 1910: 51.2 % Roman Catholic, 19.1 % Greek Catholic, 27.8 % Jewish. See Rudolf M. Mark, *Galizien unter österreichischer Herrschaft. Verwaltung – Kirche – Bevölkerung*, (Marburg: Herder Verlag, 1994) 109.

69 »Gdyby między członkami rady miejskiej nie znachodziło się ośiemdziesięciu (80) radnych religii chrześcijańskiej, natenczas utworzoną będzie według postanowień § 24. ordynacyi wyborczej rada administracyjna chrześcijańska, która według przepisów niniejszego statutu zawiadywać ma specyalnemi sprawami ludności chrześcijańskiej.« Printed in *Dziennik ustaw krajowych*, 504.

70 Ibid., 513–514.

of »Jewish influence« than the Lvivians. The Christian board of Lviv was apparently more institutionalised – it had a proper name and consisted of electors, members of the municipality whose common marker was their belonging to a Christian confession.

In 1867, the Viennese newspaper *Neue Freie Presse* commented on the composition of the Lvivian Municipal Council. It observed a tendency to exclude all members of the local *intelligentsia* and to privilege artisans and merchants.[71] In this way the paragraphs discriminating against Jews could be regarded as a strategy for the old urban elite to maintain power. This segment of society often felt threatened by the entire *intelligentsia* consisting of both Christians and Jews.

The secularly educated Jews of Lviv were largely Germanised by the beginning of the 19th century.[72] Christians were therefore able to make use of convenient cultural arguments to exclude them from power. While liberalism made religious discrimination less likely, the idea of »Galician autonomy« provided the means of pushing the German language out of the local public sphere, while the Polish-speaking elite was able to acquire better social positions. Lastly, the imperial order forced the Polish elite in Lviv to open its ranks to newcomers. As a counter measure, the Polish burghers used their political influence against Germanised Jews. They decided to establish only one curia in the municipal council with the intention of appearing more egalitarian than its Krakow counterpart. In actual fact this structural equality masked anti-Jewish resentments.[73]

The debates regarding Jewish participation in the Municipal Council seemed to be more heated in Lviv than in Krakow. One can explain the more exclusive tendencies in Lviv with the different social compositions of the municipalities: Krakow was imagined as exclusively Polish, socially dominated by aristocracy, and politically conservative. The old village pact between the gentry and Jewish mediators had been transferred to the city. This pact was one basis for the

71 »Die Rede von Herrn Wild (Buchhändler) während der zweiten Wählerversammlung bei den Stadtratswahlen,« *Neue Freie Presse*, April 19, 1866, 4. The discussions held in the Municipal Council allow us to see this institution not only as a discriminatory structure but also as an arena, in which open negotiations were possible. See Karsten Holste, Dietlind Hüchtker, and Michael G. Müller, »Aufsteigen und Obenbleiben in europäischen Gesellschaften des 19. Jahrhunderts. Akteure, Arenen, Aushandlungsprozesse,« in *Aufsteigen und Obenbleiben in europäischen Gesellschaften des 19. Jahrhunderts. Akteure, Arenen, Aushandlungsprozesse*, eds. Karsten Holste, Dietlind Hüchtker, and Michael G. Müller (Berlin: Akademie Verlag, 2009), 9–19.

72 Galas and Polonsky, *Introduction*, 13.

73 Kozińska-Witt, *Die Krakauer Jüdische Reformgemeinde*, 238.

previously mentioned programme of social solidarity in Krakow.[74] In contrast, Lviv was politically more contested, egalitarian, and »bourgeois«,[75] hence the competition between Jews and Christians was stronger and influenced their interaction in self-government.

The debates on the differentiation between Christian and Jewish property allow us to understand the difficulties of creating a municipal, religiously neutral sphere in a changing, but still socially and religiously divided society.[76] First of all, the religious topography of Krakow and Lviv differed considerably: Krakow had a clear spatial division between Jewish and Christian areas in contrast to Lviv with its ethno-religiously mixed streets.[77] Svjatoslav Pacholkiv has analysed descriptions of Lviv in 19th-century city guide books (*skorowidz*). Beginning in 1870 there was no city space referred to as a »Jewish district« because of the generally mixed composition of neighbourhoods.[78] While Jewish and Christian property in Krakow could be clearly identified, this was less unequivocal in Lviv. The social composition of each municipality and especially the individual division of confessional and professional spaces affected the local interpretation and application of imperial law.[79]

Ultimately, the Municipal Statute in Lviv ignored the most recent changes in the urban landscape, namely the dissolution of religiously divided neighbourhoods. Remaining in the past, it mirrored the traditional understanding of spatial division which claimed the city centre as exclusively Christian. Communal property was defined as Christian *ex cathedra*, thus setting the scene for future conflict.[80] By maintaining the early modern order, the municipal statute created exclusively Christian and Jewish territories and properties, which in current local practice had already disappeared.

One might ask how long early modern property perceptions influenced municipal life. Krakovian customary law, which mirrored the early modern

74 Żbikowski, *Żydzi krakowscy i ich gmina*, 85.

75 See Harald Binder »Politische Öffentlichkeit in Galizien. Lemberg und Krakau im Vergleich,« in *Stadt und Öffentlichkeit in Ostmitteleuropa 1900–1939. Beiträge zur Entstehung moderner Urbanität zwischen Berlin, Charkiv, Tallin und Triest*, eds. Andreas R. Hoffman and Anna Veronika Wendland (Stuttgart: Franz Steiner, 2002), 259–280.

76 Kozińska-Witt, *Die Krakauer Jüdische Reformgemeinde*, 214–224.

77 Wood, *Becoming Metropolitan*, 30–31.

78 Svjatoslav Pacholkiv »Zwischen Einbeziehung und Ausgrenzung: Die Juden in Lemberg. 1918–1919,« in *Vertraut und fremd zugleich. Jüdisch-christliche Nachbarschaften in Warschau-Lengnau-Lemberg*, eds. Alexandra Binnenkade et al. (Köln et al.: Böhlau, 2009), 155–216, here 162.

79 Śliż, *Galicyjscy Żydzi*, 37.

80 Hein-Kircher, »*Concerning the Legal Status*, 251; Kozińska-Witt, *Die Krakauer Jüdische Reformgemeinde*, 219.

order, was still influential in efforts to exclude Jews from the office of mayor and deputy mayor. Nevertheless, this mental reservation seems to have vanished with time and the implementation of imperial power. From the very beginning of the 20th century, one of Krakow's deputy mayors was always Jewish. This practice occurred not only in Krakow, but also in smaller Galician towns. Wherever Jews constituted a considerable share of the town population, they acquired important positions in the municipal administration.[81] Usually the mayor would be a Roman Catholic and the deputy mayor a Jew.[82] At the turn of the century, Lviv, in spite of the remarkable anti-Jewish atmosphere in its city administration, also shifted with regard to this practice, falling in line with this regional trend,[83] and in 1909 a barrister named Tobiasz Askenaze was elected to the office of deputy mayor.

Conclusion

The case of the Krakow municipal statute presented here demonstrates the entanglement of diverse political impulses and their interaction in a local context. The 1860s were a time of changing orders and hierarchies: citizenship, belonging to the municipality and to the Jewish community were matters newly negotiated and redefined. The first impulses for municipal reform were precipitated by imperial law, attempting to accommodate an already altered social reality.

The implementation of civil equality opened the municipal administration to some Jews. Nevertheless, the new legal option to differentiate between exclusively Jewish and Christian spaces included certain discriminatory potential: Previously established religiously mixed spaces were at risk of disappearing again. The differences between Krakow and Lviv consisted not only in the social composition of their inhabitants. In Krakow the process of developing ethno-confessionally mixed spaces was only beginning when the municipal statute

81 Jan M. Małecki traces the generally high percentage of Jews in the magistrates of Eastern Galicia at the beginning of 20th century back to lower numbers of wealthy and educated Christians, mostly Ruthenians in this region. See Jan M. Małecki »Udział Żydów w organach samorządowych większych miast galicyjskich na początku XX wieku,« in *Polska i Polacy XIX–XX wieku. Studia ofiarowane Profesorowi Mariuszowi Kulczykowskiemu w 70. rocznicę Jego urodzin*, ed. Krzysztof Ślusarek (Kraków: Historia Iagellonica, 2002), 43–60, here 58.

82 Annamaria Orla-Bukowska, »Shtetl Communities: Another Image,« *Polin* 8 (1994): 89–113, here 103; Małecki, »Udział Żydów w organach samorządowych,« 53–60.

83 Wacław Wierzbieniec, »Lvov, Przemyśl and Rzeszów. Jewish Representation in Municipal Self-Governments,« *Simon Dubnow Institute Yearbook* 10 (2011): 255–273, here 257.

came into rule. Therefore, the religious division of property introduced anew by the statute did not meet serious resistance. In contrast, mixed spaces in Lviv were already well established. Hence, the Jewish inhabitants regarded the religious segregation postulated by the municipal statute as a discriminatory act.

The main benefactors of the liberal reforms were wealthy and secularly educated Jews who advanced in the municipal hierarchy and acquired stable positions in the administration where they could influence municipal, as well as Jewish politics. This real power over Jewish communal affairs was the reason why Orthodox Jews in Krakow finally accepted the Progressives in the administration of the Jewish community.[84] These changes can be attributed to the impact of imperial law on the traditional Krakovian municipality. The intervention of the imperial and municipal authorities forced the Orthodox to recognize the Progressives, even though they practiced modified religious rites, were not among the wealthiest, and made up less than one percent of the community.

The Orthodox decided to search for a *modus vivendi* with their new competitors which required the general acceptance of cooperation with the Progressives within the Jewish community. This cooperation concerned not only the problem of how the community should deal with the secular authorities, but also the character of relations between the different factions within the community. The acceptance of the Progressives as official representatives of the Jewish community was the fleeting result of the temporary weakness and disintegration of Orthodoxy. The Orthodox tried to reverse this development by mobilizing an opposition movement that consolidated their ranks and established a modern form of Orthodox politics, including the ability to negotiate with the secular world. Rachel Manekin describes this process as a move »from a traditional society to an Orthodox one – that is, a society that fights the danger of the modern world by employing that world's methods and tools, and by internalizing some of them«.[85]

The implementation of »foreign« imperial law stood at the beginning of the municipal and communal changes described here. It strongly influenced the municipalities by creating opportunities for Jewish participation. As a consequence, some elements of the traditional social order collapsed. Nevertheless, these changes built upon local needs for modern regulation in urban topo-

84 Hanna Kozińska-Witt »The Association of Progressive Jews in Kraków, 1864–1874,« in *Polin* 23 (2010): 119–134; eadem, »Stowarzyszenie Izraelitów Postępowych, 1864–1874,« *Biuletyn Żydowskiego Instytutu Historycznego* 192 (1999): 19–32. These articles summarize the results of my doctoral thesis. See Hanna Kozińska-Witt, *Die Krakauer Jüdische Reformgemeinde 1864–1874*, Ph.D. thesis, Tübingen 1996.

85 Manekin, *Orthodox Jewry*, 174 and 179.

graphy and legal orders, as the old ones had become outdated. For example, strict divisions between Jewish and non-Jewish spaces no longer existed in their original sense. The traditional segregation was seen as an obstacle to the development of the municipalities into modern cities as it excluded part of their inhabitants from participating in local administration and by segregating areas by religion.

Imperial law provided a structural framework for changes, which were negotiated in various arenas among the representatives of different local milieus and groups. The results of this process differed depending on the social context of each municipality. Nevertheless, imperial law served to influence every level of regional administration and every dimension of local reality, including citizenship and confessional affiliation.

Hanna Kozińska-Witt

The Institute for Nationality Research (1921–1939) – A Think Tank for Minority Politics in Poland?

On the evening of May 16, 1928, more than a dozen members of the Polish parliament, an even larger number of scholars, and several journalists convened in the representative Hall of the Mazovian Dukes in Warsaw. The meeting had an informal character – it was announced as a social gathering – and no special topic or speaker was announced. Nevertheless, the meeting itself was quite special. The guests had been invited by the Institute for Nationality Research (*Instytut Badań Spraw Narodowościowych*, IBSN), which organized such events in order to:

> provide an opportunity for representatives of Polish society to come into contact with representatives of non-Polish societies in an informal atmosphere and to contribute in this way to the participants getting to know one another better.[1]

At the time, the members of these supposedly different national societies had all lived for almost ten years in an independent Polish state. Yet – as the language of this quote indicates – for many of that time it seemed to be natural that each of the national groups formed its own society within the state, societies, therefore, that needed to be brought together.

Among the guests were representatives and MPs of Polish as well as German, Jewish, and Belarusian parties, journalists of the Ukrainian newspaper *Dilo* (»The Deed«), the Jewish daily *Nasz Przegląd* (»Our Review«), and many Polish, Jewish, Belarusian, and Ukrainian scholars. Other public figures were also present, such as Stanisław Bukowiecki,[2] chairman of the Polish General Public Prosecutor's

1 »[...] dać sposobność zetknięcia się na gruncie towarzyskim przedstawicielom społeczeństwa polskiego z przedstawicielami społeczeństw niepolskich i przyczynić się w ten sposób do wzajemnego bliższego poznania się,« in: »Zebranie towarzyskie Instytutu,« in: *Sprawy Narodowościowe* 2, no. 2 (1928): 310.

2 Stanisław Bukowiecki (1867–1944), lawyer, publicist, minister of justice of the Polish Regency Council 1917–1918, organizer and chairman of the Polish Office of the Attorney General 1919–1939. *Encyklopedia Historii Drugiej Rzeczypospolitej*, s.v. »Stanisław Bukowiecki.«

office, historians Marceli Handelsman,[3] Ignacy Schiper,[4] and Majer Bałaban,[5] linguists Roman Smal-Stocki[6] and Ivan Ohienko,[7] the rabbi of the Great Synagogue in Warsaw and director of the Institute for Judaic Studies (*Instytut Nauk Judaistycznych*), Mojżesz Schorr,[8] as well as Stanisław Thugutt,[9] former vice premier and director of the IBSN, and its secretary general, Stanisław Józef Paprocki,[10] to mention only a few. As reported in a short note in *Sprawy*

3 Marceli Handelsman (1882–1945), one of the most influential and internationally recognized Polish historians of that time, professor of Warsaw University, worked several times as an advisor to the government in international negotiations. Originally from a Jewish family, he converted to Catholicism. *Polski Słownik Biograficzny*, s.v. »Marceli Handelsman.«

4 Ignacy Schiper (1884–1943), historian of Polish-Jewish economic and cultural history and Zionist politician. From 1922 to 1927 member of the Sejm, from its founding in 1927, lecturer at the Institute for Judaic Studies (Instytut Nauk Judaistycznych – INJ) in Warsaw. *Encyclopaedia Judaica*, 2nd ed., s.v. »Ignacy Schiper.«

5 Majer Bałaban (1877–1942), one of the most influential historians in Polish-Jewish history, active Zionist, 1920–1930 head of the *Tahkemoni* rabbinical Seminar in Warsaw, one of the founders and later director of the INJ, first professor for Jewish History at a Polish University. *Encyclopaedia Judaica*, 2nd ed., s.v. »Meir Balaban.«

6 Roman Smal-Stocki (1893–1969) born in Chernivitsi, scholar, politician and diplomat, after WWI representative of the Western Ukrainian National Republic (1918–1919) and later special envoy of the Ukrainian National Republic (1921–1923) to Berlin, 1923–1924 professor of Slavic linguistics in Prague, 1925 lecturer, later professor at Warsaw University, secretary of the Ukraiński Instytut Naukowy in Warsaw (1930–1939). *Encyclopedia of Ukraine*, s.v. »Roman Smal-Stotsky.«

7 Ivan Ohienko (1882–1972), in Polish also Jan Ogijenko, monastic name Ilarion, scholar, politician, Orthodox metropolitan, co-organizer and first rector of the Kamianets-Podilskyi University in 1918, minister of education and then minister of religious affairs 1919–1924 (from 1920 in exile) of the Ukrainian National Republic, from 1926–1932 professor of Church Slavonic at Warsaw University. *Encyclopedia of Ukraine*, s.v. »Ivan Ohiienko.«

8 Mojżesz Schorr (1874–1941), historian, orientalist and rabbi, professor for Semitic languages and history of the ancient Orient first at Lviv and later at Warsaw University, from 1923 rabbi at Warsaw's Great Synagogue, founder and first director of the Institute for Judaic Studies, member of the Polish Academy of Arts and Sciences, from 1935 to 1938 member of the Polish Senate. *Encyclopaedia Judaica*, 2nd ed., s.v. »Mojżesz Schorr.«

9 Stanisław August Thugutt (1873–1941), politician and leader of the Polish cooperative movement, 1918–1919 minister of interior, 1922–1927 member of the Sejm, and 1924–1925 vice premier and minister without portfolio in the government of Władysław Grabski. *Kto był kim w Drugiej Rzeczypospolitej*, s.v. »Stanisław August Thugutt.«

10 Stanisław Józef Paprocki (1895–1976), lawyer, political and social activist, follower of Józef Piłsudski, initiated the founding of the Union for the Reform

Narodowościowe (»Nationality Affairs«), the institute's journal, the meeting lasted until midnight due to the »animated conversations«.[11]

The meeting took place a few months after the IBSN – originally founded as a private initiative in 1921 – had been thoroughly restructured, professionalized, and integrated into a network of governmental and semi-governmental institutions dealing with minority questions. The aim of the event was to present the institute as an institution that not only researched minority issues but which was also able to function as an intermediary between the minorities' representatives, on the one hand, and the government and state administration, on the other. In this manner, the IBSN showed that it was able to create a space where the political and social elites of different national groups could come together with Polish politicians and state administrators on an informal basis. This made it possible to work toward an atmosphere of trust for possible future cooperation. And trust was an important factor in the political system of Piłsudski's Poland, where the achievement of a balance of interests through parliamentary struggle was not considered appropriate as a means of serving the ›interests of the state‹. Men of trust *(mężowie zaufania)* in turn had considerable influence on governmental decision making.[12]

The issue of national minorities and their integration into the Polish state, which emerged after World War I, was one of the most difficult political questions of the time. In fact, it remained unresolved throughout the twenty years of the Second Polish Republic's existence. When the state was invaded by German and Soviet troops in September 1939, there was no solution in sight that would have satisfied all sides. Nevertheless, despite the relatively short time and the great economic and political problems the new independent state had to face, various ideas and concepts for a solution were developed, proposed, and discussed, with some of them being enacted. The Institute for Nationality Research was an important actor in this field and set the stage for many such attempts.

In this article I will focus on a group of people – mainly scholars, politicians, and officers of the higher ministerial administration – who are not all widely known, but were well networked and, as experts[13] on minority issues, had

of the Republic (*Związek Naprawy Rzeczypospolitej* – ZNR) in 1926 and was its secretary general from 1926–1929, from January 1926 secretary of the IBSN, which he directed from April 1927 to September 1939 as secretary general. *Polski Słownik Biograficzny*, s.v. »Stanisław Józef Paprocki.«

11 »Zebranie towarzyskie Instytutu,« *Sprawy Narodowościowe* 2, no. 2 (1928): 310.

12 Andrzej Chojnowski, *Piłsudczycy u władzy: Dzieje Bezpartyjnego Bloku Współpracy z Rządem*(Wrocław et al.: Ossolineum, 1986), 33–36.

13 On the role of experts and their influence on politics in Poland and other countries of Central and Eastern Europe of that period, see Martin Kohlrausch,

considerable influence on the Polish minority politics of the time. In this context, I present the IBSN as an institution that would today be called a think tank[14] for minority policy. In the first part of the article I will show how the IBSN emerged and how it developed as an institution for minority research and related policy advice in the years before and soon after the coup d'état of Józef Piłsudski in May 1926. In the second part, I will examine its function as an intermediary between the state and minorities by analyzing how the research, discussions, and gatherings organized by the IBSN influenced the development of laws concerning religious groups in Poland.

The legal status of the Orthodox Church and the Jewish community in Poland – the two largest non-Catholic religious communities – was widely unregulated due to the process of transformation after World War I.[15] At the same time, the vast majority of those from different religious groups affected by the lack of regulations were considered to belong to a different nationality than the ethnic Poles,[16] and thus the issue was one of the most important within the field of minority policy. During the law-making process the IBSN did not only provide its expertise to the lawmakers, but also offered Jewish and Ukrainian political groups a forum to articulate their expectations concerning this legis-

Katrin Steffen, and Stefan Wiederkehr, »Introduction,« in *Expert Cultures in Central Eastern Europe: The Internationalisation of Knowledge and the Transformation of Nation States after World War I*, eds. Martin Kohlrausch, Katrin Steffen, and Stefan Wiederkehr (fibre: Osnabrück, 2010), 9–30, here 9–25 (online in: http://www.perspectivia.net).

14 On the definition of think tanks, see Diane Stone, »Think Tanks and Policy Analysis,« in *Handbook of Public Policy Analysis: Theory, Methods, and Politics*, eds. Frank Fischer, Gerald J. Miller, and Mara S. Sidney (New York: Marchel Dekker Inc., 2006), 149–158. Similar institutions also existed in other fields, such as the Instytut Wschodni in Warsaw and the Instytut Naukowo-Badawczy Europy Wschodniej in Vilnius which worked in the field of Eastern policy and the Instytut Bałtycki in Toruń, which dealt with the development of the north-western parts of Poland.

15 The legal basis of the Orthodox church had been completely unclear until the Provisional Regulations on the Relationship of the Government to the Orthodox Church in Poland (*Tymczasowe przepisy o stosunku rządu do Kościoła prawosławnego w Polsce*) was issued on 30 January 1922 although, even afterwards, many questions – especially concerning the property of the church remained unsolved. Krzysztof Krasowski, *Związki wyznaniowe w II Rzeczypospolitej, studium historyczno-prawne* (Warszawa–Poznań: PWN, 1988), 128–158. The legal situation of the Jewish communities was even more complicated, as the different legal regulations of the former partition power remained at least partly in force, leading to the legal situation of the Jewish communities differing quite strongly between the former partitions of Poland. Ibid., 179–190.

16 A small number of Jews and Orthodox Christians considered themselves to be Poles of Mosaic or Orthodox confession.

lation and to come into contact with Polish politicians and the country's ministerial bureaucracy. Through this constellation, I argue, the IBSN's work had a considerable impact on the political process of constructing and partly establishing a legal basis for the relations between the religious communities and the state.

The Emergence of the Institute for Nationality Research

In the first years after WWI the public debate over national minorities and their role in the Polish state was quite tense, especially after Poland was forced to sign the 1919 Minorities Treaty in order to receive international recognition as an independent state. This was, regardless of the treaty's content, perceived as a great injustice by all Polish political camps, as the regulations for minority protection were only imposed on certain countries and were not universally binding for all states. The debates on minority rights in the constitutional Sejm were also heated, especially between the right-wing National Democrats and the Jewish deputies.[17] In this atmosphere, a circle of politicians and scholars, including people such as Szymon Askenazy,[18] Stanisław Thugutt, Marceli Handelsman, Tadeusz Hołówko,[19] Stanisław Stempowski[20] and Leon Wasilewski,[21] came

17 The 11 Jewish and 8 German MPs were the only representation of national minorities in the constitutional Sejm; Paweł Korzec, »Der Block der Nationalen Minderheiten im Parlamentarismus Polens des Jahres 1922,« *Zeitschrift für Ostforschung* 24, no. 2 (1975): 193–220, here 198.

18 Szymon Askenazy (1866–1935), Polish historian and diplomat, member of the Jewish Assimilationist Party, chair of modern history at Lviv University before WWI. During WWI in Switzerland, where he supported the struggle for Polish independence as editor of the *Moniteur Polonais*, 1920–1923 Polish representative at the League of Nations. *YIVO Encyclopedia of Jews in Eastern Europe*, s.v. »Szymon Askenazy,« http://www.yivoencyclopedia.org (accessed August 1, 2014).

19 Tadeusz Hołówko (1889–1931), politician and journalist, until 1926 member of the Polish Socialist Party, follower of Józef Piłsudski, vice president of the Nonpartisan Bloc for Cooperation with the Government (*Bezpartyjny Blok Współpracy z Rządem* – BBWR), from 1927–1930 director of the Eastern Department in the Ministry of Foreign Affairs, murdered by Ukrainian nationalists in summer 1931 in Truskawec, Galicia. *Polski Słownik Biograficzny*, s.v. »Tadeusz Hołówko.«

20 Stanisław Stempowski (1870–1952), politician, social activist, journalist, and translator of several books into Polish, supporter of the Polish Socialist Party before WWI, 1920–1921 Minister of Agriculture and later Minister without Portfolio in several governments of the Ukrainian National Republic, 1924–1939 director of the Library of the Ministry of Agriculture. *Polski Słownik Biograficzny*, s.v. »Stanisław Stempowski.«

21 Leon Wasilewski (1870–1936), scholar, politician, and diplomat, 1918–1919 Polish Minister for Foreign Affairs, 1920–1921 Polish ambassador to Estonia,

together, sharing the conviction that minority questions in Poland should be solved peacefully and in mutual agreement with the respective groups. In order to better realize this goal, they promoted the foundation of an institute for research on nationalities. In this context, minority issues could be researched and discussed on a scholarly basis outside the political arena. At a meeting on December 4, 1921, Marceli Handelsman, who had proposed the formation of such an institute, stressed its necessity due to:

> the short-lived tenure of our ministerial offices, the underdevelopment of views on ethnic minorities in society and political parties, the lack of knowledge about them from the point of view of Polish foreign interests and especially because of the ignorance towards these issues, even among Poland's most distinguished citizens.[22]

While Handelsman's initiative for such an institution found support among the group, his original idea that the institute, in addition to its scholarly work, should develop political programs and support the government in policy-making, was rejected due to the political diversity of those attending the meeting. At another meeting later that month, the plans became more concrete: The institute was to mainly organize lectures and discussions on topics related to its activities, while the members of the institute were to form commissions on each national minority living in Poland. They were then to research the problems of the respective group and discuss them with its members.[23] However, over the first few years of its existence, the activities of the IBSN did not in fact extend beyond a number of lectures and the publication of one single pamphlet.[24] By 1924 the work of the institute had already come to a halt, mainly due to a lack of funds.[25]

1921 delegate at the Treaty of Riga negotiations, member of the Polish Socialist Party, from 1924 head of the Institute of Modern Polish History, died in Warsaw 1936. *Kto był kim w Drugiej Rzeczypospolitej*, s.v. »Leon Wasilewski.«

22 »krótkotrwałość istnienia naszych gabinetów ministerialnych, niewyrobienie poglądów na sprawę mniejszości narodowych wśród społeczeństwa i partji [sic] politycznych, nieinformowanie o nich z punktu widzenia interesów państwowych polskich zagraniczy, a zwłaszcza ze względu na nieznajomość tych spraw nawet pośród najwybitniejszych ludzi w Polsce.« Biblioteka Uniwersytecka w Warszawie, Dział Rękopisów, sygnatura (file) 1562, kartka (folio) 43.

23 Ibid.

24 Among others, the following lectures and discussions were held: Tadeusz Hołówko on the nationality policies of the PPS, Stanisław Thugutt on the question of eastern Galicia, and Edward Maliszewski on relations among nationalities in Poland. See ibid.; Mirosław Boruta, »Instytut Badań Spraw Narodowościowych (1921–1939). Z dziejów polskich badań naukowych nad problematyką etniczną,« *Przegląd Polonijny* 11, no. 2 (1985): 63–85, here 65. Maliszewski's lecture was published by the IBSN: Edward Maliszewski, *Stosunki narodowościowe w Polsce* (Warszawa: Instytut Badań Spraw Narodowościowych w

The following year, however, attempts were undertaken to revive the IBSN. When Władysław Grabski's government appointed an expert committee[26] on minority questions in 1925, the situation seemed to be promising for an institution that could provide expertise in the field and thus influence politics, especially as, of its three members, Aleksander Zwierzyński,[27] Leon Wasilewski, and Henryk Loewenherz,[28] the latter two had been connected to the institute.[29] In order to revive the institute, Tadeusz Hołówko began as director in December 1925,[30] and in early spring 1926, the IBSN sent a short announcement to the press, which presented the institute to the public and invited minority parties and organizations in Poland as well as Polish institutions dealing with minority issues to cooperate on the project.[31] The description of the institute's activity had also been expanded somewhat, as it now explicitly mentioned its interest in Polish minorities abroad. The major difference from the early 1920's was that the IBSN now also aimed at becoming a political actor. In the attached description this was phrased in the following way:

> The Institute for Nationality Research in Poland aims at providing the Polish society with an understanding of the life of national minorities in Poland through the publication of collected material, the submission of memoranda to the state authorities and legislators, and the organization of lectures and conferences. In

Polsce, 1923), while Hołówko published a pamphlet on his own: Tadeusz Hołówko, *Kwestia narodowościowa w Polsce* (Warszawa: Księgarnia Robotnicza, 1922). This was at least partly based on his lecture in the IBSN.

25 Boruta, »Instytut Badań Spraw Narodowościowych,« 66.

26 »Dokumenty w sprawie polityki narodowościowej władz Polskich po przewrocie majowym,« *Dzieje Najnowsze* 3 (1972): 137–169, here 152.

27 Aleksander Zwierzyński (1880–1958), politician and journalist, 1922–1935 member of the Sejm, first for the *Związek Ludowo-Narodowy*, later for the *Stronnictwo Narodowe*, 1920–1938 editor of the *Dziennik Wileński*. *Encyklopedia Historii Drugiej Rzeczypospolitej*, s.v. »Aleksander Zwierzyński.«

28 Henryk Loewenherz (1871–1936), lawyer, politician, member of the Polish Sejm and Senate, until 1922 member of the Polish Socialist Party, delegate to the Paris peace conference, where he took part in the negotiations on the eastern Border of Poland, 1928 elected to the Sejm and 1930 to the Senate, both times on the list of the BBWR. *Polski Słownik Biograficzny*, s.v. »Henryk Loewenherz.«

29 Both of them were connected to the IBSN and the circles that had founded it, though their names were not mentioned in the declaration of 1926. They did however appear on the first published list of members of the institute of 1928. »Z Instytutu Badań Spraw Narodowościowych, Członkowie Rzeczywiści Instytutu,« *Sprawy Narodowościowe* 2, no. 2 (1928): 309–310.

30 Stanisław J. Paprocki, »Ś. p. Tadeusz Hołówko wobec problemów narodowościowych,« in *Sprawy Narodowościowe* 5, no. 4–5 (1931): 381–398, here 381.

31 The declaration probably appeared in several journals and newspapers around April 1926. See »Instytut dla Badań Spraw Narodowościowych w Polsce,« *Droga*, no. 3–4 (1926): 80–81; »Instytut Badań Spraw Narodowościowych w Polsce,« *Głos Prawdy*, April 17, 1926.

> this way the institute intends to take part in the creation of the conditions necessary for the friendly and harmonious co-existence of the nationalities that are part of the Republic.[32]

However, the real turning point came half a year later with the coup d'état of Józef Piłsudski, when the political conditions in Poland changed fundamentally and seemed to open up the opportunity for a different nationality policy.

The Redesign of the Institute after the Coup d'État of 1926

When Piłsudski and his followers seized power in May 1926 with a platform of »moral renewal« (*odnowa moralna*) and »recovery« (*sanacja*), expectations were high for the new administration. Among the problems to be solved by the new government, minority issues took a prominent place. As the representatives of national minorities perceived Piłsudski as generally friendly towards citizens of non-Polish nationality, the hope for a change in nationality policy seemed to be justified. Despite these hopes, however, the new government in fact remained silent on the topic.[33]

In response to this silence, on June 16, 1926, the IBSN organized a discussion with Sejm members and other representatives of the Ukrainian and Belarusian population in Poland. Following this discussion and based on its outcome Hołówko held a lecture a week later, in which he developed a program of how the *Sanacja* – as Piłsudski's government was called referring to its slogan – should act in regard to the *Kresy*,[34] as the eastern territories of the Polish state were known, and to Eastern Galicia in order to satisfy the needs of their Ukrainian and Belarusian inhabitants.[35] He suggested a reform of the administration, the

32 »Instytut badań spraw narodowościowych w Polsce ma na celu przez publikowanie zgromadzonego materiału, składanie memoriałów do władz państwowych i ustawodawczych, urządzenie odczytów, wykładów i konferencyj przyczyniać się do bliższego poznania się społeczeństwa polskiego z życiem mniejszości narodowych w Polsce i w ten sposób współdziałać w wytworzeniu warunków przyjaznego i zgodnego współżycia narodowości wchodzące w skład Rzeczypospolitej,« »Instytut dla Badań Spraw Narodowościowych w Polsce,« *Droga*, 81.

33 Andrzej Chojnowski, *Koncepcje polityki narodowościowej rządów Polskich w latach 1921–1939* (Wrocław et al.: Ossolineum, 1979), 73–74.

34 The term *Kresy* literally means borderlands and has a somewhat mythical meaning, as it refers not only to the eastern territories of the Second Republic but also to the far larger eastern part of early modern Poland-Lithuania. Werner Benecke, »Die Kresy – Ein Mythos der polnischen Geschichte,« in *Politische Mythen im 19. und 20. Jahrhundert in Mittel- und Osteuropa*, eds. Heidi Hein-Kircher and Hans Henning Hahn (Marburg: Verlag Herder Institut, 2006), 257–266.

35 »Dyskusję z mniejszościami narodowemi w Pałacu Książąt Mazowieckich,« *Głos Prawdy*, Juli 3, 1926. A reworked version of his lecture appeared as: Tadeusz

educational system and the regulation of religious questions. The Ukrainians and Belarusians were to be allowed to develop a »full national and cultural life according to the western European model.«[36]

In August 1926, when the Council of Ministers dealt with minority issues, it became clear that there was no reason to expect rapid change. The Minister of Internal Affairs, Kazimierz Młodzianowski, enthusiastically presented his guidelines for the minority policy, which were based on the concept of »state assimilation« (*asymilacja państwowa*). Its basic idea was that minorities should not be forced to become Poles by assimilation but instead loyal citizens of the Polish state, who enjoy the freedoms of cultural and social development in exchange for their loyalty. Młodzianowski's plan therefore specified numerous measures intended to accommodate the different minorities.[37]

However, Piłsudski did not show much interest in pursuing political activism on the issue. As the protocol of the meeting recorded, he advised »not to overestimate the importance of this [minority] problem«, as the state could not »allow its vital interests to take a back seat«.[38] He was especially unwilling to make any compromises with regard to Polish being the sole state language, which had »to be taught in every school within the state's territory,« in which »all state activities« had to be conducted, and which had to be used by »courts, administration, and the local government.«[39] Taking into consideration that no political decision could be made without Piłsudski's consent after the May coup, his clear standpoint meant the end of any forthcoming reform regarding minority politics. Still, he pointed out that the government would need more detailed information on minority issues in order to make later decisions.[40]

However, as was the case with most other political plans, such decisions were not communicated to the public. As Prime Minister Kazimierz Bartel stated, his government wanted to »keep quiet and work«.[41] When Aleksander Zwierzyński, the representative of the National Democrats, resigned from the expert committee, Hołówko took his place,[42] which could be understood as a reaction to

Hołówko, »Metody i drogi sanacji stosunków we wschodnej Galicji i województwach wschodnich,« *Droga*, no. 6–7 (1926): 46–55.

36 »życia narodowego i kulturalnego, na wzorach Zachodnej Europy,« ibid., 47.

37 Madajczyk, »Dokumenty w sprawie polityki narodowościowej,« 140–142, 148–160.

38 »radzi nie przeceniać znaczenia tego problemu. Przy jego regulowaniu państwo nie może usuwać na drugi plan swoich zasadniczych interesów,« ibid., 143.

39 Ibid.

40 Ibid., 144.

41 Kazimierz Bartel, *Mowy parlamentarny* (Warszawa: Drukarnia Państwowa, 1928), 19. Quoted from Chojnowski, *Koncepcje polityki narodowościowej*, 74.

42 Chojnowski, *Koncepcje polityki narodowościowej*, 81 (for more details see footnote 57).

Hołówko's criticism. Henceforth all members of the committee were linked to the IBSN. However, this did not mean that the government was taking any of the steps Hołówko suggested concerning the politics in the *Kresy* and Galicia. Not being able to see any progress in the issue, he published several articles criticizing the lack of activity despite the fact that he was part of the Piłsudski camp himself.[43] Leon Wasilewski also made critical remarks in the press, although more measured ones.[44]

As the discussions organized by the IBSN under Hołówko as well as its proactive support for a rapid reform of minority policy show, the institute was poised to establish itself as a driving force in the public debate on minority issues. This, of course, was not in the interest of the government, which did not want to be faced with a discussion on its minority policies. The government therefore set out to take steps to solve this dilemma: When Hołówko became director of the Eastern Department of the Ministry of Foreign Affairs (*Ministerstwo Spraw Zagranicznych*, MSZ) in early 1927, the post was surely an advancement to his career. Yet, as Andrzej Chojnowski pointed out, it was actually meant to deflect his activism in the inner-Polish debate on minority questions.[45] Hołówko's resignation as director of the IBSN soon after his appointment to the ministry post suggests that he accepted this compromise.[46]

Around the time of Hołówko's resignation as director, there was a complete overhaul of the IBSN. It appears that government circles offered the institute an arrangement which seemed to be beneficial for both sides. Several ministries ensured stable financial support to the institute in exchange for access to its expertise and – just as importantly – for the institute to agree to cease any political activity.

The IBSN was thus included in a process of strategic realignment of the state's infrastructure for minority politics. While the aforementioned experts' committee was dissolved in 1927, the structure of the Ministry of Internal Affairs (*Ministerstwo Spraw Wewnętrznych*, MSW) was reorganized and a special Nationalities' Section (*Wydział Narodowościowy*) was established in 1927.[47] It was responsible for the supervision of the political and social lives of minority groups in Poland, as a means of keeping the government agencies informed, but

43 Ibid., 82–83.

44 *EPOKA*, May 3, 1927.

45 Chojnowski, *Koncepcje polityki narodowościowej*, 85–86.

46 At the meeting of the IBSN's Board of April 7, 1927, Hołówko's resignation as director of the institute was announced as a result of his new post in the MSZ. *Sprawy Narodowościowe* 1, no 2 (1927): 216.

47 ST. J. B., »O kompetencje Wydziału Narodowościowego Ministerstwa Spraw Wewnętrznych,« *Przełom* 1, no. 9 (1926): 5–8.

was also responsible for the preparation of and advisement on laws and other legal measures concerning minorities. Still, the Nationalities' Section mostly acted at the administrative level, which led to certain restrictions to its outreach.

In this context, the IBSN seemed a promising partner, especially as many of its founders had been connected to the new government's camp.[48] The IBSN's task in this new network was indeed manifold. On the one hand, the institute was meant to make up for the lack of data on minorities, as Piłsudski had indicated. On the other hand, the informal contact the institute maintained with researchers and politicians from the different minority groups could be helpful with regard to new efforts in this field. This was especially important if one takes into account how politics functioned under Piłsudski, who despised the parliament along with party politics, and preferred matters to be regulated behind the scenes by men of trust.[49] In this regard, the IBSN was meant to function as a kind of intermediary between the minorities and the state agencies. In addition, the institute took on several functions in the sphere of international minority politics, which are beyond the scope of the present discussion.[50] To fulfill these functions in the intended way, the IBSN formally remained an independent institution. However, it changed in practice from a civil society initiative into a semi-official institution, which was almost entirely financed by state agencies, most prominently including the MSW, the MSZ, and the Ministry of Religion and Education (*Ministerstwo Wyznań Religijnych i Oświecenia Publicznego*, MWRiOP),[51] and as such the institute had to remain neutral in the political debate.

The person mainly responsible for that transformation was Stanisław Józef Paprocki, who had been the councilor (*radca*) in charge of press supervision at the MSW from October 1925, and who joined the IBSN in January 1926 to run the institute's office. When it became clear in early 1927 that Hołówko would resign as director of the IBSN, Paprocki left the MSW and succeeded Hołówko as secretary general of the institute. From the middle of 1926 through 1929, Paprocki also served as the secretary general of the Union of the Reform of the Republic (*Związek Naprawy Rzeczpospolitej*, ZNR),[52] which was the organization

48 This included Hołówko, Wasilewski, Handelsman, Loewenherz, and many more.

49 Chojnowski, *Piłsudczycy u władzy*, 33–36.

50 In this context the IBSN also observed the situation of the Polish minority abroad, the minority policy in other countries and neighboring countries in particular, and the international development of minority rights and the minority issue; see Boruta, »Instytut Badań Spraw Narodowościowych,« 66–68.

51 Stanisław J. Paprocki, interview, *Wiedza i Życie*, no. 2 (1931): 181–184; Boruta, »Instytut Badań Spraw Narodowościowych,« 66.

52 Archiwum Akt Nowych (hereafter AAN), Prezydium Rady Ministrów (hereafter PRM), sygn. *akta grupowe* 46–40, k. 10.

of the left-wing, democratic fraction of the Piłsudski camp.[53] Moreover, Paprocki was one of the proponents of the concept of »state assimilation«. As Paprocki put it in an article on the minority question in the ZNR Journal *Przełom* (»Breakthrough«) in February 1927, this meant that: »it is in the interest of the state that citizens who belong to national minorities should want to accept the interests of the state as their own.«[54]

Under Paprocki, the institute reformed its statutes and outlined its fields of research in the following areas: 1. Minority issues in the international sphere, as well as in international law; 2. minority questions in Poland; and 3. minority problems outside Poland.[55] The IBSN created its three sections in line with these three areas.[56] In the context of this article, I will focus on the work of the second section dealing with *inner*-Polish affairs. That section was organized in several commissions, with one each for Jewish, Ukrainian, and German affairs, as well as one Russian and Czech and one for Lithuanian and Belarusian matters.[57] These commissions were usually composed of IBSN members as well as researchers and politicians of the respective minority groups. The commissions, which organized lectures and discussion events, were again subdivided into thematic groups. Aside from the above-mentioned meetings, the commissions were the most effective tool to gain representatives of certain minority groups for the institute.

With Paprocki at the head of the IBSN, the institute became more professional, changed its statutes, and began to publish the journal *Sprawy Narodowościowe* (SN). Many articles published in the journal also appeared in the abridged French edition *Questions Minoritaires*, which the institute began publishing in 1928. The SN, which is still a widely used source for researchers, also demonstrated the close links between the IBSN and the Nationalities' Section of the Ministry of Internal Affairs. The officials of the Nationalities' Section regularly published articles in *Sprawy Narodowościowe*, though without mentioning who their employer was. Aside from Aleksander Hafftka,[58] head of

53 On the ZNR, see Przemysław Waingertner, *»Naprawa« (1926–1939): z dziejów obozu pomajowego* (Warszawa: Semper, 1999).

54 Stanisław J. Paprocki, »Interes państwa i mniejszości narodowe,« *Przełom* 2, no. 4 (1926): 2.

55 AAN, Ministerstwo Spraw Zagranicznych (hereafter MSZ), sygn. 5314, k. 21.

56 Boruta, »Instytut Badań Spraw Narodowościowych,« 66–67.

57 Ibid.

58 Aleksander Hafftka (1892–1964), Polish state official, publicist, 1920–1922 official in the Central Lithuanian Ministry of Foreign Affairs, 1924–1925 editor of the daily *Głos powszechny* (General Voice) in Częstochowa, 1927–1937 councilor for Jewish affairs in the Ministry of Internal Affairs; *Yidisher Gezelshaftlekher Leksikon*, s.v. »Aleksander Haftka.«

the Jewish division of the Nationalities' Section from 1927 to 1937, the articles were all published under pen names,[59] even those written by the officials of other ministries. Another hint pointing to close ties was a chronicle of events for the various minorities in Poland, published as a regular section of the SN. The reports published in the journal often seem to be shortened – and thus less detailed – versions of those that were written by the Nationalities' Section.[60]

In October 1927, according to its new statute, the IBSN board of directors appointed 34 full members, a number which roughly doubled by the time the institute ceased to exist in September 1939. Many of its founders remained members, including Handelsman, Thugutt, Hołówko, and Wasilewski, to be joined by other well-known scholars like Stanisław Kutrzeba[61] and Florian Znanecki.[62] Membership was also a tool to strengthen ties to a number of representatives of minority groups such as Majer Bałaban, Mojżesz Schorr, Stefan Lubliner,[63] Roman Smal-Stocki, and Ivan Ohienko.[64] While most of the IBSN's work was conducted by the institute's office, managed by Paprocki, its members took part in several commissions, organized and held lectures, and wrote articles for the SN.

In summer 1929, Paprocki described the outcome of the institute's changes in a letter to the Minister of Foreign Affairs, asking for more subsidies:

59 Zygmunt Kalksein, responsible for Germans in Poland, published articles in *Sprawy Narodowościowe* and a book in the IBSN series as Zygmunt Stoliński; Rajmund Różycki, dealing with Ukrainians, published in *Sprawy Narodowościowe* as M. Feliński; Stanisław Łaniewski, who worked on Belarusians in the MSW, published as Stanisław Ełski.

60 Some of the reports in *Sprawy Narodowościowe* on the Jews in Poland were even signed by Aleksander Hafftka, who was responsible for the reports on Jewish affairs in his ministry office. It seems very unlikely that he wrote two completely different reports on the same questions.

61 Stanisław Kutrzeba (1876–1946), scholar and politician, professor at the Jagiellonian University in Kraków and head of the Polish Acadamy of Arts and Sciences (1939–1946), in 1918 member of the Polish delegation to the Treaty of Versailles negotiations. *Encyklopedia Historii Drugiej Rzeczypospolitej*, s. v. »Stanisław Kutrzeba.«

62 Florian Znaniecki, born 1882 in Świątniki, founder of the Polish Sociological Institute in Poznań in 1921 and 1920–1939, professor at the Adam Mickiewicz University there, being in New York when WWII began, he stayed in the USA; *Internationales Soziologenlexikon*, 2nd ed., s. v. »Florian Znaniecki.«

63 Stefan Lubliner (1890–1942), journalist, editor of the monthly Polish-Jewish *Rozwaga* (Reflection), volunteer in Piłsudski's Legions during World War I. *Getto Warszawskie*, s. v. »Stefan Lubliner,« http://www.getto.pl (accessed August 8, 2014).

64 »Z Instytutu Badań Spraw Narodowościowych, Członkowie Rzeczywiści Instytutu,« in: *Sprawy Narodowościowe* 2, no. 2 (1928): 309–310.

> The well planned organization of the institute had, on the one hand, ensured its *social* nature [emphasis in the original text], which allowed for unofficial contact with representatives of national minorities and related institutions abroad, while on the other hand, it placed the institute's work on the right track, eliminating political aspects (the establishment of a program in the field of nationality policy), and replaced them by strictly scholarly work. This had the aim of enabling the institute to determine the relevant factors necessary for the establishment of political proposals, while leaving the formulation of such proposals to political organizations and government agents.[65]

What Paprocki expressed in the bureaucratic language of the time was not necessarily the description of the IBSN as it worked – as it was surely not as apolitical as described by Paprocki – but rather as the Polish government agencies considered it to be expedient for their means: an institution providing the government with scholarly collected data. At the same time, it served as an unofficial channel of communication, through which it was possible to obtain information on the state of affairs of minority communities and to stay in contact with all of the political camps among them, regardless of government policies.

From the perspective of the minorities, however, the IBSN was expected to become an institution that would communicate their interests to Polish society and to political decision makers. This notion was demonstrated in an article by Natan Szwalbe,[66] in the Jewish daily *Nasz Przegląd*, which appeared a few days after the IBSN meeting mentioned at the beginning of this article. Szwalbe expressed his hope that the IBSN would function as an intermediary not only with regard to Poland's Jews but also to Germans, Belarusians, and most of all Ukrainians.[67] He argued that the IBSN could play a:

> valuable role if it initiated a broad campaign to raise awareness in Polish society and demonstrated the need for the quickest possible counteraction to the Soviet

65 »W ten sposób pomyślana organizacja instytutu z jednej strony zapewniła mu charakter *społeczny*, umożliwający nieoficialny kontakt z przedstawicielami mniejszości narodowych i instytucjami pokrewnemi zagranicą, z drugiej zaś strony wprowadziła prace instytutu na właściwe tory, eliminując momenty polityczne (ustalenia programu w zakresie polityki narodowościowej) a na ich miejsce wprowadzając prace ściśle badawcze, mające na celu ustalenie elementów niezbędnych dla wyprowadzenia wniosków politycznych, pozostawiając sformulowania tych wniosków organizacjom politycznym i czynnikom rządowym.« AAN, MSZ, sygn. 5314, k. 22.

66 Natan Szwalbe, born 1883, journalist, editor at the Jewish daily *Nasz Przegląd*, head of the press office of the Zionist Organization in Poland. *Baza osób polskich – Polnische Personendatenbank*, s.v. »Natan Szwalbe,« http://baza-nazwisk.de (accessed August 2, 2014).

67 *Nasz Przegląd*, May 25, 1928.

> influence, which would be a positive and constructive cultural and educational measure among the Ukrainians living in Poland.[68]

Concerning the other nationalities, especially Jews and Germans, the task of the IBSN

> »would be much easier if only the decision makers (*sfery miarodajne*) listened to the discussions and conversations held by the institute's direction in a sincere and friendly atmosphere«.[69]

Szwalbe's article shows that the approach of the IBSN – not only towards the discussion of and research into the problems of the different national minorities in Poland but also in terms of having their representatives participate in that process on equal terms – was quite successful as a means of gaining the trust of those circles that were in favor of cooperating with the Polish government to find a balanced solution to the minorities question. Still, they also were aware that the actual influence of the IBSN on the political leadership was rather limited and uncertain. Or, as Szwalbe summarized, »[...] for the moment, this is only wishful thinking. We are still far from fulfilling the promises of the May coup slogans in the field of nationality policy.«[70]

In contrast to Szwalbe's suggestions, the IBSN did not especially aim at influencing public opinion. Instead it provided the government and its ministries with processed information on the respective issues and – much more importantly – it organized gatherings and lecture series, thus providing a space, where »both sides of the barricade« could meet and exchange their thoughts in an informal manner, and where minorities could lobby for their interests.

The legal regulation of the status of religious communities was a field of minority policy that touched the vital interests of a large portion of the national minority population. This was caused by the correlation of religious and national belonging: Lutheran Christians were usually German in national terms, while Greek Catholics were Ukrainian, and Roman Catholics were considered to be Poles and vice versa.[71] Therefore, attempts to regulate the legal basis of religious

68 »Instytut Badań' mógłby w tym przypadku odegrać wdzięczną rolę, gdyby rozwinął wśród społeczeństwa polskiego szeroką akcję uświadamiająca i uwidocznił potrzebę najrychlejszego przeciwdziałania wypływom sowieckim za pomocą pozytywnej, twórczej pracy kulturalno-oświatowej wśród ukraińców zamieszkujących państwo polskie.« Ibid.

69 »miałby znacznie łatwiejsze zadanie, gdyby sfery miarodajne zechciały się przysłuchiwać dyskusjom i rozmowom, prowadzonym w atmosferze szczerej i życzliwej.« Ibid.

70 »Są to jednak na razie pobożne tylko życzenia, jesteśmy wciąż jeszcze dość dalecy od realizacji haseł, głoszonych podczas przewrotu majowego w dziedzinie polityki narodowościowej.« Ibid.

71 This rule, of course, had many exceptions and its perception was stronger in the minds of the people than was its reality. For example, there were also Jews who

communities were inseparably connected with nationality politics. This was a field in which the ISBN possessed sound expertise and access to the relevant personalities from the religious communities, and the government – in need of such knowledge and connections – made use of what its think tank had to offer.

As mentioned above, except for the Catholic Churches, whose legal status was settled in the Concordat with the Vatican of 1925,[72] the status of the other confessions was still only partly or provisionally regulated in the late 1920s. Many regulations concerning the Jewish community and Orthodox Church were not in fact issued until the 1930s. Apart from their strictly religious tasks, the two institutions also fulfilled cultural and social roles for their adherents so that they were also of great interest to Ukrainian and Jewish politicians in Poland, as they held the potential to serve as important forms of support for national movements. In both cases, the IBSN was involved in the gathering of information for such law-making processes. While the members of the institute provided Polish officials with expertise on relevant topics, the institute also served as a forum for Ukrainian and Jewish representatives to make their suggestions known and to lobby for their positions.

The Ukrainization of the Orthodox Church

In 1927, *Sprawy Narodowościowe* already printed an article on the »The Nationality Dispute in the Orthodox Church in Poland«.[73] In the article, Mykola Kovalevskyi,[74] an exiled Ukrainian politician and a regular IBSN collaborator,

considered themselves to be Poles of Mosaic faith, Lutheran Ukrainians, Greek Catholic Poles, and most of all many who did not define themselves in national terms, as for example the so-called *tutejsi* (literally meaning locals). Felix Ackermann argues in his study on the city of Grodno that the categorization of the population along national lines resulted from the founding of Poland as a nation state, which created the need to assign every person to a national group. The Polish administration thus often applied the categories of native language and confession as ethnic factors to this end. Felix Ackermann, *Palimpsest Grodno. Nationalisierung, Nivellierung und Sowjetisierung einer mitteleuropäischen Stadt 1919–1991* (Wiesbaden: Harrassowitz, 2010), 25–27.

72 On the concordat, see Krasiewski, *Związki Wyznaniowe*, 73–82.

73 Mikołaj Kowalewski, »Spór narodowościowy w Cerkwi Prawosławnej w Polsce,« Sprawy Narodowościowe 1, no. 3 (1927): 259–269.

74 Mykola Kovalevskyi, pol. Mikołaj Kowalewski (1892–1957), politician and publicist, activist of the Ukrainian national movement in tsarist Russia, member of the Central Rada of the Ukrainian National Republic, 1917–1918 Minister of Food Supply, 1918–1920 Minister of Agriculture in the Directorate government, after the failure of Ukrainian independence émigré in Poland, worked for the Promethean »Agencja Telegraficzna Express« and the Instytut Wschodni. Mykola Kovalevs'kyi, *Pry Dzherelakh Borotby* (Innsbruck: Maria Kovalevska, 1960), dust jacket text.

described the conflict between the Orthodox Church hierarchy, whose members were mainly of Russian nationality, and Ukrainians from Wolhynia. According to Kovalevskyi, the Ukrainian Orthodox wanted to bring about certain ecclesiastical reforms such as the introduction of the Ukrainian language for sermons and at mass. Laymen also demanded a return to the historical Ukrainian tradition of the Orthodox Church in the Polish-Lithuanian Commonwealth, which would have allowed for more lay influence on the development of the church, »for in the times before the partitions, when the borders of the Polish state reached to the Dnieper, democratic principles dominated in the governance of church matters and in the life of the Orthodox Church.«[75] As the text argues further, this practice had only been replaced later under tsarist rule by a more authoritarian system which suppressed the Ukrainian national character of the church. In »reborn Poland«, Kovalevskyi continued, the desire to return to the old tradition and free itself from the paternalism of the Russian hierarchy was brewing among the Ukrainian population.[76]

The conflict within the Orthodox Church became visible at a time when the legal status of the Church was still unclear and was only based on the »Provisional Regulations on the Relations of the Government to the Orthodox Church in Poland« of 1922.[77] After the May coup, Orthodox Ukrainian church activists hoped that the new government would introduce a more elaborated legal basis for Orthodoxy. As they saw it, of course, this change was hoped to meet their interests rather than those of the predominantly Russian hierarchy, so that they promoted a reform process from within. By 1924 the church had already achieved autocephalous status, i.e. it was an autonomous Orthodox Church in Poland that had cut its ties to the Moscow Patriarchate.[78] As described by Kovalevskyi, the aim was mainly to strengthen the role of the Ukrainian language – and thus of the Ukrainians – within the church and to establish a structure based on the traditions of conciliarity (*sobornist'*), which guaranteed greater lay influence within the church.[79]

75 »W czasach przedrozbiorwych bowiem, kiedy granicy państwa polskiego sięgały po Dniepr, w życiu cerkwi prawosławnej dominowała zasada demokratycznego rządzenia sprawami cerkiewnemi.« Kowalewski, »Spór narodowościowy,« 261.

76 Ibid., 261.

77 Cornelia Schenke, *Nationalstaat und nationale Frage. Polen und die Ukrainer in Wolhynien (1921–1939)*, (Hamburg–München: Dölling und Galitz, 2004), 194–199; Werner Benecke, *Die Ostgebiete der Zweiten Polnischen Republik. Staatsmacht und öffentliche Ordnung in einer Minderheitenregion 1918–1939* (Köln–Weimar–Wien: Böhlau, 1999), 202.

78 Benecke, *Die Ostgebiete der Zweiten Polnischen Republik*, 201–204.

79 Mirosława Papierzyńska-Turek, *Między tradycją a rzeczywistością. Państwo wobec prawosławia* (Warszawa: PWN, 1989), 207.

However, the ideological underpinnings of this grassroots movement in Wolhynia had been prepared by scholars such as Ivan Ohienko, who had been a professor at the Institute for Orthodox Theology (*Studium Teologii Prawosławnej*, STP)[80] at Warsaw University since 1926. In August 1928 he was joined by Oleksandr Lototskyi,[81] who became a professor at the STP as well. After the February Revolution of 1917, they had been ministers in different Ukrainian governments. After Ukrainian independence had failed, both became professors in Prague in the early 1920s, before they resettled in Warsaw. There they became members of the IBSN.[82] In their work, they tried to demonstrate the original Ukrainian character of the Orthodox Church in Kievan Rus, which in their view was only later subordinated by force to the Moscow Patriarchate. According to Lototskyi, who was among the founders of the Autocephalous Ukrainian Orthodox Church in 1919,[83] having a particular national character was in fact one of the distinctive elements of the eastern churches.[84]

When the conflict between the Ukrainization movement and the Russian-oriented camp – to a large extent a conflict between laymen and clerics – surfaced in early 1927, Metropolitan Dionizy[85] tried to mediate in the conflict but ultimately took the side of those closer to the clerics. The advocates of Ukrainization in turn organized a Ukrainian Orthodox Church Congress, which took place in Lutsk in April 1927. The event outraged the leadership of the

80 Ibid., 82.

81 Oleksander Lototskyi, in Polish also Aleksander Łotocki (1870–1939), politician, theologian and church historian, minister of Religion in the Ukrainian government in 1918, one of the founders of the Ukrainian Autocephalous Orthodox Church in 1919, after 1920 émigré in Vienna and Prague, member of the government in exile of the Ukrainian National Republic, since 1929 professor for church history at the Institute for Orthodox Theology (STP) of Warsaw University, 1930–1939 director of the Ukrainian Scientific Institute in Warsaw. *Encyclopedia of Ukraine*, s.v. »Oleksander Lotocky.«

82 Ohienko was a member of the institute since 1928 already. See »Z Instytutu Badań Spraw Narodowościowych, Członkowie Rzeczywiści Instytutu,« *Sprawy Narodowościowe* 2, no 2 (1928): 309; Lotockyi's name appears in the member list of the IBSN of 1932, which was printed in: *Dziesięciolecie działalności Instytutu Badań Spraw Narodowościowych 1922–1932* (Warszawa: Instytut Badań Spraw Narodowościowych, 1932).

83 Andre Partykevich, *Between Kyiv and Constantinopole. Oleksander Lotocky and the Quest for Ukrainian Autocephaly* (Edmonton: Canadian Institute of Ukrainian Studies, 1998), 27–42.

84 Aleksander Łotocki, *Autokefalia, Zasady Autokefalii* (Warszawa: Biblioteka Polska, 1932), 121–122.

85 Dionizy, secular name Konstanty Waledyński (1876–1960), Orthodox bishop, Metropolitan of Warsaw and all Poland, head of the Polish Autocephalous Orthodox Church from 1924–1948. *Kto był kim w Drugiej Rzeczypospolitej*, s.v. »Konstanty Waledyński.«

church even more, who repudiated the lay right to convene such an assembly. Consequently the Synod of Bishops of the Polish Autocephalous Orthodox Church prohibited all clergy members from participating. However, the congress did convene and was composed exclusively of laymen who demanded more rights for the Ukrainians as well as an all-Polish council (*sobór*). Its resolutions were printed in *Sprawy Narodowościowe*.[86] The church leadership reacted with an eparchial assembly two months later, which proclaimed more or less the opposite of the Ukrainian demands. Finally, in summer 1927 both sides started extensive petition campaigns that aimed to win the support of the Ministry of Religion and Education.[87]

The IBSN was another possible channel to influence the government in favor of support for the Ukrainian side. Among its members was – in addition to Ohienko and Lototskyi – Kazimierz Okulicz,[88] who served from August 1926 to October 1928 as director of the Department for Non-Catholic Confessions in the Ministry of Religion and Education. The first visible activity in this context was the previously mentioned article by Mykola Kovalevskyi, who described the conflict with a strong preference for the Ukrainian side. This account was nevertheless published in a Polish scholarly journal, which was probably one of the main sources of information for vast parts of the administration concerned with these matters, so that its impact should not be underestimated. Another occasion, which the supporters of Ukrainization supposedly used to promote their cause, was the »social gathering« of the IBSN in May 1928, at which Okulicz, Ohienko, and Kovalevskyi were present.[89] Though it is not documented who talked to whom or what had been the content of the »animated conversations,« the participants most likely used the occasion to exchange their ideas on the shape and legal basis of the Orthodox Church in Poland.

Indeed the idea of Ukrainization of the Orthodox Church found some support within the Ministry of Religion and Education during the year 1928. In the same issue that reported about the »social gathering«, another article on

86 *Sprawy Narodowościowe* 1, no. 4 (1927): 398–405.

87 Benecke, *Die Ostgebiete der Zweiten Polnischen Republik*, 225–229.

88 Kazimierz Okulicz (1890–1981), politician, journalist and government official, worked for several institutions of the short-lived Republic of Central Lithuania (1920–1922), from 1926–1928 Director of the Confessional Department of the MWRiOP, 1928–1930 member of the Sejm, 1928–1939 member of the editorial board of »Kurier Wileński.« Paweł A. Leszczyński, *Centralna administracja wyznaniowa II RP. Ministerstwo Wyznań Religijnych i Oświecenia Publicznego* (Warszawa: Semper, 2006), 262.

89 »Z Instytutu Badań Spraw Narodowościowych, Członkowie Rzeczywiści Instytutu,« *Sprawy Narodowościowe* 2, no. 2 (1928): 310.

the nationalities issues and system of the Orthodox Church in Poland appeared.[90] It was published under the pen name Wiktor Lubicz, which was used by Wiktor Piotrowicz,[91] who in 1928 for a short time was head of the section for Christian Confessions in the ministry.[92] In his article Piotrowicz evaluates the developments in the Orthodox Church and the pros and cons of the conciliar system from the Polish state's point of view. He came to the conclusion that the nationalization – he also included the much weaker movement for Belarusization in his considerations – would be generally beneficial for the state. He argued that the nationalization of the church would bind the population closer to it and thus lead to the »distraction of the population from the negative influences of communist and seditious propaganda.«[93] He stressed, however, that a campaign of nationalization through the introduction of Ukrainian and Belarusian into ecclesiastical life as well as its democratization through the introduction of the *sobornist'* would also strengthen the national movements of the respective population groups:

> And that is exactly where the need emerges – seen from the state's point of view – to distinguish between the church's objectives and political goals and to direct the national movements within the church along a path of loyalty towards the state.[94]

Still, Piotrowicz advocated the reform of the Orthodox Church more or less along the lines the Ukrainization movement had drawn, as he considered it to be a return to the historical tradition of the Polish Orthodox Church. That was, for him, a way to sever the church's connection to Russian Orthodoxy. The importance of this point for the Polish state originated mainly in the fear that Russia could try to interfere with Polish internal matters under the pretext of supporting Orthodoxy, as it had in 18th-century Poland-Lithuania.[95]

90 Wiktor Lubicz [Piotrowicz], »Z zagadnień narodowościowych i ustrojowych w Cerkwi Prawosławnej w Polsce,« *Sprawy Narodowościowe* 2, no. 2 (1928): 169–190.

91 Wiktor Piotrowicz (1900–1954), publicist and government official, head of the Confessional Department of the Vilna Province administration, in the second half of the 1930s councilor for in the Press Office of the MSW, author of essays and books on confessional questions. *Polski Słownik Biograficzny*, vol. 26, 453–454.

92 Leszczyński, *Centralna administracja*, 269.

93 »do odwrócenia uwagi tej ludności od ujemnych wpływów propagandy komunistycznej i wywrotowej,« Lubicz, »Z zagadnień narodowościowych,« 182.

94 »I tu właśnie powstała potrzeba – z państwowego punktu widzenia – odróżnienia celów cerkiewnych od politycznych i skierowania tego ruchu narodowościowego w Cerkwi na drogę państwowej lojalności.« Ibid., 184.

95 Ibid., 178–179, 189.

This positive evaluation of the Ukrainization movement was also supported by Gustaw Dobrucki, the minister in charge of religious affairs. At a conference of referents for the religious affairs of the eastern provinces, he pleaded for the friendly treatment of the Orthodox Church and acknowledged his support for the democratization of the Orthodox Church as well as the introduction of the languages of the respective population groups into ecclesiastical life.[96] A few days later, however, Prime Minister Piłsudski stepped down from his office and dismissed his government. Under the new Prime Minister, Kazimierz Bartel, the office of the Minister for Religion and Public Education was taken by Kazimierz Świtalski, who had less liberal views on the issue than Dobrucki. In the course of the following months Piotrowicz and Okulicz also left the ministry.[97]

The loss of these officials, who had supported the Ukrainization movement, was a severe throwback, as lobbying had to start anew under different circumstances. Another attempt was undertaken by Ivan Ohienko on January 28, 1929 with a lecture organized by the IBSN as a part of a lecture series on the Ukrainian question. Its title was »The Fate of the Ukrainian Church and Her Current State«.[98] Ohienko's attempt to win over Polish government officials for a policy of Ukrainization was mainly based on a twofold argumentation: First, he idealized the historic relations between an Orthodox Church, as he describes it, of Ukrainian national character and the early modern Polish rulers. According to him, the early modern *Rzeczpospolita* was »extremely important in the history of the Ukrainian church«.[99] Ohienko presented it as a period in which church life flourished and was able to develop its full Ukrainian character with Ukrainian as the language of the Orthodox Church and a fully developed system of conciliarity as the church's inner system of organization. He connected the image of positive historical relations between Poland and the Orthodox Church of Ukrainian character to the present, referring to the recognition of the autocephalous state of the Polish Orthodox Church in 1924 as an act of historical justice:

> We Ukrainians have finally received satisfaction [...] It is on November 13, 1924 that autocephaly was established in Poland. [...] The Muscovite church is not entitled to the Orthodox Church in Poland. Almost 300 years have passed since the violation of the Ukrainian Church but satisfaction was received.[100]

96 Papierzyńska-Turek, *Między tradycją a rzeczywistością*, 239–240.
97 Leszczyński, *Centralna administracja*, 239, 262, 269.
98 The text, including the following discussion, was printed in *Sprawy Narodowościowe*. Jan Ogijenko (Ivan Ohienko), »Losy Cerkwi ukraińskiej i jej stan obecny,« *Sprawy Narodowościowe* 3, no. 1 (1929): 175–183.
99 »nader ważne w historii cerkwi ukraińskiej,« ibid., 175.
100 »My Ukraińcy, otrzymaliśmy satysfakcję. [...] Jest [to] z dnia 13 listopada 1924 r. zaprowadzenie autokefalii w Polsce. [...] cerkiew moskiewska nie ma żadnych

In this quote the second part of Ohienko's argumentation line surfaces as well, in which he emphasizes the anti-Russian sentiment of the Ukrainization movement in order to demonstrate its common interest with the Polish state. But while many Poles saw the Russian Orthodox Church as a part of the tsarist Russification policy of the Polish lands – an attitude manifested in the demolition of the Orthodox Cathedral at Saxon Square in Warsaw as an act of symbolic liberation in the first years of Polish independence[101] – Ohienko claimed that the originally Ukrainian Orthodox Church had been a victim of the same Russification policy: In the former territories of the *Rzeczpospolita*, the church had been destroyed by the Tsars and Russian Orthodox hierarchy, a policy that the Soviet rulers had recently repeated after the short period of Ukrainian independence, which resulted from the February Revolution of 1917.[102]

Even though this argumentation was more or less based on the same ideas the Ukrainization movement had used before, Ohienko changed the strategy to some extent: He did not openly demand the Ukrainization of the Orthodox Church. Instead he tried to give new direction to the aims of the movement and avoided the word »Ukrainization«:

> I reject this term, because it is not about Ukrainization, but exclusively about *de-Russification* [emphasis in the original]: The Ukrainian population is longing for the state of affairs of pre-partition Poland. [...] It is mainly about the return to that rightful ecclesiastical system and culture that once already existed in Poland; it is foremost about sermons in the people's language, education in their native language.[103]

The fear that support for the movement could foster a Ukrainian national movement which could possibly be hostile to Poland was one of the main concerns of Polish politicians. Ohienko took this fear seriously, introducing a historical angle, which was meant to prove that the Orthodox Church in Poland should ideally have a Ukrainian character. This strategy culminated in his final appeal:

> The Polish nation always says: Poland has risen from the dead. Yes, Poland has risen from the dead. We, the Ukrainians, expected that the Ukrainian Orthodox Church would also receive the opportunity to rise from the dead, but until today

uprawień w stosunku do cerkwi prawosławnej w Polsce. Prawie 300 lat minęło od czasu pogwałcenia cerkwi ukraińskiej ale satysfakcja nastąpiła.« Ibid., 179.

101 Benecke, *Die Ostgebiete der Zweiten Polnischen Republik*, 199–201.

102 Ogijenko, »Losy Cerkwi ukraińskiej,« 175–180.

103 »ten termin odrzucam, ponieważ nie o ukrainizację chodzi, a chodzi wyłącznie o *derusyfikację* [emphasis in the original]: pragnie ludność ukraińska tego co było w Polsce przedrozbiorowej. [...] chodzi głównie o przywrócenie tego prawnego ustroju i kultury cerkwi, które już były w Polsce; chodzi przedewszystkiem o kazaniu w języku ludowym, o nauczanie w języku macierzystym.« Ibid., 181.

> that did not happen. Poland has risen from the dead but it left all the Russian remnants in the Ukrainian Church just as they had been in the times of [Tsar] Peter [I.] and [Tsarina] Catherine.[104]

Though the precise extent of the influence of this lecture cannot be evaluated, the struggle for structural reform and the introduction of the Ukrainian language would attain some success in the following years, mainly in Wolhynia, where Voivode Henryk Józewski adopted and supported this policy and even established a Ukrainian bishop.[105] Another success was the convocation of an all-Polish council (*sobór*) in 1930 by Polish President Ignacy Mościcki, with Ivan Ohienko even preparing a series of memorials for the event.[106] Since the mid-1930s, however, the Polish government withdrew from this type of policy, instead enforcing the Polonization of the Orthodox Church.[107]

The IBSN's Research on the Jewish Community and the Development of its Legal Status

One of the first announcements in the newly created Journal *Sprawy Narodowościowe* involved the Jewish section of the institute, which was preparing a survey of the Jewish communities in Poland. The decision to do so was made during a session of the Jewish section in late March 1927.[108] Roughly two months later, the section agreed upon the text of the accompanying questionnaire, which was printed in the following issue.[109] The background of the study was the fact that five different bodies of legislation governing Jewish communities were then in force in Poland at the same time.[110] The questionnaire

104 »Naród Polski wszędzie mówi: Polska zmartwychstała. Tak, Polska zmartwychstała. Ale my, Ukraińcy, oczekiwaliśmy, że będzie dana możność wstać z martwych również i prawosławnej cerkwi ukraińskiej w Polsce, ale do dziś dnia to nie nastąpiło. Polska zmartwychstała ale pozostawiła wszystkie pozostałości rosyjskie w ukraińskiej cerkwi, tak, jak były one za czasów Piotra i Katarzyny.« Ibid. 182.

105 Timothy Snyder, *Sketches from a Secret War. A Polish Artist's Mission to Liberate Soviet Ukraine* (New Haven and London: Yale University Press, 2005), 147–167. The administration in other regions, however, did not support such a policy. Papierzyńska-Turek, *Między tradycją a rzeczywistością*, 240–242.

106 AAN, MWRiOP, sygn. 997, k. 3–102.

107 Schenke, *Nationalstaat und nationale Frage*, 271–281.

108 »Z Instytutu Badań Spraw Narodowościowych,« *Sprawy Narodowościowe* 1, no. 2 (1927): 216.

109 »Z Instytutu Badań Spraw Narodowościowych, Komisja żydowska,« *Sprawy Narodowościowe* 1, no. 3 (1927): 328–329.

110 As the laws of the former partitioning powers remained in force with only minor restrictions, the legal status of the Jewish Communities differed between the former Prussian Greater Poland, the former Austrian Lesser Poland, the former

elicited data such as the size of each community, the number of taxpayers and the range of the amounts paid, the political composition of the community and its administrative board, as well as the date of the last community board elections. It also contained specific questions concerning Lesser Poland (*Małopolska*) and the western provinces. The questionnaire was sent to over 500 Jewish communities in western, central, and southeastern Poland in March 1928.[111]

The background for this was the government's effort to regulate the legal basis of the Jewish communities, which the pre-May governments had failed to accomplish despite several initiatives launched by Jewish Sejm deputies.[112] The Jewish section of the institute wanted to support the new legislative initiative with information on the structure and functioning of the Jewish communities. As the authorities had not collected any such data,[113] the survey was introduced to fill the gap and provide the legislators with information.

As neither the IBSN's archive nor the files concerning the Jewish communities of the Ministry of Religion and Public Education have been preserved, it is not possible to reconstruct which information and suggestions, if any, the IBSN sent to the ministry apart from the summary published in *Sprawy Narodowościowe*.[114] Nor can its possible influence on law-making be quantified. Nevertheless, it is a good example to demonstrate the functions of the IBSN. The Jewish Commission of the IBSN, along with others, consisted not only of members of the institute but also of a number of outsiders. Among them were many Jewish politicians such as the Bundist Wiktor Alter,[115] the Zionists

Russian territories in the east and northeast, and the Kingdom of Poland. Yet another body of legislation applied to Upper Silesia, which came under Polish rule after the partition of that region between Germany and Poland in 1922.

111 Izaak Bornstein, »O działalności żydowskich gmin wyznaniowych w Polsce« *Sprawy Narodowościowe* 2, no. 6 (1928): 707–718, here 709. In the northeastern territories, no communities existed at the time, or at least as legal bodies, as they had no legal basis in the Russian Empire (except for the Kingdom of Poland). In Poland this legal basis was only introduced in 1927 and the communities there were recognized as organizations under public law the following year.

112 Jolanta Żyndul, *Państwo w Państwie? Autonomia narodowo-kulturalna w Europy środkowowschodniej* (Warszawa: DiG, 2000), 112–122.

113 Bornstein, »O działalności żydowskich gmin wyznaniowych,« 708.

114 Ibid.

115 Wiktor Alter (1890–1943), politician, leader of the Jewish »Bund« Socialist Party, and secretary general of the General Council of Jewish Trade Unions in Poland, from 1927–1936 alderman in the Warsaw City Council. *YIVO Encyclopedia of Jews in Eastern Europe*, s.v. »Wiktor Alter,« http://www.yivoencyclopedia.org (accessed August 1, 2014).

Apolinary Hartglas,[116] Ignacy Schiper, and Fiszel Rottenstreich,[117] Izaak Rubinstein[118] of the *Mizrahi* religious Zionists, and Aron Lewin[119] of the orthodox *Agudas Yisroel*. The last two were also rabbis – Rubinstein in Wilna and Lewin in Sambor – as was Mojżesz Schorr at the Great Synagogue in Warsaw.[120] Such public figures were obviously much better suited to gain the trust of Jewish communities than any state officials would, as they were much better informed about their ways of working and, most of all, were not considered to be complete outsiders. The different political backgrounds of the commission members, moreover, made it clear that a variety of approaches was represented in the commission with regard to how Jewish communities should be organized and what their roles should be.

The social role of the Jewish community was highly controversial, not only within Jewish political circles, but also between Polish state institutions and Jewish politicians. While the dispute among Jewish representatives over the communities' character mainly arose from the question of whether it should be an institution only accessible to religious Jews – as the Orthodox saw it – or whether it should be an institution that serves all those who considered themselves to be of Jewish nationality, although not necessarily religious. The latter position was shared by almost all non-religious Jewish parties, including the Zionist Organization (often known as the General Zionists), the two *Po'ale Zion* parties, the Folkists, and the socialist, anti-Zionist *Bund*. Consequently, all Jewish parties, regardless of their views on religion, ran for community board elections to secure their influence on Jewish life. This led to fierce power struggles within the community boards between secular and religious Jewish

116 Apolinary Hartglas (1883–1953), politician and lawyer, member and in the 2nd half of the 1930s president of the Zionist Organization in Poland, member of the Sejm from 1919–1930. *YIVO Encyclopedia of Jews in Eastern Europe*, s.v. »Apolinary Hartglas,« http://www.yivoencyclopedia.org (accessed August 1, 2014).

117 Fiszel Rottenstreich (1880–1938), lawyer, politician, and publicist, member of the Galician Zionist Organisation, from 1922–1928 member of the Senate and 1930–1935 of the Sejm, also director of the Department of Trade, Industry and Finance of the World Zionist Organisation. Szymon Rudnicki, *Żydzi w parlamencie II Rzeczypospolitej* (Wydawnictwo Sejmowe: Warszawa, 2004), 417.

118 Izaak Rubinstein (1880–1945), rabbi, politician, member and chairman of the party committee of Mizrahi, Polish senator from 1922–1939. *YIVO Encyclopedia of Jews in Eastern Europe*, s.v. »Yitshak Rubinstein,« http://www.yivoencyclopedia.org (accessed August 1, 2014).

119 Aron Lewin, (1879–1941), politician and Orthodox rabbi, member of Agudah Yisroel, from 1927 chief rabbi of Rzeszów, member of the Sejm from 1930–1935. *YIVO Encyclopedia of Jews in Eastern Europe*, s.v. »Lewin Brothers,« http://www.yivoencyclopedia.org (accessed August 1, 2014).

120 »Z Instytutu Badań Spraw Narodowościowych,« *Sprawy Narodowościowe* 1, no. 1 (1927): 87–89, here 88–89.

parties, which were mainly concentrated on the allocation of funds for organizations attached to the different parties.[121] Despite this conflict, however, there was a consensus that the activities of the Jewish community should not only be restricted to religious affairs but should also include a wide variety of matters such as education, culture, and social welfare. Many Jewish politicians, especially secular politicians, also believed that the Jewish community should serve as a basis for the establishment of Jewish cultural autonomy,[122] though the specifics of how such autonomy should work were – like many other issues in Jewish politics – still disputed.

In the newly created Polish state after World War I, such a concept could not win the support of Józef Piłsudski, who was then the country's head of state, nor could Jewish politicians persuade members of the Polish parliament of it.[123] In the decree on the changes in the organization of Jewish religious communities, issued by Piłsudski on February 7, 1919, the competences of the Jewish communities were strictly limited to religious functions with some minor exceptions for social welfare.[124] After the May coup, however, many Jewish politicians saw the chance to renegotiate the communities' status. The IBSN must have seemed quite a promising avenue to prepare for this campaign. Two members of the Jewish Commission of the IBSN, Aleksander Hafftka and Samuel Adalberg,[125] would indeed be directly involved in the preparation of laws in the field as those responsible for Jewish affairs in the Ministry of Internal Affairs and in the Ministry of Religion and Education.[126] The close ties of the institute to several influential politicians and to the administration raised the hope that the IBSN would be the right forum to begin negotiations on the community issue.

However, despite these incipient informal discussions at the institute involving Jewish leaders of various political backgrounds and state officials, the government already in fall 1927 decided to introduce legal regulations for the

121 Gershon C. Bacon, *Politics of Tradition. Agudat Yisroel in Poland 1916–1939* (Jerusalem: Magnes Press, 1996), 178–224.

122 Żyndul, *Państwo w Państwie?*, 106–122.

123 Ibid., 109–114.

124 The decree is printed in: Józef Dawidsohn, *Gminy Żydowskie (z tekstami ustaw i rozporządzeń)* (Warszawa: Klub Posłów Sejmowych Żydowskiej Rady Narodowej, 1931), 53–55.

125 Samuel Adalberg (1868–1939), Polish state official and Jewish folklorist, advocate of Jewish assimilation, 1918–1930 referent for questions of Mosaic confession and later head of the section for Mosaic confession in the MWRiOP. *YIVO Encyclopedia of Jews in Eastern Europe*, s.v. »Samuel Adalberg,« http://www.yivoencyclopedia.org (accessed August 1, 2014).

126 »Z Instytutu Badań Spraw Narodowościowych,« *Sprawy Narodowościowe* 1, no. 1 (1927): 87–89, here 88.

communities without any further consultations or even awaiting the results of the survey undertaken by the IBSN. In October 1927, President Ignacy Mościcki and Gustaw Dobrucki, the Minister for Religion and Public Education, issued several decrees based on Piłsudski's decree of 1919 that extended the legal basis for Jewish communities to the eastern territories of Poland, while adjusting it in former Galicia to reduce the differences between the various regions.[127] It also contained minor modifications, and granted the communities the status of organizations under public law. The restrictions mainly limiting these community activities to religious functions would, however, remain unchanged.[128]

Why did the government decide to end the consultations with Jewish experts and politicians, issuing legislation affecting the Jewish communities without their consent instead? With no documentation available, one can only guess what the reasons were. The most probable explanation is that the government officials present at the debates on the Jewish communities in the IBSN's Jewish section – Hafftka and Adalberg – noticed a lack of will among the Jewish leadership to find a compromise on that issue. This unwillingness was not so much meant in relation to the government as it was within Jewish society itself. There was no end in sight to the ongoing power struggles or to the debate over whether the communities should be religious or secular institutions and not much in fact changed until the beginning of World War II.[129] Under these circumstances the government's support for either side in this internal Jewish conflict would have worsened their relations with the other. And in this context, the government decided to only solve the most urgent problems by basically extending the status quo in the former Kingdom of Poland to the rest of the country. This did not place one particular side in a favorable position, but improved the situation of a vast part of the Jewish population, especially in the eastern parts of the country.

Jewish society reacted to these regulations with various degrees of disappointment.[130] This feeling was addressed by Izaak Bornstein,[131] a Jewish statistician who had been in charge of the IBSN's survey on the communities, who

127 Żyndul, *Państwo w Państwie?*, 178–224.

128 Dawidsohn, *Gminy Żydowskie*, 56 f.

129 Bacon, *Politics of Tradition*, 128.

130 While for instance the Lemberg Zionist Ignacy Schwarzbart considered at least the »smaller half« of their demands fulfilled (*Chwila*, April 25, 1928), his fellow Zionist Wolf Schmorak (*Chwila*, May 8, 1928) regarded the new law as an absolute obstacle to the successful functioning of the communities.

131 Izaak Bornstein (1895–1943), economist and statistic, from 1926 secretary of the JDC (American Jewish Joint Distribution Comitee) Office in Poland, Co-founder of the CEKABE (Centrala Kasa Bezprocentowych), the Central Organisations of Jewish Free Loan Banks. *Yidisher Gezelshaftlekher Leksikon*, s.v. »Izaak Bornstein.«

presented his findings on November 8, 1928 during a session of the institute's Jewish Commission. During the following discussion it was Adalberg who suggested the publication of the report.[132] It appeared in number 6/1928 of *Sprawy Narodowościowe*. At the beginning Bornstein stated that:

> the law on Jewish communities issued on the basis of the presidential decree of October 14, 1927 (amended March 6, 1928), was criticized by the Jewish public, which demanded a community that would cover a broad field of educational and social activities while, at the same time, serving as a nucleus of national autonomy, and not – as it is at present – be restricted only to meeting the religious needs of certain parts of the Jewish population.[133]

He therefore expressed quite openly the dissatisfaction of the Jews with the current situation as well as their expectations that a new law would grant the communities broader competences with regard to social and cultural work. In his analysis, however, he stressed that many of the existing Jewish communities were already engaged in social and cultural activities that went far beyond a narrow understanding of religious functions. His data demonstrated that Jewish communities with more than 5,000 members had been spending about one third of their budgets on social and educational efforts.[134] This showed that despite the letter of the law, Jewish communities were actually active in much broader spheres of endeavor.

In another article on that issue in the official *Kwartalnik Statystyczny* (Statistical Quarterly), Bornstein went even further and declared that, contrary to the official restrictions on secular purposes, the communities were acting as de facto Jewish national self-governing bodies. As he argued, this was due to their newly acquired status as institutions under public law:

> The Jewish community is thus not only a philanthropic institution, which distributes certain funds among the poor of their place. It is also an autonomous body of this nationality to meet its cultural and social needs and even has the right to impose obligatory taxation on its members [...].[135]

132 »Z Instytutu Badań Spraw Narodowościowych,« *Sprawy Narodowościowe* 2, no. 5 (1928): 621–623, here 623.

133 »Ustawa o gminach wyznaniowych żydowskich, wydana na podstawie rozporządzenia Prezydenta z dnia 14 października 1927 r. (znowelizowana dnia 6 marca 1928 r.) spotyka się z krytyką opinji żydowskiej, która domaga się gminy, któraby miała szeroki zakres działania w żydowskich sprawach oświatowych i społecznych i mogła być temsamem zaczątkiem autonomji narodowej, a nie ograniczała się – jak jest obecnie – do zaspokajania tylko potrzeb religijnych pewnej części ludności żydowskiej.« Bornstein, »O działalności żydowskich gmin wyznaniowych,« 708.

134 Ibid., 714.

135 »Gmina żydowska bowiem nie jest tylko instytucją filantropijną, zajmującą się podziałem pewnych funduszów wśród ubogich swej miejscowości; jest ona

Bornstein's assumption was not completely wrong. Especially the right to tax its members granted the Jewish communities a stable financial basis and the means to fund cultural and social activities. Still, his assumptions were generally far too optimistic. The reason why the communities could act as they did and expand their legal boundaries was mainly due to the fact that the state bureaucracy, and the Ministry of Religion and Education in particular, which was charged with the supervision of the communities, turned a blind eye to their practices. There was no guarantee, however, that this would remain as it was in the late 1920s. In 1930 – the year when Adalberg retired – the Ministry of Religion and Education already decided to implement a bill on new voting regulations for the communities. The decree strengthened the religious character of the Jewish communities, by dint of introducing a rule that allowed community boards to remove voters from the electoral rolls if they were accused of taking a public stand against the Jewish religion.[136]

This regulation was often interpreted as a favor to the Orthodox party *Agudas Yisroel* to reward it for its support of the Nonpartisan Bloc for Cooperation with the Government (*Bezpartyjny Blok Współpracy z Rządem*)[137] in the 1928 and 1930 elections. The regulation enabled *Agudas Yisroel* to strengthen its power in community elections by deleting large numbers of especially secular Jewish voters from the communities' electoral rolls.[138]

Soon after that, the supervision of the Jewish communities by the Ministry of Religion and Education and its counterparts in the voivode administration strengthened its control over the communities, and it criticized any large expenditures made on tasks not related to religion. This development along with the community board election regulations provoked continual critique from Jewish politicians and social activists. Even in the two-volume collection

jednocześnie organem autonomji tej narodowości na polu zaspokojenia jej potrzeb kulturalnych i społecznych, działając z prawem przymusowego opodatkowania ludności […].« Izaak Bornstein, »Budżety gmin wyznaniowych żydowskich w Polsce,« *Kwartalnik Statystyczny* 6, no. 3 (1929): 1361–1391, here 1361.

136 The decree is printed in: Dawidsohn, *Gminy Żydowskie*, 69–87. The regulation to remove voters from the electoral rolls is to be found in § 20.

137 The Nonpartisan Bloc for Cooperation with the Government was formed prior to the elections of 1928 as the party of the Piłsudski camp. On the Bloc, see Chojnowski, *Piłsudczycy u władzy.*

138 Żyndul, *Państwo w Państwie?*, 116–118. This regulation seemed to have been abused quite often, especially in smaller communities, as can be seen from an interpellation of Sejm deputy Icchak Grünbaum on March 11, 1931. In it, he mentions cases, when for example a person has been removed under the § 20 rule for »reading a newspaper on the Sabbath with an uncovered head at home« or »talking to a girl.« The text of the interpellation is printed in: Dawidsohn, *Gminy Żydowskie*, 108–110; the examples are given on page 109.

Jews in Reborn Poland, published in 1932 and 1933, which was meant to underline the positive attitude of Jews towards Poland, the chapter on »Legislation concerning the Jewish communities in Reborn Poland« was strongly critical.[139]

Conclusion

In the course of the 1920s, the IBSN, at first a private initiative of scholars and politicians considered to be experts on minority questions, developed into a semi-governmental think tank. It therefore exchanged its independence for better material conditions and direct access to decision-making state agencies. It served not only as a provider of policy advice but also as an intermediary between the representatives of the minorities, Polish politicians, and the state administration. The institute thus had considerable influence on the development of minority policies in Poland during the late 1920s. However, this does not mean that the IBSN had the power to decide on the general direction of these policies, even as it did provide input into the debates of the time. Thanks to its large network, which included the intellectual and political elites of the minorities, the institute was able to contribute information to these debates, which would probably not have otherwise been accessible to the state administration. Even more, it served as a forum in which minority representatives, Polish politicians, and state officials could exchange their ideas in an informal atmosphere and without being widely visible to the press or political opponents.

As the example of the Orthodox Church shows, such activities could have a considerable impact on law-making and the political process. However, it also indicates that the success of the intermediaries always depended on the attitudes of the people involved in the process. Whenever the ministerial staff changed – quite a common event during this period – relations between the institute, the respective minority representatives, and the decision-makers were thrown out of balance and had to be reconfigured.

The debates on the Jewish communities, in turn, clearly delineated the limits of the policy advisement process. Without the political will to find a common position among Jewish politicians, it was impossible to convince the government to change the status quo, if only since no clear alternative was being put forward. Still, the government had not been eager to introduce major changes in the first place, and used the disagreement among Jewish politicians to cement this position. The government did not see any political benefit to be gained by

139 Michał Ringel, »Ustawodawstwo Polski Odrodzonej o gminach żydowskich,« in *Żydzi w Polsce Odrodzonej*, vol. 2, eds. Aleksander Hafftka, Ignacy Schiper and Arje Tartakower (Warszawa; Żydzi w Polsce Odrodzonej, 1933), 242–248.

granting the Jewish communities broader autonomy with the risk of becoming embroiled in an inner-Jewish conflict. Their broader ability to act in practical terms instead reflected the good will of the particular official in charge and could change when he left office. The Orthodox Church was regarded as instrumental with regard to the Ukrainian and Belarusian populations of the eastern borderlands, who were to be tied closer to the state. The support of the Ukrainization movement by the state was considered – at least by some officials – to be a step towards strengthening the loyalty of the Ukrainian population to the state. The relations between the Jewish population and the state were clearly not viewed as particularly critical by the officials in charge, who therefore did not see a need to change the status quo.

This in turn shows that the nationality policies of the Piłsudski camp, despite any great hopes for improvements in the new state for the non-Polish population in Poland, were not aimed at finding a single suitable system for all its citizens without regard to their nationality. Steps were only taken in cases in which it would serve short-term political interests – and even then they were taken very cautiously. Institutions like the IBSN, by contrast, depended on the official will to reform in order to work successfully.

Stephan Stach

Competing Laws – Competing Loyalties

Enlightenment versus Religious Law: Debating Jewish Burial in the Hebrew Press of Late Imperial Russia

> Religion is valid as long as its followers believe in its divine provenance, while the idea of amendment can enter the heart only after this belief was lost, and the human mind no longer fears to approach the sanctum and find faults with it which require mending by human hands.
>
> (Aḥad Ha-Am, »An Open Answer to a Private Letter,« *Ha-Melits*, October 31, 1894)

> Often the less there is to justify a traditional custom, the harder it is to get rid of it.
>
> (Mark Twain, The Adventures of Tom Sawyer, Ch. 5)

An ancient Jewish custom requires that the burial of the deceased be performed without hindrance, preferably on the same day that death occurs before nightfall or otherwise – if unforeseen obstructions are encountered – with as little delay as possible. Consequently, a burial intentionally deferred for any given reason, as in the Christian tradition of a funeral-wake, is considered an insult to the honor of the deceased, and is termed in the corpus of Jewish law (*Halakhah*) as ›keeping the dead for the night‹ (*Halanat ha-met*, hereafter *Halanah*). Abiding by this old religious custom contained an element of risk, for those who seemed to have passed away while being actually unconscious or in a coma could have been placed in their graves prematurely.

By the end of the 18th century, medical science in Europe acknowledged that failing to recognize signs of a pulse or breathing with an unconscious individual was not a sure indication of his or her demise. It was therefore concluded, with no reliable means with which the certainty or exact time of death could be determined, and in order to avoid tragic accidents, that burials should be postponed for a few days until clear signs of decomposition appeared on the body. In some 18th-century German states such new scientific realizations, combined with new ideas and attitudes brought forth by the Enlightenment, inspired a set of new regulations requiring the suspension of burial for three days, as well as a new »Gothic« literary genre, portraying the horrifying images of those who woke up in their graves after being mistakenly interred. The new legislation terminated the long-held monopoly of religion and the church in determining the time of death, and placed it for the first time within the jurisdiction of the state through its certified representatives – medical doctors.[1]

While in some German states legislation forced the Jews, if only *de jure*, to accept the supremacy of science over religion in such matters of life and death already at the end of the 18th century, in the case of the Jews of the Russian Empire – the largest Jewish community in the world in the 19th century – change was slower to set in. There, traditional Jewish society remained for the most part unmoved by the European Enlightenment and unaffected by new regulations in its spirit, so that the fear of *Halanah* transgressions was rife, and the custom of burying the dead as quickly as possible (*Kvurah mehirah*) continued. However, the juridical-halakhic reasoning behind this traditional custom, as well as the medical soundness of the prohibition of *Halanah*, came under intensified scrutiny and criticism in the Hebrew press of the Russian Empire. Around 1860, a number of Jewish newspapers appeared that used Hebrew – the ancient language of scripture and of the rabbinical elite – as opposed to Yiddish, which was the everyday language of the majority of Russian-Polish Jewry. The newspapers catered exclusively to Jews, and succeeded with time in creating a public sphere in which the most prominent problems and concerns of the Jews in Russia were addressed and debated openly.[2]

In 1880 a journalistic discussion emerged that was to last for over a decade and which mirrored a great ideological divide within the Jewish society of the period.

1 Edicts requiring Jews to postpone the burial of their dead for three days were issued by the duke of Mecklenburg-Schwerin in 1772 and by Friedrich Wilhelm III of Prussia in 1798. Falk Wiesemann, »Jewish Burials in Germany – Between Tradition, the Enlightenment and the Authorities,« *Leo Baeck Institute Year Book* 37 (1992): 17–31, ibid., 18–19; Andreas Reinke, »Zwischen Tradition, Aufklärung und Assimilation: die Königliche Wilhelmsschule in Breslau, 1791–1848,« *Zeitschrift für Religions- und Geistesgeschichte* 43, no. 3 (1991): 193–214.

2 Since Yiddish was much more prevalent than Hebrew, it was regarded as politically dangerous in the eyes of imperial censorship, hence the development of a Yiddish press was harshly restricted until 1902. See David E. Fishman, *The Rise of Modern Yiddish Culture* (Pittsburgh, PA: Pittsburgh University Press, 2005), 21–24. For a more in-depth view regarding censorship policies: Dmitrii A. El'iashevich, *Pravitel'stvennaia politika i evreiskaia pechat' v Rossii, 1797–1917* (St. Petersburg: Mosty kul'tury, 1999), 396, 401, 435, 444, 447. The 1860s also saw the appearance of a Jewish press in both Russian and Polish. See Yehuda Slutsky, *Ha-itonut ha-yehudit-rusit ba-me'ah ha-tesha-esreh* (Jerusalem: Mosad Bialik, 1970); Marian Fuks, *Prasa żydowska w Warszawie 1823–1939* (Warszawa: Państwowe Wydawnictwo Naukowe, 1979).

The world around was changing and modernizing at a previously unknown rapid pace, challenging Jewish society, and creating a dilemma concerning the amount of change and external influence that Jews could, or should, absorb without compromising their unique identity. Some were willing to forgo religious conservatism, to varying degrees, in order to embrace what modernity had to offer them as a minority group in Russia, so they could better integrate into Christian society and improve their social standing. State-regulated education, with its choice of new professions, and the expanding urban centers of the Russian Empire with their secularizing lifestyles, held a special appeal, and were viewed by a growing number of Jews as instrumental in achieving their aspirations in terms of improving their social condition. And so the well-known Yiddish folk-saying, »Seven miles around Odessa burn the fires of Hell«, represents the common conception of the aggressively secularizing powers of big towns during that period, in which those who approach them even from a distance are affected.[3] On the other hand, there were those who faced no dilemma and rejected modernity with its secular influences as being dangerous. For them, Judaism was defined in strictly religious terms with no scope for compromise, and with the understanding that most, if not all outside influence should be blocked.

The part of the Jewish intelligentsia that was non-conservative and to a large extent responsible for creating the Hebrew press, were called *Maskilim* in the language of the period. This term denoted their identification with the ideas of the Jewish Enlightenment – the *Haskalah* – which, as the late Jonathan Frankel summarized, »was not a homogeneous movement but rather a broad concept which covered an entire spectrum of different groups and ideas«, basically sharing »a general agreement that Jewish life had to adapt itself to the modern world, intellectually through an educational revolution and economically through ›productivization,‹ a radical change in Jewish occupational patterns«.[4] The Hebrew press in Russia and Congress Poland was, from its very beginning, meant to serve as a Maskilic mouthpiece and was considered a part of the state-approved ›three-part Maskilic establishment‹ in Russia. This establishment included, in addition to the press, the rabbinical seminaries in Zhitomir and Vilna, and the Society for the Spread of Enlightenment among the Jews of Russia (OPE), all of which were founded in the 1860s.[5] With this said, it is

3 Steven Zipperstein, *The Jews of Odessa* (Stanford, CA: Stanford University Press, 1985), 1.

4 Jonathan Frankel, *Prophecy and Politics: Socialism,* Nationalism *and the Russian Jews, 1862–1917* (London–New York: Cambridge University Press, 1981), 30.

5 Eli Lederhendler, The *Road to Modern Jewish Politics* (New York–Oxford: Oxford University Press, 1989), 111–112.

important to note that while a ›Maskilic rhetoric‹ was very apparent in the Hebrew press, preaching for the rationalization, modernization, and Europeanization of Jewish society, the Maskilim were by no means striving to abolish Jewish tradition. Rather, they sought to reform Jewish society while drawing, as Israel Bartal put it, »on an internal Jewish root,« basing themselves on Jewish tradition and on »immanent Jewish sources«.[6]

The opposition to the Maskilim, generally termed ›Orthodox‹ in the language of the period, grouped together those representatives of Jewish society who viewed modernity as posing a set of threats to its traditional existence, »and whose awareness of those threats and its attempts to cope with them, [left] a deep imprint on its whole being.«[7] Here too there was scope for leniency and, as I will demonstrate later, certain Orthodox representatives were willing to use distinctly modern tools – like newspapers – to do battle with their Maskilic nemeses, while others of this group adapted parts of Maskilic ideology, like secular education and proto-nationalism, to the point that they were described by some contemporary scholars as ›Maskilic rabbis.‹[8] Of all the Hebrew newspapers that addressed the subject of the *Halanah* prohibition, two are of particular interest: *Ha-Melits*, whose loyalties lay with the Maskilim; and its rival, *Ha-Levanon*, which served as the formal mouthpiece for Jewish Orthodoxy of the ›Lithuanian persuasion.‹[9] Among all the editors of the different newspapers, the man who was the most instrumental in initiating the journalistic discussion concerning *Halanah* and cultivating the controversy around it was Alexander Tsederboym, the publisher-editor of *Ha-Melits* and a central figure in the world of the Hebrew press from the 1860s.[10]

6 Israel Bartal, *The Jews of Eastern Europe 1772–1882* (Philadelphia, PA: Philadelphia University Press, 2005), 92.

7 For a definition of »Jewish Orthodoxy«, see Immanuel Etkes, »Parashat ha-›haskalah mi-ta'am‹ ve-ha-tmurah be-ma'amad tnuat ha-haskalah be-rusiyah,« in *Ha-dat ve-ha-hayyim: tnu'at ha-haskalah be-mizraḥ eyropah*, ed. idem (Jerusalem: Merkaz shazar, 1993), 167–216, here 214.

8 Yosef Salmon, »Ha-ortodoksiya ha-yehudit be-mizraḥ eyropah: kavim le-aliyata,« in *Ortodoksiyah yehudit: hebetim ḥadashim*, eds. Yosef Salmon et al. (Jerusalem: Magnes, 2006), 367–379, especially 367–368.

9 All quotations from the Hebrew press are dated according to the Gregorian calendar, as indexed by the Early Hebrew Newspapers site of the National and University Library in Jerusalem: http://jnul.huji.ac.il/dl/newspapers/index1024.html. For a historical and cultural overview of the »Litvaks«, see Vital Zajka, »The Self-Perception of Lithuanian-Belarusian Jewry in the Eighteenth and Nineteenth Centuries,« *Polin* 14 (2001): 19–30.

10 *Ha-Melits* (»The Advocate«) ed. in Odessa and St. Petersburg from 1860 to 1904 was the most prominent Hebrew newspaper of the period. *Ha-Levanon*, ed. in Jerusalem, Paris, Mainz, and London from 1863 to 1886, was ›adopted‹ as the formal mouthpiece for Jewish Orthodoxy in 1868. Otherwise, *Ha-Maggid* (»The

Tsederboym (Erez) – a publisher and a lobbyist

Alexander Ha-Levi Tsederboym (1816–1893) was a journalist, publicist, and lobbyist (*shtadlan*) for the Jewish cause in Russia. Born in Zamość in the province of Lublin, an important center of the early Haskalah in Congress Poland, he was brought up and educated by his father, who was a watchmaker and a Hebrew poet, in a home that was a meeting place for the local Maskilic intelligentsia. Tsederboym moved to Odessa sometime around 1840, where he made his living in different occupations within the textile business, and where he turned his home into a meeting place for the local Maskilim. At the same time he dabbled in local Jewish politics and cultivated personal contacts with different high-ranking Russian officials. Those connections in high places, as well as his commercial and political skills, enabled him to establish and manage one of the first Hebrew newspapers in Russia which he edited, until his dying day, for 33 years. Writing mainly under the pen-name *Erez* (cedar tree), Tsederboym was known as a controversial figure: a highly opinionated, at times impulsive publicist with a cumbersome, pseudo-intellectual literary style and unrealized aspirations of becoming an influential figure in St. Petersburg's Jewish political circles, which were dominated at the time by Jewish banking and railway magnates, the likes of the Gintsburg and Poliakov families.[11] Yet with all his apparent professional and personal shortcomings, Tsederboym succeeded in harnessing the influence and prestige that his profession earned him in order to support various Jewish causes, both on a local and a national scale. He approached members of the Russian authorities directly in order to intervene on behalf of poor Jews who had been expelled from their villages; he secured stay permits for Jewish university students in St. Petersburg allowing them to live in the town legally, and lobbied that more Jews be granted entrance to universities all over the country, above and beyond the »Jewish quota« imposed by Russian

Herald«), ed. in Lyck, Berlin, Cracow, Vienna, and London from 1856 to 1903, was the first modern Hebrew newspaper to appear and cater to the Jews of the Russian Empire. Finally, *Ha-Tsfirah* (»The Dawn«), ed. in Warsaw from 1862 to 1931, began as a periodical dedicated to scientific topics, and at the close of the 19th century became the formal organ representing the young Zionist movement. For a historic overview, see Menuha Gilbo'a, *Leksikon le-toldot ha-itonut ha-ivrit ba-me'ot ha-18 ve-ha-19* (Jerusalem: Mosad Bialik, 1992), 117–135 (*Ha-Maggid*), 137–157 (*Ha-Melits*), 167–181 (*Ha-Tsfirah*), and 186–195 (*Ha-Levanon*). The latest reference to premature burial that I am aware of is to be found in *Ha-Melits*, February 13, 1893, probably marking the most far-reaching echo of the *Halana* prohibition debate.

11 For a survey of Jewish political sphere in Russia, and specifically in St. Petersburg, see Benjamin Nathans, *Beyond the Pale: The Jewish Encounter with Late Imperial Russia* (Berkeley, CA: University of California Press, 2002), 165–198.

authorities in 1886. Tsederboym's greatest contributions to the national Jewish cause were his success in securing a formal license for *Ḥibat-Tsiyon* (Lovers of Zion), the proto-Zionist movement, and his relentless fight against slander and accusations aimed at the Jews by the Judophobic press in Russia.

It is important to note that as a publisher-editor Tsederboym encouraged open debate and, from an early stage in the evolution of *Ha-Melits*, did not deny those who opposed him or his newspaper's formal ideological stance from writing in his paper. Moreover, his candid approach led him at times to unwittingly publish information that showed him in a less-than-favorable light.[12] Despite being one of the founding fathers of modern Hebrew journalism and his high standing as a public figure among the Jews of Russia, Tsederboym was almost forgotten after his death. His biography has yet to be written, while for the most part only fragmented memoirs – some of his own, some written by others – remain.[13]

Alexander Tsederboym placed himself at the forefront of the opposition to the prohibition of *Halanah*, promulgating a call for a change of what he recognized to be a dangerous custom. The public debate which followed was possibly one of the most intriguing in the Hebrew press at the time, and it was certainly one of the longest, reaching into the 1890s and exceeding the boundaries of newspaper

12 Perhaps the best example of editorial openness is the heated journalistic debate between the Maskilim and the Orthodox in Russia concerning the need for religious reforms (*Pulmus ha-tikunim ba-dat*), which preoccupied the Hebrew press from 1868 to 1871. Orthodox writers were well represented in this public debate and published their views openly in *Ha-Melits* (September 10, 1868), and in other newspapers like *Ha-Maggid* (April 14, 1869). For an overview of this debate, see Shmuel Feiner, *Haskalah ve-historiyah* (Jerusalem: Merkaz Shazar, 1995), 403–416. Publishing opinions that opposed the newspaper's formal ideological line continued in *Ha-Melits* even after Tsederboym's death, as in a set of articles by Yehoshua Yosef Freyl, a former publicist in *Ha-Levanon*, who opposed *Hibat-Tsiyon*, while *Ha-Melits* was the movement's ardent supporter: *Ha-Melits*, June 15, 17, and 20, 1894. For Tsederboym admitting to an embarrassing incident in which he was denied access to the house of Baron Goratsii Gintsburg for previously writing unfavorably about the family, see *Ha-Melits*, May 2, 1882.

13 For a partial list see Tsederboym's own autobiographical essays in *Ha-Melits*, September 8, 1886; October 3, 1890. For monographs, see Reuven Braynin, *Zikhronot: sirtutim mi-ḥayey A. Tsederboym ve-tkhunato* (Kraków: Y. S. Fuks, 1899); Shmuel Leyb Tsitron, *Di geshikhte fun der yidishe prese: fun yor 1863 biz 1889* (Vilnius: Farayn fun Yiddish literatn un zhornalistn, 1923); *Iz arkhiva sem'i Tsederbaum*, ed. V. L. Telitsyn, Iu. Ia. Iakhnina and G. G. Zhivotovskii (Moskva: Sobranie, 2008). To date, the best overview in English is still Alexander Orbach, *New Voices of Russian Jewry: A Study of the Russian-Jewish Press of Odessa in the Era of the Great Reforms, 1860–1871* (Leiden: E. J. Brill, 1980).

journalism, as it appeared in at least three Hebrew books printed in Russia between 1881 and 1892.[14]

The outline of the debate

The *Halanah* debate represented two »spheres of confrontation«: The first was internal to the Jewish community; the second positioned the Jews as an ethnic minority against the imperial state, its law and administration. In the internal Jewish sphere, the Maskilim advocated banning the custom of immediate burial and adapting an alternative procedure that would both pose no danger to those who were only seemingly dead, and at the same time would conform with the state law that required postponing burials for three days. The Orthodox, in response, fought to preserve the old custom out of fear that losing the battle on either front would further destabilize traditional Jewish society, which by 1880 had already been losing ground to the influence of external forces: the spread of secular education and the influence of Russian revolutionary ideology on Jewish youth; the internal Jewish migration to large towns; emigration abroad spurred by harsh living conditions and pogroms, were all persistently driving Jews away from their traditional, religious way of life.[15] The polemical tactics chosen by the Maskilim were to simultaneously attack the Orthodox stance with halakhic and scientific arguments. Initially they sought to demonstrate that the prohibition of *Halanah* did not stand on solid halakhic ground, and should therefore not have been regarded as taboo. Secondly, the Maskilim opposed the custom of immediate burial from a scientific-medical point of view, while specifically targeting Jewish burial societies who were in charge of organizing and administering traditional burials. The Orthodox, on their part, denied that there was any kind of danger inherent to the old custom. Consequently, if there was no problem then there was certainly no need for change.

14 Alexander Tsederboym, *Mishlo'aḥ manot* (St. Petersburg: Tsederboym and Goldblum Press, 1881); David Elazar Finkel, *Meytsarey she'ol* (Warszawa: M.Y. Halter Press, 1889), translated from German; Dov Ber Yehuda Leib Ginzburg, *Emunat ḥakhamim* (Vilnius: Orlozorov Press, 1892), in which the 3rd chapter polemicized against Finkel's book.

15 For a concise review of the different challenges that Jewish Orthodoxy faced in the 19th century, and the various responses to modernity it created, see Mordechai Breuer, »Ortodoksiyah: mats'a le-vedek bayyit histori«, in *Ortodoksiyah yehudit: hebetim ḥadashim*, eds. Yosef Salmon, Aviezer Ravitzky, and Adam S. Ferziger (Jerusalem: Magnes Press, 2006), 79–85. For the influence of secular, and especially university education on Jewish youth, see Nathans, *Beyond the Pale*, 201–256; Yvonne Kleinmann, *Neue Orte – neue Menschen. Jüdische Lebensformen in St. Petersburg und Moskau im 19. Jahrhundert* (Göttingen: Vandenhoeck & Ruprecht, 2006), 100–110.

In the second sphere, that of confrontation between Jews and the state, traditional Jewish society was retaliating against the efforts exerted by the imperial authorities to enforce secular burial legislation as inscribed in state law. This action was perceived by Jewish Orthodoxy as yet another in a string of attempts, which already began during the reign of Nicolas I (1825–1855), to weaken the juridical and administrative autonomy of the Jewish community in Russia, and the Orthodox accordingly sought to either ignore or evade state legislation.[16] The state, which was not initially concerned with traditional Jewish ways of handling the dead, began to show growing interest in the subject once it became clear that it involved an ongoing and blatant breach of law on the part of Jews.

The internal Jewish sphere – maskilic criticism

On November 30, 1880, *Ha-Melits* published a news item that had appeared earlier that month in the *Frankfurter Zeitung*, depicting how during the funeral procession of a Parisian fur merchant in St. Ouen Catholic Cemetery, screams for help were heard from within the coffin which, once opened, revealed the fur merchant in a deep state of shock, yet very much alive. This near tragedy which befell a Catholic who was undoubtedly buried after a funeral vigil of some length, prompted Tsederboym to add an explosive footnote in small print. In a few short paragraphs he delivered a scorching attack on those whom he termed ›our Orthodox brothers‹ (*aḥeynu ha-ḥaredim*), who, in order to refrain from committing the sin of *Halanah*, practiced the custom of »bringing the dead quickly to their graves while their flesh was still warm«.[17]

It is both interesting and important to note that Tsederboym's point of departure for his attack reflected the realization that premature burial was not merely a vague possibility, but rather a gruesome reality. Once he asserted that particular point, he went on to strike at the heart of its religious justification: He argued that there *was* no unequivocal Jewish law forbidding delayed burial, but instead that immediate burial was a custom which was based on mere superstitions mixed with kabbalistic nonsense. Then he pointed an accusing finger at the leading rabbis of Russian-Polish Jewry, posing the rhetorical question: Seeing that Jewish law very explicitly commanded that one should strive to do all in one's power to save the life of even *one* human being, how can the rabbis remain

16 For the juridical autonomy of the Jews in Russia, see Michael Stanislawski, *Tsar Nicholas I and the Jews: The Transformation of Jewish Society in Russia, 1825–1855* (Philadelphia, PA: Jewish Publication Society in America, 1983), 127; Eli Lederhendler, *The Road to Modern Jewish Politics*, 50–52.

17 *Ha-Melits*, November 30, 1880.

indifferent to this dangerous custom, if there was a danger that even one in a thousand could accidentally be buried alive?[18]

Finally, *Ha-Melits*' publisher-editor delivered a blow to the scientific validity of the halakhic procedure of determining the certainty of death, and especially the old custom in which signs of breathing were checked by placing a feather to the nose or mouth of the individual suspected to be deceased.[19] He noted that specialists and doctors could not recognize any other definite sign of death save the appearance of signs of decay on the body, which are known to appear only a few days after the moment of death. At times even a prolonged delay of burial was not enough to determine death with absolute certainty, as the above-mentioned story of the fur merchant illustrated. With this in mind, he asked, how can Jews rely on the »feather test« and then assume certain death based upon the experience – not of a doctor or a paramedic – but that »of the Jewish undertaker and the Jewish layabout?«[20]

By March 1881 Tsederboym had expanded his footnote into a 26-page-long essay which was printed as a booklet titled *Mishlo'aḥ manot* and distributed among *Ha-Melits*' subscribers as a supplementary gift for the Purim holiday in hundreds of copies.[21] This was a somewhat hastily composed essay in which Tsederboym repeated and expanded his previously stated arguments, while at the same time unabashedly attacking Jewish Orthodoxy and criticizing the custom of hasty burial from both halakhic and scientific points of views.

18 Ibid. The reference Tsederboym evoked was that of *Piku'aḥ nefesh*, a halakhic term which places the sanctity of human life and the need to save it even above observing Jewish law (*Babylonian Talmud*, Yoma, 85).

19 The halakhic reasoning for the use of a feather to test »the breath of the nose« (*Nishmat apo*) was a deduction from a case in which a man was buried under a pile of rocks on a Sabbath, and this is the continuation of the above-mentioned debate. It was then permitted to violate the sanctity of the Sabbath and dig him out (*Piku'aḥ nefesh* surpasses the Sabbath), and accordingly check for vital signs all over his body, »all the way up to his nose.« Ibid. Yoma, 86:71.

20 *Ha-Melits*, November 30, 1880. This is a play on words which rhymes in Hebrew: *Ha-kavran ve-ha-batlan*.

21 *Mishlo'aḥ manot* is the name given to the customary gift of food and sweets which Jews exchanged with each other during Purim. The number of *Ha-Melits* subscribers in 1881 is unknown; in 1885–1886 it fluctuated between 1,600 and 2,700 due to harsh competition with the first Hebrew daily which appeared in St. Petersburg at the time. See Tsederboym's letter published in *He-Avar* 2 (1954): 148. Hundred of copies thus seems like a conservative estimate for the distribution of *Mishlo'aḥ manot*, given the fact that it was supposedly attached as a gift to each newspaper issue sent to subscribers. For a study of the distribution of Hebrew literature and the Hebrew press in our period of interest, see Hagit Cohen, *Be-ḥanuto shel mokher ha-sfarim: ḥanuyot sfarim yehudiyyot be-mizraḥ eyropah ba-maḥatsit ha-shniyyah shel ha-me'ah ha-19* (Jerusalem: Magnes, 2006).

The opening part of *Mishlo'aḥ manot* was dedicated to a meticulous study of the various references to Jewish burial procedures in Halakhah.[22] It is important to note that there are not many references to the prohibition of delaying burial in Jewish law, so that even an individual with an average knowledge of Halakhah could have a good grasp of the topic without a great deal of effort. This certainly aided the Maskilic stance in what otherwise would have been one of its weakest points, as only a halakhic sage – in other words, a rabbi – who dedicated his whole life to the study of Jewish law and was ordained by another rabbi, could claim the authority to comment or rule on such important issues. The Maskilim, with whom Tsederboym sided, with their affinity to foreign, secular ideals and philosophies, could not claim the same authority. Furthermore, as Tsederboym argued before, the sum of halakhic references to *Halanah* does not imply a decisive ruling on the matter, allowing space for different interpretations, and there have indeed been halakhic sages throughout the ages who took a strict stance on the matter, and others who were more lenient.[23] Once again, this fact played into the hands of the Maskilim, for if Halakhah showed itself to be irresolute in such a serious matter concerning life and death, it could not serve as an authoritative source.

Initially, Tsederboym noted, the prohibition of *Halanah* appeared in the Pentateuch (*Deuteronomy* 21:22–23), but this clearly referred and applied only to executed criminals. In later centuries, Tsederboym continued, this restriction was expanded to include all those who died, and the custom of burying the deceased on the day of death was already well established during the Second Temple Era, i.e. roughly from the 6th century BCE. This custom was later codified in the Talmud (3rd century CE), albeit with the reservation that delaying burials was possible in order to prepare shrouds or coffins. The burial custom in its most uncompromising form eventually found its way into various kabbalistic works which further strengthened its authority as the sole burial practice.[24] In the 11th and 12th centuries, prominent medieval commentators like Rabbi

22 Tsederboym, *Mishlo'aḥ manot*, 2–4.

23 For a contemporary exploration of the halakhic background of the *Halanah* prohibition, which agrees with Tsederboym's study, see Moshe Samet, »Halanat metim: le-toldot ha-pulmus al kvi'at zman ha-mavet,« *Asufot* 3 (1989): 413–465, and especially 463 for the above-mentioned observations. Samet's article is thus far the most comprehensive study of the *Halanah* debate in the 18th and 19th centuries. Unfortunately, he did not dedicate more than a short footnote to the 19th century debate as it appeared in the Hebrew press of our period of interest.

24 Tsederboym, *Mishlo'aḥ manot*, 2–3; Samet, »Halanat metim,« 415, with source references. For the reservation concerning shrouds and coffins, see *Babylonian Talmud*, Sanhedrin, 46: 71.

Shlomo ben Itshak (Rashi) and Rabbi Moshe ben Maimon (Maimonides) offered strict interpretations of the biblical passage, requiring all burials to be performed without delay while disallowing leniency.[25]

Yet, by the 16th century, when Yosef Karo's *Shulḥan arukh* was adopted as the handbook for Jewish religious conduct by Ashkenazi Jews – and thus by East European Jewry[26] – some additional reservations were introduced to soften the strict law: If, for example, the Sabbath or a holy day were approaching, in which working at a grave would represent a transgression, then the burial was to be deferred until the Sabbath or holy day ended. Furthermore, the funeral could be postponed if the shrouds were not ready, or members of the deceased family had to arrive from far away, or if mourners were to be hired. Furthermore, Jewish burial societies had the right to delay funerals if the deceased's relatives refused to pay for them.[27] Such mitigations that were clearly to be found in Halakhah supported yet another of Tsederboym's initial arguments, in which he claimed that the taboo associated with delaying Jewish burials did not originate in formal law, but rather in the mystical traditions of the Kabbalah. The obligation to hasten the burial of the dead, he emphasized, was a folk custom that evolved from a very selective reading of religious law. Those mystical traditions, asserting that the soul of the deceased would find no rest until his or her body was interred in the ground, could be traced back to the Middle Ages and the *Zohar*.[28] They probably gained special popularity among Ashkenazi Jews with the appearance of handbooks for the ritualization of death and dying, the likes of the 17th century compilation *Ma'avar yabok*.[29]

Moving on to criticize »the feather test«, and in an attempt to strengthen his initial claim that premature burial was not a rare occurrence, Tsederboym repeated tales he knew from his younger years in Zamość concerning Jews from different small Polish towns in the Lublin area who were mistakenly believed to have died and then buried, or who were nearly buried alive. He

25 Tsederboym, *Mishlo'aḥ manot*, 2–3. See Rashi's commentary to *Deuteronomy* 21: 22–23; Rambam, *Book of Commandments*.

26 The *Shulḥan arukh* was adapted to the Ashkenazi ritual by rabbi Moshe Isserles (The »Rema«, 1520–1572) of Kraków. For a discussion of the *Halanah* prohibition in *Shulḥan arukh*, see Avraham S. Avraham, *Nishmat Avraham: Hilkhot ḥolim, rof'im ve-refu'ah* (Jerusalem, 1983).

27 *Shulḥan arukh*, Yoreh de'ah, 357; Hoshen mishpat, 107: 4.

28 Tsederboym, *Mishlo'aḥ manot*, 12; *Zohar*, Trumah: 141.

29 *Ma'avar Yabok* (Mantova, 1626) was a collection of 112 prayers and ceremonies dedicated to the sick and the dying. Written by the Kabbalist Aharon Brakhya of Modena (d. 1639), the book was later translated from Hebrew into Yiddish and gained tremendous popularity among the Jews of Eastern Europe. See Avriel Bar-Levav, »Ritualisation of Jewish Life and Death in the Early Modern Period,« *Leo Baeck Institute Year Book* 47 (2002): 69–82, especially 75.

complemented those old tales with more recent stories of premature burials quoted from newspapers, other than his own, that involved non-Jews and occurred in Hungary, France, and Romania.[30] In an almost casual manner, Tsederboym then brought forth what could have been one of his strongest arguments against Jewish Orthodoxy: The custom of immediate burial opposed state law, which required a waiting period of three days before burial. On that point he noted ironically that he recommended that Jews refrain from trying to »influence« state officials, like doctors and policemen, to register the time of death of the deceased as earlier than it actually was.[31] Tsederboym was referring to a well-known procedure in which dates of death were recorded retroactively, so as to avoid the transgression of *Halanah* while appeasing the authority's requirements for delaying burial, and it was clear from Tsederboym's words that he was hinting that »influencing« the authorities meant bribing them.[32]

Tsederboym's essay concluded somewhat strangely with a reprint of the three-way correspondence from 1772 between Moses Mendelssohn (1729–1786), Rabbi Jacob Emden (1698–1776), and Rabbi Mordechai Yaffe of Mecklenburg-Schwerin debating the prohibition of *Halanah*.[33] Despite the seemingly odd choice of conjuring up a century-old debate which had taken place among Jewish rabbis in German lands, it served a double purpose. First, Tsederboym used Mendelssohn and his support for a delayed Jewish burial procedure, expressed in that three-way correspondence, as a stamp of approval for the

30 Tsederboym heard of a case of the near premature burial of a Jew in Rejowiec from his father. He heard of a similar case that allegedly happened in Tyszowce from the poet and mathematician Jacob Eichenbaum. *Mishlo'aḥ manot*, 4–6.

31 Ibid., 14.

32 Bribing state officials so they would falsify the recorded time of death was widespread among Jews in the German states at the end of the 18th and the beginning of 19th centuries, see Wiesemann, »Jewish Burials in Germany,« 23. Recent studies have shown that the Jews in 19th-century Congress Poland were no strangers to this practice of »retroactive registry« either. See Agnieszka Jagodzińska, »Kaddish for Angels: Revisioning Funerary Rituals and Cemeteries in 19th Century Jewish Warsaw,« *Jewish Cultural Studies* 3 (2011): 265–289, here 273; Jan Paweł Woronczak, *Cmentarz żydowski w Kromołowie jako tekst kultury*, Ph.D. thesis, University of Wrocław, 1999, v.

33 For the historical background for this correspondence and the 18th-century premature burial controversy between the German *Maskilim* and their Orthodox rabbi opponents, which evolved into a long journalistic debate in the maskilic periodicals at the turn to the 19th century, see Shmuel Feiner, *The Jewish Enlightenment* (Philadelphia, CA: Philadelphia University Press, 2002), 331–335; Moshe Pelli, *The Age of Haskalah* (Leiden: Brill, 1979), 207–211; Moshe Samet, »Halanat metim,« 418–423. For an index of the German Haskalah essays on the subject, published (in Hebrew) in the maskilic periodicals of the period in question, see Pelli, *The Age of Haskalah*, 185.

halakhic stance voiced in *Mishlo'aḥ manot*. Mendelssohn was considered to be the founding father of the Jewish Enlightenment, and his stance in regard to the issue of *Halanah* – his only attempt at religious reform – was later adapted by the Maskilim of Central and Eastern Europe as a symbol of their aspirations toward modernizing religious practices.[34]

Secondly, in reviving the old journalistic debate concerning the practice of immediate burial, which preoccupied the old Maskilic periodicals in German-speaking lands on and off for over three decades, Tsederboym was implying that *Ha-Melits* was a direct successor to those old and prestigious Hebrew periodicals. Now that *Ha-Melits* was picking up the discussion where the old periodicals left off, Tsederboym was metaphorically donning the halo of the pioneering Maskilim of a century before by spearheading the Maskilic camp in its struggle against Orthodoxy on the issue of *Halanah* prohibition.

The ramifications of these actions were very clear: This was a frontal attack on Halakhah itself and a public declaration of war that the representatives of Jewish Orthodoxy in Russia could not remain indifferent to. Accordingly, they retaliated against Tsederboym and *Ha-Melits* with a journalistic counterattack that appeared in *Ha-Levanon*, which was published in Mainz at the time, and which had already begun to serve as the formal mouthpiece for Jewish Orthodoxy in Russia.

The internal Jewish sphere – the Orthodox response

As fate would have it, the Orthodox response to the journalistic debate initiated by Tsederboym lasted only a short time, from June to October 1881, after which *Ha-Levanon* and its publisher-editor Yeḥiel Bril (1836–1886) encountered a series of difficulties that affected the paper's frequency of publication, leading to the *Halanah* controversy being dropped in favor of other topics of discussion.[35]

34 Samet, »Halanat metim,« 463. Tsederboym copied the three-way correspondence between Mendelssohn and the rabbis from an old maskilic periodical called *Bikurey ha-itim*, published in Vienna from 1820 to 1831 and 1844 to 1845, which he knew from his youth. *Mishlo'aḥ manot*, 14. See Moshe Pelli's annotated index. *Bikurey ha-itim: bikurey ha-haskalah* (Jerusalem: Magnes, 2005), with an extensive English abstract.

35 Bril left Mainz – the home of the newspaper's editorial and sponsors – to visit the Jewish Pale of Settlement after the pogroms of spring 1881. Consequently, *Ha-Levanon* turned from a weekly into a monthly periodical, and 1882 was the last year in which it appeared regularly. This period also marked Bril's warming up to *Ḥibat-Tsiyon*, the proto-Zionist movement in Russia, which may have somewhat diminished his devotion to the Orthodox camp. For the newspaper's history during those years, see Gilbo'a, *Leksikon le-toldot ha-itonut ha-ivrit*, 194–195 (*Ha-Levanon*). For a survey of *Ha-Levanon*'s political inclinations, its Ortho-

Bril's withdrawal meant that, by the end of 1881, only those newspapers which were associated with the Maskilic camp were left to continue the public debate; yet even during that short period of active Orthodox response, *Ha-Levanon* published a rebuttal of Tsederboym's publications that represented both an example of classic Orthodox apologetics and a formal statement of defense on the subject of *Halanah*.

The man who stepped into the journalistic ring to confront the Maskilic attack was Rabbi Israel Ḥayyim Daykhes (1850–1937), a descendant of a prominent line of Vilna rabbis who, despite his relatively young age, was already considered a halakhic authority thanks to his published commentary on the Jerusalem Talmud. In addition, Daykhes was proficient in Haskalah literature and clearly did not oppose journalism in principle, as he was familiar with the debates in the Hebrew press, and at some point became a journal editor himself.[36] In a four-part essay appearing in installments all through June 1881, Daykhes conducted a direct and scorching attack on *Mishlo'aḥ manot* and its publisher, arguing the following main points:[37]

1) The Jews were loyal subjects to the Tsar and obeyed state law, and thus regularly delayed the burial of their dead as the law demanded. Consequently, the journalistic discussion involving hasty burial was purely theoretical, and all of Tsederboym's insinuations concerning bribes and falsifications of registries were nothing but baseless accusations – a fact that revealed Tsederboym to be a slanderer, an informer, and a traitor to his people.

2) Daykhes strongly opposed not only the contents of Tsederboym's publication but even his very attempt to deal with halakhic matters. The right to publish a halakhic commentary was reserved exclusively to ordained rabbis, and a newspaper editor-journalist had no halakhic authority whatsoever. Daykhes argued that Tsederboym lacked the proper training to write commentaries, and that this essay also showed the lack of a basic understanding of the law. *Mishlo'aḥ manot* was therefore completely off the mark in its halakhic claims, and worse – it was a dangerous essay because it sought to destabilize the very foundations of Jewish religion. Daykhes then offered a meticulous halakhic discussion of his

dox, anti-maskilic stance, and Bril's ideological shift, see Gideon Kouts, *The Hebrew and Jewish Press in Europe* (Paris: Suger Press, 2006), 43–59.

36 For a short biography of Daykhes, rabbi of Vladislavov (Suwałki province) from 1885, and of Leeds from 1901, publisher of a Hebrew periodical dedicated to Jewish thought and biblical commentary (London, 1902–1904), and a list of his publications, see Elyakim G. Kressel, *Leksikon ha-sifrut ha-ivrit ba-dorot ha-aḥaronim*, vol. 1 (Merḥavia: Sifriyat po'alim, 1965–1967), 549.

37 »Ha-gam erez ba-hora'ah?« *Ha-Levanon*, June 8, 15, 22, and 29, 1881.

own, proving the *Halanah* prohibition to be thoroughly based on sound law, rather than custom, and therefore clearly obligatory for any observant Jew.

3) In the last part of his essay, Daykhes addressed the claim concerning the inherent danger of premature burial in the prohibition of *Halanah*, and offered his own explanation for the journalistic reports of people who were thought to be dead before they miraculously recovered. The experienced functionaries and undertakers of the Jewish traditional burial societies, he claimed, knew how to tell the difference between those who were unconscious and those who were dead. Furthermore, if the ancient sages of blessed memory had not specifically required a delayed burial, it meant that they had not deemed the delay necessary or important for determining the certainty of death. Finally, while he reluctantly accepted the possibility that in certain cases a few Christians had indeed almost been buried alive as different newspapers reported, Daykhes concluded that the traditional handling of the dead protected Jews from such tragic consequences, and that even if such tragic misfortunes did occur, they did so »once in a thousand years and therefore are not worth relating to«.[38]

It is interesting to note that Daykhes did not address Tsederboym's memories of premature and near-premature burials of Jews from the Lublin area that were mentioned in *Mishlo'aḥ manot*, though he could have legitimately claimed that they were unreliable hearsay testimonies, especially as Tsederboym never showed them to be anything more than that. Then again, during summer 1881, when Daykhes challenged Tsederboym's Maskilic criticism, expressing utter denial regarding the possible dangers inherent in hasty burial, no journalistic reports concerning the suspected premature burial of Jews were known from the Pale of Settlement,[39] yet a dramatic change came that autumn when contemporary, first-hand reports, began to trickle in and appear in the newspaper in the form of letters sent in by a very specific group of readers, who were commonly known as »the correspondents«.

The correspondents of the Hebrew press: journalistic importance and social role

The correspondents, or field reporters, were Hebrew-writing Jews who sent their reports, for the most part on a volunteer basis, to the newspapers' editorial boards from all over the Russian Empire, describing various features of daily life within the Jewish sphere – from both central areas and the peripheries. During

38 Repeated twice in his essays on June 22 and 29, 1881.

39 According to the 1897 census, over 95% of all Jews in the tsarist empire lived within the limiting borders of the Pale of Settlement, see Yaakov Leshchinski, *Dos yidishe folk in tsifern* (Berlin: Klal-Farlag, 1922), 21.

their humble beginnings in the 1860s, the Hebrew newspapers were not able to finance a network of news correspondents, so they had to rely on the good will of whoever was able to write news stories in Hebrew and could afford to post them.[40] Those volunteers, who were sometimes referred to as *pirḥey sofrim* (»cadet writers«), were driven by the deep traditional reverence for the written word found among both the Maskilim and the Orthodox, and were motivated by the enormous esteem in which Jewish society held those who published – virtually any text – in Hebrew. Sixteen was a typical age for a budding correspondent, and many were the complaints leveled at the youngsters whose writing showed neither respect for their elders nor reverence for Hebrew grammar.[41] Nonetheless, this group of young people included some of the future publicists, novelists, and even national-movement activists of the period that extended to World War I. In addition, the correspondents fast became a central and at times vociferous segment of Jewish public opinion, and served as an important force in their local communities in unmasking and warning against social wrongs. The social implications for those who managed to have their work published and see their names printed »in square script« were often dramatic, and their social status and »value« on the match-making market frequently rose almost overnight.[42]

The fact that editors had to rely on their readers to produce news from the Jewish sphere turned the question of correspondent reliability into a critical one. Professional reporters who were on the editors' payroll were just beginning to emerge in the 1880s, but even then the Hebrew papers were still dependent on news sent in by casual, and sometimes unknown, contributors whose trust-

40 In the very first issue of *Ha-Maggid* – the first modern Hebrew periodical to appear – editor Eliezer Lipman Zilberman called upon his readers to write the editorial about »any matter that concerns the good of the Jewish people, or that concerns an individual that he alone, or more people like him, would like to inform the public about«. *Ha-Maggid*, June 4, 1856. The system of correspondents was thus established as an informal journalistic institution that was active well into the 1890s.

41 For instance *Ha-Maggid*, February 12, 1885.

42 Ḥayyim Tchernovits (1870–1949), professor of theology, Hebrew publicist, and sometime deputy state rabbi of Odessa, recalled in his memoirs how his correspondence, published in *Ha-Melits* when he was only sixteen, won him a seat of honor in a meeting of the elders of his town, see idem, *Pirkey Ḥayyim* (New York: Bitsaron, 1954), 112. For a similar story, see Mordekhay ben Hilel Ha-Cohen's memoirs *Me-erev ad-erev* (Vilnius: Greber press, 1904), 130. Publishing a correspondence in the Hebrew press and thus becoming a ›lucrative catch‹ for well-off fathers-in-law, held the promise of a comfortable living for a young Maskil: Y. D. Bayerski, »Sod baḥurim,« *Ha-Melits*, May 12, 1884; Elyakim G. Kressel, *Toldot ha-itonut ha-ivrit be-erets israel* (Jerusalem: Ha-sifriyah ha-tsiyonit, 1964), 13.

worthiness was hard to verify.[43] Hence, if a spurious report was ever accidentally published, it would be discovered by one of the readers – usually a person involved in the matter at hand – who would send a rebuttal to the editorial board. The renegade correspondent would then be blacklisted by the editor in order to prevent any additional publications based upon his false reports.[44] This system of self-correction, which relied on the feedback of the reading public, worked well enough, but the unintentional publication of unreliable news items that could only be detected in retrospect, urged the editors to adapt a series of preventive measures to help them protect their newspapers' credibility from being undermined by such reports: Correspondence sent to the newspaper editors by unfamiliar people had to be authenticated by the local Crown Rabbi or by one of his deputies with an official governmental stamp. In cases in which this was not possible, the correspondent would be requested to have his letter authenticated by someone whom the editors regarded as a reliable witness such as another correspondent or a newspaper distribution agent. Even if the protective system was not entirely flawless, it seemed to have produced satisfactory results on the whole.[45]

Consequently, when examining a journalistic debate in the Hebrew press of the period through the prism of correspondence, and in order to get a satisfactory overview of the matter at hand, it is necessary to consider both the reports that appeared and the rebuttals that were possibly published at a later

43 »As we are far away from the place of occurrence«, wrote Tsederboym after a falsified report from Ekaterinoslav was accidentally published, »and we cannot discuss the details of all the deeds that we are informed of, we can only depend on the reports of our correspondents when we know them to be trustworthy men.« *Ha-Melits*, February 17, 1888.

44 Avraham Tsvi Brodsky from Bessarabia, for instance, was denounced publicly by another reader in *Ha-Melits* for copying old reports from *Ha-Melits* and sending them to another Hebrew newspaper. Tsederboym reassured his readers that he already knew all about Brodsky and his nefarious deeds, indicating that he had already been ›blacklisted‹. *Ha-Melits*, January 24, 1887.

45 See Tsederboym's accusatory footnote in which he raged against »the lying informants from Borisov« (Minsk province), who misled him with a false report. He publicly threatened that no more correspondences from Borisov would be published unless they were to be properly authenticated by the Crown Rabbi, or by »a familiar man« (to the editorial board), see *Ha-Melits*, December 28, 1886. The Crown Rabbi (*Kazennyi ravvin*) was more often than not a mere government bureaucrat, as opposed to the »Spiritual Rabbi« (*Dukhovnyi ravvin*), who was the halakhic authority in the Jewish congregations, see ChaeRan Y. Freeze, *Jewish Marriage and Divorce in Imperial Russia* (Hanover–London: Brandeis University Press, 2002), 95–130. On one rare occasion, talented forgers managed to have a falsified letter published with a fake signature of the substitute Crown Rabbi of Antopol (Grodno province), see *Ha-Melits*, November 17, 1890.

date. Otherwise, another feature typical of the Hebrew press was its uncanny ability to preserve the impulse for heated debates concerning specific topics over long periods of time, often spanning whole decades.[46] This was due to the fact that quite in contrast to the familiar cliché that »today's newspaper wraps tomorrow's fish«, Hebrew newspaper issues were carefully collected at the end of every year, bound in hardcover, and sold at bookstores as sought-after collectors' items even years after they were published. As those yearly volumes became an indispensable part of both personal and public libraries, they enabled their owners to read them again and again as if they were classical literature, while new generations of young enthusiasts became to varying degrees familiar with discussion topics of the past.[47]

The reports supplied by the correspondents therefore assisted both in supporting the debate concerning the *Halanah* prohibition and maintaining it as an engaging topic of discussion for years to come. No less importantly, the appearance of correspondences dealing with the question of Jewish burial traditions signified a shift of venue for the journalistic discussion, which in turn reflected a change in the public debate. Once the discussion exhausted itself in the »high«, intellectual, journalistic sphere, in which editors and rabbis polemicized about halakhic matters, the debate entered the sphere of »current affairs«, with common people using the language of facts to report news.

A short time after Tsederboym published his *Mishlo'aḥ manot*, a steady trickle of reports began to appear in the Hebrew press – mainly in *Ha-Melits*, but also in *Ha-Tsfirah* and *Ha-Maggid* – containing descriptions of confirmed mishandlings of Jews whose death had not been fully determined, and reporting on both Jews and Christians who were supposedly dead but woke up before they were buried. Reports about Christian cases were usually copied from the non-Jewish press. Those concerning Jewish cases were testimonies from the field, describing for the first time how unconscious people, mistaken for dead, were almost buried

46 The *Etrog* – a lemon-like fruit of the citron family, used for ritualistic purposes on the Jewish holiday of *Sukkot* – was the center of a heated journalistic debate that started in the late 1860s, and was still alive and kicking in the 1890s, for it involved the halakhic question (which later turned political) of which type of *Etrog* was preferable, that of Corfu or that of Palestine, see Salmon, »Ha-ortodoksiyah ha-yehudit be-mizraḥ eyropah,« 375; *Ha-Melits*, January 17, 1894.

47 As E. G. Kressel put it: »The newspaper was not only read, it was *studied*.« Kressel, *Toldot ha-itonut ha-ivrit*, 12 (emphasis in the original). One of those young fans of the Hebrew press was Israel's national poet, Ḥayyim Naḥman Bialik (1873–1934), who reminisced in his childhood memoirs on how he used to delve secretly into old copies of *Ha-Melits* and *Ha-Tsfirah* that he discovered in the attic of his home. »*Ha-Melits*, *Ha-Tsfirah* ve-tseva ha-niyyar,« *Kol kitvey Ḥ. N. Bialik* (Tel Aviv: Dvir, 1951), 268–272.

alive, increasing the realization that premature burial was not so infrequent after all, and indeed not a misfortune that occurred »once in a thousand years«.

The case of Shmuel Vonizenski

Among all the reports dealing with suspected premature burials which appeared in the 1880s, the burial ordeal of the unfortunate Shmuel Vonizenski received the widest exposure. All of the first-hand witnesses to this incident who sent their reports to the Hebrew newspapers agreed upon the following details: Vonizenski, a sixty-five-year-old Jew »with a constitution of iron«, visited the public bathhouse in his native town of Smorgon in Vilna province, on a certain Friday afternoon in September 1881.[48] After spending some time in the hot steam he felt unwell and proceeded to the corridor to cool down, where he lost consciousness and collapsed. The doctors who had rushed in could not revive him with smelling salts, and several attempts at bloodletting failed as well due to the »freezing« of the blood in his veins. Once all resuscitation attempts proved futile, a feather was brought and placed against Vonizenski's nostrils, and since no signs of breathing were detected, he was declared dead. Preparations for an immediate funeral then ensued in order to complete his burial before the Sabbath set in. As custom obliged, Vonizenski's body was wrapped in shrouds, shards of clay were put over his eyes and mouth, and he was interred without a coffin, still wearing his prayer shawl (*talit*). Once buried, his body was covered in planks, yet the earth that was put over it was not poured into the grave itself, leaving the body in an enclosed space. According to the reports in *Ha-Melits*, the local spiritual rabbi flew into a rage when he heard of the haste involved with the burial, but there was no turning back.[49]

As opposed to the rabbi, the local chief of police in whose absence – and without his approval – Vonizenski's burial took place, had no qualms about opening the grave when he returned to town two days later. The gruesome sight which unfolded was described both in *Ha-Melits* and *Ha-Levanon* thus: The deceased was found lying a small distance away from his shrouds and prayer shawl which were both stained in blood and vomit. The shards which had been placed on his eyes and mouth were cast aside, and »the face and throat of the body were extremely swollen, while many marks testified that the poor wretch had died quite recently of asphyxia«.[50]

48 David Kupelevitch [a correspondence from Smorgon], *Ha-Melits*, September 13, 1881.

49 Ibid., For a survey of Jewish burial customs, see *Encyclopaedia Judaica*, 1st ed., s.v. »Burial.«

50 *Ha-Melits*, September 13, 1881. Tederboym noted that he had an additional correspondence from Smorgon, which he did not publish, testifying to the

Denials of Vonizenski's alleged premature burial appeared in *Ha-Levanon* a few weeks later when Tsvi Hirsh Fridzon, Deputy Crown Rabbi of Smorgon, wrote a correspondence claiming that none of the reports portraying the state of the body in the grave were true, and that all of the newspaper coverage had been the result of a personal feud between the correspondent, David Kupelevitch, and Vonizenski's son-in-law. Furthermore, he noted, six hours elapsed before the deceased was buried, during which he showed no signs of life, making it highly unlikely that he could have regained consciousness later on.[51]Alongside Fridzon's report there was another correspondence sent in by an anonymous writer using the pseudonym Sh.L.Y., with additional information and a more balanced approach: The deceased had a short neck, he claimed, which made him especially susceptible to strokes. The majority of details concerning the state in which the body was found were true, but – he explained – according to the doctors who examined the deceased, it was not unusual for digested food to spew out of a lifeless body, and the blood which stained Vonizenski's prayer shawl must have trickled out of his severed veins that were cut by the doctors after he collapsed in the bathhouse. There were no signs that the body »moved« in the grave, he concluded, though he admitted that it could have been advisable to postpone the burial for a longer period of time in order to refute any doubts regarding the certainty of Vonizenski's death.[52]

Seen from a 21st-century medical point of view, the reports at hand do not present us with enough information with which to determine that Vonizenski was buried alive. Assuming that all the signs mentioned in the correspondences as proof of his awakening and suffocation in his grave indeed appeared, they could just as well indicate a physiological activity that is known to occur postmortem. The »Vonizenski affair« will thus, for the time being, remain an enigma.[53]

What is clear in this journalistic context is that, in contrast to the uncompromising stance and sweeping denial offered by Rabbi Daykhes as a representative of the Orthodox intelligentsia, the journalistic discussion initiated by reporters moved away from the halakhic and into the scientific sphere. Both supporters and opponents of the custom of immediate burial considered the facts at hand without attempting to interpret present occurrences in accordance

alarming state of the body. The correspondence in *Ha-Levanon* agreed with the publication in *Ha-Melits*, except that it was reported that the deceased was found »lying on his side.« *Ha-Levanon*, September 14, 1881.

51 *Ha-Levanon*, October 7, 1881.

52 Ibid.

53 I am indebted to Dr. Jack Horner, M.D., for examining the journalistic evidence and offering his professional input.

with the past, and without denying a reality that contradicted or opposed the world as it was framed and interpreted by Halakhah. It is intriguing that such a factual discussion mainly took place in a newspaper that was committed to uphold the Orthodox cause, which may possibly suggest that segments of *Ha-Levanon*'s readership were not as conservative as their rabbis.

While criticism of the *Halanah* prohibition concerned itself with the scientific validity of the halakhic ruling, it also addressed the medical and moral qualifications of the officers whose task was to implement religious law. This part of the discussion centered on the Jewish burial societies, and similarly to the whole *Halanah* debate, it too represented an old Maskilic complaint about Orthodox Judaism, for which the Hebrew press offered a new venue of expression.

Administers of burial and death

The institution of *ḥevrah kadisha* (Holy Society) already existed in Talmudic times and was to be found all over the Jewish world – with slight variations – in different centuries and geographical locations, but its fundamental functions remained the same. The duty of its members was to take care of all matters, logistical and otherwise, connected with the handling of the deceased, from their last hours on their deathbeds through their final interment. The *ḥevrah kadisha* performed the ritual cleansing of the corpse, wrapped it in shrouds, carried it to the burial site to the allotted plot, and carried out the actual burial. Their actions were considered to be the greatest religious obligation (*mitsvah*) one could perform, and it was termed a *ḥesed shel emet*, »a true act of grace«, for this was a favor that the receiving party could never pay back.

Among the Jews of tsarist Russia, the *gabayim* (»managers«) of the burial societies were usually the leaders and dignitaries of their congregations. Formally, they were expected to volunteer for service without pay, and they were required to be elected to their office every year. Further down the chain of command were different laborers who belonged to the less prestigious and educated classes, and among them were the *shamashim* (beadles) who were in charge of the manual labor involved, such as carrying the dead and digging graves. A corresponding society of »righteous women« volunteered to offer exactly the same services for deceased women, attending to the sick on their deathbeds, cleansing bodies, and sewing shrouds.[54] Thanks to the high social

54 For the history and role of *the ḥevrah kadisha* in early modern Ashkenazi society, and its position among other religious-philanthropic organizations within Jewish congregations, see Jacob Katz, *Tradition and Crisis: Jewish Society at the End of the Middle Ages* (New York: Schocken Books, 1971), 157–167. For

ranking of its leaders, the *ḥevrah kadisha* was considered to be a prestigious organization, and this prestige very often wielded considerable political power which at times was exploited in dubious manners. Such was the contempt that some burial societies incurred, that Maskilic discourse turned the *ḥevrah kadisha* into a literary topos representing pure evil, and which the novel *Kvurat ḥamor* (»A Donkey's Burial«) by Perets Smolenskin is probably its most outstanding example.[55]

Accusations against burial society *gabayim* extorting considerable sums of money from bereaved relatives who were obligated to bury their loved ones, as well as complaints concerning their vindictiveness in settling personal scores with members of their congregation, punishing them for their »unacceptable lifestyles« after they died, were heard in Congress Poland as early as the 1820s.[56] Reports in the Hebrew press of the last two decades of the 19th century seem to suggest that not much had changed, as a biting editorial in *Ha-Melits* of December 1890 indicated with a summary of the burial societies' transgressions.

There was nothing »holy« about the *ḥevrah kadisha*, the anonymous writer claimed. Its managers avoided any contact with the deceased, leaving the »dirty work« to the *shamashim*, and instead concentrated mainly on assessing how much money they could demand from the bereaved families, very often above and beyond their financial means.[57] Some *gabayim*, the writer argued, were ruthless enough to delay the burial of the deceased as a means of exerting pressure on those relatives who were reluctant to pay, and the allotment of burial

the burial society's role among Polish Jews, see François Guesnet, *Polnische Juden im 19. Jahrhundert: Lebensbedingungen, Rechtsnormen und Organisation im Wandel* (Köln: Böhlau, 1998), 357–386; Anna Michałowska-Mycielska, *The Jewish Community: Authority and Social Control in Poznań and Swarzędz,* 1650–1793 (Wrocław: Wydawnictwo Uniwersytetu Wrocławskiego, 2008), 143–153.

55 Smolenskin (1842–1885), depicted a young Maskil who was persecuted by his coreligionists for stealing the cakes from the *ḥevra kadisha* banquet. This led him to financial ruin and divorce, so in order to survive he was forced to become an informer for the tsarist authorities. This incited the members of his congregation to have him killed, and their revenge was completed when they buried him as they would a beast of burden. The novel was published in installments in Smolenskin's periodical *Ha-Shaḥar* 4 (1872), and printed as a book only after his death (Warszawa: Katsenelbogen, 1901).

56 Marcin Wodziński, *Haskalah and Hasidism in the Kingdom of Poland: A History of Conflict* (Oxford: The Littman Library of Jewish Civilization, 2005), 9–115; Jagodzińska, »Kaddish for Angels,« 268–269.

57 The correspondent from Novgorod-Severskiy (Chernigov province), who went by the pseudonym *Gerve-toshav,* described the unabashed corruption that accompanied elections for public office in Jewish congregations. Victory in the elections was bought, he claimed, »with money, with vodka, and with the fist.« *Ha-Melits*, September 18, 1885.

plots by the *ḥevrah kadisha* very often involved the sale of prestigious locations at elevated prices, even though the cemeteries were public property owned by the congregation as a whole. The money collected from bereaved families often lined the pockets of the *gabayim* themselves, while they were sometimes used to finance the traditional yearly banquets of the burial societies, which, the author claimed, occasionally turned into an outrageous display of gluttony and debauchery. Finally, the author reported that the beadles, whose job it was to handle the corpses, were prone to alcoholism and violence, which was often directed at mourning relatives, or even at other members of the *ḥevrah kadisha*.[58]

The burial societies' exclusiveness in handling the dead and their monopoly on administering funeral arrangements, with all it involved, meant that in practice they – and no one else – determined the certainty of death. Seen in this wider context, the abhorrence found in Maskilic discourse towards the *ḥevrah kadisha* is easier to understand, and all the more so Tsedeboym's aversion towards »the Jewish undertaker and Jewish layabout« who, using their »feather test«, decided who was to be considered dead and ready for burial. Here there were matters of life and death entrusted into the hands of those who were both corrupt and ignorant while they – and not trained men of science and medicine – were the ones who decided not just where one's final resting place would be, but also when one's death became definite. Consequently, reports that depicted the *ḥevrah kadisha* as carelessly – if unintentionally – killing people who happened to lose consciousness in one way or another are numerous, and the following is a partial yet informative list.

One report from Medzhibozh (Podolia province), told of a baby that had received an overdose of prescribed medicinal wine and fallen into a deep sleep. His mother called one of the beadles of the burial society, who rushed to begin funeral procedures before nightfall, but the baby luckily woke up while being ritually cleansed.[59] Similarly, an eighteen-year-old from Lakhva (Minsk province), who was known to suffer from heart problems, lost consciousness and was assumed dead. Fortunately for him, one of beadles who cleansed his body

58 *Ha-Melits*, December 2, 1890. For correspondences depicting drunk and violent *ḥevrah kadisha* beadles, see *Ha-Melits*, June 10, 1883 (from Balta, Podolia province); October 31, 1883 (from Aleksandria, Kherson province); April 28, 1885 (from Vetka, Mogilev province). Tsederboym himself, it was reported after his death, served as one of the managers of the *ḥevrah kadisha* in St. Petersburg for many years, yet it did not prevent him from publicly criticizing his peers when in 1884 one of the *gabayim* attempted to extort money from a bereaved family, see *Ha-Melits*, September 14, 1893; February 1, 1884.

59 *Ha-Melits*, June 12, 1885.

thought he recognized some vital signs, stopped the burial preparations and called a doctor who managed to revive the young man.[60]

A seventeen-day-old infant from Riga who was born prematurely was, however, not as lucky. Thought to be stillborn, the baby was left in a drafty funeral room for the night in order to delay its decay. Come morning the beadles arrived to conduct the burial and realized the child was alive, and the doctor who was rushed in managed to revive it. However, the child did not survive the exposure to the cold and died the same evening.[61] Similarly, the wife of a local rich man in Vorontsova (Kiev province), fell victim to the over-diligent »righteous women« of the local *ḥevrah kadisha*. As she had suffered a second stroke in ten days, the women decided – based on the »feather test« – that this time she was not in a »lethargic sleep« as she had been a week before, so they promptly set off to bury her without consulting a doctor. The correspondent Baruch Kritzstein reported that the »body« swallowed its saliva and groaned while being cleansed, but the pious women attributed those symptoms to the machinations of an »evil spirit«, and the woman was placed in her grave.[62]

The concerns of the imperial authorities

As mentioned before, the *Halanah* debate involved two main spheres of confrontation: The first was a discussion that was internally Jewish; the second pitted the Jews and their religious traditions against the Russian state and its secular laws and regulations. In general, Jewish burial was regarded by the state as a traditional religious custom which the Jews, not unlike other denominations in the Russian Empire, could practice freely according to their ancient law – very much like marriage, divorce, and circumcision. The state lacked the motivation to intervene unless the custom somehow interfered with imperial law or regulations, or if an action was considered to be a transgression by the standards of the denomination itself.[63] The Imperial Medical Codex (*Vrachebnyi ustav*) required that every individual assumed dead would not be buried before he or she was examined by a doctor, or alternatively by a policeman or a priest. Burials were required to be postponed for three days, while there were

60 *Ha-Melits*, February 18, 1887.

61 *Ha-Melits*, May 31, 1886. This tragic story was reported both in the *Rigasche Zeitung* and the *Rigasche Polizei Zeitung* of the same week, and supplemented by an eyewitness account in *Ha-Melits*.

62 *Ha-Melits*, August 15, 1884.

63 As in the case of bigamy, a transgression according to Jewish law, and therefore punishable by the state; see Freeze, *Jewish Marriage and Divorce*, 227.

recognizable exceptions to the law in which urgent burials were permitted, or indeed – vital.[64]

Nonetheless, the Jewish custom of immediate burial represented a clear breach of state law, and the picture that emerges in the Hebrew press reflects a growing interest in Jewish burial customs on the part of the imperial authorities in the 1880s, though the few relevant correspondences dealing with the topic report only local regulations of governors. This might imply local initiatives toward reinforcing state laws with regard to the Jews rather than an imperial policy that was dictated from above. Unfortunately, it is hard to identify what triggered such local legislation, but it seems justifiable to speculate that at least some of these initiatives were spurred on by provincial occurrences and internal conflicts among various Jewish communities.

For instance, the newspapers reported in 1885 that the governor of Podolia province had ordered that all the Jews under his jurisdiction delay the burial of their dead for three days without, however, any clear explanation given for that decision. On the other hand, similar orders were handed down in the province of Bessarabia and in Warsaw in 1887, while in the former case it was specifically noted that the legislation was initiated in reaction to Jews informing on each other.[65] The sporadic nature of these reports seems to suggest that there was generally no strict enforcement of burial regulations with regard to the Jewish congregations, at least as long as no special attention was needed and no suspicion of foul play was raised. As stated before, the arrangement in which the date of death was registered »retroactively« was convenient for both Jewish traditionalists and state bureaucrats, and the prevailing trend seems to have been that such falsified registration was more common in peripheral towns and in the countryside, where the Jewish population was generally more observant and kept to traditional burial customs. In the large cities of Russia and Poland, where police supervision was more pronounced and a greater portion of the Jewish

64 *Svod zakonov Rossiiskoi Imperii*, vol. 11, part 1 (St. Petersburg, 1906), article 1327, 127. Sub-clause no. 4 relates that no burial should take place before the time stipulated by medical regulations. The medical regulations (*Svod zakonov*, vol. 13, book 2, part 1, ch. 4.) provided for a three day delay, yet permitted urgent burial in cases of epidemics (article 713), or in times of warm weather when at least 24 hours passed since the assumed time of death, and clear signs of decomposing were detected (article 714).

65 For Podolia, see *Ha-Melits*, August 10, 1885 (a memorandum issued by the governor to the Crown Rabbis of Balta); for reports from Soroka (Bessarabia) and the reports of mutual informing among the Jews, see *Ha-Melits*, June 21, 1887; for Warsaw, see *Ha-Tsfirah*, November 6, 1887.

population tended to be less attached to religious tradition, Jews seemed to have abided more by state law in this particular regard.[66]

Jewish tradition came into harsh conflict with state law in cases which necessitated special treatment, such as sudden inexplicable death – as in the case of Vonizenski cited above – or when death was known or suspected to have been a result of violent action. An autopsy would then have to be performed before burial, and if the deceased had already been interred, the body would be exhumed for inspection.[67] Jewish Orthodoxy viewed autopsy as a profane action which resulted in *nivul ha-met* (desecration of the dead) so that autopsies performed on Jews were to be avoided at all cost, even if a direct confrontation with the authorities would follow.[68]

Thus, when the body of a ninety-year-old Jew from a village near Liubeshov (Minsk province) who had been murdered sometime before, was discovered on the road to town, his relatives from his native village were not too concerned with informing the police of the murder so those responsible might be found, but instead rushed to bury the old man in Liubeshov, lest the police find out about the body and order an autopsy.[69] Conditions in Russia in this period were such that the number of professional doctors was small, their workload unmanageable, and the support they received from the state meager. Consequently, it is not hard to imagine how the shortage of doctors, especially in rural areas, enabled the Jews to bury their dead in accordance with their customs.[70]

66 For Poland, see Jagodzińska, »Kaddish for Angels,« 273. For postponed Jewish burials in Grodno, St. Petersburg, and Riga, see *Ha-Melits*, January 15, 1894; April 20, 26, and 28, 1893. This tendency toward more conservative Jewish conduct in the countryside and more liberal conduct in towns was known in Germany as well; see Wiesemann, »Jewish Burials in Germany,« 26.

67 *Svod zakonov Rossiiskoi Imperii*, vol. 11, part 1, (St. Petersburg, 1906), article 1327, 127. Sub-clause no. 4, *Vrachebnyi ustav*, in: *Svod zakonov*, vol. 13, book 2, part 1, ch. 4 (article 715).

68 For a discussion of *Nivul ha-met* with extensive halakhic references, see Michael Greyber, *Nitu'aḥ ha-metim le-tsorkhey limud ve-ḥakirah: mi-nekudat hashkafat ha-dat ha-israelit* (Jerusalem: Mad'a, 1943).

69 Eventually word got out and the body had been exhumed and checked by the authorities; see Moshe Epstein [a correspondence from Liubeshov], *Ha-Melits*, September 3, 1888.

70 As late as 1900, there were no more than 19,842 qualified doctors (including military medics) in the Russian Empire, and even less than that in earlier decades. The law required doctors, in the public and private sectors alike, to perform an autopsy in every case that required special attention, and they were obliged to testify in court if foul play was involved. This duty very often obliged doctors to travel long distances at their own expense, see Nancy Mandelker Frieden, *Russian Physicians in an Era of Reform and Revolution, 1856–1905* (Princeton, NJ: Princeton UP, 1981), 266–267, 323.

A rather extreme case, which is nonetheless illustrative for the clash of tradition and state law, was reported in *Ha-Melits* on September 8, 1886: The police commander at Shpola (Kiev province) set out to fetch a doctor from a nearby town to examine a Jew who had died suddenly, and left his deputy in charge of the corpse.[71] The deceased's relatives managed to trick the deputy, however, and conduct a secret burial, while placing an old tombstone over his grave to camouflage it. Two days later, when the commander returned with the doctor, he could not find the grave or even enter the graveyard as the Jewish congregation was physically blocking the way. It took the humiliated state official six weeks before he managed to assemble thirty armed Cossacks and force his way into the cemetery, but even after he dug up a fair portion of it and exhumed an unknown number of corpses, he could not identify the Jew in question. He then had to console himself with arresting members of the family of the deceased and some of the Jews who had obstructed the entrance to the cemetery six weeks previously.

It would generally seem that political rule and medical conditions in Russia during the period in question enabled the majority of Jews who still lived according to their ancient traditions to continue and practice their age-old burial customs. It is also likely that this went on without extracting too high a price from the Jewish congregations who sometimes managed to brazenly ignore state law, or alternatively utilize persuasive measures in dealing with the local authorities. The same pattern of behavior was to be found among Orthodox Jewish congregations in other countries, as in the German states and the Austrian Empire, where laws forbidding premature burial had already been constituted in the 18th century, and there too the issue remained unresolved generations later. Only in times and places where state enforcement was uncompromising – mainly in the second half of the 19th century – did the Orthodox yield to secular legislation, which in turn prompted them to find »halakhic bypasses« to justify their need to delay the burial of their dead.[72]

Conclusion

The shift from religious to scientific thought, inspired by the Enlightenment, spurred on state legislation imposed from above, which in the case of Jewish

71 The term used here for »police commander« is *pakid*, which means »clerk« in modern Hebrew, but this more likely referred to the *stanovoi pristav* (police commander) who was in charge of the local police force, as *pakid* in the Hebrew of that period probably simply meant »officer«. See the translation from Hebrew to Russian suggested in contemporary newspapers, e.g. *Ha-Tsfirah*, July 12, 1892; *Ha-Melits*, October 6, 1893; *Ha-Melits*, November 5, 1894.

72 Samet, »Halanat metim,« 450–451, 455.

burial customs clashed with a two-thousand-year-old tradition and – in the particular case of Russian-Polish Jewry in the 1880s and 1890s – infringed upon the vestiges of a 400-year-old Jewish religious autonomy. In this general context the debate over the *Halanah* prohibition becomes a convenient test case through which it is possible to examine Jewish responses to both external and internal pressures – those that had been applied by the state and its regulations on the one hand, and those which originated from internal Jewish conflicts on the other.

Orthodox Jewry was faced by a threat to one of its foundations, the infallibility of Halakhah, which was a system of conduct designed to encompass virtually every aspect of Jewish life. If this system could be shown to be undecided on such weighty matters as life and death, if it could not remain outside the jurisdiction of scientific criticism – or indeed of any type of criticism – it might no longer be regarded as the perfect, flawless, and timeless system it was thought to be. By further deduction, if Halakhah was not perfect and flawless, it just might show itself to be redundant and irrelevant, and all the more so in a world that was constantly changing and modernizing. From that point on, the road to apostasy, as far as the Orthodox were concerned, seemed wide open.

Consequently, Jewish Orthodoxy could not but act with unfailing suspicion towards any imposed change in traditional customs, even if a halakhic justification for such a change could be found within Jewish juridical sources. That is why even rabbis with some Maskilic inclinations such as Rabbi Daykhes, refused to acknowledge the possible dangers inherent within the ancient burial custom so as not to admit Halakhah's lack of soundness on matters of life and death.[73] Locally, with regard to the burial societies, it is easy to imagine how they feared that tampering with the well established procedures of caring for the dying and handling the dead would somehow compromise their monopoly, threatening their political and economic grip on their congregations.

Not unlike the imperial state, the Hebrew press of Russian-Polish Jewry also served as an agent of change. By reflecting anti-Orthodox ideological approaches and cultivating a new modernized discourse in which novel and non-halakhic solutions for various problems were considered, it succeeded over time to influence and mold public opinion. The special status the Hebrew press enjoyed among its Jewish readers, which categorized it as a literary genre of sorts,

73 A collection of *responsa* (rabbinical correspondence) from the last two decades of the 18th century, from Italy and elsewhere in Europe, shows that the rabbinic elite was not unaware of the dangers of premature burial. But their conservatism eventually won out, and the furthest they were willing to go was to instruct those in charge of the burial procedures to »take extra care« to notice vital signs in those presumed dead. Ibid., 453–455.

preserved the relevancy of the *Halanah* debate for over a decade. While Tsederboym's role in this process was central, it would seem, ironically, that his decision to revive the burial controversy in 1880 was spontaneous, as it was probably triggered by that particular report about the French fur merchant who had almost been buried alive. Tsederboym's familiarity with the *Halanah* debate a hundred years before increased his and his newspaper's prestige as direct heirs to the founders of Haskalah, yet unlike the Orthodox rabbis at the end of the 18th century who disregarded the journalistic discussion, the rabbis in Russia understood the importance of trying to influence public opinion and had no qualms about trying to do so through the printed media. Still, if the Orthodox were doing their best to resist change and avoid the implementation of state law when it conflicted with their religious customs to the point of using, in extreme cases, violence at the local level, they could not stop a journalistic debate from penetrating public discourse and reaching down to the »lower echelons« of Jewish society. Since halakhic debates were no longer an issue restricted to the rabbinical elite and its halakhic correspondence (*responsa*), the weaknesses of religious law on critical issues were now openly discussed and denounced.

At its core, the *Halanah* debate reflects Jewish society's slow, and to a large extent self-propelled mentality shift towards non-traditional modes of thought. The public journalistic debate – in itself an innovation among Russian-Polish Jewry of this period – offered a unique opportunity to advance this process. The rift was growing steadily between those segments of Jewish society that placed science at the center of their system of beliefs and thought, and those who chose religion, with its mystical traditions and the conviction that no new or relevant knowledge could be found outside Jewish lore. Though the journalistic sources do not disclose the extent to which the abolition of the traditional burial custom was successful at the end of the 19th century, it is clear that a fundamental change was well on its way.

Dror Segev

Civil Law and Jewish Halakhah: Problems of Coexistence in the Late Russian Empire*

Russia was, and still is, known for a lack of respect for written law. However, as in every modern European state, the rule of law in the Russian Empire was considered obligatory for everyone, at least in theory. On the other hand, the Jewish subjects of the empire, faithful to their religion, had their own law, *Halakhah*, which they regarded as of divine origin. In some cases, as also happens in every modern state – including the State of Israel – civil and religious laws contradicted each other.[1] The aim of this article is to explore how both law systems interacted and coexisted in late imperial Russia, and to examine particular issues and general approaches which defined this coexistence. I look at the interaction of both bodies of law as reflected in the memoranda produced by hundreds of rabbis and the evaluation of those memoranda by local governors, written in 1908, during preparations to the Rabbinic Commission of 1910. This unique corpus of documents presents an integral and perhaps the fullest possible picture of relationships between state law and Halakhah, as it was practiced in the last decade of the Russian Empire. As I intend to argue, the rabbis' memoranda clearly showed that the Russian Empire was a relatively hospitable place for Jews observing religious laws and traditions, and the problems – rather marginal – were caused by the inconsistency of Russian legislation, as will be demonstrated below.

An institution known as the *Rabbinic Commission* was established within the Ministry of the Interior in 1848 in order to serve as a kind of central consistory that would be able to provide the government with information concerning the Jewish religion and to decide on halakhic issues. The seven members of the

* I am grateful to Yvonne Kleinmann, Anna Berezina, Shaul Stampfer, Alex Valdman, and Theodore Weeks who read this article and made very useful comments and suggestions.

1 For overview of contradictions between the modern state law and Halakhah, see chapter 9 in Leo Landman, *Jewish Law in the Diaspora: Confrontation and Accommodation* (Philadelphia, PA: The Dropsie College for Hebrew and Cognate Learning, 1968), 135–148 and Gil Graff, *Separation of Church and State: Dina de-Malkhuta Dina in Jewish Law, 1750–1848* (Tuscaloosa, AL: University of Alabama Press, 1985).

Commission were nominated by the minister from a list of candidates elected by Jewish communities. However, the Commission did not become a permanent body and was convened irregularly, between long intervals, while its deliberations were confined to the questions proposed by the ministry.[2]

In early February 1908, the Ministry of the Interior announced the convocation of the sixth Rabbinic Commission, which after several postponements met in 1910.[3] In sharp contrast to previous practice, when the ministry itself formulated the questions for the Commission, this time it was interested in hearing the opinions of local rabbis. In the aftermath of the Revolution of 1905–1907, Prime Minister and Minister of the Interior Peter Stolypin adopted a new mode of governing, giving a certain weight to public opinion.[4] The convocation of the Rabbinic Commission in 1908–1910 was apparently a first stage in Stolypin's vague plan to reorganize Jewish communal life in order to eliminate unnecessary tensions between the Jewish population and the Russian state. Therefore, the announcement of the sixth Commission in 1908 was accompanied by instructions to the officially recognized rabbis to convene meetings and formulate questions for the Commission's deliberations, without any restrictions.[5]

The issue of the official recognition of rabbis in the Russian Empire was not an easy one and differed in the two major regions where the Jewish population was concentrated: the Pale of Jewish Settlement, which consisted of the fifteen western provinces, annexed to Russia in 1772–1812, and the Kingdom of Poland, which was annexed in 1815 and governed in a manner distinctive from the rest of the empire. In the Kingdom of Poland, the only legal requirement for

2 For a general survey of Rabbinic Commissions, see Moisei Kreps, »Ravvinskaia komissiia,« *Evreiskaia entsiklopediia*, vol. 13, eds. A. Harkavi and L. Katsenel'son (St. Petersburg: Brockhaus-Efron, 1912), 233–238. For more details on the commissions, their elections and aspirations, see Eli Lederhendler, *The Road to Modern Jewish Politics: Political Tradition and Political Reconstruction in the Jewish Community of Tsarist Russia* (Oxford: Oxford University Press, 1989), 73–74, 150–152; ChaeRan Y. Freeze, *Jewish Marriage and Divorce in Imperial Russia* (Hanover, NH: Brandeis University Press, 2002), 84–95, 245–256.

3 On the Rabbinic Commission of 1910 and the preparations for it, see Vladimir Levin, *Ha-politikah ha-yehudit ba-imperiyah ha-rusit be-eydan ha-reaktsiyah, 1907–1914*, Ph.D. thesis, Hebrew University of Jerusalem, 2007, 224–272.

4 On Stolypin, see Peter Waldron, *Between Two Revolutions: Stolypin and the Politics of Renewal in Russia* (DeKalb: Northern Illinois University Press, 1998); Abraham Ascher, *P. A. Stolypin: The Search for Stability in Late Imperial Russia* (Stanford: Stanford University Press, 2001); A. P. Borodin, *Stolypin: reformy vo imia Rossii* (Moskva: Veche, 2004).

5 Russian State Historical Archives, St. Petersburg (hereafter RGIA), collection (*fond*) 821, inventory (*opis'*) 9, file (*delo*) 63, folio (*list*) 1; inv. 8, file 293, fol. 12–20.

the official recognition of rabbis was a minimal knowledge of the Russian language. This requirement allowed almost all traditional communal rabbis to be recognized by the state authorities. In the Pale of Settlement, in contrast, the state demanded that a rabbi have a secondary or higher secular education. Therefore, communities had no other choice but to hire so-called crown (*kazionnyi*) rabbis, who had the necessary educational qualifications and were recognized by the state. They performed the duties which the state demanded of rabbis, i.e. keeping population records and arranging the oaths of Jews in imperial institutions; less formally they often acted as representatives of the community before the state authorities. At the same time, communities continued, as in the past, to hire traditional rabbis to perform traditional rabbinic functions, i.e. deciding on halakhic questions, presiding over religious courts, etc. These so-called »spiritual« (*dukhovnyi*) rabbis were well versed in Talmud and rabbinic law, but rarely spoke any Russian and functioned semi-legally due to the absence of recognition by the state.

The existence of the »double rabbinate« found its reflection in the preparatory work to the Rabbinic Commission of 1910. Since the Ministry of the Interior asked for the opinions of officially recognized rabbis, the traditional rabbis of Poland could send their memoranda directly to the ministry. In the Pale of Settlement, in contrast, the »spiritual« rabbis could not voice their opinions directly, with many of them instead joining the gatherings of the crown rabbis in 1908 or influencing them in other ways. As the following discussion demonstrates, the memoranda prepared by crown rabbis in the Pale during their meetings included many views quite similar to the proposals of the Orthodox rabbis of Poland. Therefore, the matters of disagreement between the crown and »spiritual« rabbinates go beyond the scope of this article.

As a result of the governmental initiative, 125 memoranda from individual rabbis and the gatherings of rabbis in each province in the Pale of Settlement and the Kingdom of Poland were sent to the ministry in the course of 1908.[6] In addition, two special assemblies of Orthodox rabbis convened: Polish rabbis met in Warsaw in late December 1908; and about 20 prominent »spiritual« rabbis from the Pale of Settlement met in Vilna (today Vilnius) in April 1909.[7] Rabbis submitted the most important questions and problems that they had drawn up to the Commission and proposed desired solutions. The rabbinical memoranda were accompanied by reports of the local governors who expressed their

6 For the rabbinical proposals sent to the Ministry of the Interior see RGIA, coll. 821, inv. 9, file 51. Consulted as microfilm in the Central Archives for the History of Jewish People, Jerusalem (hereafter CAHJP), HM2/8003.1; RGIA, coll. 821, inv. 9, file 66.

7 RGIA, coll. 821, inv. 9, file 66, fol. 38–69; file 51, fol. 310–329.

opinions about the suggested measures.[8] These documents provide insight into the interaction between Halakhah and civil law in the late Russian Empire, as seen by Orthodox rabbis – bearers of Jewish tradition, and by governors – bearers and executors of Russian imperial law.

The aims of the rabbis: harmonizing civil law with Halakhah

When the Ministry of the Interior announced the conventions of rabbis as a preparatory step leading to the Rabbinic Commission, the joy of the Orthodox activists was almost boundless. »I have read the news item – wrote an Orthodox publicist in Warsaw – once, twice, three times, and my eyes could not have their fill of looking at those letters, printed black on white.« The reason for his joy was obvious: »Those who know how to read between the lines, understand that this time the Minister of the Interior is almost begging the rabbis to meet and to unite for the sake of strengthening Judaism [*ḥizuk ha-yahadut*].«[9]

Rabbis interpreted the ministry's invitation to express their opinions as the readiness of Stolypin's government to make a kind of alliance with Jewish Orthodoxy, which presented itself as a loyal ally of the tsarist administration in its struggle with revolutionary-minded Jewish youth. In their communications with the government, Orthodox rabbis constantly stressed that they were willing »to impel the backward, lost young Jews to return to the true path of religion, and [...] to tear them from various anti-governmental associations, into which godless and adroit agitators had drawn them.«[10] Orthodox rabbis needed governmental support to perform this task, for example to strengthen their position in the communities and remove the obstacles to the complete observance of religious commandments. According to Orthodox rhetoric, strict adherence to Jewish religious observance led Jews to be loyal subjects of the Tsar, while secularization made Jews receptive to revolutionary ideologies. Therefore, it was in the interest of the Russian government to eliminate obstacles to the full-scale observance of all halakhic norms. If state law did not contradict Halakhah, Jews would find it easier to observe religious rules. Convenient conditions for strict observance would prevent secularization, and Jews would remain religious and loyal.[11] Orthodox rabbis thus made maximal demands; and by meeting

8 RGIA, coll. 821, inv. 9, file 63.
9 Ari Sho'eg [Yehuda Leib Volnerman], »Ha-hashgaḥah ha-ne'elamah,« *Ha-Kol*, no. 9, February 28, 1908, 65.
10 RGIA, coll. 821, inv. 8, file 293, fol. 51.
11 For the relationship between Orthodoxy and the government after the 1905 Revolution, see Vladimir Levin, »Orthodox Jewry and the Russian Government:

them the state could produce an ideal situation for the strict observance of Halakhah.

Not all of the issues raised by the rabbis were halakhic ones. Their most essential demand was official recognition of »spiritual« rabbis and even providing them with significant power over the community, ranging from the supervision of traditional private teachers (*melamdim*) and ritual slaughter to the rabbinic censorship of all Hebrew and Yiddish books.[12] However, these demands had nothing to do with Halakhah: there is no halakhic prohibition of a general secular education, which the state demanded in order to recognize a person as a crown rabbi. Indeed, the early 20th century saw an increasing number of »spiritual« rabbis in the Pale who acquired the necessary educational qualifications and became state-recognized rabbis. Therefore, the issue of the double rabbinate will be left aside, as it does not concern Halakhah, and the article will exclusively discuss the proposals concerning the reconciliation of state and religious laws. The collection of those proposals presents a full range of frictions between the civil and religious systems of law and articulates the most acute problems of Jewish law in Russian imperial reality, as seen by the Jewish religious authorities.

The first field in which the rabbis asked for change was the conditions in military service and prisons. Both soldiers and prisoners in Russia found themselves in frameworks which made it difficult to observe Halakhah. Moreover, disconnection from the observant Jewish community for several years of military service or detention was a significant factor in the process of secularization.[13] Russian law recognized the basic religious needs of Jewish soldiers. It ordered commanders to provide them with rooms for prayer,[14] to free them from labor on Saturdays and holidays, and to allow leaves of absence on some Jewish holidays.[15] However, unsurprisingly, those provisions bore a character

An Attempt at Rapprochement, 1907–1914,« *East European Jewish Affairs* 39 (2009): 187–204.

12 See, for example, Aharon Surasky and Avraham Mordechai Segal, *Rosh golat ariel: toldot ḥayav u-foalo shel* [...] *rabi Avraham Mordekhai Alter* [...] *mi-gur*, vol. 2 (Jerusalem: Machon Amudei Ha-or – Maasehen shel tsadikim, 1995), 472.

13 Yohanan Petrovsky-Shtern, *Jews in the Russian Army, 1827–1917: Drafted into Modernity* (Cambridge: Cambridge University Press, 2009), 9–17.

14 In the majority of the cities outside the Pale of Settlement the first synagogues were opened in local military barracks. For example, see the history of synagogues in St. Petersburg, Vladimir Levin, »Istoriia dorevoliutsionnykh evreiskikh molitvennykh uchrezhdenii Peterburga,« *Ami – Narod Moi* 55, no. 2 (1993), 2–3. See also Petrovsky-Shtern, *Jews in the Russian Army*, 69–73.

15 For the text of the law see *Zakony o evreiakh*, eds. Ia. I. Gimpelson and L. M. Bramson (Petrograd: Iurisprudentsiia, 1914–1915), 711. For discussion see Petrovsky-Shtern, *Jews in the Russian Army*, 64–66.

more suitable to Christianity, not to traditional Judaism, since the main emphasis was put on prayer and not on observing everyday religious commandments and complicated dietary laws. Nuances were completely omitted: for example, while the Ministry of War published an annual calendar of Jewish holidays, it consistently failed to mention that they begin at sunset the previous day. As a result, many commanders, being faithful to orders, were not ready to release their Jewish soldiers on the eve of a holiday. Therefore, many rabbis asked for legislation allowing Jewish soldiers to take leave from the very beginning of a holiday.[16]

Orthodox rabbis were especially interested in creating conditions in which Jewish soldiers would be able to continue an observant way of life.[17] The assembly of Polish Orthodox rabbis in Warsaw proposed, for example, releasing Jewish soldiers from any work on Saturdays, maintaining kosher kitchens,[18] permitting the wearing of *tsitsit* (fringed undergarments) under the uniform, and keeping *tfillin* (phylacteries) and *talit* (prayer shawls) in military kit-bags. Moreover, they proposed, that military uniforms would not contain *sha'atnez* – a mixture of wool and linen prohibited by Halakhah.[19]

16 RGIA, coll. 821, inv. 9, file 51, fol. 1 (meeting of rabbis in Nikolaev in 1904), 255 (rabbis of Minsk province), 264 (rabbis of Ekaterinoslav province), 269 (rabbis of Grodno province), 328 (the assembly in Vilna); file 66, fol. 9–11 (rabbis of Kielce province), 18–20 (rabbis of Płock province), 21–22 (rabbis of Suwałki province), 26–27 (the rabbi of Mariampol in Suwałki province), 55 (the assembly in Warsaw). Petrovsky-Shtern also states that the military legislation was inconsistent, but he entirely overlooked the issue of the beginning of holidays, which turned out to be so important for both traditional and crown rabbis in 1908. See Petrovsky-Shtern, *Jews in the Russian Army*, 65.

17 In this context it should be mentioned that although all males were obliged to serve in the military from 1874, only a small percentage of them, selected by lot, was actually drafted. For example, in the town of Korets, Volyn' province, 501 young men were called to appear in the conscription department (of them 122 Jews) in 1887, but only 149 (38 Jews) were actually drafted – *Ha-Melits* 278, December 29, 1887 (January 10, 1888), 2957. Cf. tables 7–10 in Petrovsky-Shtern, *Jews in the Russian Army*, 139–141, which show that only 10–20 % of Jews registered for the draft were actually called for service.

18 Having separate eating arrangements for Jewish soldiers was explicitly prohibited in 1887–1888. Petrovsky-Shtern, *Jews in the Russian Army*, 195.

19 RGIA, coll. 821, inv. 9, file 66, fol. 39v, 55–56v. Cf. Surasky and Segal, *Rosh golat ariel*, vol. 2, 472 (rabbi Avraham Bornstein of Sochaczew); RGIA, coll. 821, inv. 9, file 51, fol. 104 (»spiritual« and »crown« rabbi Yehuda Leib Tsirelson of Priluki in Poltava province and »spiritual« rabbi Shmariyahu Noaḥ Schneersohn from Bobruisk); file 66, fol. 9–11 (rabbis of Kielce province), 18–20 (rabbis of Płock province), 28–33 (rabbis of Łomża, Kolno, Szczuczyn, and Mazowieck districts in Łomża province).

Similar issues were raised concerning Jews in prisons. Many rabbis asked for the assignment of special rooms for prayer and for the provision of kosher food,[20] while one memorandum mentioned that, until 1889, kosher food had been delivered for Jewish prison inmates in Kovno province.[21] The general assembly in Warsaw, however, did not ask for prayer rooms but stressed the release of Jewish prisoners from work on Saturdays, kosher kitchens, permission for the use of *tfillin* and *tsitsit*, as well as the supply of books of »religious-moral content.«[22]

The second field in which the rabbis asked for change was that of marital laws.[23] Here a difference existed between the Kingdom of Poland and the rest of the empire. While in Poland marriages were registered by civil officials after the performance of religious ceremonies and divorce was the prerogative of civil courts, in the Pale of Settlement (and the rest of the empire) the performance of both those rituals and their registration were delegated to the crown rabbis, who were required to act according to Jewish law. However, difficulties in both regions were similar.

One problem was the validity of marriages conducted according to Halakhah but not registered by the civil authorities in Poland or by the crown rabbis in the rest of the empire. While such a marriage was binding from the halakhic point of view, the civil law did not recognize unregistered marriages and considered them null and void. The problem, however, arose mostly not from a contradiction between the state and Jewish systems of law, but from the widespread

20 RGIA, coll. 821, inv. 9, file 51, fol. 257v (rabbis of Minsk province), 279 (rabbis of Kovno/Kaunas, Rossieny/Raseiniai, and Shavli/Šiauliai districts in Kovno province); file 66, fol. 9–11 (rabbis of Kielce province), 12–17 (rabbis of Siedlce province), 18–20 (rabbis of Płock province). It is needless to mention that only a very limited number of Jews were actually imprisoned.

21 RGIA, coll. 821, inv. 9, file 51, fol. 279 (rabbis of Kovno, Rossieny, and Shavli districts in Kovno province).

22 RGIA, coll. 821, inv. 9, file 66, fol. 56v. The logic behind not asking for prayer rooms presumably followed the relative importance of commandments from the halakhic point of view: Sabbat, *kashrut*, *tfillin*, and *tsitsit* are more important than praying in an especially designated room. It could also be supposed that the rabbis were not fond of keeping Torah scrolls in Russian prisons or saw the establishment of prayer rooms there as too similar to Christian practice and to the practice of Reform communities in Germany.

23 For the laws concerning Jewish marriage and divorce see the last guidebook to legislation affecting Jews to be published in the Russian Empire: *Zakony o evreiakh*, eds. Gimpelson and Bramson, 622–680. For various practices and problems see Freeze, *Jewish Marriage and Divorce*. For a general overview of Russian marital laws and attempts to change them see William G. Wagner, *Marriage, Property, and Law in Late Imperial Russia* (Oxford: Clarendon Press, 1994), 61–223.

reluctance of Jews to register their vital events.[24] Another issue was connected to divorce and the possibility of remarriage. This problem usually affected women, since Halakhah prohibited them from remarrying without receiving a divorce letter (*get*) from their husbands. Although Halakhah principally prohibited polygamy for Ashkenazi Jews, wedding a second wife without divorcing the first one was nonetheless valid *post factum* and could not be simply annulled, as state law demanded. In such a case, a halakhic divorce was no less obligatory. The striking feature of the halakhically valid *get* is that a husband must consent to grant his wife a divorce of his own free will. In contrast to Christian or civic laws, where the church or the court could annul the marriage, there is no Jewish authority which could annul a marriage that had been conducted in accordance with Jewish law. The same free will is demanded for the *ḥalitsah* – a ceremony by which a brother of the deceased husband releases his childless sister-in-law from the Biblical obligation to marry him (levirate marriage). Only the performance of the *ḥalitsah* in the presence of a Jewish religious court allows such a widow to remarry.

Rabbinical proposals all featured the desire to give priority to halakhic norms over civic ones in every detail. This approach was consistent with imperial law, which sought to deal with marital issues according to religious laws. In the Pale of Settlement, the rabbis' memoranda stressed the need to legitimatize unregistered marriages as well as to resolve the relatively minor issues which sometimes caused crown rabbis legal problems. For example, many rabbinical meetings asked for the legal recognition of the halakhic procedure of divorce from a mentally ill wife, which contradicted the civil approach, since in such a case the wife's consent to receive the *get* was overruled by the opinion of 100 rabbis, recognizing her mental illness (without any medical examination).[25] They also asked for the legal recognition of divorce by messenger – a situation in which the husband does not deliver the *get* personally but via a proxy.[26] The failure of the

24 On the registration of Jewish vital statistics see Eugene M. Avrutin, »The Power of Documentation: Vital Statistics and Jewish Accommodation in Tsarist Russia,« *Ab Imperio* 2003, no. 4: 271–300; idem, »The Politics of Jewish Legibility: Documentation Practices and Reform During the Reign of Nicholas I,« *Jewish Social Studies* 11 (2005): 136–169; idem, *Jews and the Imperial State: Identification Politics in Tsarist Russia* (Ithaca, NY: Cornell University Press, 2010).

25 RGIA, coll. 821, inv. 9, file 51, fol. 88 (rabbis of Chernigov province), 104 (rabbis Tsirelson and Shmariyahu Noaḥ Schneersohn), 255 (rabbis of Minsk province), 301 (the rabbi of Lida in Vilna province). Cf. RGIA, coll. 821, inv. 9, file 66, fol. 73 (rabbis of Płońsk district in Warsaw province). On divorce on grounds of insanity see Freeze, *Jewish Marriage and Divorce*, 185–188.

26 RGIA, coll. 821, inv. 9, file 51, fol. 70 (the rabbi of Mozyr' in Minsk province), 88 (rabbis of Chernigov province), 138 (rabbis of Kiev province), 297 (rabbis of Oshmiany district in Vilna province), 328 (the assembly in Vilna).

state authorities to recognize such divorces, conducted in the absence of the husband, had become a pressing problem. The mass emigration of Jews overseas led to situations in which husbands in America sent halakhically valid writs of divorce to their wives remaining in the Russian Empire, but those were not officially recognized. The rabbis also looked for civil support in pressuring brothers-in-law to perform the *ḥalitsah* ceremony. They proposed that state law could oblige such a person to support his sister-in-law financially throughout the entire time he refuses to perform the *ḥalitsah* »of his own free will.«[27]

The proposals of the Polish rabbis were similar, involving official recognition of halakhically binding marriages and divorces[28] and state pressure to perform *ḥalitsah*.[29] One gathering of rabbis simply asked for »governmental support in cases of resistance to the laws of the *Shulḥan arukh*[30] concerning marriage, divorce, and *ḥalitsah*.«[31] The assembly in Warsaw, not going as far, wished to reduce the involvement of civil authorities in Jewish matrimonial matters and proposed doing away with civil court divorce trials in cases in which the involved spouses had no contradictory claims to each other.[32] By contrast, another meeting of Polish rabbis followed a minimalistic approach and proposed changing only the existing law prohibiting women from remarrying for ten months after their divorce, since it contradicted the Talmudic rule allowing marriage after three months.[33] In other words, the rabbis asked for consistency

27 RGIA, coll. 821, inv. 9, file 51, fol. 50 (rabbi of Simferopol in Taurida province), 75 (rabbis of Poltava province), 125 (rabbis of Vitebsk province), 128 (Rabbi Maze of Moscow), 130 (Barats, the »learned Jew« in Kiev), 255 (rabbis of Minsk province), 300 (rabbi of Lida in Vilna province). A similar decision was accepted by the Rabbinical Commission of 1893–1894, see *Zakony o evreiakh*, eds. Gimpelson and Bramson, 674. Cf. Freeze, *Jewish Marriage and Divorce*, 238–239.

28 RGIA, coll. 821, inv. 9, file 66, fol. 9–11 (rabbis of Kielce province), 18–20 (rabbis of Płock province), 21–22 (rabbis of Suwałki province), 28–33 (rabbis of Łomża, Kolno, Szczuczyn, and Mazowieck districts in Łomża province), 66 (the assembly in Warsaw), 73 (rabbis of Płońsk district in Warsaw province).

29 RGIA, coll. 821, inv. 9, file 66, fol. 18–20 (rabbis of Płock province), 68–68v (the assembly in Warsaw), 70–72 (rabbis of Lublin province).

30 The *Shulḥan arukh* is a codification of Halakhah in brief and authoritative form, completed in 1563 by Rabbi Yosef Caro. Its combination with Rabbi Moshe Isserles' gloss »Ha-Mapah,« representing the Ashkenazi tradition, constituted in practice a binding code of halakhic law. See Elimelech Westreich, »Shulḥan 'arukh,« in *The YIVO Encyclopedia of Jews in Eastern Europe*, ed. Gershon David Hundert (New Haven and London: Yale University Press, 2008), 1742.

31 RGIA, coll. 821, inv. 9, file 66, fol. 74–75 (rabbis of Nieszawa district in Warsaw province).

32 RGIA, coll. 821, inv. 9, file 66, fol. 66.

33 RGIA, coll. 821, inv. 9, file 66, fol. 28–33 (rabbis of Łomża, Kolno, Szczuczyn, and Mazowieck districts in Łomża province).

in applying the existing legislative principle that marital issues were to be decided by religious functionaries according to religious laws.

Rabbis paid special attention to cases in which a husband had converted to Christianity, while his wife remained Jewish. In such a situation the wife had difficulties in getting a halakhic divorce from her baptized husband, thus becoming an *agunah* – a wife who could not remarry (an apostate is considered by Halakhah a sinner but nonetheless a Jew).[34] The imperial law stated that if the spouse remaining Jewish did not want to convert and refused to continue living with the convert, the marriage was dissolved. However, in the second half of the 19th century some Russian Orthodox bishops and some governors insisted on the dissolution of the Jewish marriages of converts according to Jewish law, while others allowed them to remarry without a Jewish divorce. An end was put to this ambivalence in 1892, when the Holy Synod, the governing body of the Russian Orthodox Church, unequivocally decided that a baptized Jew could receive permission to remarry without any divorce procedure with the spouse who remained Jewish.[35] Other Christian Churches also took a stricter position toward the performance of Jewish religious rituals by a convert, when the baptized husband was ready to grant the *get* to his Jewish wife.[36] This approach caused, of course, irresolvable problems for the deserted wives, who found themselves in a situation where they could never marry again. Therefore, many rabbis asked the government to prohibit the baptism of Jews before arranging a Jewish divorce, or to force the future convert to grant a Jewish divorce before the baptism ceremony.[37]

34 See Ellie R. Schainker, *Imperial Hybrids: Russian-Jewish Converts in the Nineteenth Century*, Ph.D. thesis, University of Pennsylvania, 2010, 81–100; Freeze, *Jewish Marriage and Divorce*, 188–190. Various attempts to estimate the number of Jewish converts to Christianity show that the majority of converts were unmarried women, and that the percentage of married men was not high. See Michael Stanislawski, »Jewish Apostasy in Russia: A Tentative Typology,« in *Jewish Apostasy in the Modern World*, ed. Todd M. Endelman (New York: Holmes & Meier, 1987), 189–205, here 200; Schainker, »Imperial Hybrids,« 63.

35 Schainker, »Imperial Hybrids,« 97–99; *Zakony o evreiakh*, eds. Gimpelson and Bramson, 673.

36 See, for example, the complaint of the Evangelical Lutheran consistory against the rabbi of Kiev, who arranged the divorce of a couple, one of whom converted to Lutheranism, without the consistory's agreement, *Rassvet*, no. 46, November 24, 1907, 20; or the court prosecution of a rabbi for divorcing a husband who converted to Lutheranism from his Jewish wife, *Vestnik evreiskoi obshchiny*, no. 1, January 1914, 57–58.

37 RGIA, coll. 821, inv. 9, file 51, fol. 75 (rabbis of Poltava province), 125 (rabbis of Vitebsk province), 138 (rabbis of Kiev province), 149 (the rabbi of Kamenets-Podolsk in Podolia province), 153 (the rabbi of Novo-Ushitsa in Podolia province), 172 (the rabbi of Khmel'nik in Podolia province), 255 (rabbis of

The third field of the rabbis' concern was the Sabbath. The prohibition of various kinds of work on the Sabbath is one of the main elements of Jewish law and as it was put by a Polish rabbi in 1908, »the weakening of the Jewish faith begins with breaking the Sabbath [laws].«[38] The rabbis' memoranda touched upon issues both small and large, and their goal was, as phrased by the assembly in Warsaw, »to grant Jews such conditions that they would not be compelled to break Sabbath rules.«[39]

Some rabbis called for a policy of not summoning Jews to courts of law on Saturdays, because court procedures often involve writing, and especially because Halakhah prohibits swearing oaths on the Sabbath.[40] Russian imperial law also prohibited taking oaths in synagogues on Saturdays, and the oaths during court trials had to be arranged by rabbis according to the same rules. However, a judge could administer the oath of Jewish witnesses when no rabbi was present in the building of the court of justice, i.e. taking the oath administered by a judge became a widespread practice. In such cases, the oath could be taken legally on a Saturday if the Jewish witness had no objections.[41] While there are no known statistics on the matter, one could suppose that many Jews agreed to take this oath. The rabbis believed that the inclusion of a prohibition to swear an oath on a Saturday in civil law would prevent a situation in which it is easier to break Halakhah than to keep it, thus strengthening religious observance.

Another request involved the Sabbath law that prohibits carrying objects from household to household and from homes to the street. In order to overcome this prohibition, Halakhah provides for the symbolic linking of all households with a cord that surrounds a town or a neighborhood, called an *eruv*, thus allowing for objects to be moved within those boundaries. The *eruv* was explicitly prohibited in the Kingdom of Poland in the 1860s[42] and therefore requests to permit the installation of an *eruv* took a prominent place in the

Minsk province); file 66, fol. 18–20 (rabbis of Płock province), 68 (the assembly in Warsaw). Cf. Freeze, *Jewish Marriage and Divorce*, 267.

38 RGIA, coll. 821, inv. 9, file 66, fol. 43 (Rabbi Ber Graubart of Będzin in Piotrków province).

39 RGIA, coll. 821, inv. 9, file 66, fol. 52.

40 RGIA, coll. 821, inv. 9, file 66, fol. 7–8 (rabbis of Piotrków province), 9–11 (rabbis of Kielce province), 18–20 (rabbis of Płock province), 34–35 (rabbis of Łomża province), 54 (the assembly in Warsaw); file 51, fol. 75 (rabbis of Poltava province).

41 *Zakony o evreiakh*, eds. Gimpelson and Bramson, 699.

42 François Guesnet, *Polnische Juden im 19. Jahrhundert: Lebensbedingungen, Rechtsnormen und Organisation im Wandel* (Köln et al.: Böhlau, 1998), 260–262.

memoranda of many Polish rabbis.[43] Others, such as Rabbi Shalom Dov Ber Schneersohn of Lubavitch and his representatives at the Warsaw assembly, considered the *eruv* problem unimportant. The Lubavitcher *Rebbe* pointed out that one should not »connect the serious with the simple, so that only the simple might be granted,« fearing that the authorities would permit the *eruv*, as a simple measure, thus showing their acceptance of rabbis' wishes, but at the same time would reject rabbinic requests about a much more serious problem – Sunday trade.[44]

Indeed, the most serious matter in the field of Sabbath observance was the issue of trade on Sundays. During the 19th century it was customary that Jewish shops in the Pale of Settlement were closed only on Saturdays, while they opened after the end of church service on Sundays and major Christian holidays.

The first restriction on Jewish trade was included in the notorious Temporary Rules of 3 May 1882, issued after the wave of anti-Jewish pogroms of 1881–1882. The rules aimed at protecting the Christian population and especially peasants from Jewish »exploitation« consisted of three articles, which prohibited Jews from newly settling in the countryside of the Pale of Settlement, acquiring land in the countryside, and »performing trade on Sundays and the Twelve Great Feasts.« However, this last article contained a provision that the closing of Jewish shops would be practiced according to the same rules that applied to Christian shops.[45] Thus, Jewish trade on Sundays was not actually eliminated and the ability to open shops on Sundays depended on each municipality and its policy concerning Christian shops. In the majority of cities and towns in the Pale, shops could be opened on Sundays for five hours in the afternoon.[46]

43 Surasky and Segal, *Rosh golat ariel*, vol. 2, 472 (Rabbi Avraham Bornstein of Sochaczew); RGIA, coll. 821, inv. 9, file 66, fol. 9–11 (rabbis of Kielce province), 12–17 (rabbis of Siedlce province), 18–20 (rabbis of Płock province), 34–35 (rabbis of Łomża province), 53–54 (the assembly in Warsaw).

44 The *Rebbe* even thought that the absence of an *eruv* makes Jews more cautious about Sabbath observance. Shalom Dov Ber Schneersohn, *Igrot-kodesh* [...] *me-et* [...] *admor maharshav* [...] *mi-Lubavitch*, vol. 2 (Brooklyn: Kehot Publication Society, 1982), 439.

45 Cited according to Gr. Vol'tke, »Vremennye pravila 3 maia 1882 goda,« *Evreiskaia entsiklopediia*, vol. 5, eds. L. Katsenel'son and D. Gintsburg (St. Petersburg: Brockhaus-Efron, 1910), 815–822, here 816.

46 Gr. Vol'tke, »Subbotnii, prazdnichnyi otdykh (po russkomu zakonodatel'stvu),« Ibid., vol. 14, ed. L. Katsenel'son (St. Petersburg: Brockhaus-Efron, 1913), 597–599, here 598. For restrictions on Muslim commerce see Robert Geraci, »Sunday Laws and Ethno-Commercial Rivalry in the Russian Empire, 1880s–1914,« National Council for Eurasian and East European Research 2006, 1–42, https://www.ucis.pitt.edu/nceeer/2006_819_Geraci.pdf (accessed July 16, 2015).

The closure of all shops on Sundays was mandated by the government in November 1906 as a step towards improving the working conditions of shop assistants and other employees in the trade, by providing them with one day off every week. However, these 1906 rules also allowed local authorities to permit limited Sunday trade, depending on local conditions, i.e. the presence of a significant non-Christian population. Thus, in some cities or provinces the old order remained intact, with Jewish shops open on Sundays for five hours, while in other places different case-by-case provisions were made, while in yet other localities Sunday trade was completely prohibited.[47] The introduction of such a measure was considered by the rabbis to be a very serious threat to Jewish religious observance. The strict implementation of Sunday closures would force Jews to abstain from work for two days a week, leading to devastating economic consequences, or to open their shops on Saturday and thus break the Sabbath rest. Therefore, many rabbinic gatherings, including the major assemblies of Orthodox rabbis in Warsaw and Vilna, asked for permission for Jews to replace the mandatory Sunday closure with a Saturday closure.[48]

Another issue involving Sabbath observance touched upon Jewish pupils in state schools. A provision allowing Jewish children to abstain from writing on Saturdays existed in the 1860s and 1870s, but was rescinded in 1882.[49] Several attempts to reinstall this provision in the following decades were unsuccessful.[50] This meant that the benevolent approach toward Jewish religious customs was replaced in the 1880s by an insistence on the uniform application of norms. Therefore, many rabbinic gatherings, especially those of the crown rabbis in the Pale of Settlement, asked for Jewish children to be excused from writing in state schools on Saturdays.[51] The most conservative Orthodox leaders, like Rabbi

47 See, for example, the order of the governor general of the provinces of Vilna, Kovno, and Grodno allowing five hours of trade on Sundays, *Rassvet*, no. 11, March 22, 1907, 23; *Severo-zapadnyi golos*, no. 635, January 6, 1908, 2; the complete prohibition of trade on Sundays by the Bessarabian governor, *Der Fraynd*, no. 171, August 2, 1907, 3; permission for Jewish artisans to work on Sundays but without selling their products or accepting new orders in Ekaterinoslav, *Der Fraynd*, no. 168, July 30, 1907, 3. For the Zionists' and rabbis' protests over the complete closing of shops in Poland see *Rassvet*, no. 8, March 2, 1907, 25–26; *Svoboda i ravenstvo*, no. 21, April 5, 1907, 17.

48 RGIA, coll. 821, inv. 9, file 66, fol. 7–8 (rabbis of Piotrków province), 18–20 (rabbis of Płock province), 21–22 (rabbis of Suwałki province), 34–35 (rabbis of Łomża province), 52v–53 (the assembly in Warsaw); file 51, fol. 35 (rabbis of Kherson province), 320–321v (the assembly in Vilna).

49 RGIA, coll. 821, inv. 9, file 63, fol. 37.

50 Solomon Pozner, *Evrei v obshchei shkole* (St. Petersburg: Razum, 1914), 52–53.

51 RGIA, coll. 821, inv. 9, file 66, fol. 21–22 (rabbis of Suwałki province), 26–27 (the rabbi of Mariampol in Suwałki province); file 51, fol. 75 (rabbis of Poltava province), 88 (rabbis of Chernigov province), 125 (rabbis of Vitebsk province),

Shalom Dov Ber Schneersohn, thought, however, that any simple permission to abstain from writing would be inadequate since the classroom behavior of Christian pupils would influence the Jewish ones.[52] Under Schneersohn's influence the assembly of Orthodox rabbis in Vilna decided to request the complete release of Jewish children from attending state schools on Saturdays.[53]

In addition to those three major fields – service conditions for Jewish soldiers, marital issues, and the Sabbath rest – some rabbinic gatherings asked for further adjustments of state laws to Halakhah. By Jewish law and custom, burials were to take place on the day of death, but Russian law postponed it for three days out of a concern for the premature burial of people who were still alive. Although the medical codex containing this clause was published in 1857, the local authorities, as it would seem, only began to insist on such a delay in burial in the 1880s.[54] Nonetheless, it did not become a serious problem as only two rabbis' gatherings requested that burials be allowed on the day of death.[55]

Another problem was raised by the practice of *sheḥitah* – Jewish ritual slaughter. According to Halakhah, ritual slaughterers have to inflate the lungs taken from the animal, in order to ensure that the lungs have no scarring that would render the animal not kosher. One gathering of rabbis requested permission to inflate the lungs by mouth, as was customary in Jewish tradition but contradictory to the medical laws of the empire.[56] It is noteworthy that not a single rabbi raised the issue of *metsitsah* – oral suction of blood from the circumcision wound, which suggests that the custom was practiced without hindrance.[57]

138 (rabbis of Kiev province), 279 (rabbis of Kovno, Rossieny, and Shavli districts in Kovno province). Similar demand was included into the program of the first Orthodox political organization, »Knesset Israel,« in 1907 – *Ustav obshchestva »Knesset Israel«* (Vilna, 1908), 2. On »Knesset Israel« see Vladimir Levin, »›Kneset israel‹ – ha-miflagah ha-politit ha-ortodoksit ha-rishonah ba-imperiyah ha-rusit,« *Zion* 76 (2011): 29–62.

52 *Der Fraynd*, no. 96, April 29, 1909, 2. For the negative opinion of the *Rebbe* from Ger (Góra Kalwaria), Avraham Mordechai Alter, see Schneersohn, *Igrot-kodesh*, vol. 4, 307.

53 RGIA, coll. 821, inv. 9, file 51, fol. 322. Cf. also fol. 104 (Rabbis Tsirelson and Shmariyahu Noaḥ Schneersohn).

54 On the issue of burials see Dror Segev's article in this volume.

55 RGIA, coll. 821, inv. 9, file 66, fol. 9–11 (rabbis of Kielce province); file 51, fol. 88 (rabbis of Chernigov province).

56 RGIA, coll. 821, inv. 9, file 66, fol. 18 (rabbis of Płock province).

57 On the controversy over oral suction see Jacob Katz, »Pulmus ha-metzitzah« in idem, *Ha-halakhah be-meytzar: Mikhsholim al derekh ha-ortodoksiyah be-hithavutah* (Jerusalem: The Magnes Press, 1992), 150–183, especially 175–176, mentioning the prohibitions of oral suction by the authorities in Hungary, Hessen-Darmstadt, Baden, and Frankfurt in 1899, and 179–180 on the practice in Lithuania without any direct contact of the *mohel*'s mouth with the wound.

The last issue raised by the rabbis involved the contradiction of civil law not with Halakhah in its strict sense, but with tradition and common sense. The Imperial Law of 1835 obliged rabbis (outside of Poland) to personally perform circumcisions, marriages, divorces, and funerals, and prescribed punishment for all others who performed them. This clause was perfectly suited to the Christian clergy, who indeed performed baptisms, marriages, and funerals, but did not correspond with Jewish practices. According to Halakhah and Jewish tradition, a rabbi was not involved in any of the rites: circumcision was carried out by a specialist (*mohel*); marriage could be officiated by anyone knowledgeable in Jewish law, while crown rabbis often had no religious education at all; divorce was arranged by a Jewish court (*beit din*) of three Talmudic scholars; and burial rites were carried out by a voluntary association called *ḥevrah kadisha*. In reality, the crown rabbi only registered events, while the rituals were performed by others. Therefore, the majority of meetings of crown rabbis in the Pale of Settlement proposed a change in imperial law so as to enable them to legally delegate those duties to other persons.[58]

As they were written in the midst of a wave of optimism concerning governmental support for Jewish Orthodoxy, we can see that the rabbis' memoranda, and the proposals therein, which were discussed collectively during the rabbis' gatherings, touched on all of the main points of contention between the state law and Halakhah in the late Russian Empire. Although the lists of desired changes were long, in reality they showed that Jewish religious laws could in fact generally be observed. This seems especially striking since Jews in Russia were often seen as a persecuted minority – a view quite widespread from the last quarter of the 19th century.

Thus, a secular Hebrew journalist could write in 1909: »[Our government] struggles only with Jews, not with the Jewish religion,«[59] and the future leader of Lubavitch Hasidism, Rabbi Yosef Yitsḥak Schneersohn, wrote in 1907: »Thank God, we have not yet seen that our government is against religion, God forbid.«[60]

58 RGIA, coll. 821, inv. 9, file 51, fol. 9v–10 (meeting of rabbis in Nikolaev in 1904), 19v–20 (rabbi Ḥaim Chernovits from Odessa), 44v (rabbis of Kherson province), 80v (rabbis of Poltava province), 89 (rabbis of Chernigov province), 110 (Rabbi Tsirelson of Priluki), 128v–129 (Rabbi Yakov Maze of Moscow), 142 (rabbis of Kiev province), 195–196 (rabbis of Volyn' province), 259 (rabbis of Minsk province), 266 (rabbis of Ekaterinoslav province), 269v (rabbis of Grodno province), 340–343 (rabbis of Bessarabia province).

59 Editorial in *Hed ha-zman*, no. 55, March 6 (19), 1909, 1.

60 Schneersohn, *Igrot-kodesh*, vol. 1, 34.

The aims of the imperial authorities: the supremacy of civil law

The memoranda elaborated in rabbis' gatherings and written up by individual rabbis were sent to the Ministry of the Interior via the provincial authorities, and each provincial governor added his opinion on the measures proposed by the rabbis of his province. These accompanying letters offer us a glimpse into the attitude of the governors, who were the most important officials in supervising the implementation of state law.

In general, the attitudes of provincial authorities towards Jewish traditional practices varied in accordance with the *Weltanschauung* of each governor. More liberal or pragmatic governors were inclined to permit or tolerate some practices that more centralistic or nationalistic governors would ban. This could be seen in connection with the aforementioned example of the implementation of obligatory Sunday rest. However, none of the governors expressed general support for the rabbis' memoranda on halakhical matters, although some did support a number of the more insignificant points.

Some governors discussed the proposed measures from the state's point of view. For example, the governor general in Kiev, Vladimir Sukhomlinov, a future Minister of War, after receiving the proposal to oblige those converting to Christianity to divorce their Jewish wives and to coerce the performance of *ḥalitsah*, wrote to St. Petersburg that *ḥalitsah* should be abolished altogether and that rabbis should be obliged to arrange for the divorce of baptized Jews »without hindrance.«[61] In essence, he adopted a position that completely contradicted that of the rabbis. While the rabbis believed in an unchangeable Halakhah and asked for civil laws to be changed, Sukhomlinov and his office believed in superiority of imperial law and demanded changes in Halakhah to fit it. His colleagues in other provinces held similar opinions. The governor of Poltava province and the governor general in Vilna asked the ministry not to exempt Jewish children from writing on Saturday.[62] The governor in Suwałki opposed Sunday trade,[63] and the governor in Łomża opposed all of the proposals except for the reduction of the period before remarriage for divorced women from ten to three months.[64]

Other governors did not bother themselves with detailed discussions. For example, the governor of Kielce province wrote that »all of the projects fail to fit with existing laws and contradict the general order of the administration.«[65] His colleague from neighboring Piotrków also insisted that the majority of the

61 RGIA, coll. 821, inv. 9, file 63, fol. 7.
62 Ibid., fol. 5, 31–36.
63 Ibid., fol. 23–25.
64 Ibid., fol. 26–27.
65 Ibid., fol. 18.

rabbis' proposals contradicted the law, while the governors of Ekaterinoslav (today Dnipropetrovs'k) and Siedlce provinces stressed that Jews in general evaded imperial law.[66] The governor of Bessarabia stated that all but two of the proposals submitted by the rabbis of his province were »inadmissible for discussion [in the Rabbinic Commission] since they do not concern the matters prescribed in law [about the commission] and many of them are extremely undesirable.«[67]

Almost all of the governors' letters included passages that testified to their deep suspicions, if not hostility, towards Jews in general and towards what they regarded as the real intentions of the rabbis' memoranda. Some appeared to perceive traditional rabbis as »fanatics with backward views on modern culture,«[68] while others were afraid of Jews as a distinctive and hostile group and stressed the dangers of a »consolidation of Jews,« of the »traditional aspiration of Jews for isolation [and the] formation of a state within the state,« and of suspicious »motives of Jews towards other nationalities.«[69]

In St. Petersburg, Alexander Kharuzin – director of the Department of Foreign Cults at the Ministry of the Interior, the highest official directly responsible for Jewish religious affairs and himself a former governor of Bessarabia – also did not welcome the rabbinic proposals. He rejected 32 issues for discussion in the Rabbinic Commission, among them the recognition of unregistered marriages, burials on the day of death, inflating the lungs by mouth, the *eruv*, writing on Saturdays, Sunday rest, and all of the proposals concerning Jewish soldiers. As a reason for his rejection, he claimed that the proposals »contradict [imperial] laws and have no relation to the Jewish faith« that the Rabbinic Commission was entitled to deal with.[70] Such a reaction indicated that the rabbis overestimated the readiness of the government to make »concessions« to Orthodox Jewry. They did not understand that the imperial officials of the early 20th century clearly distinguished between religious and civilian spheres of life, while such distinctions were alien to the Jewish Halakhah.

Even after Kharuzin's dismissal of a large number of issues, the ministry presented dozens of other questions to the Rabbinic Commission, which gathered in the spring of 1910, and to the *Conference of Jews on matters concerning their religious lives*, convened at the same time.[71] Most of them, however, were

66 Ibid., fol. 16 and 18.
67 Ibid., fol. 9 and 70v.
68 Ibid., fol. 60–62.
69 Ibid., fol. 5, 9–12, 31–36.
70 RGIA, coll. 821, inv. 8, file 294, fol. 62–65.
71 The Conference of Jews on matters concerning their religious lives (S''ezd evreev po delam ikh religioznogo byta) was especially convened to discuss the questions

about communal and educational problems and only a few dealt with frictions between Halakhah and imperial law.[72] The representatives of the ministry watched the proceedings carefully and immediately put an end to any discussion about Jews in non-Jewish institutions, like the issue of writing in the state schools on Saturdays.[73] In other words, the officials of the ministry, in line with Kharuzin's opinion, clearly stated that the Jewish participants of the Conference, the majority of them rabbis, were not even allowed to raise issues involving the general laws of the empire. The Commission and Conference were convened in order to provide the Ministry of the Interior with a plan for the reorganization of Jewish communities, but none of the measures proposed after long and sometimes stormy deliberations were implemented in practice and not a single step towards implementation was taken by the authorities.

The attitude of the governors and other officials in the Ministry of the Interior towards the rabbis' memoranda and their behavior during and after the convention of the Commission clearly showed that the imperial authorities of the early 20th century did not recognize the importance of the frictions between Halakhah and secular law. Their reaction demonstrates that Orthodox rabbis' rhetoric regarding the link between religious observance and political loyalty fell on deaf ears. None of the governors were ready to facilitate the observance of Halakhah and the majority showed only incomprehension as to why the state should change its laws »in favor« of the Jews. A combination of a deep-rooted suspicion of Jews and Jewish intentions with general conservatism prevented many officials from engaging in a favorable discussion of the rabbinic memoranda. Even more pragmatically inclined officials were ready to take only very minor steps toward reconciling the imperial and Jewish legal systems. The superiority of the general civil law over any particular religious law was not to be questioned.

submitted by the rabbis to the ministry, since the Rabbinic Commission of seven members could not cope with such a large number of questions. The conference was composed of 40 participants: all candidates elected to the Rabbinic Commission in the Pale of Settlement with the addition of representatives from the Kingdom of Poland, St. Petersburg, and Moscow.

72 For the proceedings of the Rabbinic Commission see *Sbornik reshenii Ravvinskoi Komissii sozyva 1910 goda* (St. Petersburg: Ministerstvo vnutrennikh del, 1912). On the work of the Commission and the Conference see Levin, »Ha-politikah ha-yehudit,« 267–272.

73 Protocol of the »Conference of Jews on matters concerning their religious lives,« April 1, 1910. Russian National Library (St. Petersburg), Manuscript Department, coll. 183, file 34, fol. 146–157.

Halakhah and Russian imperial law from a European perspective

The problems raised by Russian and Polish rabbis in their memoranda were in no way unique to the Russian Empire. Some of them existed for centuries and were never resolved, like the inability to receive a divorce or *ḥalitsah* from Jewish converts to Christianity who did not want to cooperate.[74] Other problems, like those connected with military service and civil marriages, were caused by advancing modernity.

Jewish soldiers were prevented from a complete observance of Jewish halakhic norms in all of Europe's armies. Using the Talmudic principle of *dina de-malkhuta dina* (the law of the state is the law), the rabbinic authorities released Jewish soldiers from fulfilling religious obligations incompatible with the conditions of military service. In the Russian Empire this was explicitly stated, for example, in the book *Maḥaneh Israel* published in 1881 by Rabbi Israel Meir Ha-Cohen, widely known as the Ḥafets Ḥaim.[75] Nonetheless, the main topic of *Maḥaneh Israel* was in fact the importance of observing *all* religious commandments, as long as they do not contradict military duty.[76] The proposals of the Orthodox rabbis discussed above were directed to the same purpose.

There were also precedents when it came to caring for the religious needs of imprisoned Jews. In Berlin, for example, Jewish prayer rooms existed in the Moabit and Plötzensee prisons beginning in 1852 and 1882, respectively.[77] As

74 On halakhic attempts to allow widows to remarry without *ḥalitsah* in the medieval period, see Simḥa Goldin, *Ha-yiḥud ve-ha-yaḥad: ḥidat hisardutan shel ha-kvutsot ha-yehudiyot be-yamei ha-beinayim* (Tel Aviv: Ha-kibbuts ha-me'uḥad, 1997), 92–93. On converted Jews who did grant a *get* to wives who remained Jewish in the 12th century, see David Malkiel, *Reconstructing Ashkenaz: The Human Face of Franco-German Jewry, 1000–1250* (Stanford: Stanford University Press, 2009), 120, 138 and bibliography cited there. On the insistence of the Catholic Church that converts grant a *get* to wives who remained Jewish in 18th-century France, see Elisheva Carlebach, *Divided Souls: Converts from Judaism in Germany, 1500–1750* (New Haven–London: Yale University Press, 2011), 138–140. I am indebted to Efraim Shoham-Steiner for his help on medieval issues.

75 Israel Meir Ha-Cohen, *Maḥaneh israel* (Third edition, Warszawa 1881). For the attitude of rabbis in the Russian Empire to the issue of military service, see Mordechai Zalkin, »Bein ›bnei elohim‹ li-›vnei adam‹: rabanim, baḥurei yeshivot ve-ha-giyus la-tsava ha-rusi ba-meah ha-tesha-esreh,« *Shalom u-milḥamah ba-tarbut ha-yehudit*, ed. Avriel Bar-Levav (Jerusalem: Zalman Shazar Center for Jewish History, 2006), 165–222.

76 Ha-Cohen, *Maḥaneh Israel*, 5, 8–9. For discussion of this book in English, see Petrovsky-Shtern, *Jews in the Russian Army*, 192–194.

77 Hermann Simon, »Jüdische Betstätten in Berliner Gefängnissen am Beispiel von Plötzensee und Moabit,« in *Beiträge zur jüdischen Architektur in Berlin: Internationales Koloquium am 12. Juni 2008 in Berlin*, eds. Aliza Cohen-Mushlin,

described above, some rabbis in the Russian Empire asked for the establishment of prayer rooms, while others did not consider prayer rooms important, and stressed the observance of other commandments instead.

Once the absolutist state began to impose control over marriage, Jews did find themselves in a problematic situation. Halakhically valid marriages were considered void by the state, and divorces issued by civil courts were not, in turn, halakhically valid.[78] Cases in which state law directly contradicted Halakhah began to arise in the Habsburg monarchy after the issuance of the Marriage Patent (*Ehepatent*) in 1783.[79] In the early 20th century, 20 to 50 percent of marriages in Austrian Galicia, where most Jews remained traditional and unacculturated, were still not registered officially.[80] In Great Britain, the civil registration of marriages, in addition to religious ceremonies, was instituted in 1836. While the established Anglo-Jewry accepted this rule easily, the unregistered religious marriages of Eastern European Jewish immigrants presented a major problem for the Board of Deputies and the Chief Rabbinate.[81] In post-

Hermann Simon, and Harmen H. Thies (Petersberg: Michael Imhof Verlag, 2009), 19–25, here 20–21. On the duties of rabbis to care for Jewish prisoners see Max Beermann, *Die Seelsorge an jüdischen Strafgefangenen* (Berlin: Druck von Arthur Scholem, 1904). I am indebted to Katrin Keßler for help on this issue.

78 For an overview of practices in different countries see Avraham Ḥaim Freiman, *Seder kidushin ve-nisu'in aḥarei ḥatimat ha-talmud: meḥkar histori-dogmati be-dinei israel* (Jerusalem: Mosad Ha-Rav Kuk, 1945), 310–397. For a recent discussion of the interrelations between Jewish and civil marriages, mainly in North America, see David Novak, »Jewish Marriage and Civil Law: A Two-Way Street?« in *Tradition in the Public Square: A David Novak Reader*, eds. Randi Rashkover and Martin Kavka (Grand Rapids et al.: William B. Eerdmans Publishing Company, 2008), 304–327. Interestingly, Novak (319, note 89) cites the Ontario law stating that anyone petitioning for a civil divorce must have »removed all barriers that are within his or her control and that would prevent the other spouse's remarriage within that spouse's faith.« It seems that such a law would have been more than welcomed by the rabbis who wrote the memoranda in 1908.

79 Lois C. Dubin, *The Port Jews of Habsburg Trieste: Absolutist Politics and Enlightenment Culture* (Stanford: Stanford University Press, 1999), 174–197; Lois C. Dubin, »Les liaisons dangereuses: Mariage juif et état moderne à Trieste au XVIIIe siècle,« *Annales. Histoire, Sciences Sociales* 149, no. 5 (1994): 1139–1170. For the halakhic discussion of the famous Trieste case, see J. David Bleich, »A 19th-Century *Agunah* Problem and a 20th-Century Application,« *Tradition* 38, no. 2 (2004): 15–48. For the situation in Galicia, see Małgorzata Śliż, »Rytualne małżeństwa Żydów w Galicji w drugiej połowie XIX wieku,« *Studia Judaica* 4 (2001): 97–110; eadem, »Prawo małżeńskie dla galicyjskich Żydów (1848–1914),« *Żydzi i judaizm we współczesnych badaniach polskich* 3 (2003): 99–115.

80 Śliż, »Rytualne małżeństwa,« 100–101.

81 David Englander, »*Stille Huppah* (Quiet Marriage) Among Jewish Immigrants in Britain,« *Jewish Journal of Sociology* 34 (1992): 85–109.

revolutionary France, the state recognized only civil marriage ceremonies, which were required to precede any religious ceremonies. In 1833, the Central Consistory looked in vain for a halakhic solution to the problem of »illegal« marriages, and the problem only increased with the collective naturalization of Algerian Jews in 1870. After the reinstitution of civil divorces in 1884, the French rabbinate tried, also unsuccessfully, to find a halakhic solution to divorces issued by civil courts and not affirmed according to Halakhah.[82] As all these examples show, in addition to the objective frictions between two systems of law, one major problem was the failure of a non-acculturated Jewish population to comply with the demands of non-Jewish, external authorities.

The situation in the Russian Empire was not essentially different, aside from the fact that there were no civil marriages. The state delegated responsibility for marital issues solely to religious institutions, which were obliged to act according to their own laws. Even in the Kingdom of Poland, where divorce issues were completely within the competence of civil courts, they had to discuss Jewish divorces according to the *Shulḥan arukh*; a digest of its rules was attached to the law code and relevant chapters from the *Shulḥan arukh* were fully translated into Polish.[83] However, the translation of Jewish religious code into a language accessible to the bureaucracy signaled a particular tendency, in which the state relied on religious law but preferred to deal with it directly, without Jewish intermediaries. A similar approach was described by Robert D. Crews in relation to the Muslim population of the empire in the mid-19th century, when »state officials intensified their search for independent sources of knowledge about Islam« as »reliable alternatives to the ›fanatical‹ and self-interested Muslim clergy,« especially in marital issues.[84]

Basing marital status on religious laws, the state supervised the procedure and punished transgressors. The foremost consequence of state control was that only marriages and divorces registered by the religious authorities were considered valid, notwithstanding the complicated aspects of Halakhah.[85] In other words,

82 Zvi Jonathan Kaplan, »The Thorny Area of Marriage: Rabbinic Efforts to Harmonize Jewish and French Law in Nineteenth-Century France,« *Jewish Social Studies: History, Culture, Society* 13, no. 3 (2007): 59–72. For an overview on Jewish marriages according to French law, see Marianne Urbah, »Le mariage des Juifs devant le droit français (1896–1967). Sa célébration,« *Archives juives* 17, nos. 3–4 (1981): 50–64.

83 *Zakony o evreiakh*, eds. Gimpelson and Bramson, 674–677.

84 Robert D. Crews, *For Prophet and Tsar: Islam and Empire in Russia and Central Asia* (Cambridge, MA–London: Harvard University Press, 2006), 177–178.

85 The same thought was expressed by the Minister of the Interior S. S. Lanskoi in a memo to the Orenburg Muhammad Ecclesiastical Assembly in 1857: »the legality of Muhammadan marriage, like the marriages of other confessions, is

although the Russian state upheld the supremacy of religious norms in marital issues, it imposed religious norms through the use of secular legislative logic.[86]

The expansion of the state role in the last quarter of the 19th century and the broadening of governmental control over the population made the contradiction between the civil and religious approaches more apparent. Russian Jews, like the traditional Galician and Algerian Jewries, often did not comply with state demands, and with the registration of their life events in particular, thus causing additional friction between civil and religious laws. However, these frictions could have become more serious after a reform of the imperial marital code that was prepared in the 1890s and 1900s, but never implemented. According to ChaeRan Freeze, if put into practice, it would have meant »the abolition of autonomy in Jewish marital laws.«[87]

Neither was the serious problem of obligatory Sunday rest exclusive to the Russian Empire. Many European states in the late 19th and early 20th centuries prohibited any trade on Sunday. These laws pushed some Jewish shopkeepers toward breaking Halakhah and opening their shops on Saturday, while others sought out halakhic solutions, such as including a non-Jew in their business or selling it for the duration of Sabbat.[88]

made conditional upon [its] registration in a parish register by an ecclesiastical representative according to the established form.« Cit. by Crews, *For Prophet and Tsar*, 184.

86 The same could be concluded, for example, about the »Anglo-Muhammedan law« in British India. As Michael R. Anderson noted, »the administration of Anglo-Muhammedan law proceeded on the basis of textual understanding [...] but it misunderstood the role of Shari'a in the life of most South Asian Muslims. The legalist ideology of colonial judges erred on the side of applying clear rules in a consistent manner, regardless of whether the people genuinely treated them as binding. When harnessed to the centralized bureaucracy of the colonial state, Shari'a principles were administered with a uniformity and rule-bound consistency that was unprecedented on the subcontinent.« Michael R. Anderson, »Legal Scholarship and the Politics of Islam in British India,« in *Perspectives on Islamic Law, Justice, and Society*, ed. R.S. Khare (Lanham, MD: Rowman and Littlefield, 1999), 65–91, here 80–81.

87 Freeze, *Jewish Marriage and Divorce*, 276–279.

88 For general questions concerning work on Saturdays, see Jacob Katz, *Goy shel shabat* (Jerusalem, 1984). For the practices of Neo-Orthodoxy in Germany, see chapter 5 in Mordechai Breuer, *Jüdische Orthodoxie im Deutschen Reich, 1871–1918: Sozialgeschichte einer religiösen Minderheit* (Frankfurt am Main: Jüdischer Verlag bei Athenäum, 1986). On Jewish workers employed on Saturdays in interwar Łódź, see Ḥaim Shalem and Zeev H. Erlich, »Tguvatam shel ḥugim ortodoksiyim be-Polin le-ḥok menuḥat yom rishon,« *Gal-ed* 20 (2006): 135–143.

In the Russian Empire, shops had to be closed on Sundays following the introduction of a government decree in 1906, even as it permitted, as explained above, limited trade on Sundays. This was, however, a temporary measure, while the permanent law on Sunday rest was only accepted by the State Duma – the lower chamber of parliament – in 1910. The Duma's version of the law included no exceptions, expressing the nationalist feeling of the Duma majority and its unwillingness to take into account the interests of Jews and Muslims. However, the upper chamber of the parliament – the State Council – revised the law in 1912, which in its final form allowed shops to open on Sunday for five hours. The State Council showed no sympathy for Judaism or Islam, but acted out of its general conservatism and desire to preserve the old order: together with the possibility of limited trade on Sunday the State Council reinstated a 15-hour working day for shop assistants, abolished by the Duma's version of the law. Jewish needs were satisfied nonetheless by this legislative revision.[89]

Another major threat to Jewish observance in Europe was the prohibition of *sheḥitah* – Jewish ritual slaughter. Beginning in the 1850s, animal protectionists in Britain and Switzerland demanded that animals be kept from suffering by stunning them before they were slaughtered – a demand that was generally regarded as prohibited by Halakhah.[90] This idea was adopted by anti-Semites and the combined lobbying of both of these groups brought about the prohibition of *sheḥitah* first in St. Gallen in 1866 and then all throughout Switzerland in 1893. In 1886–1887 the prohibition of *sheḥitah* was debated in the German Reichstag and rejected, but the Kingdom of Saxony outlawed ritual slaughter from 1892–1910.[91]

In Russia the idea of outlawing *sheḥitah* first appeared in 1876, while the Society for Protection of Animals initiated this question again in 1891. However, the energetic defense of *sheḥitah* by Isaac Dembo, who based his arguments on scientific experiments and the governmental reluctance to accept such a measure put an end to the initiative.[92] The memoranda of rabbis in 1908 did not

89 For the history of the law on Sunday rest and the attempts of Orthodoxy to prevent it, see Levin, »Ha-politikah ha-yehudit,« 278–282.

90 *Jewish Encyclopedia*, vol. 11, s.v. »Scotland«, 122; Ibid., s.v. »Switzerland,« 609–612, here 612; *Jüdisches Lexikon*, vol. 4/2, s.v. »Schächten,« 134–137, here 136; *Encyclopaedia Judaica*, vol. 14, s.v. »Sheḥitah«, 1337–1344, here 1340–1341; Elijah Judah Schochet, *Animal Life in Jewish Tradition: Attitudes and Relationships* (New York: Ktav Publishing House, 1984), 283.

91 On debates about the prohibition of *sheḥitah* in Germany, see Dorothee Brantz, »Stunning Bodies: Animal Slaughter, Judaism, and the Meaning of Humanity in Imperial Germany,« *Central European History* 35 (2002): 167–194.

92 *Evreiskaia entsiklopediia*, vol. 16, s.v. »Shekhita«, 23–26, here 25; Dembo's work was published in German: Isaak Dembo, *Das Schächten im Vergleich mit anderen Schlachtmethoden* (Leipzig: H. Roskoschny, 1894).

therefore mention the issue. In late 1913 the Extreme Right Faction of the State Duma introduced a bill explicitly prohibiting Jewish ritual slaughter, but the bill was not discussed due to the outbreak of World War I and the subsequent cessation of routine legislative work.[93]

However, in Finland – an autonomous state within the Russian Empire – the *sheḥitah* was indeed outlawed in 1909 as an inhumane method of slaughter. The term proposed by Robert Crews to describe the relationship between the Russian Empire and Islam, could be equally applied to the empire's approach to Judaism.[94] The Finnish legislature, in striking contrast to the Russian imperial Duma, accepted a great number of progressive ideas, such as women's suffrage in 1906 and animal rights in 1909. As the Hebrew newspaper *Hed ha-zman* wrote while reporting on the new law, »Until now we knew that the Russian government opposed prohibiting *sheḥitah* in Finland. [...] And now, evidently, the Russian Council of Ministers decided that it was not worth it to fight with the Finnish Senate for the sake of the Jewish religion.«[95] The aforementioned assembly of Orthodox rabbis in Vilna appealed to the Finnish Senate to revoke the prohibition,[96] but to no avail: in 1913 the Russian Jewish encyclopedia reported that »the Finnish Jews have to order their meat from St. Petersburg.«[97]

Conclusions

The failures to introduce a civil marital code, to prohibit *sheḥitah*, and to impose an obligatory Sunday rest clearly demonstrate that in spite of various anti-Jewish restrictions, the *ancien régime* in the Russian Empire was relatively hospitable to observant Jews. The level of centralization of the Russian state differed from that in the West, especially in the area of state control over its subjects and the uniform implementation of law. Imperial Russia was thus well suited to premodern Jewish tradition.

93 »Zakonodatel'noe predpolozhenie ob otmene korobochnogo sbora i ob ustanovlenii sposobov uboia domashnikh zhivotnykh,« *Vestnik evreiskoi obshchiny* 1914, no. 1: 50–53; ibid., 1914, no. 2: 42–48; Vladimir Grosman, »Bor'ba so shekhitoiu,« ibid., 1914, no. 3: 38–41; D. M., »Korobochnyi sbor v Biudzhetnoi Komissii Gosudarstvennoi Dumy,« ibid. 1914, no. 5: 19–22; Heinz-Dietrich Löwe, *The Tsars and the Jews: Reform, Reaction and Anti-Semitism in Imperial Russia, 1772–1917* (Chur et al.: Harwood Academic Publishers, 1993), 296.

94 Robert Crews, »Empire and the Confessional State: Islam and Religious Politics in Nineteenth-Century Russia,« *American Historical Review* 108 (2003): 50–83.

95 Editorial in *Hed ha-zman*, no. 55, March 6 (19), 1909: 1.

96 RGIA, coll. 821, inv. 9, file 51, fol. 326.

97 *Evreiskaia entsiklopediia*, vol. 16, s.v. »Shekhita«, 23–26, here 25.

Most frictions between Russian civil law and Halakhah – as expressed by the rabbis in 1908 – were caused by the introduction of modern institutions and norms, like the drafting of Jews into the army, state control over marital issues, secular schooling, juridical reform, etc. The increasing role of the state, growing centralization and the tightening of state control over the population in the 1880s and 1890s caused more frictions and led to the abolition of practices »favorable« to Jewish observance such as the ability of Jewish soldiers to eat separately, prohibited in 1887–1888, kosher food in prisons, eliminated in 1889, and the exception from writing in state schools on Saturdays, rescinded in 1882. Legal measures with potentially major implications for observant Jews, such as the prohibitions of Sunday trade and of ritual slaughter, were not proposed until in the last years of the empire, and were never actually implemented: not because the government was attending to Jewish needs, but solely due to the strong conservative tendencies in Russian governing circles.

At the same time, the Russian imperial legislation on Jews, while supporting their religion and recognizing halakhic norms in general, failed to include the details and subtleties prescribed by Halakhah and tradition. The laws were written by officials acquainted with Christianity, but usually ignorant of rabbinical Judaism; they relied on information from Jewish mediators, but never assimilated it completely. For example, a clause in the 1844 law on state-sponsored Jewish schools stipulated that each Jewish school would have a hall where its pupils were obliged to conduct Jewish religious rites on holidays, in a manner similar to the Christian practice in all the other state schools of the empire. However, as the principal of the Jewish school in Zhitomir informed his superiors in 1850, he could not implement the clause since none of the pupils in his school were older than 11 years, while a quorum of ten thirteen-year-old boys (*minyan*) was needed for Jewish public prayer.[98] It is logical to assume that many other Jewish schools could not comply with the law and organize separate prayers either, due to the absence of a halakhically valid *minyan*.

The most striking example of mixing recognition of Jewish religious practices with Christian perceptions was the law of 1835 defining the duties of rabbis. By obliging rabbis to perform rituals in person, as described above, the state clearly wanted to improve the registration of vital events, but in fact failed as the rabbis genuinely could not meet those requirements. Although the state of Jewish vital records had improved significantly by the early 20th century, it never reached the desired completeness and continued to suffer from numerous omissions.[99]

98 State Archives of Zhytomyr Region (DAZhO), coll. 71, inv. 1, file 958, fol. 4. Consulted as microfilm in CAHJP, H2/9344.5.

99 For different aspects of Jewish vital statistics, see Avrutin, »The Politics of Jewish Legibility,« especially 155–161, and idem, »The Power of Documentation.«

Incompatibility of the description of rabbis' duties with Jewish practice became apparent quite soon, but was never resolved. The bulk of the proposals made by the crown rabbis in 1908 reflected their difficulties in fulfilling this law. Some governors openly tolerated the existing practice and supported proposals to reformulate the obligations of rabbis in 1908,[100] while other administrators were adhering strictly to the letter of law.[101]

One salient feature of the Russian imperial legislation on Jews was its inconsistency over time. In the early 20th century, Jews still lived according to the laws introduced during the reign of Nicolas I (1825–1855), when the government actively sought to absorb Jews into the structures of the Russian state. That legislation was usually supportive of the Jewish religion in principle, but failed to take into consideration many important details. Laws introduced during the next period, the epoch of the Great Reforms of Alexander II (1855–1881), which aimed at modernization and Westernization, tended to overlook Jewish differences and to include the Jewish population into general legal norms. The judicial reform of 1864 did not thus mention Jews, instead implicitly applying to them the norm that witnesses must take an oath in the courtroom,[102] thus making it possible to swear on Saturdays. After the crisis of 1881–1882 legislative politics became mostly anti-Jewish: in addition to the introduction of various restrictions, the state was also reluctant to »improve« the situation of Jews. During the same period it began to assume more effective control over all spheres of life. Therefore, the obvious inconsistencies in the laws of two previous eras were not corrected, while the implementation of laws became stricter. The opinion of the governors given in 1908 clearly expressed their suspicion of Jews and their tendency to reject Jewish requests.

As the material that was gathered during the preparations for the Rabbinic Commission of 1910 demonstrates, the rabbis prepared a long list of frictions between the state law and Halakhah and anticipated the adjustment of civil law to the religious one.[103] These expectations were the result of the generally

100 RGIA, coll. 821, inv. 9, file 63, fol. 7 (governor general in Kiev), fol. 31–36 (governor general in Vilna).

101 RGIA, coll. 821, inv. 9, file 63, fol. 9–12 (the governor of Ekaterinoslav province).

102 See the decision of the Governing Senate, the highest judicial body in Russia, in 1870, *Zakony o evreiakh*, eds. Gimpelson and Bramson, 709.

103 It is noteworthy that the idea of adjusting Halakhah to state law was not discussed during the preparations for the Rabbinic Commission of 1910. Only a few crown rabbis proposed canceling certain »annoying« rituals, like *ḥalitsah* etc., which, in their opinion, did not fit with the *Zeitgeist*, but those proposals were not taken seriously. See RGIA, coll. 821, inv. 9, file 51, fol. 145, 158, 280. The Central Consistory in Paris, for instance, looked for halakhic means to overcome

favorable attitude of imperial legislation toward the Jewish religion and of the rabbinical expectations that the government was interested in facilitating Jewish observance after the Revolution of 1905–1907. Those expectations turned out to be unfounded because of the combination of two factors: growing anti-Semitism, which excluded almost any possibility of »favorable« or even »pragmatic« approaches to the Jews; and – probably more importantly – a growing legal awareness of the authorities. The selectivity and voluntarism of previous periods, which allowed for the toleration of particular Jewish traditional practices, were gradually replaced by a stricter and more unified approach to the enforcement of laws, thus intensifying frictions between state legislation and Halakhah. The rabbis who were requesting changes in the imperial law were not able to grasp this change.

At the same time, the rabbis' proposals also demonstrated that in spite of some inconsistencies in civil law, the tensions which they caused were of minor character. Notwithstanding the developments of the late 19th and early 20th century, the Russian legislation was still generally supportive of Judaism and allowed Jews to follow the norms of Halakhah without great obstacles or harsh economic concessions. The Russian Empire was, contrary to common perception, a relatively hospitable place for observant Jews, where Jewish religious commandments and traditional behavior could still be followed almost freely into the early 20th century.

Vladimir Levin

the contradictions between civil and religious laws, out of the understanding that there is no way to adjust French civil law to Halakhah. However, its attempts failed due to the discouragement of prominent Eastern European rabbis. See Kaplan, »The Thorny Area of Marriage.« In the late Russian Empire, by contrast, traditional rabbis were reluctant to look for general halakhic solutions, hoping for state laws to be adjusted. This issue has to be discussed separately, in the framework of research on Jewish Orthodoxy and the Reform movement in Eastern Europe.

Competing Loyalties in Galicia: The Challenges Facing Metropolitan Andrei Sheptytskyi after the Disintegration of the Habsburg Empire*

In 1900 Andrei Sheptytskyi[1] was appointed by the Vatican and the Austrian emperor Franz Joseph to lead the Greek Catholic Church as Archbishop of Lviv and Metropolitan of Halych.[2] A descendant of a Polonized family, the members of which included several Uniate bishops and archbishops, Sheptytskyi changed from the Latin rite to the Eastern, Byzantine rite and became Metropolitan at the age of 35. He led the Greek Catholic Church in the region for forty-four years, seeking a *modus vivendi* with various state and political entities.

After the collapse of the Habsburg Empire, Sheptytskyi and his church faced major changes involving the political and legal status of their land – Eastern Galicia, formerly part of the Austrian crown land (*Kronland*) of Galicia and Lodomeria. The Austro-Hungarian Confessional Laws of May 7, 1874 had regulated the rights and obligations of the Catholic Church. Subsequently in Austria-Hungary, the Greek Catholic clergy and hierarchy had enjoyed a status close to that of imperial bureaucrats, participating in many important functions of the state. The leadership of the national states proclaimed by Ukrainians and Poles in 1918 had different views as to the role and functions of the Greek

* The research in different archives for this article was made possible thanks to the support of the Petro Yatsyk Program for Study of Modern Ukrainian History and Society.

1 The most valuable among the books on Sheptytskyi are: Cyrille Korolevskij, *Le Métropolite André Szeptyckyj* (Roma, 1964); Andrii Krawchuk, *Christian Social Ethics in Ukraine: The Legacy of Andrei Sheptytsky* (Edmonton et al.: Canadian Institute of Ukrainian, 1997); *Morality and Reality. The Life and Times of Metropolitan Andrei Sheptyts'ky*, ed. Paul Magosci (Edmonton et al.: Canadian Institute of Ukrainian, 1989).

2 For more on the circumstances of Andrei Sheptytskyi's appointments, see: Giovanni Coco, »Tra la Galizia e la Russia: la Nomina Episcopale di Andrej Szeptycki nell'ambito dell'Unionismo di Leone XIII,« in *Collectanea Archivi Vaticani* 61 (2006), 33–91.

Catholic Church.[3] Its spiritual leader, Andrei Sheptytskyi, until recently a loyal subject of the Emperor, was caught in the middle of a bloody struggle between two national movements, both of which claimed Eastern Galicia as an important part of their states. His personal quandary symbolized the painful dilemma of those inhabitants of Galicia who were of mixed ancestry, or who shared the legacy of more than one culture.[4] For a long time after the collapse of the Habsburg Empire, Sheptytskyi's line of thought continued to be dominated by the imperial legacy. One can argue that, for such public figures, the multiethnic empire with its complicated balance of powers, was rather more explicit and predictable than any national state. The metropolitan needed time to realize the implications of the national state concept and to reshape his own attitudes towards it. The other very problematic issue for him was the leftist, socialist orientation of the mainstream Ukrainian national movement, which often linked social and national issues.

This article will focus on the changes in the national and political loyalties of Andrei Sheptytskyi. The Ukrainian-Polish War (1918–1919), and the years of international discussions on the Eastern Galician problem in Paris (1919–1923) became a test for the metropolitan's national and political loyalties. My research, based on recently discovered archival sources, shows that his support for the Ukrainians during the Ukrainian-Polish War over Eastern Galicia derived from his very broad understanding of his own pastoral mission and duties.

Multiple identities and loyalty towards the Habsburg dynasty

Under Austrian rule, Sheptytskyi had rendered great services to the Ukrainian cause – though he generally abstained from involvement in current politics – through the tactful use of his legal status as member of the Upper House of the Austro-Hungarian Parliament and as *ex officio* member of the Galician Diet. Before the First World War, his chief political concerns were the opening of a separate Ukrainian University in Lviv and reaching a Ukrainian-Polish agreement over electoral reform in Galicia.

3 The clergy and laity of the Greek Catholic Church were almost entirely of Ukrainian nationality.

4 The Metropolitan's brother Stanisław Sheptytskyi became a general in the Polish army and defended Polish independence. At the same time, his other brother, Kazimir-Klymentii Sheptytskyi, who became a Greek Catholic monk, shared Andrei Sheptytskyi's stance. The greater part of his extended family supported Polish independence. The metropolitan's second cousin, Władysław Skrzyński, served as Polish envoy and ambassador to the Apostolic See in 1921–1937.

It took Sheptytskyi, a Galician nobleman, a considerably long time to reconsider his multiple identities and political loyalties, and to support the national aspirations of his Ukrainian congregation. In many respects, up to the beginning of the First World War, he tried to preserve his multiple identities, which did not come into conflict with his loyalty to the Habsburg Empire. For a rather long time, he saw himself as a representative of old Ruthenian nobility, drawing on the legacy of the Polish-Lithuanian Commonwealth.

In his first pastoral letter as Bishop of Stanislaviv[5] he declared himself to be »of Ruthenian kin.«[6] In the early twentieth century he was not ready to think in strictly national terms. In a 1908 letter to one of his relatives, he revealed his reasoning on issues of nationality: First of all, he saw himself as a transmitter of the legacy of the Polish-Lithuanian Commonwealth, for whom the Ruthenian and the Polish components of his identity were equally important.[7] When Sheptytskyi assumed higher ecclesiastical posts, he was mindful of his role in the reconciliation of the Polish and Ukrainian inhabitants of Galicia. In the Austro-Hungarian Empire he became an active patron of Ukrainian culture and education, as well as a champion of the economic emancipation of the Ukrainian community in Galicia. His charitable initiatives gained him popularity among the Ukrainians of Galicia before the First World War.

The war became a true watershed for Sheptytskyi, as he was now obliged to take sides. His choice to become an active player in Ukrainian politics did not weaken his loyalty to the Habsburg dynasty. In the early weeks of the war he repeatedly urged his followers to maintain their loyalty to Emperor Franz Josef and their Austro-Hungarian motherland. Thus, in his address to the Greek Catholic population of the villages on the border between the Russian and Austro-Hungarian Empires, he argued that »the Russian Tsar cannot tolerate that we have freedom of faith and of nationality in the Austrian state, and wants to take away that freedom.«[8] Sheptytskyi was convinced that the Habsburg dynasty, after the victory over the Russian Empire, could guarantee the national and

5 Sheptytskyi's first pastoral letter had the title »Our Program« and was issued on August 2, 1899.

6 Mytropolyt Andrei Sheptyts'kyi, *Pastyrs'ki poslannia 1899–1914* (L'viv: Apriori, 2007), 20.

7 Central State Historical Archive of Ukraine in Lviv/Tsentral'nyi Derzhavnyi Istorychnyi Arkhiv Ukrainy u Lvovi (hereafter TsDIAL), collection/coll. (fond) 358, inventory/inv. (opis) 2, file (sprava) 35, folio/fol. (arkush) 30–31.

8 »Bo moskovs'kyi Tsar ne mih toho sterpity, shcho v Avstriis'kii derzhavi maiemo svobodu viry ta narodnosty; hoche nam vyderty tu svobodu, zakuvaty v kaidany«. Andrii Kravchuk, ed., *Mytropolyt Andrei Sheptyts'kyi: Zhyttia i Dialnist', Tserkva i Suspil'ne Pytannia. Dokumenty i Materialy 1899–1944*, vol. 2, part 1 (L'viv: Misioner, 1998), 443.

cultural development of Ukrainians, even beyond the current borders of the Austro-Hungarian Empire.

From the beginning of the First World War, the metropolitan paid special attention to the consolidation of different Ukrainian political groups and movements, thus inviting leaders of the Ukrainian parties to discuss the current political situation in his palace on St. George Hill.[9] Perhaps influenced by these meetings, Sheptytskyi wrote and submitted a memorandum to the Austrian foreign ministry, where he laid out some ideas for the possible future reorganization of the Ukrainian lands of the Russian Empire, which he believed would be conquered by the Austrians. Essentially, he proposed the creation of a separate political entity from these territories »independent from [...] and alien to the Tsarist Empire.«[10] He thought that such a Ukrainian entity under Habsburg rule could be created in the traditional form of a hetmanate.[11] He also stressed the importance of legal reform for the new Ukrainian part of the empire, and suggested the use of Ukrainian lawyers from Galicia to facilitate the translation and rapid implementation of Austrian civil and criminal law.[12]

In church matters, Sheptytskyi contemplated using a future Austrian victory for his plans to create an Eastern-rite Ukrainian Catholic Church under the Roman Pope.[13] Towards that end, he was prepared to assume the title of Metropolitan of Kyiv and all Ukraine. He regarded the Austrian Empire as the best ally for Ukrainians in Galicia, as well as for those who still lived under tsarist rule. He also perceived an Austrian victory as a precondition for the fulfillment of his grand plans to convert the Slavic population of the Russian Empire to Catholicism. He assumed that war between the Russian Empire and Austria-Hungary could offer a unique opportunity to spread the Catholic faith of the Eastern rite among the subjects of the Romanov Empire, particularly among the Orthodox Ukrainians.

The tsarist authorities regarded Sheptytskyi as a Ukrainian nationalist, as well as an Austrian loyalist, and, more generally, as an enemy of the Russian Empire.

9 *Tsarskyi viazen' 1914–1917* (L'viv: Stavropigiiskyi Instytut, 1918), 5–6.

10 Kravchuk, ed., *Mytropolyt Andrei Sheptyts'kyi: Zhyttia i Dial'nist', Tserkva i Suspil'ne Pytannia*, vol. 2, part 2 (L'viv: Misioner, 1998), 610.

11 The *Hetmanate* was a Cossack state in today's Central Ukraine and a small part of Russia (former Starodub region of Chernigov province) between 1649 and 1764. It was founded by Hetman Bohdan Khmelnytskyi during the so-called Khmelnytskyi Uprising (1648–1657). In the 18th century the territory of the Hetmanate was limited to Left-Bank Ukraine. In 1764 Catherine II of Russia officially abolished the autonomy of the Cossack state.

12 Ibid., 610–611.

13 Ibid., 611–612. Kravcheniuk Osyp, *Veleten so Sviztoiurs'koi hory* (Yorkton, SK: Redeemer's Voice Press, 1963), 124–126.

They arrested him in September 1914 and imprisoned him in various Russian Orthodox monasteries for two and a half years.[14] Sheptytskyi's efforts on behalf of the Ukrainian national movement before the war and his wartime arrest strengthened his authority among the majority of Galician Ukrainians. He was released from tsarist imprisonment after the February Revolution in Russia and triumphantly returned to Lviv on September 10, 1917.

Sheptytskyi and Ukrainian statehood in Eastern Galicia

On the eve of the collapse of the Habsburg Empire, Sheptytskyi, together with two other Greek Catholic bishops, became a member of the Ukrainian National Council, which, in its meeting of October 18, 1918 resolved to proclaim the creation of a separate political entity consisting of the Ukrainian lands of the Austro-Hungarian Empire. Among the members of the Ukrainian National Council, formed on the initiative of Ukrainian deputies to the Austrian Parliament and the Galician Diet, Greek Catholic clergy represented an important group. The council decided that the future of the Ukrainian part of Galicia lay with Austria and was not seeking full independence, at least for the moment.[15]

Sheptytskyi thought that a demand for independence from Austria would be »careless and even dangerous, and first of all disadvantageous« and therefore supported the idea of an autonomous Ukrainian political entity under the auspices of Austria.[16] The Ukrainians' seizure of power in Lviv and other Galician towns initiated the Ukrainian-Polish War over Eastern Galicia. On November 1, 1918, Ukrainian officers informed Sheptytskyi of the Ukrainian coup.[17] In his response, he expressed his satisfaction that the city had been taken without serious bloodshed. By the force of the events he was prompted to declare his support for the Ukrainian takeover and on November 3, 1918 celebrated a mass of thanks »for the foundation of the Ukrainian state from

14 For more on Sheptytskyi's imprisonment in Russia see: Athanasius D. McVay, »A Prisoner for his People's Faith: Metropolitan Andrei Sheptytskyi's Detentions under Russia and Poland«, *Logos: A Journal of Eastern Christian Studies* 50, no. 1–2 (2009): 13–54.

15 *Dmytro Paliiev. Zhyttia ta Dial'nist'*, ed. Oleh Kupchyns'kyi (L'viv: NTSH, 2007), 106–125.

16 »Zhadannia vidluchennia Halychyny vid Avstrii [...] bulo by, po moiemu, neostorozhno, v danim sluchaiu, nebezpechne; a peredusim – bezhosenne.« Kravchuk, ed., *Mytropolyt Andrei Sheptyts'kyi: Zhyttia i Dial'nist', Tserkva i Suspil'ne Pytannia*, vol. 2, part 2, 669.

17 Orest Subtelny, *Ukraine: A History* (Toronto: Canadian Institute of Ukrainian Studies, 1994), 367–368.

the Ukrainian lands of the former Habsburg Empire.«[18] The metropolitan was not prepared for the course of events, which developed rather rapidly. It was probably somewhat later that he took the view that the Ukrainian takeover was a manifestation of Ukrainian political maturity, and was ready to share with his congregation the responsibility that went with it.

The Ukrainian-Polish War challenged Sheptytskyi's multiple loyalties. When the empire disintegrated, he faced a difficult personal choice. In November 1918 he decided to lend his support to the Ukrainian side within the Ukrainian-Polish conflict in Galicia, because, as he believed, his people had the right, like other nations, to demand a separate political entity. The form »our people« was his term of choice, and he frequently used it instead of »Ukrainians« or »the Ukrainian people.« Such vocabulary shows his inclination to avoid identification in national terms.[19] In the years prior to the First World War, Sheptytskyi also tried to refrain from referring to his Greek Catholic followers as either Ukrainian or Ruthenian, using the inclusive formulation »our people«. Such an approach irritated the leaders of the Ukrainian national movement and was discussed in the Ukrainian press.[20]

For his choice to side with the Ukrainians, Sheptytskyi faced charges of betraying Polish national interests, leveled at him by members of the Polish community in Galicia, and by leaders of the independent Polish state. Józef Bilczewski, the Roman Catholic Archbishop of Lviv, thought him to have become an »ardent Ukrainian«.[21] However, Sheptytskyi's choice in favor of Ukrainian allegiance was precipitated by the collapse of the Habsburg Empire, whereby he found himself in a situation, in which it became impossible or at least very difficult to identify with more than one national group. His pro-Ukrainian stance, and his support of the Ukrainian efforts to build a Ukrainian state in Eastern Galicia, was determined above all by his office as Metropolitan of the Greek Catholic Church, whose congregation consisted almost exclusively of Ukrainians. But even when acting in favor of the latter, Sheptytskyi avoided making any overt statement regarding his own national identity. As a young

18 *Dilo*, November 4, 1918.

19 For such references see for example the letter to Count M. Tyshkevich in Kravchuk, ed., *Mytropolyt Andrei Sheptyts'kyi: Zhyttia i Dialnist', Tserkva i Suspil'ne Pytannia*, vol. 2, part 2, 647. In a letter to the Apostolic visitator, G. Genocchi, Sheptytskyi used instead »Galician ruthenian people«. See ibid., 717.

20 Volodymyr Doroshenko, *Velykyi mytropolyt* (Yorkton, SK: 1958), 26. Semen Vityk, *Shcho dali robyty?* (L'viv, 1902), 46.

21 *Nieznana korespondencja Arcybiskupów Metropolitów Lwowskich Józefa Bilczewskiego z Andrzejem Szeptyckim w czasie wojny Polsko-Ukraińskiej 1918–1919*, ed. Józef Wołczański (Lwów–Kraków: Wydawnictwo Bł. Jakuba Strzemię Archidiecezji Lwowskiej ob. łac., 1997), 84.

man, Sheptytskyi had been strongly influenced by the ideas of Ultramontanism,[22] and as a church leader, he regarded national issues as secondary to Christian values. His support for the Ukrainian cause was secondary to his Catholicism.

The challenge of the Ukrainian-Polish War

The Ukrainian-Polish War led to enormous atrocities visited upon Ukrainian, Polish, and Jewish civilians. Both the Ukrainian and Polish sides perpetrated numerous brutalities. The Ukrainian troops and armed volunteers committed many crimes against the Polish population, while the victorious Polish troops launched their own campaign of mass persecution against the Ukrainian population of Galicia. Jewish inhabitants of the city of Lviv were caught in the middle of the conflict,[23] and accusations that they had sided with the Ukrainians prompted a three-day pogrom.[24] When combat reached the streets of Lviv, Sheptytskyi was concerned for the lives of civilians. He addressed the magistrate, urging the city officials to normalize life for the residents. On November 12, in the midst of the fiercest battle in the streets of Lviv, he officially addressed the Ukrainian National Council with the initiative to stop fighting, and open peace talks with the Poles.[25]

Upon the offer of Roman Catholic Archbishop Bilczewski, Sheptytskyi composed an official letter from both archbishops to the commanders of the Ukrainian and Polish armed units, urging them to exchange prisoners and wounded combatants.[26] He himself led the Ukrainian delegation in the Ukrainian-Polish talks, which concluded with a brief armistice. When warfare intensified in the outskirts of Lviv, Sheptytskyi demanded on March 10, 1919 that the Ukrainian troops stop bombarding the city. The Ukrainian commander Victor Kurmanovych fulfilled his request. In this way, using his standing among

22 A religious philosophy within the Roman Catholic community that places strong emphasis on the prerogatives and powers of the Pope. In particular, Ultramontanism may consist of the assertion that the superiority of Papal authority supersedes the authority of local, secular or spiritual hierarchies.

23 Wacław Wierzbieniec, »The Process of Jewish Emancipation and Assimilation in the Multiethnic City of Lviv during the Nineteenth and Twentieth Centuries,« *Harvard Ukrainian Studies* 24 (2000): 229–253, here 239.

24 According to the memoirs of Joseph Tenenbaum, Sheptytskyi was very distressed by Tenenbaum's information concerning pogroms and gave 500 korons to help the victims. See: Joseph Tenenbaum, *In Search of a Lost People: The Old and the New Poland* (New York: Beechhurst Press, 1948), 115.

25 Kravchuk, ed., *Mytropolyt Andrei Sheptyts'kyi: Zhyttia i Dial'nist', Tserkva i Suspil'ne Pytannia*, vol. 2, part 2, 692.

26 Ibid., 693.

Ukrainians, Sheptytskyi played an important role in easing the suffering of the local population. Nevertheless, Polish authorities and church hierarchs openly accused him of having a passive attitude toward the war atrocities, and of unequivocally supporting Ukrainian military actions. Sheptytskyi was even charged with these accusations before the Roman Curia.[27] In those official documents, signed by Polish state authorities and members of the Roman Catholic hierarchy he was also accused of supporting the pro-Ukrainian political activities of his clergy.

During the Ukrainian-Polish war, the church and clergy themselves became victims of abuse, as both sides viewed the clergy of the enemy side as an element of national agitation. For this reason, acts of sacrilege against church buildings, arrests, and even executions of priests of both rites, took on a mass character. Although sources and figures vary, the statistics that testify to the scale of repressions of the clergy are striking: Six Roman Catholic priests were killed and 85 arrested or detained by Ukrainian forces;[28] the Polish side killed five priests and arrested or confined around 500 Greek Catholic priests and monks in prisons and camps.[29]

In this situation, on February 27, 1919, Sheptytskyi addressed the government of the Western Ukrainian National Republic (hereafter WUNR), asking the Ukrainian authorities to release members of the Roman Catholic clergy who had been arrested or detained. The WUNR government released a great number of detained Catholic priests of Polish nationality.[30] Sheptytskyi probably expected the same step to be taken by the Roman Catholic hierarchy of Lviv. But the Ukrainian clergy was released only thanks to the intervention and assistance of the Vatican, represented by the apostolic nuncio Achille Ratti.[31]

The Ukrainian Greek Catholic Church did indeed take an active part in the state-building efforts of the Western Ukrainian National Republic. Some priests even became officials of this new Ukrainian state. Ivan Latyshevskyi, a priest, who later became auxiliary bishop of Stanislaviv, headed the Department for

27 Among others, such accusations against Sheptytskyi were put forward by Archbishop Józef Bilczewski and Lviv Armenian-rite Archbishop Józef Teodorowicz. See Archivio Segreto Vaticano (hereafter ASV), Affari Ecclesiastici Straordinari (hereafter A.E.S.), Russia, positione (hereafter pos.) 634. Also the Polish Ministry of Foreign Affairs made such accusations. See ASV, Archivio Nunziatura Varsavia (hereafter Arch. Nunz. Varsavia), vol. 194, fol. 1049–1111.

28 ASV, A.E.S., Polonia, pos. 634.

29 Actually 498 Greek Catholic priests, monks, and seminarians, according to the list presented to the apostolic nuncio by Sheptytskyi through Josaphat Jean. See ASV, Arch. Nunz. Varsavia, vol. 200, fol. 94–103.

30 TsDIAL, coll. 408, inv. 1, file 574, fol. 6.

31 ASV, Arch. Nunz. Varsavia, vol. 200, fol. 64–65, 69–69v.

Religious Affairs in the WUNR government, and many parish priests were among the members of the local branches of the Ukrainian National Council in Galician towns and villages. At the same time, relations between the Greek Catholic clergy, headed by Sheptytskyi, and the government of the WUNR, were not free of disagreement and controversy. The leftist and atheistic faction enjoyed considerable influence among the members of the Ukrainian National Council, and, among other matters, discussed the secularization of Church property, as well as elimination of religious education from school curricula.[32]

Diplomacy on behalf of the Western Ukrainian National Republic

Despite the anticlerical sentiments of some of the WUNR's leaders, Sheptytskyi assumed the role of an informal diplomat and spokesman for the unrecognized Eastern Galician state. He suggested that only a neutral international commission would be able to resolve the Ukrainian-Polish armed conflict in Galicia in accordance with the principles of international law. In January 1919 he had a conversation with a member of the Inter-Allied mission to oversee an armistice between Poles and Ukrainians, in the course of which he demanded that Woodrow Wilson's principles of self-determination be extended to Eastern Galicia. He also tried, albeit in vain, to meet with Józef Piłsudski, the head of the independent Polish state.[33]

The metropolitan's international defense of the rights of Galician Ukrainians culminated during his long journeys abroad. In the fall of 1920 he obtained permission from the Polish authorities to pay an official visit to the Holy See. During his travel and stay abroad he held, in addition to his Polish passport,[34] a diplomatic passport of the Western Ukrainian National Republic.[35] While in Rome, he tried to obtain the Pope's support for the Ukrainian cause in Eastern Galicia. Pope Benedict XV offered his support for a peace settlement of the Ukrainian-Polish conflict, and humanitarian help to the Ukrainian Catholics. For these purposes, the Roman Curia decided to send an apostolic delegate, Giovanni Genocchi, to the Ukrainian National Republic (hereafter UNR), and charged him with a special mission in Eastern Galicia. The objectives of

32 Bohdan Budurowycz, »The Greek-Catholic Church in Galicia, 1914–1944,« *Harvard Ukrainian Studies* 26, no. 1–4 (2002–2003): 291–375, here 302.

33 ASV, A.E.S., Russia, pos. 634. Budurowycz, »Greek-Catholic Church in Galicia,« 302.

34 Sheptytskyi obtained a Polish passport on December 16, 1920 and traveled to Rome with Ermenegildo Pellegrinetti, auditor of the nunciature in Warsaw. McVay, »A Prisoner for His People's Faith,« 39.

35 *Western Ukrainian National Republic, 1918–1923: Illustrated History* (Lviv et al.: Manuskrypt-Lviv: 2008), 302.

Genocchi's mission, which were of prime concern to the Vatican, had to be kept secret because of the opposition of the Polish government to the idea of a separate apostolic diplomat for Eastern Galicia. Genocchi's appointment was a major success of Sheptytskyi's efforts at the Vatican.

Genocchi, a well-known missionary, scholar, and diplomat became a great admirer of Sheptytskyi, regarding him as a true leader of his flock, and defended him against Polish accusations of using his pastoral mission in a politically instrumental way.[36] He did not manage to travel to Eastern Galicia or to Ukraine because of the warfare, though he spent some time in Vienna and Warsaw. The Polish government did not allow the apostolic diplomat to travel to Galicia. Genocchi distributed the voluminous humanitarian aid of the Vatican through officials of the Greek Catholic Church. Even after the termination of his mission, Genocchi remained Sheptytskyi's friend, and was regarded by the Polish authorities as a supporter of Ukrainian claims to Eastern Galicia.[37]

Benedict XV demonstrated his sympathy to Sheptytskyi personally, and in an official letter to the Greek Catholics, dated February 24, 1921, in which he praised the »heroic people, who suffered so much in order to preserve its Church and rite, which at the same time are the guardians of its nationality.« The pope also expressed his desire to provide help to »the Ruthenians always so close to the Roman See«, and suggested that the Eastern Slavs could approach unity with the Apostolic See.[38] In Poland this letter resonated in a very unpleasant way for the Vatican.

Even before his trip to Rome, Sheptytskyi coordinated his actions at the Vatican with the activities of the diplomatic representatives of the Ukrainian National Republic. Count Mykhailo Tyshkevych, the first head of the Ukrainian diplomatic mission to the Apostolic See, was on friendly terms with Sheptytskyi. The metropolitan and Tyshkevych corresponded frequently, especially from 1917 to 1923.[39] On May 20, 1919, Tyshkevych addressed the Secretary of the Roman Curia with a letter declaring the intentions of the Ukrainian govern-

36 Ivan Khoma, *Apostols'kyi Prestil i Ukraina 1919–1922* (Rome: Ukrainian Catholic University Press, 1987); ASV, A.E.S., Polonia, pos. 30–33, fascicolo/fasc. (file) 37, fol. 24.

37 For more details on Giovanni Genocchi's mission, see Liliana Hentosh, *Vatykan i vyklyky modernosti. Shidnoevropeis'ka polityka papy Benedykta XV ta ukrains'ko-pols'kyi konflikt v Halychyni, 1914–1923* (L'viv: Klasyka, 2006), 308–328.

38 »Herois'koho narodu, iakyi stilky zumiv vuterpity zadlia zberezhennia svoho obriadu, shcho ie odnochasno i zaborolom ioho natsional'nosti ... [...] rusyniv, kotri zavzhdy blyz'ki Ryms'komu prestolu«. Letter of Benedict XV to Andrei Sheptytskyi, published in *L'vivs'ko-arkhyieparkhial'ni vidomosti*, April 20, 1921.

39 Mykhailo Tyshkevych's letters to Sheptytskyi can be found at TsDIAL, coll. 358, inv. 1, file 357, and at the Archive of the General Curia of the Basilian brothers in Rome, Files of Metropolitan Andrei Sheptytskyi.

ment.[40] In this document he raised several points concerning Galicia and the Western Ukrainian National Republic. The Ukrainian envoy urged the Vatican to officially condemn the abuses of the Polish government, and the atrocities of Polish troops led by General Haller in Galicia.[41] Tyshkevych also passed on a request from the government of the Ukrainian National Republic to the Roman Curia to honor Sheptytskyi's suffering for the faith by making him a cardinal.[42] The metropolitan's contacts with UNR diplomats indicate that he was indeed open to the possibility of a union of Eastern Galicia (WUNR) with Ukraine (UNR), but on the condition that the Catholic Church of the Eastern rite was granted unrestricted freedom of activity.

In 1921–1923, while traveling abroad, Sheptytskyi was preoccupied with the Ukrainian-Polish hostilities, and sought to find a solution that would prove satisfactory to both sides. In his opinion, the international authorities had to pay more attention to the Galician problem. Between April and July 1921, he traveled to Belgium, the Netherlands, France, and the United Kingdom, where among other things he tried to meet with political and civic leaders in order to attract their attention to Galicia. He also sought financial support for his impoverished church and for the numerous war orphans sheltered in orphanages under the guidance of Greek Catholic monks and nuns.[43]

At the same time, Sheptytskyi was trying to draw the attention of the foreign political leaders to the situation in Eastern Galicia and to the abuses of the Polish authorities. He stayed longer in the United Kingdom than originally planned, and, after meeting with political leaders, he hoped for British support for the Ukrainians. In Paris, on July 14, 1921, he managed to meet with French President Aristides Briand, and handed him a memorandum on the situation of Ukrainians in Eastern Galicia. In this document he argued that it would not suffice »to propose to his people the rights of a national minority in the Polish state«.[44] He tried to persuade the French president to pay more attention to the

40 ASV, A.E.S., Russia, pos. 592.

41 ASV, Protocolli della Secretaria di Stato, vol. 622, no. 92346 and 92347; vol. 623, no. 93573. ASV, A.E.S., Russia, pos. 592.

42 ASV, A.E.S., Russia, pos. 592.

43 Sheptytskyi received the support of the Vatican for his fundraising activities. The Congregation for Eastern Churches granted its support to the Metropolitan in a letter from January 24, 1921. In this document, Cardinal Niccolo Marini, Prefect of the Congregation, encouraged Catholic believers to help »Ruthenians, hoping that they will play a pivotal role in the conversion of the Russians to unity in one flock of Jesus Christ«. See Andrii Kravchuk, ed., *Mytropolyt Andrei Sheptyts'kyi: Zhyttia i Dial'nist', Tserkva i Tserkovna Iednist'*, vol. 1 (L'viv: Svichado, 1995), 188.

44 Maria Klachko, »Podróż Metropolity Szeptytckiego do Zachodniej Europy i Ameryki w latach 1920–1923,« in *Metropolita Andrzej Szeptycki. Studia i materiały*,

problem of Eastern Galicia, which he believed had to be seen beyond the so-called Little Treaty of Versailles, the Polish Minorities Treaty of June 28, 1919. Sheptytskyi thought that his activities could bring about a more favorable approach from the United Kingdom and France towards Ukrainian claims in the Ukrainian-Polish conflict. But he also took into consideration a possible unfavorable decision in Paris and wanted »to secure for his people positive public opinion in the West, and the support of Western Christianity«.[45]

In August 1921 he traveled overseas to visit Canada and the United States. He spent more than two months in Canada, where his main interest was to collect money for orphans in Galicia. However, it was in the United States that he managed to attract the attention of the highest state authorities. In November 1921 he rushed to Washington, where he met with leading politicians – President Warren G. Harding, Secretary of State Charles Hughes, and Secretary of Commerce Herbert Hoover. His meeting with US leadership focused on the situation of Ukrainians in Eastern Galicia, and the Ukrainian-Polish conflict. Sheptytskyi also presented his interlocutors with a memorandum on Eastern Galicia, urging the political leaders of the United States to reconsider their attitude towards the issue. During the meeting with Hoover, he expressed his gratitude for the humanitarian help sent to Eastern Galicia and pleaded for more aid for the suffering civilian population.[46]

During his trip to Canada and the United States the metropolitan's activities were followed by representatives of the Polish diplomatic corps and secret service. Władysław Skrzyński, the Polish representative at the Vatican, asked the Roman Curia to order Sheptytskyi to avoid making any political statements. On January 1, 1922 the Cardinal Secretary of State sent a telegram to Giovanni Bolzano, the apostolic nuncio to Washington, instructing him to ask the metropolitan to refrain from further political declarations.[47]

From late March until July 1921, Sheptytskyi, as apostolic delegate, visited Ukrainian Greek Catholic communities in Brazil and Argentina. By the end of the year he was back in Europe where he visited Belgium, the Netherlands, and France. During all these trips and in meetings with politicians, social and cultural leaders, and representatives of the press, he stressed that, in his opinion, the Entente powers were at that time the legitimate authorities in Eastern Galicia. In order to underscore his position he did not visit Polish diplomatic

ed. Andrzej Zięba (Kraków: Poligrafia Inspectoratu Towarzystwa Salezjańskiego, 1994), 155–168, 161.

45 Kravchuk, ed., *Mytropolyt Andrei Sheptyts'kyi: Zhyttia i Dial'nist', Tserkva i Tserkovna Iednist'*, vol. 1, 192.

46 Klachko, »Podróż Metropolity Szeptytckiego,« 162–163.

47 Ibid., 163.

representatives abroad. He recognized the government of the Western Ukrainian National Republic as the representative of the Ukrainian claims to Eastern Galicia and kept in close touch with the WUNR's representatives abroad. Polish diplomats in the Vatican complained to the Cardinal Secretary of State about the metropolitan's stance of ignoring Polish diplomatic representatives.[48]

Sheptytskyi's criticism of the Polish state and Polish military authorities was not an expression of his attitude towards the Polish people. Contrary to how his activities of 1920-1923 were seen by the Polish authorities and in the Polish media, he was not hostile to the Polish people in general. He hoped for an arrangement of future peaceful relations between the two peoples. In his opinion the international powers were obliged to create circumstances favorable to a Ukrainian-Polish agreement. Among the main responsibilities of the Entente in such a scenario would have been to guarantee the rights of the Ukrainian population within the borders of the Polish state. Sheptytskyi undoubtedly had much hope in international authorities; he did not believe in the possibility of a direct Polish-Ukrainian agreement, nor could he find anyone genuinely interested in a Ukrainian-Polish compromise from among the Ukrainian and Polish leaderships.[49]

Sheptytskyi supported the Ukrainian side in the Ukrainian-Polish conflict to the last. On the eve of a crucial meeting of the Council of Ambassadors in Rome, he received a telegram from Kost Levytskyi, head of the WUNR government, asking him to travel to Paris immediately.[50] He rushed to Paris and managed to meet with the chairman of the Council of Ambassadors Jules Cambon, whom he tried to persuade to change or postpone the decision to place Eastern Galicia under Polish sovereignty. In a letter to the Basilian prior Lazar Berezowski, written the night before the decision, he wrote that he still hoped and prayed to God that »our cause would be solved in a way that could guarantee our people freedom of development«.[51] He made a final effort, but the future of Eastern Galicia was decided by the Allied powers in favor of Poland.

The metropolitan's diplomatic activity in support of the Western Ukrainian National Republic was very much connected to his ideas regarding the defense

48 Maciej Mróz, *W kręgu dyplomacji watykańskiej, Rosja, Polska, Ukraina w dyplomacji watykańskiej w latach 1917–1926* (Toruń: Wydawnictwo Adam Marszałek, 2004), 208–209.

49 Ryszard Torzecki, »Sheptyts'kyi and Polish Society,« in *Morality and Reality*, 75–100, here 84–85.

50 The telegram is preserved at the Archives of the General Curia of the Basilian brothers in Rome: Collection of Metropolitan Sheptyskyi/Archive Heneral'noi Kurii Chynu Vasyliia Velykoho v Rymi: Fond Mytropolyta Sheptyts'koho, vol. 9.

51 »Dai Bozhe, shchob nasha sprava bula vyrishena po-Bozhomu, tak shchob narid nash mav bodai mozhlyvist' rozvyvatysia pryrodnio.« ibid.

of the rights and future of »his people«. He supported the government of the Western Ukrainian National Republic in its efforts abroad, because he believed that its political leaders could provide favorable conditions for a peace settlement and reconciliation in Galicia, and could encourage socio-economic development of the Ukrainian community as a whole.

Sheptytskyi and the political leadership of the Ukrainian National Republic

The metropolitan's attitude to other Ukrainian states and governments[52] was not as explicit as his unequivocal support for the Western Ukrainian National Republic. In May 1917 he traveled from Petrograd to Kyiv, where he tried to establish personal relations with the leading politicians of the Central Council. He and Mykhailo Hrushevskyi, the President of the Central Council, had very different personalities. Hrushevskyi, a professor at Lviv University, avoided contact with him, suspecting him of pro-Polish inclinations.[53] Sheptytskyi was rather persistent in his efforts to convert the leading politicians of the Central Council to his view that the rebirth of the Ukrainian state was impossible without national unity, and that national solidarity could only be built upon a foundation of religious unity. He held the opinion that such religious unity could be built around the Greek Catholic Church. His talks with Hrushevskyi and with the Council's Vice President Volodymyr Vynnychenko were less than successful. They only vaguely promised to take his views into consideration.[54] In early 1918 Sheptytskyi demonstrated his support for the idea of an independent Ukrainian National Republic. In a speech before the upper chamber of the Austrian Parliament he strongly supported the provision of the treaty, signed in February 1918 in Brest-Litovsk between the UNR and the Central powers, wherein the Chelm region was to be placed under the authority

52 After the collapse of the Russian Empire in 1917 the Ukrainian lands of the empire declared their independence. The independence movement was led by the Central Council (*Tsentral'na Rada*) in Kiev, its President, Myhailo Hrushevskyi, and Vice President Volodymyr Vynnychenko. After a coup by Hetman Skoropadski, the Central Council lost power, and the Hetman and his government ruled Ukraine with the help of German and Austrian troops from April until December 1918. In December 1918 the Ukrainian National Republic was restored, its governing body – Directory of the UNR – headed by Symon Petlura.

53 Mykhailo Hrushevskyi's letters reveal his dislike and suspicion of Andrei Sheptytskyi. Hrushevskyi could not appreciate the metropolitan's ideas and activities because of his own adherence to Orthodoxy and negative attitude to the Vatican. Mykhailo Hrushevs'kyi, »Lysty z-nad Poltvy,« *Mykhailo Hrushevs'kyi. Tvory u 50-ty tomah*, vol. 1 (L'viv: Svit, 2002), 147–164, here 148–149, 157–159.

54 Hentosh, *Vatykan i Vyklyky Modernosti*, 220–221.

of the Central Council. Sheptytskyi supported the claim that »the Chelm region is an ancient Ukrainian land, which was not only ethnically linked to Ukraine, but was incorporated into the Ukrainian state centuries ago«. He also shared the idea that the peace treaty between Austria-Hungary and the Ukrainian National Republic would be impossible without a solution for the Chelm issue.[55]

During the rule of Hetman Pavlo Skoropadsky, Sheptytskyi became involved in the affairs of Eastern Ukraine. In the second session of the all-Ukrainian Church Council held in June 1918, the pro-national group suggested his candidacy for the office of Patriarch of the Ukrainian Autocephalous Church. The metropolitan expressed his interest, but in a letter to Archduke Wilhelm von Habsburg[56] he stated that he would only accept election by a majority of the council and that such an act would be tantamount to the conclusion of a church union with Rome.[57]

His plans for spreading the activities of the Greek Catholic Church to all Ukrainian lands was met with greater understanding from within Symon Petlura's government of the Ukrainian National Republic. Petlura considered granting state support to the Greek Catholic Church in the UNR.[58] Volodymyr Chehivskyi, Minister for Education, authorized the construction of a Greek Catholic Church and a Basilian monastery with a printing house in Kamianets Podilskyi.[59] Petlura had been the first to send an official Ukrainian diplomatic mission led by the above mentioned Mykhailo Tyshkevych – a well-known Catholic activist – to the Apostolic See.

In January 1920, Petlura and Sheptytskyi exchanged letters. In his letter the metropolitan presupposed the hypothetical unification of Eastern Galician lands

55 »Pevnym, imenno, ie, shcho vsi ukraintsi uvvazhaiut' Holmshchynu staroiu ukrains'koiu zemleiu, iaka ne til'ky shcho ie etnografichno tisno poviazana z Ukrainoiu, ale takozh na protiazi stolit' bula inkorporovana v ukrains'ku derzhavu.« Kravchuk, ed., *Mytropolyt Andrei Sheptyts'kyi: Zhyttia i Dial'nist', Tserkva i Suspil'ne Pytannia*, vol. 2, part 2, 676.

56 On the life and activities of Wilhelm von Habsburg, as well as his contacts with Sheptytskyi, see Timothy Snyder, *The Red Prince: The Secret Lives of a Habsburg Archduke* (New York: Basic Books, 2008). Wilhelm von Habsburg found in Sheptytskyi a moral authority, as well as support for his plans to become the ruler of a sovereign Ukrainian entity under an Austro-Hungarian protectorate. The letters from Archduke Wilhelm to the metropolitan can be located among the documents of Andrei Sheptytskyi at TsDIAL, coll. 358, inv. 3, file 166.

57 Documents rutheno-ukrainiens (Paris: Bureau Polonais de Publications Politiques, 1919), 12–13; Kravchuk, ed., *Mytropolyt Andrei Sheptyts'kyi: Zhyttia i Dial'nist'*, Tserkva i Tserkovna Iednist', vol. 1, 137.

58 Ibid., 137–140.

59 Liliana Hentosz, »Kanadyjski duchowny o. Josafat Jean – ukraiński dyplomata,« *Biuletyn Ukrainoznawczy* no. 6 (2000): 48–60.

in a single state with Eastern Ukraine, formerly under the Tsarist Empire. One could infer that he regarded Petlura as a probable and suitable leader for a unified Ukrainian state. His approach to the Ukrainian government based in Kyiv must be viewed in light of his ideas on the reunification of Eastern Slavs with Rome. Thus, in his opinion, the best government for Ukraine would be one that could guarantee the right of free and unrestrained development for the Catholic Church of the Eastern rite in its territories.

Relations with the Polish government in 1923

Sheptytskyi's diplomatic activities in Western Europe and the United States in support of the Ukrainian cause in Eastern Galicia had hardly endeared him to the Warsaw government.[60] He became the bête noire of the Polish press and of Polish public opinion in general,[61] and experienced considerable difficulties on his way back to his archdiocese in Lviv. The Polish government demanded from him his unconditional acceptance of Polish sovereignty over Eastern Galicia, and that he withdraw from any political activity. In this complicated situation, the Apostolic See negotiated the formal conditions of the metropolitan's return. Following a decision by Pope Pius XI, Sheptytskyi wrote an official letter to declare his loyalty to the Polish state[62] and got an entry visa from the Polish Legation at the Vatican.

At that time a new political coalition came to power in Warsaw and the new government required that Sheptytskyi had to swear a formal public oath of allegiance to the Polish state.[63] The metropolitan rejected such demands, suspecting the government's »desire to compromise him in front of his nation«.[64] The Vatican also opposed these demands on the grounds that they placed the Catholic hierarchy in direct subordination to the state authorities.[65] In the opinion of the Vatican, such an act by the Polish state contradicted the essential rights of a Catholic clergyman of the hierarchy appointed by the Pope to take care of his congregation. The situation grew even more complicated

60 The Polish diplomats at the Apostolic See informed the Secretary of State of their government's attitude towards Sheptytskyi, who was regarded as an »enemy of the Polish state«, and as a »renegade, who became a fierce enemy of his former kinsmen«. Central Archives of Modern Records in Warsaw/Archiwum Akt Nowych, Ambasada RP w Londynie, file (sygn.) 879, fol. 77–80.

61 Torzecki, »Sheptyts'kyi and Polish Society,« 82–83.

62 ASV, A.E.S., Polonia, pos. 40, fasc. 48, fol. 60–60v; McVay, »A prisoner for his People's Faith,« 43.

63 ASV, A.E.S., Polonia, pos. 40, fasc. 49, fol. 52, 82–84.

64 Ibid., fol. 13.

65 Ibid., fol. 37, 69.

when the Polish government refused to guarantee the metropolitan's safety on his way to his archdiocese.[66]

Sheptytskyi was detained on the Polish border, first in the sleeping car of his train, and then taken under police guard to the hospital of the Sisters of Charity in Poznan.[67] The nunciature in Warsaw did its best to negotiate with the Polish government the formal conditions of the metropolitan's release.[68] After weeks the Polish government and the Apostolic See came to a compromise with Sheptytskyi: The metropolitan would make a written but private declaration of his loyalty to the Polish state in a letter requesting a presidential audience.[69] On October 4, 1923 he met with the Polish President Stanisław Wojciechowski in the presidential country residence in Spalla, rather than in Warsaw.[70] At that confidential meeting he declared his loyalty to the Polish state.[71] The place and the informality did enhance the private character of the meeting between the head of state and the prominent member of the church hierarchy. Sheptytskyi apparently succeeded in persuading the president of his loyalty.

It took several years to conclude the concordat between the Polish state and the Apostolic See; among other contested issues was the status of the Greek Catholic Church. Only the Concordat of 1925 provided legal grounds for its practically autonomous activity in Poland. The Greek Catholic Church was able to retain its considerable material possessions, which guaranteed financial independence.[72] On the other hand, its activities outside Galicia were sharply limited, and Sheptytskti's dreams of expanding its missionary work to Volhynia and the Chelm region – areas where the Greek Catholic Church had prospered before its suppression by the tsarist government in the 19th century – were thwarted, obstructed by the provision of the concordat that placed all Greek Catholics outside the three Galician eparchies under the spiritual jurisdiction of local Roman Catholic bishops.[73] As for the Greek Catholic Church, the Concordat of 1925 was an ambivalent compromise. It accepted such demands

66 ASV, A.E.S., Polonia, pos. 40, fasc. 48, fol. 58–58v.

67 Sheptytskyi was taken ill while traveling, in Vienna, but despite the serious nature of his illness, left for Lviv, because his passport was only valid for two more days.

68 Among the files of the Apostolic nunciature in Warsaw, there are at least 71 documents concerning Sheptytskyi's return to Lviv. ASV, Arch. Nunz. Varsavia, vol. 223, fol. 600–604v.

69 ASV, A.E.S., Polonia, pos. 40, fasc. 50, fol. 10; ASV, Arch. Nunz. Varsavia, vol. 223, fol. 539.

70 ASV, A.E.S., Polonia, pos. 40, fasc. 50, fol. 41–43.

71 ASV, A.E.S., Polonia, pos. 40, fasc. 50, fol. 41v.

72 Konkordat zawarty pomiędzy Stolicą Apostolską a Rzecząpospolitą Polską. Podpisany w Rzymie 10 lutego 1925 r. (Lwów: Światosław, 1925), 17–23.

73 Ibid., 9.

of the Polish government as patronage – a practice of control that had been used in the early modern Polish-Lithuanian Commonwealth – and limitation on land ownership by the Catholic Church, which was presented as part of agricultural reform.

Concordat of 1925 provided legal grounds for the Greek Catholic Church's practically autonomous activity in Poland. It was able to retain its considerable material possessions, which guaranteed financial independence.

Conclusion

Andrei Sheptytskyi was born in Galicia and in many aspects was shaped by life in the Habsburg Empire. Later he became a Greek Catholic archbishop and metropolitan, during a time when relations between major national and religious groups were balanced due to complex imperial legislation and structures of power in Vienna. Several agreements, concordats between the Habsburg monarchy and the Vatican had meticulously regulated the life of his church before 1918. The Roman Curia as well as the Vatican had been interested in providing equal rights for the activity of the Catholic Churches of different rites, which cared for different national groups.

The metropolitan led an almost entirely Ukrainian church congregation, which at the beginning of the 20th century started to claim cultural and national sovereignty. As a former loyal imperial subject, he extended his support to Ukrainian claims to Eastern Galicia. His stance and activities in the years 1918–1923 were not the consequence of a rediscovered Ukrainian national identity or a manifestation of his support for Ukrainian statehood as such. His support for the Ukrainians in the Ukrainian-Polish War derived from his very broad understanding of his own pastoral mission and duties.

Sheptytskyi's defense of the rights and interests of the Ukrainian congregation before the international authorities alienated him from the leadership of the Polish state and provoked negative attitudes from the Polish public in general. His detention and negotiations with the leadership of the Polish state in 1923 for his return demonstrated the lack of official regulations of the activities of the Catholic and Greek Catholic Churches in the Polish state. These events were related to the more general issue of the relations between the Vatican and the new national states emerging after the collapse of the multinational empires.

In the new setting of the national state Sheptytskyi needed time to reassess the place and tasks for his church. The idea of subordinating the pastoral mission and activity of his church to the demands of the national state, either Ukrainian or Polish, was not acceptable to him. The metropolitan had to face a difficult challenge: to lead the Greek Catholic Church of the Ukrainian national minority within the Polish state, which he perceived as a nationalizing and assimilating force, while at the same time facing the rise of Ukrainian nationalism with its radical tendencies. Throughout the interwar period Sheptytskyi attempted to find the right place and mission for the Greek Catholic Church, striking a balance between radical Ukrainian nationalism and Polish etatism.

Liliana Hentosh

Ethno-Religious Coexistence in Legal Norm and Practice

Voivodes and their Office as Agents of the Law in Christian-Jewish Coexistence: The Example of Early Modern Krakow

On June 3, 1637, Jacobus Lewkowicz Opatowczyk, the *syndicus*[1] of the Krakovian Jewish community appeared in the office of the Krakow Voivodeship.[2] He presented the clerks with a document, and asked them politely to accept it and place it in their books. Apparently, there was nothing special about this event. First, according to the voivode's regulation of 1527 each document had to be registered in order to be lawfully valid.[3] Second, registering the documents was one of the usual duties of the Jewish representative to the state authorities. Yet, the document itself was without precedent. It was an open letter (*litterae universalis*) adressed to the Elders of the Krakovian Jewish Community by the Krakovian voivode Jan Magnus Tęczyński,[4] who publicly condemned the bloody anti-Jewish tumult that had taken place in Krakow on May 22 of the same year. More precisely, the letter included a strongly worded rebuke of the violent behaviour of Christian students and townsmen as well as of the negligence of the municipality and ordered the Jews to turn to the Parliament and the King to ask for justice.

The document was not issued by the voivode in his capacity as a leader of the local parliament or a noble lord in charge of assembling local military forces. It was not written in his function as head of an appeal court either. The letter was rather a personal rebuke by the voivode who reacted beyond his regular

1 A syndicus (*syndyk*) was a representative of the local Jewish community in its interaction with gentile society and authorities holding power. Linguistically adept, he would intervene on behalf of the *kehilah* and was an integral part of the early modern communal structure and autonomy.

2 Archiwum Państwowe Miasta Krakowa (hereafter APMK), Varia 11, 935.

3 Stanisław Kutrzeba, *Zbiór aktów do historyi ustroju sądów prawa polskiego i kancelaryi województwa krakowskiego z wieku XVI–XVIII*, no. 12 (Kraków, 1909), 14. This regulation was later confirmed in the Diet's constitution of 1538.

4 Jan Magnus Tęczyński (of Topór) from a powerful noble family from Lesser Poland was a Crown cupbearer (*cześnik koronny*) from 1618 and Voivode of Krakow from 1620 to 1637.

prerogatives and acted as a representative of the law intervening in a Catholic-Jewish conflict to restore peaceful interreligious coexistence. From this perspective, both the letter and Tęczyński's reaction exemplify one of the ways in which voivodes gained relevance in interreligious communication.

This article – while reanalyzing both turbulent and peaceful times in the interreligious history of Krakow – briefly examines a number of ways in which Krakovian voivodes and their office became involved in the everyday coexistence of Jews and Catholics in the city and became active agents in their dialogue. It adapts a new perspective of multi-dimensional interfaith communication to the analysis of more and less known sources issued by the Krakovian voivodes, the kings, and the Jewish Krakovian community. This new perspective consists in paying special attention to the judicial and administrative functions of the voivode and his office, notably to the two components of the institution of the voivodeship as a legal authority dealing with religious heterogeneity. While reexamining the situation of the Jews in early modern Krakow and their relations with the voivode, the study takes a new approach to the law and legal practices as the one dimension of interreligious communication which greatly helped both the religious groups and the state representatives to overcome turbulences and failures in dialogue.[5] In a broader sense, while rethinking the interrelations between the state, the law, and religious communities, I hope to deepen the general understanding of the character and role of interreligious dialogue, coexistence, and law in religiously heterogeneous areas.[6]

The voivode's office: tradition, history and historiography

The office of the voivode is one of the oldest offices in Poland. Some chronicles, among them the Jewish chronicle *Tzemah David*, written by David Ganz in 1592, traces it back to legends about the time before the Piast dynasty:

> Lechu, Čech's brother, had also attacked in that time, together with the people of the Slovaks and the Croatians, the states of Silesia and Poland, and became their head [...] and Heinrich Rätel wrote [...] that this Lechu in the state of Poland

5 For a discussion on the importance of litigation in interreligious dialogue see David Frick, *Kith, Kin, and Neighbors. Communities and Confessions in Seventeenth-Century Wilno* (Ithaca–New York: Cornell Univ. Press, 2013), 274–289.

6 The sources mentioned in this article were collected as part of a larger project generously supported by the Vidal Sassoon International Center for the Study of Antisemitism and the Nevzlin Research Center for Russian and East European Jewry at the Hebrew University of Jerusalem. Unless indicated otherwise, all the sources in this article were translated by the author.

> established seven governors and called them voivodes, and this rule exists to this very day.[7]

In the early stages of the development of the office, the voivodes – responsible for catching criminals, assembling local military forces, and even leading troops on behalf of the duke and replacing the ruler during his absence – already became the highest officers in the splintered country. Furthermore, with the nobility's increase in power, the voivode became the *palatinus* – both a sort of administrative governor of the province *(palatinatus)* and a chief representative of the local nobility to the prince, spending a great amount of time at the royal court. Last but not least, in addition to his state and administrative functions the voivode was granted jurisdiction over the Jews, as stated in the Statute of Kalisz in 1264: »The city has no jurisdiction over the Jews, only the prince or the voivode.«[8]

After the unification of Poland under one king, the office of the voivode was not terminated although it did lose some of its old prerogatives, which were granted to the royal *starosta* (*capitaneus*).[9] Probably due to his leading position among the nobles, the voivode managed to maintain the office all through the late medieval administrative and political changes, becoming a member of the king's great council – later the senate – and preserving a number of important functions throughout the early modern period as well: (1) as the chairman of the dietine (*sejmik*), the regional parliament of the nobility, (2) as the person responsible for military recruitment in his region during times of war and »general mobilization«, (3) in granting letters of protection (*glejty*), (4) in appointing functionaries responsible for sizes, weights, and measures, and (5) as a judge in the special regional court of appeal (*sąd wiecowy*).[10] And lastly, the voivode maintained jurisdiction over the Jews:

> Likewise, if the Jews engage in an argument among themselves [...] or if a Jew and a Christian fight with each other, engage in hitting or injuring each other,

7 »Lekhu, hu ahiv shel Chehu, gam ala be-et ha-hi, im amei slovaken ve-kroaten al medinat Shleziah u- Polin ve-haya sham le-rosh [...] ve-katav Henrikus Rätel [...] she-Lekhu ze yised be-medinat Polin shiv'ah netsivim ve-kara lahem voyevodey, asher takanato nitkayma ad ha-yom ha-ze.« David Ganz, *Tsemach David* (Jerusalem: Magnes, 1983), 265.

8 Statute of Kalisz (1264), § 8. Quoted from Ludwik Gumplowicz, *Prawodawstwo polskie względem Żydów* (Kraków: Uniwersytet Jagielloński, 1867), 8.

9 Although while accepting the Statute of Kalisz, Casimir the Great (Kazimierz Wielki) charged the starost and not the voivode with jurisdiction over the Jews, this change was short-lived.

10 For more information about the function of the voivode and its historical development, see Zbigniew Góralski, *Urzędy i godności w dawnej Polsce* (Warszawa: Ludowa Spółdzielnia Wydawnicza, 1983), 66–71.

then neither the judge of the city, nor the consuls, nor indeed anybody else, but only the palatinus [voivode] of the Jews or his surrogate shall judge them [...].[11]

Despite the voivode's numerous functions, his jurisdiction over the Jews has been the most intensely studied of all his prerogatives. Nevertheless, the relations between the voivode and the Jews have usually been examined as part of the research on the judicature of the Jews, and not as an aspect of everyday interreligious coexistence. Writing before the Second World War, Stanisław Kutrzeba and Majer Bałaban generally pictured the voivode as an administrator of justice to the Jews.[12] In the 1970s, Benjamin Cohen, in his detailed research on the relations between the voivode and the Jewish community, showed that the competences of the voivode were not limited exclusively to judicial administration and extended far beyond the organization of the *wojewodzinski court* – also known as the *court of iudex iudaeorum*[13] – or presidency over the voivode's court.[14] Cohen's thorough research, however, had no immediate followers. It took another twenty years before Stanisław Grodziski revived the research on the voivode and the Jews and shed some light on the principles of law as applied in practice. This involved the analysis of the voivode's functions as portrayed in the regulations issued by the voivodes themselves, and not solely in the privileges

11 »Item si Iudaei inter se de facto discordiam contentionis commisserint, aut aliquam guerram, vel Iudaeus cum Christiano et se mutuo sic contendentes percusserint, aut vulneraverint, tunc neque iudex civitatis, neque consules, neque etiam aliquis hominum, tantummodo palatinus ipsorum Iudaeorum aut ille, qui loco eius praesidet, eosdem iudicet et illi iudicabunt taliter in iudicio locantes scabellum dum Iudaeis.« From the privilege of Casimir Jagiellończyk (1453), § 5. Quoted from Moses Schorr, »Krakovskii svod statutov i privilegii,« *Evreiskaia Starina* 2 (1910): 76–100, here 85.

12 See for example Stanisław Kutrzeba, *Sądownictwo nad Żydami w województwie krakowskim* (Kraków, 1901); idem, *Zbiór aktów do historyi*; Majer Bałaban, »Ze studiów nad ustrojem prawnym Żydów w Polsce. Sędzia żydowski i jego kompetencje,« in *Pamiętnik trzydziestolecia pracy naukowej prof. dr. Przemysława Dąbkowskiego* (Lwów: Uniwersytet Jana Kazimierza, 1927), 246–280.

13 The *wojewodzinski court*, which was probably active in Krakow from 1334 was a first instance and appeal court nominated by the voivode but presided over by a specially appointed judge (*sędzia wojewodzinski*), and not by the voivode himself. With time, this court took up the task of administering justice to the Jews so that its judge became known as »the judge of the Jews« (*iudex iudaeorum*) and the court was often called »the court of iudex iudaeorum.« The sessions of this court were usually regular and held in a synagogue in Krakow or in the Old Synagogue in Kazimierz.

14 The *voivode's court* was a first instance and appeal court for cases from the *wojewodzinski court* and Jewish court. In contrast with the *wojewodzinski court*, it was presided over by the voivode himself and appeals of its decisions could only be brought before the King's court. Whether as a first or second instance, the voivode's court took place at his residence (*curia palatine*) or at the Wawel Castle and was open in session during the voivode's stay in the city.

and statutes administered by the king or the Diet.[15] This article intends to amend the existing research by analyzing the judicial and administrative functions of the voivode and his office through the new perspective of interreligious coexistence and dialogue.

Rethinking the voivode's judicial duties

The voivode's jurisdiction over the Jews was one of his earliest prerogatives. Yet, as already defined in the Statute of Kalisz, it was not itself exclusive but shared with the prince.[16] Later on, in its elaborated version, confirmed in 1453 by Casimir Jagiellończyk and the following early modern kings of Poland, the general privilege asserted that this jurisdiction was to be hierarchically shared with the king and the judge of the *wojewodzinski court* known as »the judge of the Jews« *(iudex iudaeorum)*.[17] In this way, the privilege allotted the voivode the complex position of a second-instance judge and the highest executor of justice. Precisely due to this joint character of the jurisdiction over the Jews, the scope of the voivode's judicial authority was continually being redefined.

By the late Middle Ages the *iudex iudaeorum* had already taken on the burden of the majority of judicial activities,[18] the king had replaced the prince as the highest authority over the Jews, and the cases among Jews, i.e. minor civil cases, had been removed from the voivode's court to be judged by the Jewish court itself.[19] Despite all these changes, at the beginning of the 16th century, Krakovian voivodes carried out a number of important judicial functions

15 Stanisław Grodziski, »The Kraków Voivode's Jurisdiction over Jews: A study of the Historical Records of the Kraków Voivode's Administration of Justice to Jews,« in *The Jews in Old Poland 1000–1795*, ed. Antony Polonsky et al. (London: I. B. Tauris and Co. Ltd, 1993): 199–218.

16 Statute of Kalisz (1264), § 8.

17 Privilege of Casimir Jagiellończyk (1453), § 5.

18 In the first stage of the office development the *iudex iudaeorum* was appointed for special cases only: »*ad hoc specialiter deputatus*« (e.g. Jan Koczyński, 1436). Later, it became a permanent office, e. g. Jan Chamiec from Dobranowic, the fourth judge known to us, held the office for at least 10 years: 1459–1469.

19 The authority of the Jewish elders' court in cases among Jews was first mentioned in the privilege of Casimir Jagiellończyk of 1453. Yet, according to some scholars, the king simply granted written legitimacy to a long-existing practice, see for example Shmuel A. Cygielman, »The Basic Privileges of the Jews of Great Poland as Reflected in Polish Historiography,« *Polin* 2 (1989): 117–149, here 119–122 . The authority of the Jewish court in inner-Jewish cases was also accepted and restated in the regulations issued by the Krakovian voivode Andrzej Tęczyński in 1527, see Majer Bałaban, *Historja Żydów w Krakowie i na Kazimierzu 1304–1868* (Kraków: Nadzieja, 1931): 365.

through which they became involved in the everyday coexistence of Jews and Catholics in the city.

Most prominently, the voivode set up the entire apparatus of the *wojewodzinski court*, which was founded upon the interreligious cooperation of a Christian judge and Christian functionaries together with Jewish staff and assessors in order to satisfy the claims of both sides and safeguard the Jewish-Catholic dialogue. In establishing the court, the voivode initially appointed the aforementioned *iudex iudaeorum*,[20] who judged in cases where a Jew was involved. While in most of the royal cities this function was performed by the voivode's deputy (*podwojewodzi*), in Krakow this duty was usually undertaken by a specially appointed noble.[21] According to the privileges and the practical ruling of the voivodes, this noble had to be a Catholic and a man of means familiar with the »law of the land« (*prawo ziemskie*)[22] on the basis of which he passed sentences, for example in cases of Christian violence against a Jew.[23] Hence, by appointing the *iudex iudaeorum*, the voivode ensured the multi-religious character of the staff and the *wojewodzinski court* itself. This character was further strengthened in 1591 when King Sigismund III granted the Krakovian Jews the right to have a say in the election of the *iudex iudaeorum*. Unfortunately, there is no evidence as to how this right was put into practice. Based on examples of other communities and from later developments we can assume that the *kahal*, the executive board of the Jewish community,[24] first used

20 According to the preserved examples, appointing the Jewish judge was one of the first actions taken by a new voivode. Alicja Falinowska-Gradowska, »Sędziowie żydowscy w województwie krakowskim w XVI–XVIII wieku,« in *Żydzi w Małopolsce. Studia z dziejów osadnictwa społecznego*, ed. Feliks Kiryk (Przemyśl: Południowo-Wschodni Instytut Naukowy, 1991), 37–58, here 41.

21 See Bałaban, *Historja Żydów*, 373–375.

22 The early modern Commonwealth had a corporative legal system in which social estates had separate codes of laws. The »law of the land« was the code of the nobility in contrast to the city law (*prawo miejskie*) which applied to the burgher class. Despite serious attempts at its codification (e.g. *Łaski's Statutes*, *Formula processu*, *Correctura Iurium*) it was basically customary law and had a rather arbitrary character. Unlike the locally-oriented city law, *prawo ziemskie* had a general character and was often used as a common Polish law system. It was therefore also applied in cases concerning the Jews.

23 Statute of Kalisz, paragraph 21: »Za gwałt na żydzie wyrządzony, chrześcianin będzie karany podług prawa ziemskiego« (»For violence to a Jew, a Christian shall be judged according to the law of the land«), in Gumplowicz, *Prawodawstwo polskie*, 9.

24 The most informative record about the Krakovian Kahal and its rulings is the Community Statute of 1595; see Majer Bałaban, »Die Krakauer Judengemeinde-Ordnung von 1595 und ihre Nachträge,« *Jahrbuch der Jüdisch-Literarischen Gesellschaft* 1 (1913), 296–360; 2 (1916), 88–114; *Statut Krakowskiej Gminy Żydowskiej z roku 1595 i jego uzupełnienia*, ed. Anna Jakimyszyn (Kraków: Księgarnia Akademicka, 2005).

this privilege to ensure that the judge was a noble rather than a burgher inclined to support townspeople. Later on, Jewish influence was probably limited to the simple approval of the voivode's appointment.[25]

After assigning a judge, the voivode also appointed the scribe to the court of *iudex iudaeorum*, who prepared documents, kept records, announced rulings, and probably took part in the passing of sentences. Similarly, responsibility for the appointment of a Catholic scribe gave the voivode an active role in the establishment of the court's multireligious – and therefore more balanced – character and consequently in the creation and maintenance of Jewish-Catholic coexistence and dialogue. The Jews obtained the right to influence the appointment in this regard as well: »Another notary of a trial shall not be elected or deposed, unless his election is previously approved by a senior Jew [i.e. one of the elders].«[26]

Furthermore, according to the regulations issued by the voivode Andrzej Tęczyński in 1572, it was the voivode's right to appoint the Jewish assessors to the court of *iudex iudaeorum*: »The Jews will be judged by the vice-voivode [*iudex iudaeorum*] with the help of Jewish assessors elected and delegated by the voivode.«[27] While we do not know exactly how the dialogue between the Catholic judge and the Jewish assessors was carried out,[28] the royal legislation testifies that there were cases of disagreement between the two organs of the court and they required the voivode's mediation.[29] Consequently, the voivode was not only responsible for the bi-religious character of the court and its staff but also contributed directly to the continuation of the Jewish-Catholic dialogue. He played a crucial role in this as long as the presence of the assessors

25 Even this right was rescinded from time to time. In 1633, the constitution stated that the *iudex iudaeorum* must be a noble and an owner of rural estate (i. e. man of means) and the privilege of the kahal's consent was granted by the king to the Jews throughout the whole country; see Benjamin Cohen, »Ha-rashut ha-voyevodit ve-ha-kehilah ha-yehudit ba-meot ha-16–18,« *Gal-ed* 3 (1976): 9–32, here 12; Bałaban, *Historja Żydów*, 374–376.

26 »Notarius Iudicii alius non eligatur aut deponatur, nisi ita prius seniori Judaeo visum fuerit cuius electionem calculo suo aprobet.« Privilege of Stefan Batory (1578), § 31, quoted in Schorr, »Krakovskii svod,« 98.

27 Regulations of A. Tęczyński (1527), § 1, quoted in Bałaban, *Historja Żydów*, 365.

28 Unfortunately only a small portion of the judicial decisions from the time of Voivode Stanisław Lubomirski (1642–1647) have survived until today, see APMK, Decreta iudicii palatinalis, *Varia* 12, 1675–1766.

29 See e. g. the statute of Sigismund Augustus from March 19, 1554: »If the judge cannot not agree with the Jewish Assessors upon the sentence, the Voivode has to decide.« Quoted in Bałaban, *Historja Żydów*, 361.

– frequently required in the rulings of the voivodes,[30] the king[31] and the Jewish community[32] – remained essential to the court and to general coexistence. Even when the voivode's prerogative was later restricted to the approval of delegated elders and the securing of their participation in the trial, its significance to the bi-religious perspective was not diminished. Instead of direct appointment, the voivode provided legal legitimacy for the assessors and thus continued to secure the Catholic-Jewish composition of the court.

Lastly, the voivode worked closely with the *szkolnik* (*scolni ministerialis*), the Jewish usher of the court. Although not appointed by the voivode, the *szkolnik* was a middleman between the court, the voivode, and the Jews. He held the authority of summoning individuals to the court,[33] examined the injuries to the aggrieved Jewish party,[34] served as a witness, kept order during the trial, issued declarations, received Jewish oaths, etc. In Krakow, there were two *szkolniks* at the same time.[35] They cooperated with the gentile functionaries and their role was fundamental to the entire bi-religious apparatus, one which was established and maintained by the voivode[36] but financed by the Jewish community.[37]

Besides organizing the staff of the *wojewodzinski court*, the voivode was involved in securing peaceful cooperation in other ways as well. He was responsible for the coordination of the court's schedule in harmony with the two systems of religious holidays and religious laws, a matter that was addition-

30 Ibid., 365. The rule legislated by Andrzej Tęczyński was later confirmed by Stanisław Potocki on May 28, 1659.

31 This rule already appeared in the general privilege of Casimir IV and was confirmed by Sigismund Augustus in the Judicial Statute for Krakow of March 19, 1554, in a local privilege for the Jews – in which he asserted that in case of the assessors' absence the court session should be canceled – as well as in Stephan Batory's privilege of 1576.

32 Jakimyszyn, *Statut Krakowskiej Gminy*, XIII, § 17.

33 See the Judicial Statute of Sigismund Augustus from March 19, 1554, § 1: »A Jew should be summoned by the szkolnik two weeks before the trial.« Quoted in: Bałaban, *Historja Żydów*, 361.

34 See ibid., 380.

35 According to the two preserved texts of the szkolniks' oath of May 1640 and April 1641.

36 Benjamin Cohen, »Ha-rashut ha-voyevodit,« 15–17. For more information on the *szkolnik* and his statutes, see Feivel Hirsch Wettstein, »Divre Hefets. Dokumenta hebrajskie z pinkasów gminnych w Krakowie,« *Hameasef* (1902), quoted in Moses Schorr, »Przegląd literatury historyi Żydów w Polsce,« *Kwartalnik Historyczny* 17 (1903): 475–490, here 487–490.

37 At first, the community paid only in emergency cases but around the seventeenth century it paid annually for the activities of the voivode's office, see Falinowska-Gradowska, »Sędziowie żydowscy,« 39; Cohen, »Ha-rashut ha-voyevodit,« 28. In the eighteenth century the community paid a regular salary to the voivode, the judge, and the notary. See Bałaban, *Historja Żydów*, 383.

ally safeguarded by a Jewish statute and by royal edicts that forbade scheduling trials on Saturdays or during Jewish holidays.[38]

The voivode's judicial duties were not confined to the *wojewodzinski court*. The voivode, for example, also served as the first instance judge in severe criminal cases among Jews, between Jews and Christians, as well as in civil cases among Jews if the parties – although discouraged by the kahal – turned to the voivode's court.[39] Moreover, he was a second instance judge and head of the appeal court for decisions of the Jewish court and in cases of complaints filed against the *iudex iudaeorum*. He presided over the court and passed the sentences (*iudicium palatinale*) during his irregular stays in Krakow.[40] Lastly, the voivode served as an agent of the law in a special court (*iudicium compositum*) for cases of blood libel established in 1633 by King Władysław IV. In this court the voivode sat together with a *starosta* and a royal commissar, with his presence intended to guarantee the court's impartiality and its interest in the Jewish side of the case.

All these functions of the voivode, when analyzed from a legal or legislative perspective, may seem purely judicial. Yet, in the reality of the existence of a Jewish community within a Catholic environment, the roles of the voivode also grew meaningful in terms of everyday Jewish-Christian relations. This perspective is applicable not only to general privileges, but also to their interpretation in royal edicts and judicial statutes, to the voivodes' regulations and acts, as well as to Jewish legislation such as the Krakow Communal Statute of 1595. Analysis of these legal documents and of the above re-examined judicial functions of the voivode from an interreligious perspective shows that the voivode's jurisdiction over the Jews was designed not to alienate them, but quite the contrary, in order to support Christian-Jewish coexistence. The voivode was meant to secure the integration of the Jews into the corporative law system of the multireligious

38 See for example Jakimyszyn, *Statut Krakowskiej Gminy*, XIII, § 16: »Der *szkolnik* zol kein *pozew* an namen nayert al yom bet ve-yom hey« (»The *szkolnik* shall not accept summons for days other than Monday or Thursday«) and the Judicial Statute of Sigismund Augustus, § 3: »It is forbidden to schedule a trial for the Jews on Saturdays or Jewish holidays.«, translated from Bałaban, *Historja Żydów*, 361.

39 Hanna Zaremska, *Żydzi w średniowiecznej Europie Środkowej: w Czechach, Polsce i na Węgrzech* (Poznań: PTPN, 2005), 94. On the Jewish use of Polish courts, see also Adam Teller, »In the Land of their Enemies? The Duality of Jewish Life in Eighteenth-Century Poland,« *Polin* 19 (2007): 431–446, here 435–437. In 1659 the kahal received the voivode's order preventing the *iudex iudaeorum* from settling inter-Jewish cases within the jurisdiction of the Jewish court (*Beit din*).

40 According to the regulation of Andrzej Tęczyński (1527), § 2: »Appeals against the sentence of the vicegerent, or the sentence of the Jewish elders [in cases among Jews], should be lodged with the Voivode,« quoted in Bałaban, *Historja Żydów*, 365.

Commonwealth in which social estates and ethno-religious groups had their own privilege-based laws and courts.[41] While establishing a more balanced, Christian-Jewish judicial platform for interreligious cases and passing judgments according to the existing »law of the land«, the voivode and his »gentile-Jewish court« incorporated the Jews into the existing legal network and legally shielded them from being summoned before other, essentially Catholic, and usually hostile authorities such as the city courts.

Whether protecting their own prerogatives or acting solely as guardians of Jewish legal rights, the voivodes strove to prevent intervention by other jurisdictions in cases that involved Jews.[42] They even often became involved in capital cases and severe interreligious conflicts, including blood libels, i.e. accusations of sacrament desecration and sacrilege, in which the king himself was the highest authority. They tried – though usually unsuccessfully – to prevent other courts from taking over cases before the oft-delayed royal intervention,[43] as for example during the famous process of the church thief Piotr Jurkiewicz.

In June 1635, Jurkiewicz, a Catholic, was caught in the act of stealing silverware from a church. When subjected to torture (*quaestie*) he confessed that, persuaded by a Jew named Jacob, he had also taken sacramental bread (i.e. host) and sold it to him. Aware of the consequences of such an accusation, the aforementioned voivode Jan Magnus Tęczyński asked the kahal to bring Jacob to his court in order to place him under the voivode's jurisdiction and enable the voivode to judge his case according to the »law of the land«. Unfortunately Jacob had escaped and since the voivode failed to bring the accused to the court, the city magistrate immediately availed himself of the opportunity and intervened by arresting a randomly selected Jew with his wife and children. When this became widely known, the magistrate released the imprisoned family and the city court sentenced both Piotr Jurkiewicz and the absent Jacob to be burned at the stake. During his last confession, however, the church thief admitted that he had never stolen the host and the whole accusation of Jacob had been a lie.

The voivode intervened immediately and sent his *iudex iudaeorum* to interrogate Jurkiewicz and clear Jacob's name. The Jewish aspect of the case was registered in the voivode's acts (*księgi wojewodzińskie*) in order to place it back under the voivode's jurisdiction and the rule of the »law of the land«. Again, the voivode's intervention succeeded only partially because – despite Jurkiewicz's

41 Benjamin Cohen, »Ha-voyevoda be-torat shofet ha-yehudim be-polin ha-yeshanah,« *Gal-ed* 1(1973): 1–12, here 1–2.

42 Ibid., 3, 6.

43 Benjamin Cohen, »Ha-yurisdiktsiyah ha-voyevodit legabei ha-yehudim be-polin ha-yeshanah« in *Sefer Raphael Mahler*, ed. Shmuel Yavin (Merhavia: Sifriat Poalim, 1974), 47–66, here 58–59.

confession – the magistrate still demanded that Jacob be arrested. Finally, on the June 24, 1636, the case reached the king, who supported the voivode's attempts and concluded the process by asking the kahal to swear again that they took no part in Jacob's escape.[44]

Although royal intervention did not calm public opinion in this case, it did put an end to the jurisdictional interplay between the voivode, who was protecting the privileges of the Jews, and the magistrate, who was attempting to extend city rule over the Jewish suspect. This judicial competition resulted mainly from the weak points of the court system in the Commonwealth, such as the law of *actor sequitur forum rei*.[45] In this system, the voivode, whose authority did help to incorporate the Jews into the legal system and to preserve Christian-Jewish coexistence, could only partially protect the Jews and fight other courts and their continuous attempts to undermine Jewish legal rights. After all, even with the king's help, the voivode hardly ever managed to summon Christians to his court. As Benjamin Cohen observed so precisely:

> General privileges established the voivode as a protector of the Jews as a group, of their lives, their sacred things and possessions. On the other hand, they took from him the authority to judge or arrest those hurting the Jews.[46]

Aware of those limits to their jurisdiction, the voivodes found ways outside the court walls to support the Jewish community in conflicts with their Catholic neighbors, and thus to contribute to the maintenance of peaceful coexistence. As the above mentioned letter of Andrzej Tęczyński exemplifies, the voivode – who were not able to arrest or judge those guilty of the tumult – buttressed his judicial authority with an administrative status and used it to suggest legal procedures as means of conflict solution and compensation. This in turn allowed the Jewish community to overcome the tragedy and return to its everyday coexistence with its neighbors. In other words, the voivode combined his judicial prerogatives with the high local status arising from his administrative functions in order to act as an agent of the law beyond the court and to intervene in interreligious cases.

Administrative and other duties

In addition to the judicial duties re-examined above, the voivode had administrative and economic functions, through which he became an active agent in

44 For more details on the case, see Bałaban, *Historja Żydów*, 181–183.

45 »The actor must follow the forum of the thing in dispute.« This judicial maxim means that the plaintiff needs to sue in the jurisdiction where the subject of the lawsuit or the defendant is located.

46 Cohen, »Ha-yurisdiktsiyah ha-voyevodit,« 49.

the establishment and maintenance of Jewish-Catholic coexistence and everyday interaction. Among other things, he was responsible for issuing a price list for domestic and imported goods,[47] appointing functionaries to be in charge of sizes, weights, and measures, regulating local trade and crafts, and collecting taxes and customs. Consequently, he was often approached as the highest local state representative and an administrative authority over the Jews, especially in conflicts between the Jewish community and their neighbors, e.g. crises regarding Jewish settlement in the city, problems with trade and craft rights which he tried to settle through agreements, so-called *pacta* (ugody), between Kahal and municipality. Hence, the voivode frequently acted as an agent of the law and issued temporary regulations or signed agreements, which in turn were usually confirmed by the kings. For example, already in 1485 the voivode signed an important trade agreement between the Krakovian Jews and the municipality:

> We the signed below, the Elders of the Jewish Community in Krakow, admit and testify with the signature of our own hand, how with the consent of the entire community we have been convinced and have undertaken of our own free will and without any coercion, to abstain from trade and cease from dealing with merchandise. Likewise, not to take various commodities or merchandise and sell with our own hands to other Christians, except for our unredeemed pledges by which we lost in usury and which we can sell in our houses at any time and opportunity. We may not dare to convey and bring these pledges to sell them in the streets or markets in the city, except during two days of the week, Tuesday and Friday, restricted for markets, as well as on the fair-days [...] Likewise we shall sell only the pledges we can swear on the Torah to be ours. And if it happens that a man or a woman will maliciously go and carry old or new commodities into the city [in order] to sell them, and will be caught selling them or willing to sell them on any other day except for the two above mentioned days and the market-days, then the inhabitants of the city have the right to confiscate all his commodities. Moreover, this Jew shall be put in prison unless he pays the penalty of 3 *grzywny* to the palatines. Likewise, poor Jewesses have the right to sell on all days shawls and scarves made by their own hands and craft. This letter shall be a testimony and evidence in the hands of the burghers and city council to be fulfilled as written without cunning and without any fraud we have written and signed.[48]

We have no evidence concerning the negotiations before or right after the agreement. As far as we know, the original document was written in Hebrew and signed – after approval by the entire community[49] – by four Jewish Elders in

47 Zdzisław Kaczmarczyk and Boguslaw Leśnodorski, *Historia państwa i prawa Polski*, vol. 2, (Warszawa: PWN, 1966), 59.

48 Quoted in Majer Balaban, *Toldot ha-yehudim be-Krakov u-be-Kazhimiezh, 1304–1868*, vol. 1, transl. David Weinfeld, Asher Wilcher, Sinai Leichter and Elazar Fershker (Jerusalem: Magnes Press, 2003), picture 8.

49 See Hanna Zaremska, *Żydzi w średniowiecznej Polsce. Gmina krakowska* (Warszawa: Instytut Historii PAN, 2011), 376–377.

front of the City Council. On June 7, a few days after the conclusion, a Latin translation of the agreement was submitted by the Elders to the voivode, Jan Amor of Tarnów.[50] Afterwards, the document signed by the voivode was inserted into the collection of city laws and only this version was presented later to the kings, who all frequently referred to the agreement as if made by the voivode himself.[51] According to Bałaban, who interpreted the agreement as anti-Jewish and imposed on the Krakovian community, the document was signed and sanctioned by the voivode as »the lord of the Jews.«[52] The voivode was not in fact asked by the city council to sign and enforce the treaty upon the Jews. Quite the contrary, it was the kahal that appeared in front of the voivode and as the Latin version reveals, the Jews approached him as subjects of the voivodeship (*ditioni et potestati nostri paltinatus dediti et subjecti*)[53] and not as commoners subject to the absolute rule of »their lord«. Moreover, the representatives of the community did not ask the voivode as »their lord« or protector to cancel the »imposed« treaty. On the contrary, the elders – who were probably involved in the negotiations leading to the writing of the Hebrew original and later preserved it scrupulously – requested his recognition of the treaty and presumably paid for all the diplomatic procedures as was customary.[54]

The fact that the kahal placed extra effort and invested substantial amounts of money into the validation of the agreement by the voivode sheds new light on both the meaning of the treaty itself and on the character of the voivode's involvement in the case. First, it implies that the agreement was not entirely anti-Jewish and had a great importance to the community. Second, it suggests that the voivode was approached not as a superior authority enforcing a destructive treaty but – on the contrary – as a state representative, who could and did use his

50 Jan Amor (Młodszy) z Tarnowa (lat. Ioannis Amor de Tharnow), circa 1425–1500.

51 See e.g. the edict of Sigismund I of 1527: »Sigismund I rex Poloniae ordinationem Ioannis Amor de Tarnow palatini Cracoviensis, de mercatura Iudaeorum a. 1485 factam, ratam esse iubet.«, quoted in Piekosiński. There are many other examples of the voivode's involvement in interreligious agreements, e.g. in 1533 Piotr Kmita helped to sign a settlement agreement between the Jewish community and the municipality of Kazimierz and Stradom, see Mathias Bersohn, *Dyplomatariusz dotyczący Żydów w dawnej Polsce: na źródłach archiwalnych osnuty (1388–1782)*, (Warszawa, 1910), 53–58.

52 Bałaban, *Historja Żydów*, 60.

53 Ibid.

54 For more information on payments for office services and chancellery procedures, see for example Stanisław Kętrzyński, *Zarys nauki o dokumencie polskim wieków średnich* (Poznań: Wydawnictwo Poznańskie, 2008); Andrzej Tomczak, »Kilka uwag o kancelarii królewskiej w drugiej połowie XVI wieku,« *Archeion* 37 (1962): 235–252.

administrative prerogatives and local status to foster the mutual pact resulting from interreligious negotiations and guarantee its execution. In turn, these conclusions challenge Bałaban's interpretation and justify the re-examination of the treaty itself and of the voivode's role from the perspective of interreligious communication.

From this point of view, the treaty of 1485 reveals itself as a trade-oriented chapter in a multi-dimensional dialogue between the Jewish community and Christian burghers, through which the Jews attempted to establish themselves as an economic corporation entering new markets.[55] Consequently, by sanctioning the document, the voivode appears to have functioned as an agent of the law validating the Christian-Jewish agreement. All in all, the analysis of the signing procedure in 1485 from the perspective of interreligious communication offers an alternative interpretation of the treaty and deepens our understanding of the role of the law, the state, and its representatives as supportive and validating factors in Christian-Jewish dialogue and coexistence.

The voivode, in addition to his judicial and administrative prerogatives, also acted as a local representative of royal authority, approving, for example, the results of inner-Jewish elections on the behalf of the king.[56] Through this prerogative, the voivode granted state legitimacy to Jewish functionaries, the kahal system, and Jewish autonomy in general, thus providing crucial support for Jewish self-government.[57]

Besides representing royal authority on a permanent basis, the voivode carried out the king's ongoing orders and hence frequently intervened in cases of interreligious conflict. For example, in 1539, after Catherine Wajgel – an 80-year-old widow who had been tried and convicted by the ecclesiastic court for apostasy from Catholicism to Judaism[58] – had been burned at the stake, Voivode Piotr Kmita[59] was ordered by the king to calm the anti-Jewish atmosphere and

55 On the changes in the economic orientation of the Jewish community and its role in the urban realm of the early modern Commonwealth, see for example Elchanan Reiner, »Aliyat >ha-kehilah ha-gdola<: al shorashei ha-kehilah ha-yehudit ha-ironit be-polin ba-et ha-hadashah ha-mukdemet,« *Gal-ed* 20, no. 2 (2006): 13–37.

56 See Jakimyszyn, *Statut Krakowskiej Gminy*, VIII, § 11.

57 On the interplay between the state and Jewish autonomy, see for example Moshe Rosman, »Tiv ha-autonomiyah shel yehudei polin,« in *Kehal Yisra'el: Ha-shilton ha-atsmi ha-yehudi le-dorotav*, vol. 3, ed. Israel Bartal (Jerusalem: Merkaz Zalman Shazar, 2001), 24–42.

58 The case was described by Łukasz Górnicki, *Dzieje w Koronie Polskiej* (Wrocław: Ossolineum, 2003), 13–15.

59 Piotr Kmita (1477–1553) was a Grand Marshal of the Crown and Voivode of Krakow. A humanist and »agile« politician, he was known for his love of »big money« and close relations with Queen Bona. Consequently, both the Jews as

find those who brought the »old townswoman« to Judaism. The voivode intended to quiet the people by arresting the local cantor who, according to public opinion, had been responsible for the widow's conversion. However, when it turned out that the alleged proselytizer had escaped, Kmita received new royal orders and arrested the Jewish elders for being responsible for the man's flight.[60] Although the Jews pleaded with Kmita to free their representatives, the voivode in this case functioned as a representative of the royal authority and acted solely according to the king's orders and not in line with his ordinary prerogatives and image as being the »protector of the Jews«.

Following the kings' orders – in which the voivode's judicial authority (*arbitrium*) was interpreted quite freely – the voivodes also intervened in internal Jewish cases. In 1537, for example, after all measures had failed toward solving the inner-Jewish conflict between the Krakovian community and Czech immigrants, King Sigismund I ordered Voivode Piotr Kmita to intervene. Since the two communities – which had separate rabbis and administrations following years of squabbling over their respective supremacy – could not agree on joint use of the old synagogue or on separate fiscal representation, Piotr Kmita was ordered to grant the Czech community a suitable place for an independent synagogue and to control Jewish fiscal affairs.[61] In other words, the voivode was ordered to represent the law and the king in an inner-Jewish conflict and to provide legal tools leading to its solution as well as to the improvement of Jewish fiscal discipline.

The voivodes, who themselves lived in a religiously heterogeneous environment,[62] also occasionally intervened into interreligious conflict on their own initiative, as in the cited case of the tumult of 1637. Whether acting solely as a protector of the Jews or trying to rebuild the city's reputation[63] and underline

well as Catholic merchants bribed him to influence the royal couple on their behalf; see Bałaban, *Historja Żydów*, 123.

60 Ibid., 128.

61 For details on this case, see Bałaban, *Historja Żydów*, 111–112. For examples of the voivode's involvement in Jewish communal life, see Cohen, »Ha-rashut ha-voyevodit.«

62 For example, in the 15th century the manor of the Krakow castellan and voivode from 1438–1459, Jan of Tęczyn, was directly adjacent to the Jewish cemetary. Moreover, in the 16th century a Protestant, Piotr Zborowski, was chosen to be voivode.

63 In 1637, there was a rivalry between Krakow and Warsaw in the matter of a royal marriage ceremony and the coronation of the new queen. Voivode Tęczyński, as a noble and representative of Krakow, probably tried to defend his city and wrote that such riots had never taken place in the capital before and could have easily be suppressed, see APMK, *Varia* 11, 959.

his innocence,[64] Jan Magnus Tęczyński issued a strongly-worded letter condemning the tumult that had taken place during his absence. In this way, he used his position to legitimize Jewish claims, calm the situation, and reinstate peaceful neighborly relations. By issuing the letter and advising the Jewish community on the legal steps it should take to obtain compensation for its losses, the voivode initiated legal procedures and acted as an independent agent of the law supporting the reestablishment of Christian-Jewish coexistence.

Officium palatinum and its functions

The voivode's permanent judicial and administrative functions, accompanied by occasional duties and interventions, were undoubtedly far too numerous for one person to handle. Moreover, his position in the state and his regional authority obliged him to travel quite frequently. The burden of some of the voivode's multiple duties was therefore shared by the office of the voivode, the *officium palatinum*, at first during the voivode's absence and later on a permanent basis. Its officers took responsibility for the regular registration of Jewish merchants' deals and loans, for issuing licenses for Jewish business, and for the approval of Jewish acquisitions. The *officium palatinum* and its functionaries also occasionally became involved in interreligious cases requiring authorization and registration. As early as 1469, for example, the functionaries of *officium palatinum* – and not the voivode himself – certified a critical agreement, according to which the Jewish community sold its estates on the Jewish street to the Krakovian Academy and moved to a smaller and less central area of Krakow:

> Judge Johannes Chamiec de Dobranowice, Johannes the notary and the *subiudex* of the Jews in Krakow, and also their [Jewish] seniors, allow, accept, and ratify the exchange of synagogues, hospitals, and cemeteries for the house and land located on Spiglarska Street has been undertaken by the Krakovian Jews with Jan Długosz the Krakovian canon.[65]

Although we do not know much about the circumstances leading to the signing of this agreement, its reexamination from the perspective of multireligious communication sheds light on the role of the *officium palatinum* as a local agent

64 In his letter, the voivode – probably to clear his name – underlines his absence from the city and rebukes the municipality and its lack of intervention to stop the riots: »Nie może się tesz tego zamilczeć iako magistratus Supremus na ten czas negligentissime i tak się zda iakoby własnie umyślinie stanął. Gdysz aby iednym bramy zawarciem mogłaby się beła wielka część tumult uspokoić.« (»We should not conceal that the magistratus Supremus, rather neglectful at that time, refrained – as if deliberately – from action, while the mere closing of a gate could have calmed down a large part of the tumult.«), APMK, *Varia* 11, 959.

65 Bałaban, *Historja Żydów*, 57–59.

of law. According to Bałaban's narrative »the Jewish move to the Szpiglarska Street was almost equal to an expulsion.«[66] Yet, as Hanna Zaremska has recently suggested, the treaty was not entirely anti-Jewish. Individual Jews and the community as a whole had already acquired estates in the new area before the agreement and had even built one of their synagogues there. Moreover, although the new location was further away from the city center, it did not harm Jewish trade or residential rights. It seems therefore that the treaty was a compromise preceded by Jewish-Christian negotiations and constituted a joint attempt to reduce tensions resulting from living in close proximity.[67] In this case the *officium palatinum* was thus not in fact an apparatus imposing a »semi-expulsion« but functioned as a representative of the state, lending legitimacy to the contract. In other words, the voivode's office used its powers to validate the results of the ongoing negotiations aimed at the preservation of Christian-Jewish coexistence.

Over time and due to the demographic growth of the Jewish population as well as the improvement of the administrative and judicial system of early modern Poland, more and more of the voivode's roles were carried out by his office. Consequently, the administrative center moved from the synagogue to the *officium palatinum* and its functionaries became more involved in Christian-Jewish communication. The *officium palatinum* received the right to issue preventive orders and laws and announce them in the synagogues. The *szkolnik* became responsible for registering low-value sureties.[68] In the 17th century a newly established functionary – the *instigator* – took on a number of judicial competences and became the voivode's general prosecutor responsible for law and justice among the Jews.[69] The voivode himself henceforth passed judgment only in cases dealing with large sums.[70] In the 18th century, the voivode's authority was in fact functionally based on the *officium palatinum* which took care of all civil and petty criminal cases and served as a notary office where city

66 Ibid., 58.

67 Zaremska, *Żydzi w średniowiecznej Polsce*, 359–360.

68 The Statue of 1649 by Voivode Władysław Dominki Zasławski-Ostrogski (1618–1656), § 4, see Gumplowicz, *Prawodawstwo polskie*, 114.

69 According to Benjamin Cohen the appointment of an instigator marked a shift in the character of the voivode's jurisdiction over the Jews from their protection to persecution and close interference in communal life, a shift which was to define the relations between the voivodes and the Jews over the last centuries before the partition of Poland. Both the new function and the change in the relations could however also be ascribed to the maturing of the Polish administration and bureaucracy, demographical growth, and the decline of Jewish autonomy, see Cohen, »Ha-rashut ha-voyevodit,« 11; idem, »Ha-yurisdiktsiyah ha-voyevodit,« 54–56.

70 According to the Statute of Voivode Stanisław Potocki (1659) appeals could be lodged to the voivode's court only in claims of value higher than 250 zloty.

inhabitants registered their contracts, agreements, accusations, and testimonies. In short, by mediating in interreligious conflicts and legitimizing the outcome of Christian-Jewish dialogue »the voivode's functionaries were involved in everything that happened in the Jewish community, on the Jewish street and the market square.«[71] Moreover, they were an active party to religious coexistence and dialogue, and were not mere representatives of the state or the voivode, but actual agents of authority and law involved in these areas.[72]

The early activities of the office, its involvement in interreligious coexistence, and its growing responsibilities were the result of many factors. The very legitimacy of the office's authority, however, had its roots both in the real necessity for an administrative mechanism that could manage the burden of the voivode's multiple functions and in the understanding of the status of the Jews not as subjects to voivode's *(palatinus)* personal rule but as a social group belonging juridically and administratively to the voivodeship *(palatinatus)*.[73] Hence, both the voivode and his office represented the Krakow Voivodeship *(Palatinatus Cracoviensis)* and as such became involved in interreligious coexistence and dialogue in early modern Krakow.

Conclusion

In early modern Krakow, the voivode and the *officium palatinum* formed a common authority, the *Palatinatus Cracoviensis*, which functioned in a religiously heterogeneous reality. Through the constant redefinition and widening of their judicial as well as administrative duties they became both an intermediary between the state and its dwellers of various religious adherence, as well as agents in the interreligious communication between Catholics and Jews living in Krakow and its urban environs. Whether acting in accordance with their written prerogatives and occasional royal orders or pursuing a freer interpretation of their duties, both the voivode and his office supported and strengthened interreligious communication both in times of crisis and during periods of more relaxed relations. Their activities usually aimed at maintaining peaceful neighborliness and dialogue in spite of the fact that the religious elites supported the

71 Cohen, »Ha-yurisdiktsiyah ha-voyevodit,« 47.

72 At the time the vice-palatinus and his office (*Officium vicepalatinale*) also became more active and issued laws, e. g. laws regarding trade and guilds, Jewish tax payments, and various warnings. We unfortunately have no documents from the office and its proceedings.

73 Bałaban, *Historja Żydów*, 60.

policy of separation.[74] On an everyday basis, they formed the apparatus that incorporated the Jews into the country's legal system and tried to protect them from antagonistic courts. Buttressed with the normative law, they provided a juridical and administrative basis for Catholic-Jewish dialogue and granted it state and local legitimacy. Whenever necessary, they mediated between the sides and offered legal tools and means for preserving or re-establishing bi-religious coexistence and communication.

Through the voivodes' involvement, normative law turned into legal practice which contributed to the establishment and maintenance of peaceful neighborliness. My reexamination of the functions and actions of the voivodes and their office from the perspective of multireligious coexistence proves that Christian-Jewish communication had many dimensions and was based not only on the real necessity that resulted from sharing the same urban space, but also on the pragmatic adaptation of normative law. Through the use of law, the voivodes and their office mediated in dialogues between Christians and Jews as well as between the state and its various religious groups. This aspect of their activities and functions has rarely been noticed by historians. Without a doubt, in the developing administrative and juridical system of early modern Poland other institutions and agents were also involved in the establishment and maintenance of interreligious communication as well. Their activities also await analysis from the perspective of Christian-Jewish dialogue. Such a reexamination could further build on existing research and provide new conclusions leading to a deeper understanding of the relations between the law, religion, and the state in religiously heterogeneous areas.

Anat Vaturi

74 See for example Magda Teter, »Kilka uwag na temat podziałów społecznych i religijnych pomiędzy Żydami i Chrześcijanami we wschodnich miastach dawnej Rzeczpospolitej,« *Kwartalnik Historii Żydów*, no. 3 (2003): 327–336.

How to Safeguard a Town Constitution in Early Modern Poland: A Case Study on the Legal Status of Christians and Jews*

Legal history is one of the most active fields in research on towns as well as on the Jewish population in early modern Poland.[1] However, urban history and Jewish history are only rarely integrated into a single picture.[2] This is at least partly grounded in separate research communities and traditions of publication. For example, one of the foci in Jewish history is on editions and interpretations of so-called Jewish privileges. But what exactly is a Jewish privilege? And were there other privileges that give insight into the legal status of the Jewish population and its broader social entanglements? Thirty years ago, Jakub Goldberg pub-

* This text is a reworked and extended version of my article »Meshilut ve-hetrogenyut datit: Rzeszow ke-mikre mivḥan be-shugiyat ma'amdam ha-mishpati shel notsrim ve-yehudim,« in *Historiah mitnageshet ve-kium meshutaf: perspektivut chadashot shel ha-mifgash ha-yehudi-polani*, ed. Dani'el Blatman (Jerusalem: Magnes, 2014), 25–45.

1 To name only some more recent studies: e. g. Stanisław Grodziski et al., eds., *Z dziejów staropolskiej kultury prawnej* (Kraków: Towarzystwo Autorów i Wydawców Prac Naukowych Universitas, 2004); Ernst Eichler and Heiner Lück, eds., *Rechts- und Sprachtransfer in Mittel- und Osteuropa. Sachsenspiegel und Magdeburger Recht* (Berlin: De Gruyter, 2008); Marian Mikołajczyk, *Proces kryminalny w miastach Małopolski XVI–XVIII wieku* (Katowice: Wydawnictwo Uniwersytetu Śląskiego, 2013) – and on Jewish legal history: e. g. Anna Michałowska-Mycielska, *The Jewish Community. Authority and Social Control in Poznań and Swarzędz, 1650–1793* (Wrocław, Wydawnictwo Uniwersytetu Wrocławskiego, 2008) – esp. 124–136, 157–196 and (a small chapter on legal interaction with non-Jewish authorities) 236–249; Judith Kalik, *Scepter of Judah: The Jewish Autonomy in the Eighteenth Century Crown Poland* (Leiden–Boston: Brill 2009).

2 Integrative exceptions are Dorota Mazek, *Ku ozdobie i profitowi. Prawodawstwo miast prywatnych Wielkopolski 1660–1764* (Warszawa: Neriton, 2003), esp. 78–96; Stefan Rohdewald, *»Vom Polocker Venedig«. Kollektives Handeln sozialer Gruppen einer Stadt zwischen Ost- und Mitteleuropa (Mittelalter, frühe Neuzeit, 19. Jh. bis 1914)* (Stuttgart: Steiner, 2005); Renata Król-Mazur, *Miasta trzech nacji. Studia z dziejów Kamieńca Podolskiego XVIII wieku* (Kraków: Avalon, 2008).

lished the first volume of his lavish *Jewish Privileges in the Polish Commonwealth.*[3] This source collection and its abundant introduction up to today represent an indispensable basis for any further research into the legal history of the Jews in Poland-Lithuania – and not only of the Jews. Goldberg distinguishes four categories of privileges granted to Jews by royal, noble, and church authorities in the early modern period: general privileges, regional privileges, community privileges and – often part of the latter – privileges for individual Jews.[4]

In 2007, Adam Teller reaffirmed these categories;[5] furthermore, he began a contextualization of the privileges granted to Jews: At the local level, he compares the privileges of Jewish communities with the privileges of Christian settlers.[6] In the administrative sphere, he draws analogies between the development of an extended Jewish organisational structure and the political institutions of the Polish-Lithuanian state. Finally, in the field of legal codification he compares Moses Isserles' annotated edition of the *Shulḥan arukh*[7] structurally to the Polish translation and commentary of Saxon law for Christian burgher communities,[8] while traditionally Isserles' comment with regards to content is referred to as an Ashkenazi adaptation of Joseph Caro's Sephardic model. Based on these examples, Teller considers the Jews to be one of the constituent estates of the *Rzeczpospolita.*[9]

3 Jacob Goldberg, ed., *Jewish Privileges in the Polish Commonwealth: Charters of Rights Granted to Jewish Communities in Poland-Lithuania in the Sixteenth to Eighteenth Centuries. Critical Edition of Latin and Polish Documents with English Introduction and Notes*, vol. I (Jerusalem: Israel Academy of Sciences and Humanities, 1985). Two more volumes followed in 2001.

4 Ibid., 1–20.

5 Adam Teller, »Der Blick nach Osten. Rechtlicher Status und Rechtssystem der polnischen Judenheit vom 16. bis zum 18. Jahrhundert,« in *Juden im Recht. Neue Zugänge zur Rechtsgeschichte der Juden im Alten Reich*, eds. Andreas Gotzmann and Stephan Wendehorst (Berlin: Duncker & Humblot, 2007), 395–413, esp. 396, 400–401; idem, »Telling the Difference: Some Comparative Perspectives on the Jews' Legal Status in the Polish-Lithuanian Commonwealth and the Holy Roman Empire,« *Polin* 22 (2010): 109–141, here 120.

6 This perspective is confirmed by Jürgen Heyde in a broader perspective in his most recent study on Jewish economic elites in Poland in the 15th and 16th centuries. Jürgen Heyde, *Transkulturelle Kommunikation und Verflechtung. Die jüdischen Wirtschaftseliten in Polen vom 14. bis zum 16. Jahrhundert* (Wiesbaden: Harrassowitz, 2014).

7 Moses Isserles' comment (*HaMappah*) was first printed in the Kraków edition of the *Shulḥan arukh* in 1571.

8 The most prominent was Bartłomiej Groicki, *Artykuły prawa majdeburgskiego* (Kraków: Oficyna Łazarza Andrysowica, 1558; reprint: Warszawa: Wydawnictwo Prawnicze, 1954), and idem, *Porządek sądów i spraw miejskich prawa majdeburskiego w Koronie Polskiej*, Kraków: Oficyna Łazarza Andrysowica, 1559; reprint: Warszawa: Wydawnictwo Prawnicze, 1954).

9 Teller, »Der Blick nach Osten,« 402, 405–408.

The present study will pursue this call for contextualisation at a micro level. It focuses on the analysis of privileges from Rzeszów,[10] the administrative centre of a large noble estate halfway between Krakow and Lwow, which was ruled by several noble dynasties from the middle of the 14th century through the partitions of the Polish-Lithuanian Commonwealth in the late 18th century.[11] Intriguingly, no privilege from Rzeszów is documented in Goldberg's collection, and there is good reason for this. In general, the town lords of Rzeszów formulated the rights and duties of the Jewish community as well as those of individual Jews as part and parcel of the privileges granted to their town as a whole or to individual guilds accessible to both Christians and Jews.[12]

At a typological level, this means that a fifth – though at first glance less visible – entry has to be added to Goldberg's and Teller's categories of privileges concerning the Jewish population: that of general privileges for towns and guilds. In terms of analysis, the question has to be raised whether it made a substantial difference to define the legal status of the Jewish population within general privileges and not in separate ones. This question is related to the ongoing scholarly discussion on the place of Polish Jewry in the culture of the early modern Commonwealth, most prominently led by Gershon Hundert and Moshe Rosman. While Hundert claims a separate »Jewish cosmos«,[13] even though his own empirical works give evidence of the embeddedness of Polish Jews in the politics, economics, and culture of the multi-religious *Rzeczpospolita*,[14] Moshe Rosman argues in a postmodernist vein in favour of Jewish, Polish,

10 At least the privileges for the town are edited: Wioletta Zawitkowska and Grzegorz Zamoyski, eds., *Przywileje miasta Rzeszowa XIV–XIX wieku* (Rzeszów: Mitel, 2014) which eased my work in cases when archival manuscripts were hardly decipherable. The privileges for the guilds still wait for editing.

11 Franciszek Leśniak, »Życie gospodarcze, społeczne i kulturalne,« in Dzieje Rzeszowa, vol. 1: Rzeszów od najdawnejszych czasów do I rozboru, ed. Feliks Kiryk (Rzeszów: Krajowa Agencja Wydawnicza, 1994), 193–216, here 194–198; Maria Borowiejska-Birkenmajerowa, »Rozwój przestrzenny miasta za Mikołaja Spytka Ligęzy,« in Ibid., 259–269; eadem, »Miasto rezydencjonalne Lubomirskich,« in Ibid., 303–316.

12 For examples see Archiwum Państwowe w Rzeszowie (APRz), 1: Akta miasta Rzeszowa (AmRz), sygnatura (sygn.) 1 (parchment); ibid., sygn. 6 (parchment); ibid., sygn. 8 (parchment); ibid., sygn. 9; ibid., sygn. 11 (parchment); ibid., sygn. 12 (parchment); ibid., sygn. 27, 27–28 (copy); ibid., 46–51 (copy); ibid., 51–59 (copy); ibid., 73–81; ibid., 625–627 (copy).

13 Gershon D. Hundert, *Jews in Poland-Lithuania in the Eighteenth Century. A Genealogy of Modernity* (Berkeley–Los Angeles: University of California Press, 2004), 236.

14 See esp. the chapter »Jews and Other Poles« in Gershon D. Hundert: *The Jews in a Polish Private Town. The Case of Opatów in the Eighteenth Century* (Baltimore–London: Johns Hopkins University Press, 1992).

as well as other cultures as »polysystems; open, dynamic, heterogeneous cultural systems«[15] and explicitly avoids cultural essentialism by identifying a shared band of culture common to Poles, Jews, and other Europeans.[16] The examination of the Rzeszów privileges is a case study on this question.

It has not yet been systematically examined whether the integration of Jewish communities and craftsmen into the general legal order of their town was a common phenomenon in Red Ruthenia, or even beyond.[17] The present article concentrates on the question of how this integration was conceptualized in the Rzeszów case and what it meant for the relations of Christians and Jews and the functioning of the town itself. A brief introduction into the political and ethno-religious setting of the Rzeszów estate will offer a framework for a closer analysis of a few selected privileges for the town and its guilds.

Rzeszów – the space of reference

The latifundium of Rzeszów was, from the late Middle Ages onward, part of the sparsely populated transitional zone of Polish- and Ruthenian-speaking areas in the east of Lesser Poland and western Ruthenia. Rzeszów and its surroundings fulfilled an important function in the colonisation and frontier defence of the Commonwealth. In order to attract settlers, King Kazimierz III granted Magdeburg Law to the town of Rzeszów in 1354 and bestowed the estate on a successful warrior in his service. The endowment with Magdeburg law exempted urban dwellers from the royal *vojevod*'s and castellan courts. The latter were replaced by the burghers' town magistrate, council, and courts of lay assessors. Nevertheless, the status of the burghers' institutions was vulnerable, as supreme power in the Rzeszów estate now belonged hereditarily to the noble town lord. During the following centuries, the burghers' self-administration succumbed increasingly to the magnates' will.[18]

15 Moshe Rosman, *How Jewish Is Jewish History?* (Oxford–Portland, Oregon: Littman Library of Jewish Civilization, 2007), 93.

16 Ibid., see esp. chapters 3 and 5.

17 Forerunners are Adam Kaźmierczyk, *Żydzi w dobrach prywatnych w świetle sądowniczej i administracyjnej praktyki dóbr magnackich w wiekach XVI–XVIII* (Kraków: Uniwersytet Jagielloński, Katedra Judaistyki, 2002); Krzysztof Stopka, »Die Stadt, in der die Polen Deutsche genannt wurden: Zwischenethnische Interaktion in Kam"janec'– Podil's'kyj in der Darstellung armenischer Quellen aus der Zeit um 1600,« in *Lithuania and Ruthenia: Studies of a Transcultural Communication Zone (15th–18th Centuries)*, eds. Stefan Rohdewald, David Frick, and Stefan Wiederkehr (Wiesbaden: Harrassowitz, 2007), 67–110.

18 On administrative and court institutions in Rzeszów see Jan Pęckowski, *Dzieje miasta Rzeszowa do końca XVIII. wieku* (Rzeszów: Nakładem Gminy Miasta Rzeszowa z Drukarni Ed. Arvaya, 1913), 5, 57–60, 122, 127–140, 157–177;

From the late 16th century through the end of the 18th century, the guarantee of free religious practice and a broad range of economic options attracted many settlers:[19] craftsmen from the region and other places in the Commonwealth, German settlers from Prussia and Saxony, and, from the late 16th century on, an increasing number of Jews.[20] The religious microstructure on the Rzeszów estate was complex: The noble town lords – as well as many urban dwellers and peasants – belonged to the Roman Catholic Church. Only a few Ruthenian villages dating back to the Kievan era remained Orthodox[21] and subsequently joined the Greek-Catholic (Uniate) Church when the Orthodox bishops of the Przemyśl diocese officially accepted papal authority after a century of resistance. In religious practice, the Uniates kept Greek-Orthodox rites which, through the steady contact with Roman Catholics, took syncretistic shape.[22] The Roman Catholic Church had a high profile in Rzeszów, where it controlled several churches, monasteries, a Piarist collegium, lay brotherhoods, and several craft guilds.[23] A considerable share of the craftsmen and peddlers in town, as well as

Adam Kamiński, »Pierwsze dwa wieki dziejów miasta Rzeszowa,« in *Pięć wieków miasta Rzeszowa, XIV–XVIII w.*, ed. Franciszek Błoński (Warszawa: PWN, 1958), 10–14, 20–23.

19 Pęckowski, *Dzieje miasta Rzeszowa*, 321–325, 360–361; Maurycy Horn, *Żydzi na Rusi Czerwonej w XVI i pierwszej połowie XVII wieku* (Warszawa: PWN, 1975).

20 A (incomplete) register of the newly inscribed burghers who settled down in Rzeszów from the mid-17th through the late 18th century offers basic information on their individual geographic descent and partly on their religious affiliation. APRz, 1: AmRz, sygn. 28: Regestrz Mieczczanów Przysięgłych miasta Rzeszowa, 1665–1798.

21 Zdisław Budzyński, »Stosunki społeczne i życie kulturalne,« in *Dzieje Rzeszowa*, ed. Kiryk, vol. 1, 273–295, here 273.

22 Jacek Krochmal, »Catholic-Orthodox Relations in the Diocese of Przemyśl in the Fourteenth – Eighteenth Centuries,« in *Lithuania and Ruthenia*, eds. Rohdewald, Frick, and Wiederkehr, 210–231, here 225–227. – On the gradual Latinization of the Orthodox rite during the 17th century see Rafał Czupryk, »Relacje unicko-łacińskie w świetle kanonicznych wizytacji dekanalnych (na przykładzie diecezji przemyskich obrządku unickiego i łacińskiego w XVIII w.),« *Prace Historyczno-Archiwalne* 20 (2008): 39–52, here 39–41.

23 Zdisław Budzyński, »Życie społeczno-religijne i kulturalne,« in *Dzieje Rzeszowa*, ed. Kiryk, vol. 1, 365–380, here 365, 375–380; Józef Świeboda, »Środki materialne OO. Pijarów w Rzeszowie w XVII–XVIII w.,« in *Wkład pijarów do nauki i kultury w Polsce XVII–XIX wieku*, ed. Irena Stasiewicz-Jasiukowa (Warszawa–Kraków: ZPPP, 1993), 204–217; Innocenty Rusecki, »Z dziejów kultu bernardyńskiego sanktuarium maryjnego w Rzeszowie,« *W nurcie franciszkańskim* 17 (2008). http://www.zakonfranciszkanów.pl/index.php?option=com_content&view=article&id=381:n17h1&catid=135:nurt17hist&Itemid=553 (accessed 14 November 2015). For details on the individual buildings and institutions see Zdisław Budzyński, »Stosunki społeczne i życie kulturalne,« in *Dzieje Rzeszowa*, ed. Kiryk, vol. 1, 276–277, 283–284, 285–288.

of the leaseholders, was Jewish.[24] Protestants occur in the sources only in rare cases.[25]

The latifundium was no clearly delineable territory. Crucial for political rule and economic exploitation were the urban and rural settlements that exercised agriculture, trade, and crafts, and paid goods and taxes to the town lord. The distribution of the estate among heirs, however – as well as fires, wars, and epidemics – were able to seriously harm the holdings. From the middle of the 17th through the middle of the 18th century, Rzeszów suffered several invasions by Moscovite and Swedish troops, as well as Tatar attacks. Four serious fires devastated the town between the mid-17th and the early 18th centuries.[26] During this period, the population of Rzeszów declined to a few hundred inhabitants, and only around 1720 returned to the level of population in 1648 (some 2,500 inhabitants), again numbering among the medium-sized towns in the Commonwealth.[27]

Up until the first years of the 18th century, the noble town lords, under pressure from the Christian burghers, tried to legislatively limit the settlement of Jews in order to exclude them from trading in certain goods and to control the number and location of their houses.[28] Jewish settlers had already successfully entered the town's economy around 1600 and established their own administrative and religious infrastructure according to tradition and specific local conditions. In practice analogous to the Christian purlieus, the Jewish community was granted autonomy in internal administrative, religious, and legal matters, as long as it did not contradict the interests of the town lord. The Jewish and Christian communities were mutually responsible for certain services, such as the fortification and defence of the town.[29] Still, in contrast to many other private towns, where Jews were directly subordinate to the town lord, Jews in

24 Pęckowski, *Dzieje miasta Rzeszowa*, 263–265, 275–279, 298–302.

25 One example is the privilege for the so-called German guild from 1714, see the copy of the perished privilege in: APRz, 1: AmRz, sygn. 27, 51–59.

26 Jerzy Motylewicz, *Miasta ziemi przemyskiej i sanockiej w drugiej połowie XVII i w XVIII wieku* (Przemyśl–Rzeszów: Południowo-Wschodni Instytut Naukowy w Przemyślu, 1993), 239; Maria Borowiejska-Birkenmajerowa, »Miasto rezydencjonalne Lubomirskich,« in *Dzieje Rzeszowa*, ed. Feliks Kiryk, vol. 1, 303–339, here 303–304; Jerzy Motylewicz, »Stosunki gospodarcze,« in Ibid., 343–364, here 343–344.

27 Motylewicz, *Miasta ziemi przemyskiej i sanockiej*, 244.

28 Crucial in this regard was Hieronim Augustyn Lubomirski's privilege for the town from 1667. APRz, 1: AmRz, sygn. 8 (parchment) which will be analysed later in this article.

29 Franciszek Kotula, »Obwarowanie Rzeszowa i rozwój przestrzenny miasta w XVII i XVIII wieku,« in *Pięć wieków miasta Rzeszowa*, ed. Błoński, 159–240, here 185–186.

Rzeszów were not exempt from Magdeburg law, beyond internal community affairs.[30]

In light of repeated devastations and the consequent depopulation, the legal restrictions imposed on the Jewish population starting in the early 18th century were put less and less into practice. The town lords simply could no longer afford to choose their subjects according to religious affiliation. Approximately half of the population increase of the late 17th and early 18th centuries was due to the immigration of Jews who,[31] as in other towns,[32] acted as a »demographic reserve«.[33] Jerzy Ignacy Lubomirski, the town lord between 1706 and 1753, continuously reduced legal restrictions on his Jewish subjects. Especially in the important matter of settlement rights, he no longer differentiated between Christians and Jews: each group took the oath of loyalty in accordance with its respective religion,[34] paid taxes, contributed to the upkeep of the town, and rendered the other required services.[35]

The complex relationships between the individual religious communities and denominations and the ruling authorities on the Rzeszów estate can be mirrored in a panorama of options in order to integrate the latter into the various administrative systems of the *Rzeczpospolita*: From the perspective of the magnates Lubomirski, Rzeszów was their autonomously ruled latifundium that, in the context of the Commonwealth, made its contribution to military defence.[36] In terms of church administration, it belonged to the diocese of

30 Barbara Wizimirska, »Żydzi przed sądami Rzeszowskimi w XVII i XVIII wieku,« *Pracy Historyczno-Archiwalne* 3 (1995): 91–103, here 92.

31 See Motylewicz, *Miasta ziemi przemyskiej i sanockiej*, 249.

32 For comparison see Murray J. Rosman, *The Lords' Jews. Magnate-Jewish Relations in the Polish-Lithuanian Commonwealth during the Eighteenth Century* (Cambridge, MA: Center for Jewish Studies, Harvard University, 1990); Kaźmierczyk, *Żydzi w dobrach prywatnych*.

33 For the concept of »demographic reserve« see the introduction by Jacob Goldberg in *Jewish Privileges in the Polish Commonwealth*, ed. Goldberg, 17.

34 For the exact formulation of a Jewish oath in Rzeszów see Barbara Wizimirska, »Żydzi przed sądami Rzeszowskimi w XVII i XVIII wieku,« *Pracy Historyczno-Archiwalne* 3 (1995): 91–103, here 99. Humiliating forms of the Jewish oath, as prescribed in Magdeburg law, are documented for Rzeszów only in rare exceptions. See ibid., 100–101. For a description of such ceremony see Kaźmierczyk, *Żydzi w dobrach prywatnych*, 122–126.

35 Barbara Wizimirska, »Sytuacja prawna Żydów w Rzeszowie XVII i XVIII w.,« *Prace Historyczno-Archiwalne* 8 (1999): 3–18, here 3–9, 13; eadem, »Chrześcijanie i Żydzi w Rzeszowie w XVII i XVIII wieku,« *Pracy Historyczno-Archiwalne* 1 (1993): 75–90, here 75–76, 83–84.

36 The magnate's contribution to the royal army's mobilisation of the nobility is well documented in APRz, 519: Archiwum Lubomirskich (AL), sygn. 664–672 (Wojsko koronne).

Przemyśl, which until the late 17th century had a Greek Orthodox – as well as a competing Roman Catholic hierarchy. After that period, it had Uniate and Roman Catholic hierarchies whose spheres of authority overlapped, but were not identical.[37] According to its late medieval privilege of Magdeburg Law, the town was ruled by the Christian burgher community. In the context of Jewish administration, represented by the Council of the Four Lands (*Va'ad arba aratsot*), the community of Rzeszów constituted part of the land Rusiah (Ruthenia) until the late 17th century, then shortly belonged to the province of Przemyśl, and from 1715 was considered a »free city,« sending its own delegates to the *Va'ad*.[38] In brief – the legal authority over the population of the latifundium was in line with the principle of the personality of law that was rooted in the medieval tradition. Essentially this meant that in any legal procedure a person would be treated according to the law of the corporation – a social estate, religious community, or profession – he or she belonged to.[39] Only in cases when different groups were involved in legal interactions did specific institutions have to intervene.[40] All of the above-mentioned authorities legitimised secular claims of power on the basis of religion – in other words: religion, law, and rule were inseparable.

On this basis I consider the privileges issued by the town lords as one type of legal act regulating the coexistence of several Christian denominations as well as Jews. The focus is on the question of how the privileges expressed negotiations and conflicts between Catholics and Jews in the town, and how these negotiations had influenced the formulation of the privileges. In the particular setting of the privileges, as well as in a broader context, I will enquire to what extent the condition of religious heterogeneity found its expression in the legal system of the latifundium.

37 Krochmal, »Catholic-Orthodox Relations,« 210–231.

38 *Encyclopaedia Judaica* (Jerusalem: Encyclopaedia Judaica, 1971), s.v. »Rzeszów«; Kalik, *Scepter of Judah*, 359–360. For the case of Jonas Przemyslki, a delegate to the Va'ad in 1739, see APRz, 519 (AL), sygn. 699, 30–30v., 33–33v.

39 Gillian R. Evans, *Law and Theology in the Middle Ages* (London et al.: Routledge, 2002), 87–90.

40 I delved into this problem in »Rechtsinstrumente in einer ethnisch-religiös gemischten Stadtgesellschaft des frühneuzeitlichen Polen. Der Fall Rzeszów,« in *Konkurrierende Ordnungen. Verschränkungen von Religion, Staat und Nation in Ostmitteleuropa vom 16. bis zum 20. Jahrhundert*, eds. Johannes Gleixner, Laura Hölzlwimmer, Christian Preusse, and Damien Tricoire (München et al.: BiblionMedia, 2015), 159–199.

Genesis and significance of privileges in the Rzeczpospolita

In the nobility-ruled towns of early modern Poland-Lithuania, privileges were issued essentially on four occasions: First, this happened when a town was handed over by the king to a commendable noble. Usually the king signed a donation privilege for the recipient that specified the territory and some basic legal conditions. Later this privilege could be extended to fair rights.[41] Second, this was done as a consequence of a change in political rule. In this case the new town lord, as a signal of continuity, confirmed existing privileges but sometimes modified them.[42] Thirdly, privileges were granted in times of crisis or fundamental change, such as war and economic decline. In this situation, the granting of privileges was aimed at stabilizing the social and political system.[43] This frequently applied to Rzeszów and many other towns in the Rzeczpospolita after 1648.[44] Finally, on special occasions the town lords issued privileges for certain groups and persons in order to manage relations with and between their subjects in detail. Within this type, privileges for craft guilds[45] and privileges for the Jewish population were very prominent.[46]

As mentioned above, the town lords of Rzeszów during the 17th and 18th centuries usually issued privileges for the whole town, and defined the status of

41 Mazek, *Ku ozdobie i profitowi*, 74–76. Two examples from Rzeszów are the privilege by King Kazimierz III for Jan Pakosławic, January 19, 1354. AGAD, Metryka Koronna, sygn. 17, 247v.–248 (copy) as well as the privilege by Jan Kazimierz for Jerzy Sebastian Lubomirski, July 22, 1661. APRz, 1: AmRz, sygn. 7 (parchment).

42 Juliusz Bardach, Bogusław Leśnodorski, and Michał Pietrzak, *Historia ustroju i prawa polskiego* (Warszawa: LexisNexis, ^{5}2005), 191–192, 200, 243–244 – For example in the case of the privilege granted by King Aleksandr Jagiellończyk to the Rzeszów estate in 1502, APRz, 1: AmRz, sygn. 4; by Stefan Batory in 1578, APRz, 1: AmRz, sygn. 3; and Jan Kazimierz in 1661, APRz, 1: AmRz, sygn. 7.

43 Henryk Grajewski, *Granice czasowe mocy obowiązującej norm dawnego prawa polskiego* (Łódź–Wrocław: Zakład Narodowy im. Ossolińskich, 1970), 19–20; Tomasz Opas, »Miasta prywatne a Rzeczypospolita,« *Kwartalnik Historyczny* 28 (1971): 28–47, here 32.

44 E. g., in the case of Mikołaj Spytek Ligęza's privilege for the town of Rzeszów from June 12, 1599. APRz, 1: AmRz, sygn. 27, 625–627.

45 Examples from Rzeszów are the privilege for the cobblers' guild from June 16, 1654. APRz, 1: AmRz, sygn. 6; the privilege for the tailors' guild from July 10, 1670, APRz, 1: AmRz, sygn. 27, 51–55 (copy); the privilege for the bakers' guild from February 28, 1728, APRz, 1: AmRz, sygn. 27, 75–81 (copy), and the privilege for the butchers' guild of the same date. APRz, 1: AmRz, sygn. 11, as well as the above-mentioned privileges for the German guild in 1714.

46 See the numerous examples in *Jewish Privileges in the Polish Commonwealth*, ed. Goldberg, vol. 1–3. – For more privileges see Adam Kaźmierczyk, ed., *Żydzi polscy 1648–1772. Źródła* (Kraków: Uniwersytet Jagielloński, Katedra Judaistyki, 2001).

their Jewish subjects within them. From the late 17th century, privileges as well as other regulations were even addressed to »the magistrate and the synagogue«, the »whole community« – i. e., the Christian burgher community and the Jewish community (*sinagoga*),[47] and even to »the two nations« (*obywatele oboja narodów*).[48] This habit is intriguing, as on the level of the Commonwealth it paralleled the common notion of the »two nations« (*Rzeczpospolita obojga narodów*) in official language, which since the Union of Lublin referred to the – at least theoretically – equal legal status of Poles and Lithuanians.[49] In Rzeszów the specific local situation requires a new reading. It has to be examined to what extent the linguistic transfer from the state level to the local was synonymous with an equal – or at least similar – legal status of Christians and Jews in Rzeszów.

At first glance, the analysis of local privileges might seem extreme in its petty details. This impression fades away when one considers the evolution of the political system in Poland-Lithuania from the late 16th century onwards. The evanescence of royal power in favour of the nobility, especially of the magnates, who ruled on their large estates without royal intervention, led to a fragmentation of political rule into many regional and local orders.[50] This decentralisation of political power led to a general perception of growing legal insecurity. Therefore, various segments of the population tried to ensure the continuation of their existing rights. The inhabitants of towns, especially nobility-ruled ones like Rzeszów, aimed at the confirmation and extension of their privileges.[51] This procedure enhanced the status of local regulations, particular legal systems and legal autonomies.[52] Seen from this perspective, the stability of the *Rzeczpospolita* as a state depended on the effectiveness of local and regional rule and their respective interconnections with the crown. For these reasons it is worthwhile to delve into a microcosm like the Rzeszów estate and to scrutinise the legal culture of its heterogeneous population. A case study of the town- and guild privileges will enable us to illuminate how a single unit of the *Rzeczpospolita* functioned

47 For example APRz, 519: AL, sygn. 113, 15v.–16v. (1728); ibid. 25–30 (1730). For a general evaluation see Wizimirska, »Sytuacja prawna Żydów w Rzeszowie«, 9.

48 See Johanna Lubomirska's evaluation of a commission for the re-establishment of order in the Jewish community in Rzeszów, 1750–1756. APRz, 519: AL, sygn. 458, 2–6v., here 6v.

49 Bardach, Leśnodorski, and Pietrzak, *Historia ustroju i prawa polskiego*, 185–187.

50 Janusz Tazbir, »Rzeczpospolita wielu narodów,« in *Polska. Losy państwa i narodu do 1939 roku*, ed. idem, Henryk Samsonowicz, Tadeusz Łepkowski and Tomasz Nałęcz (Warszawa: Iskry, 2003), 135–245, here 202–203.

51 On the specific situation of the Jewish population see *Jewish Privileges in the Polish Commonwealth*, ed. Goldberg, vol. 1, 11–14.

52 Teller, »Der Blick nach Osten,« 396, 400–401.

and was embedded in a larger political and economic network.[53] The category of religion is used as a marker of difference in formulating the privileges, which should not blind us to the other categories of difference that existed. For example the institution of the Jewish community as well as the Christian burgher community can equally be considered as economic units. Nevertheless, it is worthwhile to consider to what extent privileges took religious diversity into account, especially in the interaction between Catholics and Jews.

Privileges for the town of Rzeszów – negotiations on the status of the Jews

The noble lords of Rzeszów issued a manageable number of privileges for their town. From the middle of the 14th till the end of the 18th century, only seven such privileges are passed down to us,[54] and it is unlikely that many others were lost, as the known ones are linked to each other through frequent textual interconnections. As in other places, the changing of privileges either occurred after a change in political rule or in times of serious crisis. In contrast with minor regulations, town privileges had to address the entire socially and religiously heterogeneous urban population and provide it with a political constitution that expressed continuity and flexibility at the same time. In correspondence with this challenging requirement, they were formulated in very general terms.

A basic norm that was confirmed by each of the privileges was jurisdiction in accordance with the Magdeburg (Saxon) Law code. Furthermore, each privilege revised taxes and services, imposed rules for trade activities, and granted sublicences to manufacture, distribute, and sell alcohol. Occasionally privileges redefined the territory of the estate.[55] At the same time, the early privileges tell us little about the differentiation of the population in terms of religious or denominational affiliation. A privilege issued by Piotr Kmita Lunak from 1427 that confirmed Magdeburg Law on the estate and at the same time annulled old Ruthenian law[56] might refer to a Greek-Orthodox population. In 1571, Mikołaj

53 During the last few years the study of smaller towns in the *Rzeczpospolita* has attracted at least some attention. See Mazek, *Ku ozdobie i profitowi*; Mariusz Zemło, ed., *Małe miasta. Religie* (Lublin–Supraśl: KUL, 2006); Rohdewald, *»Vom Polocker Venedig«*; Kaźmierczyk, *Żydzi w dobrach prywatnych*; Stopka, »Die Stadt, in der die Polen Deutsche genannt wurden«; Król-Mazur, *Miasta trzech nacji.*

54 13 more privileges that concerned the original granting of Magdeburg law, the transfer of rule to noble town lords and the granting of fair rights were issued by the Polish kings. See *Przywileje miasta Rzeszowa XIV–XIX wieku*, ed. Zawitkowska and Zamoyski.

55 APRz, 1: AmRz, sygn. 2 (parchment) and ibid., sygn. 27, 619–625 (copy); ibid., 625–627; ibid., 633; ibid., 628–629; ibid., 630–632; APRz, AmRz, sygn. 8.

56 APRz, 1: AmRz, sygn. 27, 620.

Rzeszowski, a successor of his, reminded the people of Ruska Wieś (Ruthenian village) and of the neighbouring villages that they had been subordinated under Rzeszowian jurisdiction by his ancestors and therefore owed him tribute.[57] Again this claim could hint at separate Greek-Orthodox settlements.

The category of religious affiliation entered the Rzeszowian privileges explicitly in the late 16th century. From this time on, the privileges mirror the noble lords' preoccupation with the growing settlement of Jews in the town and its consequences for the established order of the estate. The development of the social and economic relations between the long-established Christian burghers and the Jewish newcomers can be clearly traced in two privileges.

As early as 1599, Mikołaj Spytek Ligęza issued a privilege[58] that, through the absence of an *invocatio* and the brevity of its *intitulatio*, indicated the urgency of its purpose. Without any further digression, he formulated his motivation – the persistent misery in town and the emigration of many inhabitants, caused by the severe fires in 1576 and 1580.[59] In terms of patronage, Ligęza assumed responsibility for his subjects. He attributed the economic decline of his town to divine judgement and allegorically promised his wards shelter under his wings. In turn, he appealed to the solidarity of the urban community in times of trouble.[60] The measures for the reconstruction of the town announced in the privilege concerned his »dear subjects« without further differentiation: Ligęza fixed long-term tax exemptions for anyone who engaged in the construction of houses and the establishment of new workshops. In addition, he ceded a share of his landholdings to the inhabitants of Rzeszów so that they could set up workshops and gardens as a minimal source of income. In the same spirit he exempted the inhabitants of his town from urban customs »for eternal times« and proposed a reduction of taxes to the Crown. A single group was doubly restricted in its activities:

> I hereby order, and promise to ensure, that the Jews do not build more houses than those they already have, and that they do not buy up merchandise needed by the craftsmen for their workshops.[61]

From this passage it is evident that Jewish merchants had successfully settled down and found their way into the latifundium's economy by 1599 – apparently

57 Ibid., sygn. 27, 622–623.
58 Ibid., 625–627.
59 Motylewicz, »Przemiany gospodarcze,« 225; Tadeusz Ochenduszko, *Dzieje Rzeszowa do 1918 roku. Kalendarium* (Rzeszów: Mitel, 2006), 29.
60 APRz, 1: AmRz, sygn. 27, 625.
61 »Zakazuię y strzymać obiecuię, aby Żydowie więcey nie budowali domów ieno ci, ktorzy place maią, y aby nie przekupowali takowemi towarami, które rzemieślnicy w rzemiośle swoim używaią.« Ibid., 626. – All translations from Polish are by the author (Y. K.).

to the detriment of the long-established local guilds. The privilege was clearly the outcome of negotiations between these two competing groups, and the town lord can be considered as their mediator.[62] The fact that he forbade the Jews from further purchasing real estate and restricted certain economic strategies points to his cooperative relationship with the Christian purlieus. Nevertheless, the quoted passage at the same time implicitly contains a conservative and reaffirming aspect: The presence of Jews in town was not fundamentally called into question, and their previously acquired possessions were guaranteed. Christian inhabitants no doubt had priority in the magnate's considerations, but their rights were not exclusive. What is more, Jews were not collectively excluded from the above-mentioned amenities. As to the normative content of the privilege, in particular the definition of the Jews' legal status, it has to be admitted that it was rather negligible. No concrete punishment was fixed for new Jewish settlers who disregarded the restriction. All in all, Ligęza's privilege can be characterised as a gesture toward the Christians complainants and at the same time as an investment in the future of the latifundium. The well-being of his subjects – whether Christian or Jewish – would finally have positive consequences for his coffers and the town.

One question reaches beyond the text: how much did the restriction against the Jewish population really hinder Jews from settling down in the subsequent decades? A privilege issued almost 70 years later, in 1667, by Hieronim Augustyn Lubomirski,[63] the town lord of Rzeszów between 1667 and 1706, sheds light on the legal practices of the day. In a brief introduction, Hieronim Augustyn confirmed the privileges of his predecessors, especially the application of Magdeburg Law, but when it came to Ligęza's privilege from 1599 he made one reservation: »as far as it does not contradict the laws of succession and is in accordance with the previous privileges«.[64] In the *narratio* he gave a more precise account of the current conflict in town:

> Through these, our burghers and subjects, it has been amply proven why, in our growing town, harm creeps into our manner of community life step-by-step [...]

62 In another article I focused on the narrative aspect of the Rzeszów privileges. Yvonne Kleinmann, »Normsetzung, Narration und religiöse Symbolik. Privilegien als Grundlage der Religionspolitik auf dem frühneuzeitlichen Latifundium Rzeszów,« in *Kommunikation durch symbolische Akte. Religiöse Heterogenität und politische Herrschaft in Polen-Litauen*, ed. Yvonne Kleinmann (Stuttgart: Steiner, 2010), 249–269.

63 APRz, 1: AmRz, sygn. 8 (parchment). For this article I used a copy from the record of the court of lay assessors in Rzeszów. APRz, 1: AmRz, sygn. 27, 630–632.

64 »in quantum Iuri Haereditario non repugnat et anterioribus privilegijs est conforme approbamus.« Ibid., 631. – All translations from Latin have been edited by Sebastian Röbert.

> – namely, because the infidel Jews [...] evidently take up permanent residence there and thereby [violate] these well-known privileges. Not only does the number of the existing permanent dwellings of the heads of household exceed forty, but wherever any given roof shelters occupants, they [the Jews] strive to contribute [only] one third of the number required in fulfilling burghers' duties and keeping watch, as was the custom at the time when they had only seven [households], and this was allowed to continue out of leniency.[65]

These few lines identify Christian burghers as the claimants and initiators of the privilege, document the significantly increased number of Jewish households, and trace the antagonism between Christians and Jews back to this change. Without hesitation, the town lord took sides with his Christian subjects and claimed that the Jewish settlement practice violated the privileges of his predecessors. In this case he did not exactly refer to Ligęza's privilege from 1599, but to a separate decree from the same year that had limited the number of Jewish houses in the Old Town to seven and, in the adjacent New Town, to 40.[66] Using this information, the evolution of the conflict can be reconstructed: Hieronim Augustyn's predecessors clearly had failed to adapt the tax and service system in Rzeszów to the increasing size of the Jewish settlement. Therefore, the considerably expanded Jewish community – in comparison with the Christian burgher community – bore a relatively small share of duties. Apart from this, as the privilege continues, another quarrel occupied the Christian and Jewish inhabitants:

> Furthermore they [the Jews] pursue trade with all manner of goods within the town and beyond; most notably, they produce whole barrels of mead and presume to traffic everywhere in fish soup, other pickled goods, and salted fish. They serve imported beer and wine at will, and in town they trade in retail all kinds of grains they have purchased in the countryside in large quantities, and also publicly trade in other goods that do not compete with those of the craftsmen.[67]

65 »Cum[que] etiam eosdem cives ac subditos nostros sufficienter deductum fuerit qua ratione crescente in civitate nostra in dies infidelium iudaeorum [...], suumq[ue] inibi domicilium libere figente manifestum per hoc contra eadem privilegia praejudicium, simul et notablile civilis ratione vitae dispendium pedetentim irrepserit et emergat, ut pote cum non tantum excedens quadraginta focos fixae et statae patrum familias mansionis numerus, quolibet vero tectum aliquot fovens inquilinos, oneribus civitatis ferendis excubijs quoq[ue] peragendis, per tertia solvendi partem quemadmodum protunc cum numero erant septem tantum servari contendant usum sicq[ue] hactenus per conniventiam servatum fuerit.« Ibid.

66 Ochenduszko, *Dzieje Rzeszowa do 1918 roku*, 31.

67 »verum etiam omnis generis mercimonium tam intra, quam extra civitatem liberam sibi usurpent negotiationem, specialiter autem mellis integras cremant orcas, halecibus, alijsq[ue] murialibus, sive salsis piscibus passim mercari deprehendantur, cocturam mulsi ejusdemq[ue] ut et cerevisiae advectitiae similiter et

From this description, we can conclude that the recently immigrated Jews had ignored established trade monopolies and guild privileges and thereby unhinged the economic system of the estate.[68] With the phrase »as we want to take care of the seriously weakened and rather unstable cause of our burghers and subjects« the town lord acted in favour of the traditional economic order. The issuance of the privilege was a way to protect established practice from newcomers.

In the *dispositio*, Hieronim Augustyn decreed »that the above-mentioned infidel Jews without any exception will be urged to take a proportional share in all regular and hereditary duties and charges«.[69] This measure was an effort to re-establish an equilibrium between the size and duties of each community and thereby prevent further social unrest. In the same sense, the directive addressed at the Jewish merchants that banned them from trade with certain goods and forced them to respect the guilds' privileges supported the old order.

Economic competition between Christians and Jews notwithstanding, the privilege did not express religious antagonism. The formula *Infideles Iudaei* – as well as the Polish terms *niewierni* and *starozakonni* – was a common term for Jews in official documents that expressed their clear separation from the Christian community, but did not touch upon free religious practice. The limitation in the production of mead explicitly did not concern mead for ritual purpose:

> They [the Jews] are authorised to fabricate mead only in such quantities that seem reasonable for their Pessakh holiday. This applies anywhere within and beyond the town. Henceforth excluded are weddings and circumcisions.[70]

This precise differentiation indicates to which extent the town lord was informed by representatives of the Jewish community and had entered into negotiations with its elders. Apparently mead had also been consummated beforehand on the occasion of Jewish weddings and circumcisions, but this practice was regarded as a custom (*minhag*) – as opposed to the ritual con-

vini propinationem pro libitu exerceant, frumentum omnis generis per praedia coemptum centenis modys intra civitatem distrahant, alijs quoq[ue] mercibus, quae nonnisi mechanicis competunt palam negotientur.« APRz, 1: AmRz, sygn. 27, 631.

68 The charge was probably addressed at a couple of Jewish commissioners who had settled down in Rzeszów and purchased merchandise for wholesalers in large quantities. Pęckowski, *Dzieje miasta Rzeszowa*, 277.

69 »quatenus praefati Infideles Iudaei ad omnia onera et contributiones tam regulares, quam haereditariae [...] proportionaliter sine ulla exceptione teneantur«. APRz, 1: AmRz, sygn. 27, 631.

70 »Coctura mulsi in tantum solummodo et praecise sibi permissa quantum necessitas pro Paschate eorum rationabiliter exigere videbitur, idq[ue] congiatim tantum et extra civitatem. Nuptiarum et circumcisionis actibus prorsus exclusis.« Ibid., 631–632.

sumption of mead at the Pessakh Seder – and could be dropped. The regulation of mead fabrication should be seen as a compromise between the Jewish elders and unmentioned guild representatives.

However, in the political field, the town lord clearly prohibited the legal dissociation of the Jews from the Christian purlieus, e. g. the rules of Magdeburg law. The privilege tells us about the Jews' striving to circumvent the local court of lay assessors and to establish an exclusive legal relationship with the town lord, as is was common practice in most private towns. In this case, Hieronim Augustyn again adopted the position of the Christian burghers and reaffirmed their jurisdiction as courts of first instance. Still, the crucial factor in his decision was not the Christian character of the Magdeburg Law code, which he did not even mention, but the authority of the long-established institution.

By 1750, after several wars, fires, and epidemics, the situation in Rzeszów had significantly changed. In that year, Hiernonim Augustyn's son Jerzy Ignacy, town lord between 1706 and 1753, issued a privilege for the town that marks another shift in the legal status of his Jewish subjects.[71] The privilege was addressed to both the Catholic burgher community and the Jewish community: »equally to the town council and the whole Catholic community of my town Rzeszów, the Old and the New Town – and to the local Synagogue [Jewish community]«. In the face of his old age, his experience in rule and, perhaps, knowledge of European political thought of his time,[72] Jerzy Ignacy expressed his loyalty towards his subjects on the one hand, and on the other systematised their duties in order to hand over to his successor a functioning and well-ordered town. He requested total obedience and listed all kinds of obligations of the »orthodox Catholics« – various fees, the upkeep of public buildings and infrastructure, etc. – towards the town's *communitas* and its lord. Most revealing is the sentence concluding this passage, which obliged the Jewish community »for eternal times« to cover half of all above-mentioned expenses out of its independent tax revenue (*krupka*). In the subsequent passages, he stressed several times the common interest and responsibility of his Catholic and Jewish subjects. He entrusted only some tasks to either the Catholic or to the Jewish community exclusively, but still took care to maintain a general equilibrium. Strikingly, in the privilege of 1750, the common attribute *infidelis* for Jewish subjects had disappeared. If we read the privilegium like a will, the Catholics in Rzeszów would represent the elder son, but the Jews would still be a second

71 APRz, 1: AmRz, sygn. 12 (parchment).

72 Jerzy Ignacy Lubomirski in his function as a general of the Polish and Saxon armies during many years assembled at the Saxon court of the Polish king. Półćwiartek, »Latyfundium Rzeszowskie,« 562–563.

child. Their common inheritance consisted in a *concivilitas* based on shared responsibility without regard to religious affiliations.

In summary, it can be claimed that the privileges for the town reflect a far-reaching neutrality of the noble lords in religious matters. None of the discussed privileges contains religious polemics or uses religious identities in its argumentation. The measures decreed aimed at mitigating political and economic conflict. Solely two markers indicate the privileges' rootedness in Catholicism: the dates of issuance follow the Catholic calendar, and the decreed fines were to the benefit of charitable Catholic foundations.[73]

Religious imprinting of guild privileges

> On the occasion of *quatember*,[74] which is held four times a year, the masters and apprentices of the guild – Catholics, Lutherans, and Calvinists – are obliged to assemble and celebrate a memorial service for the departed brothers and sisters of the guild, as is also custom in other guilds. Anyone who deliberately does not appear will have to pay the guild's fine of six pounds of wax (two pounds for apprentices) [...]. (The Jews who make up part of this guild are exempt from the duty to participate in the ceremonies of the Holy Catholic Church.).[75]

This passage from the privilege for the so-called German guild, issued by the above-mentioned Jerzy Ignacy Lubomirski on 17 March 1714, is representative of many other privileges for the various guilds of Rzeszów during the early modern period. It formulates a code of behaviour for the members of the guild, differentiated according to their religious affiliation. In addition, it describes the economic and social interaction of the various religious groups in town and reflects the influence of Catholic symbols and rituals on the guild. In a larger context it tells the following story: The population of Rzeszów at the time was subdivided into three Christian denominations as well as a Jewish community,

73 APRz, 1: AmRz, sygn. 27, 632.

74 Pol. *Suchedni* (also *Suche dni*) – in the tradition of the Roman Catholic Church, fast days that are held at the beginning of the four seasons respectively. They are meant to renew faith and are accompanied by church services, expiatory sacrifices, and pastoral care. *Pastoralliturgisches Handlexikon*, ed. Rupert Berger (Freiburg et al.: Herder, ^{3}2005), s.v. »Quatembertage«.

75 »Podczas suchedni, ktorych bywa czworo w roku, wszyscy magistrowie y czeladź cechu tego, tak Katholicy, Lutrzy, iako y Kalwini powinni bydź na requialney mszy za zmarłych braci y sio[s]tr cechu tegoż odprawuiącey się, iako inszych cechow zwyczay. A ktory z umysłu nie będzie, podpadać powinien winy cechowey sześć funtow wosku, a czeladnik dwa. [...]. (Żydzi ktorzy do tego cechu należeć będą wolni od tego obligu, gdyż nie powinni bywać przy ceremoniach kościoła Świętego Katholickiego).« APRz, 1: AmRz, sygn. 27, 51–59.

who all cooperated with each other in the German guild. The name of the guild did not refer to its ethnic composition, but to the regional origin of the individual crafts assembled there.[76] All those practicing one of these crafts were obliged to join the German guild. Beyond its economic activities, the guild was a social and religious community that was dominated by the rites and values of its Catholic members. Even Lutherans and Calvinists who refused to join Catholic memorial services had to pay a wax fine that was destined for the Catholic Corpus Christi procession. All guilds were required to participate in this procession. Also, Jews were obliged to pay their membership fees to the guild, as well as fines in the form of wax, into the cash box.[77]

It is evident from this short description that the German guild was a heterogeneous joint venture with clear internal delineations and a distinctive hierarchy according to religious affiliation. A similar structure can be found in other guilds in early modern Rzeszów.[78] These efforts at delineation notwithstanding, several denominational and religious groups were united within one and the same guild in many cases – an unthinkable practice in the original late medieval understanding of guilds as a symbiotic Christian community, or *Lebensgemeinschaft*.[79] Still, against the opposition of Catholic guild members and clerics, mixed guilds were very common especially in the eastern territories of the Polish-Lithuanian Commonwealth.[80]

However, at the local level, one must ask why the town lords, in their general privileges, mostly avoided religious symbolism and the formation of explicit hierarchies among religious groups, but focused on Catholic values and rituals in guild privileges. Different functions and initiators for the two kinds of privileges are easily distinguishable: In the general privileges, the noble lord regulated the town's fundamental legal and economic matters. Therefore, they can be perceived as the core of the premodern local constitution. The town lord tried to strengthen the (admittedly) religiously heterogeneous *concivilitas* via

76 Among others blacksmiths, saddlers, lorimers, tin moulders, turners, cobblers, and tailors.

77 APRz, 1: AmRz, sygn. 27, 55–56.

78 See the privilege for the cobblers' guild from June 16, 1654. APRz, 1: AmRz, sygn. 6 (parchment); the privilege for the tailors' guild from July 10, 1670. APRz, 1: AmRz, sygn. 27, 51–55 (copy); the privilege for the bakers' guild from February 28, 1728. APRz, 1: AmRz, sygn. 27, 75–81 (copy), and the privilege for the butchers' guild from the same date. APRz, 1: AmRz, sygn. 11 (parchment).

79 For a revised analysis of the late medieval guild system as a flexible institution in historical development see Jan Lucassen, Jan Luiten van Zanden, and Tine De Moor, eds., *The Return of the Guilds* (Cambridge: Cambridge University Press, 2008), 5–18.

80 M[oses] Kremer, »Der antayl fun yidishe ba'aley-malakhot in di kristlekhe tsekhn in amolikn Poyln,« *Bleter far Geshikhte* 2 (1938): 3–32, here 6.

these privileges.[81] By contrast, guild privileges were usually initiated by a group of craftsmen who, in written form, had asked the town lord for permission to establish a guild and formulated their concept of a Christian community in work and life. If these orientations did not contradict other privileges and were not to the detriment of another group, the town lord would adopt them into a privilege and, through promulgation, give them legal force.[82]

The oldest preserved guild privilege in Rzeszów was issued in 1449 for the weavers' guild; that is, at a time when the Christian population was not yet divided by the Reformation, and Jews only started to settle down in the region. Even at this early date, this privilege prescribed an admission fee and fines in the form of wax.[83] It can be deduced from this circumstance that the community life of the Rzeszowian guilds was rooted in Christian ritual from the very beginning. Religious dissent – whether through the immigration of Jews or through the breakup of the Christian community into several denominations – inevitably challenged this order. A privilege issued by Mikołaj Rzeszowski for the cobblers' guild in 1569,[84] which referred to an older privilege, very adequately described the growing religious competition in town. This privilege reaffirmed the wax contribution and obliged new members to light candles in church on Sundays and holidays. In addition, its members were called to fabricate guild candles collectively before the Corpus Christi procession. They were obliged under threat of punishment to join the procession together with their wives and to carry the sign of the guild, along with the candles, immediately behind the sanctum throughout the streets of Rzeszów. The same requirement was applied to the Corpus Christi service, but with one exception: The privilege in that case allowed guild members to send a substitute.[85]

In comparison to the mid-15th century, the ritual activity of the guild, especially on the occasion of Corpus Christi, had grown considerably.[86] It signalled the Catholics' striving to take over public space through religious

81 On the concept of *concivilitas*, understood as collective action of various social and religious groups in one town, see Rohdewald, *»Vom Polocker Venedig«*, 16–23, especially on collective activities of early modern guilds: 263–266.

82 This procedure is explained in detail in the privilege for the German guild from 1714. APRz, 1: AmRz, sygn. 27, 51.

83 APRz, 1: AmRz, sygn. 27, 17–20, here 19.

84 Ibid., sygn. 1 (parchment).

85 Ibid., sygn. 27, 6, 8–8v.

86 Also in other parts of Europe the importance of the Corpus Christi procession was growing during the counter-reformation. Through the end of the Thirty Years' War it was the guilds' duty to organize these processions. Holger Nielen, *Prozessionsfeste und dramatische Spiele im interreligiösen Vergleich. Eine religionsphänomenologische Studie zu Fastnacht, Fronleichnam, ʿAšura und Purim* (Berlin: Logos, 2005), 134–137.

symbols and to impose themselves on unnamed competitors. The privilege was issued only one year before the so-called *Consensus Sendomirensis* concluded by the Bohemian, Helvetian, and Lutheran protestant churches in the neighbouring Sandomierz in 1570.[87] Therefore, it is most likely that the concession to send a substitute for the Corpus Christi procession was aimed at Calvinist and Lutheran members. With the aid of this strategy, the guild saved its economic cohesion even though its religious cohesion had collapsed.

Religious dissent with Jewish craftsmen was dealt with by the guilds and town lords in various ways. As the privilege for the German guild has demonstrated, Jewish craftsmen could be economically integrated, but ritually separated. Another option was the complete exclusion of Jews from Christian guilds. This happened regularly in the various regions of the Polish-Lithuanian Commonwealth,[88] though I have not found evidence for such practice in Rzeszów. Jewish craftsmen could also establish their own guilds, as occurred in other towns of the region[89] but only in a few cases in Rzeszów from the late 17th century.[90] As to the town lords, they could also force craftsmen of different religious affiliation to join a common guild. This was true for Jerzy Ignacy Lubomirski's privilege for the bakers' guild from 24 February 1728. The privilege's *inscriptio* significantly differed from previous privileges.[91] With the words »to our glorious Council and the entire Jewish Synagogue of our town Rzeszów,«[92] the noble lord addressed the administration of the Christian purlieus and the elders of the Jewish community *pari passu*. Without entering into details, he referred to an enduring conflict between Catholic and Jewish bakers in town. Therefore, he

87 About the Consensus Sendomirensis see Michael G. Müller, »Der Consensus Sendomirensis – Geschichte eines Scheiterns? Zur Diskussion über Protestantismus und protestantische Konfessionalisierung in Polen-Litauen im 16. Jahrhundert,« in *Konfessionelle Pluralität als Herausforderung. Koexistenz und Konflikt in Spätmittelalter und Früher Neuzeit*, eds. Joachim Bahlcke, Karen Lambrecht, and Hans C. Maner (Leipzig: Leipziger Universitätsverlag, 2006), 397–408.

88 See Maurycy Horn, »The Chronology and Distribution of Jewish Craft Guilds in Old Poland, 1613–1795,« in *The Jews in Old Poland, 1000–1772*, eds. Antony Polonsky, Jakub Basista, and Andrzej Link-Lenczowski (London, New York: I.B. Tauris, 1993), 249–266, here 253–254; Kremer, »Der antayl fun yidishe ba'aley-malakhot,« 4.

89 For example 1735 in Zasław (Volhynia), where Jewish tailors and blacksmiths asked the town lord for permission to establish their own guild for ritual reasons. See *Żydzi polscy 1648–1772. Źródła*, ed. Kaźmierczyk, 48–50. For a general outline on Jewish guilds see Horn, »The Chronology and Distribution of Jewish Craft Guilds,« 253–266.

90 Wizimirska, »Sytuacja prawna Żydów w Rzeszowie,« 7.

91 APRz, 1: AmRz, sygn. 27, 73–81 (copy).

92 »sławetnym urzędom mieyskim y całey synagodze żydowskiey miasta naszego Rzeszowa«. Ibid., 73.

ordered the rival craftsmen, who until then had coexisted in free competition without any guild affiliation, to establish a single common guild.[93]

Nobody had asked for this foundation. The obvious motivation for the surprising measure was the acute need to bolster the insufficient bread supply for the urban population.[94] In contrast to the older mixed guilds, which had turned into such only through immigration and religious schism, the bakers' guild was explicitly founded »in order that, with the aid of this regulation, Catholics and Jews behave and administer well in the bakers' craft«.[95] The town lord gave them a clearly defined common task – satisfying the existential need for bread in the future – and made them mutually dependent in the case that they could not meet the demand.

This equality of responsibility notwithstanding, the hierarchy of Catholics and Jews within the guild hardly differed from that of long-established guilds: Exactly 30 Catholics and eight Jewish bakers were admitted.[96] The guild statutes established numerous religiously influenced rituals and fees. For instance, on the occasion of the annual collective purchase of grain, Catholics as well as Jews were obliged to contribute a certain amount of wax to the guild's treasury for the Corpus Christi procession. This was kept in the chapel of St Valentin, the Catholic patron saint of bakers. Correspondingly, the rhythm of weeks and holidays followed the Catholic order. Neither Catholic nor Jewish guild members were allowed to buy goods on the market before the end of Sundays or holiday services,[97] whereas Jewish holidays were not even mentioned in the privilege.

It does not appear from the text, whether more than eight Jewish bakers had exercised their craft in Rzeszów beforehand. Only in this case could the limitation be interpreted as a discriminating measure. Beyond any doubt, the new order was quantitatively and qualitatively in favour of the Catholic guild members. Given the dominance of the Catholic Church on the regional and state levels,[98] as well as the personal commitment of the town lord in church

93 This measure concurs with Moses Kremer's claim, that in private towns the town lords and not the guild masters decided whether guilds were religiously heterogeneous or uniform. Kremer, »Der antayl fun yidishe ba'aley-malakhot,« 5.

94 APRz, 1: AmRz, sygn. 27, 74–75.

95 »aby według tego prawa Katholicy y Żydzi konsztu piekarskiego dobrze się sprawowali y rządzili«. Ibid., 74.

96 Ibid.

97 Ibid., 75–77.

98 This dominance was manifest in a strong Catholic public sphere, imprinted by monasteries, educational institutions, the cult of Mary and – last but not least, the Catholic king. Hans-Jürgen Bömelburg, »Politische Öffentlichkeit und Verfassung zwischen Königsherrschaft, Oligarchie und Adelsrepublikanismus,«

patronage,[99] there was most likely no other option. The close connection between the guild's activities and Catholic ritual and space must be interpreted as an act of symbolic subordination. However, Jerzy Ignacy Lubomirski formally expressed a respectful attitude towards the Jewish community in the address. At the language level, the pejorative *infidelis* of the older privileges had given way to the neutral *Żydzi* in the legal ritual at the initiation into the guild, with the Jewish oath standing alongside the Christian one. No additional, humiliating ceremony was mentioned.[100]

The guild privilege of the bakers was, in two regards, not at all an exception: Many other guild privileges were also formed by Catholic symbols and rituals.[101] Beyond this, mixed guilds for Christians and Jews were common in Rzeszów as well as in other towns of the region.[102] The first known guild privilege in Rzeszów, the privilege for the shoemakers from 1569, had already admitted Christians and Jews.[103]

Conclusions and further perspectives

Returning to the categories outlined at the beginning of this article: Did a substantial difference exist between the known privileges addressed exclusively to the Jewish community and those general Rzeszowian privileges concerning various religious groups in town? And, if yes, what does it mean in the larger setting of research in Polish-Jewish history? The answer has to be differentiated into two levels. As to the content, the town lords' privileges granted to the whole town population of Rzeszów focussed in particular on the same topics raised in exclusive royal and private privileges for regional Jewries, as well as for local Jewish communities: They addressed questions of judicial authority, religious freedoms or restrictions, and regulated tax payments and other duties, trading activity, property rights, relations between Jews and Christians, as well as the town lord's self-obligations towards his or her subjects.[104]

in *Polen in der europäischen Geschichte. Ein Handbuch*, vol. 2: *Frühe Neuzeit*, ed. idem (Stuttgart: Hiersemann, 2012), 369–396.

99 For Jerzy Ignacy's engagement in church patronage see APRz, 519: AL, sygn. 169.

100 APRz, 1: AmRz, sygn. 27, 75.

101 See for example the privilege of the butchers' guild from 1728, APRz, 1: AmRz, sygn. 11 (parchment).

102 Horn, »The chronology and distribution of Jewish craft guilds,« 258; Kremer, »Der antayl fun yidishe ba'aley-malakhot,« 3–32.

103 APRz, 1: AmRz, sygn. 1 (parchment).

104 These are the characteristics systematized by Jacob Goldberg in his collection of exclusive privileges for the Jews. See *Jewish Privileges in the Polish Commonwealth*,

The essential difference lay on the level of formal address and understanding of political rule. The issuance of a privilege for the entire population of the town – or for all members of a guild – automatically stressed the common concern of the document. Even though the privileges analysed here reflect various conflicts between Catholics and Jews, they group the two main religious communities in town into one common picture. The rights granted to the Jews were directly comparable to the rights of other groups and vice versa. One could even claim that the town lords used the privileges to mediate between antagonistic groups. It is symptomatic that they avoided broaching the issue of religious antagonism.[105] Only guild privileges emphasized clear delineations in the domain of religious ritual, but the coexistence of Catholics and Jews in one and the same guild was not thereby called into question.

On this empirical basis it can be claimed that the legal system of the Rzeszów estate – in this case town and guild privileges – reflects the close interaction and mutual dependence of Jewish and Christian inhabitants as well as the town lords at various levels. Forms of day-to-day communication, of course, could be further investigated at the level of neighbourly relations.[106] The privileges analysed indicate the flexibility and dynamics of legal regulations and practice in times of political change. They also point to the common political culture, especially negotiation strategies of Christians and Jews in Rzeszów – and elsewhere in the Commonwealth.

Coexistence and *concivilitas* must not be confused with harmony. The noble lords, who from the mid-17th century on faced a serious military threat to their existence, as well as economic and demographic decline in their town, used privileges as an integrative measure. Nevertheless, the language of the privileges – at least until the late 17th century – clearly expressed the reservations of both lords and burghers towards Jewish settlers. Jews were perceived not only as an economically harmful, but also as a morally dangerous group which had to be disciplined in favour of the Christian burghers. Religious antagonism was postponed solely for the sake of urban reconstruction and economic growth, and Jewish inhabitants were able to obtain more and more rights. Not that the

ed. Goldberg, vol. 1, 4–5, 21–22, 32–33, 42–44. For some examples, see ibid., 83–88 (Dobromil, 1612), 148–150 (Leżajsk, 1765), 313–317 (Sokołow, 1668).

105 The political role of silence is at the center of Yvonne Kleinmann, »Reden oder Schweigen über religiöse Differenz? Kommunikationsfelder eines städtischen Gemeinwesens im frühneuzeitlichen Polen,« in *Gottlosigkeit und Eigensinn. Religiöse Devianz im konfessionellen Zeitalter*, eds. Eric Piltz and Gerd Schwerhoff (Berlin: Duncker & Humblot, 2015), 353–385.

106 See the inspiring study by David Frick, *Kith, Kin, and Neighbors: Communities and Confessions in Seventeenth-Century Wilno* (Ithaca–London: Cornell University Press, 2013).

attitude towards the Jews was better than in other towns, but economic and demographic conditions were clearly worse. A truly neutral position concerning the religious affiliation of his subjects was taken only by Jerzy Ignacy Lubomirski in the mid-18thcentury.

If we, lastly, ask about the success of the arrangements between Catholics and Jews in the Rzeszów privileges (as well as in other legal regulations) we have to compare them to political strategies in other towns of the region. The described complaints of the Catholic burghers and guilds – about Jews buying up houses, harming the town's economy, etc. – were very similar to those for example documented in the royal town of Przemyśl.[107] There, upon the initiative of a royal commission, the ongoing competition and aggressions were settled in 1645 by a so called *ugoda*, a compromise solution between Christians and Jews concerning each group's rights and duties in town. This arrangement notwithstanding, complaints and conflicts did not cease, and in 1759 the reeve's (*wójt*) court even imposed the death sentence on six Jews in blood libel accusation.[108] During the entire discussed period no blood libels or accusations of host desecration occurred in Rzeszów.[109]

Yvonne Kleinmann

107 See the numerous examples given by Mojżesz Schorr, *Żydzi w Przemyślu do końca XVIII. wieku* (Lwów: Nakładem Funduszu Konkursowego, 1903), 95, 100, 102, 105–108, 114–116, 119–121.

108 Ibid., 28–29; 243–245.

109 See the documentation in Hanna Węgrzynek, *»Czarna legenda« Żydów. Procesey o rzekome mordy rytualne w dawnej Polsce* (Warszawa: Bellona, 1995), 182–194, as well as in Zenon Guldon and Jacek Wijaczka, *Procesy o mordy rytualne w Polsce w XVI–XVIII wieku* (Kielce: DCF, 1995), 96–101.

The Other Townsfolk: The Legal Status and Social Positions of the Jews in Cities of the Grand Duchy of Lithuania in the 17th and 18th Centuries

»The Jews are as much burghers as the Christian burghers are.« This was a crucial statement by Stanisław Niezabitowski, the administrator of Slutzk, one of the major towns and Jewish communities in the Belorussian part of the Grand Duchy of Lithuania.[1] The Jews constituted the largest religious minority group in the early modern Polish-Lithuanian Commonwealth and were mostly city-dwellers. At the end of the 17th century about twenty percent of the region's urban inhabitants were Jewish, and by the end of the 18th century the percentage of Jews in cities and towns had grown to fifty percent.[2] However, the Jewish population did not enjoy the same legal status as the Christian townsfolk. One could ask: What did Niezabitowski have in mind with his statement about Jewish and Christian burghers? What did it mean that the Jews were referred to in the same way as the Christian burghers in many documents? Did they have the same status as Christian burghers or did a different type of Jewish citizenship exist?

This article attempts to determine the differences in the legal status of Christian and Jewish townsfolk in the Grand Duchy of Lithuania. Its main aim is to describe what Jewish citizenship meant in practice. In order to show the most significant distinctions, I chose four issues – political rights, jurisdiction, taxes and duties, and economic activity – which in my opinion, mark the crucial differences between Christian and Jewish city dwellers.

1 Central Archives of Historical Records in Warsaw/Archiwum Główne Akt Dawnych we Warszawie (hereafter AGAD): Archiwum Radziwiłłów (hereafter AR), XXIII, teka (file) 135, plik (folder) 6, 282–283.

2 Jerzy Topolski, »Jews in the Urbanization of Poland,« in *Jews in Poland*, ed. Andrzej K. Paluch (Kraków: Wydawnictwo Uniwersytetu Jagiellońskiego, 1992), 45–51, here 47.

The sources that I draw from are handwritten documents from the Warsaw Radziwiłł Family Archive and state documents stored now in the Lithuanian Historical Archive in Vilnius. Generally speaking, this research is based on two types of sources: legal documents – Jewish and general privileges, privileges for artisans' guilds, and other legal documents – and court acts from royal and private towns. Based on the combination of both types of sources, I seek to describe the law and answer the question of how the legal status of the Jews was implemented in practice on the local level in the Grand Duchy of Lithuania. Due to excellent preservation of the relevant source material, the paper focuses mostly on two cities, Slutzk and Vilnius, which were among the most important Jewish communities in the early modern period. Both communities were prominent members of the autonomous Jewish council of Lithuania (*Va'ad medinat Lita*), featured a concentration of Jewish economic activity, and hosted famous religious scholars.[3] My choice of Lithuania as my area of interest is no coincidence. Firstly, it is important to stress that the Grand Duchy of Lithuania had a different legal system from Crown Poland. The so-called Third Lithuanian Statute, introduced as a binding law codex for the Duchy in the late 16th century, had a special importance. As I will argue further on, thanks to this codex, the Jews gained a higher social standing within Christian society.[4] Secondly, the Duchy is considered to have been more tolerant towards religious minorities.

The society of the Grand Duchy of Lithuania was very heterogeneous in terms of religion. It hosted various Christian denominations, including Greek Ortho-

3 The community of Vilnius was described in several works, see: Israel Klauzner, *Toldot ha-kehilah ha-ivrit be-Vilna* (Vilna: Ha-kehilah ha-ivrit, 1938); David Frick, »Jews and Others in Seventeenth-Century Wilno: Life in the Neighborhood,« *Jewish Studies Quarterly* 12 (2005): 8–42; idem, »Jews in public places; Further Chapters in the Jewish Christian Encounter in the Seventeenth Century Vilna,« *Polin* 22 (2009): 215–248; idem, *Kith, Kin, and Neighbors: Communities and Confessions in Seventeenth-Century Wilno* (Ithaca–London: Cornell University Press, 2013). In contrast the community of Slutzk was studied less, see: Anna Michałowska-Mycielska, »Władza dominalna a konflikt w gminie. Wybory władz gminnych i rabina w Słucku, 1709–1711,« in *Małżeństwo z rozsądku? Żydzi w społeczeństwie dawnej Rzeczypospolitej*, eds. Anna Michałowska-Mycielska and Marcin Wodziński (Wrocław: Wydawnictwo Uniwersytetu Wrocławskiego, 2007), 59–73; Barbara Pendzich, »The Jewish Community of Słuck After the Polish-Muscovite War of 1654–1667,« in *Proceedings of the 11th World Congress of the Jewish Studies* (Jerusalem: Magnes Press Hebrew University of Jerusalem, 1997), 173–180; Barbara Pendzich, »Civic Resilience and Cohesion in the Face of Muscovite Occupation,« in *Citizenship and Identity in a Multinational Commonwealth. Poland-Lithuania in Context 1550–1772*, eds. Barbara Pendzich and Karin Friedrich (Leiden and Boston: Brill, 2009), 103–127.

4 About the Third Lithuanian Statute, see Juliusz Bardach, *Statuty litewskie a prawo rzymskie* (Warszawa: Uniwersytet Warszawski, 1999); Juliusz Bardach, *O Dawnej i nie dawnej Litwie* (Poznań: Wydawnictwa Naukowe UAM, 1989).

dox, Greek Catholics, Calvinist and Lutheran Protestants, as well as non-Christian groups such as Jews, Karaites, and Tatars. Non-Catholic Christian churches had a better legal position than in Crown Poland due to the fact that the Warsaw Confederation Act of 1573, a document which guaranteed religious freedom for noble Protestants (Lutherans and Calvinists alike), was included into the Third Lithuanian Statute. While the political life of the country was dominated by Protestant families, especially in the 17th century, it can be argued that the Lithuanian Statute and the Warsaw Confederation, as part of the Statute, affected the Jewish standing there as well.[5] Finally, Lithuanian Jews constituted a separate subgroup among the Jews living in the early modern Polish-Lithuanian Commonwealth. They differed from their brethren in Poland in terms of community organization, language, and their customs.[6] Differences in the social structures of Christian society – in particular, a weaker townsfolk and a more significant position of magnates than in Crown Poland – were also of fundamental importance in the formation of the Jewish diaspora in Lithuania.[7]

5 Wojciech Kriegseisen, *Ewangelicy polscy i litewscy w epoce saskiej (1696–1763). Sytuacja prawna, organizacja i stosunki międzywyznaniowe* (Warszawa: Semper, 1996), 26–27; Józef Gierowski, »Przestrzeń etnograficzno-geograficzna Rzeczypospolitej,« in *Na szlakach Rzeczypospolitej w nowożytnej Europie*, ed. Andrzej K. Link-Lenczowski (Kraków: Księgarnia Akademicka, 2008), 557–573, here 571; Henryk Wisner, *Najjaśniejsza Rzeczypospolita. Szkice z czasów Zygmunta III i Władysława IV Wazy* (Warszawa: Neritron, 2001).

6 See: Dovid Katz, *Lithuanian Jewish Culture* (Vilnius: Baltos Lankos, 2004). About the special features of the Jewish autonomy in Grand Duchy of Lithuania, see Abba Gomer, *Beiträge zur Finanz- und Sozialgeschichte des litauischen Judentums* (Bochum, 1932); Mark Vishnitser [Wischnitzer], »Litovskii Vaad,« in *Istoriia evreyskogo naroda*, vol. 11, eds. Aleksandr Braudo et al. (Moskva: Mir, 1914), 181–204; Haim Hillel Ben-Sason, »Lithuania. The Structure and Trends of its Culture,« in *Encyclopedia Judaica Year Book 1973* (Jerusalem: Encyclopedia Judaica 1973), 120–134; Vital Zajka, »Lithuanian-Belarussian Jewry in the Eighteenth and Nineteenth Centuries,« *Polin* 14 (2001): 19–30; Maria Cieśla, »Sharing a Commonwealth – Polish Jews or Lithuania Jews,« *Gal-Ed* 24 (2015): 15–44.

7 The differences between Crown Poland and the Grand Duchy of Lithuania have been studied by Polish historians, see for example Juliusz Bardach, *O dawnej i niedawnej Litwie*, 73–119; Urszula Augustyniak, *Dwór i klientela Krzysztofa Radziwiłła 1585–1640. Mechanizmy patronatu* (Warszawa: Semper, 2001); Urszula Augustyniak, »Specyfika patronatu magnackiego w Wielkim Księstwie Litewskim w XVII w. Problemy badawcze,« *Kwartalnik Historyczny* 109 (2002): 97–111; Henryk Wisner, *Rzeczpospolita Wazów III. Sławne Państwo Wielkie Księstwo Litewskie* (Warszawa: Neritron IH PAN, 2008); Andrzej Rachuba, *Wielkie Księstwo Litewskie w systemie parlamentarnym Rzeczypospolitej 1569–1763* (Warszawa: Wydawnictwo Sejmowe, 2002); Andrzej Zakrzewski, *Sejmiki Wielkiego Księstwa Litewskiego w XVI–XVIII w. Ustrój i funkcjonowanie: sejmik trocki* (Warszawa: Liber, 2000); Maria Barbara Topolska, *Społeczeństwo i kultura w Wielkim Księstwie Litewskim od XV do XVIII w.* (Poznań: Bogucki Wydawnictwo

There has been almost no specific research on the Jewish diaspora in Lithuania. Historians have considered it to be identical with its Polish counterpart and have very seldom paid attention to the differences between Polish and Lithuanian Jews.[8] Yet, without doubt a clear distinction between the two parts of the Commonwealth needs to be drawn.

Jewish citizenship – »The Jews are as much burghers as the Christian burghers are«?

The first question is: What did it mean for the Christians to have urban citizenship? The privileges of the city burghers included freedom of economic activity, juridical independence, and political rights. Political rights meant the right to elect and to be elected to the city council that decided the internal and external policies of the city. Scholars argue that the political rights constituted the most important component of citizenship.[9] People who wanted to receive citizenship had to meet several conditions. The first and most important was that only Christians were entitled to apply for citizenship. It is clear enough that the Jews could not meet this particular condition because of their religion. However, the Jews fulfilled other requirements, such as providing a birth certificate, an oath, a fee for recording in the town's register, and in some cases having to buy a

Naukowe/Zielona Góra dystr. Oficyna Wydawnicza Uniwersytetu Zielonogórskiego, 2002).

8 Gershon D. Hundert, *Jews in Poland-Lithuania in the Eighteenth Century: A Genealogy of Modernity* (Berkeley–Los Angeles: University of California Press, 2004); See also David Ruderman, *Early Modern Jewry: A New Cultural History* (Princeton: Princeton University Press, 2010). Only in some older works was the Grand Duchy of Lithuania separated from Crown Poland, see for example Sergei Bershadskii, *Litovskie evrei. Istoriia ikh iuridicheskogo i obshchestvennogo polozheniia v Litve ot Vitolda do Lubel'skoi Unii* (St. Petersburg: Tipografiia M. M. Staciulevicha, 1883). Exceptions in the most recent research are Adam Teller, *Kesef, koaḥ, ve-hashpa'sh: yehudim be-aḥuzot beit Radzivil be-Lita ba-meah ha-18* (Jerusalem: Zalman Shazar Center for Jewish History, 2006); Jurgita Šiaučiūnaitė-Verbickienė, *Žydai Lietuvos Didžiosios Kunigaikštystės visuomenėje: sambūvio aspektai* (Vilnius: Żara, 2009).

9 Stanisław Gierszewski, *Obywatele miast Polski przedrozbiorowej* (Warszawa: PWN, 1973), 35; Maria Bogucka, »Struktury ustrojowe, społeczne i etniczne oraz konflikty grupowe w miastach,« in *Dzieje miast i mieszczaństwa w Polsce przed rozbiorowej*, eds. Henryk Samsonowicz and Maria Bogucka (Wrocław et al.: Ossolineum, 1986), 454–489, here 465; Andrzej Sulima-Kamiński, »Przestrzenie obywatelskie w wieloetnicznej, wielowyznaniowej i wielokulturowej Rzeczypospolitej,« in *Lex est Rex in Polonia et in Lithuania* [...] *Tradycje prawnoustrojowe Rzeczypospolitej – doświadczenie i dziedzictwo*, ed. Adam Jankiewicz (Warszawa: DiG, 2011), 85–99, here 90.

house in the city.[10] Nevertheless, as is obvious from the introductory quote, contemporaries spoke of there being Jewish burghers as well.

How does the situation appear if one examines the privileges more closely? A quotation from the privilege given for the town of Kiejdany, a private town that belonged to the Radziwiłłs, states that »no Christian or Jew should live, trade, or work as an artisan in the town of Kiejdany, who has not taken the oath of allegiance to the town's owner.«[11] The same rule was introduced in Slutzk, which belonged to the same family. The town privilege stipulates:

> As it is the custom in all towns it should also be here that every newcomer to the town, whether a Christian or a Jew, with due respect to its laws, should pay a fee when recording his presence in the town's register: a Christian should pay two zloty and a Jew a proper plenty.[12]

The cited documents seem to suggest that Jewish burghers had exactly the same status as did Christian burghers, who after swearing an oath of allegiance received all economic privileges. They did, however, have to pay more for the privilege, so that it would appear that the Jews had a lower social standing.

The issue of Jewish political rights is not discussed in these privileges. One has to take into consideration the sources that describe the practice. As my research has shown, Jews had no right to elect or to be elected to any position on the city council in any of the royal towns of the Grand Duchy of Lithuania.[13] In contrast, the situation seems to have been more complicated in private towns. As the election rights of Jews are not known in the Grand Duchy of Lithuania, some other privileges have to be taken into consideration.[14] After the introduction of

10 Stanisław Gierszewski, »Obywatele miast Polski przedrozbiorowej,« 32.

11 »Żadnemu chrześcijaninowi i Żydowi wolno nie być może mieszkać osiadłością abo handle odprawować abo rzemiosło robić w mieście kiejdańskim, któryby przysięgę wierności nie wykonał Panu dziedzicznemu.« *Lietuvos magdeburginių miestų privilegijos ir aktai*, vol. 3, ed. Antanas Tyla (Vilnius: Lituovos Istorijas Institutas, 2002), no. 61.

12 »Jako zwyczaj wszystkich miast niesie tako i tu kto nowo do miasta wstępuje i prawo miejskie przyjmuje bądź chrześcijanin bądź Żyd, tedy przy wpisywaniu w miejski regestr niech dwa złote przyjemszczyzny chrześcijanin a Żyd sowito do miejskiej skrzynki dołoży.« AGAD, AR XXIII, teka 133, plik 16; see also: AR XXIII, teka 134, plik 1. The governor of the city, Stanisław Niezabitowski, wrote in his memoires about Jews swearing an oath (May 21, 1695): »Jm p. wojewoda mścisławski odebrał przysięgę od mieszczan i Żydów słuckich, także od żołnierzów słuckich«, Stanisław Niezabitowski, *Dzienniki 1695–1700*, ed. Alojzy Sajkowski (Poznań: Wydawnictwo Naukowe UAM, 1998), 82.

13 Maria Cieśla, Żydzi w Wielkim Księstwie Litewskim 1632–1764. Sytuacja prawna. Demografia. Działalność gospodarcza, Ph.D. thesis, Polish Academy of Sciences: Institute of History, 2010, 131–134.

14 In some cities in Crown Poland Jews could participate in city council elections, see Tomasz Opas, »Żydzi w miastach szlacheckich województwa lubelskiego w

Magdeburg Law to Slutzk in the second half of the 17th century, the Jews had the opportunity to influence the economic policy of the city. A representative of the *kahal*, the administration of the Jewish community, had to take part in the city council session, during which the taxes were assessed. In a meeting of the city council in November 1661 the following decision was taken:

> Dawid Jakubowicz, a Jew and a subject of the Jewish community, is hereby designated to participate in the town's council sessions every Thursday as the representative of the Jewish community responsible for executing the Jewish obligations of providing accommodation to soldiers, and other duties of Jewish houses.[15]

As can be seen from the quotation, Jews could only decide in matters connected to the duties and taxes that they paid. As a result they could be sure about a fair assessment of the taxes; however, their position within the city council cannot be considered as equal to the position of the Christian burghers. The sources do, nevertheless, indicate that the Jews did indeed take part in the sessions. Moreover, if a representative of the Jewish community was missing for a session, the community was reprimanded by the Christian city governors.[16]

In connection to the issue of Jewish political rights one has to focus one's attention on the Jewish community – the *kehilah*. Every privilege for a new Jewish settlement guaranteed the right to establish a structured community. One such example was the community in Poswol, a small town in the northern part of the Grand Duchy of Lithuania that was church property. The Jews there were allowed »to elect elders in accordance with the above mentioned [rules of the] Jewish religion, just as it is in other towns and communities.«[17] Some privileges described very precisely the way in which the elders of the community were to be

XVIII w.,« *Biuletyn Żydowskiego Instytutu Historycznego* 67 (1968), 3–37; Józef Mazurkiewicz, »O niektórych problemach prawno-ustrojowych miast prywatnych w dawnej Polsce,« *Annales Universitatis Mariae Curie-Skłodowska* (Sectio G: Jus) 12 (1965): 97–119.

15 »Dawida Jakubowicza Żyda poddanego z szkoły ich żydowskiej naznaczono do stanownictwa, który ma co czwartek stawać do sesji i pilnować spraw swoich żydowskich względem stancyi i serwiz z domów swoich żydowskich.« AGAD, AR XXIII, teka 134, plik 1, 397 (October 1, 1661). Concerning the same matter see also: AR XXIII, teka 137, plik 4, 50–52 (Respons na punkta od Żydów słuckich, February 2, 1661); AR XXIII, teka 134, plik 1, 477 (Protokół sesji rady miejskiej, February 7, 1664).

16 AGAD, AR XXIII, teka 134, plik 1, 386 (Protokół sesji rady miejskiej, May 16, 1661), AR XXIII, teka 154, plik 5, 19 (Protokół sesji rady miejskiej, September 17, 1673); ibid. (Protokół sesji, February 10, 1674).

17 »Starszych według wzwyż mianowanej religii żydowskiej jako po inszych dzieje się miastach przykahałkach obrali.« Wróblewski Library of Lithuanian Academy of Sciences/Lietuvos Mokslų Akademijos Biblioteka (hereafter LMAB), fond (collection) 43, no. 14811.

elected. For instance, in the privilege for Stary Bychów issued in 1758, Michał Antoni Sapieha wrote: »two Jewish elders from one family cannot be nominated as chairs at the same time; instead, the whole community should elect the chairs among themselves by signing in the presence of an envoy of the castle.«[18]

The Jewish communities were completely independent from the Christian city council, with a structure and functions that existed »parallel to those of the city council«.[19] Salo W. Baron has argued that in »medieval and early modern Europe the Jewish community reached its apogee. In many countries and periods it came close to justifying complaints that it constituted a state within the state«.[20] Every member of the community who paid taxes could elect and be elected to the *kahal*. However, it seems that the public activity of the Jews in the *kehilah* cannot be seen in the same way as the political rights of the Christians. The Christian council decided on all of the town's regulations. This influenced the lives of Christians and Jews alike. By contrast, the *kahal* was important only for the Jewish community; it was not able to pass resolutions that were in force for both Christians and Jews. However, if the Jews had to fulfill an obligation, the role of the *kahal* was exactly the same as the role of the city council. So one could say that the two institutions were equal with regard to internal matters, but in matters concerning the whole town, they were not.

Jurisdiction – »The Jews should obey only the king and his officials within their jurisdiction«

The second important issue was that of matters of jurisdiction. If a town had Magdeburg Law its inhabitants had the right to be under the exclusive jurisprudence of the town courts. The exception was only the *jurydyki*, the parts of the city that belonged to magnate or Church owners. These parts were located within the towns but were not part of the town in terms of their organization. In terms of law and jurisdiction they were independent of the town's council. Their inhabitants were mostly judicially subject to the town's lord; however, the latter

18 »starsi żydowscy dwaj z jednej familii obrani być nie mają, ale cały gmin kreskami z porządku siebie obrać onych ma przy widzie z zamku zesłanym.« Jakub Goldberg, *Jewish Privileges in the Polish Commonwealth: Charters of Rights Granted to Jewish Communities in Poland-Lithuania in the Sixteenth to Eighteenth Centuries*, vol. 1 (Jerusalem: The Israeli Academy of Sciences and Humanities, 1985), no. 3.

19 Adam Teller, »Telling the Difference: Some Comparative Perspectives on the Jews' Legal Status in the Polish-Lithuanian Commonwealth and the Holy Roman Empire,« *Polin* 22 (2009): 109–142, here 120.

20 Saul W. Baron, The Jewish Community its History and Structure to the American Revolution (Philadelphia, PA: Westport, CT, 1942), 208.

sometimes used Magdeburg Law as well.[21] The Jewish juridical system was slightly different. The general privilege for the Lithuanian Jews confirmed that the »Jews should obey only the king and his officials within their jurisdiction.« The Jews thus had the status of free people with juridical dependence only on the king and his officials. The same principle was sanctioned in every document addressed to Jewish communities in the Grand Duchy of Lithuania, as the privilege for the community in Jurbork, issued in 1642, illustrates: »The Jews should not resolve their issues in court other than the *starosta*'s court [the royal court] in Jurbork.«[22]

Such direct dependence on the king, represented, at the local level, by his officials – was one of the features that distinguished Jews from Christians. Two other significant principles concerning jurisdiction were introduced into the general Lithuanian privilege. The first was the exclusion from the jurisdiction of the Lithuanian Tribunal. The second is the principle of *actor sequitor forum rei*, which was applied to conflicts with burghers. It prescribed that, if a Jew accused a Christian townsman of something, the conflict would be solved in the court of the town council. However, in this case the privileges granted that »not the Magdeburg but the common law [*prawo ziemskie*] should be applied; they should be judged according to the common law and the [third] land statute.«[23]

This principle seems to have been very significant for the social position of the Jews. One has to bear in mind that only the nobility had the same rights.[24] Moreover, in many cases Lithuanian law – in this case the Third Lithuanian Statute – was more advantageous to the Jews. Particularly insulting items in Magdeburg Law were not adopted in the Third Lithuanian Statute, as I will argue below based on the example of the Jewish oath.

The system of appeals was very simple in royal towns, where Jews had the right to appeal to assessorial courts. In the case of substantial conflicts, a commission (*sąd komisarski*) was arranged. One such example was the conflict between Jewish and Christian burghers in Vilnius that was resolved by a commission in 1636. The commission had to decide on the Jews' rights to trade

21 Concerning the *jurydyki*, see Józef Mazurkiewicz, *Jurydyki lubelskie* (Wrocław: Zakład im Ossolińskich – Wydawnictwo PAN, 1956); Tomasz Opas, *Własność w miastach i jurydykach prywatnych w dawnej Polsce. Studium historyczno-prawne* (Lublin: Wydawnictwo UMCS, 1990); especially about the Lithuanian cities, see Przemysław Borowik, *Jurydyki miasta Grodna w XV–XVIII wieku. Stanowy podział nieruchomości* (Supraśl: Stowarzyszenie Collegium Suprasliense, 2005).

22 »Sami też względem osób swych przed żadnym inszym sądem stawać i sprawować się we wszelkich in genere sprawach nie powinni jeno przed starostą naszym tamecznym jurborskim«. *Lietuvos magdeburginių miestų privilegijos ir aktai*, vol. 1, ed. Antanas Tyla (Vilnius: Lietuvos Istorijos Institutas, 1991), no. 98.

23 AVAK, 5, 304.

24 Ibid.

and work as artisans in the town. Due to the fact that the privileges issued to the Jews and those of the Christian townspeople were contrary to each other, the royal court could not pass a sentence, thus giving way to the establishment of a commission. In most cases the members of the commission were recruited from among local officials and priests. In the conflict described above, for instance, the commission consisted of the local bishop Abraham Wojna, the Vilnius voivode Krzysztof Radziwiłł, the Mścisław voivode Mikołaj Kiszka, the Chancellor of the Grand Duchy, Albrycht Stanisław Radziwiłł, and the Vice Chancellor, Stefan Pac.[25]

A similar development can be seen in private towns, apart from one significant difference. A good illustration is provided in the privilege for the Jewish community in Kiejdany. The document states: »On no account should Jewish cases be brought before the town court, but they should be judged by the castle court according to the Jewish privileges and laws of the Grand Duchy of Lithuania.«[26] The Jews were thus excluded from municipal jurisdiction, while they were, however, directly responsible to the court of the town owner. This rule was introduced by a general privilege granted to the nobility in 1539, which is seen as one of the most important privileges for the development of the Jewish legal position in the Polish-Lithuanian Commonwealth.[27]

In practice, Jews were judged by a different person in every single private town. Officials of the noble lord who managed the towns were generally responsible for jurisdiction over the Jews. In every estate they had different tasks, which were adjusted to the local situation and referred to by different titles. In Slutzk, which belonged to the Radziwiłł family, special officials, called *podstarosta* (vice-major) or *ekonom generalny* (general steward), were responsible for the Jewish jurisdiction. In Shklov, by comparison, which belonged to the Czartoryski family, the same obligation was given to the governor of the city.[28]

25 Lithuanian Metrika/Metryka Litewska (hereafter ML), vol. 111, 718; see also concerning other commissions ML, vol. 312, 8; ML, vol. 312, 89; ML, vol. 176, 119–120; AGAD, AR XXIII, teka 32, plik 3, 643. Stanisław Albrycht Radziwiłł, the Chancellor of the Duchy, who took part in the Vilnius commission in 1636, described his activity as following: »My komisarze królewscy doprowadziliśmy do zgody magistrat wileński z Żydami w sprawie wznieconego tumultu. Aby jednak sine było okazji do podobnych ekscesów staraliśmy się w domu wojewody znaleźć sposób na zapewnienie bezpieczeństwa. Ale nieobecność biskupa zmusiła nas do odłożenia tej sprawy do następnego dnia.« Albrycht S. Radziwiłł, *Pamiętniki o dziejach w Polsce*, vol 1. (1632–1636), eds. Adam Przyboś and Roman Żelewski (Warszawa: PIW, 1980), 561.

26 Stefan Gąsiorowski, »Żydzi w Kiejdanach w XVII i XVIII w. Rekonesans badawczy,« in *Małżeństwo z rozsądku*, 73–87, here 85.

27 Teller, »Telling the Difference,« 119.

28 Adam Kaźmierczyk, Żydzi w dobrach prywatnych w świetle sądowniczej i administracyjnej praktyki dóbr magnackich w wiekach XVI–XVII (Kraków: Księgarnia Akademicka, 2002), 93.

In the Grand Duchy of Lithuania, Jewish dependence on municipal jurisdiction was very rare. The relatively late adoption of Magdeburg Law and, to an even greater extent, a weak burgher community can be seen as the most important factors that contributed to the preservation of Jewish juridical independence from the Christian burghers.[29]

In contrast to the royal cities, the appeal system in the privately owned estates was much more complicated. In Slutzk, the jurisdiction of the office of the *ekonom generalny* served the Jews as the court of appeals. At the same time, the Jews had the right of appeal to the owner of the city. However, due to the fact that Ludwika Karolina Radziwiłł, the owner of the town, first married Frederic William of Brandenburg and, after his death, Charles III Philip Elector of the Palatinate, and lived in the Holy Roman Empire, this privilege was limited.[30] In contrast to Slutzk, Jews in Shklov had a limited right to appeal. They were allowed to go to the town lord only in vital cases.[31]

The regulations of the Third Lithuanian Statute were established as legally binding law through the Jewish privileges in the Grand Duchy of Lithuania. Furthermore, the application of Magdeburg Law was prohibited in many documents. In the present context it has to be stressed that the application of the Third Lithuanian Statute was also significant for the social position of the Jews. As mentioned above, Jews had the same position as nobles in court trials with burghers. This is supported by other examples, the first being the status of the Jews who converted to Christianity. The Statute stipulated that »if a Jewish man or a Jewish woman joins the Christian Church, every such person and their descendants should be recognized as noble.«[32] Scholarly opinion is still divided about whether this ruling was really put into practice. Doubts arise because the law quoted above was introduced in the paragraphs describing punishments for all kinds of criminal cases. The sentence about the converts seems to be taken out of context. Due to the lack of sufficient source materials it is almost impossible to find examples of converted Jews. Some scholars have maintained that this privilege never functioned in practice.[33] However, Jakub Goldberg's assumption

29 Concerning the application of the Magdeburg law in the Grand Duchy of Lithuania, see Bardach, »Ustrój miast na prawie magdeburskim,« 73–119. By contrast, cases of Jewish dependence on the Municipal Courts were known in Crown Poland, see Kaźmierczyk, *Żydzi w dobrach prywatnych*, 27–40.

30 Ibid., 127.

31 Ibid., 93.

32 »A jeśliby który Żyd albo Żydówka do wiary chrześcijańskiej przystąpili tedy każda taka osoba i potomstwo ich za szlachcica poczytani być mają« Statut Wielkiego Księstwa Litewskiego (Wilno: Nakładem Wileńskiego Towarzystwa Topograficznego, 1819), chapter 12, part 7.

33 See Marceli Janecki, Erhielten die Juden in Polen durch die Taufe den Adelstand (Berlin: J. Sittenfeld, 1888); Jerzy Michta, »Nobilitacje Żydów litewskich w

that it was a law that was in fact used very rarely seems to be more plausible, because the few known cases from the second half of the 18th century are not sufficient to confirm the hypothesis that it never was used.[34]

The second example was the punishment for killing or injuring a Jew, which was exactly the same as for killing or injuring a noble.[35] The Jews thus had a higher social position than Christian townsfolk, as the punishment for killing a Christian burgher was less severe. Contemporaries were well aware of the significance of this privilege. In a Jewish legend from the 18th century about Saul Wahl, who was supposedly king of Poland for a day, it was mentioned among the most important Jewish privileges in the Grand Duchy of Lithuania. According to the legend, it was indeed issued by the Jewish king Saul Wahl.[36]

The significance of the application of the Third Lithuanian Statute can also be shown using the example of the Jewish oath, as the Polish version of the Magdeburg Law included a number of insulting elements, which were absent in the Third Lithuanian Statute.[37] Many Jewish privileges confirmed the rules of the Lithuanian Statute. These documents often state that Jewish oaths had to be consistent with the Jewish religion.[38] Jewish internal jurisdiction also has to be mentioned as an important legal authority. Every kind of internal litigation had to be judged in Jewish courts; the Third Lithuanian Statute even allowed them to judge cases of murder.[39] However, this was limited in practice by local Jewish privileges, as in Birże by Ludwika Karolina Radziwiłł in the second half of the 17th century:

XV–XVIII w.« in Miasta ludzie, instytucje, znaki. Księga jubileuszowa ofiarowana prof. Bożeny Wyrozumskiej, ed. Zenon Piech (Kraków: Towarzystwo Naukowe Societas Vistulana, Instytut Historii UJ, 2008), 369–375.

34 Jakub Goldberg, »Die getauften Juden in Polen-Litauen im 16.–18. Jahrhundert: Taufe, soziale Umschichtung und Integration,« *Jahrbücher für Geschichte Osteuropas* 30 (1982): 161–183; David Frick, »Jews and Others in Seventeenth Century Wilno: Life in the Neighborhood,« *Jewish Studies Quarterly* 12 (2005): 8–42, here 33–34.

35 Statut Wielkiego Księstwa Litewskiego, chapter 12, part 7.

36 Concerning the Saul Wahl legend, see Tsvi Hirsch Edelman, *Gdulat Shaul* (London, 1854); Majer Bałaban, *Skizzen und Studien zur Geschichte der Juden in Polen* (Berlin: L. Lamm, 1911), 26–31; Philipp Bloch, »Die Sage vom Saul Wahl dem Eintagskönig von Polen,« *Zeitschrift der Historischen Gesellschaft für die Provinz Posen*, 4 (1889): 234–258; Moshe Rosman, *How Jewish is Jewish History?* (Oxford: Littman Library of Jewish Civilisation, 2007), 156–158.

37 Kaźmierczyk, *Żydzi w dobrach prywatnych*, 122–123.

38 Goldberg, Jewish Privileges in the Polish Commonwealth, no. 58; ML, vol. 118, 169.

39 »Gdyby Żyd Żyda na śmierć zabił, ranił, albo i zbił tedy o tym sąd i skazanie o tym ma być uczynione według prawa i przywilejów ich.«. Statut Wielkiego Księstwa Litewskiego, chapter 12, part 7.

> *Interea* [among others], it is ordered that Jews should not judge criminal cases among themselves as they belong to the castle court's jurisdiction, except matters of the Jewish religion which are to be resolved in their own courts, as is the case in other towns where Jews reside.[40]

Lastly, it is crucial to remember that the *Va'ad medinat Lita* was also accepted by the king as a court of appeal.[41] The application of the legislation also has to be taken into consideration when analyzing the issue of juridical sources. A closer investigation of different court sources shows that the written law was not always applied in practice. Still, differences between the 17th and the 18th century have to be noted. It seems that the written law was observed more conscientiously in the 17th century. Many court sources attest to trials in which Jews enforced their juridical rights.[42] In the 18th century, the situation changed and Jewish juridical privileges were no longer observed as conscientiously, with Jewish cases present in each kind of court. Jewish trials were held in the municipal courts, with even the Lithuanian Tribunal imposing sentences. Processes in which Jews brought Christians up on charges in what was deemed to be the wrong court – something typical for the 17th century – occurred very rarely in the 18th century. In fact, Jews often used Christian courts for internal litigation.[43] It seems that there were many reasons for this development. Firstly, it can be seen as a sign of assimilation of the Jews into the social and juridical system. As they mostly lived in towns, they had the same economic privileges and used the same courts as Christian burghers. Secondly, in non-Jewish courts, procedures and verdicts appeared to be more advantageous for Jews. Due to the crisis in the Jewish *kehilah*, Jews often complained that the Jewish courts were too expensive and that the judges were not fair.[44]

40 »Interea nakazuje się Żydom, aby [...] criminalia między sobą nie sądzili, bo te do nich nie należą ale do dworu krom spraw i deferencji zakonnych między nimi zachodzących, które im wolno samym rozsądzać i terminować według zwyczaju inszych miast, gdzie Żydzi mieszkają.« LMAB, f. 25, no. 167, 381.

41 ML, vol. 119, 73.

42 ML, vol. 319, 526; ML, vol. 146, 71.

43 ML, vol. 159, 95.

44 Lithuanian State Historical Archives/Lietuvos valstybės istorijos archyvas (hereafter LVIA), fond/f. (collection) 1280, signature/sign. 2070 (October 10, 1717).

Taxes – »taxes will be levied on every Jewish house in town, just like on other townsmen's houses«

The taxes and duties that Jews paid fall into two groups, the first being state taxes. Among these the Jewish poll tax (*pogłówne żydowskie*) was the most significant, while the »return tax« (*powrotne*) was of minor importance. As for the other state taxes, the Jews had to pay, together with all other state citizens, the hearth tax (*podymne*) and the general poll tax (*pogłówne generalne*).[45] City taxes and duties are especially significant for this analysis. A more detailed examination reveals that the text of the general privilege did not introduce any binding principle and that, »taxes will be levied on every Jewish house in town, just like on other townsmen's houses; Jews are not liable for other duties like the donativum[46] [...] and if they have contracts with the burghers, they should pay accordingly.«[47]

As a further analysis of examples from different places has shown, there was no generally applicable system. The Jews paid different taxes in every town and sometimes even the individual systems changed over time. In cases where the Jewish community was important and the Christian burghers weak, the Jews often succeeded in receiving tax exemptions. For instance in Grodno the community received a separate privilege in the form of an exemption from the military tax (*hiberna*), originally paid to support the army during the winter in ecclesiastical and royal estates, and later a permanent tax paid to the commander or the army *hetman*.[48]

Generally speaking, the Jews had to pay the rent (*czynsz*) for their houses in every city, but a slight difference between royal and private towns must be noted: In royal towns the Jews paid exactly the same rent as the Christian burghers,[49] whereas in the private towns of the second half of the 18th century a new »Jewish

45 Anna Filipczak-Kocur, *Skarbowość Rzeczypospolitej 1587–1648* (Warszawa: Wydawnictwo Sejmowe, 2006), 258; Roman Rybarski, *Skarb i pieniądz za Jana Kazimierza, Michała Korybuta oraz Jana III* (Warszawa: TNW, 1939), 214–235; Henryk Wisner, *Rzeczpospolita Wazów III. Sławne Państwo Wielkie Księstwo Litewskie* (Warszawa: Neritron IH PAN, 2008), 226.

46 A general tax for merchants.

47 »z domów tych, które w miastach mają podatki powinni dawać zwyczajne, iako inni mieszczanie innszym powinnościom miejskim nie zwyczajnym jako donativum nie podlegają [...], albo gdzie pakta z mieszczany mają, tedy podług ich płacić powinni.« AVAK, vol. 5, 304 (October 19, 1744).

48 ML, vol. 149, 492–497.

49 AGAD, Archiwum Roskie/Roś Archive, sygnatura (file) 831.

rent« was introduced. Jews henceforth paid more than Christians, but at the same time they were exempted from all personal duties.[50]

This process was typical for small towns, whereas in medium-sized private towns the old identical rent was paid till the end of the 18th century. In every town the buildings that were used for religious services, e.g. synagogues, ritual baths, were exempted from any tax. Usually these exemptions were introduced into the local privileges for Jewish communities as in the case of Stołpce:

> Jews from Stołpce have asked me for permission to build a synagogue and a cemetery for the purpose of their religious education and services, and I hereby grant it to them seeing that the cause is right [...] I also allow them to use a garden two *morgen* in size on the outskirts of the town [...] where they can bury their deceased, build their school and their baths. From this day on, in perpetuity, they are released from any kind of tax and obligation for the use of this land.[51]

It is worth remembering that this principle was introduced for every kind of religious institution, both Jewish and Christian. Therefore, in terms of taxation, Jewish synagogues and Christian churches were treated equally.[52]

The second important group of taxes was connected to the economic activity of the Jews. Taxes were paid, for example, for the right to produce and sell alcoholic beverages (*czopowe, szelężne*) and to trade (*donativum kupieckie*). Two general principles were introduced with regard to these taxes: First, in some towns the Jews paid a part of all taxes, proportional to the number of Jews living in the town. In Slutzk for instance, in the first half of the 17th century Jews constituted about one third of all city inhabitants so that they paid one third of all city taxes and duties. In the second half of the 17th and in the 18th century, the rapid demographic growth of the Jewish population contributed to a conflict with the Christian burghers, who tried to increase the Jewish share of the general taxes.[53] The second principle was that, instead of paying the tax, the Jews paid a

50 Teller, *Kesef, koaḥ*, 51; Adam Teller, »The Legal Status of the Jews on the Magnate Estates of Poland-Lithuania in the Eighteenth Century,« *Gal-Ed* 15–16 (1997): 41–65, here 48.

51 »Ci Żydzi stołpeccy wnieśli prośbę do mnie aby wolno szkołę dla ich nabożeństwa i ogród dla chowania ciał zmarłych Żydów mieć widząc tedy rzecz słuszną pozwoliłem im szkołę pobudować w mieście Stołpcach [...] dwa place dołączam także na ogród dwa morgi puste za miastem [...] na mogiłki dałem Żydom łaźnie i kompalnie na tychże dwóch placach przy szkole [...] z których to zajętych szkołę i ogrodem placów [...] i tej łaźni od daty tego kwitu uwalniam ich na potomne czasy od płacenia czynszów i wszelkich składanek.« Czartoryski Library Krakow, Manuscript Collection/Biblioteka Książąt Czartoryskich Kraków, Dział Rękopisów, no. 9219.

52 Abba Gomer, Beiträge zur Kultur- und Sozialgeschichte des Litauischen Judentums im 17. und 18. Jahrhundert (Köln: F. W. Fretlöh, 1930), 5.

53 AGAD, AR XXIII, teka 134, plik 1; AR XXII, teka 154, plik 5.

fixed contribution to the city council, which paid the tax money from the whole city into the state treasury. One such example was Vilnius, where the contribution was introduced in the 1630s, with the Jews there paying 300 zloty annually. It was not long, however, before the amount was raised to 600 zloty as a result of a conflict with the Christians. After paying this contribution the Jews were liberated from all taxes connected to their economic activity. All other direct taxes, as for instance the *donativum*, were paid only by Christian burghers.[54]

Personal obligations were also connected to the taxes. Military service was the first and most important obligation that the Jews had to bear together with other inhabitants. In Slutzk and Vilnius, the Jews were organized into units in the same way as the Christians. Once a year they had to take part in military displays, in which every unit had to present their weapons. Together with the Christians, they had to take care of buildings important for the defense of the town.[55] Also connected to military service was the aforementioned *hiberna tax.*[56] However, while Jews in Crown Poland paid this tax, it is not certain whether Lithuanian Jews did so as well. My own research has shown that not every Jewish community in Lithuania contributed to it.[57] The cities of Brześć and Grodno had a separate privilege, which exempted the Jews from the tax.[58] Sometimes the Jews had to provide accommodation (*stacje*) to soldiers, members of parliament, or emissaries. This obligation was significant in the capital city of Vilnius as it was the place where the Sejm and the Lithuanian Tribunal met. During their sessions, delegates there were lodged in burgher homes, whether Christian or Jewish.

The obligation to deliver money to the town's owner (*podwody*) should also be listed among personal duties. The representatives of the community were responsible for the transfer of the money collected in the city to the main treasury of the private owner and to the state treasury. Due to the Jews' economic activity and their basic economic skills it was a very common Jewish obligation,

54 Maria Łowmiańska, »Wilno przed najazdem moskiewskim 1655 roku,« in *Dwa doktoraty z Uniwersytetu Stefana Batorego w Wilnie* (Poznań: Wydawnictwo Poznańskie, 2005), 151–329, here 170.

55 Anatol Hryckiewicz, »Milicje miast magnackich na Białorusi i Litwie w XVI–XVIII wieku,« *Kwartalnik Historyczny* 77 (1970): 47–61, here 50.

56 About the hiberna tax, see Michał Nycz, Geneza reform skarbowych Sejmu Niemego. Studium z dziejów skarbowo-wojskowych z lat 1697–1717 (Poznań: PTPN, 1938), 35–47.

57 Maria Cieśla, *Żydzi w Wielkim Księstwie Litewskim*, 101.

58 Maurycy Horn, *Powinności wojenne Żydów w XVI i XVII wieku* (Warszawa: PWN, 1978), 40; ML, vol. 149, 492–497; AVAK, vol. 5, 161.

in Slutzk as elsewhere. However, as many documents indicate they employed local peasants to take care of the collection.[59]

As special attention has to be paid to the many small private towns, it is worth bearing in mind that in the Grand Duchy of Lithuania, most of them had a semi-agrarian character. The majority of the towns' inhabitants were involved in agriculture and, at the same time, had to carry out some farming work for the towns' owners.[60] Jews were always exempted from this obligation.[61] A quotation from a privilege issued by Hetman (military commander) Stanisław Denhoff on 20 April 1725 for the Jewish community of the private town of Stołpce sheds light on this issue: »I release them [the Jews] from all the duties that the burghers of my court of Kowalewszczyzna have to fulfill: from obligations of delivering mail and harvesting, filling the dikes, working in the granary, and repairing the bridges.«[62] In summing up the analysis of the tax and obligation system it should be pointed out that, in most cases, Jewish and Christian taxpayers were treated in the same way. A clear tendency to tax Jews and Christians equally is documented for many towns. In addition to taxes paid to the state and to the town owners, Jews paid internal taxes as well. Among the most significant of these were the tax for the support of Jewish autonomous institutions (*skhum*), the payment for all kinds of professional activity *(ḥazaka)*, and a tax for selling and buying products (*korobka*). Other taxes do not merit closer consideration in this context as they tended to be less important for the subject discussed.[63]

59 AGAD, AR XXIII, teka 133; AVAK, vol. 28, no. 145.

60 Concerning the specific characteristics of Lithuanian towns, see Jerzy Ochmański, »W kwestii agralnego charakteru miast WXL w XVI,« in *Studia historica w 35 lecie pracy naukowej Henryka Łowmiańskiego*, eds. Aleksander Gieysztor et al., (Warszawa: PWN, 1958), 279–295.

61 ML, vol. 159, 380–381; ML, vol. 149, 738–741.

62 »uwolniłem ich wszystkich od powinności tych które mieszczanie moje mają do dworu mego Kowalewszczyzny pełnią to jest od podwód odprawowania posyłek listownych od tłok latem do żniwa od gwałtu pospolitego do zasypywania grobel stawów od robienia spichlerzów i od poprawowania mostów na rzekach od tego wszystkiego uwalniam.« Czartoryski Library Krakow, Manuscript Collection, no. 9219.

63 Concerning internal Jewish taxation, see Gomer, *Beiträge zur Kultur- und Sozialgeschichte*, 25–26; Israel Susis, »Der yidisher seym in Lite un Vaysrusland in zayn gezetsgeberisher tetikkayt loyt zayne protokoln 1623–1761,« *Tsaytshrift*, 1928, no. 2–3: 1–73, here 14–15. See also Judith Kalik, *Scepter of Judah: The Jewish Autonomy in the Eighteenth-Century Crown Poland* (Leiden–Boston: Brill, 2009), 17.

Artisans and economic activity – »They can enjoy all liberties (...) of trade«

The last of the issues to be discussed here are the laws that influenced the economic activity of the Jews, with such rules introduced both in the general city privileges and in Jewish privileges. Formal agreements with municipal councils were of special importance.[64] Generally, the Jews enjoyed many of the rights that the Christian city burghers had. Among them, exemption from customs, the right to use wood from the nearby forest (*wychody*), and the right to meadow use were particularly significant.[65] Other regulations were introduced by the Jewish privileges as well. The general privilege for Lithuanian Jewry stated:

> They can enjoy all liberties, *in genere et in specie*, of trade [...] if there are any artisans among them, they are allowed to work freely in the professions they have learned but they should not be accepted into guilds.[66]

With regard to this quotation, it must be stressed that the Jews had the right to work in every profession, especially in trade and artisanship. Nevertheless, other types of sources must be analyzed in order to show the nature of the legal practice. The economic activity of the Jews was one of the areas that were most strictly limited. It was quite common for conflict over Jewish economic activity to break out shortly after the formation of a Jewish community. Ultimately, Jews and Christians had to reach an agreement, which in almost every case limited Jewish economic activity. In some cases, this process of limitation took a long time. In Vilnius, for instance, the first limitations were introduced in the first half of the 17th century. However, the struggle continued through the second half of the 18th century. In the first years of the 18th century, seventeen cases between Jews and the city burghers – represented by the city council or the guilds – concerning Jewish economic rights were heard by royal courts. Limitations were

64 At the end of the 18th century the formal agreements became the basis of the Jewish settlement in Polish-Lithuanian cities. See Jerzy Michalski, »Problem ludności żydowskiej w polskiej opinii publicznej w pierwszym dwudziestoleciu panowania Stanisława Augusta Poniatowskiego,« in Jerzy Michalski, *Studia Historyczne z XVIII i XIX wieku*, vol. 1 (Warszawa: Stentor, 2007), 104–123; Idem, »Sejmowe projekty reform położenia ludności żydowskiej w Polsce w latach 1782–1792«, in: Ibid., 305–323; Teller, »Telling the Difference,« 131.

65 ML, vol. 114, 282; ML, vol. 118, 169; ML, vol. 118, 219; Henryk Łowmiański, »Wychody miast litewskich,« in Henryk Łowmiański and Maria Łowmiańska, *Dwa doktoraty z Uniwersytetu Stefana Batorego w Wilnie* (Poznań: Wydawnictwo Poznańskie, 2005), 110–147. See also Stanisław Grodziski, *Obywatelstwo w szlacheckiej Rzeczypospolitej* (Kraków: UJ, 1963), 138–139.

66 »Wszystkie wolności in genere et in specie onym nadane jako to na: wolne handle, [...] Rzemieślniki, którzykolwiek są między Żydami jakie kto z nich rzemiosło umie wolno im robić bez przeszkody wszelakiej a do cechu należeć nie mają.« AVAK, vol. 5, 304.

introduced in several areas. First, the Jews were not allowed to trade in certain products:

> They are not to trade in the following products: salt, rye, flax, seeds, hemp, oil, wine, herring, wax, iron, silk, tin plate, steel, linen cloth more expensive than six zloty, expensive belts, Turkish cloth, and goods more expensive than plain woolen cloth (*falandysz*).[67]

All products listed in this quotation were crucial to Lithuania's foreign trade.[68] The merchandise of the Jewish merchants was further limited by the artisans' guilds. Generally, Jews were not allowed to trade goods produced by the members of artisans' guilds such as shoes and caps.[69] Second, restrictions on the number of Jewish market stalls and shops were very common, which can be illustrated with the example of Vilnius: Jews could have market stalls in the Jewish quarter of the city, while in other areas only some products could be sold.[70] In a 1732 agreement between the city council and the elders of the Jewish community, the Jews were reminded that they »should not bring any groceries, sugar, or other merchandise out to the streets, market squares, or courts. The foregoing applies also to people pretending to work for the nobles as advisors (*faktorzy*).«[71] Third, a limitation to the market time for Jews was introduced in some towns; in Grodno, for example, Jews were allowed to trade only after ten in the morning.[72]

The situation of Jewish artisans was different. Generally, only people who were members of artisan guilds, which were indeed also religious and professional organizations barred to Jews, could work as artisans. Nevertheless, some Jewish artisans did work in the towns. Generally speaking, Jews were allowed to work in professions that required a Jewish religious background in order to meet the needs of the community, for instance butchers, who had to observe the rules of ritual butchering (*sheḥitah*), and tailors, who were prohibited from mixing

67 »Towarami nie handlowali solą, żytem, lnem, siemieniem, pienką, woskiem, olejem, winem, śledziami, żelazem, stalą, blachą, jedwabiem, jedwabnymi materiami, suknem nad złotych sześć każdego waloru, pasami drogimi, oponami, ubraniami tureckimi [...] towarów droższych nad falendysz prosty nie sprzedawali.« ML, vol. 413, 413 (January 28, 1752).

68 Klausner, *Toldot ha-kehilah ha-ivrit be-Vilna,* 10.

69 *Akty cechów wileńskich 1495–1759*, eds. Henryk Łowmiański, Maria Łowmiańska, Stanisław Kościałkowski and Jan Jurkiewicz (Poznań: Wydawnictwo Poznańskie), nos. 96 and 280; ML, vol. 398, 285–292.

70 Klausner, *Toldot ha-kehilah ha-ivrit be-Vilna,* 10.

71 »towarów po rynku, ulicach przedmieściach, pałacach, dworach, korzeni, cukrów, et in generis kupieckich towarów nosić nie powinni etiam pod pretekstem niesienia za kimś faktorii czynić nie mają.« LVIA, Senej Aktai/Old Acts 4761, 1214.

72 ML, vol. 408, 48.

linen and wool (*sha'atnez*).[73] Jewish artisans also worked in professions that did not have a guild. Many privileges stated that »Jews can work as artisans and learn artisan professions, especially professions without a guild.«[74] Another method allowed Jews to produce only for the internal Jewish market, as it was stated in the privilege for tailors in Vilnius: »They are not allowed to manufacture, repair, or rework Polish or any other Christian dress, either for men or for women, in their workshops.«[75]

However, as closer analysis has revealed, the status of Jewish artisans did in fact change. A common practice in the late 17th century was to allow Jews to work in a chosen profession for Christians in return for payment, for which the tailors' guild in Grodno is a typical illustration. In 1649, the artisans' guilds came to an agreement with the Jewish community. Under the terms of this agreement, Jewish tailors, cap makers, and furriers were allowed to trade their goods after paying a fee to the artisan's guild. Additionally, Jews were allowed to hire Christian assistants.[76] Similar regulations were introduced to other towns such as Brześć, where this affected the butchers' guild, as in Vilnius the musicians' and medical guilds.[77]

Analyzing the issue of Jewish economic activity, we need to differentiate between private and royal towns. It seems that the differences were very significant in this area. Firstly, limitations to Jewish trade were very rare in private towns. Slutzk is a good case in point as a place where Jews had unlimited opportunity to trade.[78] Restrictions were imposed only on Jewish agents or brokers, who connected foreign merchants with the local ones. The group of Jewish brokers grew in the second half of the 17th century as a result of the pauperization of the Jewish population. The owner of the town thus decided that no more than two Jewish agents should work in Slutzk.[79]

73 Akty cechów wileńskich 1495–1759, nos. 176 and 187.

74 »rzemiosła, w których bywają Żydzi ćwiczeni, a zwłaszcza tych, których nie ma cechów wolno robić.« See as well the privilege for artisans in Mińsk: »gdzie cechy od antecessorów naszych uprzywilejowane i od nas potwierdzone nigdzie Żydzi rzemiosła cyrulickiego publice ani privatum nie zażywają.« Ibid., no. 192.

75 »Nie mają sukien Żydzi, w których chrześcijanie tak Polacy, jako cudzoziemcy chodzą oboi płci na warsztatach swoich rabiać i przerabiać żadnym sposobem i żadnym obyczajem wymyśliwszy albo wymyślając robić.« *Akty cechów wileńskich 1495–1759*, nos. 176 and 187.

76 Mark Vishnitser [Wischnitzer], »Evrei remeslnik i tsekhovaia organizatsiia,« in *Istoriia evreiskogo naroda*, vol. 11, 290.

77 Rywka Notik, »Tsu der geshikhte fun handverk bay litvisher idn,« *YIVO-Bleter* (1936): 107–118, here 112–113; Vishnitser, »Evrei remeslnik,« 290; ML, vol. 362, 244–245; *Akty cechów wileńskich 1495–1759*, nos. 376, 570, 700 and 804.

78 AGAD, AR XXIII, teka 134, plik 1, 272–273.

79 AGAD, AR XXIII, teka 154, plik 5, 307–337; AR XXIII, teka 138, plik 3, 25.

It seems that artisans also had a much better position in private towns. This is illustrated by a quotation from the privilege for the town of Kiejdany: »Jews working in artisan professions should join guilds, pay the dues, and obey every rule and law of the guild, or else they will lose the right to work in the profession.«[80] Artisans' guilds open to Jews were characteristic for every town that belonged to the Protestant Radziwiłł family, with the result that Jews could work in any profession there. However, the question whether the same principle was introduced to other private towns in Lithuania remains unanswered.

Analyzing the limitation of Jewish economic activity, one has to bear in mind that most restrictions were not in fact introduced in practice. Vilnius is a good case in point: As mentioned above the rules in the capital city were very restrictive. However, one should note that Jewish merchants and artisans continued to work there nevertheless. As every few years things changed, with new limitations being introduced and old ones removed, one is tempted to conclude that these regulations were quite temporary.

Lastly, some other issues have to be mentioned that distinguished Jewish from Christian town dwellers, as for instance the limitation of settlement, the *ḥazakah* rights. It is worth remembering that according to many privileges and agreements Jews were not allowed to settle anywhere in town, and Christian burghers especially tried to limit the settlement of Jews in the market squares. However, as the research carried out by Adam Teller and David Frick has shown, this was not translated into practice.[81] Jewish settlement was limited not only by Christians, but by the Jewish communities as well. Every Jew who wanted to settle down and work in a given community had to receive the *ḥazakah*. Due to the high payments connected to this right not every Jew could afford it.[82]

80 »Żydzi też jakimkolwiek się rzemiosłem bawiący, do cechu tegoż rzemiosła należeć składanki czynić i wszelkich postanowionych porządków i powinności postrzegać pod utraceniem rzemiosła mają.« in *Lietuvos magdeburginių miestų privilegijos ir aktai*, vol. 3: Kedainiai, ed. Antanas Tyla (Vilnius: Lietuvos Istorijas Institutas, 2002), no. 41.

81 Teller, *Kesef, koaḥ*, 57; Frick, »Jews and Others,« 8–42; Jurgita Šiaučiūnaitė-Verbickienė, »The Jewish Living Space in the Grand Duchy of Lithuania: Tendencies and Ways of Formation,« in *Jewish Space in Central and Eastern Europe: Day to Day History*, ed. eadem (Cambridge: Scholars Publishing, 2007), 7–27.

82 Concerning *ḥazakah* rights, see: Ignacy Schiper, *Dzieje handlu żydowskiego na ziemiach polskich* (Kraków: KAW, 1990), 144–145; Mojżesz Siemiatycki, *Prawa obywatelstwa w gminach żydowskich w Polsce w XVII i XVIII wieku*. Praca Magisterska, Archiwum Żydowskiego Instytutu Historycznego (ŻIH), sygnatura/sygn. (file) 7/11, 5–7; Louis I. Rabinowitz, *The Herem Hayyishub. A Contribution to the Medieval Economic History of the Jews* (London: Edward Goldston, 1945).

Considering the position of the Jews, it has to be taken into account that Jewish society was not homogenous. This is especially true for royal towns, where the Jewish advisers of the Crown (*faktorzy królewscy*) lived and were under direct jurisdiction of the king due to the services they rendered to the royal court. Sometimes, especially in the 18th century, they were exempted from the jurisdiction of Jewish courts. Often they were liberated from all payments and obligations; and what is more, their economic activity was not limited.[83] The king's advisers thus differed from other Jews in terms of their legal position, jurisdiction, economic activity, and social position.

Conclusion

In summary, let us revisit the significant features that marked the position of the Jews and the differences between the positions of the Christian and Jewish townsfolk. Firstly, the Jews had no general political rights; their public activity was restricted to the Jewish communities. Secondly, they differed from the Christian burghers in terms of jurisdiction and thus depended on the king or his officials in royal towns. This was a contrast to private estates, where the owner of the town and his officials were responsible for the Jewish jurisdiction. Furthermore, Christian and Jewish burghers were subject to different laws, the Christians to Magdeburg Law and the Jews to the Third Lithuanian Statute. In contrast, the analysis of the tax system has shown a clear tendency toward the harmonization of the Jewish and Christian systems. Thus in many places Jews had to pay exactly the same taxes as Christians. Finally, comparing the terms of economic activity of the Jewish and Christian burghers one has to bear in mind that Jewish traders and artisans were limited in their professional activity. As the different privileges show, limitations were different in every given city.

In the documents Jews are called citizens or burghers just like the Christians. The Jews lived in the city, where they concentrated their economic activity, but their legal status was not equal to that of the Christian burghers. Scholarly opinion is still divided on whether the Jews constituted a separate, second urban estate.[84] However, one has to bear in mind that Jewish citizenship was not the

83 Maria Cieśla, »Mojżeszowicz, Gordon, Ickowicz: The Jewish Economic Elites in the Grand Duchy of Lithuania (in the 17th and 18th Century),« *Acta Poloniae Historica* 107 (2013): 101–127; Maria Cieśla, »Łazarz Mojżeszowicz przykład żydowskiej kariery w Wielkim Księstwie Litewskim w połowie XVII wieku,« *Kwartalnik Historyczny* 112, no. 4 (2005): 5–29.

84 Teller, »Telling the Difference,« 121; Juliusz Bardach, »Głos w dyskusji,« in Żydzi w dawnej Rzeczypospolitej, Materiały z konferencji ›Autonomia Żydów w Rzeczypospolitej Szlacheckiej‹. Międzywydziałowy Zakład Historii i kultury Żydów w Polsce Uniwersytet Jagielloński 22.–26.9.1989, eds. Andrzej Link-

same as that of the Christians. In most cases, Jews and Christians shared only the same obligations. Some scholars argue that Jewish and Christian burghers constituted two separate urban estates, which differed legally and socially. The Christian one had a privileged position, whereas the Jewish estate enjoyed only limited rights. However, Juliusz Bardach's assumption that the Jews constituted a group outside of every estate seems to be more plausible.[85] It has to be emphasized, nevertheless, that the specific status of the Jews was nothing extraordinary in early modern Lithuanian towns, in which different people lived and every group had its own legal position,[86] its own rights, and its own duties. As an organism, the city could function only if the different groups were to cooperate.

Maria Cieśla

Lenczowki and Tomasz Polański (Wrocław et al.: Zakład Narodowy im Ossolińskich Wydawnictwo, 1991), 344–347, here 345.

85 Bardach, »Głos w dyskusji,« 345.

86 Andrzej B. Zakrzewski, »Rzeczypospolita XVI–XVIII w. Państwem Tatarów,« in *Rzeczypospolita państwem wielu narodowości i wyznań XVI–XVIII w.*, eds. Tomasz Ciesielski and Anna Filipczak-Kocur (Warszawa–Opole: DiG, 2008), 221–231; Gierszewski, *Obywatele miast Polski przedrozbiorowej*, 92. The other example were the Armenians although they lived mostly in Crown Poland and not in the Grand Duchy of Lithuania, see Renata Król-Mazur, *Miasto trzech nacji – studia z dziejów Kamieńca Podolskiego w XVIII w.* (Kraków: Avalon, 2008).

Economic Entanglements and Neighborly Disputes in the Northwest Provinces of the Russian Empire*

For the past fifteen years, historians of the Russian Empire have focused their research on either specific ethnic groups such as Russian Orthodox peasants, Muslims, and Jews or have analyzed vertical interactions between the »state« and the imperial population.[1] As a result, we know very little about how people of diverse backgrounds interacted with one another on a daily basis and we know even less about how they made sense of the world around them. There are two interrelated explanations for this striking omission. The first reason has to do with the organization of archival repositories in the former Soviet Union. Government-related records were preserved and catalogued in official state archives according to the bureaucratic division of government established during the reign of Tsar Alexander I. While it is relatively easy to locate documents on specific ethnic groups by combing through archival inventory lists to find words such as »Jew,« »Muslim,« or »Old Believer,« it is much more time consuming to find sources that reveal the day-to-day encounters between imperial communities. Second, when historians have analyzed interethnic relations, they focused their attention on events that had generated rich paper trails and therefore were easy to locate in the archives. Yet by researching highly visible topics such as pogroms, scandalous trials, and other idiosyncratic historical occurrences, scholars have largely overlooked the ways in which Jews related with their neighbors in periods of time that were not clouded by extreme political and social crisis.

* This is a revised essay that first appeared in *Journal of Modern Jewish Studies* 9, no. 1 (2010): 1–16.

1 See, for example, Robert D. Crews, *For Prophet and Tsar: Islam and Empire in Russia and Central Asia* (Cambridge, MA: Harvard University Press, 2006); Benjamin Nathans, *Beyond the Pale: The Jewish Encounter with Late Imperial Russia* (Berkeley: University of California Press, 2002); and Willard Sunderland, *Taming the Wild Field: Colonization and Empire on the Russian Steppe* (Ithaca, NY: Cornell University Press, 2004).

Drawing on a vast archive of civil court records, this essay sketches out how »neighbors« – that is, those individuals who lived and worked side-by-side with one another in small town settings – utilized the law to mediate everyday disagreements in three distinct contact zones: the neighborhood, the noble estate, and the marketplace.[2] Civil courts provided impartial forums for adjudicating disagreements, and a broad spectrum of the population, whatever their ethnic or religious origin, turned to institutions of legal justice when they were unable or unwilling to settle disputes among themselves.[3] Focusing on the northwest Russian provinces of Vil'na, Grodno, and Kovno (roughly, the territories that comprise present-day Lithuania), this essay analyzes the role that courts and the legal process itself played in the mediation of neighborly disputes between the 1830s and the 1870s.[4] In particular, I examine how Jews and their neighbors used the highly contradictory provisions of imperial law to resolve immovable property disputes, community quarrels, debts, and contractual obligations squarely within the framework of the law. In the multiethnic empire, people continued to develop pragmatic relationships with one another

2 Most of the cases analyzed in this essay are preserved in Lithuanian State Historical Archives/Lietuvos valstybės istorijos archyvas, Vilnius (LVIA), fond (collection, hereafter f.) 447, opis (inventory, hereafter op.) 2–8, beginning in 1832 and ending in the late 1870s. I have identified around 214 civil suits in which Jews appeared as either plaintiffs or defendants (sometimes both). Some of the cases are as short as four pages, whereas others are as long as 245 pages. Typically, the documents are under 100 pages.

3 On popular uses of the court system in the Russian Empire, see, for example, Jane Burbank, *Russian Peasants Go to Court: Legal Culture in the Countryside, 1905–1917* (Bloomington, IN: Indiana University Press, 2004); Cathy A. Frierson, »Rural Justice in Public Opinion: The Volost' Court Debate,« *Slavonic and East European Review* 64, no. 4 (1986): 526–545; Cathy A. Frierson, »›Must Always Answer to the Law …‹: Rules and Responses in the Reformed Volost' Court,« *Slavonic and East European Review* 75, no. 2 (1997): 308–334; and Valerie A. Kivelson, »Muscovite ›Citizenship‹: Rights without Freedom,« *Journal of Modern History* 74 (2002): 465–489. On imperial legal practices, institutions, and reform, see Richard Wortman, *The Development of a Russian Legal Consciousness* (Chicago: University of Chicago Press, 1976); Ekaterina Pravilova, *Zakonnost' i prava lichnosti: Administrativnaia iustitsiia v Rossii (vtoraia polovina xix v.–oktiabr' 1917 g.)* (S.-Peterburg: Izdatel'stvo Obrazovanie-Kul'tura, 2000); and Jörg Baberowski, *Autokratie und Justiz: Zum Verhältnis von Rechtsstaatlichkeit und Rückständigkeit im ausgehenden Zarenreich 1864–1914* (Frankfurt a. M.: Klostermann, 1996).

4 For a perceptive analysis of imperial administrative practices and nationality policies in the northwest provinces, see Darius Staliunas, *Making Russians: Meaning and Practice of Russification in Lithuania and Belarus after 1863* (Amsterdam: Radopi, 2007); and Mikhail Dolbilov, *Russkii krai, chuzhaia vera: Etnokonfessional'naia politika imperii v Litve i Belorussii pri Aleksandre II* (Moskva: Novoe literaturnoe obozrenie, 2010).

based on the distinct economic conditions and residential patterns in which they lived and operated.[5] This is not to suggest that Jews and their neighbors always lived in harmonious coexistence or that quarrels over the most trivial matters never got out of control. But the fact that neighbors articulated and worked out their differences – using the concepts and procedures dictated by the imperial legal system – suggests that, at least in most instances, people adopted practices that allowed them to live together, »if not in peace, then at least in truce.«[6]

In the northwest provinces of the Russian Empire, the lawsuits adjudicated by district or provincial courts represent only a fraction of the total number of the disagreements that took place on a daily basis between neighbors. Scholars working on civil litigation practices in other settings observe that many more disputes are resolved amicably before they ever appear in court.[7] In whatever time or place they live, in other words, people use all possible means to settle their disagreements by negotiating, persuading, and reasoning. While most Jewish neighborly feuds were resolved by informal practices, in the mid-nineteenth century, imperial Russian courts nevertheless provided popular arenas for adjudicating civil suits. This does not mean that trials did not drag on for years, that judges or the local police chiefs could not be bribed, or that the judicial system was a model of operational efficiency. In the 1850s, these and other criticisms made by educated Russians led eventually to the monumental 1864 judicial reform, introducing far-reaching changes at all levels of the legal-administrative system.[8] Yet however problematic and frustrating the imperial legal system may have been, individuals continued to turn to imperial Russian courts to settle neighborly disagreements, in part, because they had few alternatives available to them. What else could they do, to whom could they turn, if a neighbor refused to repay their debts, pay their rent, or fulfill their contractual obligations?

5 For a highly persuasive analysis of civic engagement and activism in an imperial setting, see Michelle U. Campos, *Ottoman Brothers: Muslims, Christians, and Jews in Early Twentieth-Century Palestine* (Stanford, CA: Stanford University Press, 2011).

6 I borrow this phrase from an excellent study of neighborly relations by Bruce H. Mann, *Neighbors and Strangers: Law and Community in Early Connecticut* (Chapel Hill, NC: The University of North Carolina Press, 1987), 163–164.

7 See, for example, Burbank, *Russian Peasants*, 84; and the classic study on informal ways that neighbors settle disputes by Robert C. Ellickson, *Order Without Law: How Neighbors Settle Disputes* (Cambridge, MA: Harvard University Press, 1991).

8 On the 1864 judicial reform, see Wortman, *Russian Legal Consciousness*, 237–242; and Baberowski, *Autokratie und Justiz*, 39–93.

The politics of economic exchanges

Since the early modern era, the development of a wide range of economic relationships between Jews and their neighbors allowed social contacts to broaden. Jews played visible roles in local economies by making and selling alcoholic beverages, trading and delivering various goods and products, and most importantly, managing noble estates.[9] In the Lithuanian portion of the Commonwealth, a handful of noblemen owned as much as ninety percent of the land. Jews performed such vital roles in local economies that they received communal protections, privileges, and support from the wealthy noblemen on whose estates they lived and worked. On several occasions, the lease-contracts signed between Jews and the nobility gave the Jewish leaseholders quite a bit of jurisdiction over the property on the land, as well as over the Christian proprietors (the townspeople, serfs, peasants, and boyars) who lived there. For the vast majority of Jews who lived in small market towns, however, artisanry or commercial trade in either textiles or furs were the preferred occupations. But no matter what economic activities they practiced, Jews and their Christian neighbors did not, as Robert Blobaum has recently put it, lead »separate existences.«[10] In these territories, Jews lived among and worked with a diverse conglomeration of confessional groups – Catholics, Calvinists, Lutherans, and Russian Orthodox, among others. By the end of the eighteenth century, when the Tsarist government acquired the territories that constituted the northwest provinces of the empire, economic contacts permitted Jews to interact with their Christian neighbors on a variety of different levels.

Economic activities had important implications for the types of social contacts and relationships Jews and their neighbors were able to form. Commercial exchanges led to intimate social connections, appreciation of religious

9 The literature on Polish-Jewish relations in the early modern period is quite extensive. See, for example, Jakub Goldberg, »Friends and Strangers: An Outline of the History of Polish-Jewish Relations in the Former Polish Commonwealth.« *Dialectics and Humanism* 1 (1989): 13–31; Moshe J. Rosman, *The Lords' Jews: Magnate-Jewish Relations in the Polish-Lithuanian Commonwealth during the Eighteenth Century* (Cambridge, MA: Harvard University Press, 1990); Magda Teter, *Jews and Heretics in Catholic Poland: A Beleaguered Church in the Post-Reformation Era* (Cambridge: Cambridge University Press, 2006); David Frick, »Jews and Others in Seventeenth-Century Wilno: Life in the Neighborhood,« *Jewish Studies Quarterly* 12 (2005): 8–42; idem, *Kith, Kin, and Neighbors: Communities and Confessions in Seventeenth-Century Wilno* (Ithaca–London: Cornell University Press, 2013); Adam Teller »The Shtetl as an Arena for Polish-Jewish Integration,« *Polin* 17 (2004): 25–40. The journals *Polin* and *Gal-Ed* publish articles on Jewish neighborly relations on a regular basis.

10 *Antisemitism and its Opponents in Modern Poland*, ed. Robert Blobaum (Ithaca, NY: Cornell University Press, 2005), 2.

differences, and even, on occasion, friendships.[11] At the same time, economic activities also helped to produce many of the conflicts between neighbors. The intimacy of daily commercial exchanges led to all sorts of cases over economic matters that were tried and settled in courts of law.[12] These disagreements were usually over civil matters such as contractual obligations, rent, inheritance, debt, and property (broadly conceived). But they also involved issues such as theft of and damage to property; counterfeiting, identity theft, and other acts of dishonesty; as well as insults, fights, and even murder on rare occasions.

The trial transcripts illustrate intense struggle over proprietary rights, confusion over ownership, and uncertainty over contractual obligations and compensation, with many of the cases heard by provincial courts dragging on for years.[13] In Uzhertsy, for example, a small town located in Troksk district, the landowner, Stanislav Antonovich Truzhenskii, sold a plot of land with a small home to Dovid Movshevich Al'per for eighty-four rubles. At the time of the sale, the two men agreed that, if Truzhenskii broke his promise and failed to give Al'per sole possession over the property, the landowner would compensate Al'per twice the amount that he had originally paid for the plot of land. The two men signed the contract on March 8, 1852. After some months had passed, Truzhenskii suddenly declared that the Jew had paid him only twenty-five rubles for the property and decided to levy a fine of 150 rubles. At this time, Truzhenskii also claimed to have reached another, oral agreement with Al'per: that the Jew would pay the landowner twenty-five rubles in rent for every year he resided on the property. When Al'per allegedly failed to pay, Truzhenskii filed a complaint with the Troksk district court on February 8, 1857, almost five years to the date that Truzhenskii first agreed to sell Al'per the property.[14]

During the trial, Al'per disagreed with Truzhenskii's version of the story. Al'per countered that he did, in fact, pay eighty-four rubles for the property. He even offered to give the plot of land and the home back to Truzhenskii if the landowner paid him 168 rubles, twice the amount of the original sale they had agreed upon in the first place. After a rather lengthy five-year delay, the Troksk district court finally ruled that Truzhenskii violated the terms of the agreement

11 Teller, »The Shtetl,« 37.

12 On the importance of economics for analyzing Jewish neighborly relations, see Gershon D. Hundert, »The Implications of Jewish Economic Activities for Christian-Jewish Relations in the Polish-Lithuanian Commonwealth,« in *The Jews in Poland*, ed. Chimen Abramsky et al. (New York: Basil Blackwell, 1986).

13 For similar observation for other settings in early modern and modern Russia, see, for example, Valerie A. Kivelson, *Cartographies of Tsardom: The Land and Its Meanings in Seventeenth-Century Russia* (Ithaca, NY: Cornell University Press, 2006), 46; and Burbank, *Russian Peasants*, 82–118.

14 LVIA, f. 447, op. 2, delo (file, hereafter d.) 7529.

he signed with Al'per in 1852, stipulating that the landowner (or one of his descendents) needed to pay the Jew 168 rubles for the property, as well as 68.25 rubles in court fees. At around the same time the court ruled in Al'per's favor, Truzhenskii passed away from a long illness, and his daughter, Emiliia Stanislavovna Truzhenskaia, decided to file an appeal on behalf of her father. In the appeal, Truzhenskaia claimed that the entire transaction that took place in 1852 was invalid: »The contract my deceased father signed should not be considered valid, since it was not signed in a court of law. For this reason, it should not be considered authentic and serve as proof of any transaction [between my father and Al'per.]« Truzhenskaia, in other words, argued that her father should never have been obligated to pay the 168 rubles in the first place. »The Jew Al'per does not have any legal right to own the home on that plot of land,« the daughter continued, »and consequently does not have any right to build any other additions to the house without consent.« After hearing both testimonies, the Vil'na appellate court ruled on March 19, 1865 in favor of Dovid Movshevich Al'per, awarding him 168 rubles (twice the amount that he had initially paid for the property) and 84.50 rubles in court fees. Moreover, the court stipulated that if Truzhenskaia failed to pay Al'per the entire sum then Al'per would retain sole possession of the property. As far as the rent money that her father failed to collect from Al'per, the court ruled that the oral agreement made between the two men was not valid since it was not signed on stamped government paper.[15]

Although in the northwest provinces, Jewish residence was often concentrated into certain areas, Jews did not live in hermetic isolation or in clearly demarcated communal living quarters.[16] Since the early modern period, Jewish communal leaders and Christian authorities attempted to limit Jewish-Christian contact by forbidding Jews from dwelling in non-Jewish homes and by regulating who could be employed by whom. The Catholic Church worked hard to maintain religious and social boundaries by restricting activities that led to religious negligence, moral corruption, and fraternization.[17] Despite these well-publicized efforts, as Jacob Katz pointed out for a slightly different context, authorities faced all sorts of difficulties regulating social contact between individuals »with whom economic relationships were continuous.«[18] Over the course of the nineteenth century, Jews continued to live in close proximity to

15 Ibid.

16 On neighborly contact in the early modern period, see, for example, Edward Fram, *Ideals Face Reality: Jewish Law and Life in Poland, 1550–1655* (Cincinnati: Hebrew Union College Press, 1997), 30–31; Frick, »Jews and Others,« 10–20; and idem, *Kith, Kin, and Neighbors*, 20–76.

17 Teter, *Jews and Heretics*, 68.

18 Jacob Katz, *Exclusiveness and Tolerance: Studies in Jewish-Gentile Relations in Medieval and Modern Times* (Springfield, NJ: Behrman House, 1961), 9.

Poles, Lithuanians, Germans, and Russians, with whom they socialized and engaged in commercial transactions. And it was precisely these shared communal spaces – the courtyards, homes, and apartment buildings – where so many neighborly disputes took place.

In Vil'na, the largest and most prosperous city in the northwest provinces of the empire, travelers and merchants passing through the city would on occasion rent rooms or apartments from Jews. Even though Jewish communal leaders had forbidden Jews from residing in non-Jewish homes either on a temporary or permanent basis since at least the seventeenth century, both Jews and Christians paid little attention to the regulations and rented rooms from one another.[19] In addition to upsetting prescriptive social norms, these types of living arrangements also caused conflicts on those occasions when the tenants failed to pay their rent on time. On August 8, 1853, for example, Aizik Shevemovich agreed to rent out an apartment for fifty-four rubles to Spiridon Ambelikopulo, an army officer who needed a place to stay in Vil'na. Ambelikopulo, it seems, did not have the entire sum of money, and a local resident by the name of Liudvig Martines served as a witness and guarantor when the two men signed the contract. When Ambelikopulo failed to pay the rent on time, Aizik's son Shloma quickly filed a suit against Martines on behalf of his father. »Since I am poor and have no personal property of my own, I ask the court to stop the proceedings,« Martines pleaded. He suggested that Shavemovich needed to obtain the rent money from the debtor, Spiridon Ambelikopulo, who had already returned to St. Petersburg. Martines could not understand why Shavemovich's son filed a suit against him instead of Ambelikopulo who »earned a salary, was considered well-off in society, and could pay his own debts.« In this case, the court ruled that Liudvig Martines, after having agreed to serve as the official guarantor, needed to respect the letter of the law and pay Aizik Shevemovich the entire sum owed by the army officer, along with an unspecified amount of interest.[20]

Outside of homes and apartment buildings, Jews and their Christian neighbors met, socialized, and feuded in streets and alleyways. In January 1869, a déclassé nobleman, Adol'f Matovskii, roamed the streets of Oshmiany (Vil'na province) in search of someone who would loan him a few rubles. After walking around the town without any luck, Matovskii finally stumbled upon two local moneylenders, Leizer and Itsko, who offered to loan him the money, and suggested that they sign a payment voucher in the amount of sixty rubles in Itsko Shryra's name. As soon as the men signed the voucher, Matovskii claimed that

19 As David Frick points out, since the seventeenth century, Jews also rented rooms and houses from non-Jews, see Frick, »Jews and Others,« 20–21; and idem, *Kith, Kin, and Neighbors*, 37–41.

20 LVIA, f. 447, op. 2, d. 3555.

the Jews not only ran off with the money but also with the signed voucher. Matovskii, it seems, filed a lawsuit against Shryra in hopes of avoiding having to repay his debt: the nobleman insisted that he never received either a signed voucher or the money from the Jew. Shryra, however, disagreed with Matovskii's recollection of the events. He argued that the document was signed at Rafail Vaks's home, and in front of several witnesses, at which time he handed Matovskii the sixty rubles. Matovskii did not know how to sign his own name, and so he asked Venedikt Berkovich, who became one of the key witnesses in the case, to sign the document for him. Although Shryra did not remember what type of money he gave Matovskii (whether coins or paper bills), he did remember that he kept the voucher because the nobleman never asked for it back. Moreover, Shryra also recalled that he did not have the entire amount Matovskii requested, so he proceeded to borrow forty rubles from Vaks in exchange for twelve chairs, two silver spoons, and a large samovar.[21]

Two witnesses testified in the case. The first witness, Iurii Pashkevich, testified that Matovskii pleaded with Shryra to give him the money, but he never actually saw the money exchange hands between the two men, because they walked into an adjoining room of the house to sign the voucher. The second witness, Venedikt Berkovich, produced the most damaging testimony when he declared that Shryra did not give a single kopek to Matovskii. Enraged at Berkovich's testimony, Shryra asked the court to dismiss the evidence, pointing out that both of the witnesses happened to be Matovskii's friends and therefore should not be considered credible. After hearing all the testimony, the court declared that it would not uphold Matovskii's claim. According to Article 402 of the Russian civil law code, the testimony of one witness, Berkovich, was not enough to prove either the guilt or innocence of the defendant.[22]

When compared with other lawsuits filed in the Russian Empire, the disputes between Jews and their neighbors over such issues as land, homes, contractual obligations, and debts proved in no way remarkable. As in many other places, individuals turned to civil courts in hope of protecting their possessions, economic resources, and commodities from unlawful abuse.[23] While the court cases analyzed thus far represent ordinary disagreements that could occur anywhere and between anyone in the empire, the disputes over the management of noble estates could be characterized as typically Jewish. Since the seventeenth century, noblemen leased their estates (both large and small) to Jews, who in

21 LVIA, f. 447, op. 7, d. 1696.

22 Ibid.

23 Burbank makes a similar observation in *Russian Peasants*, 84–87.

turn performed the primary managerial and lease-holding duties.[24] During the nineteenth century, most Jews abandoned lease holding in favor of occupational practices related to the craft and service sectors, and some made considerable sums of money as entrepreneurs. Despite the gradual transformation of Jewish economic life, produced in part by the forced modernization of the imperial economy and the legislation passed by the Russian government, Jews continued to appear before provincial courts to settle their disagreements with estate owners. Unlike the small claims suits over issues such as rent, contractual obligations, or debts, disputes over the management of noble property tended to involve large sums of money (well over 500 rubles), and could be appealed until they reached the Senate, the highest and most powerful court in the Russian Empire.

On April 11, 1864, Kazimir Osip Okushka, a resident of Dunilovichi, signed a three-year contract with Berk Lifshits to manage his estate. According to Okushka's version, Lifshits agreed to receive a salary of 200 rubles per year. As part of the agreement, Lifshits was required to pay Okushka rent, sow fifty-three hectares of land, and feed and maintain in healthy condition fifty cows and thirty sheep and goats. The contract also had three additional clauses: If Lifshits failed to pay the rent on time, he would not be permitted to sell foodstuffs on the property, and Okushka would be within his rights to confiscate all of Lifshits's personal property. If Lifshits did not sow the fifty-three hectares of land, Okushka would be entitled to evict Lifshits from the land without returning any of the rent. And if any of the animals died during the three-year period, Lifshits was obligated to compensate Okushka ten times the amount that he had originally paid for them. Before a year had passed, Okushka filed a complaint with the Vil'na civil court. Okushka claimed that Lifshits failed to honor *any* of the contractual obligations, and therefore sued the Jew for 1,660 rubles since he managed to pay only seventy rubles in rent, sow eighteen out of fifty-three hectares of land, and damage forty-nine out of eighty healthy animals. By the time the complaint was filed, Okushka claimed that Lifshits had vacated the property and refused to give up any of his personal belongings to compensate him for violating the terms of the contract.[25]

Yet Lifshits had a different tale to tell. According to his account, the landowner first asked him to rent the property and devote all his energies to

24 The secondary literature on Jewish lease holding is quite extensive and a bit repetitive. See, for example, Gershon D. Hundert, *Jews in Poland-Lithuania in the Eighteenth Century: A Genealogy of Modernity* (Berkeley: University of California Press, 2004), 38–44; and Adam Teller, »The Legal Status of the Jews on the Magnate Estates of Poland-Lithuania,« *Gal-Ed* 15–16 (1997): 41–63.

25 LVIA, f. 447, op. 2, d. 7842.

maintaining the estate in working order after it had suffered severe economic devastation as a consequence of the liberation of the serfs:

> When I did not agree to the initial terms [to be a lessee], Okushka nevertheless hired me to manage the property because he knew I had talent and because he maintained his permanent residence in Riga and was not able to administer the estate. And since that time, I fulfilled my duties with the utmost diligence, making sure the estate stayed solvent and did not have any unnecessary expenses. But to my misfortune, the harvest last year was not good, and most of the crop remained on the fields, as everyone knows around these parts. And because I had nothing to feed the livestock, the animals began to die off. When the landowner, Okushka, found out about the unfortunate turn of events, he blamed me for the bad harvest and the death of the livestock, withheld my salary (200 rubles), and threatened to sue me, as though his misfortunes were due to my negligence.[26]

Lifshits felt that he should not be held accountable for Okushka's losses, arguing that the contract needed to be dismissed by the court. »I never saw the contract before, agreed to the terms, or signed the document,« Lifshits testified. »Since my name and signature were written by Okushka himself, and since there were no witnesses, all of this proves that he [Okushka] forged the contract.«[27]

The trial began on October 27, 1865. Lifshits defended himself against the accusations, claiming that he served as an administrator of the estate and not as a lessee. He also filed his own petition and countersued Okushka for 200 rubles for the salary that the landowner owed him for managing the estate, as well as for 1,800 rubles for the salary of the men that Lifshits had employed on the estate. The trial continued for over a year, but on November 29, 1866, Okushka filed another petition with the Vil'na civil court. This time, he requested to drop the case due to an unexpected development: Berk Lifshits had just passed away. The case, however, did not come to an end with Lifshits's death. In an attempt to clear his good name and social standing, Okushka filed yet another petition with the court. Standing by the original version of his story, Okushka maintained that Lifshits had never managed the estate and the allegations that he, the landowner, had forged the contract were entirely unjust and untruthful. »The signature can be verified with the signature that was signed on the petition presented [originally] at court,« Okushka pleaded. »And for this sneaky attack on me, he himself should be sued. But because he died, I respectfully ask the court to stop the proceedings, since the slander of the deceased Lifshits no longer affects me.« Okushka only asked that Lifshits's estate pay for the court proceedings. After a number of witnesses were questioned, none of whom could verify the terms of the contractual obligations since no one had seen the two men sign the actual contract, the court ruled, on May 6, 1867, that the case was finally closed.

26 Ibid.
27 Ibid.

Okushka, however, was awarded 1.20 rubles, which was to be paid by Lifshits's estate, for the three sheets of stamped government used during the trial.[28]

In a similar case, in May 1866, Liutsiian Seliava, an estate owner of Polish descent, agreed to sell a home to Konstantin Skrakhovskii, a Jewish homebuilder and real estate manager, for 3,000 rubles. As part of the contractual agreement, Seliava asked Skrakhovskii to pay 400 rubles per year and build a second two-story brick home for 3,000 rubles. Shortly thereafter, Seliava fell ill and decided to undergo a mineral water cure. Skrakhovskii agreed to postpone the closing for six weeks until Seliava returned from his cure on the condition that the landowner pay a 3,000 ruble fine if he failed to honor the agreement. While away, Seliava also asked Skrakhovskii to manage his properties and collect rent monies from the tenants. After Seliava returned from his cure, Skrakhovskii filed a claim with the Vil'na civil court, arguing that, in addition to refusing to honor the agreement, Seliava had borrowed 400 rubles for his own personal use and then moved back into the home that he had originally sold. Seliava, on the other hand, countered that the Jewish homebuilder and real estate manager failed to pay the 3,000 rubles for the first home and wanted a complete account of all the rent monies collected while he was away. For these reasons, Seliava felt no obligation to pay either the 3,000 rubles for the second home or the fine that totaled 3,000 rubles. After a series of appeals lasting almost four years and finally reaching St. Petersburg, the Senate ruled that Seliava violated the terms of the contract, and awarded Skrakhovskii all the money that he was entitled, a total of 8,900 rubles.[29]

In the first half of the nineteenth century, under Alexander I and Nicholas I, most Jews continued to make a living by trading various goods and products, providing credit when credit was in short supply, offering skilled and unskilled labor, working in small workshops, and managing noble estates. But as the empire modernized along economic lines, a new generation of Jews played an increasingly visible role in the newly emerged financial markets, in industrial entrepreneurial activities, and in the trade of large-scale merchandise. By the mid-nineteenth century, a shift in Jewish economic life began to take place, which had important implications for the type of social contacts and economic relationships Jews forged with their Christian neighbors.[30] With more capital at their disposal, Jewish bankers, industrialists, entrepreneurs, and merchants (of

28 Ibid.

29 The case has been preserved in the Institute for Jewish Research, New York (YIVO), RG 12, Box 6, Folder 10 (no pagination).

30 On Jewish entrepreneurship, see Arcadius Kahan, *Essays in Jewish Social and Economic History*, ed. Roger Weiss (Chicago: University of Chicago Press, 1986), 82–100.

various wealth and social status) suddenly found themselves in a position to employ the local population for their own needs.

In Shventsian, a small market town located around eighty-four kilometers north of Vil'na, Isai Getsel' Berkovitch Bak, a Jewish merchant of the second guild, signed a contract with the townsman Evstafia Selitsev to build four general stores for 1,900 rubles (of which 150 rubles would be paid up front). The construction of the stores was scheduled to begin on February 1, 1864, and completed no later than January 1, 1866. In addition, the contract stipulated that if Selitsev did not complete the work on time Bak would be able to fire Selitsev and receive the losses from hiring additional laborers, while Selitsev would be required to return the deposit. Not long after the two men signed the contract, Bak claimed that Selitsev had not completed any of the work, and Bak wasted no time in hiring another skilled laborer to build the four stores. After around seven months had passed since the two men parted ways, Bak suddenly decided to file a lawsuit against Selitsev for 1,407 rubles. The merchant justified the sum by claiming that he lost 1,182 rubles when he was forced to hire the more expensive contractor; that Selitsev never returned the deposit; and that he needed to pay an additional seventy-five rubles in court fees when he signed the new contract.[31]

Selitsev countered by pointing out that Bak repeatedly tried to cheat an »illiterate worker« by handing over only a third of the money he agreed to pay up front. For fifty rubles, Selitsev could neither purchase the required work instruments nor hire the workers he needed to build the four stores. In spite of this, Selitsev pointed out that he stayed true to the terms of the contract, using all of his available resources to hire twenty-four workers and procure the instruments. Eventually, the men had to stop building the stores, and as soon as they did, Bak decided to fire everyone, tear up the contract, and take back twenty-five rubles. »Incapable of feeding such a large number of workers on such a small sum of money,« Selitsev remarked in his sworn statement, »Bak suggested that I turn to a Jew by the name of Beniamin for some groceries. But that shameless Jew took advantage of my dire circumstances by doubling the price of the groceries.« Selitsev did not know why Bak waited nearly seven months to file a lawsuit, but noted that when the two men went their separate ways, the merchant accepted his own responsibility for the difficulties in building the four stores, and declared that he would drop the matter altogether. While the court deliberated over the testimony offered by both litigants, Selitsev and Bak reached an agreement and decided to settle peacefully out of court.[32]

Since the early modern period, even while Jewish communities enjoyed juridical autonomy and self-government, Jews appeared both as plaintiffs and

31 LVIA, f. 447, op. 2, d. 7626.
32 Ibid.

defendants in cases involving a broad spectrum of Polish-Lithuanian society. They also used Polish and Lithuanian institutions of legal justice to resolve conflicts with their Jewish neighbors. The Jewish court system exercised authority over religious practices, the family, commerce, inter-communal disputes, and even criminal cases. But with the gradual erosion of the corporate structures of the Jewish community, more and more Jews relied on civil courts to settle matters that had once been adjudicated by rabbinic leaders. As the historian Adam Teller has recently pointed out, when Jews turned to Polish courts they expected to »receive a reasonably equitable (and enforceable) resolution to their disputes with their neighbors, both Jewish and non-Jewish.«[33]

Over the course of the nineteenth century, as the imperial Russian government intervened in Jewish life in unprecedented fashion, Jews continued to make abundant use of the legal-administrative system, displaying a remarkable consciousness of imperial Russian law and the legal process itself. Jews filed petition after petition and complaint after complaint to receive an exemption to the hundreds of statutes that regulated their precise movement, residence, and career paths. For family disputes, Jews turned to the Russian state in instances when rabbinical authorities were not able to agree on a bill of divorcement.[34] As I will demonstrate in the remaining part of this essay, for disputes over property, land, inheritance, and many other material claims, Jews relied on either district or provincial courts to resolve disagreements with their Jewish neighbors. And even in those instances when two Jewish neighbors feuded over »internal« matters such as the improper collection of communal taxes, Jews asked the imperial government to settle their disagreements.

Outside of the cases that dealt with the management of noble estates, the feuds between Jewish neighbors were caused by many of the same issues discussed above. Unpaid debts, property controversies, and various difficulties in enforcing written contracts accounted for many of the disagreements between Jews, which were eventually tried and settled in courts of law. In Minsk, two Jewish townsmen, Burn Vul'fovich Muevich and Bern Girshovich Okun, purchased a piece of land on which they agreed to construct two wooden homes. After acquiring the property, Muevich paid 200 rubles to construct the first wooden home. Shortly thereafter, Muevich and Okun got into an argument over ownership of their joint property: the second home was never built, and Okun never bothered to repay his debt to Muevich. On January 18, 1878, Muevich and Okun turned to an imperial court to resolve their small claims

33 Adam Teller, »›In the Land of their Enemies‹? The Duality of Jewish Life in Eighteenth-Century Poland,« *Polin* 19 (2007): 431–446.

34 ChaeRan Y. Freeze, *Jewish Marriage and Divorce in Imperial Russia* (Waltham, MA: Brandeis University Press, 2002).

property dispute. After listening to both sides, the judges ruled that Muevich and Okun needed to divide the property into equal halves, construct a second home as well as a fence of »sizeable« proportion that would divide the two pieces of land, and repay any outstanding debts. In addition, the court permitted Okun to store building materials on his neighbor's lawn during the construction of the second wooden home, but for no more than one week. If the litigants violated any of the terms of the settlement, the court required both Okun and Muevich to pay 200 rubles, a sum that would be donated to the Jewish hospital of Minsk.[35]

While almost all of the civil cases were over financial transactions or controversies, not all of the litigants turned to institutions of legal justice asking for large sums of money (in excess of 500 rubles). Iurii Aframovitch, a resident of Vil'na, filed a lawsuit against two of his tenants, Sholom and Ester Slobodskii, for refusing to give back fifty rubles that they had officially borrowed from him.[36] The Minsk townsman Beniamin Berkovitch claimed that Khaim Saganovich, a resident of Gorodki, failed to repay a debt that totaled exactly 152.415 rubles. In the petition filed on March 14, 1868, Berkovitch requested that Saganovich sell his home, which was appraised at fifty-five rubles, in order to return a portion of the debt. Several months later, Saganovich's two sons, Moisei and Mendel', responded by pointing out that the home in question had burned down three years ago and left their father without any savings or assets. Penniless and without any means of supporting himself, the father left Gorodki and transferred ownership of the property to his two sons. After acquiring the land, Moisei and Mendel' decided to build two homes with two small shops with their own money and without any help from their father. »Since the homes are our own personal property,« the brothers argued, »we should not be held accountable for our father's debt.« On February 13, 1868, the district court ruled in favor of the two brothers, but Berkovitch was not happy with the decision. In exactly one month and one day, the townsman filed an appeal with the Vil'na appellate court. The court, however, did not review Berkovitch's request, citing that all appeals needed to be filed no later than one month after the initial decision had been made. Instead, the court fined Berkovitch to pay 1.20 rubles in fees for the three sheets of stamped government used in transcribing the details of the case.[37]

In addition to unpaid financial debts, Jews relied on civil courts to intervene in internal disputes over one of the most important collective responsibilities of the Jewish community: the payment of taxes. In Lida, a town situated around 160 kilometers west of Minsk, Mikhail Shomovich Danishevskii and Khosel'

35 YIVO, RG 12, Box 6, Folder 10.
36 LVIA, f. 447, op. 3, d. 3564.
37 LVIA, f. 447, op. 2, d. 7839.

Davidovich Beker attempted to settle a dispute with Khaim Shmuilovich Kamenetskii over 1,600 rubles. After Danishevskii and Beker failed to pay the tax levied on the slaughter of meat and poultry (*korobka*) to the Oshmiany Jewish community, Kamenetskii reassured the communal leaders that his two neighbors would pay the money and therefore offered his home as collateral in the sum of 1,600 rubles. When Danishevskii and Beker failed to pay their taxes, the elders confiscated the home, which prompted Kamenetskii to file a complaint against his neighbors with the Lida police in February 1863. After reviewing the case on June 5, 1863, the Lida police asked Danishevskii and Beker to pay 1,600 rubles to Kamenetskii, with the stipulation that they had exactly four weeks to file an appeal. Danishevskii and Beker drafted an appeal on June 25, 1863, but, due to unforeseen circumstances not explained in the court records, the courier filed the complaint with the Lida civil court on July 10, 1863, that is, after the four-week deadline had already expired. Moreover, Danishevskii and Beker did not use stamped government paper for official correspondence; their appeal was written on plain white paper, replete with erasures, and had failed to follow the letter of the law. For these reasons, the Lida civil court declined Danishevskii's appeal. But the decision did not stop Danishevskii from appealing yet another time – in this instance, to the Vil'na civil court. In his appeal, Danishevskii argued that the fault lay with the courier who failed to deliver the documents on time. The Vil'na appellate court presided over the case, but once again ruled in favor of Kamenetskii.[38]

Neighborly relations in the nineteenth century

Transcribed in official administrative language, the court records – most of which captured male voices – rarely offer a glimpse of the mental universe that both Jews and their neighbors shared and inhabited. These sources tell us precious little about people's feelings or attitudes to the world around them. We cannot tell, for instance, what a Jewish merchant, moneylender, shopkeeper, or innkeeper really thought about the people he did business with, met on the streets, courtyards, and alleyways, or sold goods to in the marketplaces. Nor can we really comprehend a peasant's attitudes toward his Jewish neighbors, a nobleman's feelings toward the Jew who managed his estate, or a traveler's views of the Jew from whom he rented a room. We know, in short, almost nothing about ordinary people's perceptions, attitudes, and prejudices, or, for that matter, the subjective dimensions of neighborly interactions and encounters.

38 LVIA, f. 447, op. 2, d. 7544.

Whatever their limitations, a close reading of the trial records documents the persistent engagement of ordinary people with imperial Russian legal practices and system of government. Imperial institutions structured people's lives, while civil law provided the necessary framework for establishing the rules and procedures, which helped mediate neighborly conflicts. Over the course of the long nineteenth century, the Russian government continued to recognize a broad spectrum of religious and customary legal practices, even as it worked to impose a uniform legal culture on all its subjects.[39] In case after case, both Jews and their neighbors relied on either district or provincial courts to settle disagreements, in accordance with civil statute law and Russian administrative practices and documentary procedures. For cases involving litigants of different religious origin or social status, civil courts provided the most effective and straightforward means of resolving neighborly disagreements. Even in those instances when two Jews could have turned to the Jewish court system, they usually opted to settle their disputes in the civil arena. For the ordinary person, the abstract principles of Jewish law proved difficult to comprehend, while a ruling based on established commercial practices made more practical sense.[40]

Although we may never grasp the mental universe of the people who inhabited these lands, we can be certain that both Jews and their neighbors did not live in two distinct worlds. These documents offer a window, through which we can observe vibrant horizontal interactions and encounters between populations – whatever their ethnic or religious origin. As I have demonstrated, some of the cases were involved in large amounts of money, and a few even reached the Senate. But more often than not, both Jews and their neighbors turned to imperial Russian courts in hopes of recovering relatively small sums that ranged anywhere from twenty to 150 rubles, over property controversies, contract disputes, and unpaid debts – issues which caused many of the daily tensions between neighbors. Economic exchanges, in other words, brought Jews

39 For a perceptive analysis and positive appraisal of the Russian Empire's diverse legal system, see Jane Burbank, »An Imperial Rights Regime: Law and Citizenship in the Russian Empire,« *Kritika: Explorations in Russian and Eurasian History* 7, no. 3 (2006): 397–431, here 406–416. For a discussion of the problems of imposing uniform legal practices in an imperial setting, see Virginia Martin, »Kazakh Oath-Taking in Colonial Courtrooms: Legal Culture and Russian Empire-Building,« *Kritika: Explorations in Russian and Eurasian History* 5, no. 3 (2004): 483–514.

40 Michael J. Broyde and Michael Ausubel, »Legal Institutions,« in *YIVO Encyclopedia of Jews in Eastern Europe*, vol. 2, ed. Gershon D. Hundert (New Haven, CT: Yale University Press, 2008): 1007–1010, here 1008.

in constant contact with neighboring populations, without always engendering conflicts that could be described as antisemitic or overtly hostile. The dichotomy between coexistence and conflict, which has informed most historical analysis of interethnic social relations in the modern period, obscures the fact that tension was a fundamental, even productive, reality of everyday life.[41]

Eugene M. Avrutin

41 See the important and suggestive remarks made by David Nirenberg, *Communities of Violence: Persecution of Minorities in the Middle Ages* (Princeton, NJ: Princeton University Press, 1996), 9.

Notes on Contributors

Eugene M. Avrutin is Associate Professor of History and Tobor Family Scholar in the Program of Jewish Culture and Society at the University of Illinois at Urbana-Champaign. He is the author of *Jews and the Imperial State: Identification Politics in Tsarist Russia* (2010) and many articles on on documentation practices, the concept of race, religious toleration, and neighborly coexistence. Avrutin is currently completing *The Velizh Affair: Ritual Murder in a Russian Border Town*. eavrutin@illinois.edu

Maria Cieśla holds a Ph.D. in history from the Institute of History at the Polish Academy of Sciences, where she is presently a faculty member, working in the Early Modern Research Group. Since 2015 she is also a Research Fellow at the German Historical Institute in Warsaw participating in the research field *Regionalism and Region-Building*. Her work focuses on the social history of Polish-Lithuanian Jewry in the early modern period. She has published numerous articles in this field; her book *Jews in the Grand Duchy of Lithuania 1632–1764* (Pol.) is forthcoming. mariaciesla@gmail.com

Liliana Hentosh works as a senior research associate in the Institute for Historical research at the Ivan Franko National University of Lviv, Ukraine. The main area of her research is the history of the Catholic Church in the late 19th and first half of the 20th century. She has written several articles on the entanglement of Church and nationalism as well as on national and religious relations in East Central Europe. In 2006 she published the monograph *The Vatican Challenged by Modernity: Ukrainian-Polish Conflict in Galician and Eastern Politics of Pope Benedict XV (1914–1923)*. Her most recent book, the biography *Metropolitan Sheptytsky 1923–1939. Testing Ideals* (Ukr.), was published in 2015. hentosh7@gmail.com

Jürgen Heyde is Associate Professor of Eastern European history at Halle University and Research Fellow at the Center for the History and Culture of East Central Europe (GWZO) in Leipzig. His work focuses on the impact of non-dominant groups in early modern and modern societies. His publications include: *Transkulturelle Kommunikation und Verflechtung. Die jüdischen Wirtschaftseliten in Polen vom 14. bis zum 16. Jahrhundert* (2014); *Geschichte Polens* (³2011); *Bauer, Gutshof und Königsmacht. Die estnischen Bauern in Livland unter polnischer und schwedischer Herrschaft 1561–1650* (2000). juergen.heyde@uni-leipzig.de

Anna Juraschek holds a doctorate in Legal and Cultural Studies of Eastern Europe. Her research focuses on Jewish literature and thought in Central and Eastern Europe. In her Ph.D thesis *The Salvation of the Picture Through the Word. The Idea of Picture in the Prose and Artistic Work of Bruno Schulz* (Regensburg, 2016) she examined the idea of the picture in Bruno Schulz's works relating it to Walter Benjamin's philosophy. Since 2015 she is the Regional Coordinator for Poland and the Czech Republic at the Institute for External Relations (ifa) in Stuttgart. juraschek@ifa.de

Yvonne Kleinmann is Professor of East European History and Director of the Aleksander Brückner Center for Polish Studies at Halle University. In the context of the interdisciplinary research group *Pathways of Law in Ethno-Religiously Mixed Societies* she delves into the functioning of a Catholic-Jewish-Protestant town in early modern Poland. Her broader fields of research are interethnic relations and legal history in early modern Poland-Lithuania and the late Russian Empire as well as Jewish history in Eastern Europe. In 2006 she published *New Places – New People. Jewish Forms of Life in St. Petersburg and Moscow in the 19th century* (Germ.). yvonne.kleinmann@geschichte.uni-halle.de

Hanna Kozińska-Witt is Associate Research Fellow at the Aleksander Brückner Center for Polish Studies at Halle University. She specializes on Eastern Europe in the modern era, namely on the history of Polish Jews as well as on urban history of the 19th and 20th centuries. Her publications include the monographs *Die Krakauer Jüdische Reformgemeinde 1864–1874* (Frankfurt a. M. 1999) and *Krakau in Warschaus langem Schatten. Konkurrenzkämpfe in der polnischen Städtelandschaft 1900–1939* (Stuttgart 2008). Her current project is entitled *Jews in Krakow's municipal self-government in the Galician period*, for which she was awarded a *Polonez 2* Fellowship from the Polish National Science Centre (NCN). kozinska@web.de

Oksana Leskiv holds a master's degree in History from the Ukrainian Catholic University, Lviv. In her thesis she focused on the rural history of Galicia in the mid-19th century. In addition, she is certified as an Operations Manager and Business Consultant and currently works for a marketing and communications agency and manages the IT group of a Swedish company in Lviv. oksana@pixelant.se

Vladimir Levin is the Deputy Director of the Center for Jewish Art at the Hebrew University of Jerusalem and a post-doctoral fellow of the Inter University Academic Partnership in Russian and East European Studies (IUAP), assigned to Ben-Gurion University of the Negev. His Ph.D. thesis is entitled *From Revolution to War: Jewish Politics in Russia, 1907–1914* (Hebr., Jerusalem). His broader research interests comprise East European Jewish history in the 19th and 20th centuries as well as the history and architecture of synagogues in that region. vlalevin@gmail.com

Jana Osterkamp is a historian and legal scholar. She holds a Ph.D. in History, with a dissertation titled *Verfassungsgerichtsbarkeit in der Tschechoslowakei (1920 –1939). Verfassungsidee – Demokratieverständnis – Nationalitätenproblem* (Frankfurt a. M. 2009). Her current work focuses on concepts of federalism in the Habsburg monarchy stressing the topics of nation, religion, economy, law, and region. Since 2012 she is head of a research group on the history of federalism. Her lectureships at Ludwig-Maximilians-University Munich include the history of Central Europe and the history of religion. jana.osterkamp@collegium-carolinum.de

Angela Rustemeyer is University Lecturer of Eastern European History at Vienna University. In her dissertation she focused on the lives of domestic servants in St. Petersburg and Moscow, 1861–1917 (1994), in her *Habilitation* thesis she examined lese-majesty in early modern Russia (2004). Her research interests cover crime and law in Russia and France, 1500–1930, economy and culture in early-modern Eastern Europe, and ethnography and historiography in Eastern Europe. Since 2009 she has coordinated projects for the development of adult literacy at the *Deutscher Volkshochschul-Verband.* rustemeyer2002@yahoo.com

Dror Segev holds a master's degree in European and Scandinavian History. In 2016, his Ph.D. thesis *The Social Role of the Hebrew Press in the Russian Empire during the Reign of Tsar Alexander III, 1881–1894* (Tel Aviv University) won the prestigious Dan Davis Prize. Currently he is the Editorial Manager and Book Review Section Editor of the bilingual journal *Gal-Ed: On the History and Culture of Polish Jewry.* drorsege@post.tau.ac.il

Stephan Stach holds a master's degree in East European History and Slavic Studies. In 2014 he completed his Ph.D. thesis on concepts for an integrative nationality policy in independent Poland, 1926–1939 (Halle University) within the framework of the interdisciplinary research group *Pathways of Law in Ethno-Religiously Mixed Societies*. His research interests include nationality policy in interwar Poland, Polish-Jewish relations after World War II as well as Central and East European dissident movements of the 1980's. With his post-doc project *Knowledge about the Shoah in Communist Poland: The Jewish Historical Institute in Warsaw 1947–1989* he was a Rothschild Europe Research Fellow at Halle University. Currently he is a Research Fellow of the Institute of Contemporary History at the Academy of Sciences of the Czech Republic. stach@usd.cas.cz

Anat Vaturi holds a Ph.D. in History from Tel Aviv University. In her dissertation she re-examined religious toleration in early modern Poland and analysed the status of Jews and Protestants in post-Reformation Krakow. Her broader research interests are Polish-Jewish history, interreligious relations as well as early modern legal culture. Currently she is a post-doctoral researcher in the Department of Jewish History at the University of Haifa. anvaturi1@gmail.com

Tracie L. Wilson holds a Ph.D. from the Department of Folklore and Ethnomusicology at Indiana University-Bloomington. In the interdisciplinary research group *Pathways of Law in Ethno-Religiously Mixed Societies* at Leipzig University, she conducted research on the project *Legal Landscapes on the Edge of Empire: Narrating the Sex Trade in Galicia*. Her research interests include social movements and activism, gender, legal institutions, and migration in East Central Europe, and most recently assisted reproductive technologies and policymaking in Poland. Currently she is Associate Research Fellow at the Aleksander Brückner Center for Polish Studies. twilson351@gmail.com